Indian Himalaya

a Lonely Planet travel survival kit

Michelle Coxall
Paul Greenway

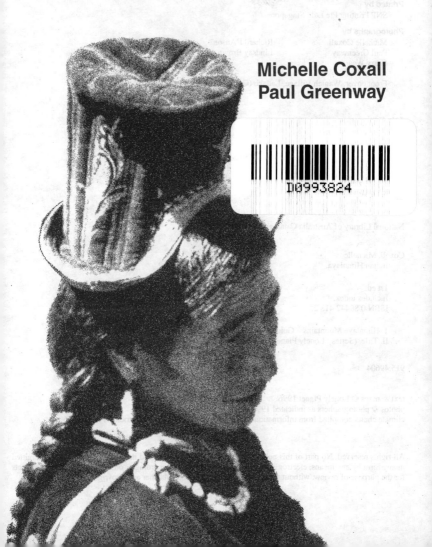

Indian Himalaya

1st edition

Published by
   Lonely Planet Publications
   Head Office: PO Box 617, Hawthorn, Vic 3122, Australia
   Branches: 155 Filbert St, Suite 251, Oakland, CA 94607, USA
                   10 Barley Mow Passage, Chiswick, London W4 4PH, UK
                   71 bis rue du Cardinal Lemoine, 75005 Paris, France

Printed by
   SNP Printing Pte Ltd., Singapore

Photographs by
   Michelle Coxall   Richard I'Anson
   Paul Greenway   Lindsay Brown
   Garry Weare

   Front cover: Wanlah Village, Ladakh (Garry Weare)

This Edition
   September 1996

National Library of Australia Cataloguing in Publication Data

Coxall, Michelle
   Indian Himalaya.

   1st ed.
   Includes index.
   ISBN 0 86442 413 2.

   1. Himalaya Mountains – Guidebooks. I. Greenway, Paul.
   II. Title. (Series : Lonely Planet travel survival kit).

915.49604

text & maps © Lonely Planet 1996
photos © photographers as indicated 1996
climate charts compiled from information supplied by Patrick J Tyson, © Patrick J Tyson, 1996

Michelle Coxall

Michelle's fascination with India began in 1989 when she spent two months travelling around the country by train. She returned in 1994 and spent seven months in India, working with the Tibetan refugees in McLeod Ganj, Himachal Pradesh and updating the Gujarat chapter of Lonely Planet's *India*. She fell under the spell of the Indian Himalaya and returned in 1995 to co-author this book. She is currently working on Lonely Planet's *Rajasthan*, a new guide to the Indian state.

Paul Greenway

It took some time for Paul to adjust from the tropical, coastal Australian city of Darwin, where he lived, to the freezing, breathless altitudes of northern India. During his research, he got stuck in snowstorms in southern Ladakh, avoided being kidnapped in Zanskar, was constantly frustrated by road closures just about everywhere, and had a really nasty cold in Shimla. Now based in Adelaide, Paul supports hopeless Australian Rules football clubs, relaxes to tuneless heavy rock and refuses to settle down. He has contributed chapters for Lonely Planet's *Indonesia*, and, for his sins, will be sent to Mongolia for a future assignment.

Special Thanks to Garry Weare

Garry Weare, author of Lonely Planet's *Trekking in the Indian Himalaya*, wrote the trekking sections of this book. He also generously contributed his expertise for the following chapters: Facts about the Region, Ladakh & Zanskar, Jammu & Kashmir and Himachal Pradesh. He is also a director of World Expeditions, and continues to return to India to research and lead treks each season.

From the Authors

Michelle Coxall Michelle would like to thank Indra Gongba (Trek-Mate) and Krishna (Hotel Tower View), both from Darjeeling; Henry Rutishauser, from Switzerland; Robert Ritchie, for his insights and help in Josimath; Garry Weare, for casting an eye over the finished product and providing invaluable help, advice and input; to the villagers of Dusallan, Himachal Pradesh, for their hospitality in 1994 and 1995; and to Theresa, who reckoned I'd do this thing even when I doubted it myself.

Thank you to Sharan Kaur for her patience and editorial guidance. Thanks also to Jo Horsburgh for her astute editing and encouragement, and to Helen Castle for her editorial input. And special thanks to my belly dancing crone Selena, her husband Serhan, and the rest of the family at Brunswick (Biddy, Cleo and Latcho) – for everything.

Paul Greenway I would like to thank the following people, who added considerably to my enjoyment and knowledge: Charlotte Hansen and Mark Breit (Australia), and Danny Shquri (Israél) in Leh; the adorable Nathalie Perrangher (Switzerland) (and her apricots), and Anna Candy (UK) around Leh and Pangong Tso; Chantel Bellou (France), Phillippe (Switzerland) and the rest of the gang in the Nubra Valley; Tim Sheridan and Lisa Bianco (Australia), Robin Murray (UK) and Seraphim Carlson (USA) for helping to fill in the long days in Sarchu; Vinay Singh (India) for assistance beyond the call of duty in Sarchu and Leh; and Padam Singh (India), from World Expeditions (India), for his invaluable help around Kinnaur and Lahaul & Spiti. Many thanks also to Garry Weare for his contribution to the sections on the western Himalaya.

At Lonely Planet, thanks to Sharan Kaur and Greg Alford; and to my senior partner, Michelle Coxall.

Acknowledgement

The extract on page 10 from *Across the Top* by Sorrel Wilby is reprinted by kind permission of Pan Macmillan Australia Pty Limited. © Sorrel Wilby 1992.

From the Publisher

This book was edited by Jo Horsburgh, and proofed by Helen Castle. Paul Piaia was responsible for the mapping, design, illustration and layout. Assistance in mapping was given by Adam McCrow and Chris Love, and some of the illustrations were contributed by Tamsin Wilson, Reita Wilson and Rachael Scott. The cover was designed by Simon Bracken and Adam McCrow.

Thanks to Bill Aitken for giving us the benefit of his knowledge of the history of the Himalayan regions.

Welcome guidance and support in editorial and design matters were given respectively by Sharan Kaur and Valerie Tellini.

Warning & Request

Things change – prices go up, schedules change, good places go bad and bad places go bankrupt – nothing stays the same. So if you find things better or worse, recently opened or long since closed, please write and tell us and help make the next edition better.

Your letters will be used to help update future editions and, where possible, important changes will also be included in an Update section in reprints.

We greatly appreciate all information that is sent to us by travellers. Back at Lonely Planet a hard-working readers' letters team of Julie Young and Shelley Preston (Australia), Simon Goldsmith (UK), Arnaud Lebonnois (France) and Sacha Pearson (USA) sort through the many letters we receive. The best ones will be rewarded with a free copy of the next edition or another Lonely Planet guide if you prefer. We give away lots of books, but, unfortunately, not every letter/postcard receives one.

Contents

Map Legend

BOUNDARIES

.... International Boundary
.... Disputed Boundary
.... Regional Boundary

ROUTES

.... Freeway
.... Highway
.... Major Road
.... Unsealed Road or Track
.... City Road
.... City Street
.... Railway
.... Underground Railway
.... Walking Track
.... Walking Tour
.... Ferry Route
.... Cable Car or Chairlift

AREA FEATURES

.... Parks
.... Built-Up Area
.... Pedestrian Mall
.... Market
.... Cemetery
.... Forest
.... Glacier, Ice Cap
.... Beach or Desert

HYDROGRAPHIC FEATURES

.... Coastline
.... River, Creek
.... Intermittent River or Creek
.... Rapids, Waterfalls
.... Lake, Intermittent Lake
.... Canal
.... Swamp

SYMBOLS

✪ CAPITAL		.... National Capital
◉ Capital		.... Regional Capital
⬤ CITY		.... Major City
● City		.... City
● Town		.... Town
● Village		.... Village
■	▼	.... Place to Stay, Place to Eat
☕	🍷	.... Cafe, Pub or Bar
✉	☎	.... Post Office, Telephone
❶	⑤	.... Tourist Information, Bank
⊖	Ⓟ	.... Transport, Parking
🏛	⌂	.... Museum, Youth Hostel
⌷	🛆	.... Caravan Park, Camping Ground
✚	⊟	.... Church, Cathedral
☪	⌂	.... Mosque, Stupa
▣	▥	.... Buddhist Gompa, Hindu Temple
✛	★	.... Hospital, Police Station

◉	🅿	.... Embassy, Petrol Station
✈	✝	.... Airport, Airfield
⌷	❀	.... Swimming Pool, Gardens
❖	🐘	.... Shopping Centre, Zoo
⚲	▤	.... Winery or Vineyard, Picnic Site
←	A25	One Way Street, Route Number
🏛	⚑	.... Stately Home, Monument
▥	▣	.... Castle, Tomb
⌢	⌂	.... Cave, Hut or Chalet
▲	☀	.... Mountain or Hill, Lookout
☗	⚓	.... Lighthouse, Shipwreck
)(	◎	.... Pass, Spring
⚐	⚑	.... Ski Field, Surf Beach
	∴	.... Archaeological Site or Ruins
		.... Ancient or City Wall
		.... Cliff or Escarpment, Tunnel
		.... Railway Station

Note: not all symbols displayed above appear in this book

Introduction

Throughout the ages, sages and mystics have travelled to the mighty Indian Himalaya to draw inspiration from its perennially snow-clad peaks, magnificent remote valleys and gorges and life-giving rivers for their meditations. The early sages who gave voice to their awe of this singularly soul-stirring mountain chain referred to it as 'the expanse of the two arms of the Great Being' – an evocative description suggesting a world locked in the Himalaya's divine snowy embrace. The Himalaya was known as 'Dhevbumi' – the abode of the gods.

Once a pilgrimage to this remote lofty realm entailed a long, arduous journey on foot from the hot Indian plains, or across the formidable high passes which were the only means of passage from the Tibetan plateau. Today it is possible to penetrate the mountain fastnesses by bus or jeep, and to some areas,

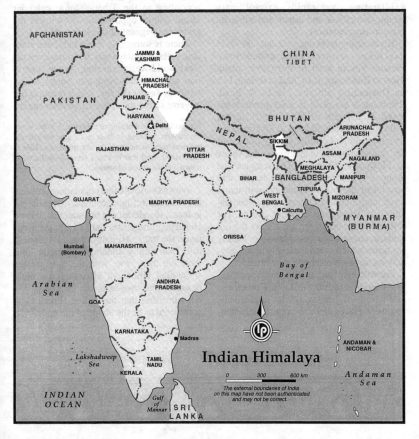

Indian Himalaya

0   300   600 km

The external boundaries of India
on this map have not been authenticated
and may not be correct.

such as Ladakh, in the north-eastern region of the state of Jammu & Kashmir, by plane – a flight which affords some of the world's most stunning aerial scenery.

It is almost too easy to get carried away with superlatives when writing about the Indian Himalaya, but after all, this region *does* have some of the most beautiful mountains in the world (and certainly some of the world's highest); the most dramatic river valleys and gorges; a profusion of wildflowers and unique fauna; quiet places for reflection and meditation; fascinating hill stations; laidback travellers' centres like McLeod Ganj, Manali and Manikaran; exhilarating river rapids; extraordinary temple complexes and ornate and colourful *gompas* (monasteries).

If you enjoy trekking, you can take short day hikes or three-week expeditions. Perhaps you're keen to learn more about Tibetan Buddhism; if so, McLeod Ganj, Leh or Darjeeling are the places to head. Rishikesh is *the* place to go if you're interested in aspects of Hindu philosophy. Wildflower buffs will head to Sikkim to see its renowned and prolific variety of orchids and rhododendrons, or to the beautiful Valley of Flowers in Garhwal. The temples and gompas scattered across the length and breadth of the Indian Himalaya will tempt those interested in architecture and manifestations of Hindu and Buddhist culture. For rest and recreation there are always the hill stations, eminently accessible – some by tiny toy trains which wend their way up gravity-defying tortuous narrow-gauge lines.

For wild elephant, tiger or rhino spotting, you'll enjoy safaris at the Rajaji, Corbett and Jaldhapara wildlife sanctuaries respectively, and these places are also home to an aston-ishing array of mammals and a great variety of birdlife.

The hustle and bustle characteristic of life on the Indian plains rapidly evaporates the further you ascend towards the soaring peaks of the Himalaya. The mountain villages are renowned for their hospitality and it's not unusual to be invited into a family home for a cup of *chai* (tea), or to a colourful village religious or harvest celebration. The Buddhist gompas of the Indian Himalaya remain repositories of rich Tibetan culture, resplendent with vibrantly coloured prayer rooms and exquisitely embroidered *thangkas*, or religious paintings. Festivals celebrated according to the Tibetan lunar calendar afford unique opportunities to witness the pomp and pageant of this living religion.

There is something about the sheer grandeur of the Himalaya which inspires even the most world-weary traveller. As the Australian author and adventurer Sorrel Wilby writes in *Across the Top*, which recounts her traverse across the entire Himalayan chain:

I do not know the meaning of existence; I do not know the answers; but here, in these mountains, for just one moment there is no need to ask questions. Life is understood. And that is why I return – will always return – to the abode of snows.

With its various tribal populations, colourful Tibetan refugee centres, magnificent gompas, wonderful old hill stations, frenetic Hindu pilgrimage sites and tiny mountain villages, the Indian Himalaya has a lot more to offer than simply stunning landscapes – but there are those, too, with the omnipresent snow-clad Himalaya affording the most beautiful and awe-inspiring backdrop. It's not surprising that the Indian Himalaya is considered to be the abode of the gods.

Facts about the Region

Fragments of implements dating from the early Stone Age (8000 BC) have been recovered from the Alaknanda Valley in Uttarakhand (Uttar Pradesh), and prehistoric implements discovered near Srinagar (Jammu & Kashmir) and further evidence from Himachal Pradesh testify to the antiquity of human habitation. With the expansion of the Indus Valley civilisation of proto-Dravidians (2500-1500 BC), migrations to the foothills followed. The Aryan invasion over the north-west passes (1500-1000 BC) drove the Dravidians back south. The four books of Aryan scriptures *(Vedas)* move from early worship of the Indus River eastwards to honour the Ganges. Where the Ganges rises in Uttarakhand is known as *devbhumi* – the land of the gods.

The Aryans propitiated their nature gods through sacrificial ritual conducted by their hereditary priests the Brahmins who have continued to dominate the social hierarchy, the indigenous inhabitants being relegated to humbler status, thus originating India's complex caste system. Around 800 BC the speculative *Upanishad* scriptures included the doctrines of Hindu philosophy and idealised the Himalayan ashram. The Buddha (born c563 BC) threatened Brahmanical orthodoxy by his rejection of the caste system. In 260 BC the emperor Ashoka declared Buddhism the state religion and official patronage saw the new faith spread both to South-East Asia and over the Himalaya to China.

The great Hindu monist philosopher Shankaracharya (born c788 AD) restored the Brahmanical order aided by his energetic missionary pilgrimages in the Himalaya. Thanks to his teaching, orthodox Hindus view physical reality as illusory *(maya)*. Hypotheses such as the Aryan invasion are rejected in favour of belief in a golden age beyond the purview of history.

The popular scriptural epics of Hinduism began to be written down around 400 BC. Specific references to the Himalaya are made in the *Mahabharata*. The semiscriptural *Puranas* are a mix of mythology and surprisingly detailed Himalayan geography. The Vedic gods were merged largely into Vishnu the preserver and Shiva the destroyer. Legendary heroes such as Ram and Krishna were deified as embodiments of Vishnu by the orthodox, but the majority of Hindus in the Himalaya stayed with the *lingam* (phallic symbol) worship of Shiva.

Western Himalaya

Ladakh & Zanskar The first inhabitants of Ladakh were the nomadic Khampas who roamed the remote grazing areas of the Tibetan plateau. The Mons, who professed Buddhism, established the first settlements on the windswept plateau. Dards from the Indus Valley introduced irrigation to make agriculture possible in the higher reaches. The Dards were gradually displaced or assimilated by migrations from Guge, a province in Western Tibet. The Indian teacher Padmasambhava (8th century) crossed the Himalaya to establish Tibetan Buddhism which was enriched by the 11th century scholar Ringchen Zangpo who founded several famous *gompas* (monasteries). In the 14th century the Gelukpa order of monks was introduced to Ladakh.

With Islam spreading up the Indus Valley, the divided upper and lower realms of Ladakh united under the Buddhist ruler Tashi Namgyal. Later, however, the Muslim ruler of Baltistan forced the Ladakhi king to marry his daughter. Ladakh enjoyed stability under Singe Namgyal, the offspring of this union. He constructed the royal palace at Leh and established gompas of the Drukpa order in Ladakh and Zanskar. The Ladakhi kingdom now included Zanskar and Spiti in addition to the Indus Valley, but these territories diminished after a war with the forces of the 5th Dalai Lama sent from Lhasa. Relations with Tibet improved after the signing of a trade agreement.

In 1846 Ladakh became part of the territory of the maharaja of J & K and remained under Kashmiri control until 1995 when it achieved partial administrative autonomy.

Jammu & Kashmir Prior to its conversion to Islam in the 14th century Kashmir was renowned as a repository of Buddhist and Brahmanical learning. Kashmiri pundits occupy a unique niche in Hindu affections and their wholesale displacement in the current agitation betrays the state's tradition of assimilation. During the Utpala and Karokta dynasties the influence of Kashmir was felt beyond the valley. Shah Mir arrived in Kashmir to found an Islamic dynasty that lasted to the Mughal era.

It was Sultan Sikandar who destroyed Kashmir's notable temples and imposed a tax on Hindus. The Mughals valued Kashmir as a reminder of their Central Asian roots. Following them the despotic Afghan Durranis held sway until the Sikh Maharaja Ranjit Singh took control. The British intervened and by the Treaty of Amritsar (1846) the Hindu Maharaja of Jammu acquired Kashmir. The new state of Jammu & Kashmir (J & K) included Hindu Jammu, Buddhist Ladakh and Muslim Kashmir and Baltistan. (The bloody outcome of this union in Kashmir's recent history will be considered later in this chapter under Government and Politics.)

For 101 years the Dogras of Hindu Jammu ruled over Kashmir. The last maharaja, Hari Singh, ruled from 1923 and was reluctant to cede his territory to either India or Pakistan after partition in 1947. While the maharaja vacillated, Pakistan dispatched Pathan tribesmen to capture Srinagar. Hari Singh called for Indian help to repel the aggressors, which resulted in war between India and Pakistan leading to a Line of Actual Control that continues to be a source of aggravated dispute.

Himachal Pradesh In 1966, Himachal Pradesh comprised a nucleus of 31 'native states' that in 1948 combined their destinies after a millennia of internecine strife. These tiny hill states enjoyed relative affluence owing to their strategic location on the trading routes between Central Asia and the Indian peninsula. Alexander the Great invaded north-west India in 327 BC and penetrated as far as the Beas River but was pushed back by Chandragupta II, the founder of north India's classic Hindu dynasty. Himachal's squabbling petty warlords overlooked the rise of Rajput power. Meru Varman had already installed himself as the Rajput ruler of the Chamba Valley in the mid-6th century. He established a kingdom with his headquarters at Brahmapuri (Brahmaur) and the Varman Dynasty survived in the valley for over 1000 years. The beautiful temples at Brahmaur and at the later capital of Chamba (founded by Raja Sahil Varman in the 10th century) are a legacy of this dynasty. Chamba's strategic position between the high Himalaya and the Kangra Valley to the south was used to great advantage by its rulers. They controlled trade across the Pangi Range where a main route linked Kullu and Lahaul with Kishtwar and Kashmir along the Chandrabhaga river.

The Kangra Valley was the domain of the Katoch Dynasty whose first capital was Nagarkot. Later it moved to Kangra. It was the fabled wealth of the Bajreshwari Temple in Kangra fort (amassed by the rulers' trading activities) that lured the notorious despoiler of Hindu temples, Mahmud of Ghazru. In 1009 the Afghan raider carried off a vast fortune in gold, silver and jewels. The Kangra rulers were renowned for their refinement and later would commission miniature paintings which, although inspired by the Mughal court developed their own distinctive Kangra style. This Pahari school of painting peaked under the patronage of Raja Sansar Chand (1775) who after the decline of Mughal influence had extended his claims, deposing the rulers of Chamba and Kullu. The rise of Sikh ambitions now threatened the hill rulers. Their warrior guru Govind Singh had won the first battles based at Paonta Saheb in the south-east, site of a famous *gurudwara* (Sikh temple). Religious persecution during Aurangzeb's long reign of intolerance drove the Sikhs to seek domination in the hill states. The situation was further complicated by the nascent Nepali power, the Gurkhas, expanding vigorously westwards. Their leader Amar Singh Thapa allied with the deposed Chamba and Kullu rulers against Kangra. To save himself, Sansar Chand had to call in the Sikhs, who halted the Gurkha invasion but now had a free hand to influence the power play in Himachal.

In 1966 Lahaul & Spiti, which had come under Punjab administration at Independence, became part of Himachal Pradesh (Land of the Snow Ranges) which attained full statehood in 1971.

Uttarakhand The situation in Uttarakhand saw similar infighting between early fiefdoms but the rivalry was later confined to a Garhwal versus Kumaon matching of arms. From the 8th to the 14th century the Katyuri Dynasty ruled from central Kumaon. It was succeeded by the Chand rajas whose first capital was at Champawat in the east, and later, more central, at Almora. Until the 14th century, Garhwal ('the place of forts') had 52 fortified fiefdoms which were united under Raja Ajay Pal, whose first capital was at Chandpur. Later the capital was moved to Srinagar on the Ganges. The Gurkhas overran both Kumaon and Garhwal and posed a threat to the British who sought to control the profitable shawl wool trade. After initial losses, the British by 1815 were able to confine the Gurkhas within the boundaries of Nepal. As the price of enlisting British help to evict the Gurkhas, the Garhwal maharaja ceded Pauri Garhwal east of the Ganges, including Srinagar, to the British. His new capital at Tehri gave the name to his truncated native state of Tehri Garhwal. The British also took over the administration of Kumaon.

The Uttarakhand hills of Garhwal and Kumaon (comprising the region between Himachal and the Nepal border) were merged in 1947 with the new and most populous Indian state of Uttar Pradesh.

Eastern Himalaya
West Bengal Hills & Sikkim The eastern Himalaya remained isolated from the concerns of northern Indian rulers. Only in 1661 did a Mughal flotilla penetrate as far as the Brahmaputra Valley. Sikkim was originally inhabited by animist tribal Lepchas who were joined in the 15th century by Bhutias fleeing religious turmoil in Tibet.

A blood brotherhood was forged between the Lepchas and Bhutias that included marriage alliances and the adoption by the Lepchas of Nyingmapa (ancient) Buddhism, which was introduced by the Bhutias. Hereditary kingship under a Buddhist chogyal (king) was instituted in 1642.

The district of Kalimpong was lost to neighbouring Bhutan in the early 18th century and in 1780 more territory was lost to the Gurkha invaders from the east. British power forced the Gurkhas back to Nepal and returned Sikkimese territory in expectation of favour and influence. In 1835, the chogyal was forced to cede Darjeeling to the British as a convalescent station. Then, in 1861, to confirm their mastery, the British made Sikkim a protectorate. This infuriated the rulers in Tibet who considered Sikkim their cultural province. Lhasa mounted an expedition in 1886 that was thrown back. Two years later the British mounted their own expedition to Lhasa. Earlier, in 1864, similar territorial claims by Bhutan had caused the British to wrest by arms Kalimpong and the Duars.

The British encouraged emigration of Nepali labour to both Darjeeling and Sikkim. Gurkha families continue to be integral to Darjeeling's famous tea estates, a lucrative revenue earner for the British that remains the most important factor in the economy of the West Bengal hills.

In 1947 India took over the protectorate status of Sikkim. With their numerical majority the Nepali Hindu settlers were dissatisfied at the conservative policies of the Chogyal and agitated for more representation. Widespread unrest resulted in 1975 in a referendum whereby the people of Sikkim voted for a democratic system. India annexed the state and replaced the chogyal with an elected legislature.

GEOGRAPHY

In that most oft-quoted verse of the *Kumar-sambhava*, by the renowned Sanskrit poet Kalidasa, the Himalaya is described as 'the King of mountains' and the 'measuring rod of the world'. These are apt appellations: the Himalaya Range extends in an arc some 2500 km from Nanga Parbat (8125m) in Pakistan in the west, to the far-eastern Indian state of Arunachal Pradesh in the east, with Namche Barwa standing at the eastern perimeter. It boasts some of the loftiest peaks in the world, with 14 peaks over 8000m high, including, of course, Everest, scraping the heavens at a staggering 8877m in Nepal, and the no-less inspiring Kangchenjunga, at 8598m, dominating Sikkim, and the highest mountain in India.

The width of the range varies from some 200 to 300 km, separating the Indian subcontinent to the south, and in part, the Tibetan plateau to the north. The range is embraced by two rivers which rise behind it in Tibet near Mt Kailash. The Indus threads its way westwards, then penetrates the mountains and proceeds across Pakistan before meeting the Arabian Sea. The Brahmaputra heads off in the opposite direction, coursing eastwards behind the Himalaya before breaching it and flowing through the north-eastern region in a south-westerly direction, entering the sea at the Bay of Bengal.

The range encompasses three more or less parallel mountain zones. At the top end of the spectrum is the Greater Himalaya, its eternally snow-clad peaks and glacial flanks forming a veritable bastion, with those mountains at the western end dividing Kashmir and Himachal Pradesh from Ladakh. Lying to the north of the Himalaya at the western end of the Indian Himalaya are the Zanskar and Ladakh ranges, referred to as the trans-Himalayan region, which marks

the transition zone between the Indian sub-continent and the Tibetan plateau. In the Greater Himalaya which falls within the geographical boundaries of Uttarakhand, or northern Uttar Pradesh, rise the major tributaries of the Ganges, as well as to the west of this region, the source of the Yamuna. The range extends east into Nepal, with the Greater Himalaya here forming the boundary between Nepal and Tibet. The mountains of Nepal become progressively more spectacular in the eastern section of Nepal and it is here that Everest makes its heaven-challenging bid. Continuing eastwards, the Himalaya threads its way in an enormous arc which embraces Sikkim, projects eastward into mountainous Bhutan, until finally culminating in the Assam Himalaya at its far-eastern extremity, forming the mountainous region of Arunachal Pradesh.

Before the Greater Himalaya lie the peaks and ridges of the Middle Himalaya, with mountain peaks averaging in height between 4000 and 5000m. This zone encompasses the Pir Panjal Range in the western Himalaya, which extends from Gulmarg in Jammu & Kashmir, enclosing the Kashmir Valley and extending to the Banihal La. Here the Pir Panjal meets the ridgeline that separates the Kashmir Valley from the Warvan Valley. From Banihal the Pir Panjal sweeps southeast to Kishtwar, and from there to the east if forms the divide between the Chandra and Ravi valleys. Further east it forms the natural divide between the Chandra and Kullu valleys. The Pir Panjal is breached only once – at Kishtwar – where the combined waters of the Warvan and Chandra rivers meet to form the Chenab River, one of the main tributaries of the Indus.

To the south of the Pir Panjal lies the Dhauladhar Range. It is most easily recognised as the snow-capped ridge behind Dharamsala, and it forms the divide between the Ravi (Chamba) and the Beas (Kangra) valleys. Further to the west it provides the divide between the Chenab Valley below Kishtwar and the Tawi Valley which twists south to Jammu. This is the range crossed at Patnitop on the Jammu-Srinagar highway.

At the bottom of the elevation profile is the Lower Himalaya, or Himalayan foothills. These are the first slopes reached by those heading north from the plains. In the west, they form the Siwalik Range, which extends from western Himachal Pradesh midway into northern Uttar Pradesh, and rises to elevations of between 1500 and 2000m. In the eastern Himalaya, the southern reaches of which are directly in the path of the monsoon which sweeps in from the Bay of Bengal, these lower slopes have been progressively buffeted and eroded over the ages to the point where they were completely levelled, and this third and lower mountain fold is absent here.

In the western Himalaya, the Indus River and its tributaries provide the principal drainage system. The catchment area is extremely large. The Kabul river system drains the Hindu Kush to the west, while the Shyok, Gilgit and Hunza river systems drain the Karakoram to the north. On its long descent to the plains, the Indus is supplemented by the Jhelum, Chenab, Ravi and Sutlej rivers whose headwaters drain the entire western Himalaya.

Eastwards from the Sutlej River, the rivers drain into the Ganges basin. First there is the Tons which joins the Yamuna. The Ganges, as the Bhagirathi, rises above Gangotri in northern Uttarakhand. It is joined by the Pindar, the Dhauliganga, the Nandakini, the Mandakini, and the Alaknanda, all of which rise in northern Uttarakhand, until finally the Ganges meets the Yamuna at Allahabad on the plains. As the sacred Ganges continues its journey eastwards across north-east India, it is fed by all the main river systems of Nepal before reaching the Bay of Bengal.

The Brahmaputra is the third major river system of the subcontinent. Like the Indus and the Sutlej it has its source close to Mt Kailash in Tibet. From here, where it is known as the Tsangpo, it flows nearly 1000 km eastwards, draining the Tibetan plateau and the headwaters of the rivers north of the Himalaya, until it sweeps around the Assam Himalaya and descends to the Bay of Bengal, meeting the Ganges en route.

GEOLOGY

The Himalaya is one of the youngest mountain ranges in the world. Geological samples retrieved from the summit of Mt Everest reveal that in millennia past, the Himalaya once formed part of an ocean bed. Its evolution can be traced to the Jurassic era (80 million years ago) when the world's land masses were split into two: Laurasia in the northern hemisphere, and Gondwanaland in the southern hemisphere. The land mass which is now India broke away from Gondwanaland and floated across the earth's surface until it collided with Asia. The hard volcanic rocks of India were thrust against the soft sedimentary crust of Asia, creating the highest mountain range in the world. It was a collision that formed mountain ranges right across Asia, including the Karakoram, the Pamirs, the Hindu Kush, the Tien Shan and the Kun Lun. The Himalayan mountains at the front of this continental collision are still being formed, with the range continuing to rise up to 0.8 cm annually.

Following this initial massive upward thrust, which took place over a period of some five to seven million years, unlike most of the rest of the earth's land masses, the Himalaya was never subsequently subjected to inundation, which has given rise to the remarkable floral and faunal diversity of the Himalayan zone.

CLIMATE

The weather will probably dictate when you travel to the Indian Himalaya. Climatically, the Indian Himalaya can be divided into three regions. The first contains the ridges and valleys to the south of the Pir Panjal Range, and the monsoonal hill states from Jammu to Uttarakhand, the West Bengal hills and the lower regions of Sikkim; the second includes the region south of the main Himalaya but beyond the Pir Panjal – it encompasses the Kashmir Valley and valleys of Lahaul & Spiti, and has a modified monsoon climate. The third region, that of Ladakh and its environs, lies beyond the Himalaya and has a high altitude desert climate.

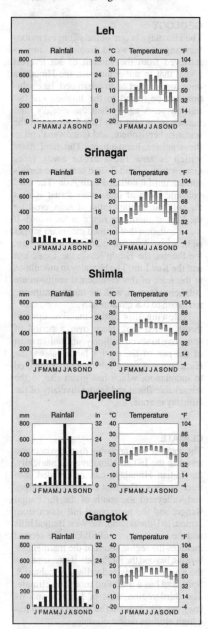

Leh

Srinagar

Shimla

Darjeeling

Gangtok

Ladakh & Zanskar

Ladakh is isolated from most of the Indian climate patterns. Humidity is always low, and rainfall no more than a few cm each year, which can fall in the peak tourist summer months of July and August. Dramatic monsoons can drift over Zanskar in summer.

In winter, it is generally dry in Ladakh and Zanskar, but a lot windier, with plenty of snow and ice in temperatures that don't go above zero for many months.

Vale of Kashmir

Spring in the Kashmir Valley begins in mid-March and continues through to the end of May. At this time Kashmir experiences its heaviest rainfall, with storms breaking over the Pir Panjal. During July and August, the valley becomes hazy and humid. During these summer months temperatures often reach 30°C. Autumn is the most settled period. The months of September and October are typically clear with a minimum of rain. The winter is from December to March.

Jammu & Himachal Pradesh

In Jammu, the Kangra Valley, Chamba district, Kullu and Parbati valleys, Manali and Shimla, the rains last from about mid-June to mid-September. The winter, often accompanied by snow and subzero temperatures, is from early December to the end of March. The ideal time to visit is between September and November. Between March and April the weather can be clear and fine, although quite chilly.

The exceptions are Kinnaur and Lahaul & Spiti, which have a modified monsoon and a severe winter. Between June and October, the days are sunny and the evenings are cool. At other times of the year, snow, and temperatures below -20°C are responsible for blocking passes and isolating the regions.

Uttarakhand

The best weather is from mid-May to mid-July and mid-September to mid-November. The Char Dham are snowbound between November and April. Summer is from June to August and winter from December to Feb-

Indian Himalaya

The external boundaries of India on this map have not been authenticated and may not be correct.

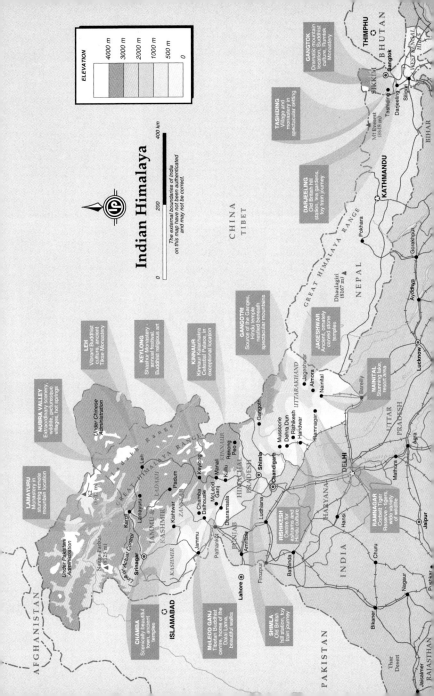

ELEVATION

	4000 m
	3000 m
	2000 m
	1000 m
	500 m
	0

0   200   400 km

GANGTOK
Dramatic mountain location, Buddhist culture, Rumtek Monastery

TASHIDING
Village and monastery in spectacular setting

DARJEELING
Old British hill station, tea gardens, toy train journey

JAGESHWAR
Ancient, ornately carved stone temples

NAINITAL
Stunning lake, resort area

GANGOTRI
Source of the Ganges, Hindu temple nestled beneath spectacular mountains

KINNAUR
Kinnaur Kalachakra Celestial Palace, in exceptional location

KEYLONG
Shashur Monastery, annual festival, Buddhist religious art

LEH
Vibrant Buddhist culture, ancient Tikse Monastery

NUBRA VALLEY
Extraordinary scenery, wildlife, picturesque villages, hot springs

LAMAYURU
Monastery in stunning remote mountain location

CHAMBA
Scenically beautiful town, ancient temples

McLEOD GANJ
Tibetan Buddhist centre, home of the Dalai Lama, beautiful walks

SHIMLA
Old British hill station, toy train journey

RISHIKESH
Centre for ashrams and Hindu culture

RAMNAGAR
Corbett Tiger Reserve – tigers, array of wildlife

AFGHANISTAN

Under Pakistani Administration

Under Chinese Administration

Nanga Parbat (8125 m)

K2 (8611 m)

Line of Actual Control

Line of Actual Control

CHINA
TIBET

Kargil
Lamayuru
Leh
Padum
Keylong
Manali
Kullu
Chamba
Dalhousie
McLeod Ganj
Dharamsala
Reking
Peo
Shimla

Srinagar
Kishtwar

Jammu

ISLAMABAD

Lahore

Firozpur

Bathinda

Amritsar

Pathankot

Ludhiana

Chandigarh

Mussoorie
Dehra Dun
Haridwar
Rishikesh

Gangotri

Jageshwar
Almora
Nainital

Ramnagar

DELHI

Mathura

Agra

Bareilly

Lucknow

Ayodhya

Gorakhpur

Pokhara

KATHMANDU

Dhaulagiri (8167 m)

Mt Everest (8848 m)

Tashiding
Darjeeling
Siliguri

THIMPHU

Gangtok

BHUTAN

SIKKIM

WEST BENGAL

BIHAR

NEPAL

GREAT HIMALAYA RANGE

JAMMU & KASHMIR

LADAKH

ZANSKAR

KASHMIR

HIMACHAL PRADESH

UTTARAKHAND

UTTAR PRADESH

PUNJAB

HARYANA

INDIA

PAKISTAN

Bikaner

Churu

Nagaur

Jaipur

Pushkar

Jaisalmer

Thar Desert

Hansi

Chittoor

PIR PANJAL RANGE

GREAT HIMALAYA RANGE

MICHELLE COXALL

MICHELLE COXALL

PAUL GREENWAY

GARRY WEARE

MICHELLE COXALL

MICHELLE COXALL

Many faces of the culturally diverse Indian Himalaya.

ruary. At the higher altitudes during the height of summer, it can be quite cool. During the monsoon (July-August), expect delays due to landslides and road closures. At this time, too, the famed views of distant snow-clad peaks are enshrouded in cloud. Rishikesh, Haridwar and the hill stations can be visited year round, although it can get quite chilly in winter when temperatures drop to single figures.

West Bengal Hills

Down on the West Bengal plains in the regions of Siliguri and Jalpaiguri, it is very hot during the summer months of May and June, and quite cool between October and February. As you begin the ascent to Darjeeling, at 2134m, the temperature drops dramatically. Darjeeling has been described as having three seasons: cold, very cold, and very, very cold!

For mountain views from Darjeeling, the best time to visit is from mid-September to mid-December, although it gets pretty cold by December. The season resumes around mid-March and continues to mid-June, but as the haze builds up the views become less clear. During the monsoon months (June-September), clouds obscure the mountains and the rain is often so heavy that whole sections of the road from the plains are washed away, though the town is rarely cut off for more than a few days at a time.

Sikkim

Given the great variation in altitudes in Sikkim (from only a few hundred metres in the bottom of river valleys, to heights of over 6000m in the Greater Himalaya), there can be a considerable variation in temperature in different places. Places found below 3000m enjoy particularly fine weather in spring (March to May) and autumn (September to November). Between November and February it can get quite chilly, even at lower elevations. As the snow-clad peaks of northern Sikkim block the passage of the monsoon, which sweeps across the state from June until August, Sikkim receives a phenomenal rainfall, particularly in the southern regions such

as Gangtok, which can register up to 325 cm per annum. It is drier further north.

ECOLOGY & ENVIRONMENT

By the turn of this century, population pressure was beginning to take its toll on the Himalayan regions, and the already limited resources were severely strained. While the density of population to land is much less than on the plains, the ratio between population and arable land is much higher, in some cases more than four times greater than down on the plains. To compound the problem, productivity of arable land is only one-quarter of what it is on the plains, and with increasing population growth, ever more land is being sought for cultivation, and wood consumption for domestic fuel is reaching dangerously high proportions. While the number of grazing animals has more than doubled in some instances since 1950, there is an ever-diminishing amount of grazing land available, and over-grazing has contributed to soil erosion.

Himalayan inhabitants, who previously depended almost solely on the bounty of the land for their requirements, have had to find alternative sources of income. This has resulted in a mass exodus of able-bodied men to the plains in search of employment, placing a greater burden on the women of the hills and the disruption of traditional cultural lifestyles. An increase in tourism to the Himalaya has provided one means of securing an alternative form of living, but unrestricted and poorly managed tourism strategies have brought their own environmental and cultural problems (see under Tourism later in this section). Poaching of the already besieged larger animals of the Himalayan regions is another means of supplementing an ever-diminishing living.

Deforestation

The Himalayan regions are acutely susceptible to environmental degradation. Precipitous slopes and torrential monsoon rains already place enormous pressure on the fragile ecosystem, and depletion of forest cover speedily accelerates this process.

Denudation of forests to clear land for cultivation, and timber extraction for commercial purposes have resulted in massive soil erosion, with the soil of the Himalaya being literally washed down onto the plains. Due to the vulnerability of the fragile hills ecosystem and the dependence of its inhabitants on the forests for fuel and fodder, a National Forest Policy stipulated that at least 60% of forest cover should be preserved in the hills, as compared to around 30% on the plains. In theory, this should be reflected in the respective ratios of timber output of these regions. However, in the state of Uttar Pradesh, for example, of which Uttarakhand forms only a very small area, the latter supplies up to about 70% of the state's timber output in any one year. Recent satellite photographs have revealed that forest cover in the Himalayan regions is now below 11%.

The devastation caused by flooding in the Himalayan region and on the plains has increased exponentially over recent years. A recent UN report estimates that over a 30 year period between 1950 and 1980, a staggering 40% of the Himalayan watershed was destroyed due to deforestation.

Hydroelectric Projects

A trend towards rapid industrialisation following the departure of the British in the 1940s has resulted in the construction of enormous hydroelectricity projects to provide power for industries and irrigation on the plains. In 1963, the Bhakra Dam project, which harnessed the Sutlej River in present-day Himachal Pradesh, was completed, with the submerging of some 371 villages and the displacement of 36,000 people. This project was followed by the construction of the Pong Dam on the Beas River, with the displacement of a further 150,000 people. Many of these people were promised land in the state of Rajasthan, the main beneficiary of the project, a promise which is yet to be fulfilled.

Controversy is now rife regarding the proposed Tehri Dam project on the Bhagirathi River in Uttarakhand, which was given the go-ahead in 1976. This dam will result in the

The Chipko Movement

Not surprisingly, it is those who depend most intimately on the Himalaya's benevolence who have commenced the struggle to halt or reverse the environmental degradation. In the 1970s, the women of Uttarakhand embarked on a grassroots environmental movement to save the forests of the central Himalaya. Conforming to the Gandhian doctrine of *ahimsa*, or nonviolence, these Garhwali women founded the tree-hugging, or Chipko movement (*chipko* means 'to embrace'). These brave women, some of whom were prepared to die for their cause, literally clung to the trees which were marked for felling, held demonstrations against the auctioning of trees, or tied sacred threads around trees destined for the axe. The state government was finally compelled to issue an injunction suspending the felling of trees above altitudes of 1000m and on gradients of more than 30˚.

The women of the Chipko movement recognised that the forests are neither the preserves of those who inhabit them, nor of those with the greatest economic ability to exploit them. The slogan of the movement was 'What do the forests bear? Soil, water and pure air. Soil, water and pure air are the basis of life'. There is a recognition that the forests belong to all people and all creatures, and that whatever threatens the forests threatens all life on earth. ■

relocation of more than 85,000 people. In Sikkim, environmentalists and local inhabitants have condemned the Rathong River project of West Sikkim which will result in the relocation of tribal groups such as Lepchas and Bhutias. However, it is not just the cultural upheaval, nor even the loss of forests and land to these giant concrete monsters which most disturbs environmentalists.

The Himalaya is a seismically active area, possessing two major thrust faults, and a number of lesser faults. Periodically the Himalaya is shaken by major and minor earthquakes. In 1991, central Garhwal in Uttarakhand was devastated by a major earthquake: over 800 people were killed, thousands injured, and damages were estimated at US$130 million. The potential for a catastrophic ecological disaster on a scale never before experienced, to say nothing of the immediate loss of human and animal lives should any of these massive dam projects be damaged or destroyed in an earthquake, is chilling. Some analysts suggest that existing projects are not being managed or maintained as efficiently as they could be, with estimates of up to 30% underutilisation; productivity and power output could be increased by upgrading these projects as opposed to building new plants.

Other Environmental Threats

Road building has further added to the already considerable strain on the environment. The British wasted no time building roads and laying railway tracks in the hills region. The trend was continued following independence, motivated both by the imperative to open the region to facilitate economic exploitation, and to provide access to the Himalaya's vast border areas for the deployment of troops. However, the methods of road building have become more sophisticated: human labour has been supplemented with the introduction of explosives which have weakened pre-existing fissures and resulted in a high increase in the numbers of landslides in the region.

A further threat to the delicate ecological balance is the introduction of monoculture, generally to serve the economic interests of those on the plains. In 1988, the women of the Chamoli district of Uttarakhand staged a heated battle in protest at a government forestry department initiative to plant pine saplings in an established oak forest. Pine is a fast-growing species which can be tapped for resin and harvested for timber. Not only would the conifers have destroyed the existing oak forest, but pines inhibit undergrowth and pine needles acidify the soil. In addition, they are of little domestic use, as they produce no edible fodder, and when burnt produce too much smoke and a viscous soot. The women were ultimately successful, and the saplings were removed from the forest, which readily recovered. However, pine

plantations have been introduced into other areas of the hills, with economic advantages overriding negative ecological and social impacts.

In addition to all of the above is the introduction of chemical fertilisers and pesticides to enhance crop production and output.

Tourism

Contributing to the environmental and cultural degradation of the Himalaya is tourism. For centuries pilgrims made the long arduous trek on foot to the holy sites of the mountains, having little or no impact on the fragile ecosystem of the Himalayan zone. However, since roads have been blasted through the mountains, linking the holy sites with the plains, the situation has changed dramatically. The vast numbers of pilgrims to Badrinath are having diabolical impacts, not only ecologically, but culturally. The *chattis* (simple wooden lodgings which once accommodated pilgrims en route to the shrines) have vanished, replaced by ugly tourist guesthouses and hotels.

The negative impacts of tourism are also felt in more secular destinations such as the hill stations of Mussoorie and Darjeeling. Up to 700,000 visitors converge on Mussoorie annually, and unrestricted development has left a legacy of ugly modern highrise hotels strung across the ridgetop and visible 34 km distant from Dehra Dun. The population of Darjeeling has multiplied exponentially over recent years, and the town's ability to cope with this influx has proven to be inadequate, with chronic water shortages and power failures. With tourism as a major revenue earner, it is difficult to envisage an end to the rapid development which is disfiguring the landscape and pushing resources to the limit.

Critics also condemn the lack of foresight which saw the development of tourist amenities within the heart of Corbett National Park, with no attempt to ensure that they blend into the environment. The increase in trekking and mountaineering expeditions to the Himalaya following WWII has also taken its toll on this region. Some measures have been taken to preserve wilderness areas, for example, entry to the Nanda Devi Sanctuary is now prohibited.

In 1974, when Ladakh was officially opened to tourism, a group of seven Germans straggled into Leh and stayed at the only guesthouse. In about 20 years, over 100 guesthouses have been built in and near Leh, catering for the estimated 20,000 visitors each year. The political problems in Kashmir have also added considerably to the number of visitors who choose the safer areas of Ladakh and Zanskar. This continues to put enormous strains on the local environment, and the infrastructure: there is now obvious pollution, ineffective sewerage, and unsafe drinking water.

The almost 4000m high Rohtang Pass, in Himachal Pradesh is also suffering from the effects of pollution arising from the increasing number of visitors to this region. The pass is littered with rubbish which is carried by the high-velocity winds across the region, or finds its way into the Beas River, which has its source here.

The Green Revival

The Himalayan Environment Trust (see the boxed section on Wildlife Conservation Societies under Flora & Fauna) has initiated a project to protect the Gangotri Basin of Uttarakhand, identified as the most polluted area in the Himalaya.

Each year 250,000 pilgrims visit the sacred shrine, in addition to over 70 mountaineering expeditions and some 25,000 trekkers. A staggering 50 tonnes of rubbish and refuse lies on the trails in the vicinity of the sacred village, and between it and the source of the Ganges above it, much of which finds its way into the river system. Trees and bushes flanking the main trail up to the source of the Ganges have been stripped for fuel for campfires, and the environs of the basin have been denuded of forest cover.

The objectives of the Gangotri Conservation Project are to remove rubbish from the area with the assistance of the Indian army, mountaineering organisations and adventure tour operators, and to commence intensive

afforestation of the area. In addition, the building of rubbish dumps, the supply of more ecologically sound forms of fuel to the region, the training of officers to enforce environmental regulations and the establishment of sustainable eco-development programmes in local villages, along with other measures, will be introduced.

The trust has prepared a Code of Conduct for visitors to the Himalayan region; see the Society & Conduct section later in this chapter for details.

FLORA & FAUNA
Flora
Despite the hostile nature of the Himalayan region and its inability to support large populations, its traditional inhabitants learnt to live in harmony with their environment. The forests serve not only a material function in their provision of sustenance, fuel, timber for the construction of houses and implements, and herbs for the treatment of various ailments, but also a cultural function, forming the basis of many folk songs and ritual offerings to the gods in the form of wood, flowers and leaves.

The vegetation of the western and eastern Himalaya differs markedly: the greater and more evenly distributed humidity in the eastern zone facilitates the growth of trees, which are found up to higher elevations – over 4500m – than in the western region, where the tree line is reached at just over 3500m. Some of the tallest trees in India can be found in the eastern Himalaya.

Himalayan flora is heavily influenced by the flora of the more ancient mountains of China. Over subsequent aeons, mutations, climatic changes and concomitant vegetational adaptation (and no doubt extinction in some cases), as well as glacial movement, gave rise to the present-day vegetational wealth of the Himalaya. It is interesting to note that glaciation had no impact on the lower reaches of the Himalaya, and the Himalayan foothills therefore remain repositories of flora which can be traced back *beyond* the ice age, rendering them some of the most ancient species of vegetation on earth.

Western Himalaya There is a higher representation of conifers in the western Himalaya than the eastern Himalaya.

Subtropical The subtropical zone extends from only a few hundred metres above sea level to around 1200m, encompassing the region known as the *terai*, which extends from Kashmir to Bhutan. It includes the Siwalik Range which extends from western Himachal Pradesh to the region of the Corbett Tiger Reserve in Uttarakhand.

Forests of the hardwood sal *(Shorea robusta)* are found at lower elevations. A rare type of palm *(Phoenix acaulis)*, two forms of ground orchid belonging to the genera *Zeuxine* and *Eulophia*, and swamp forests and grasslands (savanna) are also found in this zone. Likewise the evergreen Indian laburnum *(Cassia fistula)*, which bears vivid yellow flowers between April and June is found here. Between March and May, the deciduous coral tree *(Erythrina suberosa)*, bears vivid scarlet flowers in clumps at the end of its branches. The easily identifiable flame of the forest *(Butea monosperma)* bears distinctive and vivid orange flowers between February and May.

Shrubs include the dhaula *(Woodfordia fruticosa)*, which can be seen in the lower reaches of Uttarakhand, and the evergreen bansa *(Justicia adhatoda)*, the leaves of which are used in traditional preparations to cure respiratory complaints.

The easily identifiable hemp *(Cannabis sativa)* is often seen growing on the perimeters of cultivated land and road edges. Hemp has, of course, a myriad of uses other than the more obvious one, and is used in the making of rope and the weaving of cloth.

Temperate The temperate zone extends in the western Himalaya from 1200m to the tree line. As you ascend above 1500m, a notable change is evident in the vegetation. The tropical vegetation of the lower zones gives way to dark and dank forests of oak, birch, mag-

nolia and laurel. Found between 1800 and 2400m are the deodar *(Cedrus deodara)* and blue pine *(Pinus wallichiana)*. Above 2400m is the spruce *(Picea smithiana)*, yew *(Taxus baccata)* and cypress *(Cupressus torulosa)*, and higher still, growing up to the tree line,

The *Cedrus deodora*, or deodar, is common in mid-temperate zones of the Himalaya.

The *Taxus baccata*, or yew, grows at altitudes above 2400m in the western Himalaya.

is the Himalayan fir *(Abies spectabilis)*, found between 2850 and 3600m. A high-altitude variety of oak *(Querucus semecarpifolia)* is found between 2250 and 2850m. There are substantial forests of birch *(Betula utilis)* in the Nanda Devi Sanctuary.

Floral species include the fragrant white columbine *(Aquilegia fragrans)*, which grows profusely in Himachal Pradesh and is found up to 3500m. Found at slightly lower elevations is the columbine *(Aquilegia pubiflora)*, which has bell-shaped purplish-white flowers. The wild strawberry *(Fragaria nubicola)* is a welcome find along the middle-altitude trekking trails of Garhwal. The Himalayan mayapple *(Podophyllum hexandrum)*, found at high altitudes throughout the western Himalaya, has long been revered for its medicinal properties.

The ethereal *Ainsliaea aptera* flowers prior to the monsoon between March and May and is found up to 2800m. The dainty pink flowers are suspended from long, slim stems.

There are numerous species of rhododendron in this zone. Between March and May the hillsides are ablaze with the deep red

flowers of the most common tree rhododendron, or *Rhododendron arboreum*. Belonging to the same species is the *Rhododendron lepidotum*, a hardy shrub which clings to rocky ground and can be found both above and below the treeline.

Alpine Beyond the treeline, up to the snow line, taller stands of forest give way to low shrubs, Himalayan grasses and flowering herbs. As the snows begin to melt at the end of the long winter, the high-altitude grazing grounds known as *bugyals*, and valleys, are carpeted with a multitude of wildflowers which remain in bloom until early summer. With the onset of the monsoon, in July, a second and even more vibrant flowering occurs, which extends until the end of the monsoon, in late August or early September. Some of the varieties found at these higher elevations include anemones, forget-me-nots, dwarf irises, dwarf rhododendrons, primulas, delphiniums and ranunculus, among others. The beautiful blue poppy *(Meconopsis aculeata)* flowers during the monsoon on the bugyals.

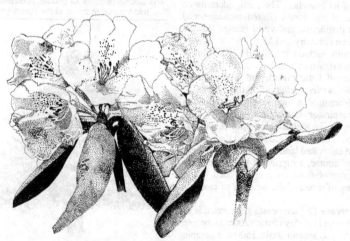

Many varieties of rhododendron are found in both temperate and alpine zones throughout the Himalaya.

Distributed throughout the Himalaya is the common *Primula denticulata*, with its distinctive tooth-edged leaves and pinkish or purplish blooms which grow in densely compacted heads. It can be found growing up to elevations of 4200m, and flowers between April and June.

Eastern Himalaya In the eastern Himalaya, the vegetation profile extends from tropical (just above sea level to around 1000m), subtropical (from around 900m to 1800m), temperate (from 1800m to 3500m), subalpine (3500 to 4500m) and alpine (4500 to 5500m – the snow line). It hosts an astonishing array of flora – over 4000 different species – some of which can be found in the western Himalaya, and some of which bear elements of Chinese and Malaysian influence. There are over 30 species of rhododendron, including the *Rhododendron niveum* which is the state tree of Sikkim, and more than 600 species of orchid. Orchids are found up to 2100m, although some hardy species thrive at up to 3000m.

Subtropical & Tropical Tropical evergreen forests found up to elevations of 800m are repositories of unique biodiversity. Much of the rich vegetation at these lower elevations has been cleared for pasture and cultivation. In the next vegetational zone are the subtropical grasslands and forests, found between 900 and 1800m. As in the western Himalaya, the tree rhododendron is found in this zone. Also found here are forests of oak, walnut and sal, and some varieties of orchid.

Temperate Temperate rainforests are found between 1800 and 3500m, and include varieties of conifer (including India's only deciduous conifer, *Larix griffithiana*), magnolia, rhododendron, birch, maple and oak.

Subalpine & Alpine The subalpine zone extends from 3500 to 4500m, and supports varieties of rhododendron and ground flora

such as primulas and anemones. Beyond the treeline and up to the snow line (5500m), tree species give way to low shrubs, lichens, mosses and alpine flowers such as the tiny *Rhododendron nivale*, edelweiss *(Leontopodium himalaynum)*, and varieties of primula, while the arid desertscapes found over 4500m support the hardy androsace.

Fauna
Some species of wildlife are distributed across the Himalaya, although there are regional variations.

In the temperate regions of the eastern Himalaya, many animals bear distinct relationships with those of the countries extending to the east, such as Myanmar (Burma) and southern China, while others bear affinities with those which live in the moist, tropical regions of Asia, such as fruit bats, flying foxes and the oriental squirrel. This zone forms the zoogeographical region known as the Oriental region.

The Oriental influence is negligible in the western Himalaya. Here, distinct Indian species are found. Some of these are also found on the Indian plains. As well, mammals bearing relationships to those found beyond India's borders to the north and west, with a greater European influence, are found here.

Mammals of the Tibetan Plateau In the icy and desolate conditions which prevail on the Tibetan plateau, which incorporates the eastern regions of Ladakh, mammals have to survive in frequently freezing conditions, with scant vegetation and minimal rainfall. Here can be found the yak, braving out the elements at elevations of some 4200 to over 6000m, and the largest mammal to be found in these icy areas. Other species include the bharal, or blue sheep, which is rarely found below 3660m in winter, and in summer, ascends as high as 4880m, its blue coat making it almost indistinguishable from the rocks and boulders which litter its grazing grounds.

Although the habitat of the beautiful (and endangered) snow leopard is vast, extending across the entire Himalaya Range and further north into Tibet and Central Asia, it is rarely seen, as it inhabits one of the most desolate places on earth, on the high Tibetan plateau some 3660 to 3965m above sea level. In the winter months, with the retreat of the mammals on which it preys to lower elevations, the snow leopard can be found at elevations as low as 1850m. The snow leopard has a soft grey lightly spotted coat and a pure white underbelly. The Tibetan antelope, or chiru, is sometimes found in the northern and eastern regions of Ladakh.

Deer Below the treeline in the western Himalaya are various forms of deer, including the barking deer, or muntjac, and the sambar (the largest Indian deer with correspondingly imposing horns). Both are found in densely forested hill areas. In India, found only in or near the Kashmir Valley, is the Kashmir stag, or hangul. In summer it is found in regions extending from 2700m up to the snow line. The diminutive, and endangered, musk deer is found in forested regions extending across central and north-eastern Asia.

Primates Mammals belonging to the monkey family found below the treeline include the common rhesus macaque, with its distinctive reddish fur on its loins and rump, the Assamese macaque, found in the Himalayan foothills extending eastwards from Mussoorie to Assam, and the long-limbed black-faced langur, found throughout India. The langurs found in the Himalayan regions are generally heavier than their cousins from the plains, weighing up to 21 kg, and have bushier whiskers.

The Cat Family Apart from the snow leopard, mentioned earlier, other mammals belonging to the cat family found in the Himalayan regions are the lynx and Pallas' cat. The lynx is found in the upper reaches of the Indus Valley and parts of Ladakh. Pallas' cat, with its distinctive low, broad head and low-set ears, about the size of your average domestic moggy, is found in Ladakh. The forests and grasslands surrounding Dhikala, in the Corbett Tiger Reserve, are home to the Indian tiger.

Varieties of civets, closely related to the cat family, found in the Himalayan foothills include the common palm civet, which is distributed right across the length of the lower ranges from Kashmir to Assam, as well as in most regions of the Indian peninsula, and the Himalayan palm civet, distinguishable from the common variety by its white whiskers and plain (as opposed to spotted or striped) coat.

The lynx, found in parts of the western Himalaya, is an endangered species.

Pandas & Bears The red panda, or cat bear, is found only in the eastern Himalaya in India, although its habitat extends further east through the upper reaches of Myanmar and southern China. This cute little nocturnal fellow spends its nights foraging for food and its days sleeping high up in the treetops. Its coat is a distinctive reddish chestnut, while its face is white, but has a reddish stripe on the forehead. Its tail is ringed with red bands.

The brown bear, found in the western Himalaya, may be seen above the treeline. It is distinguishable from its cousin the Himalayan black bear, which is found across the Himalaya, by its distinctive brown coat and

The endangered Himalayan brown bear dwells in the higher altitudes of the western Himalaya.

heavier build. The black bear inhabits steep and densely forested hillsides. It may be found near the treeline in summer, but retreats well below the treeline in winter.

The Dog Family The red fox and the hill fox are both found in the Indian Himalaya. The hill fox enjoys a diet of smaller mammals including marmots and Himalayan mouse-hares. Belonging to the same family is the predatory wolf, which is found in parts of Kashmir and Ladakh, and follows the seasonal migration of flocks and game on which it preys in winter, dining on smaller mam-

mals and birds in the summer. Wolves have also been known to attack and devour humans.

Goats & Antelopes The ibex is found in the western Himalaya above the treeline. The male stands to a height of about one metre, and has a creamy, slightly brown-tinged coat in winter, which becomes darker brown in summer, and a great beard. In spring, ibex retreat below the snow line in search of fresh grass. Also belonging to the goat family is the Himalayan tahr, which is found across the Indian Himalaya at elevations of between 2500 and 4400m. It has backward tilting short horns and a dense coat of long flowing hair, including a distinctive ruff. The markhor is found below the snow line in Kashmir, its absence of underwool restricting it from venturing to the icy regions further north. Bucks stand to one metre and have a long flowing beard and mane, and enormous horns which bear distinct differences across this species, according to locality, from tight corkscrew forms to open spirals.

The serow belongs to the goat-antelope family and can be found in both the eastern and western Himalaya. It is a thick-set animal whose coat comes in a variety of

The red fox can be recognised by the white tip on its tail.

The ibex inhabits higher altitudes than any other Himalayan mountain goat.

hues, from almost black, to red. It is usually found in temperate zones between 1850 and 3050m in heavily wooded gorges. Also belonging to this family is the smaller goral, with small, backward-tending horns. The grey goral is found in the western Himalaya, but the brown goral is found only in the eastern Himalaya and Assam. The goral inhabits elevations of from 900 to 2750m, although has been seen above the treeline, and the grey goral is often seen in the environs of hill stations.

Belonging to the same group is the heavy-set takin, found in limited numbers in the eastern Himalaya. It is found at temperate elevations and inhabits densely wooded regions.

Other Mammals Mammals found both in the lower reaches of the Himalaya and throughout the Indian peninsula include the Asiatic jackal, common red fox, Indian hare and Indian crested porcupine.

Herds of wild Indian elephant can also be seen at the Corbett National Park, as well as the Rajaji National Park. The low-lying savanna on the northern plains of West Bengal is one of the last homes of the Indian rhinoceros.

Birdlife There is a profuse variety of birdlife in the Indian Himalaya. As with its mammal population, the species in the eastern Himalaya have a distinct relationship to species of the Oriental region. This influence becomes less marked as you proceed further westwards, until it is supplanted by birdlife of the Palaearctic regions.

The Himalaya is the home of a variety of endemic bird species, including broadbills, finfoots, honey guides and parrotbills. The chir pheasant and mountain quail, both belonging to the pheasant family, are found only in the Himalayan regions of India, as is the cardueline finch, which is found below the treeline in moist temperate forest conditions.

In the western Himalaya are 14 species which can be traced back *beyond* the period of extensive glaciation which occurred during the Pleistocene epoch. These include two species of bullfinch, the woodsnipe, Himalayan pied woodpecker, pied ground

The Yeti

A discussion of the animal life of the Himalaya would be incomplete without reference to its most enigmatic and mysterious inhabitant – the Yeti. *Yeti* is a Sherpa word, and the yeti invokes collective fear and awe among both Sherpas and Tibetans. Who or what is the yeti? Various theories have been proposed about the Himalaya's most infamous inhabitant. It has been suggested that the yeti, or Abominable Snowman, is a link between homosapiens and our primate ancestors. Sceptics have suggested it's a case of mistaken identity – the yeti is nothing more than a Himalayan bear.

So how do you identify a yeti? Completely covered with hair, the yeti reputedly has feet spanning some 30 cm long and 15 cm wide, and is almost 2½m tall. It is a malevolent creature possessing supernatural powers and is known for its blood-curdling call, although yetis have been known to provide sustenance to meditating hermits. A little known fact about the yeti is its penchant for chocolate. According to Sonam Wangyal, a respected mountaineer and climber of Mt Everest, he and his climbing team witnessed a gigantic hairy creature of humanoid appearance stalking across the snow near their camp. After the creature had disappeared from sight, the stunned witnesses went to the spot where it had last been spotted. While no evidence of the creature remained (footprints had been concealed beneath a heavy snowfall), on their return to the campsite, they discovered to their amazement the inexplicable absence of a large box of chocolates!

While this event took place in the Nanda Devi Sanctuary of Garhwal, most of the sightings of creatures conforming to yeti dimensions have been almost wholly restricted to the eastern Himalaya. If there is one thing that all mountain inhabitants believe about this creature, it is that

thrush, blackthroated jay and smoky leaf warbler.

Birds of Prey Birds of prey include the Himalayan golden eagle, an awe-inspiring sight as it soars overhead in search of prey. Its enormous size – up to one metre in length – cruel talons and beak enable it to prey on the young of even large creatures such as lambs and musk deer fawns. It can be found well above the treeline, even as far north as the snow line in summer months. The Himalayan bearded vulture, or lammergier, is less massive but no less spectacular, found at elevations above 1200m up to an extraordinary 7000m. It is notable for bearing aloft

The golden eagle has a golden brown plumage on its back.

The lammergier, a vulture, has a pale breast and black feathers around its bill.

it should be avoided at all costs. This is not some long-lost ancestor who will be readily welcomed into the family home for a cup of chai!

While it is only comparatively recently that the yeti has aroused the imaginations of those of the west, finding its way into the distinguished pages of Britain's _Times_ newspaper in 1931, the Tibetan Buddhist saint and poet, Milarepa, who lived in the 11th and 12th centuries, recounts in one of the songs of his _Mgur Abum_ (Hundred Thousand Songs of Milarepa) of a strange Himalayan-dwelling creature which is referred to as _mitre_.

Can the legend of the yeti be easily discounted? The Himalaya encompasses some of the most desolate and inaccessible environs on the face of the earth. Of those creatures which science has, in its inimitable way, tracked down and recorded, there are vast gaps in our knowledge of their habits and habitats. It is not outside the realms of possibility that there are not just yetis, but other creatures living in remote and inaccessible regions of the Himalaya of which we have no knowledge.

While the yeti might easily be dismissed as simply the stuff of legend and lore, actual photographs of enormous footprints taken by the respected and renowned mountaineer Eric Shipton will give sceptics food for thought. Photographs of unidentifiable large footprints and sightings of a large hairy beast by members of a mountaineering expedition to Annapurna in Nepal have further compounded the mystery.

So what do you do if you are confronted by a yeti? Well, unless you're in possession of a decent supply of chocolates or resemble a wandering ascetic, the best strategy is to run like hell! ∎

large bones which are dropped mid-flight from heights of up to 50m above the ground, whereupon they are shattered on the rocks, exposing the marrow on which this bird feeds.

Pheasants Found in the eastern Himalaya are various types of Himalayan pheasant, including the blood pheasant, an exotic bird with crimson-coloured blotches on its plumage and a crimson throat, which can be seen near the snow line. Belonging to the same family, and also found only in the eastern regions, are the peacock pheasant and eared pheasant. In the densely forested regions of the western Himalaya is found the Impeyan or Himalayan monal pheasant, which is resplendent, in the males at least, with a beautifully coloured plumage of green, purple and blue. The western tragopan, a type of horned pheasant, is a highly endangered species found only in the western Himalaya. Also found in the western Himalaya is the koklas pheasant, which can be seen on the forested slopes of hillsides. Oddly, it is absent in the eastern Indian Himalaya, but reappears further east in China and Mongolia.

Distributed across the lower regions of the Himalaya are various types of kaleej, also belonging to the Himalayan pheasant family, which feature a bright crimson head and a deep black plumage in the male, and russet-brown in the female. In the extreme north-eastern Himalaya is the eared pheasant, a large bird with a blue-grey plumage, which is sometimes found in the vicinity of gompas where it has been known to take food offered by monks.

In Sikkim, the peacock pheasant is found only at lower elevations in tropical jungle.

Other Species The redbilled blue magpie, found at lower elevations between Himachal Pradesh and further east to eastern Sikkim, is frequently seen around hill stations. The tiny redbilled leiothrix has a distinctive yellow throat and breast, black wings trimmed with yellow and red and, as its name suggests, a bright red bill. It is often seen

around tea plantations. The rare orange-rumped honey guide is notable for its ability to digest beeswax. Its curious name is derived from its usefulness in guiding animals and humans to honeycombs, flying before them and uttering distinctive calls which lead honey seekers to the object of their search. After the honey has been extracted by these guests, the bird completes the meal, dining on the wax, remnants of honey and larvae. It is found between 1500 and 3500m across the Himalaya.

Migratory Birds Apart from its endemic species, the Himalaya also hosts a temporary population of some 300 transient species which migrate from Central Asia to the Indian peninsula during the autumn and spring. For many years ornithologists doubted the ability of birds to cross over the top of the high Himalaya, theorising that birds penetrated the range through river valleys. However, it has now been discovered that not only large birds, but even some mid-size to small species fly *over* the Himalaya on their annual migration. The return journey poses more difficult challenges, and many come to grief traversing the desolate and freezing glaciers of the upper realms of the Himalaya. These high-altitude migrators include ducks, geese and cranes. Even crows and finches have been observed above 7000m.

There are also many species which breed high up in the Himalaya, and descend to the foothills or the Indian peninsula in winter. Wall creepers generally don't venture far beyond the southern perimeters of the foothills, and the beautifully plumed grandala retreats only down to about 3000m in winter. Various types of flycatchers, thrush, woodcock and the blue chat migrate in winter to southern India. Some, such as the woodcock, fly virtually nonstop – a journey of some 2000 km!

Some species of birds found in the southern regions of the Indian peninsula bear distinct resemblances to or are almost identical with those found in the Himalaya. A case in point is the laughing thrush, which is found across the Himalaya, and nowhere else on the peninsula other than in the hills region of southern India!

Endangered Species

Human encroachment is now taking its toll, in both direct and indirect ways, and the Himalaya now has the highest concentration of endangered mammals in India. The high rate of endemism makes protection of these species critical.

The greatest threat to the larger wild inhabitants of the Himalaya is poachers. The record prices set for the pelts of some of these magnificent creatures in the world market due to continued demand has resulted in the hunting of many of the Himalaya's wild animals almost to the point of extinction. And the more rare these animals become, the higher are the prices fetched by unscrupulous fur traders. In Kathmandu, a coat made from the fur of the highly endangered snow leopard can fetch up to US$3000. Other protected species which are destined to end their days draped around the shoulders of the rich and stupid include Tibetan wolves and the highly prized lynx. The musk deer is one of the most highly sought creatures in the Himalaya, with the lucrative trade in the musk gland, used in the preparation of perfume, affording a keen incentive for the slaying of this beast. Some measures have been taken to protect this creature, such as the establishment of the Kedarnath musk deer sanctuary in Uttarakhand.

Hunting of protected and/or endangered species for sport or meat continues unabated in the high Himalaya, and previously inaccessible regions are now within easy distance of roads which have been pushed ever further up into the hills. The border tensions between India and China have resulted in the dispatchment of troops to these remote regions, and hunting is a pleasant recreational diversion from border patrol. The problem is exacerbated by the supply of firearms to local people sent out by army personnel to obtain meat for the army encampments. The temptation to dispatch endangered species must prove practically irresistible to villagers who barely manage to scratch a subsistence living.

The beautiful red panda of Sikkim is highly sought after by illegal animal dealers. It is easily tamed, and sought by some keepers of private zoos around the world.

Animals threatened due to illegal hunting include the markhor, a type of wild goat, the ibex, the tahr and the rare hangul, or Kashmir stag, which has also suffered from human encroachment on its habitat. Populations of the hangul are estimated as low as 200 animals, down from an estimated 5000 in the 1920s. Populations of the urial, or shapu, which is found in Ladakh, have declined drastically due to hunting by army personnel in this region. The Tibetan antelope, or chiru, no longer ventures into this region, where it was once found, due to the military presence here. Also no longer found in Ladakh is the Tibetan gazelle. The military is also responsible for the reduction in numbers of the rare Sikkim stag. The heads of wild ass (kyang) are at risk of being more frequently seen adorning the space above mantelpieces than on the beast in question, and the stag is also hunted for its meat.

The elimination of some species is facilitated by the reduction in the species on which they prey. The Tibetan wolf falls into this category.

Endangered species of birdlife include the western tragopan, a type of pheasant which is found in the western Himalaya, which is now a totally protected species. The Darjeeling zoo has announced plans to try to breed this bird in captivity. It's probably too late for the mountain quail, also a member of the pheasant family, which hasn't been spotted since the 1870s. It resides now only in a stuffed capacity in a few select museums in England and the USA. It was discovered in Uttarakhand. The honey guide is another rare species of bird.

The establishment of wildlife reserves and sanctuaries has gone some way in stabilising animal numbers, but more reserves need to be created. Unfortunately for some creatures, such as the snow leopard, the only chance of survival may be the breeding of these animals in captivity. Unfortunately, success rates are very low (see the West Bengal Hills chapter), and even if successfully bred, there is no guarantee that these animals can be successfully returned to the wild. Project Tiger has been established to arrest the diminishing number of tigers in India. The red panda has also proved to be extremely difficult to breed in captivity.

A new agreement between China and India may help stop the lucrative trade in tiger parts.

National Parks & Wildlife Sanctuaries

National parks and wildlife sanctuaries are legion in the Indian Himalaya. Some, such as the Dachigam Wildlife Sanctuary in Kashmir, represent the last and only habitat of some of their inhabitants. Others, such as Corbett Tiger Reserve, have a well developed infrastructure for visitors including a range of accommodation and safaris. Others were originally founded as game reserves, with the interests of hunters, not the protection of animals, as the primary motivation for their establishment, and little has been done to enhance the preservation prospects of their inhabitants.

Dachigam Wildlife Sanctuary (Jammu & Kashmir)
This sanctuary is in a very scenic valley with a large meandering river. The surrounding mountain slopes are possibly the last home of the rare Kashmir stag (hangul), as well as black and brown bears. There are also populations of musk deer. The instability in Kashmir in recent years has seriously endangered the wildlife of Dachigam. The sanctuary is 22 km by road from Srinagar, and is certainly worth a visit. The best time to visit is between June and July.

Kanji Game Reserve & Hemis High Altitude National Park (Ladakh & Zanskar)
The Kanji Game Reserve is not far from Kargil; the Hemis National Park is accessible from Hemis. These are

inhabited by some of the Himalaya's most rare and endangered species, such as the ibex and snow leopard. These parks and others in this region are generally for the protection of animals and not for the pleasure of humans.

Great Himalayan National Park (Himachal Pradesh) This park encompasses some 1700 sq km to the south-east of Kullu, and is known for its abundant birdlife. It also has a good representative population of mammals found across the western Himalaya. The best time to visit is between April and June, and September and October, outside the monsoon season.

Daran Ghati Sanctuary (Himachal Pradesh) The Daran Ghati Sanctuary is accessible from Rampur, and encompasses 167 sq km. Here, there are various species of pheasant, as well as musk deer, rarely seen bears and leopards, and goral. The best time to visit is between April and July, and September and October.

Kanawer Sanctuary (Himachal Pradesh) Accessible from Manikaran is the Kanawer Sanctuary. With an elevation profile extending from 1800m to above the treeline, a range of mammals can be seen here, including the serow, tahr, goral, musk deer and bharal, with occasional sightings of leopards. It is best visited between May and June, and September and October.

Kalatope Wildlife Sanctuary (Himachal Pradesh) This small sanctuary is in the Chamba Valley, only 8½ km from Dalhousie. It is home to a variety of species including the black bear and barking deer (muntjac), as well as an abundant variety of birdlife. The best time to visit is between May and June, and September and November.

Rakchhalm Chitkul Sanctuary (Himachal Pradesh) In the remote Kinnaur district, this sanctuary encompasses an area of 140 sq km. Special permission is required to visit this sanctuary.

Corbett Tiger Reserve (Uttarakhand) The Corbett National Park and adjacent Sonanadi Wildlife Sanctuary are collectively known as the Corbett Tiger Reserve. Covering an area of 1318 sq km, it was established in 1936 as India's first national park. Encompassing part of the Siwalik Range and traversed by the Ramganga River, in which anglers test their wits against the mahseer, Corbett is famous of course for its tigers, and boasts a population of one tiger per five sq km. Other mammals seen here include barking deer and sambar, and there is also abundant birdlife. The reserve has come under some criticism for permitting the construction of a hydroelectric project which submerged one-tenth of the park, severely disrupting the traditional migration route of herds of wild elephant. The tiger reserve is open between 15 November and 15 June.

Kedarnath Sanctuary (Uttarakhand) Kedarnath Sanctuary covers an area of 957 sq km, and contains populations of musk deer, tahr, serow and leopard. It is in Chamoli district, in Garhwal.

Nanda Devi Sanctuary (Uttarakhand) The beautiful Nanda Devi Sanctuary covers an area of 630 sq km in Chamoli district, in Garhwal, in the upper watershed of the Alaknanda River. It is presently closed to visitors due to the detrimental environmental impact of the large number of trekking and mountaineering expeditions which passed through the region. The sanctuary is inhabited by serow, musk deer, bharal and goral.

Valley of Flowers (Uttarakhand) The Valley of Flowers, known as the 'garden on top of the world' was designated as a national park in 1981. It is accessible from Govind Ghat, a small village on the main Josimath to Badrinath road, and its profuse wildflowers are best seen during the monsoon, from July to early September, particularly between mid-July and mid-August.

Rajaji National Park (Uttarakhand) The Rajaji National Park encompasses 820 sq km and is easily accessible from Haridwar or Rishikesh, and is known for its herds of wild elephants. Other mammals include the occasional tiger, as well as sloth bears, sambar, chital, barking deer and jungle fowl. The sanctuary is open between 15 November and 15 June.

Jaldhapara Wildlife Sanctuary (West Bengal) The Jaldhapara Wildlife Sanctuary, encompassing 116 sq km in Jalpaiguri district, 135 km from Siliguri, is home to the endangered Indian rhinoceros (rhinoceros unicornis). It is possible to take elephant safaris from Hollong, within the sanctuary. The sanctuary is open between October and May, but the best animal sightings are between March and April.

Buxa Tiger Reserve (West Bengal) Accessible from either Jaldhapara or Siliguri is the newly designated Buxa Tiger Reserve, covering 761 sq km. The reserve was recently adopted into Project Tiger, and forms part of the migration corridor for elephants between Bhutan and Assam. It is best visited between November and April.

Kangchenjunga National Park (Sikkim) Entrance into the heart of this magnificent alpine wilderness is prohibited to visitors, although treks

along the Dzongri Trail from Yuksom enter the southern periphery. The park is bordered on the north by the Zemu Glacier; to the west rears the massive bulk of Kangchenjunga and the Nepal Peak. The southern boundary is formed by the Chhurong and Bokto rivers.

Fauna found in the park include the beautiful snow leopard, the muntjac, or barking deer, the Himalayan black bear, and the red panda, among other species. Much of this pristine wilderness remains unexplored, and harbours a profuse variety of flora and bird species.

Fambonglho Wildlife Sanctuary (Sikkim) The Fambonglho Wildlife Sanctuary lies only 25 km from Gangtok, and it is possible to visit it with a special permit issued by the District Forestry Officer in Gangtok. The Himalayan black bear and red panda are found here, together with a wide variety of other animal and bird species. The sanctuary is open between October and April.

GOVERNMENT & POLITICS

India has a parliamentary system of government, with an upper house and a lower house. There are also state governments. There is a strict division between the activities handled by the states and by the national government. The police force, education, agriculture and industry are reserved for the state governments. Certain other areas are jointly administered by the two levels of government.

In the May 1996 national elections, the Congress (I) Party, which has ruled India for all but four years since Independence in 1948, lost its majority. At the time of writing, the Hindu nationalist Bharatiya Janata Party (BJP) had been invited to form a coalition government. However, because no party has a majority, a period of instability is likely.

Ladakh & Zanskar

The state of Jammu & Kashmir has also faced other internal disputes, as inhabitants of districts with a distinct cultural and ethnic identity such as Ladakh and Kargil also struggle to find a voice in the troubled region. In 1995, the Leh Autonomous Hill Development Council was formed according to the terms of a presidential order. The

formation of the council represents the culmination of a struggle against what has been perceived as regional discrimination, which first found expression in violent uprisings in 1969. Relations between the Buddhist and Muslim communities have been strained since 1989 when the majority Buddhists imposed a social boycott on the Muslims. However, tensions between the Buddhist and Muslim communities have eased with the establishment of the council, with members from both the Ladakh Buddhist Association and the Ladakh Muslim Association having dual control.

The district of Kargil has not been agitating for an increase in autonomy, the majority Muslim community arguing that geographically and economically (and no doubt culturally) the district is linked to the Kashmir Valley (with its Muslim majority). However, in Zanskar, a subdistrict under the administration of Kargil, problems derived from tension between the majority Buddhist inhabitants of Zanskar and the predominantly Muslim inhabitants of Kargil remain to date unresolved. In mid-1995, there was a local political protest in Zanskar, and in order to draw attention to their cause, foreign trekkers were discouraged from trekking in the region. It now seems that the situation has been resolved and Zanskar leaders issued a statement in January 1996 that there will be no further impediment for foreign tourists who may 'come and go freely as before'.

Kashmir

Throughout the British era, India had retained many 'princely states', and incorporating these into independent India proved to be a considerable headache. Guarantees of a substantial measure of independence encouraged most of them to accept inclusion in either Pakistan or India, but at the time of independence, there were still three holdouts. One was Kashmir, a predominantly Muslim state with a Hindu maharaja. In October 1948, the maharaja had still not opted for India or Pakistan when a rag-tag Pathan (Pakistani) army crossed the border, intent on racing to Srinagar and annexing Kashmir without provoking real India-Pakistan conflict. Unfortunately for the Pakistanis, the Pathans had been inspired to mount their invasion by the promise of plunder, and they did so much plundering on their way that India had time to rush troops to Srinagar and prevent the town's capture. The indecisive maharaja finally opted for India, provoking the first, although brief, India-Pakistan war.

The UN was eventually persuaded to step in and keep the two sides apart but the issue of Kashmir has remained a central cause for disagreement and conflict between the two countries ever since. With its overwhelming Muslim majority and its geographic links to Pakistan, many people were inclined to support Pakistan's claims to the region. But by then, Kashmir had become a *cause célèbre* in the Congress Party and, despite a promised plebiscite, India has, until quite recently, consistently avoided holding such a vote. To this day, India and Pakistan are divided in this region by a demarcation line (known as the Line of Actual Control) yet neither side agrees that this constitutes the official border.

The Kashmir issue again moved onto centre stage during the early 1990s with demonstrations on both sides of the Line of Actual Control and an alarming increase in Jammu & Kashmir Liberation Front (JKLF) guerrilla activities in the Vale of Kashmir. Pakistan was almost certainly involved in encouraging, funding and supplying arms to the militants on the Indian side of the 'border' (which, of course, is denied) but reports suggest that the over-zealous activities of the Indian Army are also partially responsible for the upsurge in militancy. Mutual suspicions brought India and Pakistan to the brink of war yet again in early 1992. It was averted in the nick of time following a meeting between the leaders of the two countries in Switzerland, and Pakistani Army intervention in preventing Kashmiri radicals from attempting to cross the Line of Actual Control.

Pakistan's support of the Kashmiri militants, on both sides of the 'border' and in the

Vale itself, have rebounded. By early 1992, Kashmiri militants and their supporters on both sides were demanding nothing short of *azadi*, independence from both India and Pakistan. In 1995, a split in the JKLF led to the removal of its chairperson and founder, Amanulla Khan, who was still advocating total accession with Pakistan despite popular calls for azadi. Yasin Malik, president of the Kashmir unit of the JKLF, took over. Yasin Malik has moved his headquarters to Srinagar where he plans to spearhead the movement towards the goal of azadi.

Clashes between the JKLF and the pro-Pakistan Hizbul Mujahideen have resulted in the deaths of dozens of their active workers. Calls for azadi by the JKLF have provoked sharp reprisals from the Hizbul Mujahideen, with the kidnapping of many of the former's top leaders.

Analysts suggest that the calls for azadi by the JKLF could pave the way for fresh dialogue with the Indian government. In this way, a measure of autonomy for the people of Kashmir could be attained within the framework of the Indian constitution. In July 1995 the governor general of Jammu & Kashmir, KV Krishna Rao, announced that elections to the state assembly would be held before 18 January, 1996, the date when President's Rule expires in the state. However, as with previous announcements, the election date has again been postponed.

The escalation of violence in Jammu & Kashmir makes visiting the the troubled region unviable. In 1995, a little-known guerilla group known as Al-Faran took six foreign tourists hostage – one was murdered and one escaped. At the time of writing, the other four hostages remained captive. Al-Faran has refused to relinquish the hostages until the Indian government has acceded to its demands to release political prisoners, which the government has to date refused to do.

Himachal Pradesh

Himachal Pradesh came into being as a separate hills province only eight months after India attained independence. In 1956 the region was declared a Union Territory, and in 1966 the remote districts of Lahaul & Spiti, previously part of the Punjab, were incorporated into the new state of Himachal Pradesh. In 1996, the Congress party was returned to power headed by Chief Minister Virbhadra Singh. In contrast to most other parts of India, here Congress polled well against the Bharatiya Janata Party (BJP).

Himachal Pradesh is predominantly populated by Hindus, but it has a rich ethnic and religious composition of Tibetan Buddhists, Muslims, Sikhs and some Christians. Although the Congress party retains power, there is widespread support for the radical BJP. In April 1994, in a poorly concealed endeavour to garner votes, the BJP whipped up anti-Tibetan refugee sentiments following unrest between Tibetan refugees and the Hindu community in McLeod Ganj, with agitators demanding the removal of the Tibetan refugees and their leader, the Dalai Lama. Conciliatory gestures were quickly offered to the Tibetan community and the Dalai Lama by the Congress party and local leaders, with the Dalai Lama imploring his people to express goodwill towards their Hindu neighbours. The potentially volatile situation was defused, although some analysts suggest that relations between the two communities remain strained.

Uttarakhand

Many of the inhabitants of the hills regions of the Indian Himalaya feel isolated from mainstream central government politics and removed from the decision-making processes of the plains. Hills inhabitants are poorly represented in the corridors of power; the eight districts which comprise Uttarakhand, for example, have only 19 elected members in the Vidhan Sabha (Legislative Assembly), as compared to 14 MLAs from the single district of Gorakhpur, on the Uttar Pradesh plains, although Uttarakhand's population is over five times greater.

Inhabitants of Uttarakhand have a long history of defiance and protest in the face of what they perceive as state and central gov-

ernment interference in the central Himalayan region, particularly in relation to commercial forestry. Present day unrest in the hills can be traced to state forestry policies of the late 19th century, which resulted in the traditional consumers of the forest being denied access to large tracts which had been earmarked for felling. To add insult to injury, hills inhabitants were compelled to supply unpaid labour, called *begar*, to forestry officials. Dissatisfaction resulted in the calling of a general strike in January 1921 which brought the administration to a standstill, and resulted in the abolition of the unpaid labour system. There was also widespread support for the nationwide independence movement, particularly in the Kumaon district, which came under direct British rule.

Today the battle against 'outside' rule has taken the form of agitation for a separate state. The inhabitants of Uttarakhand feel that the central and state (UP) governments are out of touch with the needs of those who reside in the hills. Separatists cite the geographical, cultural and traditional distinctions of the hills as compared to the plains, and propose a separate state named Uttarakhand, comprising the two Uttarakhand districts of Garhwal and Kumaon.

The alienation of the hills people was no better exemplified than in the decision to impose on the hills region of Uttar Pradesh the Mandal Commission's recommendation in 1994 to reserve 27% of government jobs for the socially and economically disadvantaged castes and classes. What was greeted as a positive reform on the plains resulted in violent unrest in the hills, where only 2% of inhabitants could be classified within the official designation.

In the early 1990s, the agitation for separate statehood was revived. Widespread *bhands* (strikes) were called, with separatist sentiments further inflamed by anti-statehood statements made by the Chief Minister of Uttar Pradesh, Mulayam Singh. A number of violent clashes with police have ensued, and agitation for a separate state continues.

West Bengal Hills

The establishment of autonomous hill councils does not always guarantee a successful resolution to the problems which arise due to the differing interests of ethnic groups which reside there.

In 1988, the Darjeeling Gorkha Hill Council was established in the hope that it would offer a solution to the widespread discontent of the majority Nepali-speaking community whose ancestors were brought to the district in the 1840s to clear land and work as labourers on the tea gardens. Friction was caused by the central and state government policy of only employing Bengali-speaking people for government positions, and this perceived discrimination resulted in widespread riots, the crippling of the administration and the loss of hundreds of lives. The Gurkhas were led by the Gurkha National Liberation Front (GNLF), with Subhash Ghising at the helm, who demanded a separate state to be known as Gurkhaland.

In December of 1988, the GNLF gained 26 of the 28 seats in the hill council, with Ghising retaining the leadership as the chairperson of the council. Separate statehood aspirations were relinquished in return for greater autonomy for the Darjeeling district, which remains part of West Bengal.

However, in mid-1995, widespread dissatisfaction with the council and its leader, Ghising, and accusations of financial mismanagement and even misappropriation of funds manifested in bhands and demonstrations across the district, led by the revived Akhil Bharatiya Gorkha League (ABGL). Calls for statehood, and even secession from India, are again resounding around the hills of West Bengal.

Sikkim

The state of Sikkim, annexed by the Indian Union in 1975, is enjoying unprecedented economic prosperity and stability. Prior to its merger with India, Sikkim was in economic decline due to the closure of trade routes with Tibet.

Central government assistance in the form of tax concessions has enabled the growth of flourishing industries, and Sikkim proudly boasts new roads, bridges and (more controversially) hydroelectric plants. It has not, however, all been smooth sailing for India's 22nd state. Corruption charges are currently pending against former chief minister Nar Bahadur Bhandari, who remained at the helm almost continuously from 1979 when his Sikkim Sangram Parishad (SSP) party came to power, until early 1994, when a vote of no confidence was passed, and he was ousted. Sikkim's current chief minister is Pawan Kumar Chamling, leader of the SSP.

ECONOMY

Despite the vagaries of the climate, the steep terrain, poor irrigation and the limited area available for cultivation, agriculture is still the mainstay of the Himalayan economy. Cereals such as rice, wheat and maize are generally grown to meet subsistence requirements. Vegetables are grown across the lower and middle hills, and form important cash crops. In Himachal Pradesh and most of the eastern Himalaya, over 90% of the working population are engaged in agriculture. In Uttarakhand, more than 80% depend on agriculture as the primary means of living, while in Jammu & Kashmir, the figure is about 42%. In contrast to other regions in India, in the Himalayan region, most of those people engaged in agriculture are owner-cultivators.

The Himalaya is also an important fruit-growing region. Fruits grown here include stone fruits such as apricots, peaches and plums, lemons, oranges, pineapples, and most importantly, apples. Climatic conditions in the western Himalaya are conducive to the growth of edible mushrooms. They are cultivated in Jammu & Kashmir, Himachal Pradesh and Uttarakhand. In the West Bengal hills region, tea cultivation is the most important economic activity. Animal husbandry is an important occupation in the Himalaya. The Gujar, Bakrawala and Gaddi tribes of the western Himalaya are traditionally semipastoralist, seminomadic herders of sheep, goats and buffalo, and also cultivate maize in the summer month, and wheat during the winter.

Cottage industries thrive throughout the Himalayan region. A network of cooperative stores in the major cities of India ensure a ready domestic market for many of the crafts and textiles of the Himalaya. Tourism is also a major money earner with large numbers of people deriving income from the associated industries of accommodation, food, tours and entertainment. Mountaineering and trekking provides employment for guides and porters.

Forestry-based industries are found throughout the Himalaya other than in the higher reaches where timber is scarce. Saw mills supply timber for local use, and in Himachal Pradesh, they have a thriving industry supplying fruit packing cases. A subsidiary of forestry-based industry is the production of turpentine and resin.

Across the Indian Himalaya, the hills inhabitants' exploitation of its wealth of herbs used in traditional medicine for economic purposes is minimal, with herbs being gathered only to supply domestic needs. This is, however, a lucrative revenue earner which hasn't escaped plains entrepreneurs, but economic returns to local inhabitants are

negligible. According to one estimate, production of herbal medicine in India represents a staggering eight billion dollar industry.

Industrial development has been minimal in the hills, although there are some heavy industries in the lower regions, including those at Jammu and Dehra Dun. The primary fruit growing industries have given rise to a healthy fruit preservation industry, including canning and the production and distribution of juices.

Since independence was attained in 1947, the government, in a massive modernisation and industrialisation drive, has increasingly turned towards the Himalaya to exploit its hydroelectricity potential. The first project was the Bhakra Nangal project of Bilsaspur (now part of Himachal Pradesh), which entailed the construction of the large Govind Sagar Dam. The project provides irrigation for 3.5 million hectares in Rajasthan and the Punjab, supplying 13,000 million units of energy. This was followed by the construction of the Pong Dam on the Beas River, which irrigates 1.62 million hectares down on the plains. Both of these projects required the resettlement of nearly 190,000 people and the submerging of nearly 50,000 hect-

Monasteries & Money

It is interesting to consider the economic role played by monasteries *(gompas)* in those areas where Tibetan Buddhism was established in the Himalayan region. Many gompas found themselves in a contradictory role, in which, while they were supposed to be concerned with matters spiritual, were compelled to adopt a secular role alleviating the economic distress of the inhabitants of surrounding regions. From around the mid 1500s, gompas served an economic role in the form of usury, trade, bartering and other commercial transactions. During periods of drought or famine, gompas distributed grain on a loan or exchange basis, and became progressively more affluent, evident in their large and ornate buildings, and beautiful religious statues and other paraphernalia, the construction and execution of which provided jobs for the laity. Affluent gompas procured large tracts of land, and in some cases, even entire villages, in the form of endowments. In some instances, land was made available to the laity under a crop-sharing basis.

The amount of power or degree of respect invested in gompas bears a direct relation to the degree of economic influence held over the laity. This is still evident in the regions of Ladakh and Spiti, where the gompas are very affluent and the gompas command a great deal of respect; conversely, in Lahaul and parts of Kinnaur, gompas are much poorer, and wield power to a much lesser degree over the populace. ■

ares of land. In Uttarakhand, two barrages have been built on the Yamuna and one of its tributaries, the Giri, with water being directed through a system of canals, tunnels and drops to increase velocity and generate electricity at a series of power houses. Barrages are also under construction on the Ganges and its tributary, the Alaknanda, and a dam has been constructed on the Ramganga River. A dam in the Bhagirathi river valley at Tehri will require the resettlement of some 85,000 people and the submerging of the ancient capital of Tehri.

In the West Bengal hills, the Jaldhaka project supplies electricity to this region, although frequent power failures are a testament to the ineffectiveness of this project.

The relative isolation and inaccessibility of the Himalayan region has been seen as a barrier to effective exploitation of its vast resources. Rather than taking advantage of this perceived geographical hindrance to promote decentralised development, the focus of development has been on making the region more readily accessible to the plains. This priority is the predominant reason for the construction of roads (and several railway lines) in this region.

Jammu, Kashmir & Ladakh

The Kashmir Valley is a major vegetable producing region, and apples are the most important fruit grown here. The valley also produces substantial quantities of saffron, and has a very old silk growing and weaving industry.

With its minimal rainfall, most water for irrigation in Ladakh comes from melted snow from the highlands, which is then carefully and skilfully shared through *yura*, or irrigation channels, between families and their farms. Farming in Ladakh revolves around crops of *nas* (barley), *dro* (wheat), *kushu* (apples) and *chuli* (apricots). Animal husbandry comprises mainly sheep, goats and cows.

Ladakhis often live on small farms which have been handed down from one generation to the next. But with the introduction of western technology in the form of heavy,

expensive machinery, as well as fertilisers, and Indian Government policies of specialising in cash crops, the farmer *(sonampa)* has become less important and effective, and staple foods are sometimes imported into the region.

Himachal Pradesh

Only about 10% of land in Himachal Pradesh is cultivated. In 1975, the cultivation of hops was introduced into Lahaul on an experimental basis, and Lahaul is now the only area in which hops are grown in India. Other major bread earners of the Lahaul Valley are peas and potatoes, which form a major part of cash crops, earning Rs 57 million and Rs 33 million respectively. Other vegetables such as red cabbage, celery and leek are also produced here.

Himachal Pradesh is also a major apple growing area, and this agricultural sector has grown considerably over recent years. In 1950-51, orchards covered an area of only 400 hectares. By 1981-82, that area had expanded to some 91,350 hectares. The state is the largest producer of quality seed potatoes, and also has a considerable share in the high quality ginger market. Wheat and vegetables form other major cash crops, and Himachal Pradesh has found a market niche with the production of edible mushrooms. With a burgeoning population and a paucity of arable land, subsistence farmers have been forced to break ever more rocky ground from which they manage to produce barely enough to support even a frugal existence. Industry has yet to take off in this state, with only small scale industries here. A number of workers have found employment in mines and quarries supplying the nascent construction industry. Revenue derived from forest extraction represents about one-third of that of the state economy.

Uttarakhand

Subsistence agriculture has traditionally formed the basis of the economy of the UP hills, with over 80% of the population dependent on agriculture. This is despite the fact that land under cultivation represents an average of only 14.5% of the total geographical area. With the reduction in the size of land holdings, and the decreasing productivity of land due to soil erosion, the men have been increasingly compelled to seek employment on the plains, giving rise to a mail-order economy.

The Dehra Dun district in Uttarakhand is renowned for its high-quality basmati rice.

West Bengal Hills
In the Darjeeling hills, tea cultivation forms the most important economic activity, with over 40,000 people employed on its 78 tea gardens, which produce almost a quarter of India's tea. In Darjeeling itself, over half of the population is dependent on tourism. In Kalimpong, an important economic activity is the cultivation of flowers, particularly orchids and gladioli; the orchards are almost exclusively owned by one family. Cut flowers are supplied to both the domestic and international markets.

Sikkim
Prior to the closing of the borders between India and Tibet, trans-border trade formed a large component of economic activity in Sikkim, with tribes such as the Lachen and Lachung in the northern regions also occupied as pastoralists. With the closure of the border, herds have been seriously depleted, as communities relied heavily on the grazing grounds in Tibet.

Subsistence agriculture and horticulture now form important activities, with the cultivation of buckwheat, potatoes and barley. In the lower elevations, rice is grown, and in higher elevations, maize is cultivated. Cardamom and oranges are the two main cash crops. By and large, agriculture is not sufficient to supply food requirements, and some staples, such as rice, are now imported from the plains. Road building and maintenance provides employment for a number of workers, although immigrant labourers from the plains engaged in road building have contributed to Sikkim's food deficit. With the merger of Sikkim with India in 1975, extensive industrialisation has taken place,

facilitated by generous central government subsidies in the form of tax concessions.

POPULATION & PEOPLE
There is evidence to suggest that the lower Himalayan region may have supported one of the earliest human habitations dating from the middle Pleistocene period. The Himalaya formed a bridge between central and south Asia, with entire population groups crossing the many passes of the high Himalaya. Migration to the Himalayan region has been motivated variously by politics, economics, climate and spirituality. This movement is reflected in the region's ethnic diversity. Traces of paleo-Mongoloid, Mongoloid, Mediterranean, Alpine and Nordic strains are all represented across the diverse human panorama, which encompasses three main ethnic groupings, Mongoloids, Negroids and Aryans. Supporting a population of some 50 million people, today the majority of the inhabitants of the Indian Himalaya dwell at elevations of between 1000 and 2500m. In the high altitude zone, there are very few settlements, with most of the inhabitants, who are generally of Mongoloid origin, engaged in a semipastoralist, seminomadic lifestyle.

Jammu, Kashmir & Ladakh
The people of the Jammu region are predominantly Hindu and of Dogra origin. In the Kashmir Valley, the people are mainly Muslim and have a distinctly central Asian appearance.

Ladakh's diverse ethnic composition comprises four main groups. The Mons, who profess Buddhism, migrated from northern India; the Baltis, a predominantly Muslim people, settled in and around Kargil from an unknown central Asian area. The Dards settled near Kargil, where they converted to Islam, and in the Dha-Hanu region, where they are also known as Drukpas and remain mainly Buddhist. The Tibetans are the dominant group. Most Tibetans migrated to Ladakh over the centuries, but in more recent times, others have arrived as refugees following China's occupation of Tibet. Other groups professing Buddhism include the

Bedas, some of whom may also be Muslims, and the Garas.

Himachal Pradesh

Himachal Pradesh is inhabited by two groups of seminomadic people – the Gaddis and the Gujars. The Gujars, originally from Gujarat, live in Jammu & Kashmir and in some parts of Uttarakhand. What forced them to leave their homeland on the plains is not known, nor has the precise period of their permanent migration to the north been established. The Gujars converted to Islam from Hinduism during the reign of Aurangzeb. The initial migration originally brought the Gujars to Kashmir, but the paucity of grazing areas compelled some of them to migrate eastwards into the area now encompassed within the boundary of Himachal Pradesh, and there is a sizeable community of Gujars in the Chamba district of this state.

The traditional home of the Gaddis is the village of Brahmaur, the ancient capital of the princely state of Chamba, in the upper Ravi Valley, although there are substantial populations around Dharamsala in the Kangra Valley.

The Gaddis are Hindus, and are traditionally Shaivites, worshippers of the god Shiva.

The inhabitants of Lahaul are known as Lahulas.

In the remote Kinnaur Valley of Himachal Pradesh, the majority of the inhabitants are Kinnauris. The Kinnauri Rajputs, known as Khosias, profess either Hinduism or Buddhism, according to the region in which they dwell. Buddhism is more prevalent in those regions of Kinnaur which lie near the Tibetan border.

Uttarakhand

The Jaunsaris live in the Jaunsar-Bawar area of the Yamuna Valley in north-western Garhwal. The Jaunsaris claim that they are the ancestors of the Pandavas, the heroes of the *Mahabharata*. Sculptures retrieved from this area show a Greco-Roman influence leading to speculation that the origins of the inhabitants of this region can be traced to Kushan and Hun invaders.

The Jadhs, of Mongoloid origin, live in Uttarkashi district in the north-west region of Uttarakhand, to which they migrated from Tibet several centuries ago.

Bhotiyas, also of Mongoloid origin, are found near India's frontiers. There are several communities of Bhotiyas in the northern regions of the eastern part of Uttarakhand. They share a common Mongoloid origin, but possess distinct cultural and linguistic characteristics. In the Johar Valley, in the Munsiyari area to the north of Pithoragarh, are the Malla Johar Bhotiyas, with the highest concentration living in the village of Milam. Marchas, an ethnically distinct group of Bhotiyas originally from Tibet and of Mongoloid origin, reside in the Vishnuganga Valley. Isolated from the Malla Johar Bhotiyas by the Panchachuli Range are the Bhotiyas of Dharchula, whose traditional lands bear frontiers with both Tibet and Nepal. This region supports three groups of Bhotiyas who reside in three separate valleys after which they are known: the Darma, Byans and Chandans valleys.

The closure of the Indo-Tibetan border in 1962 had a dramatic impact on the lives of the Bhotiyas of this region. Many former Bhotiya villages at higher elevations are now abandoned, with Bhotiyas now residing for the most part in villages in the lower valleys, only returning to the higher tracts in the summer.

West Bengal Hills & Sikkim

The Lepcha people of Sikkim live in the area extending west to Bhutan, east to Nepal, and south to the Darjeeling hills. It is possible that the Lepchas may have migrated north from south-eastern Asia in the fifth century AD, although some scholars suggest their origins may lie in central Nepal or the far north-eastern states of India. The Lepchas themselves believe they were created from two balls of snow taken from the summit of Kangchenjunga and fashioned into human form by the god Rom. The Lepchas' language differs in kind from most of the other indigenous languages of this region and is extremely ancient.

Prior to their conversion to Buddhism in the 17th century, the Lepchas practised a form of animism reflected in the worship of local spirits and deities. Even today, elements of this ancient worship can be discerned in contemporary religious practice in Sikkim. The main dichotomy is between the *rums*, which are benevolent spirits, and the more diabolical *mungs*, which have been known to possess human beings and work their malignant mischief, until dispatched by a *bongthing*, or exorcist.

The second important ethnic group in Sikkim are the Bhutias, who originated from Tibet in the 15th century, bringing Tibetan Buddhism in their wake. The word Bhutia is derived from Bod or Bhote, meaning Tibet. They share some ethnic similarities with the Bhutiyas of the western Himalaya. Isolation from Tibet has resulted in some regional differences in the Tibetan language, and the language spoken by those of Bhutia origin is now referred to as Sikkimese. In the high northern reaches of Sikkim are two groups of Bhutias known as the Lanchens and Lanchungs, their names derived from the valleys they inhabit.

Sikkim's Nepali community is predominantly found in the eastern, western and southern regions of Sikkim. The vast majority of Nepalis were brought by the British to the Darjeeling hills to work on the tea gardens. Most of the Nepalis of the West Bengal hills and Sikkim profess Hinduism, although some have adopted Buddhism, and to a lesser degree, Christianity. The Gurkhas originate from central Nepal.

EDUCATION

Across the Himalaya, there is a sharp and probably self-evident distinction in the degree of literacy between rural and urban areas. However, what *is* surprising is the degree of female literacy in the Himalayan regions, which in some cases is well above the national average. Lower literacy levels are found in those areas where Buddhism predominates, including parts of Himachal Pradesh and Sikkim. However, in those regions of Himachal Pradesh where Hindu-

ism is practised, both male and female literacy is above the national averages, both in rural and urban areas. Those areas of Jammu & Kashmir where Hinduism predominates also have higher female literacy rates. In Uttarakhand, the combined rural and urban literacy rate stands at 57%, with the percentage fairly evenly distributed across the two districts of Garhwal and Kumaon.

ARTS
Music, Dance & Drama
Ladakh & Zanskar Music and dance are an integral part of any gompa festival or family ceremony in Ladakh. Dances are often complicated series of steps, retelling Buddhist stories, accompanied by traditional trumpets *(thumpchen)* and drums. Mask dances, called *chaams*, if performed by monks, are slow, intricate and mesmerising. They can be seen at most festivals throughout Ladakh. During the festival at Matho Gompa in Ladakh, some monks go into a trance, and inflict wounds on themselves which appear to miraculously and spontaneously heal.

Himachal Pradesh Folk dances are an important part of the cultural life of Himachal Pradesh. In the Bilaspur and Solan regions of Himachal Pradesh, a solo dance called a *gidha* is performed. Other solo dances of Himachal Pradesh include the *cherri*, *natarambah* and *prekshani*. Accompanied by singers and musicians, one or several men commence dancing, their places being taken by other performers as the music progresses.

The most well known dance of Himachal is the *natti*, in which an entire village can participate. Accompanied by musicians playing a variety of instruments including drums and cymbals, the dancers clasp each others hands and form a circle, revolving slowly at first, but quickening their steps as the music increases its tempo.

Dancing forms an important role in the lives of the Gaddi shepherds of Himachal Pradesh, and this is particularly evident at wedding celebrations. Men and women always dance separately, the women exhibiting extraordinary poise and grace, while the men engage in apparently abandoned movements and gestures, threatening at every moment to topple earthwards, but maintaining a gravity-defying and impressive vertical equilibrium.

At the Tibetan Institute of Performing Arts (TIPA) in McLeod Ganj, students are taught the traditional *lhamo* folk opera. Accompanied by a chorus, the performers, in traditional dress, portray episodes from Buddhist scriptures and events from Tibetan history, accompanied by drums and cymbals. The lhamo originally took place over many days, but abridged operas are performed periodically at the institute for guests and visitors.

Uttarakhand Folk dances are also an important feature of the culture of Uttarakhand. In Jaunsar, in Uttarakhand, dances recreate scenes from the *Mahabharata*, particularly those episodes pertaining to the Pandavas, who are highly revered by the Jaunsaris. In the *mandavna* dance, villagers are possessed by the Pandavas, and the ensuing performance plays an important role in healing and divinatory rituals. During the *khelwar*, performers mimic people known to the audience in a comic way. The *barada nati* is also performed in this district on the eve of important religious festivals, with both boys and girls participating in the dance in traditional costume. In the Tehri Garhwal region of Uttarakhand, the *langvir nritya* is performed by men, who rotate on their stomachs on top of a long bamboo pole, accompanied by musicians. The distinctive *dhurang* and *dhuring* dances are performed by Bhotiyas at funeral ceremonies in order to release the spirit of the deceased from habitation in an animal.

Sikkim Music and dance are vital parts of the dominant Buddhist culture of Sikkim, and take a similar form to their Ladakhi counterparts (see above). Chaams are performed on auspicious dates according to the Tibetan lunar calendar at the gompas of Sikkim. In Sikkim, a chaam performed around Losong

(Sikkimese New Year), known as the *kagyat* dance, involves the burning of effigies which represent the triumph of good over evil.

The Lepchas' close affinity with their environment has given rise to a wealth of unique dances, songs and folk tales, all of which rely on the natural world for their inspiration. They celebrate the harvest with the *limboo chyabrung* dance. During the Panglhapsol Festival, the warrior dance is performed by masked dancers. Kangchenjunga, the guardian deity of Sikkim, is portrayed by a dancer wearing a blood red mask featuring five human skulls, and his supreme commander, Yabdu, is depicted by a dancer in a black mask. Other dancers are adorned in traditional battle garb. The festival is dedicated to Kangchenjunga, the war god, and is believed to have been first performed to celebrate the brotherhood pact between the Lepchas and Bhutias.

Architecture
Domestic Dwellings Typical Himalayan domestic dwellings are of stone and wood. On the lower half of the dwelling, two parallel courses of beams are laid horizontally and the intervening space filled with stone. Above this is built a dwelling entirely of wood, which overhangs the lower storey, and is usually roofed with slate depending on local availability. The lower stone and wood storey traditionally not only afforded a strong foundation for the domestic quarters upstairs, but also provided a sturdy defence against adversaries. There are few, if any, windows in this lower storey, and where windows are employed, they are usually very small. Livestock is kept in the ground floor, with grain stored on the next level, and above this, the wooden domestic dwelling which contains the sleeping quarters and the hearth. There are no chimneys; smoke is released by the removal of a tile from the roof. A deep wooden verandah on the upper storey provides protection from the heavy monsoon rains.

In the lower foothills of the western Himalaya, domestic dwellings are often made of compacted earth, or of brick, with roofs of galvanised iron, thatch or slate. Rooms encompass a central open-air compound which is encircled by a verandah. In the higher regions of Himachal Pradesh, which are subjected to heavy snowfalls, either sloped slate roofs or flat terrace roofs are found. The latter are formed by beaten earth placed over a platform of wooden planks. They are used for recreation and, more importantly, for drying grain.

Dwellings in Lahaul & Spiti are more typically Tibetan in their architecture. Of two or three storeys, a dwelling would usually feature thick walls of sun-baked bricks, a flat roof and an internal courtyard. The upper floors are quite small, with tiny windows to reduce the loss of heat.

The nomadic Khampas of Ladakh live in large tents called *rebos*, which are lined with yak wool, or in mud brick huts with minimal, if any, ventilation.

Temples Temple architecture in the hills conforms to various styles, with shrines ranging from tiny crude shelters of leaves and branches over the image of the deity to vast temple complexes such as those seen at Chamba, Jageshwar and Brahmaur. Some of the most ancient temples can be seen at Brahmaur, such as the Lakhna Devi temple, which was built in the 7th century AD. The walls are of rubble masonry, and the temple features a gable roof. Shikhara-style temples can be found in many areas of the western Himalaya. The *mandapa*, or inner sanctum, is surmounted by a large stone spire (the *shikhara*), which is frequently topped by a fluted stone medallion-shaped disk called an *amalaka*. The amalaka is often protected by an ornate square wooden edifice with a pyramidal roof, generally of wood or slate. The most notable examples of this style of temple can be found at Chamba and Brahmaur, in the Chamba Valley, at Baijnath, in the Kangra Valley, and at Jageshwar in the Kumaon region of Uttarakhand.

A third temple style is the pagoda form, which is found in various regions of Himachal Pradesh, particularly in the Kullu Valley, around Shimla, and in Kinnaur. Fine examples are evident at Mandi, Manali and Shimla. At Masrur, in the Kangra Valley of Himachal Pradesh can be seen the only rock-cut temples of the Himalaya, which are frequently found in southern and western India, such as those at Ellora in Maharashtra state. The shrines at Masrur are actually hewn out of the rocky escarpment, and date from the 8th century AD.

The Himalaya also has some fine temples featuring ornate wooden sculpture. The 12th century Khajjinag temple at Khajiar has ancient carvings featuring the Pandavas. The ceiling of the forechamber at the Chamunda Devi Temple in Chamba has intricate and ornate wooden carvings. Other excellent specimens can be seen at the Mirkula Devi Temple in Lahaul and the Magru Mahadev Temple of Mandi.

Gompas & Chortens Buddhist architecture, evident in gompas and *chortens*, draws its inspiration from Tibet. Gompas are frequently found on hilltops, requiring an arduous climb to get to them. This relative isolation, lofty aspect and difficulty of access served several purposes: merit could be derived from the difficult climb up to the gompa – the gompas were considered to be closer to the gods – and the resident monks in their cloistered lofty perches were removed from the temptations of the flesh posed by the villages in their environs. Gompas are generally oriented towards the east, although if this is restricted by geographical considerations, they can be found oriented towards the south-east or the south. The main prayer hall is known as the *dukhang*, and is surrounded by auxiliary buildings such as the monks' quarters and kitchen. The approach to the gompa is flanked by rows of tall prayer flags.

Dukhangs are usually two storeys high, with walls of whitewashed stone, fronted by a vibrantly painted facade. In the vestibule can be seen colourful frescoes featuring the kings of the four cardinal directions, who protect the universe and the heavens from outer demons. Also usually seen in the vestibule is a depiction of the wheel of life, which represents the cycle of existence, and is held by a gruesome monster representing the clutching of humanity to existence. Brightly painted, and often carved, doors give access to the dukhang, the ceiling of which is supported by large pillars which, if wooden, feature intricately carved cornices. The walls are completely covered in frescoes depicting the deities of Buddhism. The altar is known as the *chwa-shyam*, and generally enshrines three enormous gilt statues. In Sikkim, these deities traditionally comprised Shakyamuni in the centre, flanked by Chenresig to the right and Padmasambhava (Guru Rinpoche) to the left. The outside wall of the dukhang is often completely encompassed by a series of prayer wheels (*manichorkor*), which are spun by devotees when circumambulating the building. The second storey enshrines images of lesser deities, and the walls are usually also richly painted, frequently with demonic images representing the protectors of Tibetan Buddhism.

In the environs of the gompa can be seen whitewashed chortens, which were originally reliquaries (chorten means 'receptacle for offerings'), but are now frequently erected as cenotaphs commemorating Buddha or Buddhist saints. They are formed of five distinct sections representing the elements of which human beings are composed. The square foundation, or plinth, represents the earth, the spherical middle section represents water, and the conical upper structure represents fire. The whole edifice is surmounted by a spire topped by a crescent, which represent respectively air and ether.

Also seen in the environs of gompas are *mani* walls. These are formed by flat stones set upright, and engraved with sacred inscriptions, the most common of which is the sacred mantra, *'Om Mani Padme Hum'* ('Hail to the Jewel in the Lotus'). Mani stones are erected by devotees, and are often also seen on high passes, where they were placed by travellers traversing the traditional trading routes to ensure that the deities would grant them safe passage on their long journeys.

Painting

Pahari Miniatures

The Chamba and Kangra valleys of Himachal Pradesh are renowned for their miniature paintings, often referred to as Pahari paintings. In the mid-18th century following the invasion of Delhi by Nadir Shah, many artists fled to the western Himalaya where they found employment under the patronage of local rajas. Paintings were also produced for the courts by local craftspeople who were descended from families of artisans.

Unlike in the west, paintings were not seen as expressions of individual artists, but were produced anonymously by artists who took their inspiration from the sacred scriptures and infused their paintings with the purples and greens of the hills environment in which they found themselves. Unlike Mughal miniatures, which depicted the exploits of the Mughal emperors and glorified their subjects, Pahari miniatures revolved predominantly around depictions of the incarnation of Vishnu, the god Krishna. To reflect the great reverence in which the deities were held, artists aspired to technical excellence in their representations. Exposure of the local Rajput rulers to the Mughal courts also influenced the quality of the paintings and their expectations of the artists who produced them.

The raja of Guler, in Kangra, Goverdhan Singh (1744-1773) was a keen patron of the arts, and provided commissions for a number of artists at his court, as did Maharaja Sansar Chand of Kangra (1775-1823). Finely executed works commissioned by these rulers soon adorned their palaces, with Sansar Chand's fort at Kangra attracting lovers of art from far and wide. Later he shifted his capital to Nadaun, near Jawalamukhi, which soon became a thriving cultural capital for the production of finely executed works of Kangra art. The capital was again shifted, this time to Sujanpurtira, on the banks of the Beas River, and Pahari miniatures reached their apotheosis here. The demise of Sansar Chand in 1823 heralded the decline of the Kangra school of painting. Unfortunately, many of the thousands of paintings and murals which adorned the temples here were destroyed in the 1905 earthquake. Today, the finest examples of Pahari art can be seen in the museum at Chamba, and there is also a small collection in the museum at Dharamsala.

During the 18th century, miniature painting also flourished in Garhwal, where it was introduced by the master painter Maularam Tomar from the region to the west of present-day Uttarakhand, beyond the Sutlej River.

Thangkas Thangkas are Buddhist religious paintings executed on cloth with vegetable dyes, and often surrounded by fine silk brocade. The cloth is pre-stiffened with starch or clay, and the religious motif is drawn with charcoal and then filled in using coloured dyes. A range of motifs can be employed on thangkas, but generally there is a large central image of a Buddhist deity surrounded by four smaller images. The design may encompass a narrative, with the edges of the thangka depicting episodes from the life of Buddha or of Buddhist saints. Thangkas can range in size from less than 40 cm square to enormous thangkas which cover entire gompa walls. They can be used as meditational prompts, and some, such as those which depict Mahakala, are believed to possess occult powers. Thangkas can also be richly embroidered in silk.

SOCIETY & CONDUCT
Traditional Culture
Jammu, Kashmir & Ladakh The Bakrawalas are goat herders, who reside during winter in the environs of Jammu, and from late April or early May proceed with their flocks to the high valleys in search of grazing grounds. The Shia Muslims of Kargil and the Kashmir Valley are both owner-cultivators and waged agricultural labourers.

The Mons and Bedas are traditionally musicians, while the Garas fulfil the role of blacksmiths in Ladakhi society. The Muslim Baltis and Argons are owner-cultivators, and the Khampas, who graze their yaks and goats on the high Ladakhi plains during the summer, are nomadic people.

Ladakhi women wear woollen dresses called *nambus* and *phumets*, which are covered with silk or brocade by more affluent women. For more formal and festive occasions, they may wear a *perak*, a squarish hat made from lambskin and studded with turquoise jewellery. The multipurpose *bok*, or shawl, is used to carry various items and infants. Men wear thick robes, often of red and maroon shades, called *gonchas*, which are tied at the waist with a *skerag*, or rope. Beneath the robe are worn coarse woollen leggings known as *kangphyings*. A cap of sheepskin with a rear flap which protects the neck is also worn. Worn by both sexes, but only formally, are woollen shoes called *papu*, which are brightly coloured and curled at the front. Everyday footwear consists of felt boots, sometimes ornamented with pieces of coloured cloth.

Polyandry was, and is still in some pockets to a small degree, practised by the Ladakhis, with one woman married to several brothers. Primogeniture, or the passing of the ancestral

A man of Khampa origin. The nomadic Khampas were the first inhabitants of Ladakh.

lands upon the death of the father to the eldest son, ensures that land holdings remain intact and are not reduced to unmanageable levels.

One week following the birth of a child a birth feast, called *tsan ton* is celebrated. The mother remains indoors for one month following her confinement. One year after birth the naming ritual known as *ming ton* is held. The child is taken before a lama who, upon receipt of payment or produce, bestows a name on the child, after which a feast concludes the ceremony.

The *bag ton*, or marriage ritual, proceeds following presentation of the man at the bride's family bearing a bowl of *chang*, and negotiations regarding the offer proposed by the groom to the family of the bride. The ceremony is performed at the home of the groom, officiated by lamas, and the celebrations concluding the ceremony continue for several days.

The funeral ritual, known as *shid ton* can be a modest or elaborate affair according to the relative affluence or importance of the deceased. Cremation can take place up to 20 days following death, during which time prayers are recited and a piece of cloth suspended over the doorway signifies the period of mourning. Following the cremation of a highly revered man, the ashes are collected and formed into an image of the deceased, which is interned in a *chorten*. High lamas are placed in coffins with the knees drawn up against the body and personal and religious effects placed around it.

The traditional form of disposing of the body in Tibet, where wood for cremation was scarce, was the sky burial. The body, after being dissected and ground in a mortar with parched maize, was taken to a lofty site and left for wild animals and birds of prey to devour.

Himachal Pradesh The seminomadic Gaddis and Gujars move their livestock to different climatic regions according to the season. The Gujars traditionally reared buffaloes.

The Gujars are polygamous, with men sometimes taking more than one wife. During the summer they push their herds to high alpine pastures, covering distances of up to 20 km each day along traditional trails, or, more recently, along roads, and camping en route. Temporary dwellings known as *deras* provide shelter on the grazing grounds, and these are either destroyed or abandoned when the Gujars complete the next stage of the migration. The long descent commences in early Autumn, and during winter, the Gujars reside on the plains at the foot of the lower Himalayan slopes. Fresh milk is traded at the villages along the migration routes, or butter and ghee are produced which is sold further afield. The entire family is involved in this cycle of migration, with women sharing in the burden of carrying utensils and infants, and even giving birth during the annual migration.

In addition to their pastoralist activities, the Gaddis are also agriculturalists. During the annual summer migration when the men bring their flocks of sheep and goats to the high altitude pastures, the women in some cases remain in the village and undertake the onerous task of tending the fields. Livelihood is derived thus both from agriculture and trade in milk and animal products.

During migration the Gaddis generally sleep exposed to the elements among their flocks for warmth. A pillow is afforded by the multipurpose *dora*, a long length of black woollen rope traditionally worn around the waist by all Gaddis, including children. It also serves to tether sheep or goats together, or to secure items to the body. Essential items such as implements and grain supplies are carried, including the *hookah*, or tobacco water pipe, and a *lathi*, or wooden staff. Women who undertake the migration carry loads, including infants, in many cases equivalent to those of the men. Dogs also make the migration, serving the dual function of keeping wild animals at bay and containing the flock.

Gaddi men wear a *chola*, a loose grey or white coat with large pockets at the front in which are carried newborn lambs and kids, domestic utensils and foodstuffs. Beneath the chola they wear woollen trousers which are baggy to the knees, and tight at the shins and ankles. Gaddi women wear a cotton dress called a *luanchari* which has a voluminous ankle-length cotton skirt, and a headdress known as a *chadru*.

Gaddis are generally monogamous. Following preparatory ceremonies in the village of the groom, the marriage party removes to the village of the bride, where the marriage ceremony is performed. The bride then returns to live in the groom's village. Naming ceremonies are performed six months after birth, and Gaddis cremate their dead. As with many inhabitants of the hills, Gaddis fear evil spirits. Held in particular dread are *autars*, the spirits of people who die childless. In order to placate autars, they are accorded the status of local deities and propitiated accordingly.

The Lahulas are primarily agriculturalists and pastoralists. The pastoralists, like the Gaddis and the Gujars, are compelled to adopt a seminomadic lifestyle; sheep and goats are pushed to the high altitude grazing grounds in the summer, and led across the Rohtang Pass to lower elevations in winter.

Like the Ladakhis, the Lahulas traditionally practised polyandry, with the household headed by the eldest male who is known as the Yunda. Lahauli society is divided by clans called *rhus*, and marriages are contracted across, but not within, clans. Unlike most regions of India, society is not stratified by caste divisions, and due to the relative isolation of the Lahaul Valley and its distinct ethnic and linguistic characteristics, marriage was rarely contracted outside the valley.

The Kinnauris are agriculturalists, other than in the Puh district, where, due to the short growing season, the limited livelihood afforded through agriculture is supplemented by animal husbandry. Possessing a position lower in the social hierarchy than the Kinnauri Rajputs, known as Khosias, are the Berus, which comprise the artisan castes. Marriages within *khandans*, or clans, are forbidden.

Uttarakhand The Jaunsaris practise polyandry. There are three castes forming the social

hierarchy. At the bottom of the rung are the Doms, who were traditionally compelled to work as bonded labourers for the Rajputs and the Brahmins.

Most of the inhabitants are engaged in agriculture, and grain crops of barley, wheat, maize and rice are dependent on the monsoon rains.

The Jadhs of the small settlements of Uttarkashi district derive their living primarily from animal husbandry, which entails a seminomadic existence requiring a retreat to the lower foothills region in the winter months. Trans-border trade also formed an important part of the local economy until it was terminated with the closure of the Indo-Tibetan border. Trade is still conducted between the Indian plains and the Janhvi Valley, with wool being exchanged for commodities such as salt, oil, and to a lesser degree, consumer goods.

The Marchas, an ethnically distinct group of Bhotiyas, once supplemented their incomes with seminomadic pastoral activities. However, with the closure of the Indo-Tibetan border, this now takes precedence. Some income is also derived from the weaving of carpets, or supplying goods and services to the pilgrims en route to Badrinath.

Bhotiyas traditionally supported their lifestyles through trans-border trade. Due to the paucity of arable land, populations of Bhotiyas in the northern regions of Uttarakhand remain small, and this population deficit has resulted in flexibility in cross-clan marriages, with some marriages even contracted with non-Bhotiya immigrants.

Before the closure of the border, villages flanked the main trade route into Tibet, and during trading expeditions, the families of the male Bhotiyas who were engaged in trade would accompany the men to the last village before the border, where they would remain until the men returned from Tibet's market centres.

During winter, the Darma, Byan and Chandan Bhotiyas migrate to the lower reaches of Dharchula, during which time cultural, trade and social transactions take place, including marriage contracts.

West Bengal Hills & Sikkim Lepchas are traditionally agriculturalists, although many Lepchas now reside in the larger population centres of Sikkim where they are engaged in government service, business and commerce. Only in the Dzongu area of north and central Sikkim can Lepchas still be found engaged in their traditional lifestyles and relatively isolated from contemporary life.

The Bhutias are traditionally shepherds, although they have lost large tracts of grazing ground in Tibet following the closure of the border. Agriculture, and to a lesser degree, pastoralism, now constitute their primary occupations.

The Gurkhas are traditionally a warrior race whose main occupation is soldiering.

The Gurkha divisions have played important roles in the armies of Britain, Nepal and India.

Responsible Tourism

Travellers and trekkers can lessen their impact on the culture and the environment by observing the 'Code of Conduct' and the several additional points not covered by that document which are given below.

Environment Avoid buying anything in plastic bags and bottles. Don't throw them away; keep them and use them again. Try water purification tablets rather than buying plastic bottles of mineral water. Bury your personal waste and do not urinate in streams.

Code of Conduct

The Himalayan Environment Trust, based in Delhi, has compiled a Code of Conduct for visitors to the India Himalaya:

- Camp site: Remember that another party will be using the same camp site after you have vacated it. Therefore, leave the camp site cleaner than you found it.

- Limit deforestation: Make no open fires and discourage others from doing so on your behalf. Where water is heated by scarce firewood, use as little as possible. When possible, choose accommodation that uses kerosene or fuel-efficient firewood stoves. You will help the cause greatly by taking some saplings with you and planting these on your trail.

- In a safe place burn dry paper and packets. Bury other waste paper and biodegradable material including food. Carry back all non-biodegradable litter. If you come across other peoples' rubbish, remove their rubbish as well.

- Keep local water clean and avoid using pollutants such as detergents in streams or springs. If no toilet facilities are available, make sure you are at least 30m away from water sources, and bury or cover wastes.

- Plants should be left to flourish in their natural environment: taking cuttings, seeds and roots is illegal in many parts of the Himalaya.

- Help your guides and porters to follow conservation measures. Do not allow the cooks or porters to throw garbage into the nearby stream or river.

- When taking photographs, respect privacy: ask permission and use restraint.

- Respect holy places: Preserve what you have come to see, never touch or remove religious objects. Remove shoes when visiting temples and shrines.

- Refrain from giving money to children since it will encourage begging. A donation to a project, health centre or schools is a more constructive way to help.

- Respect for local etiquette earns you respect: Loose, light clothes are preferable to revealing shorts, skimpy tops and tight fitting action wear. Hand holding or kissing in public are disapproved of by local people. ■

Dress Modesty rates highly in India, as in most Asian countries. Although men – or women – wearing shorts is accepted in most of the large cities on the plains as a western eccentricity, they should at least be of a decent length. In the hill stations, you can get away with wearing this gear, but in the more remote regions of the Himalaya, you should be more comprehensively covered. Wearing shorts or a T-shirt in a more formal situation, in a remote village, or in any sacred place such as a temple, mosque or gompa, is definitely impolite.

Food Etiquette Never throw food into a fire whether at a campsite or in a home. It is also expedient not to touch food or cooking utensils that local people will use, particularly in Hindu regions. You should use your right hand for all social interactions, whether passing money or food or any other item. The hearth is the sacred centre of the home, so never approach it unless you have been invited to do so.

Religious Etiquette For religious reasons, do not touch local people on the head and similarly never direct the soles of your feet at a person, religious shrine, or image of a deity, as this may cause offence.

Washing Nudity is completely unacceptable and a swimsuit must be worn even when bathing in a remote locality.

Bargaining Always be fair in a bargaining situation and always keep your word. For example, if you have promised to pay a porter for six stages which you discover later you could complete in two, so be it. The porters must be paid the agreed amount. The same applies to staff and horsemen.

Photography Never offer money for photographs unless there is a particular sign in a gompa requesting a donation. Some gompas prohibit photography in the *dukhang*, or main prayer hall; obtain permission before whipping your camera out.

Visiting Gompas
The following etiquette should be observed when visiting gompas.

- Always circumambulate Buddhist gompas in a clockwise direction. If you approach a gompa from behind, this means walking to your left around the building to gain the entrance.

- Some gompas, including many in Ladakh, require an entrance fee. This money is used for the maintenance of gompas, so don't begrudge the small amount asked. All visitors, not just foreigners, give donations.

- Do not use flash photography in the prayer rooms. It will destroy ancient murals. (A flashlight is handy for examining murals.)

- Do not touch or remove any object in gompas.

- Remove your shoes when you enter a prayer hall. (You can leave your socks on, which is a good idea because the floors can sometimes be dirty or cold.) You are allowed to wear shoes within the general gompa compound.

- If you hire a guide to show you around the gompa, make sure they are authorised, knowledgeable, and preferably from the local area.

- Do not insist on accommodation in gompas. Some places do offer small rooms, but they are usually for the benefit of genuine Buddhist students.

- Do not disturb any monks while they are praying. Ask them, if you want to see a *puja* (an offering). ■

Top Left: A novice monk of the Nyingmapa Buddhist order.
Top Right: A sadhu in McLeod Ganj, Himachal Pradesh.
Bottom: A Tibetan Buddhist monk, Sangachoeling Gompa, West Sikkim.

Scenes from the Ladakh festival. Masked children imitate the masked monk (top centre) who leads a chaam.

RELIGION

The Himalaya has been revered for millennia as Dhevbumi, or the home of the gods. Many of the great Hindu scriptures draw upon the Himalaya for their inspiration, or weave their narratives around the exploits of the gods in the lofty Himalayan realm. It was here that Shiva, widely revered in the hills regions, married Parvati, and here that he led the heroes of the *Mahabharata*, the Pandavas, on a merry dance as he endeavoured to elude them after they sought his atonement following the slaying of their kinsfolk, the Kauravas. Two of the great battles recorded in the *Rigveda*, the Shambar Yuddha and the Dasarajna Yuddha are believed to have been fought in the Himalaya.

Buddhism made great inroads in the Himalayan region, both with Buddhists crossing the high Himalaya from Tibet and spreading the tenets of the religion throughout the Indian Himalaya, and due to the endeavours of Buddhism's greatest convert, Ashoka, who lived in the 3rd century AD and left a legacy of rock-carved edicts throughout his empire, at least one of which was installed in the Himalaya.

There are also sizeable Muslim communities, particularly in the state of Jammu & Kashmir, and Sikhism and Christianity are also professed by some inhabitants.

Hinduism

Hinduism is the dominant religion of the Himalayan region, particularly in Himachal Pradesh, where over 87% of the inhabitants profess this religion, and in Uttarakhand. About 60% of the population of Sikkim and the West Bengal hills are Hindu, with the Gurkha populations professing either Hinduism or Buddhism. Hinduism is also professed by the Dogra people from the hills beyond Jammu in Jammu & Kashmir state.

Despite its colourful appearance, Hinduism is actually one of the oldest extant religions, with firm roots extending back to beyond 1000 BC.

The Indus Valley civilisation developed a religion which shows a close relationship to Hinduism in many ways. Later, it further developed through the combined religious practices of the southern Dravidians and the Aryan invaders who arrived in the north of India around 1500 BC. Around 1000 BC, the Vedic scriptures were introduced and gave the first loose framework to the religion.

Hinduism today has a number of holy books, the most important being the four *Vedas* (Divine Knowledge) which are the foundation of Hindu philosophy. The *Upanishads* are contained within the *Vedas* and delve into the metaphysical nature of the universe and the soul. The *Mahabharata* (Great War of the Bharatas) is an epic poem containing over 220,000 lines. It describes the battles between the Kauravas and Pandavas, who were descendants of the Lunar race. In it is the story of Rama, and it is probable that the most famous Hindu epic, the *Ramayana*, was based on this. The *Ramayana* is highly revered by Hindus. The *Bhagavad Gita* is a famous episode of the *Mahabharata* where Krishna relates his philosophies to Arjuna.

Basically the religion postulates that we will all go through a series of rebirths or reincarnations that eventually lead to *moksha*, the spiritual salvation which frees one from the cycle of rebirths. With each rebirth you can move closer to or further from eventual moksha; the deciding factor is your karma, which is literally a law of cause and effect. Bad actions during your life result in bad karma, which ends in a lower reincarnation. Conversely, if your deeds and actions have been good you will reincarnate on a higher level and be a step closer to eventual freedom from rebirth.

Dharma, or the natural law, defines the total social, ethical and spiritual harmony of your life. There are three categories of dharma, the first being the eternal harmony which involves the whole universe. The second category is the dharma that controls castes, the relations between castes, and behaviour appropriate to individuals within castes. The third dharma is the moral code which an individual should follow.

The Hindu religion has three basic practices. They are puja, or worship, the cremation of the dead, and the rules and regulations of the caste system. There are four main castes: the Brahmin, or priest caste; the Kshatriyas, or soldiers and governors; the Vaisyas, or tradespeople and farmers; and the Sudras, or menial workers and artisans. These basic castes are then subdivided into a great number of lesser divisions. Beneath all the castes are the Dalits (formerly known as Harijans), or untouchables, the lowest caste-less class for whom all the most menial and degrading tasks are reserved.

Westerners may have trouble understanding Hinduism principally because of its vast pantheon of gods. See The Hindu Gods in this section for more information on the most interesting and frequently encountered gods, their associated creatures and consorts, and religious terminology.

A variety of lesser gods and goddesses also make up the Hindu pantheon. Most temples are dedicated to one or other of the gods, but curiously there are very few Brahma temples – perhaps just two or three in all of India. Most Hindus profess to be either Vaishnavites (followers of Vishnu) or Shaivites (followers of Shiva). The cow is, of course, the holy animal of Hinduism.

Hinduism is not a proselytising religion, since you cannot be converted. You're either born a Hindu or you are not; you can never become one. Similarly, once you are a Hindu

---

The Hindu Gods

There are many Hindu gods, and related auspicious beings. You can look upon all these different gods simply as pictorial representations of the many attributes of a god. The one omnipresent god usually has three physical representations: Brahma is the creator, Vishnu is the preserver and Shiva is the destroyer and reproducer.

Incarnations, Manifestations & Aspects There are subtle differences between an incarnation, a manifestation and an aspect. Vishnu has incarnations, 10 of them in all. They include Narsingha, the man-lion, Krishna the cowherd and Buddha the teacher. Shiva, on the other hand, may be the god of 1000 names but these are manifestations – what he shows himself as – not incarnations.

Vehicles Each of the gods is associated with a particular animal which can either be an attendant or a vehicle on which the god may ride. These creatures are a clue to identifying a god. Ganesh's vehicle, for example, is the rat or shrew; a statue of a rat will indicate that you are in a Ganesh shrine.

Shiva Shiva is creator and destroyer – so it's important to keep on his good side! Shiva is often represented by the phallic lingam, symbolic of his creative role. The symbol most often seen in Shiva's hand is the trident. Shiva rides on the bull Nandi and his matted hair is said to have Ganga, the goddess of the river Ganges, in it.

Shiva is also known as Nataraja, the cosmic dancer whose dance shook the cosmos and created the world. Shiva's home is Mt Kailash in the Tibetan Himalaya. He has various manifestations including peaceful Pashupati and destructive Bhairab. Usually his fearsome side is handled by Shakti.

Shiva

Shakti While Shakti the goddess is Shiva's consort, *shakti* is the creative/reproductive energy of the gods which often manifests in their consorts. A Hindu god's consort is also known as his shakti, as she is far more than just a companion. A shakti often symbolises certain parts of a god's personality, so while Shiva is the god of both creation and destruction, it is often his shakti Parvati, manifesting as Kali or Durga, who handles the destructive business and demands the blood sacrifices. She is also the energetic and dominant partner in their sexual relationship, and shakti has come to mean any goddess in her energetic and dynamic mode.

Parvati Shiva's shakti is Parvati the beautiful and she is the dynamic element in their relationship. Just as Shiva is also known as Mahadev, the Great God, so she is Mahadevi, the Great Goddess. Just as Shiva is often symbolised by the phallic lingam, so Parvati's symbol is the *yoni*, representing the female sex organ. Their relationship is a sexual one and it is often Parvati who is the energetic and dominant partner.

Parvati has as many forms as the Great God himself. She may be the peaceful Parvati but she may also be fearsome Kali, the black goddess, or Durga, the terrible. In these terrific forms she holds a variety of weapons in her 10 hands, struggles with demons and rides a lion. As Kali, the fiercest of the gods and goddesses, she demands sacrifices and wears a garland of skulls.

Parvati

Vishnu Vishnu is the preserver and also plays a role in the original creation of the universe. Narayan is the reclining Vishnu, sleeping on the cosmic ocean, and from his navel appears Brahma, who creates the universe.

Vishnu has four arms and can often be identified by the symbols he holds – the conch shell or *sankha*, the disc-like weapon known as a *chakra*, the stick-like weapon known as a *gada* and a lotus flower or *padma*. Vishnu's shakti is Lakshmi, the beautiful goddess of wealth and prosperity who came from the sea.

Vishnu has 10 incarnations starting with Matsya, the fish. Then he appeared as Kurma, the tortoise on which the universe is built. Number three was his boar incarnation as Varaha, who destroyed a demon who would have drowned the world. Vishnu was again in a demon-destroying mood in incarnation four as Narsingha, half man and half lion. Still facing difficulties from demons, Vishnu's next incarnation was Vamana, the dwarf who reclaimed the world from the demon-king Bali. In his sixth incarnation Vishnu appeared as Parasurama, a warlike Brahman. Incarnation seven was as Rama, the personification of the perfect man and the hero of the *Ramayana* who, with help from Hanuman the monkey god, rescued his beautiful wife Sita from the clutches of Rawana, evil king of Lanka. Incarnation eight was a gentle and much-loved one when Vishnu appeared as Krishna, the fun-loving cowherd, who dallied with the milkmaids, danced, played his flute and still managed to remain devoted to his wife Radha. Krishna is often blue in colour. For number nine Vishnu

Vishnu

appeared as the teacher, the Buddha. Of course the Buddhists don't agree that Buddha was just an incarnation of some other religion's god.

Incarnation 10? Well we haven't seen that one yet but it will be as Kalki, a white horse, when Vishnu wields the sword which will destroy the world at the end of the Kali-Yuga, the age which we are currently in.

When Vishnu appears as Vishnu, rather than one of his incarnations, he sits on a couch made from the coils of a serpent and in his hands he holds two symbols, the conch shell and the discus. Vishnu's vehicle is the half-man half-eagle known as the Garuda.

Ganesh With his elephant head, Ganesh is probably the most easily recognised of the gods and also the most popular. Ganesh is the god of prosperity and wisdom. Ganesh's parents are Shiva and Parvati and he obtained his elephant head due to his father's notorious temper. Coming back from a long trip, Shiva discovered Parvati in bed with a young man. Not pausing to think that their son might have grown up a little during his absence, Shiva lopped his head off! He was then forced by Parvati to bring his son back to life but could only do so by giving him the head of the first living thing he saw – which happened to be an elephant.

Hanuman Hanuman is the monkey god, the important character from the *Ramayana* who came to the aid of Rama and helped to defeat the evil Rawana and release Sita from his grasp. Hanuman's characteristics are trustworthiness and alertness.

Garuda The Garuda is a firm do-gooder and has a deep dislike of snakes. A winged Garuda statue will often be found kneeling reverentially in front of a Vishnu temple.

Brahma Brahma, despite his supreme position, appears much less often than Shiva or Vishnu. Like those gods, he has four arms but Brahma also has four heads, to represent his all-seeing presence. The four *Vedas* are supposed to have emanated from his mouths.

Saraswati The goddess of learning and consort of Brahma. She rides upon a white swan and holds the stringed musical instrument known as a *veena*. ■

Hanuman

Garuda

Brahma

Saraswati

you cannot change your caste – you're born into it and are stuck with it for the rest of that lifetime. Nevertheless, Hinduism has a great attraction to many westerners and India's 'export gurus' are many and successful.

A *guru* is not so much a teacher as a spiritual guide, somebody who by example or simply by their presence indicates what path you should follow. In a spiritual search, one always needs a guru. A *sadhu* is an individual on a spiritual search.

Sadhus

Sadhus are an easily recognised group, usually wandering around half-naked, smeared in dust with their hair and beard matted. Sadhus following Shiva will sometimes carry his symbol, the trident. A sadhu is often someone who has decided that his business and family life have reached their natural conclusions and that it is time to throw everything aside and go out on a spiritual search. He may previously have been the village postman, or a businessman. Sadhus perform various feats of self-mortification and wander all over India, occasionally coming together in great pilgrimages and other religious gatherings. Many sadhus are completely genuine in their search, but others are simply beggars following a more sophisticated approach to gathering in the rupees. ∎

A peculiar phenomenon in the western Himalaya is the institution of village and household gods, many of whom are manifestations of Shiva, Durga (Parvati) and Vishnu, as well as *nagas*, or snake-spirits, which are worshipped in various forms in thousands of villages. Worship of the five Pandava brothers is also common in the hills regions. Worship of household gods is motivated more by fear than by abject devotion, as household gods are believed to wreak havoc on the families to which they belong if they are not afforded due respect and placated with appropriate reverence and worship. In the case of trouble or misfortune, a shaman

is consulted who advises how it can be averted, and how the household god can be appropriately appeased.

Village gods, in contrast to household gods, are worshipped collectively by entire villagers in a village temple, with worship conducted by a Brahmin. They are less universally feared than household gods, although as with household gods, they are worshipped according to the degree of trouble they are capable of inflicting upon the village. Village gods speak through a *gur*, or oracle, who is possessed by the god, generally at festivals held in its honour, causing the object of their possession to dance and speak with the god's voice. They are an integral part of the cultural life of the village, directing marriage and death rituals and controlling the destinies of the villagers.

Other supernatural phenomena which play important roles in the lives of the hills inhabitants are ancestor spirits and ghosts, or *bhuts*. Ancestor spirits may demand worship according to various conditions. A common reason for ancestor worship is to appease a deceased person who returns in spirit form if it feels it did not receive appropriate burial rites, or who has returned to torment family members for indiscretions during its lifetime. A shaman diagnoses the source of the affliction for the family members, and the ancestors are worshipped as household gods.

Ghosts can also be the spirits of deceased people; the ghosts are thought to roam at night and are held responsible for inexplicable occurrences such as strange noises, rockslides and the like. They have also been thought to possess hapless victims, so causing disability, illness, insanity, and even death, and are sometimes considered responsible for the inability of women to bear children, or stillbirths. Unlike household gods, ghosts can strike randomly, and their malevolent machinations are not necessarily punishments for perceived slights or indiscretions. Charms and incantations can keep them at bay, and ghosts who possess people can be driven out with the aid of an exorcist.

Sprites, or *matris*, are invisible beings which do not deliberately attack their

The Ganesh Miracle

Ganesh received worldwide renown in 1995 when statues of the elephant god in Hindu temples around India, and even as far away as London, were allegedly imbibing milk offered to them on teaspoons by delighted devotees. The miracle, witnessed by hundreds of thousands of devotees who queued for days to offer milk to the god, ceased as quickly as it began, and sceptics and scientists are still busy offering rational explanations for the event. Some analysts have suggested that it was a case of collective religious hysteria; others propose gravitational theories for the occurrence. Devout Hindus believe that it was a clear message from the gods that they still reside in the divine realm, and are keeping an eye on their human charges. Whatever precipitated the miracle, an awful lot of milk was sold in India in the latter half of 1995, which dairy producers probably consider something of a miracle in its own right. ■

Ganesh

victims; victims are simply afflicted from having inadvertently wandered across their path. They cannot be avoided or appeased with worship, and the maladies with which they strike their unfortunate victims frequently cannot be cured or dislodged by a shaman. Sprites do not possess people, but they can cause illness, disability or insanity. Fractures resulting from tripping over a branch or similar obstruction could be attributed to the playful but not malicious machinations of sprites.

Buddhism

There are only about five million Buddhists in India, but the religion is of great importance and there are many reminders of its historic role. Strictly speaking Buddhism is not a religion, since it is not centred on a god, but a system of philosophy and a code of morality.

Buddhism was founded in northern India about 500 BC when Siddhartha Gautama, born a prince, achieved enlightenment. Gautama Buddha was not the first buddha but the fourth, and is not expected to be the last 'enlightened one'. Buddhists believe that the achievement of enlightenment is the goal of every being, so eventually we will all reach buddhahood.

The Buddha never wrote down his teachings or dharma, and a schism later developed, so today there are two major Buddhist schools. The Theravada (Doctrine of the Elders), or Hinayana, holds that the path to *nirvana*, the eventual aim of all Buddhists, is an individual pursuit. In contrast, the Mahayana school holds that the combined belief of its followers will eventually be great enough to encompass all of humanity and bear it to salvation. Today it is chiefly practised in Vietnam, Japan and China, while the Hinayana school is followed in Sri Lanka, Myanmar (Burma), Cambodia and Thailand. There are other, sometimes more esoteric, divisions of Buddhism, such as the Vajrayana, or Tantrism, a development of Mahayana that has particular relevance to Tibet, and which you can see in Ladakh and other parts of the Indian Himalaya.

The Buddha renounced his material life to search for enlightenment but, unlike other prophets, found that starvation did not lead to discovery. Therefore, he developed his rule of the 'middle way', moderation in everything. The Buddha taught that all life is suffering but that suffering comes from our sensual desires and the illusion that they are important. By following the 'eight-fold path', these desires will be extinguished and a state of nirvana, where we are free from their delusions, will be reached. Following this process requires going through a series of rebirths until the goal is eventually reached and no more rebirths into the world of suffering are necessary. The path that takes you through this cycle of births is karma, but this is not simply fate. Karma is a law of cause and effect; your actions in one life determine the role you will play and what you will have to go through in your next life.

In India, Buddhism developed rapidly when it was embraced by the great emperor Ashoka in the 3rd century BC. As his empire extended over much of India, so was Buddhism carried forth. He also sent out missions to other lands to preach the Buddha's word, and his own son is said to have carried Buddhism to Sri Lanka. Later, however, Buddhism began to contract in India because it had never really taken a hold on the great mass of people. With the revival of Hinduism in the 9th century, predominantly due to the efforts of the philosopher and theologian Shankaracharya, Buddhism in India was gradually reabsorbed into the older religion. To Hindus, Buddha is another incarnation of Vishnu.

At its peak, Buddhism was responsible for magnificent structures erected wherever it held sway.

Although Buddhism was to gain favour after the kings of Tibet invaded Ladakh in the 8th and 9th centuries, it took many generations for the Buddhist teachings to capture the local imagination. The sage Naropa is said to have founded one of the earliest gompas at Lamayuru high above the Indus. Legend has it that the Lamayuru Valley was once filled by a lake that was drained by Naropa to found the gompa. The original building, situated below the main gompa, was built in the 10th century. The gompa at Sani, close to Padum in the Zanskar Valley, also dates from this period, with its origins again attributed to the miraculous deeds of Naropa.

During the 11th century, Buddhist monks began migrating over the Himalaya in search of patronage. The artistic designs in gompas such as Alchi, dating from the 11th century, still provide some of the best surviving examples of Buddhist art of this period. From now on the movement and inspiration of Buddhist thought would be initiated from the far side of the Himalaya.

One of the greatest influences came from Tibet in the 14th century when the saint Tsongkhapa propounded a new order that restored much of the original teachings. His Gelukpa order was to become the dominant cultural force in Tibet; in Ladakh, the gompas of Tikse, Likir and Stakna were founded by this order in the early half of the 15th century. It was headed by the Dalai

Padmasambhava

The sage Padmasambhava (750-800 AD) was to have a remarkable influence on the development of Buddhism in the Himalaya and was one of the foremost proponents of Tantric Buddhism.

Padmasambhava is revered as the founder of Buddhism in Tibet. According to tradition, he was summoned to Tibet by King Trisong Deutsan, the son of a Chinese Buddhist princess. The king, who wanted to install Buddhism as the state religion in Tibet, proceeded to build a gompa at Samye. However, construction of the gompa was plagued by a succession of earthquakes, which were attributed to the malicious machinations of the local demons. In order to eliminate these spirits, the king dispatched a messenger to the great Indian gompa of Nalanda to fetch Padmasambhava. The Indian sage and mystic immediately set out on the long journey to Tibet, via Kathmandu in Nepal. Armed with his *dorje* (thunderbolt), he speedily overcame the demons and completed the construction of the gompa, installing in it the first community of lamas.

The lives of the local inhabitants were dominated by the elements, and Padmasambhava enabled their beliefs, which included animism, to be integrated with Buddhism. ■

Important Figures of Tibetan Buddhism

The following is a brief guide to some of the gods and goddesses of the Tibetan Buddhist pantheon. It is neither exhaustive nor scholarly, but it may help you to recognise a few of the statues you encounter in the many gompas of the Indian Himalaya.

Padmasambhava

Sakyamuni

Tara

Padmasambhava – the 'lotus-born' Buddha – assisted in establishing Buddhism in Tibet in the 8th century. He is regarded by followers of Nyingmapa Buddhism as the second Buddha. He is also known as Guru Rinpoche.

Avalokitesvara – 'glorious gentle one' – one of the three great saviours or Bodhisattvas. He is the Bodhisattva of compassion and is often pictured with 11 heads and several pairs of arms. His Tibetan name is Chenresig. The Dalai Lama is considered an incarnation of Avalokitesvara.

Manjushri – the 'princely lord of wisdom' – is regarded as the first divine teacher of Buddhist doctrine. He is also known as Jampel.

Vajrapani – 'thunderbolt in hand' – is one of the three great saviours or Bodhisattvas. He is also known as Channadorje. The thunderbolt represents indestructibility and is a fundamental symbol of Tantric faith; it is called a *dorje* in Tibetan and a *vajra* in Sanskrit.

Sakyamuni – the 'historical Buddha' – born in Lumbini in the 6th century BC in what is now southern Nepal, he attained enlightenment under a pipal (Bo) tree and his teachings set in motion the Buddhist faith. In Tibetan-style representations he is always pictured sitting cross-legged on a lotus flower throne.

Maitreya – the 'Buddha of the future'. He is passing the life of a Bodhisattva and will return to earth in human form 4000 years after the disappearance of Sakyamuni Buddha.

Milarepa – a great Tibetan magician and poet who is believed to have attained the supreme enlightenment of buddhahood in the course of one life. He lived in the 11th century and travelled extensively throughout the Himalayan border lands. Most images of Milarepa picture him smiling, holding his hand to his ear as he sings.

Tara – 'the saviouress' – has 21 different manifestations. She symbolises fertility and is believed to be able to fulfil wishes. Statues of Tara usually represent Green Tara, who is associated with night, or White Tara, who is associated with day. ■

Lama, and even today the 14th Dalai Lama undertakes regular visits to the gompas in Ladakh and Zanskar.

The teachings of the Tantric sages, too, were revised in the 16th century. A new gompa at Hemis was founded with the patronage of the Ladakhi royal family. Affiliated gompas at Stakna and in the King's palace at Leh also date from this period. The traditions of Padmasambhava were revered, and today the annual festival at Hemis during the time of the June/July full moon is held in his honour.

Buddhism was introduced into Sikkim by

The Eight Auspicious Symbols
The Eight Auspicious Symbols are associated with gifts made to the Sakyamuni upon his enlightenment and appear as protective motifs throughout Tibetan influenced regions.

Precious Parasol – usually placed over Buddha images to protect them from evil infuences; it is a common Buddhist motif and can be seen as far away as Thailand and Japan.

Banner of Victory – heralds the triumph of Buddhist wisdom over ignorance.

White Conch Shell – blown in celebration of Sakyamuni's enlightenment.

Two Golden Fishes – shown leaping from the waters of their captivity; thus they represent liberation from the Wheel of Life.

Vase of Great Treasures – a repository of the jewels of enlightenment.

Knot of Eternity – a commonly seen Tibetan motif, representing the entwined, never-ending passage of harmony and love.

Eight-Spoked Golden Wheel – represents the Noble Eightfold Path, and is also referred to as the Wheel of Dharma.

Lotus Flower – represents Sakyamuni's purity and his compassion.

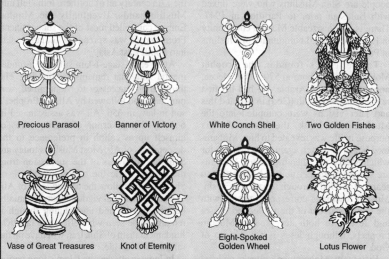

Precious Parasol   Banner of Victory   White Conch Shell   Two Golden Fishes

Vase of Great Treasures   Knot of Eternity   Eight-Spoked Golden Wheel   Lotus Flower

three Tibetan lamas, Lhatsun Chempo, Kathok Rikzin Chempo and Ngadak Sempa Chempo, in the 17th century, who belonged to the Nyingmapa order. The lamas left Tibet following the schism between the various orders, in which the Gelukpa was beginning to emerge as the dominant order. The establishment of Buddhism in the former kingdom was believed to have been foretold by Padmasambhava when he travelled through the region en route to Tibet. The three lamas consecrated Sikkim's first king, or *chogyal*, Phuntsog Namgyal, in 1642.

Islam

Muslims, followers of the Islamic religion, are India's largest religious minority. They number about 75 million in all, over 10% of the country's population. This makes India one of the largest Islamic nations in the world.

In the Himalayan region, Muslims predominate in the Kashmir Valley. Some 92% of the valley's population is Muslim, the majority of whom are Sunnites. To the east of the Kashmir Valley, in the upper valleys of the Drass, Suru and Bodhkarbu, the people are Shia Muslims who were linked with Baltistan prior to Partition in 1947. There is also a sizeable Muslim community in Leh, and a small community of Muslims in Padum.

The religion's founder, the prophet Mohammed, was born in 570 AD at Mecca, now part of Saudi Arabia. He had his first revelation from Allah (God) in 610 and this and later visions were compiled into the Muslim holy book, the *Koran*. As his purpose in life was revealed to him, Mohammed began to preach against the idolatry for which Mecca was then the centre. Muslims are strictly monotheistic and believe that to search for God through images is a sin. Muslim teachings correspond closely with the Old Testament of the Bible, and Moses and Jesus are both accepted as Muslim prophets, although Jesus is not the son of God.

Eventually Mohammed's attacks on local business caused him and his followers to be run out of town in 622. They fled to Medina, the 'city of the Prophet', and by 630 were strong enough to march back into Mecca and take over. Although Mohammed died in 632, most of Arabia had been converted to Islam within two decades.

The Muslim faith was more than a religion; it called on its followers to spread the word – if necessary by the sword. In succeeding centuries Islam was to expand over three continents. The Arabs, who first propagated the faith, developed a reputation as being ruthless opponents but reasonable masters, so people often found it advisable to surrender to them. In this way the Muslims swept aside the crumbling Byzantine Empire, whose people felt no desire to support their distant Christian emperor.

Islam only travelled west for 100 years before being pushed back at Poitiers, France, in 732, but it continued east for centuries. It regenerated the Persian Empire, which was then declining from its protracted struggles with Byzantium, and in 711, the same year the Arabs landed in Spain, they sent dhows up the Indus River to India. This was more a casual raid than a full-scale invasion, but in the 12th century all of northern India fell into Muslim hands. Eventually the Mughal Empire controlled most of the subcontinent. From here it was spread by Indian traders into South-East Asia.

At an early stage Islam suffered a fundamental split that remains to this day. The third caliph, successor to Mohammed, was murdered and followed by Ali, the Prophet's son-in-law, in 656. Ali was assassinated in 661 by the governor of Syria, who set himself up as caliph in preference to the descendants of Ali. Most Muslims today are Sunnites, followers of the succession from the caliph, while the others are Shias, or Shi'ites, who follow the descendants of Ali.

Despite its initial vigour, Islam eventually became inertial and unchanging though it remains to be seen what effect the fanatical fundamentalism of Shia Iran will have on the religion worldwide.

In India itself, despite Islam's long period of control over the centuries, it never managed to make great inroads into Hindu society and religion. Converts to Islam were principally made from the lowest castes, with the result that at Partition, Pakistan found itself with a shortage of the educated clerical workers and government officials with which India is so liberally endowed. Although it did not make great numbers of converts, the visible effects of Muslim influence in India are strong in architecture, art and food. Converts to Islam have only to announce that 'There is no God but Allah and Mohammed is his prophet' and they become Muslims. Friday is the Muslim holy day and the main mosque in each town is known as the Jami Masjid or Friday Mosque. One of the aims of every Muslim is to make the pilgrimage *(hajj)* to Mecca and become a *hajji* (a Muslim who has made the pilgrimage).

Sikhism

The Sikhs in India number 13 million and are predominantly located in the Punjab, although they are found all over India. They are the most visible of the Indian religious groups because of the five symbols introduced by Guru Govind Singh so that Sikh men could easily recognise each other. They are known as the five *kakkars* and are: *kesh* (uncut hair), *kangha* (the wooden comb), *kachha* (shorts), *kara* (the steel bracelet), and *kirpan* (the sword). Because of their kesha, Sikh men wear their hair tied up in a bun and hidden by a long turban. Wearing kachha and carrying a kirpan came about because of the Sikhs' military tradition – they didn't want to be tripping over a long dhoti or be caught without a weapon. Normally the sword is simply represented by a tiny image set in the comb.

The Sikh religion was founded by Guru Nanak, who was born in 1469. It was originally intended to bring together the best of the Hindu and Islamic religions. Its basic tenets are similar to those of Hinduism with the important modification that the Sikhs are opposed to caste distinctions and pilgrimage to rivers. They are not, however, opposed to pilgrimages to holy sites.

They worship at temples known as *gurudwaras*, baptise their children, when they are old enough to understand the religion, in a ceremony known as *pahul*, and cremate their dead. The holy book of the Sikhs is the *Granth Sahib* which contains the works of the 10 Sikh gurus together with Hindu and Muslim writings. The last guru died in 1708.

In the 16th century, Guru Govind Singh introduced military overtones into the religion in an attempt to halt the persecution the Sikhs were then suffering. A brotherhood, known as the *khalsa* was formed, and entry into it was conditional on a person undergoing baptism *(amrit)*. From that time the majority of Sikhs have borne the surname Singh which means Lion (although just because a person has the surname Singh doesn't mean they are necessarily a Sikh; many Rajputs also have this surname).

Sikhs believe in one god and are opposed to idol worship. They practise tolerance and love of others, and their belief in hospitality extends to offering shelter to anyone who comes to their gurudwaras. Because of their get-on-with-it attitude to life they are one of the better-off groups in Indian society. They have a well known reputation for mechanical aptitude and specialise in handling machinery of every type, from jumbo jets to autorickshaws.

The most sacred site in the Himalayan region for Sikhs is the lake of Hem Kund, in Uttarakhand, near the Valley of Flowers. In the *Granth Sahib*, Govind Singh recalled that he meditated on the shores of a lake, surrounded by seven snow-capped mountains; only this century was the lake identified as Hem Kund.

LANGUAGE

Hindi and Urdu are the most widely understood languages in northern India. As spoken languages there is little difference between them. However, Hindi is a Sanskrit-based language, written in Devanagiri script, while Urdu is essentially a Persian language written in Arabic script.

In all of the main towns of northern India, including the hill stations, English is widely spoken. However, higher up in the mountains this is not the case and any attempt at speaking a little of the local language will be to your advantage.

In Darjeeling and Sikkim, and most parts of Uttarakhand and Himachal Pradesh, Hindi is widely understood. It is also the language of the Gujar and Bakrawala shepherds found roaming the hills of the western Himalaya in the summer months.

In the outlying villages of the Kashmir Valley, the people only speak and understand Kashmiri; similarly Ladakhi, a Tibetan-based language, is the only language understood in the more remote valleys of Ladakh and Zanskar. In Himachal and Uttarakhand, Pahari and Garwhali respectively are widely used in the village areas. A list of Hindi words and phrases are included below to get you started. For a full introduction to the language and pronunciation refer to Lonely Planet's *Hindu/Urdu phrasebook*. Refer to the Ladakh & Zanskar chapter in this book for details on Ladakhi.

Greetings

The traditional Hindu greeting *namaste* is said with one's hands together in a prayer-like gesture. Muslims, on the other hand, give the greeting *salaam alekum*, literally 'peace be on you'. The reply is either the same or *valekum as salaam*, meaning 'and also on you'.

Hindus also say *namaste* for 'goodbye', while Muslims say *kudha hafiz*, literally 'may God bless you'.

When addressing a stranger, particularly if the person is of some standing, use the polite suffix *ji* – it's almost like 'sir'. This term can also mean 'yes' in reply to a question. Beware of *acha*, that all-purpose word for 'OK'. It can also mean 'OK, I understand what you mean, but it isn't OK'.

Basics

Excuse me.
  maaf kijiyeh
Please.
  meharbani seh

Thank you.
  shukriyaa
Yes.
  haan
No.
  nahin

big
  bherra
small
  chhota

Do you speak English?
  kya aap angrezi samajhte hain?
I don't understand.
  meri samajh men nahin aaya
How much?
  kitneh paiseh/kitneh hai?
What is the time?
  kitneh bajeh hain?
What is your name?
  aapka shubh naam kya hai?
How are you?
  aap kaiseh hain?
Very well, thank you.
  bahut acha, shukriya

Getting Around & Accommodation

How do I get to ...?
  *... kojane ke liyeh kaiseh
  jaana parega?*

Where is the ...?
  ... kahan hai?
bank
  baink
bus stop
  bas staap
chemist/pharmacy
  davai ki dukaan
post office
  daak khana
ticket office
  tikat aaphis

When will the next bus leave?
  agli bas kab jaayehgi?
Can I change money here?
  *kyaa yahaan paise badlae jaa
  sakte hain?*

Where is a hotel?
hotal kahan hai?
Do you have a room?
aap kai paas ek kamraa hai?
Is there (breakfast/hot water)?
(naashta/garam paani) hai?

Trekking

Will you come with me?
mere saath chalengeh?
What do you charge per day?
ek din kaa kyaa lete hain?
How many days will it take?
kitne din lagengeh?
Is there a place to spend the night?
raat ko rehneh kii jagaa hai?
Is food/water available?
khaanaa/paanii miltaa hai?
I have to rest.
aaraam karnaa hai

Health & Emergencies

I need a doctor.
mujhe doktar chaahiye
It hurts here.
yahaan daradh hai
I'm allergic to penicillin
mujhe penicilin se elargii hai
Help!
bachaao!
Thief!
chorr!
police station
thaanaa
I've been robbed.
merii chori ho gai hai

Time & Days

today
aaj
tonight
aaj raat
yesterday/tomorrow
kal
day
din
night
raat

week
haftah
month
mahina
year
saal

Numbers

Instead of counting in tens, hundreds, thousands, millions and billions, the Indians count in tens, hundreds, thousands, hundred thousands, and ten millions. A hundred thousand is a *lakh*, and 10 million is a *crore*.

These two words are almost always used in place of their English equivalent. Thus, you will see 10 lakh rather than one million and one crore rather than ten million.

1	ek
2	do
3	tin
4	char
5	panch
6	chhe
7	saat
8	aath
9	nau
10	das
12	baranh
13	teranh
14	chodanh
15	pandranh
16	solanh
17	staranh
18	aatharanh
19	unnis
20	bis
21	ikkis
30	tis
35	paintis
40	chalis
50	panchaas
60	saath
70	sattar
80	assi
90	nabbe
100	so
1000	ek hazaar
100,000	lakh
10,000,000	crore

Facts for the Visitor

PLANNING

When to Go

The weather will probably be your most important consideration in determining when you plan to visit the Indian Himalaya. For more information, see the Climate section in the Facts about the Region chapter. Also, it's a good idea to give all of the hill stations a miss during school holidays and the Dussehra and Diwali festivals (September and October), when it can be difficult to find accommodation, and prices increase threefold. An exception is Kullu, which is a great place to visit during Dussehra. It hosts one of the most colourful celebrations of this festival that you'll see anywhere in India.

Jammu & Kashmir Lonely Planet does not recommend travel to this region while the violence due to political unrest continues. The best weather in Jammu & Kashmir is from September to November.

Ladakh & Zanskar Ladakh receives few visitors during its bitter winters (mid-October to late May). The peak tourist season falls in July and August, although there can be occasional heavy rains at this time. In September the weather is fine and clear, and remains so until mid-October, when the first winter snows block the passes into the region. The best time to visit Zanskar is between June and September.

Himachal Pradesh In the Kangra, Chamba, Kullu and Parbati valleys, and the towns of Manali and Shimla, the combination of the best weather, lower prices and smaller crowds is from mid-September to November. Another good time to visit is from April until the rains set in, around mid-June; however, it's also the peak season when accommodation is not only expensive but difficult to find. The remote regions of Lahaul & Spiti and Kinnaur are best visited between June and October. Lahaul is totally cut off from December to March, as is north Spiti, and upper Kinnaur. But a daily bus from Shimla to Kaza (the capital of Spiti) usually manages to run – except during periods of heavy snowfall in January and February. The same applies to Kinnaur where Kalpa and Sangla are accessible, except in deep winter.

Uttarakhand The best time to visit the hill station areas of Uttarakhand (the Uttar Pradesh hills) is from mid-May to mid-July and mid-September to mid-November. Further north, the Char Dham are snowbound between November and April. The beautiful Valley of Flowers is best visited during the monsoon (mid-July to mid-August).

Corbett Tiger Reserve and Rajaji National Park are open between 15 November and 15 June. Rishikesh and Haridwar can be visited year round, although it can get quite chilly during the winter months.

West Bengal Hills The clear air between mid-September and mid-December guarantees the best mountain vistas from Darjeeling, although in November and December it can get bitterly cold. The best season to view wildlife in the Jaldhapara Wildlife Sanctuary of West Bengal is between March and April, although the sanctuary is open from October to May.

Sikkim Sikkim is best visited in spring (March to May) and autumn (September to November). Sikkim's orchids are in bloom towards the end of September/beginning of October, and between April and May.

What Kind of Trip?

In most parts of the Himalaya it is possible to travel around independently, and in many regions reputable trekking agents can tailor treks to individual requirements. If you'd prefer to join a tour, the state government tourist authorities in Delhi and Calcutta have a range of tour options, including pilgrimage tours, river rafting, trekking, skiing and other activities. A list of reputable adventure tour operators in Delhi is listed under Activities later in this chapter.

Maps

Lonely Planet's *India travel atlas* breaks the country down into over 100 pages of maps, and so gives unequalled coverage. It is fully indexed and the book format means it is easy to refer to. It gives you plenty of detail on small towns and villages to help speed along those long bus or train trips.

The Government Map Office (Survey of India) produces a series of maps covering all of India. In Delhi their shambolic office is opposite the Government of India tourist office on Janpath. The headquarters of the Survey of India, which was established in 1767, is in the Hathibarkala Estate, off Rajpur Rd in Dehra Dun. The maps are generally not all that useful since the government will not allow production of anything at a reasonable scale which shows India's sea or land borders, and many of them date back to the 1970s. They do, however, have some good city maps. It is illegal to take any Survey of India map of a scale larger than 1:250,000 out of the country.

The Survey of India's Trekking Map Series includes *Badari-Kedar* (1:250,000), a colour map of the northern Garhwal region. Their *Kumaun Hills* map is also at a scale of 1:250,000.

The Survey's *Hill Ranges & Rivers* (1:5,000,000) covers the entire country, and has an elevation profile of the peaks of the Greater Himalaya, and their *Sikkim* is a fine state map, with a scale of 1:150,000, but it's difficult to procure.

Nest & Wings (PO Box 4531, New Delhi; ☎ 644-2245) publishes a good series of maps, including both trekking and touring maps. Trekking maps include *Ladakh, Jammu & Kashmir* (Rs 50); *Himachal Pradesh*, including Lahaul & Spiti; and *Zanskar, Ladakh & Nubra Valley* (both Rs 75). *Tso Moriri & Pangong Tso, Ladakh, Jammu & Kashmir* (Rs 50) is a smaller map, and *Darjeeling Area, Sikkim & Bhutan* (Rs

20) is a road and trekking map. Their tourist maps include *Himachal Pradesh* and the *Garhwal & Kumaon Himalayas* (both Rs 30 and neither to scale).

Nelles Verlag has good maps on all of the Indian Himalaya, as well as Tibet, Nepal and Bhutan, at a scale of 1:1,500,000, but they are not widely available in India.

The Government of India tourist offices have a number of excellent giveaway city maps and also a reasonable all-India map. State tourist offices do not have much in the way of maps, but the Himachal Pradesh state tourist office has three excellent trekking maps which cover the trekking routes in that state.

What to Bring

The usual travellers' rule applies – bring as little as possible. It's much better to have to buy something you've left behind than find you have too much and need to get rid of it.

Clothes In the Himalayan regions, it can be quite cool in the evenings at the hill stations, even in the summer months, and further north it will get down to freezing, so you will need all the cold-weather gear you can muster.

For colder climates, the 'layers theory' is your best bet – start with thermals and add successive layers of clothes. If you're travelling to Ladakh, be prepared for dramatic temperature changes and for the extreme burning power of the sun in Ladakh's thin air. A cloud across the sun can change the air temperature from T-shirt to sweater level in seconds. Without a hat and/or sunscreen you'll have sunburn, a peeling nose and cracked lips in no time at all.

A reasonable clothes list would include:

- underwear (including thermals for higher elevations)
- swimming gear (summer months only)
- one pair of cotton trousers (summer and for lower elevations)
- one pair of warmer and more durable trousers (winter and for higher elevations)
- jacket (of high-quality fabric, such as a Gore-Tex, for high elevations)

- down vest (high elevations)
- one pair of shorts
- one long cotton skirt (women)
- a few T-shirts or short-sleeved cotton shirts
- thick sweater or woollen shirt for cold nights
- one pair of sneakers or shoes, plus socks; good, comfortable walking boots with ankle support if you're planning to trek
- sandals
- thongs (flipflops; handy to use when showering in common bathrooms)
- lightweight jacket or raincoat (essential during the monsoon; a more heavyweight jacket for higher elevations)
- gloves & balaclava (Both items can be purchased locally. A balaclava is particularly important at higher elevations, as considerable body heat is lost through the head.)
- a set of 'dress up' clothes (for dining in Raj-era hotels!)

Bedding A sleeping bag can be a hassle to carry, but can serve as something to sleep in (and avoid unsavoury-looking hotel bedding), a cushion on hard train seats, a pillow on long bus journeys or a bed top-cover (since cheaper hotels rarely give you one).

If you're trekking in the north then a sleeping bag will be an absolute necessity. Sleeping bags are becoming more readily available, particularly in areas which attract trekkers. However, they are generally not great quality. Sleeping bags can be rented in Leh, and are very useful even if you're not trekking or camping. The nights can get very cold, and visiting many of the remote *gompas* (monasteries) by public transport will require an overnight stop, often in basic guesthouses. If you're planning to trek, you'll also require a sleeping mat, which can be readily hired (Rs 5 per day), or can be purchased in centres such as McLeod Ganj.

A sheet sleeping bag can be very useful, particularly on overnight train trips or if you don't trust the hotel's sheets. They can also be used as liners if you hire a sleeping bag. Mosquito nets are rare, so your own sheet or sheet sleeping bag will also help to keep mosquitoes at bay. Mosquitoes are less of a hassle in the hills than down on the plains, although Siliguri and Gangtok are notorious mosquito zones.

Some travellers find that a plastic sheet is useful for a number of reasons, including to bedbug-proof unhealthy-looking beds. Others have recommended an inflatable pillow as a useful accessory. These are widely available for Rs 30.

Toilet Paper Indian sewerage systems are generally overloaded enough without having to cope with toilet paper as well. However, if you can't adapt to the Indian method of a jug of water and your left hand, toilet paper is widely available in the hill stations; it is less readily available further north in the more remote regions. A receptacle is sometimes provided in toilets for used toilet paper – use it!

Toiletries Soap, toothpaste and other toiletries are readily available, although hair conditioner usually comes in the 'shampoo and conditioner in one' format, so if you don't use this stuff, bring your own conditioner. Astringent is useful for cleaning away the grime at the end of the day – bring cottonballs for application. A universal sink plug is worth having since few cheaper hotels have plugs. A nailbrush can be extremely useful. Tampons are not readily available in the Himalayan regions – bring a supply. Sanitary pads are widely available in the hill stations, but not in the more remote regions.

Men can safely leave their shaving gear at home. One of the pleasures of Indian travel is a shave in a barber shop every few days. With AIDS becoming more widespread in India, however, choose a barber shop that looks clean, and make sure that a fresh blade is used. For just a few rupees you'll get the full treatment – lathering, followed by a shave, then the process is repeated, and finally there's the hot, damp towel and sometimes talcum powder. If you're not quick you'll find that before you know it you're also in for a scalp massage.

How to Carry It Where to put all this gear? Well, for budget travellers the backpack is still the best carrying container. Many packs these days are lockable, otherwise you can make it a bit more thief-proof by sewing on tabs so you can padlock it shut. It's worth paying the money for a strong, good quality pack, as it's much more likely to withstand the rigours of Indian travel.

An alternative is a large, soft, zip bag with a wide shoulder strap. This is obviously not an option if you plan to do any trekking. Suitcases are only for jet-setters! If you're travelling in the Indian Himalaya during the monsoon, a waterproof cover for your pack is essential.

Lots of plastic bags will keep your gear in some sort of order and will also be invaluable for keeping things dry should your pack get rained on.

Miscellaneous Items It's amazing how many things you wish you had with you when you're in India. Useful items include washing gear, medical and sewing kits, and sunglasses. A length of clothesline and a handful of clothes pegs are also worth considering if you're going to do your own laundry – elastic 'pegless' clotheslines are extremely handy; they usually have hooks at either end which make them easy to secure to just about anything. For budget travellers, a padlock is a virtual necessity. Most cheap hotels and quite a number of mid-range hotels have doors locked by a flimsy latch and padlock. You'll find having your own sturdy lock on the door does wonders for your peace of mind. Other uses are legion. Many trains have loops under the berths which you can padlock luggage to, for example. It may not make it thief-proof, but it helps. You can buy a reasonable lock in India for Rs 25 to Rs 50.

A universal sink plug is also useful, as sinks never have them. Ever tried to wash your underwear in a sink without a plug? A knife (preferably Swiss Army) finds a whole field of uses, in particular for peeling fruit. Some travellers rhapsodise about the usefulness of a miniature electric element to boil water in a cup. A sarong is a handy item. It can be used as a bed sheet, an item of clothing, an emergency towel, and a pillow on trains!

Insect repellent can also be extremely useful. Pick up an electric mosquito zapper in Delhi or Calcutta before heading north. Power cuts are common in the Indian Himalaya ('load shedding' as it is euphemistically known) and there's little street lighting at night so a torch (flashlight) and candles are essential. A mosquito net can be very useful on the plains and en route to the hills (at Siliguri, in West Bengal, for example), as well as in mosquito-prone areas such as

---

Monsoon Essentials

If you're planning to travel to the Himalayan region during the monsoon, don't underestimate its ability to turn your trip into a waterlogged misery if you're not properly prepared. Monsoon essentials include:

- sturdy umbrella (available just about everywhere)
- raincoat
- full set of wet weather gear, including overpants with elasticised ankles
- waterproofing spray for boots and packs
- a plastic cover for your pack
- gumboots/Wellingtons (readily available in the hill stations, but if you have large feet, you'll need to bring a pair with you)
- plastic envelopes (for important documents)
- good, sturdy plastic bags (to keep sodden clothes separate from dry clothes in your pack)
- waterproof cover for your camera (which enables you to take pictures without having to juggle the camera *and* an umbrella) ■

Gangtok. A small rubber wedge door-stop was one suggestion; it helps keep doors both open and closed.

Bring along a spare set of specs and your spectacle prescription if you're short-sighted. Should you lose or damage your glasses, a new pair can be made very cheaply, competently and quickly in Delhi or Calcutta, but in the hills regions, if you lose or break your only pair of specs, you'll find yourself in difficulties. Earplugs are useful for light sleepers, and even heavier sleepers can have difficulty shutting out the din in some hotels. Eye shades can also be handy.

For hot weather and for the snow zones, a sun hat and sunglasses are essential. If you're planning to trek or spend time in or near the snow zones, consider a pair of snow goggles. A water bottle should always be by your side; and also, if you're not drinking bottled water, have water purification tablets (which also reduces the amount of plastic bottles seen on dumps around India). You'll also need something with long sleeves, particularly if you're going to ride a bicycle very far. High-factor sunscreen cream is becoming more widely available, but it's *expensive*! Lip balm is especially useful in regions such as Ladakh, where the air is thinner and the sun can really pack a punch.

Other miscellaneous items worth considering are calamine lotion or an anti-itch preparation in the event of bites by bed bugs and mosquitoes. Some travellers bring a reasonably heavy duty chain to secure their pack to the luggage racks of trains and buses. Some women carry a high-pitched whistle which may act as a deterrent to would-be assailants. See the Health section later in this chapter for details about medical supplies.

SUGGESTED ITINERARIES

The Indian Himalaya is a vast region and, ideally, you could spend months here exploring tiny mountain villages, ancient gompas and pilgrimage sites. There is a danger in prescribing suggested itineraries, as part of the pleasure of travelling in the Indian Himalaya is the element of surprise. Nevertheless, if your time is limited, the following outlines might give you a place to start. The idea is to use these as a guideline only; deviating from the main tourist centres is recommended.

Most of these itineraries will take about three weeks, but they can of course be extended or incorporated according to your time and interests.

Himachal Pradesh & Ladakh
Delhi – McLeod Ganj – Kullu – Parbati Valley – Kullu – Naggar – Manali – Leh – Delhi

First port of call is McLeod Ganj, home to thousands of Tibetan refugees, and headquarters of the Tibetan Government in Exile. You can spend days here, visiting Tsuglagkhang, the Dalai Lama's temple, attending meditation classes, tucking into the best food you'll find just about anywhere, walking up to the grassy ridge of Triund, which has magnificent views of the Dhauladhar Range, and shopping for Tibetan artefacts in the town centre. Next stop is Kullu, from where you can head out along the Parbati Valley to the laidback village of Manikaran, renowned for its hot springs and fine Hindu and Sikh shrines. Then it's back to Kullu and on to Manali, stopping off at beautiful Naggar, ancient capital of the Kullu Valley, where you can visit temples built during the reign of the *rajas* (kings).

Manali has been a centre for travellers in search of the cosmic since the 1970s. It's still a good place to spend a few days, with fine old guesthouses and some interesting temples. After you're well rested, it's time to embark on one of the classic trips in India – the two day haul by bus to the capital of Ladakh, Leh*. In the town of Leh and environs are some spectacular and colourful gompas, rich repositories of Buddhist art. You can also study aspects of Buddhist philosophy here. From Leh you can reduce the long journey back to the capital to a couple of hours by flying back to Delhi.

* Before heading north to Leh, if you have the time, you could travel east from Gramphu to the remote Lahaul & Spiti region. A permit is required to visit this restricted area.

Himachal Hill Stations
Delhi – Pathankot – Dalhousie – Khajiar – Chamba – McLeod Ganj – Mandi – Shimla – Delhi

Take the overnight train to Pathankot from the capital, from where it's a 3½ hour trip by bus to the old British hill station of Dalhousie. There are some fine walks in the environs of the town, and you can walk in a day to the grassy meadow of Khajiar, spend the night in a guesthouse here and catch the afternoon bus on the following day to Chamba, renowned for its extraordinary and ancient temple complexes.

It's then a long 10 hour haul to McLeod Ganj (see below)*, where you can easily spend four or five days. Then it's on to the gateway of the Kullu Valley, Mandi, with the fine 16th century Bhutnath Temple, among others, before proceeding to the pleasant hill station of Shimla**, which still retains fine old colonial buildings, as well as two interesting bazaars. There's enough to keep you busy here for days. From Shimla, you can catch the toy train to Kalka, and then proceed from there to Delhi.

* If you have the time and inclination, it's possible to trek from the Chamba Valley to McLeod Ganj over the high Indrahar Pass across the Dhauladhar mountain range. Alternatively, you could continue down the Chamba Valley to the end of the road at ancient Brahmaur, which also has a beautiful group of ancient temples.

**From Shimla, it is possible to head north-east to the remote region of Kinnaur which shares its eastern border with Tibet. A permit is required to visit this area.

UP Hill Stations
Delhi – Haridwar – Rishikesh – Mussoorie – Haridwar – Nainital – Ranikhet – Kausani – Almora – Delhi

Catch the overnight train to Haridwar, with its hundreds of ashrams and modern temples, and take a day trip out to the Rajaji National Park (open mid-November to mid-June) and then continue to Rishikesh, where serious students of Hindu philosophy can study at the feet of the masters. From Rishikesh it takes little over an hour to Dehra Dun, from where there are numerous buses up to the nearby hill station of Mussoorie. Catch the cable car up to Gun Hill for fine Himalayan panoramas and have your fortune told by astrologers back down on The Mall.

Next it's a long day's journey to Nainital via Haridwar, where you can row around the beautiful lake and visit scenic viewpoints on horseback. Between mid-November and mid-June, take a day trip out to the Corbett Wildlife Reserve for an elephant-back tiger-spotting safari. A couple of days at either Ranikhet, Kausani or Almora* (or all of them) will have you relaxed and ready to face the chaos back down on the plains.

* From Kausani, it's only a short bus ride north to the ancient temple group at Baijnath, and from Almora, you can visit the beautiful village of Jageshwar, which has fine walks in the environs and a stunning group of ancient stone temples.

Char Dham
Delhi – Haridwar – Rishikesh – Mussoorie – Yamunotri – Gangotri – Kedarnath – Badrinath – Rishikesh – Delhi

If you're really pressed for time, you could take the 13 day *yatra* (pilgrimage) run by UP Tourism to the four shrines of Yamunotri, Gangotri, Kedarnath and Badrinath. However, you'd do better to make your own leisurely way around this region. Ideally, the best way to visit these remote shrines is by taxi; you can complete the yatra by public bus, but they tend to leave the sacred spots at ungodly hours of the morning.

After paying homage to the holy Ganga at Haridwar and Rishikesh, proceed to Mussoorie, and if you're a carnivore, enjoy your last chicken *korma* (a creamy curry) before proceeding to the holy shrines further north. It's a long and nerve-shattering trip to Hanumanchatti, roadhead for the 14 km trek to Yamunotri. If you're really keen, you'll make it to Yamunotri in a day's trek; the less energetic can stop overnight at Jankibaichatti, and if the thought of the remaining five km *uphill* trek to the holy site still doesn't thrill after a good night's sleep, you can complete the last leg on a mountain pony.

It's a long haul to Gangotri, via the pleasant town of Uttarkashi, but at least the bus will drop you practically at the door of the sacred shrine. From Gangotri you can trek in two days to the source of the Ganges (technically the Bhagirathi), at the Gangotri Glacier. The next stage of the yatra, to Kedarnath, will require an overnight halt en route – probably at Srinagar. On arrival at Gaurikund, roadhead for the 14 km trek to the holy shrine, you'll be assailed by pony owners vying for your custom. In fact, it's not such a bad way to traverse the steep trail to Kedarnath, but if you'd prefer to walk, you can stay overnight at the village of Rambara, halfway up the trail, or plough on upwards to reach Kedarnath at dusk.

It's possible to reach Gangotri in a day from Gaurikund, but the bus leaves at an obscenely early hour of the morning. After 12 long, dusty hours it will drop you in the large village of Badrinath where you can dine at the Quality restaurant, pay homage to Vishnu the following morning at the temple, and walk to the tribal village of Mana, three km distant.

How you make your way back to Delhi is up to you. You might like to stop at Govind Ghat, between Badrinath and Josimath, and trek (or take a pony) out to Ghangaria, from where you can take day trips into the beautiful Valley of Flowers National Park. At Josimath you can arrange a guide to take you on some of the fine treks in this region. If you're not a trekker, head down to the Kumaon region with its renowned hill stations, or backtrack to Rishikesh.

West Bengal Hills & Sikkim

Calcutta (or Delhi) – Siliguri – Darjeeling – Gangtok – West Sikkim – Kalimpong – Siliguri – Calcutta (or Delhi)

Find your way to Siliguri on the northern West Bengal plains, then catch the toy train for the nine hour journey to the queen of the hill stations – Darjeeling. Check out the snow leopards at India's only snow leopard breeding programme, imbibe the beverage

for which Darjeeling is famous (and visit the tea plantations), have a spot of badminton at the Gymkhana Club, then proceed to Gangtok, capital of Sikkim (with your easily obtained tourist permit, of course).

Tee up your trekking permit for West Sikkim at a reputable travel agent, then head off under your own steam to the beautiful Phodang and Labrang gompas in North Sikkim. During your stay in Gangtok, take a day trip to Rumtek Gompa, headquarters of the Kagyupa order. Then set forth for West Sikkim (on your organised trek)*, taking in the stunning gompa at Pemayangtse and the beautiful Tashiding Gompa, before heading for Yuksom, roadhead for the Dzongri Trail.

After you've completed your trek, set off for Jorethang and proceed to Kalimpong, back in West Bengal, where you can visit the ornate Zong Dog Palri Fo-Brang Gompa, and then return to Siliguri and back to Calcutta or Delhi.

* Note: 15 day permits are available for Sikkim, and are rarely extendible. The above itinerary will allow four or five days for trekking in the Dzongri region. If you're a keen trekker and would prefer a longer trek, you might have to forego a visit to East and North Sikkim.

HIGHLIGHTS
Faded Touches of the Raj

Although the British left India almost 50 years ago, there are many places in the hills where you'd hardly know it. You can relax in true British style for afternoon tea at Glenary's Tea Rooms in Darjeeling and later retire for a preprandial cocktail in front of the open fire in the lounge of the Windamere Hotel to await the gong which summons you to dinner. The Nainital Boat Club is an old British club with a lakeside ballroom which was once the preserve of only true-blue Brits (the famous British hunter Jim Corbett, having been born in Nainital, was refused membership). The Gymkhana Club in Darjeeling still has its original snooker tables, Raj ghosts and cobwebs. Cricket, polo, picnics and gymkhana are still enjoyed at places around Shimla, including The Glen, Summer Hill and Annandale.

Hindu Pilgrimage Sites

The northern hills region of Uttar Pradesh has the highest concentration of sacred pilgrimage sites in the Indian Himalaya. At Haridwar, you can watch dusty pilgrims having their sins washed away while bathing off the *ghats* (steps) on the banks of the holy Ganga, or observe the evening Ganga Aarti (river worship) ceremony, performed by priests who set floating lamps adrift on the current.

Only 24 km north is Rishikesh, which must have the highest concentration of ashrams in the world. These elaborate and often brightly coloured edifices flank the banks of the Ganges, and are resplendent with enormous statues featuring scenes from the Hindu scriptures.

Garhwal, the western region of Uttarakhand, is the site of the Char Dham, or four holy pilgrimage sites of Yamunotri, Gangotri, Kedarnath and Badrinath. At Gangotri and Badrinath, buses laden with pilgrims will drop you practically at the doorstep of their respective sacred shrines, the first dedicated to the holy Ganga, and the second to Lord Vishnu. To reach Yamunotri and Kedarnath requires a 14 km trek from their respective roadheads, and you can join pilgrims on foot or horseback for the long (but not difficult) trek to the shrines of the goddess Yamuna, and of Lord Shiva.

Kedarnath is one of the Panch Kedar, five sites sacred to Shiva. The other four shrines are located at Tunganath (with a fantastic Himalayan panorama stretching in an arc to the north), Rudranath, Madmaheshwar and Kalpeshwar, all of which are in Garhwal. You can also pay homage at the Panch Prayag, the five holy *sangams*, or confluences, formed by the meetings of the tributaries of the Ganges. These can be found at Deoprayag, Rudraprayag, Karanprayag, Nandprayag and Vishnuprayag, also all in Garhwal.

Ancient Temple Complexes

The former rajas of the various princely states which once formed parts of the Indian Himalaya have left a legacy of beautiful stone temple complexes, groups of elaborately carved temples, frequently conforming to the *shikhara* style, where the sacred inner sanctum is topped by a large stone spire. The great prestige and wealth of the Varman Dynasty which ruled over much of the Chamba Valley in Himachal Pradesh is evident in fine temple groups in the beautiful town of Chamba, and in the earlier capital of the princely state at ancient Brahmaur. The Katyuri and Chand dynasties of Kumaon, the eastern district of Uttarakhand, were responsible for the construction of the fine temple complexes at Baijnath, Bhageshwar and Jageshwar, with most of the temples dedicated to Lord Shiva. The main temple at Jageshwar enshrines a *jyoti lingam* (most important Shiva shrine), one of the 12 'lingams of light' in India.

Buddhist Gompas & Temples

Ladakh is renowned for its ancient Buddhist gompas. Forty-five km from Leh is the famous Hemis Gompa, with fine, well preserved wall paintings and ornate images of the deities. Matho Gompa, also in Ladakh, has beautiful *thangkas* (religious paintings) and hosts extraordinary oracle festivals around Losar (Tibetan New Year), during which *lamas* (Tibetan Buddhist priest) enter a trance and, while possessed by the deities, inflict wounds on themselves which appear to instantaneously (and miraculously) heal.

The idyllically sited Tikse Gompa is a very fine Buddhist edifice housing an important collection of ancient Tibetan manuscripts. Between Leh and Kargil are the interesting gompas of Alchi and Rizong. In the Zanskar region are several other notable gompas, including the Sani and Karsha gompas.

In the remote Kinnaur region of Himachal Pradesh, particularly those areas lying close to the Tibetan border, are more historic gompas, including the 11th century gompa at Nako. In the Spiti Valley is the beautiful 16th century Ki Gompa with a stunning collection of ancient thangkas, some of silk, depicting the life of Padmasambhava, the

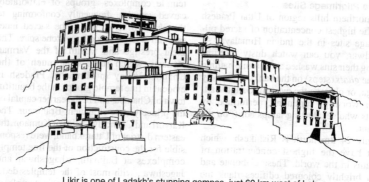
Likir is one of Ladakh's stunning gompas, just 60 km west of Leh.

Indian sage who introduced Buddhism to Tibet.

In McLeod Ganj, the headquarters of the Tibetan Government in Exile and home of His Holiness the Dalai Lama, is Tsuglagkhang, the Dalai Lama's temple. Compared with some other Buddhist temples, it is a relatively unassuming edifice, but houses some beautiful images of Tibetan deities, including Avalokitesvara, or Chenresig, of whom the Dalai Lama is considered to be an incarnation.

Manali and the West Bengal hills regions also have sizeable communities of Tibetan and Bhutanese Buddhists. There are several gompas in Darjeeling, including the Yogachoeling Gompa, which enshrines an image of the Maitreya Buddha (the coming Buddha), who is unconventionally seated as if on a chair. In Kalimpong is the beautiful, ornate Zong Dog Palri Fo-Brang Gompa, a modern edifice featuring extraordinary wall paintings and a three-dimensional *mandala* (circular symbol of the universe), one of only three in the world.

Like Ladakh, Sikkim is known for its ancient gompas. Some of the more notable gompas here include Rumtek, near Gangtok, which has an elaborate golden reliquary *stupa* (Buddhist religious monument) enshrining the remains of the late 16th Karmapa, and at which *chaam* dances (lama dances) are staged during Losar; the extraordinarily ornate Pemayangtse Gompa, and beautiful Tashiding Gompa, both in West Sikkim.

Hill Stations
The greatest number of hill stations in India are naturally found in the foothills of the Himalaya, where the sahibs and memsahibs sweltering down on the plains during the era of the Raj could retreat during the summer months for rest and relaxation. Shimla became the official summer capital of British India in 1864, and still retains some fine old Raj vestiges, such as the Christ Church, as well as stately homes over 100 years old. It's a great place to spend some time.

In Himachal Pradesh, McLeod Ganj, or Upper Dharamsala, today supporting a thriving community of Tibetan refugees who have fled from their country following its invasion by China, is also an excellent place to spend some time, particularly if you're interested in studying Buddhist philosophy. Himachal's other hill station is Dalhousie, in the Chamba Valley. Few western travellers find their way here, but it's a favourite holiday spot for vacationing Indians, and there are some fine walks in the area, as well as some dilapidated but interesting old Raj-era buildings.

In Uttarakhand is Mussoorie, the closest hill station to Delhi. Another favourite with Indian holiday makers, its fine mountain vistas and pleasant climate, together with a startling variety of places to stay, including some grand old hotels, make this a good place to visit. In the Kumaon district of Uttarakhand is Nainital, spread around the eastern side of a beautiful crater lake. While it's not quite Venice, eager boatmen will vie for your custom and nothing could be more pleasant than being rowed around the lake. Then if you can rustle up the energy, there's an astonishing variety of restaurants, or you could plod around the trails in the wooded environs of the hill station on the back of a fine mountain pony.

If you really want to escape the madding crowds, also in Kumaon are the pleasant hill stations of Almora, Ranikhet and Kausani, far less frenetic than Mussoorie or Nainital, but with stunning mountain vistas.

Then there's the queen of the hill stations: Darjeeling, in the West Bengal hills. While the queen is looking slightly the worse for wear these days, and this is not really the place to head if you're looking for peace and solitude, there's enough to keep you occu-pied here for days, including fine Buddhist gompas, pleasant walks in the environs of the hill station, several museums, a zoo, and you can visit nearby tea gardens. Travelling to Darjeeling from Siliguri on the West Bengal plains by the historic toy train shouldn't be missed.

Freak Centres

India has been the ultimate goal of the on-the-road hippie dream for years and somehow the 1960s still endures in India. The technicolour Tibetan outlook on life (they've got a way with hotels and restau-rants too) works well in Kathmandu so why not in India – you'll find McLeod Ganj, Manikaran and Manali, all in Himachal Pradesh, have long-term populations of vis-itors, as do the environs of Almora, in Uttarakhand, which captured the imagination of Timothy Leary, psychedelic interpreter of a generation. Rishikesh, with its numerous ashrams, attracts its fair share of those intent on transcending the mundane.

When the rains sweep over Himachal, the annual migration of the seriously mind-altered proceeds further north to Leh, where an altered state of consciousness can be

Chortens are found throughout Buddhist areas and commonly enshrine
sacred relics, eg a hair of the Buddha.

effected by simply viewing the wall paintings in the extraordinary gompas there.

National Parks & Wildlife Sanctuaries

Corbett Tiger Reserve, in the Kumaon district of Uttarakhand, is probably India's best known wildlife sanctuary, and is India's oldest national park. Corbett Tiger Reserve provides the opportunity to see both tigers and numerous other species in their natural habitat. Further west in Garhwal is the Rajaji National Park, known for its herds of wild elephants.

On the plains at the foot of the West Bengal hills is the Jaldhapara Wildlife Sanctuary, one of the last homes of the endangered one-horned rhino (*Rhinoceros unicornis*). Sikkim also has several wildlife sanctuaries, including the Fambonglho Wildlife Sanctuary, close to Gangtok, which has small populations of Himalayan black bear, red panda and other mammals, as well as prolific birdlife. Wildlife sanctuaries are located in the remote regions of Ladakh but are virtually inaccessible.

TOURIST OFFICES
Local Tourist Offices

Within India the tourist office story is somewhat blurred by the overlap between the national and state tourist offices. Some states, such as Uttar Pradesh, even have divisional offices for separate districts, such as Garhwal and Kumaon in Uttarakhand.

Government of India tourist offices in the four international gateways to India include:

Calcutta
　Sandozi Bldg, 26 Himayat Nagar, Hyderabad
　(☎ (0842) 63-0037)
Delhi
　88 Janpath, New Delhi
　(☎ (011) 332-0005)
Madras
　154 Anna Salai
　(☎ (044) 852-4295)
Mumbai (Bombay)
　123 Maharishi Karve Rd, Churchgate
　(☎ (022) 203-2932)

Beware that, particularly in New Delhi, touts

hanging around the national tourist office will try to hustle you into nearby privately operated tourist concerns while claiming that these are the official Government of India tourist offices. Note the above address.

The state tourist offices vary widely in their efficiency and usefulness. Some of them are very good, some completely hopeless. In many Himalayan states the state tourism ministry also runs a chain of tourist bungalows and large, sometimes colonial, hotels, which generally offer good accommodation at very reasonable prices. They also have good tourist bus services, sightseeing tours, and skiing packages, as well as other travel services. State tourist offices will usually be in the tourist bungalows (where there is one). Offices are listed at the beginning of each regional chapter.

Tourist Offices Abroad

The Government of India Department of Tourism maintains a string of tourist offices in other countries where you can get brochures, leaflets and some information about India. The tourist office leaflets and brochures often have high quality information and are worth getting hold of. However, some of the foreign offices are not always as useful for obtaining information as those within India. There are also smaller 'promotion offices' in Osaka (Japan) and in Dallas, Miami, San Francisco and Washington DC (USA).

Australia
　Level 1, 17 Castlereagh St, Sydney NSW 2000
　(☎ (02) 9232-1600; fax 9223-3003)
Canada
　60 Bloor St West, Suite No 1003, Toronto
　Ontario M4W 3B8 (☎ (416) 962-3787; fax 962-6279)
France
　8 Blvd de la Madeleine, 75009 Paris (☎ (01) 42-65-83-86; fax 42-65-01-16)
Germany
　Kaiserstrasse 77-III, D-6000 Frankfurt-am-Main-1 (☎ (069) 23-5423; fax 23-4724)
Italy
　Via Albricci 9, 20122 Milan (☎ (02) 80-4952; fax 7202-1681)

Japan
  Pearl Bldg, 9-18 Ginza, 7-Chome, Chuo ku, Tokyo 104 (☎ (03) 571-5062; fax 571-5235)
Malaysia
  Wisma HLA, Lot 203 Jalan Raja Chulan, 50200 Kuala Lumpur (☎ (03) 242-5285; fax 242-5301)
The Netherlands
  Rokin 9-15, 1012 KK Amsterdam (☎ (020) 620-8991; fax 38-3059)
Singapore
  United House, 20 Kramat Lane, Singapore 0922 (☎ 235-3800; fax 235-8677)
Sweden
  Sveavagen 9-11, S-III 57, Stockholm 11157 (☎ (08) 21-5081; fax 21-0186)
Switzerland
  1-3 Rue de Chantepoulet, 1201 Geneva (☎ (022) 732-1813; fax 731-5660)
Thailand
  Kentucky Fried Chicken Bldg, 3rd floor, 62/5 Thaniya Rd, Bangkok 10500 (☎ (02) 235-2585)
UK
  7 Cork St, London W1X 2AB (☎ (0171) 437-3677; fax 494-1048)
USA
  30 Rockefeller Plaza, 15 North Mezzanine, New York NY 10112 (☎ (212) 586-4901; fax 582-3274)
  3550 Wilshire Blvd, Suite 204, Los Angeles CA 90010 (☎ (213) 380-8855; fax 380-6111)

VISAS & DOCUMENTS
Passport
You must have a passport with you all the time; it's the most basic travel document. Ensure that your passport will be valid for the entire period you intend to remain overseas. If your passport is lost or stolen, immediately contact your country's embassy or consulate in Delhi or Calcutta.

Visas
Virtually everybody needs a visa to visit India. The application is (in theory) straightforward and the visas are usually issued with a minimum of fuss.

Tourist visas come in a variety of flavours and are shown in the visa table below.

Note that with a three month visa, your entry to India must be within 30 days from the date of issue of the visa. Also, the six month vixa is valid from the date of issue of the visa, not the date you enter India. This means that if you enter India five months after the visa was issued, it will be valid only for one month, not the full six months. If you enter India the day after it was issued, you can stay for the full six months. We get many letters from travellers who get caught out, thinking a six month visa gives them a six month stay in India.

The cost of the visa varies depending on your nationality. Currently, for a 15 day/three month/six month visa, Brits pay UK£3/13/26, and Aussies pay A$17/40/70. Most other nationalities are charged much the same.

Pakistan The high commission in Islamabad is quite efficient, although if there is an Indian embassy in your home country they may have to fax there to check that you are not a thief, wanted by the police or in some other way undesirable. The process takes a few days, and of course you have to pay for the fax.

Visa Extensions Only six month tourist visas are extendible. If you want to stay in India beyond the 180 days from the date of issue of your visa, *regardless of your date of entry into India*, you're going to have to try to extend your visa. Extensions are not given as a matter of routine. If you have already been in the country for six months, it can be difficult to get an extension, and then you may only be given a month. If you've been in India less than six months the chances are much better. A one month extension costs anything from Rs 600 to Rs 800, and four photos are required.

Applications for visa extensions can be made at Foreigners' Registration Offices (see below), and in all state and district capitals at the office of the Superintendent of Police.

If you stay beyond four months you are also supposed to get an income tax clearance before you leave. See the upcoming Tax Clearance Certificates section for details.

Duration	Valid From	Entries	Extendible
15 days	entry to India	single	No
15 days	entry to India	double	No
3 months	entry to India	multiple	No
6 months	issue of visa	multiple	Yes

Foreigners' Registration Offices Visa extensions are issued by the Foreigners' Registration Offices. The main offices include:

Calcutta
237 Acharya J C Bose Rd (☎ (033) 247-3301)
Delhi
1st floor, Hans Bhavan, Tilak Bridge, New Delhi (☎ (011) 331-9489)
Madras
Shashtri Bhavan Annexe, 26 Haddows Rd (☎ (044) 827-8210)
Mumbai (Bombay)
Special Branch II, Annexe 2, Office of the Commissioner of Police (Greater Mumbai), Dadabhoy Naoroji Rd (☎ (022) 262-0446)

Tax Clearance Certificates

If you stay in India for more than 120 days you need a 'tax clearance certificate' to leave the country. This supposedly proves that your time in India was financed with your own money, not by working in India or by selling things or playing the black market.

Basically all you have to do is find the Foreign Section of the Income Tax Department in Delhi, Calcutta, Madras or Mumbai (Bombay) and turn up with your passport, visa extension form, any other similar paperwork and a handful of bank exchange receipts (to show you really have been changing foreign currency into rupees officially). You fill in a form and wait for anything from 10 minutes to a couple of hours. You're then given your tax clearance certificate and away you go. We've never yet heard from anyone who has actually been asked for this document on departure.

Photocopies

It's a good idea to carry photocopies of your important travel documents, which obviously should be kept separately from the originals in the event that these are lost or stolen.

Take a photocopy of the first page of your passport (ie with your personal details and photograph), as well as a copy of the page with your Indian visa and any additional permits, such as that for Sikkim. A photo-copy of your travel insurance policy could be handy. Keep a record of the travellers' cheques you have exchanged, where they were encashed, the amount and serial number. Encashment receipts should also be kept separate from your travellers' cheques. Photocopy your airline ticket and your credit card. It's not a bad idea to leave photocopies of your important travel documents with a friend or relative at home.

Travel Permits

Even with a visa you are not allowed everywhere in the Indian Himalaya. Certain places require special additional permits. These are covered in the appropriate sections in the relevant chapters, but briefly they are:

Ladakh While you don't require a special permit to visit Leh, or to travel along the Manali-Leh and Srinagar-Leh highways, permits are required for four regions in Ladakh which have been recently opened to foreign visitors. These are the Nubra Valley, Pangong Tso, Tso Moriri and the Dha-Hanu region. Permits are valid for seven days and can be obtained from the District Magistrate's Office in Leh. As a result of the formation of the Ladakh Autonomous Hill Council, an entry tax has been levied on foreign tourists visiting Ladakh. See the Ladakh & Zanskar chapter for more details.

Sikkim Fifteen day permits are issued either while you wait or within two or three hours (depending on where you apply for them). See the Sikkim chapter for full details.

Lahaul & Spiti, & Kinnaur Permits are required to visit these remote north-eastern regions in the state of Himachal Pradesh. They can be easily obtained from the District and Sub-District Magistrates in most regional centres in eastern Himachal Pradesh, and are valid for seven days. See the relevant section in the Himachal Pradesh chapter for more details.

Onward Tickets

Many Indian embassies and consulates will

not issue a visa to enter India unless you are holding an onward ticket, which is taken as sufficient evidence that you intend to leave the country.

Travel Insurance

A travel insurance policy to cover theft, loss and medical problems is a wise idea. There is a wide variety of policies and your travel agent will have recommendations. The international student travel policies handled by STA Travel, Council Travel and other student travel organisations are usually good value. Some policies offer lower and higher medical-expense options but the higher one is chiefly for countries like the USA which have extremely high medical costs. Check the small print:

- Some policies specifically exclude 'dangerous activities' which can include motorcycling and even trekking. If such activities are on your agenda you don't want that sort of policy.
  A locally acquired motorcycle licence may not be valid under your policy.
- You may prefer a policy which pays doctors or hospitals direct rather than you having to pay on the spot and claim later. If you have to claim later make sure you keep all documentation. Some policies ask you to call back (reverse charges) to a centre in your home country where an immediate assessment of your problem is made.
- Check if the policy covers ambulances, an emergency helicopter airlift out of a remote region, or an emergency flight home. If you have to stretch out you will need two seats and somebody has to pay for them!

Driving Licence & Permits

If you are planning to drive in India, get an International Driving Permit from your local national motoring organisation. In some centres, such as Delhi and Mussoorie (the latter during the season only) it's possible to hire motorcycles. An International Permit can also be used for other identification purposes, such as plain old bicycle hire.

Other Documents

A health certificate, while not necessary in India, may well be required for onward travel. Student cards are virtually useless these days – many student concessions have either been eliminated or replaced by 'youth fares' or similar age concessions. Similarly, a Youth Hostel (Hostelling International – HI) card is not generally required for India's many hostels, but you do pay slightly less at official youth hostels if you have one.

It's worth having a batch of passport photos for visa applications and for obtaining permits to remote regions. If you run out, Indian photo studios will do excellent portraits at pleasantly low prices.

Visas for Neighbouring Areas & Countries

If you're heading to other places near the Indian Himalaya, the visa situation is as follows.

North-Eastern Region Foreigners must have a permit for these remote north-eastern states, although at the time of writing, restrictions for entry into Assam were under review, and could be dropped altogether in the near future.

In theory it's possible to visit all of the north-eastern states as long as you are part of a group of four. In practice things are, predictably, a lot different; you might get into Assam and Meghalaya, but getting permission to go any further is extremely difficult.

To enter the remote and predominantly tribal area of Arunachal Pradesh, foreigners need to apply for a Protected Area Permit (PAP), by writing to The Under Secretary, Home Affairs, Lok Nayak Bhawan, Car Market, New Delhi. You should apply from your home country and write at least one month in advance. When making your application, you must specify your exact date of entry into Arunachal.

A minimum of four people is required, and the permit is valid for one week only.

The Government of Arunachal Pradesh charges US$150 per person per day including transport, board and lodging within Arunachal Pradesh. The quality of accommodation in this package is very basic. If you make your own arrangements through a recognised travel agency, the charge levied by the government is US$50 per person per day, which includes a compulsory guide. It's possible to arrange your own accommodation on arrival in Arunachal Pradesh, subject to availability. Travel arrangements must be made through a recognised travel agent who can liaise with the Indian Government on your behalf.

There is a checkpost at Banderdewa, 18 km from the capital of Arunachal, Itanagar. Travellers need to make their own arrangements to the checkpost, where they will be met by a guide from Arunachal Pradesh Tourism. Visitors must be accompanied by the guide at all times, and can visit two defined sectors in one week. The first sector includes Itanagar, Ziro, Along and Pasighat; the second sector covers the Tirap district, to the south-west of Itanagar, and includes Margharita (where there is a checkpost), Miao and Namdapha. Margharita is the entry point for this district.

Myanmar (Burma) The embassy in Delhi is fast and efficient and issues four week visas. There is *no* Burmese consulate in Calcutta, although there is one in Kathmandu in Nepal and Dhaka in Bangladesh.

Nepal The Nepalese Embassy in Delhi is on Barakhamba Rd, New Delhi, quite close to Connaught Place, not out at Chanakyapuri like most other embassies. It is open Monday to Friday from 10 am to 1 pm. Single entry, 30 day visas take 24 hours and cost US$25 (payable in rupees). A 30 day visa is available on arrival in Nepal for US$25, and can be extended, but doing so involves rather a lot of form filling and queuing – it's better to have a visa in advance if possible.

There is also a consulate in Calcutta, and they issue visas on the spot. You'll need one passport photo and the rupee equivalent of US$25.

Bhutan Although Bhutan is an independent country, India has firm control over foreign policy and most other things. Applications to visit Bhutan must be made through the Director of Tourism, Ministry of Finance, Tachichho Dzong, Thimpu, Bhutan; or

through the Bhutan Foreign Mission (☎ (011) 60-9217; fax 687-6710), Chandragupta Marg, Chanakyapuri, New Delhi 110021, India; or through the Bhutanese mission in New York. And don't hold your breath – unless you have high-up Indian connections or a personal friend in the Bhutanese aristocracy, you needn't expect to get a permit. Very few permits are issued for overland travel. The only way around these restrictions is to book an organised tour, and these don't come cheap.

EMBASSIES
Indian Embassies Abroad
India's embassies, consulates and high commissions include:

Australia
    3-5 Moonah Place, Yarralumla, ACT 2600
    (☎ (06) 273-3999; fax 273-3328)
    Level 27, 25 Bligh St, Sydney, NSW 2000
    (☎ (02) 9223-9500; fax 9223-9246)
    13 Munro St, Coburg, Melbourne, Vic 3058
    (☎ (03) 9386-7399; fax 9384-1609)
    The India Centre, 49 Bennett St, Perth, WA 6004
    (☎ (09) 221-1485; fax 221-1206)
Bangladesh
    120 Road 2, Dhamondi, Dhaka
    (☎ (02) 50-3606; fax 86-3662)
    1253/1256 O R Nizam Rd, Mehdi Bagh,
    Chittagong (☎ (031) 21-1007; fax 22-5178)
Belgium
    217 Chaussee de Vleurgat, 1050 Brussels
    (☎ (02) 640-9802; fax 648-9638)
Bhutan
    India House Estate, Thimpu, Bhutan
    (☎ (0975) 22-162; fax 23-195)
Canada
    10 Springfield Rd, Ottawa K1M 1C9
    (☎ (613) 744-3751; fax 744-0913)
China
    1 Ri Tan Dong Lu, Beijing
    (☎ (01) 532-1908; fax 532-4684)
Denmark
    Vangehusvej 15, 2100 Copenhagen
    (☎ (045) 3118-2888; fax 3927-0218)
Egypt
    5 Aziz Ababa St, Zamalek, Cairo 11511
    (☎ (02) 341-3051; fax 341-4038)
France
    15 rue Alfred Dehodencq, 75016 Paris
    (☎ (01) 4050-7070; fax 4050-0996)
Germany
    Adenauerallee 262, 53113 Bonn 1
    (☎ (0228) 54-050; fax 54-05154)

srael
4 Kaufman St, Sharbat House, Tel Aviv 68012
(☎ (03) 58-4585; fax 510-1434)

taly
Via XX Settembre 5, 00187 Rome
(☎ (06) 488-4642; fax 481-9539)

Japan
2-2-11 Kudan Minami, Chiyoda-ku, Tokyo 102
(☎ (03) 3262-2391; fax 3234-4866)

Jordan
1st Circle, Jebel Amman, Amman
(☎ (06) 62-2098; fax 65-9540)

Kenya
Jeevan Bharati Bldg, Harambee Ave, Nairobi
(☎ (02) 22-2566; fax 33-4167)

Korea
37-3 Hannam-dong, Yongsan-ku, Seoul 140210
(☎ (02) 798-4257; fax 796-9534)

Malaysia
20th Floor West Block, Wisma Selangor Dredging, 142-C, Jalan Ampang 50450, Kuala Lumpur
(☎ (03) 261-7000)

Myanmar (Burma)
545-547 Merchant St, Yangon (Rangoon)
(☎ (01) 82-550; fax 89-562)

Nepal
Lainchaur, GPO Box 292, Kathmandu
(☎ (071) 41-1940; fax 41-3132)

The Netherlands
Buitenrustweg 2, 252 KD, The Hague
(☎ (070) 346-9771; fax 361-7072)

New Zealand
180 Molesworth St, Wellington
(☎ (04) 473-6390; fax 499-0665)

Pakistan
G5 Diplomatic Enclave, Islamabad
(☎ (051) 81-4371; fax 82-0742)
India House, 3 Fatima Jinnah Rd, Karachi
(☎ (021) 52-2275; fax 568-0929)

Russia
6 Ulitsa Obukha, Moscow
(☎ (095) 297-0820; fax 975-2337)

Singapore
India House, 31 Grange Rd
(☎ 737-6777; fax 732-6909)

South Africa
Sanlam Centre, Johannesburg
(☎ (011) 333-1525; fax 333-0690)

Sri Lanka
36-38 Galla Rd, Colombo 3
(☎ (01) 421-605; fax 44-6403)

Sweden
Adolf Fredriks Kyrkogata 12, 11183 Stockholm
(☎ (08) 10-7008; fax 24-8505)

Switzerland
Effingerstrasse 45, CH-3008 Berne
(☎ (031) 382-3111; fax 382-2687)

Syria
40/46 Adnan Malki St, Yassin, Damascus
(☎ (011) 71-9581; fax 71-3294)

Tanzania
NIC Investment House, Samora Ave, Dar es Salaam
(☎ (051) 28-198; fax 46-747)

Thailand
46 Soi 23 (Prasarnmitr), Sukhumvit Rd, Bangkok
(☎ (02) 258-0300; fax 258-4627)
113 Bumruangrat Rd, Chiang Mai 50000
(☎ (053) 24-3066; fax 24-7879)

UK
India House, Aldwych, London WC2B 4NA
(☎ (0171) 836-8484; fax 836-4331)
8219 Augusta St, Birmingham B18 6DS
(☎ (0121) 212-2782; fax 212-2786)

USA
2107 Massachusetts Ave NW, Washington DC 20008
(☎ (202) 939-7000; fax 939-7027)
3 East 64th St, Manhattan, New York, NY 10021-7097
(☎ (212) 879-7800; fax 988-6423)
540 Arguello Blvd, San Francisco, CA 94118
(☎ (415) 668-0662; fax 668-2073)

Foreign Embassies & High Commissions in India

Most foreign diplomatic missions are in the nation's capital, Delhi, but there are also quite a few consulates in the other major cities of Mumbai (Bombay), Calcutta and Madras. Embassies and consulates in Delhi and Calcutta are as follows (telephone area codes are (011) for New Delhi and (033) for Calcutta):

Afghanistan
5/50-F Shantipath, Chanakyapuri, New Delhi
(☎ 60-3331; fax 687-5439)

Australia
1/50-G Shantipath, Chanakyapuri, New Delhi
(☎ 688-8223; fax 687-4126)

Austria
EP-13 Chandergupta Marg, Chanakyapuri, New Delhi (☎ 60-1238; fax 688-6929)

Bangladesh
56 Ring Rd, Lajpat Nagar-III, New Delhi
(☎ 683-4668; fax 683-9237)
9 Circus Ave, Calcutta (☎ 247-5208)

Belgium
50-N Shantipath, Chanakyapuri, New Delhi
(☎ 608-295; fax 688-5821)

Bhutan
Chandragupta Marg, Chanakyapuri, New Delhi (☎ 60-9217; fax 687-6710)
48 Tivoli Court, Pramothesh Barua Sarani, Calcutta (☎ 241-301)

Canada
7/8 Shantipath, Chanakyapuri, New Delhi (☎ 687-6500; fax 687-0031)

China
50-D Shantipath, Chanakyapuri, New Delhi (☎ 60-0328; fax 688-5486)

Denmark
11 Aurangzeb Rd, New Delhi (☎ 301-0900; fax 301-0961)
3 N S Rd, Calcutta (☎ 248-7478)

Finland
E-3 Nyaya Marg, Chanakyapuri, New Delhi (☎ 611-5258; fax 688-6713)

France
2/50-E Shantipath, Chanakyapuri, New Delhi (☎ 611-8790; fax 687-2305)
26 Park St (inside the courtyard on the right-hand side of Alliance Française), Calcutta (☎ 29-0978)

Germany
6/50-G Shantipath, Chanakyapuri, New Delhi (☎ 60-4861; fax 687-3117)
1 Hastings Park Rd, Calcutta (☎ 479-1141)

Indonesia
50-A Chanakyapuri, New Delhi (☎ 611-8642; fax 688-4402)

Iran
5 Barakhamba Rd, New Delhi (☎ 332-9600; fax 332-5493)

Iraq
169-171 Jor Bagh Rd, New Delhi (☎ 461-8011; fax 463-1547)

Ireland
13 Jor Bagh Rd, New Delhi (☎ 461-7435; fax 469-7053)

Israel
3 Aurangzeb Rd, New Delhi (☎ 301-3238; fax 301-4298)

Italy
50-E Chandragupta Marg, Chanakyapuri, New Delhi (☎ 611-4355; fax 687-3889)
3 Raja Santosh Rd, Calcutta (☎ 479-2426)

Japan
4-5/50-G Shantipath, Chanakyapuri, New Delhi (☎ 687-6581)
12 Pretoria St, Calcutta (☎ 242-2241)

Kenya
66 Vasant Marg, Vasant Vihar, New Delhi (☎ 687-6540; fax 687-6550)

Malaysia
50-M Satya Marg, Chanakyapuri, New Delhi (☎ 60-1297; fax 688-1538)

Myanmar (Burma)
3/50-F Nyaya Marg, Chanakyapuri, New Delhi (☎ 60-0251; fax 687-7942)

Nepal
Barakhamba Rd, New Delhi (☎ 332-8191; fax 332-6857)
19 Sterndale Rd, Calcutta (☎ 479-1003)

The Netherlands
6/50-F Shantipath, Chanakyapuri, New Delhi (☎ 688-4951; fax 688-4856)
18-A Brabourne Rd, Calcutta (☎ 26-2160)

New Zealand
50-N Nyaya Marg, Chanakyapuri, New Delhi (☎ 688-3170; fax 687-2317)

Norway
50-C Shantipath, Chanakyapuri, New Delhi (☎ 687-3532; fax 687-3814)

Pakistan
2/50-G Shantipath, Chanakyapuri, New Delhi (☎ 60-0603; fax 637-2339)

Russia
Shantipath, Chanakyapuri, New Delhi (☎ 687-3799; fax 687-6823)
31 Shakespeare Sarani, Calcutta (☎ 247-4982)

Singapore
E-6 Chandragupta Marg, Chanakyapuri, New Delhi (☎ 688-5659; fax 688-6798)

South Africa
B-18 Vasant Marg, Vasant Vihar, New Delhi (☎ 611-9411, 611-3505)

Spain
12 Prithviraj Rd, New Delhi (☎ 379-2085; fax 379-3375)

Sri Lanka
27 Kautilya Marg, Chanakyapuri, New Delhi (☎ 301-0201; fax 301-5295)

Sweden
Nyaya Marg, Chanakyapuri, New Delhi (☎ 687-5760; fax 688-5401)

Switzerland
Nyaya Marg, Chanakyapuri, New Delhi (☎ 60-4225; fax 687-3093)

Syria
28 Vasant Marg, Vasant Vihar, New Delhi (☎ 67-0233; fax 687-3107)

Thailand
56-N Nyaya Marg, Chanakyapuri, New Delhi (☎ 60-5679; fax 687-2029)
18B Mandeville Gardens, Calcutta (☎ 76-0836)

UK
50 Shantipath, Chanakyapuri, New Delhi (☎ 687-2161; fax 687-2882)
1 Ho Chi Minh Sarani, Calcutta (☎ 242-5171)

USA
Shantipath, Chanakyapuri, New Delhi (☎ 60-0651)
5/1 Ho Chi Minh Sarani, Calcutta (☎ 242-3611)

CUSTOMS

The usual duty-free regulations apply for

ndia; that is, one bottle of whisky and 200 cigarettes.

You're allowed to bring in all sorts of western technological wonders, but big items, such as video cameras, are likely to be entered on a 'Tourist Baggage Re-Export' form to ensure you take them out with you when you go. This also used to be the case with laptop computers, but some travellers have reported that it is no longer necessary. It's not necessary to declare still-cameras, even if you have more than one.

Note that if you are entering India from Nepal you are not entitled to import anything free of duty.

MONEY

Costs

Whatever budget you decide to travel on, you can be assured that you'll be getting a whole lot more for your money than in most other countries – it's fantastic value.

If you stay in luxury hotels, fly to the hills regions (or hire a helicopter!) and see a lot of the Himalaya in a very short trip, you can spend a lot of money. There are plenty of hotels in the hill stations at US$50 or more a day and some where a room can cost US$100 plus. At the other extreme, if you scrimp and save, stay in dormitories or the cheapest hotels, always travel in ordinary public buses, and learn to exist on *dhal* (curried lentil gravy) and rice, you can see the Indian Himalaya on less than US$7 a day.

Most travellers will probably be looking for something between these extremes. If so, for US$15 to US$20 a day on average, you'll stay in reasonable hotels, eat in regular restaurants but occasionally splash out on a fancy meal, and take autorickshaws rather than a bus. Fully inclusive tours to the Himalayan region will cost you a good deal more; a fully inclusive trek including transport, meals, guides, porters, cook, tent and sleeping mat could cost upwards of US$30 per day, depending on the number of trekkers.

As a rule of thumb, the higher up you get in the Himalaya, the cheaper it gets – you wont find five-star luxury hotels at the source of the Ganges in Uttarakhand!

(Although you will have five-star-plus views!)

Carrying Money

A money belt worn around your waist beneath your clothes is probably one of the safest ways of carrying important documents such as your passport and travellers' cheques on your person. It's not a bad idea to place these documents inside a plastic bag in the money belt to protect them if you should be caught in a sudden downpour. 'Bum bags' – pouches which are worn around your waist *outside* your clothes – are popular and more readily accessible, but extremely conspicuous. Some travellers prefer a pouch attached to a string which is worn around the neck, with the pouch against the chest concealed beneath a shirt or jumper. It is now possible to purchase innocuous looking leather belts from travel goods suppliers which a have a secret compartment in which you could hide your 'emergency stash'.

Travellers' Cheques

Although it's usually not a problem to change travellers' cheques, it's best to stick to the well known brands – American Express, Visa, Thomas Cook, Citibank and Barclays – as more obscure ones may cause problems. It also happens occasionally that a bank won't accept a certain type of cheque – Visa and Citibank in particular – and for this reason it's worth carrying more than one flavour. At the time of writing, it was difficult to exchange anything other than Thomas Cook and American Express cheques in some areas of the Himalayan regions.

A few simple measures should be taken to facilitate the replacement of travellers' cheques, should they be stolen. See Stolen Travellers' Cheques in the Dangers & Annoyances section later in this chapter.

Credit Cards

Credit cards are widely accepted at the curio shops and hotels in the hill stations, but outside these areas, forget it.

With American Express, MasterCard or Visa cards you can use your card to obtain cash rupees in Delhi and Calcutta, as well as at some of the larger hill stations, including Dharamsala and Shimla. With Amex you can get dollar or sterling travellers' cheques in Delhi or Calcutta, or get cash rupees locally from an Amex office, but you must have a personal cheque to cover the amount, although counter cheques are available if you ask for them.

International Transfers

Don't run out of money in India unless you have a credit card against which you can draw travellers' cheques or cash. Having money transferred through the banking system can be time consuming, and there are very few banks in the hills regions which offer this service. You might have luck at some of the larger centres such as Shimla and Dharamsala in Himachal Pradesh, and Dehra Dun in Uttarakhand. It's usually straightforward if you use a foreign bank, Thomas Cook or American Express in Delhi or Calcutta; elsewhere it may take a fortnight and will be a hassle.

If you do have money sent to you in India, specify the bank, the branch and the address you want it sent to.

Currency

The rupee (Rs) is divided into 100 paise (p). There are coins of five, 10, 20, 25 and 50 paise, Rs one, two and five (rare), and notes of Rs one, two, five, 10, 20, 50, 100 and 500.

You are not allowed to bring Indian currency into the country or take it out of the country. You are allowed to bring in unlimited amounts of foreign currency or travellers' cheques, but you are supposed to declare anything over US$10,000 on arrival.

One of the most annoying things about India is that no-one ever seems to have *any* change, and you'll find on numerous occasions you'll be left waiting for five minutes while a shopkeeper hawks your Rs 100 note around other shops to secure change.

Currency Exchange

In major cities you can change most foreign currencies or travellers' cheques – Australian dollars, Deutschmarks, yen or whatever – but up in the hills it's best to stick to US dollars or pounds sterling. Thomas Cook and American Express are both popular travellers' cheques, and can be exchanged readily in most major tourist centres, such as the hill stations.

At the time of going to press, the exchange rates were as follows:

A$1	=	Rs 27.01
C$1	=	Rs 25.06
DM1	=	Rs 22.36
FFr1	=	Rs 6.62
Jap ¥100	=	Rs 32.47
Nep Rs100	=	Rs 60.02
NZ$1	=	Rs 23.43
Sin$1	=	Rs 24.31
US$1	=	Rs 34.06
UK£1	=	Rs 51.45

Changing Money

Outside the main cities, the State Bank of India is usually the place to change money, although occasionally they'll direct you to another bank, such as the Bank of India, the Punjab National Bank or the Bank of Baroda. In the more remote regions, few banks offer exchange facilities, so utilise the banks in the hill stations before heading further north, particularly in the northern reaches of Uttarakhand or to the remote regions of Zanskar, and Lahaul & Spiti, and Kinnaur in Himachal Pradesh, as well as outside Gangtok in Sikkim. Some banks charge an encashment fee, which may be levied for the entire transaction, or on each cheque. Check the fee before you sign your cheques.

Many people make the mistake of bringing too many small-denomination cheques. Unless you are moving rapidly from country to country you only need a handful of small denominations for end-of-stay conversions. In between, change as much as you feel happy carrying. This applies particularly in India where changing money can take time – especially in the smaller towns. You can also spend a lot of time finding a bank which will change money. The answer is to change money as infrequently as possible and to change it only in big banks in big cities or at the hill stations.

Banks in New Delhi & Calcutta

Details of banks which will exchange foreign currency are listed in individual chapters. Banks in Delhi and Calcutta include the following:

Algemeene Bank Nederlands
    18-A Brabourne Rd, Calcutta
American Express
    A Block, Connaught Place, New Delhi
    21 Old Court House St, Calcutta
ANZ Grindlays
    E Block, Connaught Place, New Delhi
    41 Jawaharlal Nehru Rd & Shakespeare Sarani, Calcutta
Bank of America
    Hansalaya Bldg, Barakhamba Rd, New Delhi
    8 India Exchange Place, Calcutta
Bank of Tokyo
    2 Brabourne Rd, Calcutta
Banque Nationale de Paris
    Hansalaya Bldg, Barakhamba Rd, New Delhi
    4-A BBD Bagh East, Calcutta
Central Bank
    Ashok Hotel (24 hours), 50 B Chanakyapuri, New Delhi
Citibank
    Jeevan Bharati Bldg, Outer Circle, Connaught Place, New Delhi
    43 Jawaharlal Nehru Rd, Calcutta
Hongkong Bank
    ECE House, 28 Kasturba Gandhi Marg, New Delhi
Standard Chartered
    Sansad Marg (Parliament St), New Delhi
    4 Netaji Subhash Rd, Calcutta
State Bank of India
    Indira Gandhi International Airport (24 hours), New Delhi
    43 Jawaharlal Nehru Rd, Calcutta
Thomas Cook
    Imperial Hotel, Janpath, New Delhi
    Chitrakoot Bldg, 230 AJC Bose Rd, Calcutta

Black Market

The rupee is a fully convertible currency, ie the rate is set by the market not the government. For this reason there's not much of a black market, although you can get a couple of rupees more for your dollars or pounds cash. In the major tourist centres you will have constant offers to change money. There's little risk involved although it is officially illegal; the major advantage is it's much quicker than changing at a bank. If you do decide to change on the black market, do it off the street rather than in the open. US$100 bills in good condition (ie with no rips or tears) fetch the best rates. Always check the quality of the notes you receive during any transaction; the slightest tear can render a note worthless.

Encashment Certificates

All money is supposed to be changed at official banks or moneychangers, and you are supposed to be given an encashment certificate for each transaction. In practice, some people surreptitiously bring rupees into the country with them – they can be bought at a discount price in places such as Singapore or Bangkok. Indian rupees can be brought in fairly openly from Nepal and again you can get a slightly better rate there.

Banks will usually give you an encashment certificate, but occasionally they don't bother. It is worth getting them, especially if you want to re-exchange excess rupees for hard currency when you depart India.

The other reason for saving encashment certificates is that if you stay in India longer than four months, you have to get an income tax clearance. See Tax Clearance Certificates earlier in this chapter for details.

Baksheesh

In most Asian countries tipping is virtually unknown, but India is an exception to that rule – although tipping has a rather different role in India than in the west. The term *baksheesh*, which encompasses tipping and a lot more besides, aptly describes the concept of tipping in India. You 'tip' not so much for good service, but to get things done.

Judicious baksheesh will open closed doors, find missing letters and perform other small miracles. Tipping is not necessary for taxis nor for cheaper restaurants, but if you're going to be using something repeatedly, an initial tip will ensure the standards are kept up. Keep things in perspective though. Demands for baksheesh can quickly become never-ending. Ask yourself if it's really necessary or desirable before shelling out.

In tourist restaurants or hotels, where service is usually tacked on in any case, the normal 10% figure usually applies. In smaller places, where tipping is optional, you need only tip a few rupees, not a percentage of the bill. Hotel porters usually get about Rs 1 per bag; other possible tipping levels are Rs 1 to Rs 2 for bike-watching, Rs 10 for train conductors or station porters performing miracles for you, and Rs 5 to Rs 15 for extra services from hotel staff.

Although most people think of baksheesh in terms of tipping, it also refers to giving alms to beggars. Wherever you turn in India you'll be confronted by beggars – many of them (often handicapped or hideously disfigured) genuinely in dire need, others, such as kids hassling for a rupee or a pen, obviously not.

Beggars

All sorts of stories about beggars do the rounds of the travellers' hang-outs, many of them with little basis in fact. Stories such as rupee millionaire beggars, people (usually kids) being deliberately mutilated by their parents so they can beg, and a beggars' Mafia are all common.

It's a matter of personal choice how you approach the issue of beggars and baksheesh. Some people feel it is best to give nothing to any beggar, believing it 'only encourages them' and preferring to contribute in a voluntary capacity; others give away loose change when they have it; some benevolent souls have even been known to exchange large notes for handfuls of rupees so that they always have change on hand specifically for this purpose; unfortunately, others insulate themselves entirely and give nothing in any way. It's up to you. ∎

POST & COMMUNICATIONS
Post

The Indian postal and poste restante services are generally excellent. Expected letters al-

most always are there and letters you send almost invariably reach their destination, although they take up to three weeks. American Express, in its major city locations, offers an alternative to the poste restante system.

Have letters addressed to you with your surname in capitals and underlined, followed by the poste restante, GPO, and the city or town in question. Many 'lost' letters are simply misfiled under given (Christian) names, so always check under both your names. Letters sent via poste restante are generally held for one month only, after which, if unclaimed, they are returned to the sender.

You can often buy stamps at good hotels, saving a lot of queuing in crowded post offices.

Postal Rates Aerogrammes and postcards cost Rs 6.50, airmail letters Rs 12.

Posting Parcels Most people discover how to do this the hard way, in which case it'll take half a day. Go about it as described below, which can still take up to an hour:

• Take the parcel to a tailor and tell him you'd like it stitched up in cheap linen. Negotiate the price first.
• Go to the post office with your parcel and ask for the necessary customs declaration forms. Fill them in and glue one to the parcel. The other will be stitched onto it. To avoid excise duty at the delivery end it's best to specify that the contents are a 'gift'. Be careful with how much you declare the contents to be worth. If you specify over Rs 1000, your parcel will not be accepted without a bank clearance certificate. You can imagine the hassles involved in getting one of these so always state the value as less than Rs 1000.
• Have the parcel weighed and franked at the parcel counter.

If you are just sending books or printed matter, these can go by bookpost, which is considerably cheaper than parcel post, but the package must be wrapped a certain way: make sure that the package can either be opened for inspection along the way, or that it is just wrapped in brown paper or cardboard and tied with string, with the two ends exposed so that the contents are visible. To protect the books, it might be worthwhile first wrapping them in clear plastic. No customs declaration form is necessary for such parcels.

Be cautious with places which offer to mail things to your home address after you have bought them. Government emporiums are usually OK. In Delhi and Calcutta, some places offer a comprehensive parcel packing service and will also offer to post the parcel for you. No matter how many travellers' testimonies you are shown guaranteeing that parcels arrived at their destinations, it pays to take the parcel to the post office yourself.

Sending parcels in the other direction (to you in India) is an extremely hit-and-miss affair. Don't count on anything bigger than a letter getting to you. And don't count on a letter getting to you if there's anything worthwhile inside it.

Telephone & Fax

The telephone system in India is generally very good. Most places are hooked up to the STD/ISD network, and so making local, interstate and international calls is simplicity itself from even the smallest town.

Everywhere you'll come across private 'STD/ISD' call booths with direct local, interstate and international dialling. These phones are usually found in shops or other businesses, but are well signposted with large 'STD/ISD' signs advertising the service. A digital meter lets you keep an eye on what the call is costing, and gives you a printout at the end. You then just pay the shop owner – quick, painless and a far cry from the not so distant past when a night spent at a telegraph office waiting for a line was not unusual. Direct international calls from these phones cost around Rs 70 per minute, depending on the country you are calling. To make an international call, you will need to dial the following:

00 (international access code from India) + country code (of the country you are calling) + area code + local number

In some centres, STD/ISD booths may offer

a 'call back' service – you ring your folks or friends, give them the number of the booth and wait for them to call you back. The booth operator will charge about Rs 2 to Rs 3 per minute for this service, in addition to the cost of the preliminary call. Advise your callers how long you intend to wait at the booth in the event that they have trouble getting back to you. The number your callers dial will be as follows:

(caller's country international access code) + 91 (international country code for India) + area code + local number (booth number)

The Central Telegraph Offices/Telecom offices in major towns are usually reasonably efficient. Some are open 24 hours.

The Indian government has set up modern, 24 hour communications centres in the four main cities, and these can be handy. The government company which runs these centres is VSNL (Videsh Sanchar Nigam Ltd), and the addresses are:

Calcutta
    Videsh Sanchar Bhavan, Poddar Court, 18 Ravindra Sarani, Calcutta 700 001 (☎ (033) 30-3266; fax 30-3218)
Delhi
    Videsh Sanchar Bhavan, Bangla Sahib Rd, Delhi 110001 (☎ (011) 374-6769; fax 374-6769)
Madras
    Videsh Sanchar Bhavan, 5 Swami Sivananda Salai, Madras 600 002 (☎ (044) 56-1994; fax 58-3838)
Mumbai (Bombay)
    Videsh Sanchar Bhavan, Mahatma Gandhi Rd, Mumbai 400 001 (☎ (022) 262-4001; fax 262-4027)

Also available is the Home Country Direct service, which gives you access to the international operator in your home country. You can then make reverse charge (collect) or credit card calls, although this is not always easy, and beware in hotels of exorbitant connection charges on these sorts of calls. You may also have trouble convincing the owner of the telephone you are using that they are not going to get charged for the call. The countries and numbers to dial are listed in the Home Country Direct Phone numbers table.

Home Country Direct Phone Numbers	
Country	Number
Australia	0006117
Canada	000167
Germany	0004917
Italy	0003917
Japan	0008117
The Netherlands	0003117
New Zealand	0006417
Singapore	0006517
Spain	0003417
Taiwan	00088617
Thailand	0006617
UK	0004417
USA	000117

Fax
Many of the STD/ISD booths also have a fax machine for public use.

E-Mail
It is possible to send and receive e-mail messages at McLeod Ganj in Himachal Pradesh. See the Orientation & Information section in the Himachal Pradesh chapter for details.

BOOKS
Most books are published in different editions by different publishers in different countries. As a result, a book might be a hardcover rarity in one country, while it's readily available in paperback in another. Fortunately, bookshops and libraries search by title or author, so your local bookshop or library is best placed to advise you about the availability of books recommended in this section.

India is one of the world's largest publishers of books in English. After the USA and the UK, it's up there with Canada and Australia as a major English-language publisher. You'll find a great number of interesting books on India by Indian publishers, which are generally not available in the west.

Foreign-language titles are harder to come by, but you'll often find second-hand copies of French, German and Japanese editions in popular travellers' centres such as Leh, McLeod Ganj, Shimla and Darjeeling.

Indian publishers also do cheap reprints of western bestsellers at prices far below western levels. A meaty Leon Uris or Alex Hailey novel, ideal for an interminable bus trip, will often cost less than US$3. Compare that with your local bookshop prices.

Recently published British and American books also reach Indian bookshops remarkably quickly and with very low mark-ups. If a bestseller in Europe or America has major appeal for India the publisher will often rush out a paperback in India to forestall possible pirates. These books generally don't take long to find their way to the second-hand booksellers in the hill stations.

Lonely Planet
It's pleasing to be able to claim that for more information on India and its neighbours, and for travel beyond India, most of the best guides come from Lonely Planet! Lonely Planet's award-winning *India* is now in its 6th edition. One of Lonely Planet's most successful and popular titles, this is the most comprehensive guide to the country you'll find.

Lonely Planet's *Trekking in the Indian Himalaya*, by Garry Weare, and this new *Indian Himalaya* regional guide have been written to complement each other. Garry has spent years discovering the best trekking routes in the Himalayan region, and his guide is full of practical descriptions and excellent maps. Lonely Planet's city guide *Delhi* has all the information you need to find your way around this often chaotic city.

Other Lonely Planet guides are: *Nepal, Trekking in the Nepal Himalaya, Tibet, Karakoram Highway, Pakistan, Bangladesh, Myanmar, Sri Lanka, Maldives & Islands of the East Indian Ocean*, and *South-East Asia*.

Guidebooks
While several guidebooks cover the entire Himalayan region, there is a paucity of guides which concentrate only on the Indian

Himalaya. Insight Guides' *India's Western Himalaya* (1992) deals only with the states of Jammu & Kashmir and Himachal Pradesh. While it's a great souvenir to carry home with you, it's a bit short on practical travel information. In a similar vein is Nelles Guides' *Northern India* (1990). The coverage of the Himalaya is not extensive, and practical travel information is limited.

Fodor's *The Himalayan Countries* (1990) covers Bhutan, Nepal, North India, North Pakistan and Tibet. The coverage of the entire Himalayan zone means that the focus on the Indian Himalaya is not extensive.

The Himalayas: Playground of the Gods (1983) by the affable Captain MS Kohli is primarily a trekking book, short on cultural notes (and good maps!), and now slightly out of date. This book may be difficult to obtain outside India.

Travel
Frank Smythe's *Valley of Flowers* (Hodder & Stoughton, 1938) is a classic travelogue, and fascinating reading for anyone interested in the western Himalaya's prolific flora. *Valley of Flowers* is much more a travelogue than a scholarly botanical treatise, and is an excellent read on this beautiful region of the Himalaya.

GD Khosla's *Himalayan Circuit: A Journey in the Inner Himalaya* (OUP, Delhi; first published 1956; reprinted 1990) recounts the author's travels as part of an official tour through the remote tribal regions of Lahaul & Spiti in the 1950s. The author writes evocatively of the magnificent landscapes and their isolated inhabitants.

Account of Koonawaur in the Himalaya by Captain Alexander Gerard is an old British stiff upper-lip account of the 'discovery' of the Kinnaur region.

Sorrel Wilby records in *Across the Top* (Pan Macmillan, Australia, 1992) an account of her traverse of the entire length of the Himalaya from Pakistan to Arunachal Pradesh accompanied by her husband, Chris Ciantar. It makes compelling, if sometimes overly graphic, reading, and includes some of Sorrel's fine colour photographs.

An adventurer of a similar calibre is Eric Newby, whose *Slowly Down the Ganges* borders at times on sheer masochism!

Kulu: The End of the Habitable World (Allied Publications, Delhi, 1980) by Penelope Chetwoode is an entertaining story of a woman's travel on horseback through the region.

While the following books will be almost impossible to secure outside India, you might be able to find some of these titles in the better bookshops of the hill stations and in large cities. All were originally published in the mid to late 1900s, some reprinted in the 1970s and 1980s in an endeavour to preserve these classic accounts of forays into the Himalayan regions during the British Raj era.

Western Himalayas & Tibet by Thomas Thomson details the author's travels through the Indian Himalaya in the mid-1800s. It includes some fine old B&W plates.

Sikkim: Among the Himalayas by Austine Waddell (out of print for nearly 100 years) is an account of the former independent and isolated kingdom complemented with original illustrations and maps.

Travels in Nepal & Sikkim: 1875-76 by Sir Richard Temple. This fine old hardcover edition includes contemporary B&W illustrations and several maps.

Wonders of the Himalaya is a classic account of the Himalaya by Francis Younghusband, who led the British expedition to Lhasa in 1904. It was recently reprinted in 1993.

History & General Interest
If you want a thorough introduction to Indian history then look for the Pelican two-volume *A History of India*. Volume 1 by Romila Thapar follows Indian history from 1000 BC to the coming of the Mughals in the 16th century. Volume 2 by Percival Spear follows the rise and fall of the Mughals through to India since Independence. More cumbersome, but offering more detail, is the 900 page paperback *Oxford History of India* by Vincent Smith (OUP, Rs 140).

Himalayan Environment & Culture (Indus, Delhi, 1990) edited by NK Rustomji & Charles Ramble is a collection of scholarly essays on subjects ranging from ecological issues (including the effects of tourism on the Indian Himalaya) to the artistic and literary heritage of the Himalayan region, including chapters on the architecture of the western Himalaya and miniature painting of the Kangra Valley.

The *Gazetteer of Sikkim* was first published in 1894, but was reprinted in 1989 by the Sikkim Nature Conservation Foundation. Only available in Gangtok, it is the definitive volume on the former kingdom of Sikkim. For readers interested in Tibetan Buddhism, the chapters dealing with its manifestation in Sikkim are astonishing and detailed. It's not cheap, at Rs 400, but is truly a collector's item. There is a cheaper edition for Rs 200, printed on poor quality paper.

A similar reference on the Kumaon region of Uttarakhand is GW Traill's *Statistical Sketch of Kamaon* (1828). One of the best references on Uttarakhand is ET Atkinson's *The Himalayan Districts of the North-Western Provinces of India* (1882), published in three volumes.

Kumaon Himalaya Temptations (1993) is published by Kumaon Mandal Vikas Nigam (KMVN), the regional division of UP Tourism in the Kumaon district of Uttarakhand. The text is by Shekhar Pathak, complemented with photos by Anup Sah. You'll find copies in good bookshops in Nainital.

A weighty tome is the beautiful *Garhwal Himalayas: Ramparts of Heaven* (Lustre Press, 1987), with text by Pushpesh Pant. The foreword is by Sir Edmund Hillary. The magnificent colour photographs are by Ashok Dilwali.

Mountain Delight (English Book Depot, Dehra Dun, 1994) is a collection of published articles by prolific writer and mountain lover Bill Aitken who has resided in Garhwal for over 30 years. This collection includes little-known facts about the British presence in the Garhwal Himalaya, as well as essays on contemporary issues. He also writes evocatively of the lakes and mountains of Garhwal and Kumaon.

Simla: Summer Capital of British India by Raja Bhasin is a great account of the colonial history of this hill station. Other readable books on Shimla include *Imperial Shimla* by Pamela Kanwar, which includes some lovely old photos of the colonial era, and *Simla: A Hill Station in British India* by Pat Barr & Ray Desmond.

SC Bajpai's *Kinnaur: A Restricted Land in the Himalaya* and *Lahaul-Spiti: A Forbidden Land in the Himalayas* are mines of information about the local customs, language, lifestyle and history.

There are many good books about Ladakh, but these may be difficult to find outside India, or even outside Leh. *Ladakh Through the Ages* (1992) by Shridhaul Kaul & HN Kaul is a good study of regional history and culture. A coffee-table book at a moderate price is *Ladakh: Nubra, the Forbidden Valley* (1987) by Major HPS Ahluwalia. It has plenty of good photos and essays on historical and contemporary themes pertaining to Ladakh, with particular emphasis on the Nubra Valley.

Ladakh (1994) by Neetu & DJ Singh is a wonderful collection of information on Ladakhi history and culture, with great photos of the area.

The Cultural History of Ladakh, Vols 1 & 2 by Snellgrove & Skorupski (Vikas, Delhi, 1977 & 1980) provide the most comprehensive cultural background on Ladakh.

Ancient Futures: Learning from Ladakh (1991) by Helena Norberg-Hodge is available in many languages, and can be found outside India. It is an enjoyable contemporary study of Ladakh, and an analysis of what the future holds. Michael Peissel's *Zanskar: the Hidden Kingdom* (1979) is one of the very few good books on Zanskar.

Kashmir by Rughubir Singh is the best illustrated book on the Kashmir Valley, followed by *Kashmir* by Francis Brunel (Rupa, 1979).

This is Kashmir by Pearce Gervis (Universal Publications, Delhi, 1974) is a storehouse of historical information on the valley. *Travels in Kashmir* by Bridgid Keenan (OUP, 1989) provides a highly readable account of the history and handicrafts of the Kashmir Valley.

Probably the best contemporary collection of essays on the Himalaya is *The Himalaya: Aspects of Change* (OUP, 1995). Edited by JS Lall, this paperback volume includes essays by various scholars on Himalayan flora & fauna, art, population and society, and the effects of development.

An Introduction to the Hill Stations of India (Indus, 1993) by Graeme D Westlake is probably the most comprehensive history of the former British hill stations you'll find anywhere. This book is widely available in northern India, including good bookstores in Delhi and Calcutta.

Also widely available is *Plain Tales from the Raj* edited by Charles Allen. It consists of interviews with people who took part in British India on both sides of the table. It's extremely readable and full of fascinating little insights into life during the British Raj.

Man-Eaters of Kumaon (OUP) by the great white hunter-turned-conservationist Jim Corbett is an immensely readable account of his experiences dispatching tigers in the lower reaches of Uttarakhand early this century. This book was first published in 1944, but has been reprinted numerous times over the years. Corbett's second book *Temple Tiger*, first published in 1954, continues the tradition with a further five hunting tales.

Sikkim (1994), with text by Earl Kowall and photographs by Nazima Kowall, is a good coffee-table souvenir. It's short on text, but the beautiful photographs are well captioned.

Freedom in Exile (Rupa, Delhi) is an account by His Holiness, the Dalai Lama, of the Chinese occupation of his country and his subsequent exile and endeavours to preserve the culture and traditions of the Tibetan people in exile.

Art

Unfortunately there is not a great selection of titles dealing with the rich artistic heritage of the Indian Himalaya. JC French's *Himalayan Art* (Neeraj, Delhi), first published in 1931 and reprinted in 1983, focuses mainly on Kangra miniatures, with detailed descriptions of the paintings in the Kangra and Chamba museums. With the same name, *Himalayan Art* by Madajeet Singh (Macmillan, New York, 1968) is an excellent guide to the various art styles that have evolved in the Himalaya.

The art historian MS Randhawa's *Travels in the Western Himalayas* (Thomson Press, 1974) deals predominantly with Kangra miniatures, but also discusses cultural aspects of the Chamba and Kangra valleys.

People & Culture

A brilliant, but scholarly, discussion of the lifestyles and customs of the inhabitants of Garhwal is *Hindus of the Himalaya* by Gerald D Berreman (OUP, Delhi). It was first published in 1963, and the current edition, reprinted in 1993, includes a prologue on the village a decade following the initial study.

SS Shashi's *The Gaddi Tribe of Himachal Pradesh* (Sterling Publishers, Delhi, 1977) is a similar ethnographic exposition of this seminomadic tribal group.

Christina Noble's *Over the High Passes: A Year in the Himalaya* (Collins, 1987) details the author's travels with the Gaddis as they traverse their traditional migration routes in Himachal Pradesh. In Noble's later book *At Home in the Himalayas* (Collins, London, 1991), she writes with great insight and affection of the hill people of Himachal Pradesh.

Alice Elizabeth Dracott spent years early this century faithfully recording the folktales of the inhabitants of the Himalaya. Her work, *Folk Tales from the Himalayas* (Vintage Books, Delhi), was first published in 1906 as *Simla Village Tales*, and is now available in a limited edition published in 1992.

Bill Aitken's *The Nanda Devi Affair* (Penguin, 1994) is an account of the history and lore of Nanda Devi, the patron goddess of Garhwal and Kumaon, who is worshipped in the form of the beautiful Nanda Devi mountain.

Tibetan Astronomy & Astrology: A Brief Introduction is a tiny pocket-sized booklet produced by the Astrological Department of the Tibetan Medical & Astrological Institute.

Fundamentals of Tibetan Medicine, published by the Tibetan Medical Centre, Dharamsala, outlines the various diagnostic and therapeutic techniques employed by traditional Tibetan doctors.

Fauna & Flora

100 Himalayan Flowers (Mapin, Ahmedabad, 1991), with text by Professor PV Bole and 150 colour photos by Ashvin Mehta, is a handy field guide to the prolific flora of the Himalaya.

Sikkim Himalayan Rhododendrons (1991) by UC Pradhan & ST Lachungpa is another useful guide for those visiting the eastern Himalaya, with colour photos and B&W illustrations.

Rupin Dang's *Flowers of the Western Himalayas* (Indus, Delhi, 1993) is a practical guide to the flora of Kashmir, Himachal Pradesh and Uttarakhand. Field notes are complemented with full-colour photos.

Indian Hill Birds (OUP, Delhi) by the late Indian ornithologist Sálim Ali was first published in 1949 (current edition 1994). It is the definitive guide to the birdlife of the Himalaya.

Also by Sálim Ali is *The Birds of Sikkim* (OUP), first published in 1962 (current edition 1989).

The best guide to India's fauna is SH Prater's *The Book of Indian Animals* (OUP, Delhi), first published in 1948 (current edition 1993).

Insight Guides' *Indian Wildlife* (1987) is another excellent guide to India's wildlife, with a very good chapter on the wildlife of the Indian Himalaya.

Religion

If you want a better understanding of India's religions there are plenty of books available in India. The English series of Penguin paperbacks are among the best and are generally available in India. In particular, *Hinduism* by KM Sen (Penguin, London, 1961) is brief and to the point. If you want to read the Hindu holy books, these are available in translations: *The Upanishads* (Penguin, London, 1965) and *The Bhagavad*

Gita (Penguin, London, 1962). *Hindu Mythology*, edited by Wendy O'Flaherty (Penguin, London), is an interesting annotated collection of extracts from the Hindu holy books. Penguin also has a translation of the Koran.

A Classical Dictionary of Hindu Mythology & Religion by John Dowson (Rupa, Delhi, 1987) is an Indian paperback reprint. There's also *Indian Mythology* by Jan Knappert (HarperCollins, Delhi, 1992), a paperback encyclopedia.

A Handbook of Living Religions edited by John R Hinnewls (Pelican, London, 1985) provides a succinct and readable summary of all the various religions you will find in India.

The recently published *Guru – the Search for Enlightenment* by John Mitchiner is excellent for anyone interested in the relevance and contribution of Indian gurus to contemporary thought and experience.

Dorf Hartsuiker's *Sadhus: Holy Men of India* (Thames & Hudson) is a fine paperback volume which examines the compulsions and lifestyles of India's wandering ascetics.

To gain some insight into Buddhism, Guy Claxton's *The Heart of Buddhism* (Aquarian Press, London, 1992) is a good place to begin. *The Power of Compassion* (Indus, Delhi, 1994) is a collection of essays by His Holiness, the Dalai Lama. It's available in bookshops in McLeod Ganj and other parts of Himachal Pradesh, as well as in Delhi. Also by the Dalai Lama, *The Way to Freedom* (Snow Lion, 1994), outlines the essence of Tibetan Buddhism in an accessible form.

The Tibetan Book of Living & Dying (Rupa, Delhi, 1995) by Sogyal Rinpoche is a lucid and erudite discussion of the principles of Tibetan Buddhism. It should not be confused with the original *Tibetan Book of the Dead*, or *Bardo Thödol*, translated by WY Evans-Wentz, which deals with the experience of death and the nature of existence after death.

Political & Cultural Analysis

Mary Craig's *Tears of Blood* (HarperCollins,

1993) is a moving and evocative commentary on the Chinese occupation of Tibet and the Tibetan's struggle for independence.

Tibet: The Facts (1990) is a report prepared by the Scientific Buddhist Association for the UN Commission on Human Rights, detailing the history of Tibet as an independent nation and its subsequent occupation by the Chinese.

Ronald Segal's *The Crisis of India* (1965) is written by a South African Indian on the theme that spirituality is not always more important than a full stomach.

Unveiling India by Anees Jung is a contemporary documentary on women in India. For an assessment of the position of women in Indian society, it is well worth getting hold of *May You Be the Mother of One Hundred Sons* (Penguin, 1991) by Elizabeth Bumiller. Her book offers some excellent insights into the plight of women in general and rural women in particular.

For those interested in the continuing and often shocking and sad story of India's tribal people, there is the scholarly *Tribes of India – the Struggle for Survival* (1982) by Christoph von Fürer-Haimendorf.

Ecological Issues

Himalaya: A Regional Perspective: Resources, Environment & Development (Daya, Delhi, 1993) edited by MSS Rawat, considers the ramifications of development for the fragile ecosystem of the Himalaya and its effects on the traditional cultural practices of its inhabitants.

Novels

Partly set in the Himalaya, Rudyard Kipling's classic novel *Kim* recounts the tale of a young streetwise anglo-Indian boy who devotes himself to a Tibetan lama who is searching for the river of immortality. In the process, recruited by the British secret service, Kim finds himself immersed in political intrigue. In this, and other books, such as *Plain Tales from the Hills*, Kipling, who lived and worked in Shimla for many

years, proves himself as the Victorian English interpreter of India *par excellence*.

Mountaineering

Where Men and Mountains Meet and *The Gilgit Game*, both by John Keay (John Murray, 1977 & 1979) are two indispensable books on the history of exploration in the western Himalaya during the 19th century.

The *Abode of the Snows* by Kenneth Mason (Diadem Books, reprint 1987) is the classic on Himalayan exploration and climbs.

Mountain Travel (Diadem Books, 1985) and *The Mountaineers* (Seattle, 1985) both by Eric Shipton & HW Tilman are highly recommended for reading on exploration in the Indian Himalaya and beyond.

Phrasebooks

Lonely Planet has the subcontinent well covered, with phrasebooks for Hindi/Urdu, Bengali and Sinhalese.

Helen Norberg-Hodge co-publishes a largish Ladakhi-English dictionary. *Getting Started in Ladakhi* (Melong Publications, Leh, 1994; Rs 75) by Rebecca Norman is a useful pocket-sized phrasebook. Both books are available in Leh.

There are many phrasebooks and teach-yourself books available in India if you want to learn more of a language.

Journals

Himal, published bi-monthly in Nepal and distributed internationally, contains good essays on cultural and ecological issues pertaining to the Himalaya. It is available by subscription. Distributors can be found in Japan, Australia, the USA, UK, the Netherlands, Switzerland, Germany and India. For their addresses contact Himal, PO Box 42, Lalitpur, Nepal (☎ 977 1 52-3845; fax 977 1 52-1013; e-mail: himal@himpc.mos.com.np).

The Tibetan Government in Exile produces a range of journals, some of which are available on subscription. See the McLeod Ganj section in the Himachal Pradesh chapter for more details.

ONLINE SERVICES

There are numerous online services relevant to India. The list in the box below is a by no means exhaustive selection.

NEWSPAPERS & MAGAZINES

English-language dailies include the *Times of India*, the *Hindustan Times*, the *Indian Express* and the *Statesman*; many feel the *Express* is the best of the bunch. The *Times* has its headquarters in Mumbai (Bombay) and the *Statesman* in Calcutta, but there are many regional editions of both. The *Independent*, which is published in Mumbai, is an excellent quality broadsheet. The *Times of India* is the largest selling English daily, with a circulation of 643,000.

International coverage is generally pretty good. However, when it comes to national news, the copy is invariably strewn with a plethora of acronyms and Indian words, the majority of which mean nothing to the uninitiated. One exception is the *Independent*.

In the hill stations, English-language dailies generally arrive after 11.30 am. In larger centres further north, you'll be able to get hold of day-old English-language papers after noon.

There's an excellent variety of meaty weekly magazines which include *Frontline* (possibly the best of the lot), *India Today, The Week, Sunday* and the *Illustrated Weekly of India*. They're all available at bookshops, especially those at major railway stations, and are interesting for the different slant which they give to political and social issues of worldwide concern.

RADIO & TV

The revolution in the TV network has been the introduction of cable TV. It's amazing to see satellite dishes, even in the remotest vil-

---

Online Services

Online Service	Information	Address
Indolink	links covering Indian business, travel, astrology and matrimonial ads	http://www.genius.net/indolink/
India Online		http://IndiaOnline.com/
Guide to India	recommendations for guidebooks	http://hubcap.clemson.edu/~nsankar/india/guide.to.india.html#Section 15
Indiaworld	festival dates and links to domestic airline schedules	http://www.indiaworld.com.index.html
The India Homepage	general information, useful travel tips and a huge number and variety of links	http://spiderman.bu.edu/misc/india/
The West Bengal Home Page	language, culture and attractions	http://ds1.gl.umbc.edu/~achatt1/wbengal.html
The Hindu	Indian news	http://www.webpage.com/hindu/index.html
The Global Hindu Electronic Network	Hindu religion, text of the *Ramayana, Mahabharata* and other scriptures	http://rbhatnagar.csm.uc.edu:8080/hindu_universe.html
The Transcendental Gallery	Indian art	http://www.best.com/~rayk/html/kamkr.html
The Batish Institute of Fine Arts & Music	Indian music (including sitar lessons)	http://hypatia.ucsc.edu:70/0h/RELATED/Batish.topopen.html
The India Travelogue	travel information	http://Alpha.Solutions.Net/rec-travel/asia/india/trip.leeper.html
Travelers' Tales	travel stories	http//www.best.com/~bradley/best
Books of South Asian Writers	bibliography of Indian (and other) writers	http://www.ntu.ac.sg:80/~mmurali/sabooks.html

lages. The result is that viewers can tune in to the BBC, and, broadcasting from Hong Kong, Murdoch's Star TV, Prime Sports and V (an MTV-type Hindi music channel). Z TV is a local Hindi cable channel.

The national broadcaster, Doordarshan, which prior to the coming of satellite TV used to plod along with dry, dull and generally dreadful programmes, has lifted its game and now offers some good viewing.

Most mid-range and all top-end hotels have a TV in every room with a choice of satellite or Doordarshan.

PHOTOGRAPHY

Film

Colour print film processing facilities are readily available in the hill stations and popular tourist centres such as Leh. Film is relatively cheap and the quality is usually (but not always) good. Kodak 100 colour print film costs around Rs 140 for a roll of 36. Always check the use-by date on local film stock. The humidity during the monsoon can play havoc with film, even if the use-by date hasn't been exceeded. Developing costs are around Rs 25, plus Rs 5 per photo for printing.

If you're taking slides bring the film with you. Colour slide film is only available in the major cities. Colour slides can be developed only in Delhi, and quality is not guaranteed. A better bet is to carry your film home with you. Kodachrome and 'includes developing' film will have to be sent overseas. It's up to you whether you send it straight back and face the risk of delay or damage, or carry it back with you at the end of your trip.

Equipment

Carrying a tripod means extra bulk, but may be the only way you'll be able to take reasonable photos in dimly lit interiors, such as gompas (those where photography is permitted). A UV filter permanently fitted to your lens will not only cut down ultraviolet light, but will protect your lens. Spare batteries should be carried at all times.

Serious photographers will consider bringing a macro lens for shots of wildflow-ers, a telephoto lens for dramatic mountain shots, and a wide-angle lens for gompa interiors, mountain panoramas and village profiles.

Photography

In the mountains you should allow for the extreme light intensity, and take care not to overexpose your shots. In general, photography is best done in the early morning and late afternoon. Some fast film, up to ASA 400, is useful if you're using a zoom or telephoto lens in low light conditions.

Restrictions & Photographing People

Be careful what you photograph. India is touchy about places of military importance – this can include railway stations, bridges, airports, military installations and sensitive border regions. Some gompas prohibit photography in the main prayer chambers. If in doubt, ask. In general most people are happy to be photographed, but care should be taken in pointing cameras at Muslim women. Again, if in doubt, ask. A zoom is a less intrusive means of taking portraits – even when you've obtained permission to take a portrait, shoving a lens in your subject's face can be disconcerting. A reasonable distance between you and your subject will help to reduce your subject's discomfiture, and will result in more natural shots.

Protecting Your Film

Film manufacturers warn that once exposed, film should be developed as quickly as possible; in practice the film seems to last, even in India's summer heat, without deterioration for months. If you're going to be carrying exposed film for long, consult a specialist photography handbook about ways of enhancing preservation. Try to keep your film cool, and protect it in water and air-proof containers if you're travelling during the monsoon. Silicone sachets distributed around your gear will help to absorb moisture.

It's worthwhile investing in a lead-lined (X-ray proof) bag, as repeated exposure to X-ray (even so-called 'film proof' X-ray) can damage film. Some airport officials may let you pass your film stock to them and will hand it back when you have cleared the X-rays. Often they'll insist that the film must be put through the baggage X-ray, but it's worth asking. Temporarily take your films out of their canisters and place them in a clear plastic bag so that the contents are immediately obvious. *Never* put your unprocessed film in baggage which will be placed in the cargo holds of aeroplanes. It will probably be subjected to large doses of X-ray which will spoil or completely ruin it.

In Delhi and Calcutta there are plenty of camera shops which should be able to make minor repairs should you have any mechanical problems, but up in the hills if you break or damage your camera you're in trouble. It's worthwhile having your camera serviced by a reputable outfit before you leave home. Places such as Shimla, Manali, Darjeeling and Dharamsala sell small basic cameras.

TIME
India is 5½ hours ahead of GMT/UTC, 4½ hours behind Australian EST and 10½ hours ahead of American EST. It is officially known as IST – Indian Standard Time, although many Indians prefer to think it stands for Indian Stretchable Time!

ELECTRICITY
Voltage & Cycle
The electric current is 230-240 V AC, 50 cycles. Electricity is widely available in the lower regions of the Indian Himalaya, but in the more remote regions, such as Yamunotri and Gangotri in Uttarakhand, the electricity supply is either nonexistent or connected to only a few establishments. In some parts of Lahaul & Spiti, and most of Ladakh, there is electricity in the evenings only. Breakdowns and blackouts ('load shedding') are endemic, particularly in the hills regions. Darjeeling is notorious for being plunged into darkness regularly, and many mid-range and top-end hotels have their own (noisy) backup generators in the event of power failure.

Plugs & Sockets
Sockets are of a three round-pin variety, similar (but not identical) to European sockets. European round-pin plugs will go into the sockets, but as the pins on Indian plugs are somewhat thicker, the fit is loose and connection is not always guaranteed.

You can buy small immersion elements, perfect for boiling water for tea or coffee, for Rs 30. For about Rs 70 you can buy electric mosquito zappers. These are the type that take chemical tablets which melt and give off deadly vapours (deadly for the mosquito, that is). There are many different brands and they are widely available – they come with quaint names such as Good Knight.

WEIGHTS & MEASURES
Although India is officially metricated, imperial weights and measures are still used in some areas of commerce. A conversion chart is included on the inside back cover of the book.

LAUNDRY
Getting your laundry done in the main hill stations is usually no problem, even though washing machines are in short supply. At even the smallest hotel you'll be able to hand in your dirty clothes in the morning and have them back freshly laundered and pressed in the evening. The secret lies in the *dhobiwallahs*, the people who still do this enormous task by hand. The charge is around Rs 10 per item.

HEALTH
Travel health depends on your predeparture preparations, your day-to-day health care while travelling and how you handle any medical problem or emergency that does develop. While the list of potential dangers can seem quite frightening, with a little luck, some basic precautions and adequate information, few travellers experience more than upset stomachs.

Travel Health Guides
There are a number of books on travel health:

Staying Healthy in Asia, Africa & Latin America by Dirk Schroeder (Moon Publications, 1994). Probably the best all-round guide to carry, as it's compact but very detailed and well organised.

Travellers' Health by Dr Richard Dawood (Oxford University Press, 1992). Comprehensive, easy to read, authoritative and also highly recommended, although it's rather large to lug around.

Where There is No Doctor by David Werner (Macmillan, 1994). A very detailed guide intended for someone, such as a Peace Corps worker, going to work in an undeveloped country, rather than for the average traveller.

Travel with Children by Maureen Wheeler (Lonely Planet Publications, 1995). Includes basic advice on travel health for young children.

Predeparture Planning

Medical Kit A small, straightforward medical kit is a wise thing to carry. A kit should include:

- Aspirin or paracetamol (acetaminophen in the USA) for pain or fever.
- Antihistamine (such as Benadryl) – useful as a decongestant for colds and allergies, to ease the itch from insect bites or stings, and to help prevent motion sickness. There are several antihistamines on the market, all with different pros and cons (eg a tendency to cause drowsiness), so it's worth discussing your requirements with a pharmacist or doctor. Antihistamines may cause sedation and interact with alcohol so care should be taken when using them.
- Antibiotics – useful if you're travelling well off the beaten track, but they must be prescribed and you should carry the prescription with you.
  Some individuals are allergic to commonly prescribed antibiotics such as penicillin or sulpha drugs. It would be sensible to always carry this information when travelling.
- Loperamide (eg Imodium) or Lomotil for diarrhoea; prochlorperazine (eg Stemetil) or metaclopramide (eg Maxalon) for nausea and vomiting. Antidiarrhoea medication should not be given to children under the age of 12.
- Rehydration mixture – for treatment of severe diarrhoea. This is particularly important if travelling with children, but is recommended for everyone.
- Antiseptic such as povidone-iodine (eg Betadine), which comes as a solution, ointment, powder and impregnated swabs – for cuts and grazes.
- Calamine or other 'anti-itch' lotion – to ease irritation from bites or stings.
- Bandages and Band-Aids – for minor injuries.
- Scissors, tweezers and a thermometer (note that carrying mercury thermometers on aeroplanes is prohibited by airlines).
- Insect repellent, sunscreen, lip balm and water purification tablets.
- A couple of syringes, in case you need injections, as local medical hygiene may be lacking. Ask your doctor for a note explaining why they have been prescribed.

Ideally, antibiotics should be administered only under medical supervision and should never be taken indiscriminately. Take only the recommended dose at the prescribed intervals and continue using the antibiotic for the prescribed period, even if the illness seems to be cured earlier. Antibiotics are quite specific to the infections they can treat. Stop immediately if there are any serious reactions and don't use the antibiotic at all if you are unsure that you have the correct one.

In India and many developing countries, if a medicine is available at all it will generally be available over the counter and the price will be much cheaper than in the west. However, be careful if buying drugs in these places, particularly where the expiry date may have passed or correct storage conditions may not have been followed. Bogus drugs are common and it's possible that drugs which are no longer recommended, or have even been banned, in the west are still being dispensed in many developing countries.

It may be a good idea to leave unwanted medicines, syringes etc with a local clinic, rather than carry them home.

Various so-called 'AIDS kits' are available in the UK and other western countries, and these have all the gear necessary for blood transfusions and injections. If you are going to be in India for a long time and intend to get off the beaten track, they can be a good idea. In fact even in many places where there are plenty of tourists, eg Leh, the medical facilities are extremely basic. Having your own sterile equipment could be worthwhile if you have an accident and are hospitalised. For such a kit to be useful for a blood transfusion, however, it needs to have the plastic tube which carries the blood from the bag or bottle, as well as the intravenous needle which actually goes into the arm – some kits have the latter but not the former.

Health Preparations Make sure you're healthy before you start travelling. If you are embarking on a long trip make sure your teeth are OK; there are lots of places where a visit to the dentist would be the last thing you'd want.

If you wear glasses take a spare pair and your prescription. Replacing your glasses can be a real problem in the Indian Himalaya, although in many of the larger cities on the plains you can get new spectacles made up quickly, cheaply and competently.

If you require a particular medication take an adequate supply, as it may not be available locally. Take the prescription or, better still, part of the packaging showing the generic rather than the brand name (which may not be locally available), as it will make getting replacements easier. It's a wise idea to carry a legible prescription or letter from your doctor to show you legally use the medication – it's surprising how often over-the-counter drugs from one place are illegal without a prescription or even banned in another.

Immunisations Vaccinations provide protection against diseases you might meet along the way. For some countries no immunisations are necessary, but the further off the beaten track you go the more necessary it is to take precautions.

It is important to understand the distinction between vaccines recommended for travel in certain areas and those required by law. Currently yellow fever is the only vaccine subject to international health regulations, however, vaccination as an entry requirement is usually only enforced when coming from an infected area.

Occasionally travellers face bureaucratic problems regarding cholera vaccine even though all countries have dropped it as a health requirement for travel. Under some circumstances it may be wise to have the vaccine despite its poor protection, eg for the trans-Africa traveller.

On the other hand a number of vaccines are recommended for travel in certain areas. These may not be required by law but are recommended for your own personal protection.

All vaccinations should be recorded on an International Health Certificate, which is available from your physician or government health department.

Plan ahead for getting your vaccinations: some of them require an initial shot followed by a booster, while some vaccinations should not be given together. It is recommended you seek medical advice at least six weeks prior to travel.

Most travellers from western countries will have been immunised against various diseases during childhood but your doctor may still recommend booster shots against measles or polio, diseases still prevalent in many developing countries. The period of protection offered by vaccinations differs widely and some are contraindicated if you are pregnant.

In some countries immunisations are available from airport or government health centres. Travel agents or airline offices will tell you where. Vaccinations include:

Meningococcal Meningitis
> The risk area for this disease is northern India (from about the level of Delhi, and then north) and Nepal. The vaccination is usually recommended for those who will be in the risk area for seven days or longer. A single injection will give good protection against the A, C, W and Y groups of the bacteria for at least a year. The vaccine is not, however, recommended for children under two years, because they do not develop satisfactory immunity from it.

Smallpox
> Smallpox has now been wiped out worldwide, so immunisation is no longer necessary.

Cholera
> Not required by law but occasionally travellers face bureaucratic problems on some border crossings. Protection is poor and it lasts only six months. It is contraindicated in pregnancy.

Tetanus & Diphtheria
> Boosters are necessary every 10 years and protection is highly recommended.

Typhoid
> Available either as an injection or oral capsules.

Protection lasts from one to five years depending on the vaccine and is useful if you are travelling for long in rural tropical areas. You may get some side effects such as pain at the injection site, fever, headache and a general unwell feeling. A new single-dose injectable vaccine, which appears to have few side effects, is now available but is more expensive. Side effects are unusual with the oral form but occasionally an individual will have stomach cramps.

Hepatitis A

The most common travel-acquired illness, which can be prevented by vaccination. Protection can be provided in two ways – either with the antibody gamma globulin or with a new vaccine called Havrix.

Havrix provides long-term immunity (possibly more than 10 years) after an initial course of two injections and a booster one year later. It may be more expensive than gamma globulin but certainly has many advantages, including length of protection and ease of administration. It is important to know that being a vaccine it will take about three weeks to provide satisfactory protection – hence the need for careful planning prior to travel.

Gamma globulin is not a vaccination but a ready-made antibody which has proven very successful in reducing the chances of hepatitis infection. Because it may interfere with the development of immunity, it should not be given until at least 10 days after administration of the last vaccine needed (ie it should be the last); it should also be given as close as possible to departure because it is at its most effective in the first few weeks after administration and the effectiveness tapers off gradually between three and six months.

Polio

A booster of either the oral or injected vaccine is required every 10 years to maintain our immunity after childhood vaccination. Polio is a very serious, easily transmitted disease which is still prevalent in the Indian Himalaya and many developing countries.

Tuberculosis

TB risk should be considered for people travelling for more than three months. As most healthy adults do not develop symptoms, a skin test before and after travel to determine whether exposure has occurred is recommended. Vaccination for children who will be travelling for more than three months is also recommended.

Basic Rules

Care in what you eat and drink is the most important health rule; stomach upsets are the most likely travel health problem (between 30% and 50% of travellers in a two-week stay experience this) but the majority of these upsets will be relatively minor. Don't become paranoid; trying the local food is part of the experience of travel, after all.

Water The number one rule is *don't drink the water* and that includes ice. Reputable brands of bottled water or soft drinks are generally fine, although in some places bottles refilled with tap water are not unknown. Only use water from containers with a serrated seal – not tops or corks. Take care with fruit juice, particularly if water may have been added. Milk should be treated with suspicion, as it is often unpasteurised. Boiled milk is fine if it is kept hygienically and yoghurt is always good. Tea or coffee should also be OK, since the water should have been boiled.

Water Purification The simplest way of purifying water is to boil it thoroughly. Vigorously boiling for five minutes should be satisfactory; however, at high altitude water boils at a lower temperature, so germs are less likely to be killed.

Simple filtering will not remove all dangerous organisms, so if you cannot boil water it should be treated chemically. Chlorine tablets (Puritabs, Steritabs or other brand names) are not available in India. They will kill many but not all pathogens. They will not kill giardia and amoebic cysts (hepatitis, giardiasis and amoebic dysentery). Iodine is very effective in purifying water and is necessary if you are trekking and drinking stream water. It is available in tablet form (such as Potable Aqua), but follow the directions carefully and remember that too much iodine can be harmful. Iodine is contraindicated in pregnancy.

If you can't find tablets, tincture of iodine (2%) can be used. Four drops of tincture of iodine per litre or quart of clear water is the recommended dosage; the treated water should be left to stand for 20 to 30 minutes before drinking. Iodine crystals can also be used to purify water but this is a more complicated process, as you have to first prepare a saturated iodine solution. Iodine loses its effectiveness if exposed to air or damp, so keep it in a tightly sealed container. Flavoured powder will disguise the taste of treated water and is a good idea if you are travelling with children.

Food There is an old colonial adage which says: 'If you can cook it, boil it or peel it you can eat it...otherwise, forget it'. Salads and fruit should be washed with purified water or peeled where possible. Ice cream is usually OK if it is a reputable brand name, but beware of street vendors and of ice cream that has melted and been refrozen. Thoroughly cooked food is safest but not if it has been left to cool or if it has been reheated. Undercooked meat, particularly in the form of mince, should be avoided.

If a place looks clean and well run and if the vendor also looks clean and healthy, then the food is probably safe. In general, places that are packed with travellers or locals will be fine, while empty restaurants are questionable. The food in busy restaurants is cooked and eaten quite quickly with little standing around and is probably not reheated.

Paranoia about food in India can spoil what could otherwise be an enjoyable (or at least interesting) culinary experience. Some of those gloomy little *dhabas* (basic restaurants) might look particularly unhygienic, but, unless the food has been precooked and left to stand in the heat, you probably won't encounter too many problems. Often the food is cooked before your eyes. There's nothing as tasty as a freshly cooked and steaming hot samosa, and nothing more unappetising than a greasy samosa which has sat for hours smeared with congealed oil and been subjected to the attentions of dozens of flies.

Nutrition If your food is poor or limited in availability, if you're travelling hard and fast and therefore missing meals, or if you simply lose your appetite, you can soon start to lose weight and place your health at risk.

Make sure your diet is well balanced. Eggs, tofu, beans, lentils (dhal in India) and

nuts are all safe ways to get protein. Fruit you can peel (bananas, oranges or mandarins for example) is usually safe and a good source of vitamins. Try to eat plenty of grains (rice) and bread. Remember that although food is generally safer if it is cooked well, overcooked food loses much of its nutritional value. If your diet isn't well balanced or if your food intake is insufficient, it's a good idea to take vitamin and iron pills.

In hot climates make sure you drink enough – don't rely on feeling thirsty to indicate when you should drink. Not needing to urinate or very dark yellow urine is a danger sign. Always carry a water bottle with you on long trips. Excessive sweating can lead to loss of salt and therefore muscle cramping. Salt tablets are not a good idea as a preventative, but in places where salt is not used much adding salt to food can help.

Everyday Health Normal body temperature is 37°C (98.6°F); more than 2°C (4°F) higher indicates a high fever. The normal adult pulse rate is 60 to 100 per minute (children 80 to 100, babies 100 to 140). You should know how to take a temperature and a pulse rate. As a general rule, the pulse increases about 20 beats per minute for each 1°C (2°F) rise in fever.

Respiration (breathing) rate is also an indicator of illness. Count the number of breaths per minute: between 12 and 20 is normal for adults and older children (up to 30 for younger children, 40 for babies). People with a high fever or serious respiratory illness (such as pneumonia) breathe more quickly than normal. More than 40 shallow breaths a minute usually means pneumonia.

In western countries with safe water and excellent human waste disposal systems we often take good health for granted. In years gone by, when public health facilities were not as good as they are today, certain rules attached to eating and drinking were observed, eg washing your hands before a meal. It is important for people travelling in areas of poor sanitation to be aware of this and adjust their own personal hygiene habits.

Clean your teeth with purified water rather than straight from the tap. Avoid climatic extremes: keep out of the sun when it's hot, dress warmly when it's cold. Avoid potential diseases by dressing sensibly. You can get worm infections through walking barefoot. You can avoid insect bites by covering bare skin when insects are around, by screening windows or beds and by using insect repellents. Seek local advice; in situations where there is no information, discretion is the better part of valour.

Medical Problems & Treatment

Potential medical problems can be broken down into several areas. Firstly there are the problems caused by extremes of temperature, altitude or motion. Then there are diseases and illnesses caused through poor environmental sanitation, insect bites or stings, and animal or human contact. Simple cuts, bites and scratches can also cause problems.

Self-diagnosis and treatment can be risky, so wherever possible seek qualified help. Although we do give drug dosages in this section, they are for emergency use only. Medical advice should be sought where possible before administering any drugs.

An embassy or consulate can usually recommend a good place to go for such advice. So can five-star hotels, although they often recommend doctors with five-star prices. (This is when that medical insurance really comes in useful!) In some places, standards of medical attention are so low that for some ailments the best advice is to get on a plane and go somewhere else.

Environmental Hazards

Sunburn At high altitudes, you can get sunburnt surprisingly quickly, even through cloud. Use a sunscreen and take extra care to cover areas which don't normally see sun – eg your feet. A hat provides added protection, and you should also use zinc cream or some other barrier cream for your nose and lips. Calamine lotion is good for mild sunburn.

Prickly Heat Prickly heat is an itchy rash caused by excessive perspiration trapped under the skin. It usually strikes people who have just arrived in a hot climate and whose pores have not yet opened sufficiently to cope with greater sweating. Keeping cool but bathing often, using a mild talcum powder or even resorting to air-conditioning may help until you acclimatise.

Heat Exhaustion Dehydration or salt deficiency can cause heat exhaustion. Take time to acclimatise to high temperatures and make sure you drink sufficient liquids. Wear loose clothing and a broad-brimmed hat. Do not do anything too physically demanding.

Salt deficiency is characterised by fatigue, lethargy, headaches, giddiness and muscle cramps and in this case salt tablets may help. Vomiting or diarrhoea can deplete your liquid and salt levels. Anhydrotic heat exhaustion, caused by an inability to sweat, is quite rare. Unlike the other forms of heat exhaustion it is likely to strike people who have been in a hot climate for some time, rather than newcomers.

Heat Stroke This serious, sometimes fatal, condition can occur if the body's heat-regulating mechanism breaks down and the body temperature rises to dangerous levels. Long, continuous periods of exposure to high temperatures can leave you vulnerable to heat stroke. You should avoid excessive alcohol or strenuous activity when you first arrive in a hot climate.

The symptoms are feeling unwell, not sweating very much or at all and a high body temperature (39°C to 41°C). Where sweating has ceased, the skin becomes flushed and red. Severe, throbbing headaches and lack of coordination will also occur, and the sufferer may be confused or aggressive. Eventually the victim will become delirious or convulse. Hospitalisation is essential, but in the interim get the victim out of the sun, remove their clothing, cover them with a wet sheet or towel and then fan continually.

Fungal Infections Fungal infections, which occur with greater frequency in hot weather, are most likely to occur on the scalp, between the toes or fingers (athlete's foot), in the groin (jock itch or crotch rot) and on the body (ringworm). You get ringworm (which is a fungal infection, not a worm) from infected animals or by walking on damp areas, for example shower floors (use thongs – flipflops).

To prevent fungal infections wear loose, comfortable clothes, avoid artificial fibres, wash frequently and dry carefully. If you do get an infection, wash the infected area daily with a disinfectant or medicated soap and water, and rinse and dry well. Apply an antifungal powder like the widely available Tinaderm. Try to expose the infected area to air or sunlight as much as possible and wash all towels and underwear in hot water.

Hypothermia Too much cold is just as dangerous as too much heat, particularly if it leads to hypothermia. If you are trekking at high altitudes or simply taking a long bus trip over mountains, particularly at night, be prepared.

Hypothermia occurs when the body loses heat faster than it can produce it and the core temperature of the body falls. It is surprisingly easy to progress from very cold to dangerously cold due to a combination of wind, wet clothing, fatigue and hunger, even if the air temperature is above freezing. It is best to dress in layers; silk, wool and some of the new artificial fibres are all good insulating materials. A hat is important, as a lot of heat is lost through the head. A strong, waterproof outer layer is essential, as keeping dry is vital. Carry basic supplies, including food containing simple sugars to generate heat quickly and lots of fluid to drink. A space blanket is something all travellers in cold environments should carry. A space blanket is a plastic insulating material coated with aluminium foil.

Symptoms of hypothermia are exhaustion, numb skin (particularly toes and fingers), shivering, slurred speech, irrational or violent behaviour, lethargy, stumbling, dizzy spells, muscle cramps and violent bursts of energy. Irrationality may take the form of sufferers claiming they are warm and trying to take off their clothes.

To treat mild hypothermia, first get the person out of the wind and/or rain, remove their clothing if it's wet and replace it with dry, warm clothing. Give them hot liquids – not alcohol – and some high-kilojoule, easily digestible food. Do not rub victims, instead allow them to slowly warm themselves. This should be enough to treat the early stages of hypothermia. The early recognition and treatment of mild hypothermia is the only way to prevent severe hypothermia, which is a critical condition.

Altitude Sickness Acute Mountain Sickness or AMS occurs at high altitude and can be fatal. The lack of oxygen at high altitudes (over 2500m) affects most people to some extent. It may be mild (benign AMS) or severe (malignant AMS) and occurs because less oxygen reaches the muscles and the brain at high altitude, requiring the heart and lungs to compensate by working harder.

Symptoms usually develop during the first 24 hours at altitude but may be delayed up to three weeks. Symptoms of benign AMS include headache, lethargy, dizziness, difficulty sleeping and loss of appetite. Malignant AMS may develop from benign AMS or without warning and can be fatal. These symptoms include breathlessness, a dry irritative cough (which may progress to the production of pink, frothy sputum), severe headache, lack of coordination and balance, loss of appetite, confusion, irrational behaviour, vomiting, drowsiness and unconsciousness.

In benign AMS the treatment is to remain resting at the same altitude until recovery, usually a day or two. Paracetamol or aspirin can be taken for headaches. If symptoms persist or become worse, however, descent is necessary; even 500m can help. The treatment of malignant AMS is immediate descent to a lower altitude. There are various drug treatments available but they should never be used to avoid descent or enable further ascent by a person with AMS.

A number of measures can be adopted to prevent acute mountain sickness:

- Ascend slowly – have frequent rest days, spending two to three nights at each rise of 1000m. If you reach a high altitude by trekking, acclimatisation takes place gradually and you are less likely to be affected than if you fly direct.
- The altitude at which a person sleeps is an important factor. It is always wise to sleep at a lower altitude than the greatest height reached during the day. Also, once above 3000m, care should be taken not to increase the sleeping altitude by more than 300m per day.
- Drink extra fluids. The mountain air is dry and cold and moisture is lost as you breathe.
- Eat light, high-carbohydrate meals for more energy.
- Avoid alcohol as it may increase the risk of dehydration.
- Avoid sedatives.
- The drugs acetazolamide (Diamox) and dexamethasone have been recommended for prevention of AMS. They can reduce the symptoms, but they also mask warning signs; severe and fatal AMS has occurred in people taking these drugs. In general they are not recommended for travellers.

Even with acclimatisation you may still have trouble adjusting. Any one of the symptoms mentioned earlier, even just a persistent headache, can be a warning. There is no hard and fast rule as to how high is too high: AMS has been fatal at altitudes of 3000m, although 3500 to 4500m is the usual range.

Motion Sickness Eating lightly before and during a trip will reduce the chances of motion sickness. If you are prone to motion sickness try to find a place that minimises disturbance – near the wing on aircraft, close to midships on boats, near the centre on buses. Fresh air usually helps; reading and cigarette smoke don't. Commercial motion-sickness preparations, which can cause drowsiness, have to be taken before the trip commences; when you're feeling sick it's too late. Ginger (available in capsule form) and peppermint (including mint-flavoured sweets) are natural preventives.

Jet Lag Jet lag is experienced when a person travels by air across more than three time zones (each time zone usually represents a one-hour time difference). It occurs because many of the functions of the human body (such as temperature, pulse rate and emptying of the bladder and bowels) are regulated by internal 24 hour cycles called circadian rhythms. When we travel long distances rapidly, our bodies take time to adjust to the 'new time' of our destination, and we may experience fatigue, disorientation, insomnia, anxiety, impaired concentration and loss of appetite. These effects will usually be gone within three days of arrival, but there are ways of minimising the impact of jet lag:

- Rest for a couple of days prior to departure; try to avoid late nights and last-minute dashes for travellers' cheques, passport etc.
- Try to select flight schedules that minimise sleep deprivation; arriving late in the day means you can go to sleep soon after you arrive. For very long flights, try to organise a stopover.
- Avoid excessive eating (which bloats the stomach) and alcohol (which causes dehydration) during the flight. Instead, drink plenty of noncarbonated, nonalcoholic drinks such as fruit juice or water.
- Avoid smoking, as this reduces the amount of oxygen in the aeroplane cabin even further and causes greater fatigue.
- Make yourself comfortable by wearing loose-fitting clothes; bring an eye mask and ear plugs to help you sleep.

Infectious Diseases

Diarrhoea A change of water, food or climate can all cause the runs; diarrhoea caused by contaminated food or water is more serious. Despite all your precautions you may still have a mild bout of travellers' diarrhoea but a few rushed toilet trips with no other symptoms is not indicative of a serious problem. Moderate diarrhoea, involving half-a-dozen loose movements in a day, is more of a nuisance.

Dehydration is the main danger with any diarrhoea, particularly for children where dehydration can occur quite quickly. Fluid replacement remains the mainstay of management. Weak black tea with a little sugar, soda water, or soft drinks allowed to go flat and diluted 50% with water are all good. With severe diarrhoea a rehydrating solution is necessary to replace minerals and salts. Commercially available oral rehydration salts (ORS) are very useful; add the contents of one sachet to a litre of boiled or bottled water. In an emergency you can make up a solution of eight teaspoons of sugar to a litre of boiled water and eat salted cracker biscuits at the same time. You should stick to a bland diet as you recover.

Lomotil or Imodium can be used to bring relief from the symptoms, although they do not actually cure the problem. Only use these drugs if absolutely necessary – eg if you *must* travel. For children under 12 years Lomotil and Imodium are not recommended. Under all circumstances fluid replacement is the most important thing to remember. Do not use these drugs if the person has a high fever or is severely dehydrated.

In certain situations antibiotics may be indicated:

- Watery diarrhoea with blood and mucous. (Gut-paralysing drugs like Imodium or Lomotil should be avoided in this situation.)
- Watery diarrhoea with fever and lethargy.
- Persistent diarrhoea not improving after 48 hours.
- Severe diarrhoea, if it is logistically difficult to stay in one place.

The recommended drugs (adults only) would be either norfloxacin 400 mg twice daily for three days or ciprofloxacin 500 mg twice daily for three days.

The drug bismuth subsalicylate has also been used successfully. It is not available in some countries. The dosage for adults is two tablets or 30 ml and for children it is one tablet or 10 ml. This dose can be repeated every 30 minutes to one hour, with no more than eight doses in a 24 hour period.

The drug of choice for children would be co-trimoxazole (Bactrim, Septrin, Resprim) with dosage dependent on weight. A five day course is given. This is a sulpha drug and must not be used by people with a known sulpha allergy.

Giardiasis The parasite causing this intestinal disorder is present in contaminated water.

The symptoms are stomach cramps, nausea, a bloated stomach, watery, foul-smelling diarrhoea and frequent gas. Giardiasis can appear several weeks after you have been exposed to the parasite. The symptoms may disappear for a few days and then return; this can go on for several weeks. Tinidazole, known as Fasigyn, or metronidazole (Flagyl) are the recommended drugs for treatment. Either can be used in a single treatment dose. Antibiotics are of no use.

Dysentery This serious illness is caused by contaminated food or water and is characterised by severe diarrhoea, often with blood or mucus in the stool. There are two kinds of dysentery. Bacillary dysentery is characterised by a high fever and rapid onset; headache, vomiting and stomach pains are also symptoms. It generally does not last longer than a week, but it is highly contagious.

Amoebic dysentery is often more gradual in the onset of symptoms, with cramping abdominal pain and vomiting less likely; fever may not be present. It is not a self-limiting disease: it will persist until treated and can recur and cause long-term health problems.

A stool test is necessary to diagnose which kind of dysentery you have, so you should seek medical help urgently. In case of an emergency the drugs norfloxacin or ciprofloxacin can be used as presumptive treatment for bacillary dysentery, and metronidazole (Flagyl) for amoebic dysentery.

For bacillary dysentery, norfloxacin 400 mg twice daily for seven days or ciprofloxacin 500 mg twice daily for seven days are the recommended dosages. If you're unable to find either of these drugs then a useful alternative is co-trimoxazole 160/800 mg (Bactrim, Septrin, Resprim) twice daily for seven days. This is a sulpha drug and must not be used by people with a known sulpha allergy.

In the case of children the drug co-trimoxazole is a reasonable first-line treatment. For amoebic dysentery, the recommended adult dosage of metronidazole

(Flagyl) is one 750 mg to 800 mg capsule three times daily for five days. Children aged between eight and 12 years should have half the adult dose; the dosage for younger children is one-third the adult dose.

An alternative to Flagyl is Fasigyn, taken as a two gram daily dose for three days. Alcohol must be avoided during treatment and for 48 hours afterwards.

Cholera Cholera vaccination is not very effective. The bacteria responsible for this disease are waterborne, so attention to the rules of eating and drinking should protect the traveller.

Outbreaks of cholera are generally widely reported, so you can avoid such problem areas. The disease is characterised by a sudden onset of acute diarrhoea with 'rice water' stools, vomiting, muscular cramps, and extreme weakness. You need medical help – but treat for dehydration, which can be extreme, and if there is an appreciable delay in getting to hospital then begin taking tetracycline. The adult dose is 250 mg four times daily. It is not recommended for children aged eight years or under nor for pregnant women. An alternative drug is Ampicillin. People allergic to penicillin should not take Ampicillin. Remember that while antibiotics might kill the bacteria, it is a toxin produced by the bacteria which causes the massive fluid loss. Fluid replacement is by far the most important aspect of treatment.

Viral Gastroenteritis This is caused not by bacteria but, as the name suggests, by a virus. It is characterised by stomach cramps, diarrhoea, and sometimes by vomiting and/or a slight fever. All you can do is rest and drink lots of fluids.

Hepatitis Hepatitis is a general term for inflammation of the liver. There are many causes of this condition: drugs, alcohol and infections are but a few.

The discovery of new strains has led to a virtual alphabet soup, with hepatitis A, B, C, D, E and a rumoured G. These letters identify specific agents that cause viral hepatitis. Viral hepatitis is an infection of the liver, which can lead to jaundice (yellow skin), fever, lethargy and digestive problems. It can have no symptoms at all, with the infected person not knowing that they have the disease. Travellers shouldn't be too paranoid about this apparent proliferation of hepatitis strains; hep C, D, E and G are fairly rare (so far) and following the same precautions as for A and B should be all that's necessary to avoid them.

Viral hepatitis can be divided into two groups on the basis of how it is spread. The first route of transmission is via contaminated food and water, and the second route is via blood and bodily fluids. The following types of hepatitis are spread by contaminated food and water:

Hepatitis A This is a very common disease in most countries, especially those with poor standards of sanitation. Most people in developing countries are infected as children; they often don't develop symptoms, but do develop life-long immunity. The disease poses a threat especially to travellers from developed countries, who are unlikely to have been exposed to hepatitis A.

The symptoms are fever, chills, headache, fatigue, feelings of weakness and aches and pains, followed by loss of appetite, nausea, vomiting, abdominal pain, dark urine, light coloured faeces, jaundiced skin and the whites of the eyes may turn yellow. In some cases you may feel unwell, tired, have no appetite, experience aches and pains and be jaundiced. You should seek medical advice, but in general there is not much you can do apart from resting, drinking lots of fluids, eating lightly and avoiding fatty foods. People who have had hepatitis must forego alcohol for six months after the illness, as hepatitis attacks the liver and it needs that amount of time to recover.

The routes of transmission are via contaminated water, shellfish contaminated by sewerage, or foodstuffs sold by food handlers with poor standards of hygiene.

Taking care with what you eat and drink

can go a long way towards preventing this disease. But this is a very infectious virus, so if there is any risk of exposure, additional cover is highly recommended. This cover comes in two forms: Gamma globulin and Havrix. Gamma globulin is an injection where you are given the antibodies for hepatitis A, which provide immunity for a limited time. Havrix is a vaccine, where you develop your own antibodies, which gives lasting immunity.

Hepatitis E This is a very recently discovered virus, of which little is yet known. It appears to be rather common in developing countries, generally causing mild hepatitis, although it can be very serious in pregnant women.

Care with water supplies is the only current prevention, as there are no specific vaccines for this type of hepatitis. At present it doesn't appear to be too great a risk for travellers.

The following strains are spread by contact with blood and bodily fluids:

Hepatitis B This is also a very common disease, with almost 300 million chronic carriers in the world. Hepatitis B, which used to be called serum hepatitis, is spread through contact with infected blood, blood products or bodily fluids (eg through sexual contact, unsterilised needles and blood transfusions or via small breaks in the skin). Other risk situations include having a shave or tattoo in a local shop, or having your body pierced. The symptoms of type B are much the same as type A except that they are more severe and may lead to irreparable liver damage or even liver cancer.

Although there is no treatment for hepatitis B, a cheap and effective vaccine is available; the only problem is that for long-lasting cover you need a six month course. The immunisation schedule requires two injections at least a month apart followed by a third dose five months after the second. Persons who should receive a hepatitis B vaccination include anyone who anticipates

contact with blood or other bodily secretions, either as a health-care worker or through sexual contact with the local population, and particularly those who intend to stay in the country for a long period of time.

Hepatitis C This is another recently defined virus. It is a concern because it seems to lead to liver disease more rapidly than hepatitis B.

The virus is spread by contact with blood – usually via contaminated transfusions or shared needles. Avoiding these is the only means of prevention, as there is no available vaccine.

Hepatitis D Often referred to as the 'Delta' virus, this infection only occurs in chronic carriers of hepatitis B. It is transmitted by blood and bodily fluids. Again there is no vaccine for this virus, so avoidance is the best prevention. The risk to travellers is certainly limited.

Typhoid Typhoid fever is another gut infection that travels the faecal-oral route – ie contaminated water and food are responsible. Vaccination against typhoid is not totally effective and it is one of the most dangerous infections, so medical help must be sought.

In its early stages typhoid resembles many other illnesses: sufferers may feel like they have a bad cold or flu on the way, as early symptoms are a headache, a sore throat, and a fever which rises a little each day until it is around 40°C or more. The victim's pulse is often slow relative to the degree of fever present and gets slower as the fever rises – unlike a normal fever where the pulse increases. There may also be vomiting, diarrhoea or constipation.

In the second week the high fever and slow pulse continue and a few pink spots may appear on the body; trembling, delirium, weakness, weight loss and dehydration are other symptoms. If there are no further complications, the fever and other symptoms will slowly diminish during the third week. However you must get medical help before this because pneumonia (acute infection of the lungs) or peritonitis (perforated bowel) are common complications, and because typhoid is very infectious.

The fever should be treated by keeping the victim cool and dehydration should also be watched for.

The drug of choice is ciprofloxacin at a dose of one gram daily for 14 days. It is quite expensive and may not be available. The alternative, chloramphenicol, has been the mainstay of treatment for many years. In many countries it is still the recommended antibiotic but there are fewer side affects with Ampicillin. The adult dosage is two 250 mg capsules, four times a day. Children aged between eight and 12 years should have half the adult dose; younger children should have one-third the adult dose.

People who are allergic to penicillin should not be given Ampicillin.

Plague There was an outbreak of pneumonic plague in 1994 in Surat, Gujarat, although the risk to travellers is tiny.

Meningococcal Meningitis This is a bacterial infection of the lining of the brain. The risk area for this disease is northern India (from about the level of Delhi, and then north) and Nepal. The vaccination is recommended for those who will be in the area for seven days or longer.

Trekkers to rural areas should be particularly careful, as the disease is spread by close contact with people who carry it in their throats and noses (spreading it through coughs and sneezes) and who may not be aware that they are carriers. Lodges in the hills where travellers spend the night are prime spots for the spread of infection.

This very serious disease attacks the brain and can be fatal. A scattered, blotchy rash, fever, severe headache, sensitivity to light and neck stiffness which prevents forward bending of the head are the first symptoms. Death can occur within a few hours, so immediate treatment is important.

Treatment is large doses of penicillin given intravenously, or, if that is not possible, intramuscularly (ie in the buttocks). Vaccination offers good protection for over a year,

but you should also check for reports of current epidemics.

Tuberculosis (TB) There is a worldwide resurgence of TB. It is a bacterial infection which is usually transmitted by coughing, but may be transmitted through unpasteurised milk. Milk that has been boiled is safe to drink; the souring of milk to make yoghurt or cheese also kills the bacilli. Most infected people never develop symptoms. In those who do, especially infants, symptoms may arise within weeks of the infection occurring and may be severe. In most, however, the disease lies dormant for many years until, for some reason, the infected person becomes physically run down. Symptoms include fever, weight loss, night sweats and coughing.

Diphtheria Diphtheria can be a skin infection or a more dangerous throat infection. It is spread by contaminated dust contacting the skin or by the inhalation of infected cough or sneeze droplets. Frequent washing and keeping the skin dry will help prevent skin infection. The mainstay of treatment of the diphtheria throat infection is an intravenous infusion of diphtheria antitoxin. The antitoxin is produced in horses so may be associated with allergic reactions in some people. Because of this it must be administered under close medical supervision. Antibiotics such as erythromycin or penicillin are then given to eradicate the diphtheria bacteria from the patient so that it is not transmitted to others. A vaccination is available to prevent the throat infection.

Sexually Transmitted Diseases Sexual contact with an infected sexual partner spreads these diseases. While abstinence is the only 100% preventative, using condoms is also effective. Gonorrhoea, herpes and syphilis are the most common of these diseases; sores, blisters or rashes around the genitals, discharges or pain when urinating are common symptoms. Symptoms may be less marked or not observed at all in women. Syphilis symptoms eventually disappear completely but the disease continues and can cause severe problems in later years. The treatment of gonorrhoea and syphilis is by antibiotics.

There are numerous other sexually transmitted diseases, for most of which effective treatment is available. However, there is no cure for herpes and there is also currently no cure for AIDS (Acquired Immune Deficiency Syndrome).

HIV/AIDS HIV, the Human Immunodeficiency Virus, may develop into AIDS. HIV is a major problem in many countries. Any exposure to blood, blood products or bodily fluids may put the individual at risk. In many developing countries transmission is predominantly through heterosexual sexual activity. This is quite different from industrialised countries where transmission is mostly through contact between homosexual or bisexual males, or via contaminated needles shared by IV drug users. Apart from abstinence, the most effective preventative is always to practise safe sex using condoms. It is impossible to detect the HIV-positive status of an otherwise healthy looking person without a blood test.

HIV/AIDS can also be spread through infected blood transfusions; some developing countries cannot afford to screen blood for transfusions. It can also be spread by dirty needles – vaccinations, acupuncture, tattooing and ear or nose-piercing can potentially be as dangerous as intravenous drug use if the equipment is not clean. If you do need an injection, ask to see the syringe unwrapped in front of you, or better still, take a needle and syringe pack with you overseas – it is a cheap insurance package against infection with HIV.

Fear of HIV infection should never preclude treatment for serious medical conditions. Although there may be a risk of infection, it is very small indeed.

The AIDS situation in India is quite serious; an article in *Navbharat Times* a few years ago estimated that 30% of the 100,000 prostitutes in Mumbai (Bombay) are HIV positive. Further, a random survey of truck drivers revealed that 25% were HIV positive and most did not know anything about AIDS.

Worms These parasites are most common in rural, tropical areas and a stool test when you return home is not a bad idea. They can be present on unwashed vegetables or in undercooked meat and you can pick them up through your skin by walking in bare feet. Infestations may not show up for some time, and although they are generally not serious, if left untreated they can cause severe health problems. A stool test is necessary to pinpoint the problem and medication is often available over the counter.

Tetanus This potentially fatal disease is found in undeveloped tropical areas. It is difficult to treat but is preventable with immunisation. Tetanus occurs when a wound becomes infected by a germ which lives in soil and in the faeces of horses and other animals, so clean all cuts, punctures or animal bites. Tetanus is also known as lockjaw, and the first symptom may be discomfort in swallowing, or stiffening of the jaw and neck; this is followed by painful convulsions of the jaw and whole body.

Rabies Rabies is a fatal viral infection found in many countries and is caused by a bite or scratch by an infected animal. Dogs are noted carriers, as are monkeys and cats. Any bite, scratch or even lick from a warm-blooded, furry animal should be cleaned immediately and thoroughly. Scrub with soap and running water, and then clean with an alcohol or iodine solution. If there is any possibility that the animal is infected, medical help should be sought immediately to prevent the onset of symptoms and death. In a person who has not been immunised against rabies, this involves having five injections of vaccine and one of immunoglobulin over 28 days starting as soon as possible after the exposure. Even if the animal is not rabid, all bites should be treated seriously as they can become infected or can result in tetanus. A rabies vaccination is now available and should be considered if you are in a high-risk category – eg if you intend to explore caves (bat bites can be dangerous) or work with animals.

Insect-Borne Diseases

Malaria The mosquitoes which carry malaria are not prevalent in the Himalayan region, but the following information is included in the event that you are planning to travel to other areas of India or other Asian countries.

If you are travelling in endemic areas, which in India is everywhere except the Himalayan region, it is extremely important to take malarial prophylactics. Symptoms include headaches, fever, chills and sweating which may subside and recur. Without treatment malaria can develop more serious, potentially fatal effects.

Antimalarial drugs do not prevent you from being infected but kill the parasites during a stage in their development.

There are a number of different types of malaria. The one of most concern is falciparum malaria. This is responsible for the very serious cerebral malaria. Falciparum is the predominant form in many malaria-prone areas of the world, including Africa, South-East Asia and Papua New Guinea. Contrary to popular belief cerebral malaria is not a new strain.

The problem in recent years has been the emergence of increasing resistance to commonly used antimalarials like chloroquine, maloprim and proguanil. Newer drugs such as mefloquine (Lariam) and doxycycline (Vibramycin, Doryx) are often recommended for chloroquine and multidrug-resistant areas. Expert advice should be sought, as there are many factors to consider when deciding on the type of antimalarial medication, including the area to be visited, the risk of exposure to malaria-carrying mosquitoes, your medical history, and your age and pregnancy status. It is also important to discuss the side-effect profile of the medication, so you can work out some level of risk versus benefit ratio. It is also very important to be sure of the correct dosage of the medication prescribed to you. Some people have inadvertently taken weekly medication (chloroquine) on a daily basis, with disastrous effects. While

discussing dosages for prevention of malaria, it is often advisable to include the dosages required for treatment, especially if your trip is through a high-risk area that would isolate you from medical care.

Mosquito-Avoidance Measures

The mosquitoes that transmit malaria bite from dusk to dawn, and during this period travellers are advised to:

- wear light coloured clothing
- wear long pants and long sleeved shirts
- use mosquito repellents containing the compound DEET on exposed areas (overuse of DEET may be harmful, especially to children, but its use is considered preferable to being bitten by disease-transmitting mosquitoes)
- avoid highly scented perfumes or aftershave
- use a mosquito net – it may be worth taking your own. ■

While no antimalarial is 100% effective, taking the most appropriate drug significantly reduces the risk of contracting the disease.

No one should ever die from malaria. It can be diagnosed by a simple blood test. Symptoms range from fever, chills and sweating, headache and abdominal pains to a vague feeling of ill-health, so seek examination immediately if there is any suggestion of malaria.

Contrary to popular belief, once a traveller contracts malaria he/she does not have it for life. Two species of the parasite may lie dormant in the liver but this can also be eradicated using a specific medication. Malaria is curable, as long as the traveller seeks medical help when symptoms occur.

Dengue Fever There is no prophylactic available for this mosquito-spread disease; the main preventative measure is to avoid mosquito bites. A sudden onset of fever, headaches and severe joint and muscle pains are the first signs before a rash starts on the trunk of the body and spreads to the limbs and face. After a further few days, the fever will subside and recovery will begin. Serious complications are not common but full recovery can take up to a month or more.

Filariasis This is a mosquito-transmitted parasitic infection which is found in many parts of Africa, Asia, Central and South America and the Pacific. There is a range of possible manifestations of the infection, depending on which filarial parasite species has caused the infection. These include fever, pain and swelling of the lymph glands; inflammation of lymph drainage areas; swelling of a limb or the scrotum; skin rashes and blindness. Treatment is available to eliminate the parasites from the body, but some of the damage they cause may not be reversible. Medical advice should be obtained promptly if the infection is suspected.

Typhus Typhus is spread by ticks, mites or lice. It begins with fever, chills, headache, muscle pains and a body rash. There is often a large painful sore at the site of the bite and nearby lymph nodes are swollen and painful. Treatment is with tetracycline, or chloramphenicol under medical supervision.

Seek local advice on areas where ticks pose a danger and always check your skin carefully for ticks after walking in a danger area. A strong insect repellent can help, and serious walkers in tick areas should consider having their boots and trousers impregnated with benzyl benzoate and dibutylphthalate.

Japanese B Encephalitis This viral infection of the brain is transmitted by mosquitoes. It is usually a severe illness with a high mortality rate. Most cases occur in rural areas because part of the life cycle of the virus takes place in pigs or wading birds. Symptoms include fever, headache, vomiting, neck stiffness, pain in the eyes when looking at light, alteration in consciousness, seizures and paralysis or muscle weakness. Correct diagnosis and treatment requires hospitalisation. Vaccination is recommended for those intending to spend more than a month in a rural risk area during the rainy season, for those making repeated trips into a risk area or who are planning to stay for a year or more in a risk area, and for those visiting an area where there is an epidemic. The disease is not common in travellers.

Cuts, Bites & Stings
Cuts & Scratches Skin punctures can easily become infected in hot climates and may be difficult to heal. Treat any cut with an antiseptic such as providone-iodine. Where possible, avoid bandages and Band-Aids, which can keep wounds wet.

Bites & Stings Bee and wasp stings are usually painful rather than dangerous. Calamine lotion or Stingose spray will give relief and ice packs will reduce the pain and swelling. There are some spiders with dangerous bites but antivenenes are usually available. Again, local advice is the best suggestion.

Snakes To minimise your chances of being bitten always wear boots, socks and long trousers when walking through undergrowth where snakes may be present. Don't put your hands into holes and crevices, and be careful when collecting firewood.

Snake bites do not cause instantaneous death and antivenenes are usually available. Keep the victim calm and still, wrap the bitten limb tightly, as you would for a sprained ankle, and then attach a splint to immobilise it. Then seek medical help, if possible with the dead snake for identification. Don't attempt to catch the snake if there is even a remote possibility of being bitten again. Tourniquets and sucking out the poison are now comprehensively discredited.

Bedbugs & Lice Bedbugs live in various places, but particularly in dirty mattresses and bedding. Spots of blood on bedclothes or on the wall around the bed can be read as a suggestion to find another hotel. Bedbugs leave itchy bites in neat rows. Calamine lotion or Stingose spray may help.

All lice cause itching and discomfort. They make themselves at home in your hair (head lice), your clothing (body lice) or in your pubic hair (crabs). You catch lice through direct contact with infected people or by sharing combs, clothing and the like. Powder or shampoo treatment will kill the lice and infected clothing should then be washed in very hot water.

Leeches & Ticks Leeches, which attach themselves to your skin and suck your blood, may be present in damp rainforest conditions; they are notoriously prevalent in parts of West Sikkim. Trekkers often get them on their legs or in their boots. An insect repellent may keep them away. You should always check your body if you have been walking through a potentially tick-infested area, as ticks can cause skin infections and other more serious diseases. Applying salt or the heat of a lighted cigarette end will make them fall off. Avoid pulling the rear of the body as this may squeeze the tick's gut contents through the attached mouth parts into the skin, increasing the risk of infection and disease. Smearing chemicals on the tick will not make it let go and is not recommended.

Women's Health

Gynaecological Problems Poor diet, lowered resistance due to the use of antibiotics for stomach upsets and even contraceptive pills can lead to vaginal infections when travelling in hot climates. Keeping the genital area clean, and wearing skirts or loose-fitting trousers and cotton underwear will help to prevent infections.

Yeast infections, characterised by a rash, itch and discharge, can be treated with a vinegar or lemon-juice douche, or with yoghurt. Nystatin miconazole or clotrimazole suppositories are the usual medical prescription. Trichomoniasis and gardnerella are more serious infections; symptoms are a smelly discharge and sometimes a burning sensation when urinating. Male sexual partners must also be treated, and if a vinegar-water douche is not effective medical attention should be sought. Metronidazole (Flagyl) is the prescribed drug.

Pregnancy Most miscarriages occur during the first three months of pregnancy, so this is the most risky time to travel as far as your own health is concerned. Miscarriage is not uncommon, and can occasionally lead to severe bleeding. The last three months should also be spent within reasonable distance of good medical care. A baby born as early as 24 weeks stands a chance of survival, but only in a good modern hospital. Pregnant women should avoid all unnecessary medication, but vaccinations and malarial prophylactics should still be taken where possible. Additional care should be taken to prevent illness and particular attention should be paid to diet and nutrition. Alcohol and nicotine, for example, should be avoided.

Women travellers often find that their periods become irregular or even cease while they're on the road. Remember that a missed period in these circumstances doesn't necessarily indicate pregnancy. There are health posts or Family Planning clinics in many urban centres in developing countries, where you can seek advice and have a urine test to determine whether or not you are pregnant.

Hospitals

Although India does have a few excellent hospitals such as the All India Institute of Medical Sciences in Delhi, most Indian cities do not have the quality of medical care available in the west. Usually, hospitals run by western missionaries have better facilities than government hospitals where long waiting lines are common. Unless you have something very unusual, these Christian-run hospitals are the best places to head for in an emergency. In remote areas, medical services are less than adequate and even nonexistent, and if you require hospitalisation, evacuation should be considered. In many remote areas, playing fields double as helipads, and in extreme medical emergencies, it may be possible to be airlifted to Delhi or Calcutta.

India also has many qualified doctors with their own private clinics which can be quite good and, in some cases, as good as anything available anywhere in the world. The usual fee for a clinic visit is about Rs 80; Rs 200 for a specialist. Home calls usually cost about Rs 100.

In centres where there is a large Tibetan population, such as McLeod Ganj, you may be able to avail yourself of traditional Tibetan medicine. Some travellers swear by some Tibetan herbal remedies for minor stomach complaints, but check your symptoms against those listed under the more serious gastric disorders in this health section. For more information on traditional Tibetan medicine, see under McLeod Ganj in the Himachal Pradesh chapter.

Toilets
'Western' hotels have a sit-up-style toilet; 'Indian' ones usually (but not always) have the traditional Asian squat style, which is a toilet bowl recessed into the floor with foot-pads on the edge of the bowl!

WOMEN TRAVELLERS
Foreign women travelling in India have always been viewed by Indian men as free and easy, based largely on what they believed to be true from watching cheap western soapies. Women have been hassled, stared at, spied on in hotel rooms, and often groped, although these situations were rarely threatening.

Recently, however, the situation has become more difficult for women travellers, mainly because the 'sexual revolution' which swept the west 25 years ago has now hit India. Movies and magazines are much more explicit, and the widespread billboard advertisements for condoms often quote passages from the Kama Sutra and depict naked or seminaked women and men. The message getting through to the middle-class Indian male is that sex before and outside of marriage is less of a taboo than in the past, and

so foreign women are more vulnerable than before.

It should be noted, however, that many western women have observed that the untoward attentions of Indian males decreases rapidly once they hit the hills. While women travelling alone in the Indian Himalaya are still disconcertingly stared at constantly, the attention is usually due to sheer curiosity rather than any more sinister motives. The 'hassle factor' decreases proportionately the higher you get!

Close attention to standards of dress will go a long way to minimising problems for female travellers. The light cotton draw-string skirts that many foreign women pick up in India are really sari petticoats and to wear them in the street is rather like going out half dressed. Ways of blending into the Indian background include avoiding sleeveless blouses, skirts that are too short and, of course, the bra-less look.

Getting stared at is something you'll have to get used to. Don't return male stares, as this will be considered a come-on; just ignore them. Dark glasses can help. Other harassment likely to be encountered includes obscene comments, touching-up and jeering, particularly by groups of youths.

Getting involved in inane conversations with men is also considered a come-on. Keep discussions down to a necessary minimum unless you're interested in getting hassled. If you get the uncomfortable feeling he's encroaching on your space, the chances are that he is. A firm request to keep away is usually enough. Firmly return any errant limbs, put some item of luggage in between you and if all else fails, find a new spot. You're also within your rights to tell him to shove off!

Being a woman also has some advantages. There is often a special ladies' queue for train tickets or even a ladies' quota and ladies' compartments. One woman wrote that these ladies' carriages were often nearly empty, another said that they were full of screaming children. Special ladies' facilities are also sometimes found in cinemas and other places.

Hazards of Spiritual Quests

Most of India's *sadhus*, the wandering ascetics who can be seen throughout the country, and in high concentrations in the holy centres of the Indian Himalaya, have embarked on their quest of worldly renunciation from purely spiritual motives. However, small numbers of western women have met with some sadhus and 'gurus' whose interest in them and whose attentions derive from causes other than in their spiritual well being. Some women have found themselves confronted with a situation where sex is introduced onto the agenda ostensibly as a means of attaining spiritual liberation, often following weeks of speculations and discussions of a more metaphysical nature. How they deal with this is up to the woman in question, but maintaining clarity and mental peace of mind is essential, and extricating yourself from such a situation is strongly advisable. It is definitely not wise to place your trust in anyone who recommends an isolated retreat for two in some remote mountain fastness, thus placing yourself in an extremely vulnerable situation. ■

GAY & LESBIAN TRAVELLERS

While overt displays of affection between members of the opposite sex, such as cuddling and hand-holding, are frowned upon in India, it is not unusual to see Indian men holding hands with each other or engaged in other close affectionate behaviour. This does not necessarily suggest that they are gay. The gay movement in India is confined almost exclusively to larger cities such as Delhi and Mumbai (Bombay). As with relations between heterosexual western couples travelling in India – both married and unmarried – gay and lesbian travellers should exercise discretion and refrain from displaying overt affection towards each other in public.

DISABLED TRAVELLERS

Travelling in the Indian Himalaya can entail some fairly rigorous challenges, even for the able-bodied traveller – long bus trips in crowded vehicles along rough, unsealed mountain roads can test even the hardiest traveller. For the mobility impaired traveller, these challenges are increased many-fold. Few, if any, buildings in the Indian Himalaya have ramps or lifts (elevators); toilets have certainly not been designed to accommodate wheelchairs; footpaths, where they exist (only in larger towns) are generally riddled with potholes and crevices, littered with obstacles and packed with throngs of people, severely restricting mobility. If, despite these impediments, you are still determined to travel to the Indian Himalaya, if your mobility is restricted you will require a strong, able-bodied companion to accompany you, and you should definitely consider hiring a private vehicle and driver.

SENIOR TRAVELLERS

Unless your mobility is impaired (see above under Disabled Travellers), or you are vision impaired or in any other way incapacitated, and are in reasonable health, there is no reason why the senior traveller should not consider the Himalaya as a potential holiday destination and select a more pedestrian destination. Octogenarian Indian travellers heading for the high Himalaya are not an uncommon sight on pilgrim-packed buses throughout the hills. It may be helpful to discuss your proposed trip with your local GP.

TRAVELLING WITH CHILDREN

The numbers of intrepid souls travelling around India accompanied by one, or even two, young children, seems to be on the increase. Children can often enhance your encounters with local people, often possessing little of the self-consciousness and sense of the cultural differences which can inhibit interaction between adults. Nevertheless, travelling with children can be hard work, and the rigours of travel in the Himalaya can be tiring at the best of times. Ideally the burden needs to be shared between two adults. For more information, see the Health section earlier in this chapter, and get hold of a copy of Lonely Planet's *Travel with Children* (1995), by Maureen Wheeler.

DANGERS & ANNOYANCES
Theft

Having things stolen is a problem in India, not because it's a thief-ridden country – it isn't – but because you can become involved in a lot of hassles getting the items replaced. If your passport is stolen you may have a long trip back to an embassy to replace it. Likewise, you may be able to replace stolen travellers' cheques in major cities. Always lock your room, preferably with your own padlock in cheaper hotels. Lock it at night, as well; people have had things stolen from their rooms when they've actually been in them.

Carry your valuables (passport, tickets, health certificates, money, travellers' cheques) with you at all times. Either have a stout leather passport wallet on your belt, or a passport pouch under your shirt, or extra internal pockets in your clothing. On trains at night keep your gear near you; padlocking a bag to a luggage rack can be useful, and some of the newer trains have loops under the seats which you can chain things to. Never walk around with valuables casually slung over your shoulder. Take extra care in crowded public transport.

Train and bus departure time, when the confusion and crowds are at their worst, is the time to be most careful. Just as the train or bus is about to leave, you are distracted by

WARNING
Carbon-Monoxide Poisoning

Tragically, a number of people have died of carbon-monoxide poisoning due to burning charcoal in their poorly ventilated hotel rooms. Avoid lighting charcoal-fuelled fires; ask the proprietor for more blankets if you need to get warm. If you do wish to light a fire, ensure that the room is well ventilated and that the fuel you use does not give off toxic fumes. ■

someone, while his or her accomplice is stealing your bag from by your feet. Airports are another place to be careful, especially when international arrivals take place in the middle of the night, when you are unlikely to be at your most alert. Chaining your backpack to the roof racks on buses is a good idea, or better still, insist that the bag be carried on board with you.

From time to time there are also drugging episodes, which often seem to take the following form: A traveller meets somebody on a train or bus or in a town, starts talking and is then offered a cup of tea or something similar. Hours later they wake up with a headache and all their gear gone, the tea having been full of sleeping pills. Don't accept drinks or food from strangers no matter how friendly they seem, particularly if you're on your own.

Beware also of some of your fellow travellers who make the money go further by helping themselves to other people's. Remember that backpacks are very easy to rifle through. Don't leave valuables in them, especially during flights. Remember also that something may be of little or no value to a thief, but to lose it would be a real heartbreak to you, such as film. Finally, a good travel insurance policy helps.

If you do have something stolen, you're going to have to report it to the police. You'll also need a statement proving you have done so, if you want to claim on insurance. Most policies insist that the stolen item must be reported within a limited amount of time, which can pose problems if you're in a remote region days away from the nearest police post. Unfortunately the police are generally less than helpful, and at times are downright unhelpful, unsympathetic and even disbelieving, implying that you are making a false claim in order to defraud your insurance company.

Insurance companies, despite their rosy promises of full protection and speedy settlement of claims, are just as disbelieving as the Indian police and will often attempt every devious trick in the book to avoid paying out on a baggage claim.

Stolen Travellers' Cheques If you're unlucky enough to have things stolen, some precautions can ease the pain. All travellers' cheques are replaceable but this does you little immediate good if you have to go home and apply to your bank to get them. What you want is instant replacement. Furthermore, what do you do if you lose your cheques and money and have a day or more to travel to the replacement office? The answer is to keep an emergency cash-stash in a totally separate place. In that same place you should keep a record of the cheque serial numbers, proof of purchase slips and your passport number.

American Express makes considerable noise about 'instant replacement' of their cheques but a lot of people find out, to their cost, that without a number of precautions 'instantly' can take longer than you think. If you don't have the receipt you were given when you bought the cheques, rapid replacement will be difficult. Obviously the receipt should be kept separate from the cheques, and a photocopy in yet another location doesn't hurt either. Chances are you'll be able to get a limited amount of funds on the spot, and the rest will be available when the bank has verified your initial purchase of the cheques. American Express has a 24 hour number in Delhi (☎ (011) 687-5050) which you must ring within 24 hours of the theft.

One traveller wrote that his travellers' cheques were stolen and he didn't discover the loss for a month. They had been left in his hotel room and the thief (presumably from the hotel) had neatly removed a few cheques from the centre of the cheque pouch. Explaining that sort of theft is really difficult and, of course, the thief has had plenty of time to dispose of them.

LEGAL MATTERS

If you find yourself in a sticky legal predicament, contact your embassy. You should carry your passport with you at all times.

In the Indian justice system it seems the burden of proof is on the accused, and proving one's innocence is virtually impossible. The police forces are often corrupt and will pay 'witnesses' to give evidence.

Drugs

For a long time India was a place where you could indulge in all sorts of illegal drugs (mostly grass and hashish) with relative ease – they were cheap, readily available and the risks were minimal. These days things have changed. Although dope is still widely available, the risks have certainly increased.

Penalties for possession, use, or trafficking in illegal drugs are strictly enforced. If convicted on a drugs-related charge, sentences are long (*minimum* of 10 years), even for minor offences, and there is no remission or parole.

BUSINESS HOURS

Indian shops, offices and post offices are not early starters. Generally, shops are open Monday to Saturday from 10 am to 5 pm. Some government offices open on alternate Saturdays and some commercial offices are open on Saturday morning. Post offices are generally open weekdays from 10 am to 5 pm, and on Saturday morning. Main city offices may be open longer hours, such as 8 am to 6 pm in Delhi. In McLeod Ganj, headquarters of the Tibetan Government in Exile, offices are open between 9 am and 5 pm on weekdays.

Banks are open for business on weekdays between 10 am and 2 pm and on Saturday morning. Travellers' cheque transactions usually cease 30 minutes prior to the official bank closing time. Shops and offices are usually closed on Sunday and public holidays.

PUBLIC HOLIDAYS & FESTIVALS

With its populations of Tibetan refugees and tribal groups, and the special reverence in which the Indian Himalaya is held as the abode of the gods, it is not surprising that some of India's most colourful and interesting festivals are held in this region. The important gompas of Ladakh and Sikkim have their own special celebrations, and in other areas of the Himalaya, the change of seasons, the sowing or reaping of crops, or devotion to a local presiding deity can all be the impetus for a colourful local festival. The festival calendar given in this section includes those which are celebrated either nationally or throughout northern India. At the beginning of each regional chapter is a list of local and village festivals which are either unique to that region, or are renowned for the exuberant or colourful celebration of a nationwide festival, such as the celebration of Dussehra at Kullu, which is *the* place to be in the Himalaya for that Hindu festival.

Hindu Lunar Months

The Hindu lunar months and their Gregorian equivalents are as follows:

Chaitra	March-April
Vaishaka	April-May
Jyaistha	May-June
Asadha	June-July
Sravana	July-August
Bhadra	August-September
Asvina	September-October
Kartika	October-November
Aghan	November-December
Pausa	December-January
Magha	January-February
Phalguna	February-March

Muslim Holidays

The dates of the Muslim festivals are not fixed; they fall about 11 days earlier each year.

Ramadan
The most important Muslim festival is a 30 day dawn-to-dusk fast. It was during this month that the prophet Mohammed had the Koran revealed to him in Mecca. Ramadan starts around 10 January 1997, 31 December 1998, and 20 December 1999.

Id-ul-Fitr
This day celebrates the end of Ramadan.

Id-ul-Zuhara
This is a Muslim festival commemorating Abraham's attempt to sacrifice his son. It is celebrated with prayers and feasts.

Muharram
Muharram is a 10 day festival commemorating the martyrdom of Mohammed's grandson, Imam Hussain.

ACTIVITIES

Cycling

A cycling tour of the Indian Himalaya is not an unrealistic proposition, but if you've never done long-distance touring before, this is probably not a good region to begin! In some of the larger hill stations, mountain bicycles are available for hire, and some local travel agencies offer mountain-

---

Festival Calendar

The holidays detailed below are celebrated throughout most of India including the Indian Himalayan regions. Interesting regional festivals are listed at the beginning of regional chapters

February-March

Shivratri – This day of fasting is dedicated to Lord Shiva; his followers believe that it was on this day he danced the *tandava* (the Dance of Destruction). Processions to the temples are followed by the chanting of mantras and anointing of lingams. Mandi, gateway for the Kullu Valley, or Baijnath, in the Kangra Valley, are the two places to be for Shivratri if you're in Himachal Pradesh at this time. Devotees make special pilgrimages to these places, at which there are week long devotions and celebrations.

Holi – This is one of the most exuberant Hindu festivals, with people marking the end of winter by throwing coloured water and red powder at one another. On the night before Holi, bonfires are built to symbolise the destruction of the evil demon Holika.

Losar – Tibetan New Year falls in either February or March according to the Tibetan lunar calendar. Colourful local festivals celebrate the commencement of the new year, and it's a good time to be in a Tibetan centre.

March-April

Ramanavami – In temples all over India the birth of Rama, an incarnation of Vishnu, is celebrated on this day. In the week leading up to Ramanavami, the *Ramayana* is widely read and performed.

April-May

Baisakhi – This Sikh festival commemorates the day that Guru Govind Singh founded the Khalsa, the Sikh brotherhood, which adopted the five *kakkars* (means by which Sikh men recognise each other), as part of their code of behaviour. The *Granth Sahib*, the Sikh holy book, is read through at *gurudwaras* (Sikh temples). Feasting and dancing follow in the evening.

May-June

Buddha Jayanti – The Buddha's birth, enlightenment and attainment of *nirvana* (final release from the cycle of existence), are all celebrated on this day. The Buddha experienced each of these on the same day but in different years.

July-August

Naag Panchami – This festival is dedicated to Ananta, the serpent upon whose coils Vishnu rested between universes. Offerings are made to snake images, and snake charmers do a roaring trade. Snakes are supposed to have power over the monsoon rainfall and keep evil from homes.

Raksha Bandhan (Narial Purnima) – On the full-moon day of the Hindu month of Sravana, girls fix amulets known as *rakhis* to their brothers' wrists to protect them in the coming year. The brothers give their sisters gifts.

Janmashtami – The anniversary of Krishna's birth is celebrated with happy abandon in tune with Krishna's own mischievous moods.

Independence Day – This holiday on 15 August celebrates the anniversary of India's independence from Britain in 1947. The prime minister delivers an address from the ramparts of Delhi's Red Fort.

August-September

Ganesh Chaturthi – This festival, held on the fourth day of the Hindu month Bhadra, is dedicated to Ganesh, the god of wisdom and prosperity. It is considered to be the most auspicious day of the year, and to look at the moon on this day is considered unlucky.

Shravan Purnima – After a day-long fast, high-caste Hindus replace the sacred thread which they always wear looped over their left shoulder.

September-October

Dussehra – Dussehra is celebrated by Hindus all over India in the month of Asvina, but a particularly colourful week-long festival is held at Kullu, in Himachal Pradesh. Dussehra celebrates the victory of Rama over the demon king of Lanka, Ravana.

Gandhi Jayanti – This is a solemn celebration of Gandhi's birthday on 2 October.

October-November

Diwali (Deepavali) – This is the happiest festival of the Hindu calendar, celebrated on the 15th day of Kartika. At night countless oil lamps are lit to show Rama the way home from his period of exile. The festival runs over five days. On the first day, houses are thoroughly cleaned and doorsteps are decorated with intricate *rangolis* (chalk designs). Day two is dedicated to Krishna's victory over Narakasura, a legendary tyrant. Day three is spent in worshipping Lakshmi, the goddess of fortune. Traditionally, this is the beginning of the new financial year for companies. Day four commemorates the visit of the friendly (but uppity) demon Bali whom Vishnu put in his place. On the fifth day men visit their sisters to have a *tikka* placed on their forehead.

Govardhana Puja – This is a Hindu festival dedicated to that holiest of animals, the cow.

Nanak Jayanti – The birthday of Guru Nanak, the founder of the Sikh religion, is celebrated with prayer readings and processions.

November-December

Christmas Day – A holiday in India. ■

bike day tours. UP Tourism offers mountain-bike tours in the Kumaon region. See the Utttarakhand chapter for details.

You can hire rattly old push-bikes in Leh, which are handy for exploring nearby gompas, and at Haridwar, on the northern plains in Uttar Pradesh. The even terrain in the environs here makes this ideal for day trips by bicycle, particularly out to the Rajaji National Park. Gurudongma Travels in Kalimpong offers extended mountain-bike tours; see the West Bengal Hills chapter for details. More information on preparing for a cycling trip and other details for cyclists is included in the Getting There & Away and Getting Around chapters.

Skiing

With the political problems and unrest in Jammu & Kashmir, the ski resort of Gulmarg is closed indefinitely, and other ski centres are being developed in the Himalayan region.

India's premier ski resort is at Auli, near Josimath in Uttarakhand. UP Tourism offers very competitive ski packages, which include ski hire, tows, lessons and accommodation. The ski season at Auli extends from the beginning of January to the end of March. See the Uttarakhand chapter for details.

There are also less developed resorts in Himachal Pradesh, at Solang Nullah, north of Manali, and near Shimla, at Kufri and Narkanda. The Himachal Pradesh Tourist Development Corporation (HPTDC) can organise courses at Solang Nullah and Narkanda, and the Mountaineering Institute & Allied Sports at Manali (see the Mountaineering section below) also runs ski courses. At Solang, the season extends from December to March; at Kufri, from December to February, and at Narkanda, from December to April. Heli-skiing can be arranged at Manali. See the Himachal Pradesh chapter for details.

Trekking

In the Ladakh and Zanskar regions is the fine 10 day Manali to Padum trek. In Himachal Pradesh is the difficult but rewarding trek across the Indrahar Pass from McLeod Ganj (Kangra Valley) to Machhetar (Chamba Valley). From Brahmaur, at the eastern end of the Chamba Valley, you can trek to the sacred lake of Manimahesh, or over the Pir Panjal Range to the Chandra Valley and Lahaul. There are some rewarding treks in the Palampur region of the Kangra Valley. In Kinnaur, a network of mountain trails affords some brilliant trekking possibilities, as does the remote region of Lahaul & Spiti, while there are numerous treks around Manali in the Kullu Valley.

Uttarakhand has some brilliant short and long treks, including those to the remote Har-ki-Dun Valley in Garhwal; treks to the Milam, Pindari and Khatling glaciers; and a short trek to the magnificent Valley of Flowers, above Josimath, among others.

The environs of Darjeeling have been a popular trekking destination for years, and this is one of the few regions where a network of rustic lodges and tea houses means that you don't need to carry a tent. West Sikkim affords some fine trekking possibilities from Yuksom along the Dzongri Trail. For more trekking details, get hold of a copy of Lonely Planet's *Trekking in the Indian Himalaya* by Garry Weare.

Warning
With the escalation of the troubles in Jammu & Kashmir, and the kidnapping of western trekkers (including the murder of a Norwegian man) in 1995, Lonely Planet strongly recommends that travellers do not visit these regions, and that they consider some of the Indian Himalaya's other fine trekking possibilities. ∎

Mountaineering

Mountaineering expeditions interested in climbing peaks over 6000m need to obtain clearance from the Indian Mountaineering Foundation (IMF) (☎ (011) 67-1211; fax 688-3412), Benito Juarez Rd, Anand Niketan, New Delhi, 110021.

For information on mountaineering expeditions to less lofty heights in Uttarakhand, contact the Trekking & Mountaineering Division (☎ (01364) 32-648), Garhwal Mandal Vikas Nigam, Laksmanjhula Rd, Muni-ki-Reti, Rishikesh. Trekking and mountaineering equipment can be hired here.

The headquarters of the Mountaineering Institute & Allied Sports (☎ (01901) 2342) at Manali in Himachal Pradesh runs beginners and advanced courses in mountaineering and other adventure activities, but a large group is required for classes (from 20 to 30 students). You can also hire trekking and mountaineering equipment here. See under Manali in the Himachal Pradesh chapter for details on the institute.

At Brahmaur in the Chamba Valley, Himachal Pradesh, the Mountaineering & Allied Sports Sub-Centre (☎ (01090) 236) can arrange guides and porters and give advice about trekking and mountaineering in this region. You can also hire two person tents here.

Mountain guides (graduates from the prestigious Nehru Institute of Mountaineering) can be organised through Mount Support (☎ (01374) 2419; fax 2459), PO Box 2, BD Nautial Bhawan, Bhatwari Rd, Uttarkashi, Garhwal, Uttar Pradesh. Graduates from the institute can also be arranged through Mansarovar Travels (☎ (S01389) 2170), Hotel Nanda Devi, Josimath, Garhwal.

The Himalayan Mountaineering Institute is based at Darjeeling, and for many years Sherpa Tenzing Norgay was the director here. There are two excellent museums here for those interested in the history of mountaineering in the Himalaya: the Everest Museum and the adjacent Mountaineering Museum.

Rock Climbing

The Mountaineering Institute & Allied Sports in Manali runs courses in rock climbing. See under Manali in the Himachal Pradesh chapter for details.

Kayaking & River Rafting

The Mountaineering Institute & Allied Sports in Manali can arrange two week kayaking trips on the Beas River in October and November for US$140. See under Manali in the Himachal Pradesh chapter for details.

River rafting expeditions are possible on the Beas River in Himachal Pradesh, on the Ganges and its tributaries in Uttarakhand, on the Indus and Zanskar rivers in Ladakh and Zanskar, and on the Teesta River in the West Bengal hills. Travel agencies in Gangtok can also organise trips on the Teesta. See the relevant chapters for details.

Horse Riding

At many hill stations it's possible to hire horses for rides around the environs, including Shimla, McLeod Ganj, Mussoorie, Nainital and Darjeeling, as well as at Kufri, near Shimla, and Solang Nullah, above Manali. Hiring a mountain pony is a fine way to head up to the sacred shrines of Yamunotri and Kedarnath in Uttarakhand, or out to Ghangaria from Govind Ghat to visit the beautiful Valley of Flowers. There are no established agencies for hiring horses and mountain ponies in Ladakh, but it's possible to hire local horses to ride out along some of the trekking routes in this region. See the Ladakh & Zanskar chapter for more details.

Golf

There's a nine hole golf course at Kalika, near Ranikhet in the Kumaon region of Uttarakhand (1820m), and a spectacular nine hole course at Naldehra, just to the north of Shimla. There's a small course at Khajiar, in the Chamba Valley of Himachal Pradesh.

Fishing

Fishing for the mahseer (*Tor putitora*) is the main attraction for anglers in Uttarakhand and West Bengal hills. In Himachal Pradesh, Katrain, along the Beas River, Larji, on the Tirthan River, and Rohru, on the Pabar River are places which afford good fishing mainly for trout. Licences are required for all fishing, but are easily obtained. See the relevant chapters for details.

Wildlife Safaris

Elephant-back safaris are possibilities at Rajaji National Park and Corbett Tiger Reserve in the lower reaches of Uttarakhand, and the Jaldhapara Wildlife Sanctuary on the northern West Bengal plains. See the relevant chapters for details.

Paragliding

During summer, it's possible to go paragliding at Solang Nullah, north of Manali. See the Himachal Pradesh chapter for details.

Hang-Gliding

Hang-gliding is being developed in Himachal Pradesh at Billing in the Kangra Valley, and around Kasauli, near Shimla.

Adventure Tour Operators

Local tour operators are listed under town headings. The following trek and tour outfits are all based in Delhi (area code: 011):

Amber Tours Pty Ltd
   Flat 2, Dwarka Sadan, C-42 Connaught Place, New Delhi (☎ 331-2773; fax 331-2984). It offers yoga and mystic tours, river rafting, trekking, fishing for the mahseer, and private jet or helicopter flights over the Himalaya.
Himalayan River Runners
   188-A Jor Bagh, New Delhi (☎ 61-5736). It offers a range of rafting expeditions in the western Himalaya.
Mercury Himalayan Explorations
   Jeevan Tara Building, Parliament St, New Delhi (☎ 31-2008). Mercury specialises in organised treks in the western Himalaya.
Shikhar Travels, 209 Competent House, 14 Middle Circle, Connaught Circus, New Delhi (☎ 331-2444; fax 332-3660). Shikhar specialises in trekking and mountaineering tours and can also organise mountaineering expeditions for beginners.
World Expeditions
   Ground Floor, MG Bhawan-1, 7 Local Shopping Centre, Madangir, New Delhi (☎ 698-3358; fax 698-3357). It has operated world-class Himalayan tours and treks since 1975. It offers some excellent fully inclusive treks to both the more popular and less visited areas of the Indian Himalaya.

Equipment Hire

A number of government-operated trekking and mountaineering divisions, as well as private operators, can provide trekking gear on hire in popular trekking regions. In Delhi, contact the following (area code: 011):

Dimension Wilderness Equipment
   E578 Basement No 4, Greater Kailash, Part II, New Delhi (☎ 644-9433)
West Coast Equipment
   (☎ 63-5498)

COURSES

Language

The Landour Language School, near Mussoorie in Uttarakhand, offers three month beginners' courses in Hindi, as well as more advanced courses. At McLeod Ganj it's possible to learn Tibetan either at the Library of Tibetan Works & Archives or from private teachers. In Darjeeling, beginners' courses in Tibetan are available at the Manjushree Centre of Tibetan Culture. For all these courses, see the relevant chapters for details.

Buddhist Philosophy

Courses in aspects of Tibetan Buddhism and culture are offered in McLeod Ganj, Darjeeling, Choglamsar (near Leh) and Leh. Indian Hinayana Buddhism can also be studied in McLeod Ganj. See the relevant chapters for details of these courses.

Hindu Philosophy, Yoga & Meditation

Rishikesh is the place to head if you're interested in staying at an ashram and learning about aspects of Hindu philosophy, including yoga and meditation. See Meditation & Yoga Courses under Rishikesh in the Uttarakhand chapter.

The Ananda Puri Ashram at Gangotri is a beautiful, peaceful place, and westerners are welcome to stay here. See the Ranikhet section in the Uttarakhand chapter for details.

Devotees of Sri Sri 1008 Hairakhan Wale Baba, more commonly known as Babaji, attend retreats at his ashram at Chiliyanaula, near Ranikhet in Kumaon, and the Hairakhan Vishwa Madadham ashram, 27 km from Haldwani, near Surat. See the Kumaon section of the Uttarakhand chapter for details.

Traditional Dance

The Tibetan Institute of Performing Arts (TIPA) at McLeod Ganj offers private tuition from teachers in traditional Tibetan dance and drama. See the Himachal Pradesh chapter for details.

The Omkarananda Ashram (Durga Mandir) at Rishikesh offers instruction in various forms of Indian classical dance. See Meditation & Yoga Courses under Rishikesh in the Uttarakhand chapter for details.

Woodcarving

With advance notice it's possible to learn traditional Tibetan woodcarving at the Tibetan Refugee Self-Help Centre in Darjeeling. See the West Bengal Hills chapter for details.

VOLUNTARY WORK

Numerous charities and international aid agencies have branches in India and, although they're mostly staffed by locals, there are some opportunities for foreigners. Though it may be possible to find temporary volunteer work when you are in India, you'll probably be of more use to the charity concerned if you write in advance and, if they need you, stay for long enough to be of help. A week on a hospital ward may go a little way towards salving your own conscience, but you may actually do not much more than get in the way of the people who work there long-term.

For information on specific charities in the Indian Himalaya, contact the main branches in your own country.

The Mahabodhi International Meditation Centre (PO Box 22, Leh, Ladakh, 194101 Jammu & Kashmir), which operates a residential school for poor children, requires volunteers to assist with teaching and secretarial work. Contact the centre at the above address, or through their head office (☎ (0812) 26-0684; fax 26-0292) at 14 Kalidas Rd, Gandhinagar, Bangalore, 560 009.

Long-term visitors at McLeod Ganj are always welcome to teach English to newly arrived Tibetan refugees. Check at the Library of Tibetan Works & Archives in Gangchen Kyishong, near McLeod Ganj.

If you have a particular interest in Ladakh and have some educational or agricultural experience, there are two organisations in Leh which may be able to use your experience and enthusiasm: the Ladakh Ecological Development Group (LEDeG) (☎ 3746; fax 2484) Leh, Ladakh, 194101; and the Student's Educational & Cultural Movement of Ladakh (SECMOL) (☎ 3676) PO Box 4, Leh, Ladakh, 194101.

In Darjeeling, the Nepali Girls' Social Service Centre may be able to offer voluntary work on an informal basis to travellers interested in teaching English, art or musical instruments. Also in Darjeeling, people interested in teaching English to Tibetan refugees should contact the Tibetan Refugee Self-Help Centre. See under Voluntary Work in the Darjeeling section of the West Bengal Hills chapter.

Aid Organisations

For long-term work, the following organisations may be able to help or offer advice and further contacts:

Voluntary Service Overseas (VSO)
    317 Putney Bridge Rd, London SW15 2PN, UK (☎ (0181) 780-2266; fax 780-1326)
International Voluntary Service (IVS)
    St John's Church Centre, Edinburgh EH2 4BJ, UK (☎ (0131) 226-6722)
Co-Ordinating Committee for International Voluntary Service
    c/o UNESCO, 1 rue Miollis, F-75015 Paris, France (☎ (01) 45-68-27-31)
Peace Corps of the USA
    1990 K St NW, Washington DC 20526, USA (☎ (202) 606-3970; fax (202) 606-3110)
Council of International Programs (CIP)
    1101 Wilson Blvd Ste 1708, Arlington VA 22209, USA (☎ (703) 527-1160)
Australian Volunteers Abroad: Overseas Service Bureau Programme
    PO Box 350, Fitzroy Vic 3065, Australia (☎ (03) 9279-1788; fax (03) 9416-1619)

ACCOMMODATION

The Indian Himalaya has a very wide range of accommodation possibilities.

Youth Hostels

There are few youth hostels in the Himalayan region, and prices are comparable for both members and nonmembers. Some offer excellent value, and some are downright shabby and should be given a miss.

Government Accommodation

Back in the days of the British Raj, a whole string of government-run accommodation units were set up with names such as Rest Houses, Dak Bungalows, Circuit Houses, PWD (Public Works Department) Bungalows, Forest Rest Houses and so on. Today most of these are reserved for government officials, although in some places they may still be available for tourists, if there is room and you have booked in advance. In an approximate pecking order, the dak bungalows are the most basic; they often have no electricity and only essential equipment in out-of-the-way places. Rest houses are next up and at the top of the tree comes the circuit houses, which are strictly for travelling VIPs.

Tourist Bungalows

Usually run by the state government, tourist bungalows often serve as replacements for the older government-run accommodation units. Tourist bungalows are generally excellent value, although they vary enormously in facilities and level of service offered.

They often have dorm beds, as well as rooms; typical prices are around Rs 30 to Rs 40 for a dorm bed, and Rs 100 to Rs 250 for a double room. The rooms have a fan, two beds and bathroom; more expensive air-con rooms are often also available. Generally there's a restaurant or 'dining hall' and often a bar. In Uttarakhand, tourist bungalows are operated by the two hills divisions of UP Tourism: Garhwal Mandal Vikas Nigam (GMVN) and Kumaon Mandal Vikas Nigam (KMVN). Mid-season and off-season discounts are normally always available. The Himachal Pradesh Tourist Development Corporation (HPTDC) offers a wide selection of interesting accommodation including that in castles, log huts and tent sites. Refer to the Himachal Pradesh chapter for details.

Tourist bungalows are good value, and often the only places available, in more remote places like Kargil, the Zanskar Valley and Kinnaur.

Railway Retiring Rooms

These are just like regular hotels or dormitories except they are at the railway stations. To stay here you are generally supposed to have a railway ticket or Indrail Pass. The rooms are, of course, extremely convenient if you have an early train departure, although they can be noisy if it is a busy station. They are often very cheap and in some places they are also excellent value. It's possible to stay in the retiring rooms at one or two stations along the narrow-gauge line between Shimla and Kalka. See the Himachal Pradesh chapter for details.

Ashrams, Gompas & Gurudwaras

Ashrams should not be treated as guest-houses – while western visitors are welcome at many ashrams, particularly in Rishikesh, they are generally for those seriously interested in learning about Hindu philosophy, and have strict rules governing visitors' stays. See under Rishikesh in the Uttarakhand chapter for more details. Visitors are also welcome at several ashrams and *dharamsalas* (pilgrims' lodgings) at the Char Dham temples of Yamunotri, Gangotri, Kedarnath and Badrinath in Uttarakhand.

Serious students of Buddhist philosophy are welcome to stay long-term at some gompas. In Himachal Pradesh, several gompas provide guesthouse-style accommodation for visitors. While you don't have to be a Buddhist student to stay at these, it should be remembered that these are holy places, and appropriate respect and decorum should be observed. The Shanti Stupa in Leh in Ladakh also offers guesthouse accommodation. See the relevant chapters for details.

Free accommodation is available at some Sikh temples (*gurudwaras*) where there is a tradition of hospitality to visitors. It can be interesting to try one, but please don't abuse this hospitality and spoil it for other travellers.

Chai Stalls & Village Hospitality

In some little-visited centres or along trekking routes, there are no guesthouses as such, but visitors may be afforded accommodation in very rustic lodgings or chai stalls. To avoid embarrassment later, establish at the outset whether payment is solicited or expected. Where you are offered free hospitality, a small gift, while not solicited, is appropriate. In popular travellers' centres, such as the villages around McLeod Ganj, in Manikaran and Manali in Himachal Pradesh, and in the environs of Almora, in the Kumaon region of Uttarakhand, many long-term visitors rent rooms in village homes, or even rent entire houses. In some of these, the distinction between a village home and a guesthouse is becoming blurred, as villagers, keen to attract this lucrative form of income, provide services such as hot water in buckets or even common geysers (tanks providing hot water).

Visitors intent on self-catering will need some form of cooking device. Gas cylinders are rare commodities in Himachal Pradesh, with waiting lists extending sometimes up to a year. In the off season, you may be able to procure a gas cylinder from a cafe which is closing over the winter season. Otherwise, it is possible to purchase electric hot plates in larger bazaars, or kerosene burners for cooking.

Hotels

Due to the high concentration of important pilgrimage sites in the Indian Himalaya, the entire region was once served by little wooden pilgrims' lodgings called *chattis*, which could be found at intervals along all the major pilgrimage routes. However, chattis have now become a thing of the past, replaced by impersonal concrete lodgings and hotels providing accommodation for the more affluent pilgrim. There are cheap hotels all over the Indian Himalaya – in larger centres, you'll find them clustered around the bus station. They can range from filthy, uninhabitable dives (but with rock bottom prices) up to quite reasonable places in both standards and prices. Ceiling fans, private toilets and bathrooms are all possibilities, even in rooms which cost Rs 120 or less per night for a double.

Throughout India, hotels are defined as 'western' or 'Indian'. The differentiation is basically meaningless, although expensive hotels are always western, cheap ones Indian. 'Indian' hotels will be more simply and economically furnished but the acid test is the toilet. You can find modern, well equipped, clean places with Indian toilets, and dirty, dismal dumps with western toilets. Some places even have the weird hybrid toilet.

Although prices are generally quoted in this book for singles and doubles, most hotels will put an extra bed in a room to make a triple for about an extra 25%. A 'family room' at some places such as Manali and at ski resorts have three to five bedded rooms, which are good value per person. In some smaller hotels it's often possible to bargain a little. During the off season in the hill stations, it's always recommended to check for a discount – prices are sometimes reduced by up to two-thirds of the peak-season price.

Expensive Hotels

You won't find many five-star hotels in the Indian Himalaya, although in the larger hill stations, there is always a range of top-end hotels, generally with rates for double rooms ranging from Rs 1000 to Rs 3000. Quite frankly, your rupee doesn't go as far up in the hills as it does on the plains, and even some of the most expensive places can be quite shabby and showing signs of wear and tear. Always ask for a discount in the off season – prices can be reduced by up to 50% or more during the winter (but not over Christmas) or monsoon in the hill stations.

Something Special

It's worth spending at least one or two nights in some of the Indian Himalaya's famous (or infamous!) grand hotels, usually old Raj relics or former maharaja's palaces. The hill stations are riddled with these wonderful old places, and a stay here could be a highlight of your trip. A night in a Raj-era hotel needn't break your budget, and you might even get more than you bargained for with a glimpse of a ghostly apparition – some of these places are reputedly haunted! A brief list of some of these special places follows. For more details, see the relevant chapters.

Himachal Pradesh
  Woodville Palace Resort, Shimla; Palace Hotel, Chail; Castle Hotel, Naggar; Circuit Rest House, Kalpa, in Kinnaur; Taragarh Palace Hotel, Kangra Valley.
Uttarakhand
  Hakman's Grand Hotel, Mussoorie; Hotel Prince, Mussoorie; Hotel Padmini Niwas, Mussoorie; Savoy Hotel, Mussoorie; Belvedere Hotel, Nainital
West Bengal Hills
  Windamere Hotel, Darjeeling; The Himalayan Hotel, Kalimpong.

Taxes & Service Charges

Most state governments impose a variety of taxes on hotel accommodation (and restaurants). At most rock-bottom hotels you won't have to pay any taxes. Once you get into the top end of budget places, and certainly for mid-range accommodation, you will have to pay something. As a general rule, you can assume that room rates over about Rs 250 will attract a 10% (sometimes just 5%) tax. Most mid-range and all luxury hotels attract a 10% loading.

Another common tax, which is additional to the above, is a service charge, which is pegged at 10%. In some hotels, this is only levied on food, room service and use of telephones, not on the accommodation costs. At others, it's levied on the total bill. If you're trying to keep costs down, don't sign up meals or room service to your room bill and keep telephone use to a minimum if you know that the service charge is levied on the total bill.

Rates quoted in this book are the basic rate only, unless otherwise indicated. Taxes and service charges are extra.

FOOD

Despite the very fine meals that can be prepared in India, you'll often find food a great disappointment. In many smaller centres there is not a wide choice and you'll get bored with *chaval* (rice), *sabzi* (mushy vegetables) and *dhal* (curried lentil gravy), although these are staples in the Indian Himalaya. In fact, in some regions, rice is a luxury and is substituted with *janghora*, a type of millet.

Contrary to popular belief, not all Hindus are officially vegetarians. Strict vegetarianism is confined more to the south, which has not had the meat-eating influence of the Aryan and later Muslim invasions, and also to the Gujarati community. For those who do eat meat, it is not always a pleasure to do so in India – the quality tends to be low (most chickens give the impression that they died from starvation) and the hygiene is not all that it might be. Beef, from the holy cow, is strictly taboo of course – and leads to interesting Indian dishes like the mutton-burger. Where steak is available, it's usually buffalo and found only in Muslim restaurants. Pork is equally taboo to the Muslims and is generally only available in areas where there are significant Christian communities (such as Goa), or among the Tibetans in Himachal Pradesh and Sikkim. If you're a nonvegetarian you'll end up eating a lot more vegetarian food in India. In some of the Indian Himalaya's particularly holy places, such as Haridwar, on the northern Uttar Pradesh plains, consuming any form of meat is forbidden by law!

Although you could travel throughout the Indian Himalaya and not eat a single curry, Indian interpretations of western cuisine can be pretty horrific; in smaller places it's usually best to stick to Indian food.

If, after some time in India, you do find the food is getting you down physically or psychologically, there are a couple of escapes. It is very easy for budget travellers to lose weight in India and feel lethargic and drained of energy. The answer is to increase your protein intake – eat more eggs, which are readily available. It also helps to eat more fruit and nuts, so buy bananas, mandarin oranges or peanuts, all easily found at bus stations or in the markets. Many travellers carry multivitamins with them. Another answer, if you're travelling on a budget, is to occasionally splash out on a meal in a fancy hotel or restaurant; compared to what you have been paying it may seem amazingly expensive, but try translating the price into what it would cost at home. Some travellers can thrive on Indian food, but crave western breakfasts – it's hard to get excited about a plate of dhal and rice first thing in the morning. Many of the flashier hotels in the hill stations offer continental breakfast buffets – they're pricey, but if you're hanging out for muesli or croissants, a great indulgence. Other hangouts, like Manali, and the Kullu and Parbati valleys, have little cafes serving great omelettes, porridge and toast.

There are considerable regional variations from north to south, partly because of climatic conditions and partly because of historical influences. In the north, as already mentioned, much more meat is eaten and the cooking is often 'Mughal style' (often spelt 'Mughlai'), which bears a closer relationship to food of the Middle East and central Asia. The emphasis is more on spices and less on chilli. In the north, grains and breads are eaten far more than rice.

In the larger centres of the Indian Himalaya, some restaurants will offer South Indian cuisine. (In the south more rice is eaten, there is more vegetarian food, and the curries tend to be hotter – sometimes very hot.) Gujarati cuisine can be found in all of the popular hill stations.

In the most basic Indian restaurants and eating places, known as *dhabas*, the cooking is usually done right out the front so you can see exactly what is going on and how it is done. Vegetables will be on the simmer all day and tend to be overcooked and mushy to western tastes. In these basic places dhal is usually free but you pay for *rotis, chapattis, parathas, puris* or rice. Vegetable preparations, dhal and a few chapattis make a passable meal for around Rs 15. If you order half-plates of the various dishes brewing out the front you get half the quantity at half the price and get a little more variety. With chutneys and a small plate of onions, which come free, you can put together a reasonable vegetarian meal for Rs 30, or nonvegetarian for Rs 40.

At the other end of the price scale there are many restaurants in the Indian Himalaya's top-end hotels that border on the luxurious and by western standards are absurdly cheap. Paying US$10 to US$15 for a meal in India seems exorbitant after you've been there for a while, but check what a meal in your friendly local Hilton would cost you.

Finally, a couple of hints on how to cope with curry. After a while in India you'll get used to even the fiercest curries and will find western food surprisingly bland. If, however, you do find your mouth is on fire, don't reach for water; in emergencies, that hardly helps at all. *Dahin* (curd or yoghurt) or fruit does the job much more efficiently.

Curry & Spice

Believe it or not, there is no such thing as 'curry' in India. It's an English invention, an all-purpose term to cover the whole range of Indian food spicing. *Carhi*, incidentally, is a Gujarati dish, but never ask for it in Kumaon where it's a very rude word!

Although all Indian food is certainly not curry, this is the basis of Indian cuisine. Curry doesn't have to be hot enough to blow your head off, although it can if it's made that way. Curry most definitely is not something found in a packet of curry powder. Indian cooks have about 25 spices on their regular list and it is from these that they produce the curry flavour. Normally the spices are freshly ground in a mortar and pestle known as a *sil-vatta*. Spices are usually blended in certain combinations to produce *masalas* (mixes), eg *garam masala* ('hot mix') is a combination of cloves, cinnamon, cardamom, coriander, cumin and peppercorns.

Popular spices include saffron, an expensive flavouring produced from the stamens of certain crocus flowers. This is used to give rice that yellow colouring and delicate fragrance. (It's an excellent buy in India, where a one gram packet costs around Rs 35 – you'll pay about 10 times more at home.) Turmeric also has a colouring property, acts as a preservative and has a distinctive smell and taste. Chillies are ground, dried or added whole to supply the heat. They come in red and green varieties but the green ones are the hottest. Ginger is supposed to be good for the digestion, while many masalas contain coriander because it is said to cool the body. Strong and sweet cardamom are used in many desserts and in rich meat dishes. Other popular spices and flavourings include nutmeg, poppy seeds, caraway seeds, fenugreek, mace, garlic, cloves, bay leaves and curry leaves.

Breads & Grains

The best Indian rice (chaval), it is generally agreed, is found in the north where Basmati rice grows in the Dehra Dun Valley. It has long grains, is yellowish and has a slightly sweetish or 'bas' smell. In the north, rice is supplemented by a whole range of breads.

Indian breads are varied but always delicious. Simplest is the chapatti/roti, which is a mixture of flour and water cooked on a hotplate known as a tawa. Direct heat blows them up but how well that works depends on the gluten content of the wheat. In restaurants featuring Punjabi cuisine, a roti is called phulka/fulka. A paratha is also cooked on the hotplate but ghee is used and the bread is rolled in a different way. There are also parathas that have been stuffed with peas or potato. Deep-fried bread which puffs up is known as a puri in the north. Bake the bread in a clay (tandoori) oven and you have naan. However you make them, Indian breads taste great. Use your chapatti or paratha to mop or scoop up your curry. It's fascinating to watch the bakers in the dhabas and bakeries, especially early in the morning – the best time to buy your Indian bread. Western-style white sliced bread is widely available, and it's generally pretty good.

Found all over India, but originating from the south, are dosas, which you'll find in restaurants featuring Madrasi cuisine. These are basically paper-thin pancakes made from lentil and rice flour. Curried vegetables wrapped inside a dosa makes it a masala dosa – a terrific snack meal. An idli is a kind of south Indian rice dumpling, often served with a spicy curd sauce (dahin idli) or with spiced lentils and chutney. Papadams are crispy deep-fried lentil-flour wafers often served with thalis or other meals. An uttapam is like a dosa.

Basic Dishes

Curries can be vegetable, meat (usually chicken or lamb) or fish, but they are always fried in ghee (clarified butter) or vegetable oil. Whether you're in the north or south, they will be accompanied by rice, but in the north you can also choose from the range of breads.

There are a number of dishes which aren't really curries but are close enough to them for western tastes. Vindaloos have a vinegar marinade and tend to be hotter than most curries. Kormas, on the other hand, are rich, substantial dishes prepared by braising. There are both meat and vegetable kormas. Navratan korma is a very tasty dish using nuts and fruit, while a malai kofta is a rich, cream-based dish. Dopiaza literally means 'two onions' and is a type of korma which uses onions at two stages in its preparation.

Probably the most basic of Indian dishes is dhal. Dhal is almost always there, whether as an accompaniment to a curry or as a very basic meal in itself with chapattis or rice. In the very small rural towns dhal and rice is just about all there is on the menu. The common green lentils are called moong; rajmaa (kidney beans) is the Heinz 57 variety of dhal!

Other basic dishes include mattar panir (peas and cheese in gravy), saag gosht (spinach and meat), aalu dum (potato curry), palak panir (spinach and cheese), and aalu chhole (diced potatoes and spicy-sour chickpeas). Some other vegetables include paat gobi (cabbage), phuul gobi (cauliflower), baingan (eggplant or brinjal) and mattar (peas).

Tandoori & Biryani

Tandoori food is a northern speciality and refers to the clay oven in which the food is cooked after first being marinated in a complex mix of herbs and yoghurt. Tandoori chicken is a favourite. This food is not as hot as curry dishes and usually tastes terrific. The humble tandoori took on a more sinister light recently, when the chopped up remains of the wife of a prominent politician were found stuffed in one!

Biryani (again chicken is popular) is another northern Mughal dish. The meat is mixed with a deliciously flavoured, orange-coloured rice which is sometimes spiced with nuts or dried fruit. A Kashmiri biryani is basically fruit salad with rice.

A *pulao* is flavoured rice, often with pulses, with or without meat.

Side Dishes

Indian food generally has a number of side dishes to go with the main meal. Probably the most popular is *dahin* (curd or yoghurt). It has the useful ability of instantly cooling a fiery curry – either blend it into the curry or, if it's too late, you can eat it straight. Curd is often used in cooking or as a dessert, and is the basic ingredient of the popular drink *lassi*. *Raita* is another popular side dish consisting of curd mixed with cooked or raw vegetables, particularly cucumber (similar to Greek *tzatziki*) or tomato. It's a particular favourite in the Kumaon region of Uttarakhand, where you'll see great terracotta bowls of raita at truck and bus halts.

Sabzi is a curried vegetable dish, and *baingan bharta* is a puréed eggplant dish. *Mulligatawny* is a soup-like dish which is really just a milder, more liquid curry. It's a dish adopted into the English menu by the Raj. Chutney is pickled fruit or vegetables and is the standard relish for a curry.

Thalis

A *thali* is the all-purpose Indian dish. Although it is basically a product of south India, you will find restaurants serving thalis or 'plate meals' (veg or nonveg) all over India. Often the sign will simply announce

'Meals'. In addition, there are regional variations like the particularly sumptuous and sweet Gujarati thalis.

The name 'thali' is taken from the dish in which the meal is served. This consists of a metal plate with a number of small metal bowls known as *katoris* on it. Sometimes the small bowls will be replaced by simple indentations in the plate; in more basic places the 'plate' will be a big, fresh banana leaf. A thali consists of a variety of curry vegetable dishes, relishes, a couple of papadams, puris or chapattis and a mountain of rice. A fancy thali may have a *pataa*, a rolled leaf stuffed with fruit and nuts. There'll probably be a bowl of curd and possibly even a small dessert or *paan* (see below under Paan).

Thalis are consistently tasty and good food value, but they have two other unbeatable plus points for the budget traveller – they're cheap and they're usually 100% filling. Thalis can be as little as Rs 8 and will rarely cost more than Rs 30. Most are 100% filling because they're normally 'all you can eat'. When your plate starts to look empty the waiter comes round, adds another mountain of rice and refills the katoris. Thalis are eaten with fingers, although you may get a spoon for the curd or dhal. Always wash your hands before you eat one – a sink or other place to wash your hands is provided in a thali restaurant.

Snacks

Samosas are curried vegetables fried in a pastry triangle. They are very tasty and are found all over India. *Bhujias* or *pakhoras* are bite-size pieces of vegetable dipped in chick-pea flour batter and deep-fried. Along with samosas they're the most popular snack food in the country.

Bhelpuri is a popular Mumbai (Bombay) snack peddled across the city, and always found in holiday resort towns around the country. *Channa* is spiced chickpeas *(gram)* served with small puris. *Sambhar* is a soup-like lentil and vegetable dish with a sour tamarind flavour. *Chaat* is the general term for snacks, while *namkin* is the name for the various spiced nibbles that are sold prepackaged.

That peculiar Raj-era term for a midmorning snack still lives – *tiffin*. Today tiffin means any sort of light meal or snack. One western dish which Indians seem to have come 100% to terms with is chips (French fries) – sometimes curried, and delicious! Unfortunately, ordering chips is very much a hit and miss affair – sometimes they're excellent, and at other times truly dreadful. Some Indian cooks call potato chips 'Chinese potatoes', and 'finger chips' is also quite common.

Himalayan Specialities
Rogan josh is lamb curry, always popular in the north and in Kashmir where it originated. *Gushtaba*, pounded and spiced meatballs cooked in a yoghurt sauce, is another Kashmiri speciality. *Chicken makhanwala* is a rich dish cooked in a butter sauce.

An indication of the influence of central Asian cooking styles on north Indian food is the popularity of *kebabs*. You'll find them all across north India with a number of local variations and specialities. The two basic forms are *seekh* (skewered) or *shami* (wrapped).

There are some local specialities which you will only find in a particular region. The staple diet in Ladakh, Garhwal and Kumaon is *dhal bhat*, but other local dishes from the Kumaon region of Uttarakhand include *aalu ke gutke* (fried potato with masala), *badeel* (chickpea paste with masala, deep fried and served in wedges with chutney/relish), and *raita* (curd with cucumber). Sweet dishes from Kumaon include *sai*, a dish consisting of semolina, curd and sugar, cooked in oil then sprinkled with shredded coconut, raisins and cashew nuts. *Sooji ke pue* is semolina, curd and sugar, rolled into balls and deep fried. *Singal* is usually made for Diwali; it consists of the same base as sooji ke pue, but the contents are forced through a bag into swirl shapes and fried.

Other sweets include *bal mithai*, a form of brown *barfi* (milk-based sweet) rolled in tiny white sugar balls. It's found in the foothills of Kumaon, especially Almora, but also in other areas. Also famous is *singauri*. Found only in Kumaon district, especially Almora, this milk-based sweet comes in two forms, the soft off-white singauri, and the tastier brown singauri.

Tibetan Cuisine
With its high concentration of Tibetan refugees and proximity to Tibet, you'll find Tibetan cuisine on many menus in the Himalayan region. While Buddhists generally espouse the virtues of vegetarian cuisine, the arid Tibetan plateau is not conducive to the cultivation of many forms of vegetable, and the Tibetan diet is frequently supplemented with meat.

The staples and other dishes of Tibet, and nearby regions such as Lakakh, Lahaul & Spiti and Kinnaur, include:

baklep – Tibetan bread.
chura – yak cheese.
detuk – rice thukpa. It's good if you're suffering from diarrhoea.
momo – you'll find the ubiquitous momo wherever there is a sizeable Tibetan population, and in Ladakh and the remote eastern regions of Himachal Pradesh. It consists of small dough parcels containing meat or vegetables, which are fried or steamed.
sanghan baklep – large momos with the edges crimped and then deep fried.
sha – meat.
sha khampo – dried yak meat.
thukpa – Tibetan noodle soup with vegetables or meat. There are various types of noodles in thukpa: *ghaytuk* – long round noodles, *thantuk* – flat square noodles, and *chitse* – long flat noodles. ■

In the Chamba Valley of Himachal Pradesh are several local dishes. *Madhra* is kidney beans with curd and ghee. The curd is fried with the ghee until dark brown, then mixed with the kidney beans along with spices including cloves and cardamom.

Khamod is the nonvegetarian form of madhra. It consists of ground mutton, curd and ghee. Also in Chamba you'll find *chukh*, a chilli sauce of red and green peppers, lemon juice, mustard oil and salt. *Jarice* is a digestive aid comprising ground coconut, cardamom, aniseed and rock sugar.

Desserts & Sweets

Indians have quite a sweet tooth and an amazing selection of desserts and sweets to satisfy it. The desserts are usually rice-based or milk-based, and consist of various interesting things in sweet syrup or else sweet pastries. Most are horrendously sweet.

Kulfi is a delicious pistachio flavoured sweet similar to ice cream and is widely available. You can, of course, also get western style ice cream all over India. The major brands, such as Kwality and Havmor, are safe and very good. *Ras gullas* are another very popular Indian dessert; they're sweet little balls of cream cheese flavoured with rose water.

Gulaab jamuns are a typical example of the small 'things' in syrup – they're fried and made from thickened boiled-down milk (known as *khoya*) and flavoured with cardamom and rose water. *Jalebis*, the orange-coloured squiggles with syrup inside, are made of flour coloured/flavoured with saffron. *Ladu* are yellow coloured balls made from chickpea flour.

Barfi is also made from khoya and is available in flavours such as coconut, pistachio, chocolate or almond. *Gajar ka halwa* is a translucent, vividly coloured sweet made from carrot, sweet spices and milk.

Mitha chaval is a special sweet which is prepared on festive occasions. It contains rice, sugar, coconut, dried fruit and ghee.

Many of the Indian sweets are covered in a thin layer of silver, as are some of the desserts. It's just that, silver beaten paper-thin. Don't peel it off, it's quite edible. There are countless sweet shops with their goodies all lined up in glass showcases. Prices vary from Rs 40 to Rs 60 for a kg but you can order 50 or 100g at a time or simply ask for a couple of pieces. These shops often sell curd, as well as sweet curd which makes a very pleasant dessert.

There are plenty of tasty western style bakeries in Shimla, and you'll also find freshly baked western cakes and breads in McLeod Ganj and Darjeeling.

Fruit

If you don't have a sweet tooth, you'll be able to fall back on India's wide variety of fruit. Apricots and other temperate-region fruits can be found in the Himalayan region. Some local specialities include cherries and strawberries in Kashmir and apricots in Ladakh and Himachal Pradesh. Apples are found all over this north-western region but particularly in the Kullu Valley of Himachal Pradesh and the higher reaches of Garhwal in Uttarakhand.

Melons are widespread in India, particularly watermelons, which are a fine thirst quencher when you're unsure about the water and fed up with soft drinks. Try to get the first slice before the flies discover it.

Cooking Back Home

There are all sorts of books about Indian cooking should you want to pursue this after you leave India. *Indian Cookery* by Dharamjit Singh is a useful paperback introduction to the art. Premila Lal is one of the country's leading cookery writers, and her books are widely available. The problem is that ingredients are only given their local name, which makes many of the recipes impractical or impossible if you don't know exactly what is being called for. Charmaine Solomon's *Asian Cookbook* is an excellent source, and includes not only Indian but also other Asian cuisine.

Himalayan Recipes is a little booklet published by the Inner Wheel Club of Darjeeling (Rs 100). Proceeds of sales are directed towards the establishment of a rehabilitation centre for alcoholics and drug addicts of the

Making Momos

If you wonder how you'll ever cope when you get back home, denied traditional Tibetan momos, or stuffed dumplings, following is a recipe supplied by the chef at the Dreamland Restaurant in McLeod Ganj:

3 cups white flour
2 onions
4-5 cloves garlic
500 g minced steak (with fat)
2 tsp salt
2 tsp garam masala

Finely chop the meat, onion and garlic, and combine with the salt and masala. Mix the flour and water to a dough with a consistency which enables it to be kneaded. Roll it flat and cut into round shapes (thicker in the centre than around the edges). Place the mixed ingredients in the centre and fold, then trim sides.

Bring the water in the *mok-tsang* (steamer) base to the boil, adding a little oil. Place momos one by one into the top section of the steamer, leaving a two cm gap between each one and steam for 15 to 20 minutes. This recipe serves four people. ∎

Darjeeling district. Recipes include both Tibetan and Nepali dishes such as momos, thukpa and *quasi* (Tibetan cookies).

Paan

An Indian meal should properly be finished with *paan* – the name given to the collection of spices and condiments chewed with betel nut. Found throughout eastern Asia, betel is a mildly intoxicating and addictive nut, but by itself it is quite inedible. After a meal paan is chewed as a mild digestive.

Paan sellers have a whole collection of little trays, boxes and containers in which they mix either *saadha* (plain) or *mitha* (sweet) paans. The ingredients may include, apart from the betel nut itself, lime paste (the ash not the fruit), the powder known as *catachu*, various spices and even a dash of opium in a pricey paan. The whole concoc-

tion is folded up in a piece of edible leaf which you pop in your mouth and chew. When finished you spit the leftovers out and add another red blotch to the pavement. Over a long period of time, indulgence in paan will turn your teeth red-black and even addict you to the betel nut. Trying one probably won't do you any harm.

Every paan seller has his or her own secret paan recipe.

DRINKS

Nonalcoholic Drinks

Tea & Coffee The Indians, for all the tea they grow, make some of the most hideously over-sweetened, murkily-milky excuses for that fine beverage that you'll ever see. Nevertheless, it's cheap, at Rs 1 or Rs 2 for a cup of *chai*, and filling. It's drunk in vast quantities in poorer regions where it serves to take away the pangs of hunger.

Better tea can be obtained if you ask for 'tray tea', which gives you the tea, the milk and the sugar separately and allows you to combine them as you see fit. Unless you specify otherwise, tea is 'mixed tea' or 'milk tea', which means it has been made by putting cold water, milk, sugar and tea into one pot and bringing the whole concoction to the boil, then letting it stew for a long time. The result can be imagined.

In Tibetan and Tibetan-influenced areas such as Ladakh, the truly intrepid and gastronomically adventurous can try *gur-gur*, or butter tea. It's traditionally made with rancid yak butter mixed with salt, milk, green leaf tea and hot water. Drink it at your peril! Kashmiri tea is fragrant and delicious.

Coffee is not as popular in the Himalayan region as in the south of the country, and it's difficult to get a decent cuppa anywhere in the hills. The branches of the Indian Coffee House are some of the few places with decent coffee.

Water In the big cities, the water is chlorinated and safe to drink, although if you've just arrived in India, the change from what you are used to drinking is in itself enough to bring on a mild dose of diarrhoea.

Outside the cities you're on your own. Some travellers drink the water everywhere and never get sick, others are more careful and still get hit with a bug. Basically, you should not drink the water in small towns unless you know it has been boiled, and definitely avoid the street vendors' carts everywhere. Even in the better class of hotel and restaurant, the water is usually only filtered and not boiled. The local water filters remove solids and do nothing towards removing any bacteria. Water is generally safer in the dry season than in the monsoon when it really can be dangerous. See the Health section for further information.

Mineral Water Most travellers to India these days avoid tap water altogether and stick to mineral water. It is available virtually everywhere along the hill station belt, although more difficult to find further north, and impossible to procure in Ladakh outside Leh, and in the remote regions of eastern Himachal Pradesh. The price ranges from Rs 12 to Rs 30, with Rs 18 being about the average. Brand names include Bisleri, India King, Officer's Choice, Honeydew and Aqua Safe. In McLeod Ganj the Welfare Department has introduced an innovative programme whereby travellers bring their plastic mineral water bottles into the Green Shop to be refilled with filtered water. It's much cheaper than buying a fresh bottle, and also serves to cut down waste.

Virtually all the so-called mineral water available is actually treated tap water. A recent reliable survey found that 65% of the available mineral waters were less than totally pure, and in some cases were worse than what comes out of the tap! Generally, though, if you stick to bottled water, any gut problems you might have will be from other sources – food, dirty utensils, dirty hands, etc.

Soft Drinks Soft drinks are a safe substitute for water although they tend to have a high sugar content. Coca-Cola got the boot from India a number of years back for not cooperating with the government, but both they and Pepsi Cola are back with a vengeance. There are many similar indigenous brands with names like Campa Cola, Thums Up, Limca, Gold Spot or Double Seven. They are reasonably priced at around Rs 7 for a 250 ml bottle (more in restaurants).

Juices & Other Drinks One very pleasant escape from soft drinks is apple juice, sold for Rs 4 per glass from the Himachal fruit stands found at many railway stations. Also good are the small cardboard boxes of various fruit juices. For Rs 6 these are excellent, if a little sweet.

Coconut milk, straight from the young green coconut, is a popular drink. Soda water – Bisleri, Spencer's and other brands are widely available. Soda water comes in larger bottles than soft drinks and is also cheaper – generally around Rs 3.50. With soda water you can get excellent, and safe, lemon squash sodas.

Falooda is a popular drink made with milk, nuts, cream and vermicelli strands. Finally there's *lassi*, that oh-so-cool, refreshing and delicious (dahin/curd/yoghurt) drink. As water is usually added to lassis, ask for a lassi without water.

Alcoholic Drinks

Alcohol is relatively expensive – a bottle of Indian beer can cost anything from Rs 23 up to Rs 160 in a flash hotel; Rs 40 to Rs 60 is the usual price range. In Sikkim it is quite cheap, but in other Himalayan regions it can be hellishly expensive. Avoid over-indulgence or you'll wake up late in the morning feeling thoroughly disoriented with a thumping headache to boot (perhaps that's where the name of the popular Thunderbolt and Turbo brands were derived!). Preservatives (sulphur dioxide in the main) are lavishly used to combat the effects of climate on 'quality'.

Beer and other Indian interpretations of western alcoholic drinks are known as IMFL – Indian Made Foreign Liquor. They include imitations of Scotch and brandy under a plethora of different brand names. The taste varies from hospital disinfectant to passable imitation Scotch. Always buy the best brand. In Himachal Pradesh, an 'English Wine Shop' is often found in each village. They are not remotely 'English', and rarely sell wine, but you can obtain cheap IMFL and beer at these places.

With the continuing freeing up of the economy, it is likely that in the near future well known foreign brands of beer and spirits will be available.

Local drinks are known as Country Liquor and include *toddy*, a mildly alcoholic extract from the coconut palm flower, and *feni*, a distilled liquor produced from fermented cashew nuts or from coconuts. The two varieties taste quite different.

Arak is what the peasants (and bus drivers' best boys) drink to get blotto. It's a clear, distilled rice or barley liquor and it creeps up on you without warning. Treat with caution and only ever drink it from a bottle produced in a government-controlled distillery. *Never, ever* drink it otherwise – hundreds of people die or are blinded every year in India as a result of drinking arak produced in illicit stills. You can assume it contains methyl alcohol (wood alcohol). In remote regions of Himachal Pradesh, *angoori* (grape) wine is traditionally drunk, especially during the long, cold winters.

Chang is Tibetan barley beer; the barley is boiled until a little soft, then placed outside until lukewarm. Yeast is added, then it is covered and left to ferment for a couple of months.

THINGS TO BUY

The Indian Himalaya is packed with beautiful things to buy. The cardinal rule when purchasing handicrafts is to bargain and bargain hard. You can get a good idea of what is reasonable in quality and price by visiting the various state emporiums, particularly in Delhi, and the Central Cottage Industries Emporiums which can be found in Delhi, Calcutta and other gateway cities. You can inspect items at these places from all over the country. Because prices are fixed, you will get an idea of how hard to bargain when you purchase similar items from regular dealers.

As with handicrafts in any country, don't buy until you have developed a little understanding and appreciation. Rushing in and buying the first thing you see will inevitably lead to later disappointment and a considerably reduced stash of travellers' cheques.

Be careful when buying items which include delivery to your home country. You may well be given assurances that the price includes home delivery and all customs and handling charges. Inevitably this is not the case, and you may find yourself having to collect the item yourself from your country's main port or airport, pay customs charges (which could be as much as 20% of the item's value) and handling charges levied by the airline or shipping company (up to 10% of the value). If you can't collect the item promptly, or get someone to do it on your behalf, exorbitant storage charges may also be charged.

Carpets

India produces and exports more handcrafted carpets than Iran, and some of them are of virtually equal quality. In Kashmir, where India's best carpets are produced, the carpet-making techniques and styles were brought from Persia even before the Mughal era. The art flourished under the Mughals and today Kashmir is packed with small carpet producers. Persian motifs have been much embellished on Kashmiri carpets, which come in a variety of sizes. They are either made of pure wool, wool with a small percentage of silk to give a sheen (known as silk touch) or pure silk. The latter are more for decoration than hard wear. Expect to pay from Rs 5000 for a good quality 120 x 180 cm carpet and don't be surprised if the vendor's initial price is more than twice as high.

Also made in Kashmir, coarsely woven woollen *numdas* and *gabbas* are appliqué-like rugs. These are more primitive and folksy than the fine carpets. *Dhurries*, flat-weave cotton warp-and-weft rugs are also found in the Himalayan regions. The many Tibetan refugees in India have brought their craft of making superbly colourful Tibetan rugs with them. A 90 x 150 cm Tibetan rug will be less than Rs 1000. Two of the best places to buy them are Darjeeling and Gangtok. Check whether the carpet is pure wool or a woollen blend. Fine New Zealand wool carpets are more expensive than those which use Indian wool. Leh has a good selection of Tibetan and Kashmiri carpets.

Unless you're an expert it is best to have expert advice or buy from a reputable dealer if you're spending large amounts of money on carpets. Check prices back home, too; many western carpet dealers sell at prices you would have difficulty matching even at the source.

Papier Mâché

Papier mâché is probably the most characteristic Kashmiri craft. The basic papier-mâché article is made in a mould, then painted and polished in successive layers until the final intricate design is produced. Prices depend upon the complexity and quality of the painted design and the amount of gold leaf used. Items include bowls, cups, containers, jewel boxes, letter holders, tables, lamps, coasters, trays and so on. A cheap bowl might cost only Rs 25, a large, well made item might approach Rs 1000.

Jewellery

Many Indian women put most of their wealth into jewellery, so it is no wonder that so much of it is available. In the Himalayan regions you'll find chunky Tibetan jewellery, which

often incorporates coral, turquoise and seed pearls. In the Muslim dominated areas of Jammu & Kashmir, silversmiths produce plain silver jewellery drawing their inspiration from Baltistan.

Leatherwork

Of course Indian leatherwork is not made from cow-hide but from buffalo-hide, camel, goat or some other substitute. *Chappals*, those basic sandals found all over India, are the most popular purchase. Chamba, in Himachal Pradesh, is renowned as *the* chappal producing region of the Indian Himalaya. In Dharamsala, men can have a pair of leather shoes made to order cheaply and efficiently. Kashmiri leather shoes and boots, often of quite good quality, are widely found, along with coats and jackets of often abysmally low quality.

Thangkas

A thangka is Tibetan religious art produced on cloth with vegetable dyes, and some thangkas are embroidered in silk. Often Tibetan Buddhist deities or compositions which are used as meditation aids are represented. Unfortunately, the quality of thangkas is nowhere near what it was 10 years ago.

Textiles

The textiles industry is still India's major industry and 40% of the total production is at the village level where it is known as *khadi*. There are government khadi emporiums (known as Khadi Gramodyog) around the country, and these are good places to buy handmade items of homespun cloth, such as the popular 'Nehru jackets' and the *kurta pajama*, bedspreads, tablecloths, cushion covers or material for clothes. Almora, in the Kumaon region of Uttarakhand, is renowned for its khadi products, and you can also purchase woollen items here.

In Kashmir, embroidered materials are made into shirts and dresses. Fine shawls and scarves of pashmina goats' wool are popular purchases in the Kullu Valley. Kullu shawls are known as *pattoos*, and are fastened with a *gachi*. Shawls from Kinnaur feature borders of bold designs which are more colourful than the muted hues prominent in Kullu shawls.

Ranikhet in Kumaon is known for its tweed. You can purchase lengths of fine tweed here, or plain gents' shawls known as *pankhis*. In Leh, traditional Ladakhi clothes, hats and shoes are available, if not a little impracticable when you get back home!

In Tibetan centres such as McLeod Ganj, Darjeeling and Gangtok, women can have the traditional Tibetan dress, or *chuba* (known in Sikkim as the *bakhu*), made to order.

The Kullu Valley is the place to find traditional Kullu jackets, shawls and *topis*, or

caps. Chamba is reputed for its finely embroidered *rumals* – small muslin cloths featuring depictions of local people or religious themes which are embroidered in satin stitch by the women of Chamba, according to a tradition which dates back over 1000 years. Rumals were traditionally used for covering religious texts, but today the craft is being revived to cater for the tourist market.

Bronze Figures

Bronze figures of the pantheon of Hindu (and Buddhist) deities can be found in all the major tourist centres of the Indian Himalaya. Figures of Shiva as dancing Nataraj are

---

The Five Mudras

Amitabha The Impartial (Sanskrit: Samahitan); the so-called 'meditative posture'. One hand is resting over the other in the lap with the palms upwards.

Ratnasambhava The Best Bestowing (Sanskrit: Varada); this posture represents charity. The right arm is fully extended, with the hand stretched downwards and the palm facing away from the body.

Akshobhya Earth-Touching (Sanskrit: Bhusparsa); this is the so-called 'witness' attitude with reference to the episode under the Tree of Wisdom, when Shakyamuni called the Earth to witness his temptations by Mara. This is the most common mudra of the seated Buddha; the right hand is directed downwards with the knuckles facing away from the body.

Vairocana The Best-Perfection (Sanskrit: Uttarabodhi); the index finger and thumb of each hand are linked and are held before the heart.

Amogha Siddhi The Blessing of Fearlessness (Sanskrit: Abhaya); the arm is raised and slightly bent, with the hand elevated and the palm facing away from the body. The fingers are directed upwards. This pose depicts the subduing of the wild elephant, which was sent out by the Buddha's brother when he returned home, fearing that he had come to claim the throne. ■

Vairocana

among the most popular, as are those of the Buddha adopting various *mudras* (postures). There are five main mudras.

Woodcarving

In Kashmir, intricately carved wooden screens, tables, jewellery boxes, trays and the like are carved from Indian walnut. They follow a similar pattern to that seen on the decorative trim of houseboats. Old temple carvings can be delightful. Traditional Tibetan woodcarvings can be purchased in McLeod Ganj and Darjeeling. Woodcarving has traditionally been employed as ornamentation on homes in Himachal Pradesh, with artisans achieving high levels of artisanship in the carving of walnut, deodar and shisham into floral and animal motifs, representations of the deities and domestic scenes. Hand-carved wooden masks used in religious rituals are also found in the lower hills region of Himachal Pradesh. In Mussoorie you can pick up finely carved wooden walking sticks.

Pottery

Red and black pottery can be found in the Kangra Valley of Himachal Pradesh, produced by local *kumbhars*, or village potters. It is decorated with motifs in black and brown, and then fired. Most regions of the Himalaya produce their own domestic utensils such as pots, pans and water pitchers which are readily available in bazaars.

Other Himalayan Buys

In curio shops in the hill stations you might be able to pick up a *khukuri* – the traditional Gurkha knife. They come in ornamented tourist models, or the more sinister-looking, and more authentic, plain model.

Darjeeling is the place to buy high quality tea. It can range in price from Rs 150 to Rs 3000 per kg! Worth trying is the unique honey available in and around Shimla. The Kangra Valley is also famous for its tea. Traditional ayurvedic medicines are a good buy in Rishikesh, as are *rudraksh melas*, puja beads made from the nuts of the rudraksh tree.

In all Tibetan centres, you can pick up a set of colourful Tibetan prayer flags for about Rs 20. Hand held Tibetan prayer wheels can be found in hill stations where there are Tibetans, such as McLeod Ganj and other regions of Himachal Pradesh, as well as Darjeeling and Sikkim. The prayer wheels consist of a small drum containing the sacred mantra *'Om Mani Padme Hum'* ('Hail to the Jewel in the Lotus') written thousands of times. The drum is rotated by means of a small chain with a weight at the end, and each rotation is equivalent to the recital of thousands of prayers!

From the abundance of apple, apricot and almond trees, especially around the Kullu Valley and Manali, there is a burgeoning local industry making delicious jams and pickles, as well as oils and shampoos made from other local fruits and nuts.

If you're keen to whip up a cuppa of yak butter tea when you get home, pick up a copper kettle and wooden tea churner, available in all Tibetan centres. (You might have trouble getting the yak through customs, though!)

Antiques

Articles over 100 years old are not allowed to be bought, sold, or exported from India without an export clearance certificate. If you have doubts about any item and think it could be defined as an antique, you can check with:

Calcutta
    Superintending Archaeologist, Eastern Circle, Archaeological Survey of India, Narayani Bldg, Brabourne Rd
Delhi
    Director, Antiquities, Archaeological Survey of India, Janpath
Madras
    Superintending Archaeologist, Southern Circle, Archaeological Survey of India, Fort St George
Mumbai (Bombay)
    Superintending Archaeologist, Antiquities, Archaeological Survey of India, Sion Fort
Srinagar
    Superintending Archaeologist, Frontier Circle, Archaeological Survey of India, Minto Bridge

Getting There & Away

No international airlines fly directly to the Indian Himalaya, so getting there is a two part journey. Therefore, the first part of this chapter deals with travel from international destinations to India. The second section concentrates on travel from Delhi and Calcutta to the Himalayan regions.

India

AIR

Your plane ticket will probably be the single most expensive item in your budget, and buying it can be an intimidating business. There is likely to be a multitude of airlines and travel agents hoping to separate you from your money, and it is always worth putting aside a few hours to research the current state of the market. Start early: some of the cheapest tickets have to be bought months in advance, and some popular flights sell out early. Talk to other recent travellers. Look at the ads in newspapers and magazines, consult reference books and watch for special offers. Then phone around travel agents for bargains. (Airlines can supply information on routes and timetables; however, except at times of inter-airline war, they do not supply the cheapest tickets.) Find out the fare, the route, the duration of the journey and any restrictions on the ticket. (See Restrictions in the Air Travel Glossary in this chapter.) Then sit back and decide which is best for you.

You may discover that those impossibly cheap flights are 'fully booked, but we have another one that costs a bit more...' Or the flight is on an airline notorious for its poor safety standards and leaves you in the world's least favourite airport in mid-journey for 14 hours. Or they claim only to have the last two seats available for India for the whole of July, which they will hold for

𝍖𝍖𝍖𝍖𝍖𝍖𝍖𝍖𝍖𝍖𝍖𝍖𝍖𝍖𝍖𝍖𝍖𝍖𝍖𝍖𝍖𝍖𝍖𝍖𝍖

Warning
The information in this chapter is particularly vulnerable to change: prices for international travel are volatile, routes are introduced and cancelled, schedules change, special deals come and go, and rules and visa requirements are amended. Air fares quoted here do not necessarily constitute a recommendation for the carrier. Airlines and governments seem to take a perverse pleasure in making price structures and regulations as complicated as possible. You should check directly with the airline or a travel agent to make sure you understand how a fare (and ticket you may buy) works. In addition, the travel industry is highly competitive and there are many lurks and perks.

The upshot of this is that you should get opinions, quotes and advice from as many airlines and travel agents as possible before you part with your hard-earned cash. The details given in this chapter should be regarded as pointers and are not a substitute for your own careful, up-to-date research. ■

𝍖𝍖𝍖𝍖𝍖𝍖𝍖𝍖𝍖𝍖𝍖𝍖𝍖𝍖𝍖𝍖𝍖𝍖𝍖𝍖𝍖𝍖𝍖𝍖𝍖

you for a maximum of two hours. Don't panic – keep ringing around.

If you are travelling from the UK or the USA, you will probably find that the cheapest flights are being advertised by obscure bucket shops whose names haven't yet reached the telephone directory. Many such firms are honest and solvent, but there are a few rogues who will take your money and disappear, to reopen elsewhere a month or two later under a new name. If you feel suspicious about a firm, don't give them full payment at once – leave a deposit of 20% or so and pay the balance when you get the ticket. If they insist on a full cash payment in advance, go somewhere else. And once you have the ticket, ring the airline to confirm that you are actually booked on the flight you paid for.

You may decide to pay more than the rock-bottom fare by opting for the safety of a better-known travel agent. Firms such as STA, who have offices worldwide, Council Travel in the USA or Travel CUTS in Canada are not going to disappear overnight, leaving you clutching a receipt for a nonexistent ticket, but they do offer good prices to most destinations.

Once you have your ticket, write its number down, together with the flight number and other details, and keep the information somewhere separate. If the ticket is lost or stolen, this will help you get a replacement.

It's sensible to buy travel insurance as early as possible. If you buy it the week before you fly, you may find, for example, that you're not covered for delays to your flight caused by industrial action.

International Airports

Delhi Delhi's somewhat chaotic, confusing and tatty Palam Airport is now officially the Indira Gandhi International Airport. The domestic terminal (Terminal I) is seven km from the centre, and the new international terminal (Terminal II) is a further nine km.

If you're arriving at Delhi airport from overseas, there's a 24 hour State Bank of India foreign exchange counter in the arrivals hall, before you go through customs and immigration. Once you've left the arrivals hall you won't be allowed back in. The service is fast and efficient.

Many international flights to Delhi arrive and depart in the small hours of the early morning. Take special care if this is your first foray into India and you arrive exhausted and jet-lagged. If you're leaving Delhi in the early hours of the morning, book a taxi the afternoon before. They'll be hard to find in the night.

When leaving Delhi with Air India (domestic or international flights) all baggage must be X-rayed and sealed, so do this at the machine just inside the departure hall before you queue to check in. For international flights the departure tax (Rs 300) must be paid at the State Bank of India counter in the departures hall, also before check-in.

Delhi Transport Corporation buses connect the international and domestic terminals for Rs 10. There is also the free IA/AI bus between the two terminals, although no one seems willing to admit such a service exists. The bus stop is just outside the domestic terminal. It only leaves every hour. EATS (see below) will also take you between terminals on their roundabout route.

There are retiring rooms at both the domestic (Terminal I: ☎ 329-5126) and international (Terminal II: ☎ 545-2011) sections of the airport. You can use them if you have a confirmed departure within 24 hours, but you'll need to ring in advance, as demand far outstrips supply. At Terminal II, they cost Rs 175 for an air-con double and Rs 40 for a dorm bed. At Terminal 1, the cost is Rs 175 for an ordinary double and Rs 250 for an air-con double. The tourist information officer at the desk at the airport may insist that the retiring rooms are 'full' and try to direct you to a hotel where the officer gets the commission.

Calcutta Calcutta's Dum Dum international airport is 20 km north of the city centre. It's possible to exchange travellers' cheques at the international terminal. In the adjacent domestic terminal, there's an accommodation booking service. There is also a railway reservation desk at the terminal. Calcutta airport has rest rooms, if you're in transit, with dorm beds for Rs 40 and singles/doubles for Rs 125/190 or Rs 175/250 with air-con. Check at the reservations desk in the terminal.

To/From the Airports

Delhi The EATS (Ex-Servicemen's Air Link Transport Service: ☎ 331-6530) has a regular bus service between both the international and domestic terminals and Connaught Place. When leaving the international terminal, the counter for the EATS bus is just to the right before you exit the building. The fare is Rs 17 and they will drop you off or pick you up at most of the major hotels en route if you ask. There is also an EATS city-to-airport service which departs regularly from opposite Palika Bazaar on Radial Rd 8 (Janpath) between 4 am and 11.30 pm.

Air Travel Glossary

Apex Tickets Apex stands for Advance Purchase Excursion fare. These tickets are usually between 30% and 40% cheaper than the full economy fare, but there are restrictions. You must purchase the ticket at least 21 days in advance (sometimes more) and must be away for a minimum period (normally 14 days) and return within a maximum period (90 or 180 days). Stopovers are not allowed, and if you have to change your dates of travel or destination, there will be extra charges to pay. These tickets are not fully refundable – if you have to cancel your trip, the refund is often considerably less than what you paid for the ticket. Take out travel insurance to cover yourself in case you have to cancel your trip unexpectedly – for example, due to illness.

Baggage Allowance This will be written on your ticket; you are usually allowed one 20 kg item to go in the hold, plus one item of hand luggage. Some airlines which fly transpacific and transatlantic routes allow for two pieces of luggage (there are limits on their dimensions and weight).

Bucket Shops At certain times of the year and/or on certain routes, many airlines fly with empty seats. This isn't profitable and it's more cost-effective for them to fly full, even if that means having to sell a certain number of drastically discounted tickets. They do this by off-loading them onto bucket shops (UK) or consolidators (USA), travel agents who specialise in discounted fares. The agents, in turn, sell them to the public at reduced prices. These tickets are often the cheapest you'll find, but you can't purchase them directly from the airlines. Availability varies widely, so you'll not only have to be flexible in your travel plans, you'll also have to be quick off the mark as soon as an advertisement appears in the press.

Bucket-shop agents advertise in newspapers and magazines and there's a lot of competition – especially in places like Amsterdam and London which are crawling with them – so it's a good idea to telephone first to ascertain availability before rushing from shop to shop. Naturally, they'll advertise the cheapest available tickets, but by the time you get there, these may be sold out and you may be looking at something slightly more expensive.

Bumped Just because you have a confirmed seat doesn't mean you're going to get on the plane – see Overbooking.

Cancellation Penalties If you have to cancel or change an Apex or other discount ticket, there may be heavy penalties involved; insurance can sometimes be taken out against these penalties. Some airlines impose penalties on regular tickets as well, particularly against 'no show' passengers.

Check In Airlines ask you to check in a certain time ahead of the flight departure (usually two hours on international flights). If you fail to check in on time and the flight is overbooked, the airline can cancel your booking and give your seat to somebody else.

Confirmation Having a ticket written out with the flight and date on it doesn't mean you have a seat until the agent has confirmed with the airline that your status is 'OK'. Prior to this confirmation, your status is 'on request'.

Courier Fares Businesses often need to send their urgent documents or freight securely and quickly. They do it through courier companies. These companies hire people to accompany the package through customs and, in return, offer a discount ticket which is sometimes a phenomenal bargain. In effect, what the courier companies do is ship their freight as your luggage on the regular commercial flights. This is a legitimate operation – all freight is completely legal. There are two shortcomings, however: the short turnaround time of the ticket, usually not longer than a month; and the limitation on your luggage allowance. You may be required to surrender all your baggage allowance for the use of the courier company, and be only allowed to take carry-on luggage.

Discounted Tickets There are two types of discounted fares – officially discounted (such as Apex – see Promotional Fares) and unofficially discounted (see Bucket Shops). The latter can save you more than money – you may be able to pay Apex prices without the associated Apex advance booking and other requirements. The lowest prices often impose drawbacks, such as flying with unpopular airlines, inconvenient schedules, or unpleasant routes and connections.

Economy Class Tickets Economy-class tickets are usually not the cheapest way to go, though they do give you maximum flexibility and they are valid for 12 months. If you don't use them, most are fully refundable, as are unused sectors of a multiple ticket.

Full Fares Airlines traditionally offer first class (coded F), business class (coded J) and economy class (coded Y) tickets. These days there are so many promotional and discounted fares available that few passengers pay full fare.

Lost Tickets If you lose your airline ticket, an airline will usually treat it like a travellers' cheque and, after inquiries, issue you with a replacement. Legally, however, an airline is entitled to treat it like cash, so if you lose a ticket, it could be forever. Take good care of your tickets.

MCO An MCO (Miscellaneous Charges Order) is a voucher for a value of a given amount, which resembles an airline ticket and can be used to pay for a specific flight with any IATA (International Air Transport Association) airline. MCOs, which are more flexible than a regular ticket, may satisfy the irritating onward ticket requirement, but some countries are now reluctant to accept them. MCOs are fully refundable if unused.

No Shows No shows are passengers who fail to show up for their flight for whatever reason. Full-fare no shows are sometimes entitled to travel on a later flight. The rest of us are penalised (see Cancellation Penalties).

Open Jaw Tickets These are return tickets which allow you to fly to one place but return from another, and travel between the two 'jaws' by any means of transport at your own expense. If available, this can save you backtracking to your arrival point.

Overbooking Airlines hate to fly with empty seats, and since every flight has some passengers who fail to show up (see No Shows), they often book more passengers than they have seats available. Usually the excess passengers balance those who fail to show up, but occasionally somebody gets bumped. If this happens, guess who it is most likely to be? The passengers who check in late.

Promotional Fares These are officially discounted fares, such as Apex fares, which are available from travel agents or direct from the airline.

Reconfirmation You must contact the airline at least 72 hours prior to departure to 'reconfirm' that you intend to be on the flight. If you don't do this, the airline can delete your name from the passenger list and you could lose your seat.

Restrictions Discounted tickets often have various restrictions on them, such as necessity of advance purchase, limitations on the minimum and maximum period you must be away, restrictions on breaking the journey or changing the booking or route etc.

Round-the-World Tickets These tickets have become very popular in the last few years; basically, there are two types – airline tickets and agent tickets. An airline RTW ticket is issued by two or more airlines that have joined together to market a ticket which takes you around the world on their combined routes. It permits you to fly pretty well anywhere you choose using their combined routes as long as you don't backtrack, ie keep moving in approximately the same direction east or west. Other restrictions are that you (usually) must book the first sector in advance and cancellation penalties then apply. There may be restrictions on how many stopovers you are permitted. The RTW tickets are usually valid for from 90 days up to a year.

Quite a few of these combined-airline RTW tickets go through India, including ones in combination with Air India which will allow you to make several stopovers within India. RTW tickets typically cost around A$1950 to A$2400, UK£560 to UK£940 and US$1250 to US$2500.

The other type of RTW ticket, the agent ticket, is a combination of cheap fares strung together by an enterprising travel agent. These may be cheaper than airline RTW tickets, but the choice of routes will be limited.

Standby This is a discounted ticket where you only fly if there is a seat free at the last moment. Standby fares are usually only available directly at the airport, but sometimes may also be handled by an airline's city office. To give yourself the best possible chance of getting on the flight you want, get there early and have your name placed on the waiting list. It's first come, first served.
Student Discounts Some airlines offer student-card holders 15% to 25% discounts on their tickets. The same often applies to anyone under the age of 26. These discounts are generally only available on ordinary economy-class fares. You wouldn't get one, for instance, on an Apex or an RTW ticket, since these are already discounted.

Tickets Out An entry requirement for many countries is that you have an onward or return ticket, in other words, a ticket out of the country. If you're not sure what you intend to do next, the easiest solution is to buy the cheapest onward ticket to a neighbouring country or a ticket from a reliable airline which can later be refunded if you do not use it.
Transferred Tickets Airline tickets cannot be transferred from one person to another. Travellers sometimes try to sell the return half of their ticket, but officials can ask you to prove that you are the person named on the ticket. This may not be checked on domestic flights, but on international flights, tickets are usually compared with passports.
Travel Periods Some officially discounted fares, Apex fares in particular, vary with the time of year. There is often a low (off-peak) season and a high (peak) season. Sometimes there's an intermediate or shoulder season as well. At peak times, when everyone wants to fly, both officially and unofficially discounted fares will be higher, or there may simply be no discounted tickets available. Usually the fare depends on your outward flight – if you depart in the high season and return in the low season, you pay the high-season fare. ■

A regular Delhi Transport Corporation bus service that runs from the airport to the New Delhi railway and the Interstate bus station; it costs Rs 20 and there is a Rs 5 charge for luggage. At New Delhi railway station it uses the Ajmer Gate side. There is also a public bus service to the airport (No 780) from the Super Bazaar at Connaught Place, but it can get very crowded.

Just outside the international terminal is a prepaid taxi booth, and a taxi to the centre costs Rs 160 when booked here. This is an excellent way to get into town if you're at all unsure of how things work. From Connaught Place to the airport you'll be asked for anything from Rs 180 upwards. Autorickshaws will run out to the airport too, but you'll be covered in exhaust fumes by the time you get there. If you can find a driver willing to take you it should cost around Rs 60.

Calcutta An airport bus costing Rs 17 runs past the Indian Airlines office and down Chowringhee Rd past Sudder St on its way in from the airport. On the way out to the

airport it departs from the Indian Airlines office at 5.30, 7.15, 9.45 and 11.15 am and 3.15 and 5.30 pm, and takes under an hour. There's also a public minibus (No S10) from BBD Bagh to the airport for Rs 3.50.

If you want to take a taxi from the airport, it's cheaper to go to the prepaid kiosk where you'll be assigned one. It costs Rs 65 to Sudder St or the Oberoi. In the opposite direction expect to pay at least 25% more. All the same, shared between four people, that's about as cheap as the airport bus.

International Airlines
Delhi Offices of international airlines in New Delhi (telephone area code: 011) are as follows:

Aeroflot
    Cozy Travels, BMC House, 1st Floor, 1 N block, Connaught Place (☎ 331-2916)
Air France
    Scindia House, Connaught Place (☎ 331-0407)
Air India
    Jeevan Bharati Bldg, 124 Connaught Circus (☎ 331-1225)

Air Lanka
    Student Travel Information Centre, Imperial Hotel, Janpath (☎ 332-4789)
Alitalia
    19 Kasturba Gandhi Marg (☎ 331-1019)
British Airways
    DLF Bldg, Sansad Marg (Parliament St) (☎ 332-7428)
Iran Air
    Ashok Hotel, Chanakyapuri (☎ 60-4397)
Iraqi Airways
    Ansal Bhawan (☎ 331-8632)
JAL
    Chandralok Bldg, 36 Janpath (☎ 332-3409)
KLM
    Tolstoy Marg (☎ 331-5841)
LOT Polish Airlines
    G-55 Connaught Place (☎ 332-4308)
Lufthansa
    56 Janpath (☎ 332-3206)
Malaysian Airline System (MAS)
    G Block, Connaught Place (☎ 332-5786)
Pakistan International Airlines (PIA)
    Kailash Bldg, 26 Kasturba Gandhi Marg (☎ 331-6121)
Royal Nepal Airlines
    44 Janpath (☎ 332-0817)
SAS
    1 Block, Connaught Place (☎ 332-7503)
Syrian Arab Airlines
    GSA Delhi Express Travels, 13/90 Connaught Place (☎ 34-3218)
Thai International
    Amba Deep Bldg, Kasturba Gandhi Marg (☎ 332-3608)

Calcutta Most airline offices in Calcutta are around Chowringhee. A number of airlines, including Gulf Air, Kuwait Airways, Philippine Airlines and TWA, are handled by GSA Jet Air (☎ 47-7783), 230A Acharya JC Bose Rd. The telephone area code for Calcutta is (033).

Aeroflot
    58 Chowringhee Rd (☎ 22-1415)
Air France
    41 Chowringhee Rd (☎ 29-6161)
Air India
    50 Chowringhee Rd (☎ 22-2356)
Bangladesh Biman
    1 Park St (☎ 29-3709)
British Airways
    41 Chowringhee Rd (☎ 29-3430)
Cathay Pacific/KLM
    1 Middleton St (☎ 47-1221)

JAL
    35-A Chowringhee Rd (☎ 24-8371)
Lufthansa
    30-A/B Chowringhee Rd (☎ 24-8611)
Qantas
    (Hotel Hindustan International), 235 Acharya JC Bose Rd (☎ 47-0718)
Royal Nepal Airlines
    41 Chowringhee Rd (☎ 29-8534)
SAS
    18-G Park St (☎ 24-9696)
Singapore Airlines
    18-D Park St (☎ 29-9297)
Swissair
    46-C Chowringhee Rd (☎ 47-4643)
Thai International
    18-G Park St (☎ 29-9846)

Travellers with Special Needs

If you have special needs of any sort – you've broken a leg, you're vegetarian, travelling in a wheelchair, taking the baby, terrified of flying – you should let the airline know as soon as possible so that they can make arrangements accordingly. You should remind them when you reconfirm your booking (at least 72 hours before departure) and again when you check in at the airport. It may also be worth ringing around the airlines before you make your booking to find out how they can handle your particular needs.

Airports and airlines can be surprisingly helpful, but they do need advance warning. Most international airports will provide escorts from check-in desk to plane where needed, and there should be ramps, lifts, accessible toilets and reachable phones. Aircraft toilets, on the other hand, are likely to present a problem; travellers should discuss this with the airline at an early stage and, if necessary, with their doctor.

Guide dogs for the blind will often have to travel in a specially pressurised baggage compartment with other animals, away from their though smaller guide dogs may be admitted to the cabin. All guide dogs will be subject to the same quarantine laws (six months in isolation etc) as any other animal when entering or returning to countries currently free of rabies such as Britain or Australia. Deaf travellers can ask for airport and in-flight announcements to be written down for them.

Children under two travel for 10% of the standard fare (or free, on some airlines), as long as they don't occupy a seat. They don't get a baggage allowance either. Bassinets should be provided by the airline if requested in advance; these will take a child weighing up to about 10 kg. Children between two and 12 can usually occupy a seat for half to two-thirds of the full fare, and do get a baggage allowance. Strollers can often be taken as hand luggage.

Cheap Tickets in India

Although you can get cheap tickets in Mumbai (Bombay) and Calcutta, it is in Delhi that the real wheeling and dealing goes on. There are a number of 'bucket shops' around Connaught Place, but enquire with other travellers about their current trustworthiness.

Fares from Delhi to various European capitals cost around Rs 5000 to Rs 7000, a bit less from Mumbai. The cheapest flights to Europe are with airlines like Aeroflot, LOT, Kuwait Airways, Syrian Arab Airways or Iraqi Airways. Delhi-Hong Kong-San Francisco costs around US$600.

Although Delhi is the best place for cheap tickets, and the closest international airport to the western Indian Himalayan regions, many flights between Europe and South-East Asia or Australia pass through Mumbai (Bombay); it's also the place for flights to East Africa. Furthermore, if you're heading east from India to Bangladesh, Myanmar (Burma) or Thailand, you'll probably find much better prices in Calcutta than in Delhi, even though there are fewer agents. Calcutta is the closest international airport to Sikkim and northern West Bengal.

Africa

There are plenty of flights between East Africa and Mumbai due to the large Indian population in Kenya. Typical fares from Mumbai (Bombay) to Nairobi are around US$440 return with either Ethiopian Air-

lines, Kenya Airways, Air India or Pakistan International Airlines (PIA, via Karachi).

Aeroflot operates a service between Delhi and Cairo (via Moscow).

Australia & New Zealand

Advance-purchase return fares from the east coast of Australia to India range from A$1250 to A$1500 depending on the season and the destination in India. Fares are slightly cheaper to Madras and Calcutta than to Mumbai (Bombay) and Delhi. Fares are slightly cheaper from Darwin and Perth than from the east coast.

Tickets from Australia to London or other European capitals with an Indian stopover range from A$1200 to A$1350 one way and A$2000 to A$2500 return, again, depending on the season.

Return advance-purchase fares from New Zealand to India range from NZ$1799 to NZ$1889 depending on the season.

STA Travel and Flight Centres International are major dealers in cheap air fares in both Australia and New Zealand. Check the travel agents' ads in the *Yellow Pages*, local newspapers and travel magazines, and ring around.

Bangladesh

Bangladesh Biman and Indian Airlines fly from Calcutta to Dhaka (US$32) and Chittagong (US$40) in Bangladesh. Many people use Biman from Calcutta through to Bangkok – partly because it's cheap and partly because it flies through Yangon (Rangoon) in Myanmar. Biman should put you up overnight in Dhaka on this route but be careful – it appears they will only do so if your ticket is specifically endorsed that you are entitled to a room. If not, tough luck – you can either camp out overnight in the hot transit lounge or make your way into Dhaka on your own, pay for transport and accommodation, and get hit for departure tax the next day.

Continental Europe

Fares from continental Europe are mostly far more expensive than from London, although

Amsterdam is edging in on the cheap air fare market, with good deals with Middle Eastern airlines from Amsterdam to Delhi.

From Amsterdam to Delhi/Mumbai, return excursion fares are about DFL2400 (UK£900). To Calcutta, expect to pay around DFL2665 (UK£1000).

From Paris to Mumbai/Delhi, return excursion fares range upwards from FF7880 (UK£980; about one-third the standard return economy fare).

From Frankfurt to Mumbai/Delhi, return excursion fares are around DM1950 (UK£820).

Malaysia

Not many travellers fly between Malaysia and India because it is so much cheaper from Thailand, but there are flights between Penang or Kuala Lumpur and Madras. You can generally pick up one-way tickets for the Malaysian Airline System (MAS) flight from Penang travel agents for around RM$780, which is rather cheaper than the regular fare. Other fares include Kuala Lumpur-Mumbai for RM$700 one way and RM$1275 return, and Kuala Lumpur-Delhi for RM$700 one way and RM$1070 return. Indian Airlines flies between Madras and Kuala Lumpur or Singapore.

The Maldives

Thiruvananthapuram (Trivandrum)-Malé costs US$63. This is cheaper than flying to the Maldives from Colombo in Sri Lanka.

Myanmar

There are no land crossing points between Myanmar and India (or between Myanmar and any other country), so if you want to visit Myanmar your only choice is to fly there. Myanma Airways flies Calcutta-Yangon; Bangladesh Biman flies Dhaka-Yangon.

If you are coming from Bangkok via Myanmar, the one-way Bangkok-Yangon-Calcutta fare is around US$240 with Thai, or US$225 on Myanma Airways.

Nepal

Royal Nepal Airlines Corporation (RNAC) and Indian Airlines share routes between

India and Kathmandu. Both airlines give a 25% discount to those under 30 years of age on flights between Kathmandu and India; no student card is needed.

Delhi is the main departure point for flights between India and Kathmandu. The daily one-hour Delhi to Kathmandu flight costs US$142.

Other cities in India with direct air connections with Kathmandu are Mumbai (US$257), Calcutta (US$96) and Varanasi (US$71). The flight from Varanasi is the last leg of the popular Delhi-Agra-Khajuraho-Varanasi-Kathmandu tourist flight.

If you want to see the mountains as you fly into Kathmandu from Delhi or Varanasi, you must sit on the left side.

There are flights to Kathmandu from Bhadrapur in eastern Nepal, accessible from northern West Bengal, with Everest Air, Royal Nepal Airlines or Necon Airways (US$99).

Pakistan

Pakistan International Airlines (PIA) and Air India operate flights from Karachi to Delhi for US$75 and Lahore to Delhi for about US$140. Flights are also available between Karachi and Mumbai on Indian Airlines.

Singapore

Singapore is a great cheap-ticket centre and you can pick up Singapore-Delhi tickets for about S$900 return.

Sri Lanka

Because the ferry service is out of operation, flying is now the only way to get to Sri Lanka. There are flights to and from Colombo and Mumbai (Bombay), Madras, Tiruchirappalli or Thiruvananthapuram (Trivandrum). Flights are most frequent on the Madras-Colombo route.

Thailand

Bangkok is the most popular departure point from South-East Asia into Asia proper because of the cheap flights from there to Calcutta, Yangon in Myanmar, Dhaka in Bangladesh or Kathmandu in Nepal. The popular Bangkok-Kathmandu flight is about US$220 one way and US$400 return. You can make a stopover in Myanmar on this route and do a circuit of that fascinating country. Bangkok-Calcutta via Myanmar is about US$270 one way.

The UK

Various excursion fares are available from London to India, but you can get better prices through London's many cheap-ticket specialists. Check the travel page ads in the *Times, Business Traveller* and the weekly entertainment guides such as *Time Out*; or check give-away papers like *TNT*. Two reliable London shops are Trailfinders (☎ (0171) 938-3939) 194 High Street Kensington, London W8 7RG, and (☎ (0171) 938-3366) 46 Earls Court Rd, London W8; and STA Travel (☎ (0171) 937-9962) 74 Old Brompton Rd, London SW7, or 117 Euston Rd, London NW1. Also worth trying are Quest Worldwide (☎ (0181) 547-3322) at 29 Castle St, Kingston, Surrey KT11ST, and Bridge the World (☎ (0171) 911-0900) at 1-3 Ferdinand St, Camden Town, London NW1.

From London to Delhi, fares range from around UK£300/342 one way/return in the low season, or UK£409/493 one way/return in the high season – cheaper short-term fares are also available. The cheapest fares are usually with Middle Eastern or Eastern European airlines. You'll also find very competitive air fares to the subcontinent with Bangladesh Biman or Air Lanka. Thai International always seems to have competitive fares despite its high standards.

If you want to stop in India en route to Australia expect to pay around UK£500 to UK£600. You might find fares via Karachi (Pakistan) or Colombo (Sri Lanka) slightly cheaper than fares via India.

Most British travel agents are registered with the Association of British Travel Agents (ABTA). If you have paid for your flight to an ABTA-registered agent who then goes out of business, ABTA will guarantee a refund or an alternative. Unregistered bucket shops are riskier but are also sometimes cheaper.

The USA & Canada

The cheapest return fares from the US west coast to India are around US$1350. Another way of getting there is to fly to Hong Kong and get a ticket from there. Tickets to Hong Kong cost about US$430 one way and around US$725 return from San Francisco or Los Angeles; in Hong Kong you can find one-way tickets to Mumbai for US$300, depending on the carrier. Alternatively, you can fly to Singapore for around US$595/US$845 one way/return, or to Bangkok for US$470/US$760 one way/return.

From the east coast you can find return tickets to Mumbai or Delhi for around US$950. The cheapest one-way tickets will be around US$660. An alternative way of getting to India from New York is to fly to London and buy a cheap fare from there.

Check the Sunday travel sections of papers like the *New York Times, San Francisco Chronicle/Examiner* or *Los Angeles Times* for cheap fares. Good budget travel agents include the student travel chains STA, and Council Travel, the travel division of the Council on International Education Exchange. The magazine *Travel Unlimited* (PO Box 1058, Allston, Mass 02134) publishes details of the cheapest air fares and courier possibilities for destinations all over the world from the USA.

Fares from Canada are similar to the USA fares. From Vancouver the route is like that from the US west coast, with the option of going via Hong Kong. From Toronto it is easier to travel via London.

The *Toronto Globe & Mail* and the *Vancouver Sun* carry travel agents' ads. The magazine *Great Expeditions* (PO Box 8000-411, Abbotsford BC V2S 6H1) is useful.

LAND

Drivers of cars and riders of motorcycles will need the vehicle's registration papers, liability insurance and an international driver's permit in addition to their domestic licence. Beware: there are two kinds of international permit, one of which is needed mostly for former British colonies. You will also need a *carnet de passage en douane*, which is effectively a passport for the vehicle, and acts as a temporary waiver of import duty. The carnet may also need to have listed any more-expensive spares that you're planning to carry with you, such as a gearbox. This is necessary when travelling in many countries in Asia, and is designed to prevent car import rackets. Contact your local automobile association for details about all documentation.

Liability insurance is not available in advance for many out-of-the-way countries, but has to be bought when crossing the border. The cost and quality of such local insurance varies wildly, and you will find in some countries that you are effectively travelling uninsured.

Anyone who is planning to take their own vehicle with them needs to check in advance what spares and petrol are likely to be available. Lead-free fuel is not available in India, and neither is every little part for your car.

Cycling is a cheap, convenient, healthy, environmentally sound and, above all, fun way of travelling. Some intrepid souls revel in the challenge posed by cycling in the Himalaya, and some agencies can even provide backup support services for touring cyclist groups. See the Getting Around chapter for information. One note of caution: before you leave home, go over your bike with a fine-toothed comb and fill your repair kit with every imaginable spare. As with cars and motorcycles, you won't necessarily be able to buy that crucial gizmo for your machine when it breaks down somewhere in the back of beyond as the sun sets.

Bicycles can travel by air. You *can* take them to pieces and put them in a bike bag or box, but it's much easier simply to wheel your bike to the check-in desk, where it should be treated as a piece of baggage. You may have to remove the pedals and turn the handlebars sideways so that it takes up less space in the aircraft's hold; check all this with the airline well in advance, preferably before you pay for your ticket.

For more details on using your own vehicle in India, see the Getting Around chapter.

Bangladesh

Unfortunately most land entry and exit points are closed, so the choice is much more limited than a glance at the map would indicate.

The main crossings are at Haridaspur/Benapol on the Calcutta route and Haldibari/Chiliharti on the Darjeeling route. The Dauki/Tamabil border crossing, in the northeast corner on the Meghalaya route, opened in 1995.

No exit permit is required to leave Bangladesh. If border officials mention anything about a permit, remain steadfast. However, if you enter the country by air and exit via land, you do need a road permit, which can be obtained from the Passport & Immigration office, 2nd floor, 17/1 Segunbagicha Rd in Dhaka, and if you are driving from Bangladesh in your own vehicle, two permits are required: one from the Indian High Commission (☎ 504-897), House 120, Road 2, Dhanmondi in Dhaka, and one from the Bangladesh Ministry of Foreign Affairs (☎ 883-260), Pioneer Rd (facing the Supreme Court), Segun Bagicha in the centre of Dhaka.

We have received in recent years letters from travellers who have crossed at Changrabandha/Bhurungamari (east of Haldibari, an alternative route from Darjeeling), Balurghat/Hili and Lalgola/Godagari, both north of Haridaspur/Benapol. These lesser crossings witness so few westerners that everyone assumes they're closed. Getting the truth from Indian and Bangladeshi officials is virtually impossible, so crossing the border on these lesser routes is never certain.

Calcutta to Dhaka The Calcutta to Dhaka route is the one used by the majority of land travellers between India and Bangladesh. Stage one is a train from Calcutta (Sealdah) to Bangaon (Rs 13, 2½ hours), the town closest to the border. From Bangaon, it's about 10 km (Rs 10, 20 minutes) by cycle-rickshaw to the border at Haridaspur on the Indian side, or Rs 50 by autorickshaw. It's possible to change money at Bangaon, and the rate is better than at the border.

Crossing the border takes an hour or so with the usual filling in and stamping of forms. From the border, it's about 10 minutes by cycle-rickshaw (Tk 5) to Benapol (the Bangladeshi border town). If you leave Calcutta in the early afternoon you should be in Benapol in time for the bus departures between 6 and 8.30 pm. There are no buses in the daytime between the border and Benapol.

Alternatively, you can take a Coaster (minibus) from Benapol to Jessore (Tk 12), from where you can proceed to Dhaka. The last 'direct' buses from Jessore leave around 1 pm.

Coming from Dhaka it's wise to book your seat on the bus at least a day in advance. The buses that operate overnight between Dhaka and the border are direct. Buses only depart from 8 to 11 pm; they reach Benapol at dawn.

From Darjeeling From Darjeeling to Siliguri, you can take the fast buses (three hours) or the slower but more picturesque toy train (about nine hours). If you take the train, it is more convenient to get off at New Jalpaiguri than at the other two stations in Siliguri.

The trip from New Jalpaiguri to Haldibari (the Indian border checkpoint) takes two hours and costs Rs 9 by train, but you have a little travelling yet before you reach Bangladesh. It's a seven km walk along the disused railway line from Haldibari to the Bangladesh border point at Chiliharti! You should, however, be able to arrange for a rickshaw from Haldibari for the first few km towards the border.

There's a railway station at Chiliharti from where you can set off into Bangladesh, although it's much quicker to take the bus. Bring some takas (the currency of Bangladesh) in with you. This is officially illegal but changing money in Chiliharti is virtually impossible. There are moneychangers at Haldibari.

From Sylhet In the early 70s, the route between Shillong in Meghalaya and Sylhet in Bangladesh was closed on the Indian side to both regional and international traffic

because of problems in Assam caused by the influx of illegal immigrants from Bangladesh. In 1995, the permit requirement was dropped; it may take a while before crossing here becomes problem free. If you're travelling by bus and border officials demand such a permit, you may have to educate them.

It takes 2½ hours to get to Tamabil from Sylhet by bus, and a 15 minute hike to the border. It is then a further 1½ km walk to Dauki in India, from where buses run to Shillong, a 3½ hour trip. From Shillong at an elevation of 1496m, if it's not cloudy, the views over Bangladesh are superb.

Europe
The classic way of getting to India has always been overland. Sadly, the events in the Middle East and Afghanistan have turned the cross-Asian flow into a trickle. Afghanistan is still off-limits but the trip through Turkey, Iran and into Pakistan is straightforward.

The Asia overland trip is certainly not the breeze it once was, but it is definitely possible. Many travellers combine travel to the subcontinent with the Middle East by flying from India or Pakistan to Amman in Jordan or one of the Gulf states. A number of the London-based overland companies operate their bus or truck trips across Asia on a regular basis. Check with Exodus (☎ (0181) 675-5550), 9 Weir Rd, London SW12 0LT, UK; Encounter Overland (☎ (0171) 370-6951), 267 Old Brompton Rd, London SW5 9LA, UK; or Top Deck Travel (☎ (0171) 370-4555) for more information.

For more detail on the Asian overland route, see the Lonely Planet guides to Pakistan, Iran and Turkey.

Nepal
There are direct buses from Delhi to Kathmandu, but these generally get bad reports from travellers. It's cheaper and more satisfactory to organise this trip yourself. There are two border entry points in the Himalayan regions covered in this book: at Banbassa, in the Kumaon district of Uttarakhand (the UP hills), which is the closest

village to the western Nepal border village of Mahendranagar; and Paniktanki, in northern West Bengal, opposite the eastern Nepal border town of Kakarbhitta.

From Siliguri, the major transport hub en route to Darjeeling and Sikkim, it is only one hour to Paniktanki. Buses run regularly on this route (Rs 6). A cycle-rickshaw across the border to Kakarbhitta costs Rs 5. Buses depart Kakarbhitta daily at 5 pm for Kathmandu (17 hours, Nepalese Rs 250).

Once in Nepal, buses travel west as far as Narayanghat on the Mahendra Highway, skirting the foothills and passing a number of interesting places and sights on the Terai (Nepalese plains); from Narayanghat the road climbs through the Shivalik Hills to Mugling and the Trisuli River valley, where you double back towards Kathmandu. If it isn't too hot, consider travelling by day, so you can see the sights and stop in Janakpur and/or the Royal Chitwan National Park.

Avalanches and floods can sometimes delay the bus. The road is in very poor condition in the vicinity of the Kosi barrage and there's another very bad section on the Prithvi Highway (the Pokhara to Kathmandu road) between Mugling and Kathmandu. Many travellers consider it to be one of the roughest bus journeys on the subcontinent!

There are day buses from Kakarbhitta that go to a number of other places on the Terai, including Janakpur (Nepalese Rs 100), and there are night buses to Pokhara (Rs 250).

It is also possible to enter Nepal from the insalubrious town of Raxaul, near Muzaffarpur, in Patna, opposite the equally insalubrious Nepal border town of Birganj. If you are heading straight to Nepal from Delhi or elsewhere in western India, then the Gorakhpur to Sunauli route is the most convenient. Gorakhpur is an important railway junction: the 783 km (14½) hour trip to or from Delhi costs Rs 64/552 in 2nd/1st class, or Rs 180 in sleeper class. There are regular departures for the Nepalese border town of Sunauli between 5 am and 8 pm (three hours, Rs 17) from the bus stand near the railway station.

It is also possible to cross the border at Nepalganj, Dhangadi and Mahendrenagar in the far west of Nepal. The entry at Mahendrenagar, just over the border from the northern Uttar Pradesh village of Banbassa, is the most interesting possibility. It may take a while for things to start operating smoothly, but when they do, this will present an interesting alternative route to/from Delhi. If the Mahendra Highway is completed by now (in theory it should be, but don't count on it) the route will be open all year; otherwise it is a dry season-only proposition, and strictly for the hardy. From Delhi to Mahendrenagar, it's a long 12 hour bus journey. From Almora, in the Kumaon region of Uttarakhand, it's seven hours (Rs 60), and from Pithoragarh, in the eastern Kumaon district, and an access point for the Milam Glacier trek, it's eight hours to Mahendrenagar (Rs 61). Banbassa is connected by rail to Bareilly.

From Banbassa, you can catch a cycle-rickshaw (20 minutes) to the border and across to Mahendrenagar. There are direct night buses from Mahendrenagar to Kathmandu, but they take a gruelling 25 hours. The countryside is beautiful and fascinating, so it's much better to travel during the day and to break the journey at Nepalganj. If you can't get a direct bus for the nine-hour trip from Mahendrenagar to Nepalganj, take a bus to Ataria (at the junction for Dhangadhi) and from there to Nepalganj. There are plenty of buses from Nepalganj to Kathmandu (day and night journeys, 16 hours) and to Pokhara (night, 15 hours).

There are other roads into Nepal from northern Bihar to the east of Birganj but they are rarely used by travellers, and a couple of them are closed. One is the crossing between Jogbani (near Purnia) and Biratnagar. Additionally, the narrow-gauge railway from Jaynagar (near Darbhanga) which crosses the border to Janakpur (an attractive Nepalese city famous as the birthplace of Sita) is also closed.

Pakistan

At present, due to the continuing unstable political situation between India and Pakistan, there's only one border crossing open.

Lahore to Amritsar The crossing at Attari is open daily to all traffic. It may be worth checking the situation in the Punjab with the Home Ministry in Delhi or the Indian High Commission in Islamabad, Pakistan, before you travel, as this could change if there are major problems either side of the border.

For the Lahore (Pakistan) to Amritsar (India) train you have to buy one ticket from Lahore to Attari, the Indian border town, and another from Attari to Amritsar. The train departs Lahore daily at 11.30 am and arrives in Amritsar at 3 pm after a couple of hours at the border passing through immigration and customs. Going the other way, you leave Amritsar at 9.30 am and arrive in Lahore at 1.35 pm. Pakistan immigration and customs are handled at Lahore railway station. Sometimes, however, border delays can make the trip much longer.

From Amritsar you cannot buy a ticket until the morning of departure and there are no seat reservations – arrive early and push. Moneychangers on the platform offer good rates for Pakistan rupees. Travellers have reported that whichever direction you're travelling, the exchange rate between Indian and Pakistan rupees is more advantageous to you on the Pakistan side of the border, but you can change Indian rupees to Pakistani rupees or vice versa at Wagah (the Pakistani border town) and in Amritsar – no matter what the Pakistanis may tell you!

Few travellers use the road link between India and Pakistan. It's mainly of interest to people with vehicles or those on overland buses. By public transport, the trip from Lahore entails taking a bus to the border at Wagah between Lahore and Amritsar, walking across the border and then taking another bus or taxi into Amritsar.

From Lahore, buses and minibuses depart from near the general bus station on Badami Bagh. The border opens at 9.15 am and closes at 3.30 pm. If you're stuck on the Pakistan side you can stay at the *PTDC Motel*, where there are dorm beds and double rooms.

South-East Asia

In contrast to the difficulties of travelling over-land in central Asia, the South-East Asian overland trip is still wide open and as popular as ever. From Australia the first step is to Indonesia – Timor, Bali or Jakarta. Although most people fly from an east-coast city or from Perth to Bali, there are also flights from Darwin and from Port Hedland in the north of Western Australia. The shortest route is the flight between Darwin and Kupang on the Indonesian island of Timor.

From Bali you head north through Java to Jakarta, from where you either travel by ship or fly to Singapore or continue north through Sumatra and then cross to Penang in Malaysia. After travelling around Malaysia you can fly from Penang to Madras in India or, more popularly, continue north to Thailand and eventually fly out from Bangkok to India, perhaps with a stopover in Myanmar. Unfortunately, crossing by land from Myanmar to India (or indeed to any other country) is forbidden by the Myanmar government.

An interesting alternative route is to travel from Australia to Papua New Guinea and from there cross to Irian Jaya, then to Sulawesi in Indonesia. There are all sorts of travel variations possible in South-East Asia; the region is a delight to travel through, it's good value for money, the food is generally excellent and healthy, and all in all it's an area of the world not to be missed. For full details see the Lonely Planet guide *South-East Asia*.

SEA

The ferry service from Rameswaram in southern India to Talaimannar in Sri Lanka has been suspended for some years due to the unrest in Sri Lanka. This was a favourite route for shipping arms and equipment to the Tamil guerrilla forces in the north of the country.

The shipping services between Africa and India only carry freight (including vehicles), not passengers.

The service between Penang and Madras also ceased some years ago.

DEPARTURE TAX

For flights to neighbouring countries (Pakistan, Sri Lanka, Bangladesh, Nepal) the departure tax is Rs 100, but to other countries it's Rs 300.

This airport tax applies to everybody, even to babies who do not occupy a seat. The method of collecting the tax varies but generally you have to pay it before you check in, so look out for an airport tax counter as you enter the check-in area.

ORGANISED TOURS

There are numerous foreign eco-travel and adventure travel companies which can provide unusual and interesting trips in addition to companies that provide more standard tours. There are too many to include them all; check newspapers and travel magazines for advertisements, and journals such as *Earth Journal* (USA) for listings. Companies that organise tours to various parts of India include the following:

Australia & New Zealand

Destinations
2nd Floor, Premier Bldg (near Queen and Durham St East) Auckland, New Zealand (☎ (09) 309 0464)
New Experience Holidays
3/131 Keen St, Lismore, NSW 2480, Australia (☎ toll-free 1-800-067-2218; fax (066) 22-2267)
Peregrine Adventures
258 Lonsdale St, Melbourne 3000, Australia (☎ (03) 9663 8611). Also offices in Sydney, Brisbane, Adelaide, Perth and Hobart.
Venturetreks
164 Parnell Rd (PO Box 37610), Parnell, Auckland, New Zealand (☎ (09) 379-9855; fax 377-0320)
World Expeditions
3rd Floor, 441 Kent St, Sydney, NSW 2000, Australia (☎ (02) 9264-3366; fax 9261-1974)
1st Floor, 393 Little Bourke St, Melbourne, Vic 3000, Australia (☎ (03) 9670-8400; fax 9670-7474)

The UK

Encounter Overland
267 Old Brompton Rd, London SW5 9JA (☎ (0171) 370-6845)
Exodus Expeditions
9 Weir Rd, London SW12 OLT (☎ (0181) 673-0859)
Imaginative Traveller (international reservation office)
14 Barley Mow Passage, Chiswick, London W4 4PH (☎ (0181) 742 3113; fax 742 3046)

The USA

Adventure Center
1311 63rd St, Suite 200, Emeryville, CA 94608 (☎ (800) 227-8747)
All Adventure Travel, Inc.
PO Box 4307, Boulder, CO 80306 (☎ (303) 440-7924)
Asian Pacific Adventures
826 S. Sierra Bonita Ave, Los Angeles, CA 90036 (☎ (800) 825-1680)
Inner Asia Expeditions
2627 Lombard St, San Francisco, CA 94123 (☎ (415) 922-0448; fax 346-5535)

The Indian Himalaya

AIR

With the deregulation of the Indian skies, Indian Airlines no longer has a monopoly on domestic air services, and at least half a dozen new airlines, known as Air Taxi Operators (ATOs), have started services, a number of which serve the Indian Himalayan regions. Compared to other modes of transport to the Himalayan regions, flights are still comparatively expensive, but are a speedy, comfortable and efficient means of covering the large distances involved (and to Leh, in winter, the *only* means of getting there).

Airlines

Addresses in New Delhi (telephone area code: 011) of airlines serving the Indian Himalaya are as follows:

Archana Airways
41-A Friends' Colony East, Mathura Rd (☎ 684-2001; airport ☎ 329-5126, ext 2354)
Indian Airlines
Malhotra Bldg, F Block, Connaught Circus (☎ 331-0517; airport ☎ 141, 144)
Jagson Airlines
12-E Vandana Bldg, 11 Tolstoy Marg (☎ 372-1593; airport ☎ 329-5126 ext 2200)
Jet Airways
3-E Hanslaya Bldg, 15 Barakhamba Rd (☎ 335-1352, 329-5404; airport ☎ 329 5406)
KCV Airways
311 Suneja Towers-1, District Centre, Janakpuri (☎ 552-9266; airport ☎ 548-1351, ext 2328)
UP Airways
A-2, Defence Colony (☎ 463-8201; airport ☎ 329-5126, ext 2389)

Addresses of airlines in Calcutta serving the eastern Himalayan regions are as follows:

Indian Airlines
    39 Chittaranjan Ave (☎ 26-2548; airport ☎ 552-8433)
Jet Airways
    2/4 Chitrakoot Bldg, 230 A AJC Bose Rd (☎ 408-192; airport ☎ 552-8836)

Booking Flights

Indian Airlines has computerised booking at all but the smallest offices, so getting flight information and reservations is relatively simple – it's just getting to the head of the queue that takes time. Nevertheless, all flights are still heavily booked and you need to plan as far in advance as possible. The private operators are all reasonably efficient, and most have computerised booking or authorised agencies in major tourist centres. Theoretically, you should be able to make reservations on all scheduled flights operating in India before leaving your home country, although your agent may not be able to issue tickets. If your agency provides this service for you, it may be necessary to reconfirm and pay for the flight on arrival in India, which should be done as soon as possible.

Buying Tickets

The following conditions apply to Indian Airlines; regulations, student discounts and restrictions applying to smaller operators should be checked when booking your ticket. All Indian Airlines tickets must be paid for with foreign currency or by credit card, or rupees backed up by encashment certificates. Change, where appropriate, is given in rupees.

Infants up to two years old travel at 10% of the adult fare, but only one infant per adult can travel at this fare. Children two to 12 years old travel at 50% of the adult fare. There is no student reduction for overseas visitors, but there is a youth fare for people 12 to 29 years old. This allows a 25% reduction.

Refunds on adult tickets attract a charge of Rs 100 and can be made at any office.

There are no refund charges on infant tickets. If a flight is delayed or cancelled, you cannot refund the ticket. If you fail to show up 30 minutes before the flight, this is regarded as a 'no-show' and you forfeit the full value of the ticket.

Indian Airlines accepts no responsibility if you lose your tickets. They absolutely will not refund lost tickets, but at their discretion may issue replacements.

Fares

The Indian Air Routes chart details the main Indian Airlines and private airlines' routes and fares throughout India. Private airlines usually charge the same as Indian Airlines on identical routes, although in some cases it can be substantially more.

If you are heading straight for the hills, it's definitely not worth considering an air pass, as you may only require one or two flights; however, if you are planning to spend a little time in other areas of India before heading home, Indian Airlines' 21-day 'Discover India' pass, which costs US$500, can be reasonable value. This allows unlimited travel on their domestic routes. There's a 25% discount if you're under 30.

Check-In

Check-in time is one hour in advance. With all flights to and from Srinagar, an extra 30 minutes is required. On some internal routes, as a security measure, you are required to identify your checked-in baggage on the tarmac immediately prior to boarding. Don't forget to do this or it won't be loaded onto the plane.

Flights & Airlines

If your point of entry into India is Calcutta, and you wish to visit the western Himalaya, the fastest and most efficient way to traverse the continent is to fly. Various operators serve this sector, with Indian Airlines offering the cheapest fares (US$132) and daily flights. Indian Airlines flight IC263 departs Calcutta daily at 7 am, arriving in Delhi at 9.05 am. There is also a daily flight (IC402)

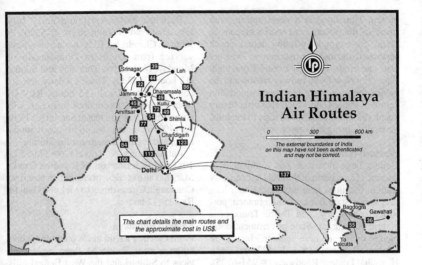

Indian Himalaya Air Routes

0   300   600 km

The external boundaries of India on this map have not been authenticated and may not be correct.

This chart details the main routes and the approximate cost in US$.

at 5.15 pm, arriving in the capital at 7.20 pm.

Following are details on flights serving the Indian Himalayan regions. For more information, including schedules and fares, see the Getting There & Away sections in the relevant regional chapters.

Jammu & Kashmir Indian Airlines has flights between Delhi and Jammu, and between Jammu and Srinagar, and Jammu and Leh. There are twice-daily flights between Delhi and Kashmir, and a weekly flight between Kashmir and Leh. Archana Airways plans to fly between Leh, Kargil and Delhi several times a week.

Himachal Pradesh Himachal Pradesh has three airports: at Gaggal, 15 km south of Dharamsala, serving the Kangra Valley; at Bhuntar, 10 km south of Kullu, serving the Kullu and Parbati valleys; and at Jubbarhatti, 23 km south of Shimla. Airlines flying to Himachal Pradesh include Archana Airways and Jagson Airlines. There are flights with Archana between Delhi and Shimla (Jubbarhatti), and with Jagson, between Delhi, Shimla, Kullu (Bhuntar) and Gaggal.

Uttarakhand Jolly Grant is the closest airport to Dehra Dun, 24 km distant, and Haridwar, 35 km to the south. Dehra Dun is 34 km south of Mussoorie, and Jolly Grant also serves Rishikesh. Other airports serving destinations in Uttarakhand are Pantnagar, 71 km from Nainital and 80 km south-east of Ramnagar, and at Pithoragarh, in eastern Kumaon. At the time of writing there were no scheduled flights to any of these airports, but this could change in the near future. Scheduled flights to Jolly Grant with UP Airways were slated at the time of writing.

West Bengal & Sikkim The closest airport serving the hills region of West Bengal and Sikkim is at Bagdogra, 12 km from Siliguri, 90 km south of Darjeeling, and 114 km south of Gangtok, in Sikkim. There are regular flights to Siliguri from both Delhi and Calcutta with Indian Airlines and Jet Airways.

BUS
Bus travel around the Indian Himalaya is covered in more extensive detail in the Getting Around chapter. Travelling by bus *to* the Himalayan regions from either Delhi (for the western Himalaya) or Calcutta (for the

eastern Himalaya) is a good option, with many of the government tourist bureaus in Delhi, for example, offering deluxe coach services to the main tourist centres. There are also numerous agencies around Connaught Place, the New Delhi railway station and the nearby popular travellers' accommodation centre of Pahar Ganj which also offer luxury coach (2x2 pushback seats) trips to the hills, generally during the season only.

Western Himalaya

Delhi's large Interstate bus terminal is at Kashmir Gate, north of the Old Delhi railway station. Facilities here include 24 hour left-luggage, a State Bank of India branch, post office, pharmacy, and Delhi Transport's Nagrik Restaurant. State government companies operating here include: Jammu & Kashmir Roadways (☎ 332-4422, ext 2243), Himachal Pradesh Roadways (☎ 251-6725), and Uttar Pradesh Roadways (☎ 296-8709).

Between early April and early July, Himachal Pradesh Tourism (☎ 32-5320), 36 Janpath, Chandralok Bldg, has a non-air-con service from Delhi to Dharamsala on Monday, Wednesday, Thursday and Sunday (12 hours, Rs 330). There's a daily non-air-con service to Manali (15 hours, Rs 400), from where you can continue on to Leh, with an overnight stop in a tent at Sarchu (ex Delhi Rs 1400, including two nights accommodation), and regular departures for Shimla.

Potala Tours & Travels (☎ 372-2552) 1011 Antriksh Bhavan, 22 Kasturba Gandhi Marg has an excellent overnight service from Connaught Circus direct to McLeod Ganj for Rs 325 (12 hours).

Eastern Himalaya

From Calcutta's Esplanade bus stand, about 800m north of Sudder St, there are bus services to Siliguri and the West Bengal hills. There are a number of private companies

Bus Services from Delhi to the Western Hills Regions

Destination	Time	Cost Luxury / State government services
Jammu & Kashmir		
Jammu	14 hours	Rs 250/120
Srinagar	24 hours (minimum)	Rs 500/173
Ladakh & Zanskar		
Leh*		
Himachal Pradesh		
Dharamsala	12 hours	Rs 425/130
Manali	16 hours	Rs 300/168
Kullu	14 hours	Rs 350/180
Shimla	10 hours	Rs 300/110
Uttarakhand		
Nainital	9 hours	Rs 230/90
Mussoorie	8 hours	Rs 230/86.50
Rishikesh	6 hours	Rs 175/60
Ramnagar	7 hours	Rs 190/68
(for Corbett National Park)		
Dehra Dun	7 hours	Rs 66 (ordinary)
Haridwar	8 hours	Rs 53.50 (ordinary)
Ranikhet	7 hours	Rs 132 (ordinary)
Almora	12 hours	Rs 112 (ordinary)

*It's possible to travel to Leh from either Srinagar or Manali. The latter is the more popular route, particularly due to the political unrest in Jammu and Kashmir. For more information, see the Ladakh & Zanskar chapter.

which have their own stands. Ordinary bus services to Siliguri's Tenzing Norgay bus terminal cost Rs 123. There are also more comfortable (and speedier!) 'rocket services', with 2x2 pushback seats (12 hours, Rs 147). For travel onwards from Siliguri (ie to the West Bengal hills and Sikkim), see the Getting Around sections in the West Bengal and Sikkim chapters. Train services to New Jalpaiguri station, eight km south of Siliguri, are a comfortable alternative.

TRAIN

While there are very few railway lines in the Himalayan regions, and those that do exist are generally narrow-gauge and of interest more for their novelty value than as a means of covering large distances, travelling *to* the hills by train from either Delhi or Calcutta is a good alternative to the buses.

The first step in coming to grips with Indian Railways is to get a timetable: *Trains at a Glance* (Rs 15) is a handy, 100 page guide covering all the main routes and trains. It is usually available at major railway stations and sometimes on news stands in the larger cities. If you can't find it, a regional timetable provides much the same information, including the local train services, and a pink section with timetables for the major mail and express trains (the fast ones) throughout the country.

There is also the 300 page *Indian Bradshaw* (Rs 50) which covers every train service throughout the country. It's more detailed than most people need and it can be frustratingly difficult to find things. It's probably only useful if you are planning to travel beyond the Himalayan regions to other parts of India. Published monthly, it's not widely available, but you can usually find it on the bookstalls at major city railway stations. Thomas Cook's *Overseas Timetable* has good train timetables for India, although it's not available in India.

The timetables indicate the km distance between major railway stations and a table at the back shows the fares for distances from one km to 5000 km for the various train types. With this information it is very easy to calculate the fare between any two railway stations.

A factor to consider with Indian trains is that getting there may not always be half the fun but it is certainly 90% of the experience. At times it can be uncomfortable or incredibly frustrating (since the trains are not exactly fast) but an experience it certainly is. Fortunately, travelling from either Delhi or Calcutta to the Himalayan regions doesn't entail some of the long, gruelling and dusty trips that it does in other parts of the country, unless you're considering taking the *long* (1628 km) trip from Delhi to New Jalpaiguri, the railhead for Siliguri, gateway to the West Bengal hills and Sikkim. All services to the railheads in the foothills of the Himalaya, or just below them, on the plains, generally take less than 12 hours.

Classes

There are generally two classes – 1st and 2nd – but there are a number of subtle variations on this basic distinction. For a start there is 1st class and air-con (AC) 1st class. The air-con carriages only operate on the major trains and routes. The fare for AC 1st class is more than double normal 1st class. A slightly cheaper air-con alternative is the AC two tier sleeper, which costs about 25% more than 1st class. These carriages are a lot more common that AC 1st class, which you won't find on any of the trains serving the Himalayan regions, but are still only found on the major routes.

Between 1st and 2nd class there are two more air-con options: the AC three tier sleeper and AC chair car. The former has three levels of berths rather than two, while the latter, as the name suggests, consists of carriages with aircraft-type layback seats. Once again, these carriages are only found on the major routes, and the latter only on day trains. The cost of AC three tier is about 70% of the 1st class fare; AC chair is about 55% of the 1st class fare.

It's possible to request a particular berth. Top berths are a good bet from the security aspect, as you can haul your pack up there (and even secure it with a chain and padlock), making it less easy to be spirited away without your knowledge.

Life on Board

It's India for real on board the trains. In 2nd class, unreserved travel can be a nightmare since the trains are often hopelessly crowded, and not only with people – Indians seem unable to travel without the kitchen sink and everything that goes with it. Combined with the crowds, the noise and the confusion there's the discomfort. Fans and lights have a habit of failing during prolonged stops when there's no air moving through the carriage, and toilets can get a bit rough towards the end of a long journey. Worst of all are the stops. Trains seem to stop often, interminably and for no apparent reason.

In 2nd-class reserved it's a great deal better since, in theory, only four people share each bench but there's inevitably the fifth, and sometimes even the sixth, person who gets the others to bunch up so they can get at least part of their bum on the seat. This normally doesn't happen at night or in 1st class, where there are either two or four people to a compartment, and the compartment doors are lockable.

Reservations

In Delhi and Calcutta there are special tourist booking facilities at the main booking offices. These are for any foreign tourists and they make life much easier. Beware of a scam at New Delhi railway station whereby a tout tells you the foreign booking office is 'closed' or under repair. He then leads you to a private agency, where you will be charged up to two times the normal price, and arranges hotels at exorbitant rates.

Reservations can be made up to six months in advance and the longer in advance you make them the better. Your reservation ticket will indicate which carriage and berth you have, and when the train arrives you will find a sheet of paper fixed to each carriage listing passenger names beside their appropriate berth number. Usually this information is also posted on notice boards on the platform. It is Indian railway efficiency at its best.

As at many bus stations, there are separate women's queues, usually with a sign saying 'Ladies' Queue'. Usually the same ticket window handles the male and female queues, taking one at a time. This means that women can go to the front of the queue, next to the first male at the window, and get almost immediate service.

If the train you want is fully booked, it's often possible to get an RAC (Reservation Against Cancellation) ticket. This entitles you to board the train and have seating accommodation. Once the train is under way, the TTE (Travelling Ticket Examiner) will find a berth for you, but it may take an hour or more. This is different from a waitlisted ticket, as the latter does not give you the right to board the train (should you be so cheeky you can be 'detrained and fined'). The hassle with RAC tickets is that you will probably get split up if there are two or more of you.

If you've not had the time to get a reservation or been unable to get one, it's worth just getting on the train in any reserved carriage. Although there's the risk of a small fine for 'ticketless travel', most TTEs are sympathetic. If there are spare berths/seats they'll allot you one, and charge the normal fare plus reservation fee. If all the berths/seats are already reserved, you'll simply be banished to the crush and confusion in the unreserved carriages. This trick only works well for day travel. At night, sleepers are generally booked out well in advance, so if you can't get one (or a RAC ticket) then sitting up in 2nd class is your only choice.

If you plan your trip well ahead, you can avoid all the hassles by booking in advance from abroad. A good travel agent who specialises in India will book and obtain tickets in advance and have them ready for you on arrival.

Refunds

Booked tickets are refundable but cancellation fees apply. If you present the ticket more than one day in advance, a fee of Rs 10 to Rs 30 applies, depending on the class. Up to four hours before, you lose 25% of the ticket value; up to three to 12 hours after departure (depending on the distance of the ticketed journey) you lose 50%. Any later than that and you can keep the ticket as a souvenir.

Tickets for unreserved travel can be refunded up to three hours after the departure of the train, and the only penalty is a Rs 2 per passenger fee.

When presenting your ticket for a refund, you are officially entitled to go straight to the head of the queue, the rationale being that the berth/seat you are surrendering may be just the one required by the next person in the queue.

Getting a Space Despite Everything

If you want a sleeper and there are none left then it's time to try and break into the quotas. Ask the stationmaster, often a helpful man who speaks English, if there is a tourist quota, station quota or if there is a VIP quota. This last option is often a good bet because VIPs rarely turn up to use their quotas.

If all that fails, then you're going to be travelling unreserved and that can be no fun at all. To ease the pain, get yourself some expert help. For, say, Rs 10 baksheesh you can get a porter who will absolutely ensure that you get a seat if it's humanly possible. If it's a train starting from your station, the key to success is to be on the train before it arrives at the departure platform. Your porter will do just that, so when it rolls up you simply stroll on board and take the seat he has warmed for you.

Women can ask about the Ladies' Compartments which many trains have and are often a refuge from the crowds in other compartments.

Railway Stations

Delhi Delhi is an important railway centre and an excellent place to make bookings. There is a special foreign tourist booking office upstairs in New Delhi railway station. This is the place to go if you want a tourist-quota allocation. It gets very busy and crowded, and it can take up to an hour to get served. If you make bookings here, tickets

must be paid for in foreign currency, and your change will be given in rupees.

The main ticket office is on Chelmsford Rd between New Delhi railway station and Connaught Place. This place is well organised, but incredibly busy. Take a numbered ticket from the counter as you enter the building, and then wait at the allotted window. Even with 50 computerised terminals, it can take up to an hour to get served. It's best to arrive first thing in the morning, or when it reopens after lunch. The office is open from 7.45 am to 1.30 pm and 2 to 9 pm Monday to Saturday. On Sunday it's open until 1.50 pm only.

Remember that there are two main railway stations in Delhi – Delhi railway station in Old Delhi, and New Delhi railway station at Pahar Ganj. New Delhi is much closer to Connaught Place, and if you're departing from the Old Delhi railway station you should allow adequate time to wind your way through the traffic snarls of Old Delhi. Between the Old Delhi and New Delhi railway stations you can take the No 6 bus for just Rs 1, or catch a rickshaw.

There are railway retiring rooms at both stations, with prices for both 24 hour and 12 hour periods. At the Old Delhi railway station, the charges are Rs 25 for a dorm bed, and Rs 100 for a double room. At New Delhi railway station it's Rs 45 in a dorm, Rs 100 in a double and Rs 150 for a double with air-con.

Calcutta Calcutta has two major railway stations. Howrah, on the west bank of the Hooghly River, handles most trains into the city, but if you're going north to New Jalpaiguri for the West Bengal hills and Sikkim, then the trains leave from Sealdah railway station on the east side of the Hooghly.

The tourist railway booking office is on the 1st floor at 6 Fairlie Place, near BBD Bagh. It's fully computerised and has a tourist quota but can be very crowded with foreigners. It's open Monday to Saturday from 9 am to 1 pm and 1.30 to 4 pm, and on Sunday between 9 am and 2 pm.

There is another booking office nearby

where you can book services which don't originate from Calcutta. It's at 14 Strand Rd, and has a satellite link. Here you can buy advance tickets on routes into and out of Delhi, Madras and Mumbai. Bookings can be made up to 60 days before departure for all trains apart from the *Shatabdi Express*, for which bookings are only open within 15 days of departure.

Both these places attract long queues and the staff at Fairlie Place office demand to see exchange certificates if you pay in rupees. There are other computerised booking offices which may be better for advance tickets out of Calcutta. The office at Tollygunge metro station is easy to get to and never seems to be very busy.

If you've just flown into Calcutta, it might be worth checking the railway reservation desk at the airport as they have an air-travellers' quota for same-day or next-day travel on some services.

There are railway retiring rooms at both stations.

Trains to the Hills

Jammu & Kashmir There is a daily express service to Jammu, the *Shalimar Express*, which leaves Delhi at 4.10 pm, arriving in Jammu at 6.15 am. Fares are Rs 145/480 in 2nd/1st class. While there are other services to Jammu, this is the only service that arrives early enough to connect with early buses travelling onward to Srinagar.

Himachal Pradesh Many travellers opt for the buses when travelling to Himachal Pradesh, but for Dalhousie or Dharamsala (for McLeod Ganj), it's possible to travel overnight by train to Pathankot, in the Punjab, from where it is only 3½ hours by bus to either of these hill stations. It's a longer trip than on the bus, but if you find you simply can't sleep on the buses, it can offer a good alternative. The *Jammu Tawi Mail* departs Delhi at 9 pm, arriving into Pathankot the following morning at 7.20 am. It costs Rs 127/421 in 2nd/1st class.

The *Himalayan Queen*, which departs Delhi at 6 am, arrives in Kalka in time to connect with the narrow-gauge Kalka-Shimla train, which departs Kalka at 10.15 am.

Uttarakhand The fastest train to Haridwar and Dehra Dun, gateways for the Garhwal district of the UP hills, is the *Shatabdi Express*, which departs Delhi at 6 am, arriving into Haridwar at 10.45 am and Dehra Dun at 11.45 am. Fares to Dehra Dun are Rs 300/600 in 1st class/AC 1st class, and to Haridwar, Rs 270/540. The overnight service is the *Mussoorie Express*, which departs Old Delhi at 10.25 pm arriving into Dehra Dun at 7.50 am, stopping at Haridwar en route. Fares to Dehra Dun are Rs 74/275 in sleeper/1st class. Rishikesh is only 24 km north of Haridwar, and the hill station of Mussoorie lies only 34 km north of Dehra Dun. There are numerous bus services connecting these towns throughout the day.

For the Kumaon district of Uttarakhand, the closest railway station is at Kathgodam, 35 km south of Nainital. There are buses throughout the day between the two centres. The *Ranikhet Express* departs Old Delhi station at 11 pm, arriving into Kathgodam at 6.30 am (Rs 97/403 in 2nd/AC 2nd class). There are also train services to Ramnagar (for the Corbett National Park) via the busy railway junction of Moradabad.

West Bengal Hills & Sikkim The *Darjeeling Mail* departs Sealdah (Calcutta) at 7 pm, arriving into New Jalpaiguri, eight km south of Siliguri, at 7 am (Rs 175/562 in 2nd/1st class). From Siliguri there are numerous modes of transport waiting to whisk you up into the hills, including (when it's operating) the nine hour toy train trip to Darjeeling. See the Getting Around and West Bengal chapters for more details.

The fastest train between Delhi and New Jalpaiguri (1628 km) is the *North East Express*, which takes 33 hours and costs Rs 214/901 in 2nd/1st class.

CAR & MOTORCYCLE

Few people bring their own vehicles to India. If you do decide to bring a car or motorcycle to India it must be brought in under a carnet, a customs document guaranteeing its removal at the end of your stay. Failing to do so will be very expensive.

Rental

Self-drive car rental in India is not widespread, but it is possible. Both Budget and Hertz maintain offices in Delhi and Calcutta. If you don't feel confident about driving on Indian roads (particularly the frequently precipitous and hair-raising roads of the Indian Himalaya), it is easy to hire a car and driver,

either from the local state tourist authority or privately through your hotel. By western standards the cost is quite low, certainly cheaper than a rent-a-car (without driver) in the west. Almost any local taxi will quite happily set off on a long-distance trip in India; enquiring at a taxi rank is the easiest way to find a car – you can also ask your hotel to book one for you although this will cost more. For more information regarding car and motorcycle travel in the Indian Himalaya, see the Getting Around chapter.

Getting Around

AIR

While there are numerous air services between the Indian Himalaya and Delhi and Calcutta (see under Air in the Getting There & Away chapter), there are only a couple of scheduled flights between centres in the hills region. Jagson Airlines has flights between Jubbarhatti airport, 23 km south of Shimla, Bhuntar airport, 10 km south of Kullu, and Gaggal airport, 15 km south of Dharamsala.

Indian Airlines operates daily services between Jammu and Srinagar, and Jammu and Leh. There is a weekly flight between Srinagar and Leh. Note that Lonely Planet recommends that you do not visit Srinagar or Jammu, while the political violence there endures. Archana Airways plans to fly between Leh, Kargil and Delhi.

Addresses and phone numbers of these airlines are included in the Indian Himalaya section of the Getting There & Away chapter. Schedules and prices are included in the Getting There & Away sections of individual chapters.

BUS

Due to the paucity of train services in the Himalayan region, unless you can afford to hire a private vehicle, you'll probably find that you'll spend a good deal of time aboard buses. Between Delhi and the more popular tourist regions such as the hill stations, there is often a choice between luxury two by two seat (2x2) services and ordinary, rattle-you-silly services. However, between the hill stations and up into the more remote regions, there's little choice other than between being squashed inside buses which would be rejected by scrap-metal merchants in some countries, or successively freezing and sweltering on their roofs.

If the weather's fine, for short trips, travelling on the roof can present a pleasant alternative to the confined conditions inside the bus. Not only is there generally more space up here, but the 360° panoramic views can be truly awe-inspiring. Bear in mind, however, that in matters of hours, you can ascend from sunny valley bottoms to thousands of metres above sea level, so make sure you have warm gear to don when it gets chilly. You should also beware of low-hanging power lines, particularly when the bus halts and you stand up to clamber down off the roof. The section of road between Manali and Dharamsala is particularly notorious for low-suspended lines, and in 1995, a westerner was electrocuted when he stood up on a bus roof at a *chai* (tea) halt along this route. Fortunately his life was saved by timely first aid, but remember to be vigilant. Also beware of low branches – if your fellow passengers suddenly collectively dive for the floor, they are probably not praying to Mecca, but are sparing themselves from being brained by a fast approaching branch. Travelling on bus roofs is not possible along the Parbati Valley or in Lahaul & Spiti and Kinnaur, due to overhanging rocks. The roads in these regions are literally carved from solid rock.

Ordinary buses generally have five seats across, although if there are only five people sitting in them consider yourself lucky! There are usually mounds of baggage in the aisles and chickens under seats. These buses tend to be frustratingly slow, are usually in an advanced state of decrepitude and stop frequently – often for seemingly no reason – and for long periods, and can take forever. They're certainly colourful and can be an interesting way to travel on short journeys; on longer trips you'll probably wish you'd stayed at home. In the Himalaya, even the longest trips are compensated for by the magnificent scenery – you'll spend half your time agonising over the centimetres which separate you from the abysses which plunge to valley floors hundreds of metres below, and the rest gazing in awe at perennially snow-covered peaks.

Government-operated bus companies operate in each state in the Indian Himalaya, and their services are usually supplemented by privately operated buses – although they may only operate on certain routes and sometimes only during season. Unlike state-operated bus companies, private operators are keen to maximise profits; therefore, maintenance is less and speed more – a dangerous combination. In addition, drivers who would have been pensioned off years before in some countries, reluctant to lose their only source of livelihood, may present an alarming spectacle straining to see through their bifocal lenses.

The thing that foreigners find hardest to cope with on the buses is the music. The Hindi pop music is usually played at maximum volume and seems to screech on and on without end. Requests to turn it down are usually greeted with amusement and complete disbelief. Just as bad are the video movies shown on many deluxe buses. Macho garbage is generally screened, also at full volume, for hours on end. If you're travelling overnight by bus, try to avoid video coaches. If you do have the misfortune to have to catch an overnight bus, you may find you have finally slipped off into a shallow slumber when you are awoken by the blaring of the bus' horn and/or the cassette suddenly turned to an ear-splitting, sleep-shattering volume. If it's any consolation, if you're awake, there's a good chance that the driver is also!

During the pilgrimage season (April to November) in the Garhwal Himalaya, you may find you've joined a group of pilgrims en route to pay homage at the four holy shrines (Char Dham) of Yamunotri, Gangotri, Kedarnath and Badrinath. In this case, you'll be assailed by collective songs in praise of the presiding deities at the shrines, which is not necessarily unpleasant. In the Kumaon district of Uttarakhand (the UP hills), buses usually stop at shrines and temples just outside major towns. The resident *pujari* (person who performs an offering) will pass a tray of *prasaad* (sacred food offerings) through the window, which will be passed from passenger to passenger, who will take a portion and smear their forehead with bright orange or red *tikka* powder, and leave a small donation.

Road Conditions

The roads in the Indian Himalaya, although remarkable feats of engineering, are, with a few exceptions (notably in the hills region of West Bengal), enough to induce terror in even the hardiest traveller. Roads are frequently unsealed, always narrow and invariably windy, and perch precariously on the sides of valleys, often with precipitous drops which plunge hundreds of metres to valley floors.

During the monsoon season (mid-June to September, with some regional variations), roads can be washed away or rendered impassable by landslides. Flexibility is the key to travelling in the Indian Himalaya during the monsoon, as the best laid plans can be hopelessly sent awry, and you may find yourself stranded for days.

In Sikkim and parts of Himachal Pradesh, frequent roadblocks have given rise to the institution of 'transshipping'. This simply means that you'll be dumped on one side of a landslide over which you and your fellow passengers will have to scramble, laden with your gear, where a veritable convoy of vehicles on the opposite side will be waiting to ferry you onwards to your destination. It's not unusual for a small settlement of chai stalls and *dhabas* (cheap restaurants) to spring up on either side of the roadblock which provide hot chai and sustenance to drenched and mud-caked passengers.

Labourers working to clear blocked roads are a ubiquitous sight throughout the Himalaya. Men, women and children, usually from the poorer areas down on the plains, frequently from Bihar, engage in the backbreaking and seemingly never-ending task of keeping the major highways of the Himalaya open to traffic.

Getting a Seat

If there are two of you, work out a bus boarding plan where one of you can guard the gear while the other storms the bus in search of a seat. The other accepted method is to pass a newspaper or article of clothing through the open window and place it on an empty seat, or ask a passenger to do it for you. Having made your 'reservation' you can then board the bus after things have simmered down. This method rarely fails.

Catching a bus involves comparatively little predeparture hassle. You can, however, often make advance reservations at bus stations for a small additional fee. You may have to ask several people before you locate the correct ticket counter, and then join the inevitable queue. A prepurchased ticket should result in a confirmed seat, and you can request a window or aisle seat. However, in the remote areas of Ladakh, Kinnaur and Lahaul & Spiti, it is every man, woman, child, goat and chicken for themselves!

Privately operated luxury coach services can be booked through travel agencies in popular tourist destinations such as hill stations. Scheduled services on popular routes are often advertised on boards outside the agency.

Baggage

Baggage is generally carried for free on the roof, so it's an idea to take a few precautions. Make sure it's tied on properly and that nobody dumps a tin trunk on top of your (relatively) fragile backpack. At times a tarpaulin will be tied across the baggage – make sure it covers your gear adequately. Some travellers even chain their pack to the roof rack – not a bad idea, although thieves have been known to simply slash packs with a knife and remove the contents. Carry your valuables on board with you. If you're travelling in the Indian Himalaya during the monsoon season, no matter how carefully you've covered your pack, there's a good chance that it will arrive sodden and drenched at your destination. Try to insist that it be placed inside the bus, even if this means you have to sit cross-legged on top of it! A drenched pack is no joke, and getting your gear dry during the monsoon will be virtually impossible – it will probably go mouldy first. If your pack must travel on the roof, cover it with a plastic bag or sheet.

Keep an eye on your bags at chai stops. There's not much you can do if potential thieves are riding on board the top of the bus. Having a large, heavy-duty bag into which your pack will fit can be a good idea, not only for bus travel but also for air travel.

If someone carries your bag onto the roof, expect to pay a few rupees for the service.

Toilet Stops

On long-distance bus trips, chai stops can be far too frequent or, conversely, agonisingly infrequent. Long-distance trips can be a real hassle for women travellers – toilet facilities are generally inadequate to say the least. Forget about modesty and do what the local women do – wander a few yards off or find a convenient bush.

TRAIN

Due to the precipitous terrain, there are few railway lines in the Himalayan regions, and those that do exist are all narrow-gauge services, meaning long, slow hauls between destinations which can be much more speedily accessed on bus services. Nevertheless, if time is not a problem, travelling along even part of these routes can be a memorable experience, and while you might disembark at your destination covered in soot and vowing never to repeat the journey again, you are guaranteed some spectacular scenery, and you'll marvel at the ingenuity of the early engineers who planned and laid these tracks.

When it's running, you can't beat the toy train trip from New Jalpaiguri or Siliguri, on the West Bengal plains, up to the hill station of Darjeeling. Construction of the line commenced in 1879, and in 1881, was finally completed through to Darjeeling. The train navigates some extraordinary loops and steep grades, covering the 90-odd km in about nine hours.

From Pathankot, in the north of the Punjab, a narrow-gauge line wends its way through the Kangra Valley to Jogindernagar, a trip taking some nine hours, passing en route the ancient capital of the valley at Kangra and the township of Baijnath, with an ancient temple dedicated to Shiva as Lord of the Physicians. The terminus at Joginder-nagar must be one of the most picturesque stations in all of India, and it's worth staying here at the railway retiring rooms before heading towards Mandi and the Kullu Valley.

The third narrow-gauge line serves Shimla, the capital of Himachal Pradesh, starting at Kalka, in Punjab & Haryana, and covering the 96 km in about five hours.

For more information on these trips, see the Himachal Pradesh and West Bengal Hills chapters for more details.

CAR

Renting

While it's possible to rent cars in major centres such as Delhi and Calcutta, if you're planning to head beyond the relatively easily accessible hill stations, it's probably not a good idea. Not only do road conditions vary from poor to impassable, roads can be treacherous, and you'll be liable for any damage sustained by the vehicle. In addition, insurance may not cover damage sustained by the vehicle in the more remote regions of the Indian Himalaya.

The hill stations can be easily accessed by bus, with good connections from airports and railway stations. Nevertheless, if you are still considering hiring a vehicle, self-drive costs around Rs 500 per 24 hours (150 km minimum) plus Rs 4 per extra km. Fuel is extra and a deposit of Rs 1000 is payable (returnable if there's no damage whatsoever to the car – a scratch constitutes 'damage', so check the car over thoroughly before you take possession of it).

All the above price examples assume you'll be driving an Ambassador. These sturdy old beasts have been known to traverse some pretty rugged country, but during the monsoon period in the higher reaches of Uttarakhand and beyond the hill stations in Himachal Pradesh, and in Ladakh and Zanskar, forget it – you'll need a four-wheel drive vehicle, and, unless you have an advance drivers' diploma in mud scrambling, you're safest bet is to hire an experienced driver who knows the terrain.

Long-distance car hire with driver is becoming an increasingly popular way of getting around parts of India. With costs shared among say, four people, it's not overly expensive and you have the flexibility to go where you want to when you want to. It is easy to hire a car and driver, either from the local state tourist authority, at a taxi stand or taxi union office, or privately through your hotel. By western standards the cost is quite low, certainly cheaper than a rent-a-car (without driver) in the west. Almost any local taxi will quite happily set off on a long-distance trip in India. Enquiring at a taxi rank is the easiest way to find a car – you can also ask your hotel to book one for you although this will cost slightly more.

A long-distance trip with driver is either 'one way', in which case it costs Rs 6 per km, or a 'running trip', which costs Rs 3 per km. This is because the one-way fare is costed on the basis of returning empty to the starting point. A running trip means a minimum of 200 km a day, so if you take a car for four days it's going to cost at least Rs 2400 (800 km at Rs 3 per km). If you're going to drive 200 km from A to B on day one, spend two days in B, then drive 200 km back to A on day four, it's exactly the same cost to take a taxi each way as to take one taxi and have the driver wait for you for two days. And it will be cheaper to take a taxi each way if 'over-night charges' apply. Overnight charges will be in addition to the hire fee. In Ladakh, for example the overnight fee is Rs 250.

Buying

Buying a car is naturally expensive in India and not worth the effort unless you intend to stay for months.

On the Road

Because of the extreme congestion in the cities and the narrow, bumpy and precipitous roads in the hills, driving is often a slow, stop-start process – hard on you, the car and fuel economy. Service is so-so in India, parts and tyres not always easy to obtain, though there are plenty of puncture-repair places.

Road Safety

In India there are 155 road deaths daily – 56,000 or so a year – which is an astonishing total in relation to the number of vehicles on the road. In the USA, for instance, there are 43,000 road fatalities per year, but it also has more than 20 times the number of vehicles.

The reasons for the high death rate in India are numerous and many of them fairly obvious – starting with the congestion on the roads and the equal congestion in vehicles. When a bus runs off the road there are plenty of people stuffed inside to get injured, and it's unlikely too many of them will be able to escape in a hurry. One newspaper article stated that 'most accidents are caused by brake failure or the steering wheel getting free'!

Many of those killed are pedestrians involved in hit-and-run accidents. The propensity to disappear after the incident is not wholly surprising – lynch mobs can assemble remarkably quickly, even when the driver is not at fault!

Most accidents are caused by trucks, for on Indian roads might is right and trucks are the biggest, heaviest and mightiest. You either get out of their way or get run down. As with so many Indian vehicles, they're likely to be grossly overloaded and not in the best of condition. Trucks are actually licensed and taxed to carry a load 25% more than the maximum recommended by the manufacturer. It's staggering to see the number of truck wrecks by the sides of the national highways, and these aren't old accidents, but ones which have obviously happened in the last 24 hours or so – if they haven't been killed, quite often the driver and crew will be sitting around, wondering what to do next.

The karma theory of driving also helps to push up the statistics – it's not so much the vehicle which collides with you as the events of your previous life which caused the accident. Therefore, the driver takes less responsibility for road safety than might normally be expected.

If you are driving yourself, you need to be extremely vigilant at all times. At night there are unilluminated cars and ox carts, and in the daytime there are fearless bicycle riders and hordes of pedestrians. Day and night there are the crazy truck drivers to contend with. Indeed, at night, it's best to avoid driving at all along any major trunk route unless you're prepared to get off the road completely every time a truck is coming in the opposite direction! The other thing you

---

Some Indian Rules of the Road

Drive on the Left Theoretically vehicles keep to the left in India – as in Japan, the UK or Australia. In practice, most vehicles keep to the middle of the road on the basis that there are fewer potholes in the middle than on the sides. When any other vehicle is encountered the lesser vehicle should cower to the side. Misunderstandings as to status can have unfortunate consequences.

Overtaking In India it is not necessary to ascertain that there is space to complete the overtaking manoeuvre before pulling out. Overtaking can be attempted on blind corners, on the way up steep hills or in the face of oncoming traffic. Smaller vehicles unexpectedly encountered in mid-manoeuvre can be expected to swerve apologetically out of the way. If a larger vehicle is encountered it is to be hoped that the overtakee will slow, pull off or otherwise make room for the overtaker.

Use of Horn Although vehicles can be driven with bald tyres or nonexistent brakes, it is imperative that the horn be in superb working order. Surveys during the research for this edition revealed that the average driver uses the horn 10 to 20 times per km, so a 100 km trip can involve 2000 blasts of the horn. In any case the horn should be checked for its continued loud operation at least every 100m. Signs prohibiting use of horns are not to be taken seriously. ∎

have to contend with at night is the eccentric way in which headlights are used – a combination of full beam and totally off (dipped beams are virtually unheard of). A loud horn definitely helps since the normal driving technique is to put your hand firmly on the horn, close your eyes and plough through regardless. Vehicles always have the right of way over pedestrians and bigger vehicles always have the right of way over smaller ones.

MOTORCYCLE

The motorcycle section is based largely on information originally contributed by intrepid Britons Ken Twyford and Gerald Smewing, with updates from Jim and Lucy Amos.

Travelling around India by motorcycle has become increasingly popular in recent years, and the number of intrepid souls who have covered the long northward haul to Leh is increasing every year. Motorcycling offers the freedom to go when and where you like – making it the ideal way to get to grips with the vastness that is India.

What to Bring

An international driving licence is not mandatory, but is handy to have.

Helmets should definitely be brought with you. Although Indian helmets are cheap, it is often hard to find one that fits well, and the quality is suspect. If required, leathers, gloves, boots, waterproofs and other protective gear should also be brought from your home country.

It is always a good idea, and vital in remote areas, to carry spare tubes and chains. A tent and sleeping bag are handy where accommodation is scarce, and essential in areas where you may be caught in bad weather (which can happen at any time of the year in some parts).

A few small bags will be a lot easier to carry than one large rucksack.

Regulations & Road Rules

Regulations may change, but currently Indian motorbike companies and traffic authorities need little, if any evidence that you have a local or foreign licence for any vehicle, or that you can even ride a motorcycle. In Delhi, helmets

are required for all drivers (but not pillion passengers), but are rarely used; helmets are not compulsory (but are advisable) in the Indian Himalayan regions.

Despite stated permit regulations, travel on a motorcycle in the restricted regions of Ladakh, Kinnaur and Lahaul & Spiti *is* allowed, either alone or in a group of less than four. However, in remote regions, travelling with a passenger, or even better, with another biker, is advisable.

Renting

Motorcycles can be rented from companies in Delhi for a negotiable price, including insurance, for about Rs 6000 per month, or from Rs 175 to Rs 250 per day. (In contrast, a Vespa scooter will cost about Rs 500 per day in Leh.) Rental companies in Delhi will want a substantial bond of about US$500 – some unused travellers' cheques will probably do.

Buying & Selling

Motorcycles can be bought and sold, or exchanged with those of other foreigners in major travel centres such as Goa, and in any major town – although the choice and prices are likely to be better in larger places like Delhi, Mumbai (Bombay) and Calcutta. In Delhi, the area around Hari Singh Nalwa St, Karol Bagh, is full of places selling, buying and renting motorcycles. One place recommended by travellers is Inder Motors (☎ 572-5879) 1744/55 Hari Singh Nalwa St.

As an example, in Delhi or Goa (and possibly Leh, but don't count on it) you could probably pick up a 1988 Enfield 500cc for US$500 to US$750 depending on its condition and your bargaining power.

To buy a new bike, you'll have to have a local address and be a resident foreign national. However, unless the dealer you are buying from is totally devoid of imagination and contacts, this presents few problems. When buying second-hand, all you need to do is give an address.

New bikes are generally purchased through a showroom. When buying second-hand it is best to engage the services of an 'autoconsultant'. These people act as go-betweens to bring buyers and sellers together. They will usually be able to show you a number of machines to suit your price bracket. These agents can be found by enquiring, or may sometimes advertise on their shop fronts.

For around Rs 500, which usually covers a bribe to officials, they will assist you in transferring the ownership papers through the bureaucracy. Without their help this could take a couple of weeks.

The overall appearance of the bike doesn't seem to affect the price greatly. Dents and scratches don't reduce the cost much, and added extras don't increase it by much.

When the time comes to sell the bike, don't appear too anxious to get rid of it. Don't hang around in one town too long, as word gets around the autoconsultants and the offers will get smaller as the days go by. If you get a reasonable offer, grab it. Regardless of which bike it is, you'll be told it's the 'least popular in India' and other such tales.

Ownership Papers A needless hint perhaps, but do not part with your money until you have the ownership papers, receipt and affidavit signed by a magistrate authorising the owner (as recorded in the ownership papers) to sell the machine. Not to mention the keys to the bike and the bike itself!

Each state has a different set of ownership transfer formalities. Get assistance from the agent you're buying the machine through or from one of the many 'attorneys' hanging around under tin roofs by the Motor Vehicles Office. They will charge you a fee of up to Rs 300, which will consist largely of a bribe to expedite matters.

Alternatively you could go to one of the many typing clerk services and request them to type out the necessary forms, handling the matter cheaply yourself – but with no guarantee of a quick result.

Check that your name has been recorded in the ownership book and stamped and signed by the department head. If you intend to sell your motorcycle in another state then you will need a 'No Objections Certificate'.

This confirms your ownership and is issued by the Motor Vehicles Department in the state of purchase, so get it immediately when transferring ownership papers to your name. The standard form can be typed up for a few rupees, or more speedily and expensively through one of the many attorneys. This document is vital if you are going to sell the bike in another state.

Insurance & Tax As in most countries, it is compulsory to have third-party insurance. The New India Assurance Company or the National Insurance Company are just two of a number of companies who can provide it. The cost for fully comprehensive insurance is Rs 720 for 12 months, and this also covers you in Nepal.

Road tax is paid when the bike is bought new. This is valid for the life of the machine and is transferred to the new owner when the bike changes hands.

On the Road

In the event of an accident, call the police straight away, and don't move anything until the police have seen exactly where and how everything ended up. One foreigner reported spending three days in jail on suspicion of being involved in an accident, when all he'd done was taken a child to hospital from the scene of an accident.

Don't try to cover too much territory in one day. As such a high level of concentration is needed to survive, long days are tiring and dangerous. On the busy national highways expect to average 50 km/h without stops; on smaller roads, where driving conditions are worse, 10 km/h is not an unrealistic average. On the whole you can expect to cover between 100 km and 150 km in a day on good roads. In the mountains, reduce this by half to one-third.

Night driving should be avoided at all costs. If you think driving in daylight is difficult enough, imagine what it's like at night when there's the added hazard of half the vehicles being inadequately lit (or not lit at all), not to mention the breakdowns in the middle of the road.

Which Motorbike?

The Yezdi 250 Classic is a cheap and basic bike. It's a rugged machine, and one which you often see in rural areas.

One of the Enfield Bullet series, usually 350cc or 500cc, is often the most popular choice for foreigners because the Bullets are easier to buy and sell, and spare parts are generally readily available. Attractions are the traditional design, thumping engine sound, and the price, which is not much more than the new 100cc Japanese bikes. They're wonderfully durable bikes, easy to maintain and economical to run, but mechanically they're a bit 'hit and miss', largely because of poorly engineered parts and inferior materials – valves and tappets are the main problem areas. Another drawback is the lack of an effective front brake – the small drum brake is a joke, totally inadequate for what is quite a heavy machine. The Bullet is also available in a 500cc single-cylinder version. It has a functional front brake and has 12-volt electrics which are superior to the 350's six-volt. If you opt for a 350cc, consider paying the Rs 4000 extra to have the 500cc front wheel fitted.

If you are buying a new Enfield with the intention of shipping it back home, it's definitely worth opting for the 500cc as it has features – such as folding rear foot-rest and longer exhaust pipe – which most other countries would require. The emission control regulations in some places, such as California, are so strict that there is no way these bikes would be legal. You may be able to get around this by buying an older bike, as the regulations often only apply to new machines. Make sure you check all this out before you go lashing out on a new Enfield, only to find it unregisterable at home. The price is around Rs 40,000, or Rs 45,000 for the 500cc model.

The Rajdoot 350 is an imported Yamaha 350cc. It's well engineered, fast and has good brakes. Disadvantages are that it's relatively uneconomical to run, and spares are hard to come by. These bikes are also showing their age badly as they haven't been made for some years now. They cost around Rs 12,000 to Rs 15,000. ∎

Repairs & Maintenance

Anyone who can handle a screwdriver and spanner in India can be called a mechanic, or *mistri*, so be careful. If you have any mechanical knowledge it may be better to buy your own tools and learn how to do your own repairs. This will save a lot of arguments over prices. In remote areas, do-it-yourself is essential. If you are getting repairs done by someone, don't leave the premises while the work is being done or you may find that good parts have been ripped off your bike and replaced with bodgy old ones.

Original spare parts bought from an 'Authorised Dealer' can be rather expensive compared to the copies available from your spare-parts-*wallah* (literally 'man').

If you buy an older machine you would do well to check and tighten all nuts and bolts every few days. Indian roads and engine vibration tend to work things loose and constant checking could save you rupees and trouble. Check the engine and gearbox oil level regularly. With the quality of oil it is advisable to change it and clean the oil filter every couple of thousand km.

Punctures Chances are you'll be requiring the services of a puncture-wallah (*punkuchawallah* in Hindi) at least once a week. They are found everywhere, often in the most surprising places, but it's advisable to at least have tools sufficient to remove your own wheel and take it to the puncture-wallah.

Given the hassles of constant flat tyres, it's worth lashing out on new tyres if you buy a second-hand bike with worn tyres. A new rear tyre for an Enfield costs around Rs 500.

Fuel

Petrol, at Rs 18 per litre, is expensive relative to the west and when compared to the cost of living in India. Diesel is much cheaper at around Rs 7.50 per litre. Petrol is usually readily available in all larger towns and along the main roads so there is no need to carry spare fuel along these routes, but bring your own along roads in remote regions. In the more remote areas, petrol supplies are often very scarce, and what little there is may be allocated for 'essential vehicles' – so take enough to get from one major town to another. (Some maps, such as those produced by Nest & Wings, indicate which places have petrol supplies.)

Should you run out, try flagging down a passing car (not a truck or bus since they use diesel) and begging for some. Most Indians are willing to let you have some if you have a hose or syphon and a container. Alternatively, hitch a truck ride to the nearest petrol station.

Road Safety

In many Himalayan regions, the roads are permanently rocky, muddy, wet, snowy or dusty, so wear wet weather gear, including a good jacket and boots – and have some protection against the sun. In case of a breakdown, you and your bike may be able to hitch a lift on a passing truck for a negotiable fee, but check how the driver ties up your bike in the back of the truck. Travelling with a passenger or another biker is advisable.

One final piece of advice: be very, very careful – roads are often windy, treacherous, narrow and rough, and most other drivers are certifiable maniacs.

BICYCLE

The cycling information from Ann Sorrel includes updates from various travellers. Every day millions of Indians pedal along the country's roads; for stalwart cyclists, a touring trip to the Himalaya is not out of the question. Nevertheless, long-distance and mountain cycling is not for the faint of heart or weak of knee. You'll need physical endurance to cope with the roads and the climate, plus you'll face cultural challenges – 'the people factor'.

Useful Information

Before you set out, read some books on bicycle touring such as the Sierra Club's *The Bike Touring Manual* by Rob van de Plas (Bicycle Books, 1993). Cycling magazines provide useful information including listings for bicycle tour operators and the addresses of spare-parts suppliers. They're also good places to look for a riding companion.

For a real feel of the adventure of bike touring in strange places read Dervla Murphy's classic *Full Tilt – From Ireland to India on a Bike*, now available in paperback, or Lloyd Sumner's *The Long Ride*, and *Riding the Mountains Down* (subtitled 'A Journey by Bicycle to Kathmandu') by Bettina Selby (Unwin Publications, 1984).

The International Bicycle Fund (IBF) (☎ (206) 628-9314), 4887 Columbia Drive South, Seattle, Washington 98108-1919, USA has two publications which may help you prepare for your cycling adventure. These are *Selecting and Preparing a Bike for Travel in Remote Areas* and *Flying With Your Bike*. Each is US$2 plus postage and handling (in the USA: US$1 for first item and US$0.50 for each additional item; other countries: US$2 for first item and US$1 for each additional item).

The IBT are also happy to help prospective long-distance cyclists with information and advice.

Using Your Own Bicycle

If you are planning to tour the Himalaya by bicycle, forget a touring bicycle – you'll need a sturdy mountain bike. Mountain bikes are especially suited to countries such as India. Their smaller, sturdier construction makes them more manoeuvrable, less prone to damage, and allows you to tackle rocky, muddy roads unsuitable for lighter machines.

I travelled 22,000 miles in South Asia by bicycle in 1982-83. I wish I had a mountain bike then. I couldn't venture down the Kargil-Padum (Zanskar) road, nor could I avail myself of all sorts of opportunities for single-track riding.

A friend later went with a mountain bike and pedalled to Everest Base Camp. While I discourage mountain biking on foot trails because of environmental degradation, a mountain bike lets you move off paved roads and onto less-used routes, confident that the machine will withstand the rougher terrain.

Ann Sorrel

Bringing your own bicycle does have disadvantages. Your machine is likely to be a real curiosity and subject to much pushing, pulling and probing. If you can't tolerate people touching your bicycle, don't bring it to India.

Spare Parts If you bring a bicycle to India, prepare for the contingencies of part replacement or repair. Bring spare tyres, tubes, patch kits, chassis, cables, freewheels and spokes. Ensure you have a working knowledge of your machine. Bring all necessary tools with you, as well as a compact bike manual with diagrams in case the worst happens and you need to fix a rear derailleur or some other strategic part. Indian mechanics can work wonders and illustrations help overcome the language barrier.

Most of all, be ready to make do and improvise.

Roads don't have paved shoulders and are very dusty, so keep your chain lubricated.

Although India is officially metricated, tools and bike parts follow 'standard' or 'imperial' measurements. Don't expect to find tyres for 700cc rims, although 27 x 1¼ tyres are produced in India by Dunlop and Sawney. Some mountain bike tyres are available but the quality is dubious. Indian bicycle pumps cater to a tube valve different from the Presta and Schraeder valves commonly used in the west. If you're travelling with Presta valves (most high-pressure 27 x 1¼ tubes) bring a Schraeder (car type) adaptor. In India you can buy a local pump adaptor, which means you'll have an adaptor on your adaptor. Bring your own pump, as well; most Indian pumps require two or three people to get air down the leaky cable.

In major cities, Japanese tyres and parts (derailleurs, freewheels, chains) are available, but pricey – although so is postage, and transit time can be considerable. If you receive bike parts from abroad, beware of exorbitant customs charges. Say you want the goods as 'in transit' to avoid these charges. They may list the parts in your passport!

There are a number of shops where you may locate parts. Try the cycle bazaar in the old city around Esplanade Rd, Delhi and Nundy & Company, Bentinck St, Calcutta. Alternatively, take your bicycle to a cycle market and ask around – someone will know which shop is likely to have things for your 'special' cycle. Beware of Taiwanese imitations and do watch out for tyres which may have been sitting collecting dust for years.

Luggage Your cycle luggage should be as strong, durable and waterproof as possible. I don't recommend a set with lots of zippers, as this makes pilfering easier. As you'll be frequently detaching luggage when taking your bike to your room, a set designed for easy removal from the racks is a must: the fewer items, the better. (*Never* leave your cycle in the lobby or outside your hotel – take it to bed with you!)

Bike luggage that can easily be reassembled into a backpack is also available, just the thing when you want to park your bike and go by train or foot.

Theft If you're using an imported bike, try to avoid losing your pump (and the water bottle from your frame) – their novelty makes them particularly attractive to thieves. Don't leave anything on your bike that can easily be removed when it's unattended.

Don't be paranoid about theft – outside the major cities it would be well-nigh impossible for a thief to resell your bike, as it would stand out too much. And not many folk understand quick-release levers on wheels. Your bike is probably safer in India than in western cities.

Buying & Selling an Indian Bicycle
Finding an Indian bike is no problem: every large town will have at least a couple of cycle shops. Shop around for prices and remember to bargain. Try to get a few extras – bell, stand, spare tube – thrown in. There are many brands of Indian clunkers – Hero, Atlas, BSA, Raleigh, Bajaj, Avon – but they all follow the same basic, sturdy design. A few mountain-bike lookalikes have recently

come on the market, but they have no gears. Raleigh is considered the finest quality, followed by BSA which has a big line of models including some sporty jobs. Hero and Atlas both claim to be the biggest seller. Look for the cheapest or the one with the snazziest plate label.

Once you've decided on a bike, you have a choice of luggage carriers – mostly the rat-trap type varying only in size, price and strength. There's a wide range of saddles available but all are equally bum-breaking. A stand is certainly a useful addition and a bell or airhorn is a necessity. An advantage of buying a new bike is that the brakes actually work. Centre-pull and side-pull brakes are also available but at extra cost and may actually make the bike more difficult to sell. The average Indian will prefer the standard model.

Reselling the bike is no problem. Ask the proprietor of your lodge if they know anyone who is interested in buying a bike. Negotiate a price and do the deal personally or through the hotel. Most people will be only too willing to help you. Count on losing a couple of hundred rupees or about 30%, depending on local prices. Retail bike stores are not usually interested in buying or selling second-hand bikes. A better bet would be a bike-hire shop, which may be interested in expanding its fleet.

Spare Parts As there are so many repair 'shops' (some consist of a pump, a box of tools, a tube of rubber solution and a water pan under a tree) there is no need to carry spare parts, especially as you'll only own the bike for a few weeks or months. Just take a roll of tube-patch rubber, a tube of Dunlop patch glue, two tyre irons and the wonderful 'universal' Indian bike spanner, which fits all the nuts. There are plenty of puncture-wallahs in all towns and villages who will patch tubes for a couple of rupees, so chances are you won't have to fix a puncture yourself anyway. Besides, Indian tyres are pretty heavy duty, so with luck you won't get a flat.

On the Road

The 'people factor' makes a bike ride in India rewarding and frustrating. Those with Indian bikes are less likely to be 'mobbed' by curious onlookers. A tea stop with an imported bike can attract a crowd of 50 men and boys eagerly commenting on the bike's operation – one points to the water-bottle saying 'petrol', another twists the shifter lever saying 'clutch', another squeezes a tyre saying 'tubeless' or 'airless', yet others nod knowingly as 'gear system', 'automatic' and 'racing bike' are mouthed. In some areas you'll even get 'disco bike'!

The worst scenario is stopping in a town centre and looking up as you are pushing off to find rickshaws, cyclists and pedestrians all blocking your way! At times, the crowd may be unruly – schoolboys, especially. If the crowd is too big, call over a *lathi* (large stick)-wielding policeman. The best advice is to keep pedalling; don't turn around or stop, and don't leave your bike and chase them, as this will only incite them further. Appeal to adults to discipline them. Children, especially boys seven to 13 years old, are unruly and dangerous in crowds. Avoid riding past a boys' school at recess.

Routes

You can go anywhere on a bike that you would on trains and buses with the added pleasure of seeing all the places in between.

Try to avoid the major highways up north like the NH1 through Haryana, and the NH2 – the Grand Trunk Road between Delhi and Calcutta. They're plagued by speeding buses and trucks. A basic knowledge of Hindi will help you to translate the signs, although at least one marker in five will be in English.

Another option is to follow canal and river paths. It's also possible in some areas to bike along railway tracks on maintenance roads. Do make enquiries before venturing off road.

I once travelled most of a day before discovering the reason I had not encountered any pedestrian traffic: a major railway bridge was down and no ferry in service to ford the raging waters!

Ann Sorrel

If mountain bicycling is your goal give serious consideration to Himachal Pradesh.

Crossing international borders with a bicycle is relatively uncomplicated. The Himalayan region has border crossings with Nepal and Bangladesh. Unlike a car or motorcycle, papers need not be presented. Do not be surprised, however, if the bike is thoroughly inspected for contraband!

Distances
If you've never before cycled long distances, start with 20 to 40 km a day. In the hills region, from 10 to 20 km a day is respectable. You can increase this as you gain stamina and confidence. Cycling long distances is 80% determination and 20% perspiration. Don't be ashamed to get off and push the bike up steep hills. For an eight-hour pedal a serious cyclist and interested tourist will average 125 to 150 km a day on undulating plains, or 80 to 100 km in mountainous areas.

Accommodation
There's no need to bring a tent. Inexpensive lodges are widely available and there are plenty of tea stalls and restaurants (called 'hotels'). When you want to eat, ask for a 'hotel'. When you want a room ask for a 'lodge'. On major highways stop at dhabas, the Indian version of a truck stop. The one with the most trucks parked in front generally has the best food (or serves alcohol). Dhabas have *charpoys* (string beds) to serve as tables and seats or as beds for weary cyclists. You should keep your cycle next to you throughout the night. There will be no bathroom or toilet facilities but plenty of road noise. Dhabas are not recommended for single women riders.

This is the best part of travelling on a bike – finding places to stay between the cities or important tourist places.

Directions
Asking directions can be a real frustration. Always ask three or four different people just to be certain, using traffic police only as a last resort. Try to be patient; be careful about 'left' *(baya)* and 'right' *(daya)* and be pre-

pared for instructions like 'go straight and turn here and there'.

Transporting your Bike
Sometimes you may want to quit pedalling. For sports bikes, air travel is easy. With luck, airline staff may not be familiar with procedures, so use this to your advantage. Tell them the bike doesn't need to be dismantled and that you've never had to pay for it. Remove all luggage and accessories and let the tyres down a bit.

Bus travel with a bike varies from state to state. Generally it goes for free on the roof. If it's a sports bike stress that it's lightweight. Secure it well to the roof rack, check it's in a place where it won't get damaged, and take all your luggage inside.

Train travel is more complex – pedal up to the railway station, buy a ticket and explain you want to book a cycle for the journey. You'll be directed to the luggage offices (or officer) where a triplicate form is prepared. Note down your bike's serial number and provide a good description of it. Again leave only the bike, not luggage or accessories. Your bike gets decorated with one copy of the form, usually pasted on the seat, you get another, and God only knows what happens to the third. Produce your copy of the form to claim the bicycle from the luggage van at your destination. If you change trains en route, *personally* ensure the cycle changes too!

Mountain-Bike Tours
Mountain-bike touring is catching on in the Himalaya. Several agencies in Dharamsala offer mountain-bike tours for visitors, as do some of the posher resorts on the outskirts of the Corbett National Park. Gurudongma Travels (☎ (03592) 55-204) in Kalimpong, in the West Bengal hills, has Indian-made 10 and 18 speed mountain-bikes for touring, and can also provide support services for cycling groups, such as backup vehicles, meals, guides and accommodation in tents and guesthouses. The innovative people at Kumaon Mandal Vikas Nigam (KMVN), a division of UP Tourism, are commencing

mountain-cycling tours in the environs of the hill station of Nainital. Some foreign travel agencies, such as Exodus Expeditions (refer to Organised Tours in the Getting There & Away chapter), organise mountain-bike tours along incredible routes such as between Leh and Manali. Snowbird Adventures in Manali will also organise mountain-bike treks to Lahaul & Spiti and Leh. And you thought the bus along this road was rough!

Final Words

Just how unusual is a cycle tourist in India? I'd venture to guess that currently 2000 foreign cyclists tour for a month or more each year somewhere on the subcontinent. That number appears to be growing rapidly. Perhaps 5000 Indians tour, as well – mostly young men and college students.

If you're a serious cyclist or amateur racer and want to contact counterparts while in India, there's the Cycle Federation of India; contact the Secretary, Yamun Velodrome, New Delhi. Last words of advice – make sure your rubber solution is gooey, all your winds are tailwinds and that you go straight and turn here and there.

HITCHING

Hitching is generally not a realistic option. There are not that many private cars streaking across India so you are likely to be on board trucks. You are then stuck with the old quandaries of: 'Do they understand what I am doing?'; 'Should I be paying for this?'; 'Will the driver expect to be paid?'; 'Will they be unhappy if I don't offer to pay?'; 'Will they be unhappy if I offer or will they simply want too much?'. But it is possible. In Ladakh & Zanskar, travelling by truck is a legitimate mode of transport, particularly along the Manali to Leh and Leh to Kargil routes.

However, it is a very bad idea for women to hitch. Remember India is a developing country with a patriarchal society far less sympathetic to rape victims than the west, and that's saying something. A woman in the cabin of a truck on a lonely road is perhaps tempting fate.

LOCAL TRANSPORT

Although there are comprehensive local bus networks in most major towns, unless you have time to familiarise yourself with the routes you're better off sticking to taxis, autorickshaws, cycle-rickshaws and hiring bicycles. The buses are often so hopelessly overcrowded that you can only really use them if you get on at the starting point – and get off at the terminus!

A basic ground rule applies to any form of transport where the fare is not ticketed or fixed (unlike a bus or train), or metered – agree on the fare beforehand. If you fail to do that, you can expect enormous arguments and hassles when you get to your destination. And agree on the fare clearly – if there is more than one of you, make sure it covers all of you. If you have baggage, make sure there are no extra charges, or you may be asked for more at the end of the trip. If a driver refuses to use the meter, or insists on an extortionate rate, simply walk away – if he really wants the job the price will drop. If you can't agree on a reasonable fare, find another driver.

Taxi & Jeep

There are taxis in most of the larger towns in the Indian Himalaya, and drivers in many centres have joined cooperatives, or unions, so long-distance fares are standardised and should be posted at the taxi booth. In Ladakh and the Kullu Valley, *all* fares are fixed, and difficult to negotiate. Nevertheless, in the off season, it's worth bargaining – fares can be reduced up to 30% or 40%.

In many centres (but not the remote regions of eastern Himachal Pradesh), share taxis or jeeps ply the major routes between important towns and hill stations. You'll find share jeep (sometimes called 'trekker') stands in Haridwar, Rishikesh and Dehra Dun, in the lower reaches of Uttarakhand, in Siliguri and some of the major towns in the West Bengal hills, such as Darjeeling and Kalimpong, and in most of the major towns in Sikkim. Jeeps generally depart when there are 11 passengers on board, and fares in the rear of the jeep are usually slightly cheaper than in the middle bench seat and in the front with the driver. Rates are up to double the cost of the equivalent bus fare, but jeeps are generally faster and relatively more comfortable.

Autorickshaw

An autorickshaw is a noisy three-wheel device powered by a two-stroke motorcycle engine with a driver up front and seats for two (or sometimes more) passengers behind. It doesn't have doors and has just a canvas top. Autorickshaws are also known as scooters or autos.

They're generally about half the price of a taxi, usually metered and follow the same ground rules as taxis. If the meter is 'broken', establish a firm rate before you set out.

Because of their size, autorickshaws are often faster than taxis for short trips and their drivers are decidedly nuttier – hair-raising near-misses are guaranteed and glancing-blow collisions are not infrequent; thrillseekers will love it!

In busy towns you'll find that, when stopped at traffic lights, the height you are sitting at is the same as most bus and truck exhaust pipes – copping dirty great lungfuls of diesel fumes

is part of the fun of autorickshaw travel. Also their small wheel size and rock-hard suspension makes them supremely uncomfortable; even the slightest bump will have you instantly airborne. The speed humps and huge potholes found everywhere are the bane of the rickshaw traveller – pity the poor drivers.

Tempo

Somewhat like a large autorickshaw, these ungainly looking three-wheel devices operate, rather like minibuses or share-taxis, along fixed routes. They are particularly conspicuous in Dehra Dun, where they are known locally as Vikrams, and ply between Rishikesh and Haridwar. Unless you are spending large amounts of time in one city, it is generally impractical to try to find out what the routes are. You'll find it much easier and more convenient to go by autorickshaw.

Cycle-Rickshaw

This is effectively a three-wheeler bicycle with a seat for two passengers behind the rider. Although they no longer operate in most of the big cities except in the old part

Cycle-rickshaws are a common form of local transport in India.

of Delhi and parts of Calcutta, you will find them in all the smaller cities and towns, where they're the basic means of transport.

Fares must always be agreed on in advance. Avoid situations where the driver says something like: 'As you like'. He's punting on the fact that you are not well acquainted with correct fares and will overpay. Invariably, no matter what you pay in situations like this, it will be deemed too little and an unpleasant situation often develops. Always settle the price beforehand.

In the well touristed places the riders are as talkative and opinionated as any New York cabby.

It's quite feasible to hire a rickshaw-wallah by time, not just for a straight trip. Hiring one for a day or even several days can make good sense.

Hassling over the fares is the biggest difficulty of cycle-rickshaw travel. They'll often go all out for a fare higher than it would cost you by taxi or autorickshaw. Nor does actually agreeing on a fare always make a difference; there is a greater possibility of a post-travel fare disagreement when you travel by cycle-rickshaw than by taxi or autorickshaw – metered or not.

Other Transport

In some places, *tongas* (horse-drawn two-wheelers) and *victorias* (horse-drawn carriages) still operate. You'll see them patiently waiting for custom in Rishikesh at the bus station. Calcutta has an extensive tramway network and India's first underground railway. Delhi has suburban trains.

Once upon a time there used to be people-drawn rickshaws but today these only exist in parts of Calcutta.

Bicycle

India is a country of bicycles – it's an ideal way of getting around the sights in a city or even for making longer trips – see the section on touring India by bicycle earlier in this chapter. Bicycles for hire in hill stations and other touristed spots, such as Haridwar and Leh, are generally low-tech bum-bruising contraptions which can be hired from around Rs 3 to Rs 5 per hour or Rs 10 to Rs 15 per day. In some places bicycle vendors may be unwilling to hire to you since you are a stranger, but you can generally get around this by offering some sort of ID card as security, or by paying a deposit – usually Rs 300 to Rs 500.

If you should be so unfortunate as to get a puncture, you'll soon spot men sitting under trees with puncture-repair outfits at the ready – it'll cost just a couple of rupees to fix it.

If you're travelling with small children and would like to use bikes a lot, consider getting a bicycle seat made. If you find a shop making cane furniture, they'll quickly make up a child's bicycle seat from a sketch. Get it made to fit on a standard-size rear carrier and it can be securely attached with a few lengths of cord.

Horse & Pony

If you're not an avid trekker, one of the finest ways to enjoy the Himalaya is astride a sturdy mountain pony. Pony-wallahs can be found at the roadheads of important pilgrimage destinations, such as those for Yamunotri and Kedarnath in the Garhwal Himalaya. As ponies represent the livelihood of their respective owners, they are generally kept in excellent condition. You'll need to engage in some heavy bargaining to negotiate a reasonable rate for your steed and its owner, who will accompany you on foot. Establish whether this rate includes extras such as horse blankets and lunch for the pony-wallah – and for the horse!

It's also possible to hire a pony for the trek to the beautiful Valley of Flowers in Garhwal. Pony treks are becoming popular in Zanskar (but you'll have to organise this yourself), and for visiting villages near Leh. Well kept horses and ponies are available for short rides in the environs of the hill stations of Shimla, Mussoorie and Nainital. There are also ponies and horses for hire at Darjeeling, in the West Bengal hills, although they appear less well groomed and in much poorer condition than their equine brethren in the western Himalaya. Yaks may also be hired at resort towns near Shimla!

TREKKING

Two-legged transport is one of the most common means of getting around, and sometimes the only way of getting to remote areas. Details of treks are included in the regional chapters. See the Facts for the Visitor chapter for information about equipment, health and issues affecting the trekker. For comprehensive coverage, pick up a copy of Lonely Planet's *Trekking in the Indian Himalaya* by Garry Weare.

ORGANISED TOURS

At almost any place of tourist interest in the Indian Himalaya, and in quite a few places where there's not much tourist interest, there will be tours operated either by the Government of India tourist office, the state tourist office or the local transport company – sometimes by all three. These tours are usually excellent value, particularly in cities or places where the tourist sights are widespread.

These tours are not strictly for western tourists; you will almost always find yourself far outnumbered by local tourists, and in many places just a little off the beaten track you will often be the only westerner on the bus. Despite this, the tours are usually conducted in English – which is possibly the only common language for the middle-class Indian tourists in any case. These tours are an excellent place to meet Indians.

The big drawback is that many of them try to cram far too much into too short a period of time. In Gangtok, for example, half and full-day tours which take in the renowned Rumtek Gompa leave you little time actually at the *gompa* (monastery) to take in the magnificent wall paintings and religious artefacts. If a tour looks too hectic, you're better off doing it yourself at a more appropriate pace or taking the tour simply to find out to which places you want to devote more time.

Ladakh & Zanskar

Population: approx 130,000
Area: approx 96,701 sq km
People per sq km: 0.74
Main Languages: Ladakhi, Purik, Balti, Tibetan and English
Best Time To Go: June to late September
Seasons:
Winter (off season) – mid-October to late May
Summer – late May to mid-October
Peak Tourist Season – July to August
Trekking Season – late May to mid-October
Rafting Season – early July to mid-September

Ladakh – the land of high passes – is the Trans-Himalaya zone which marks the boundary between the peaks of the western Himalaya and the vast Tibetan Plateau. Since it was opened up to tourism in 1974 Ladakh has been known as 'the Moonland', 'Little Tibet', and even 'the last Shangri La'. Whatever the description, Ladakh is one of the most remote regions of India.

The high culture of Ladakh is Buddhist, with its close cultural and trading connections with Tibet. This is particularly evident in the most populated region of Leh and the Indus Valley, with its many whitewashed *gompas* (monasteries) and forts perched on top of sugarloaf mountains.

Padum, the capital of the more remote Zanskar Valley shares this Buddhist heritage. Likewise, ancient gompas and tiny whitewashed villages are found in the depths of this rugged, arid mountainscape.

The region of Kargil and the Suru Valley constitutes the third main region of Ladakh. While its geography is similar to other regions of Ladakh, its people are Muslim and share a cultural affinity with Baltistan (now in Pakistan following Indian Partition in 1947).

Travel to Zanskar, Leh, and along the major routes to Srinagar and Manali is allowed without permits, as long as you don't stray too close to sensitive border areas.

HISTORY

Ladakh's rich cultural history has been well documented. Ladakh was first populated by the nomadic Khampas who grazed their yaks on the high windswept pastures. It was not until the coming of the Mons, Buddhist pilgrims from India on their way to Mt Kailash in Tibet, that settlements were established along the upper Indus.

Around Khalsi are to be found the remnant tribe of Drukpas. The Drukpas (also known in some areas as Dards) Mediterranean features and bacchanalian fertility festivals reinforce the possibility of their descent from Alexander's Macedonian army. (Other claimants live in the Pangi and Ravi valleys of neighbouring Himachal Pradesh.)

In the 7th century, Mongol influences increased with Tibetan migrants. During the

Highlights
The remote gompas set in spectacular moonscape scenery are the particular attractions of Ladakh & Zanskar. The most impressive are at Lamayuru, Hemis, Stakna, Stok, Tikse, Likir and Alchi. These and most other gompas hold fascinating annual festivals. The Ladakh Festival, held mainly in Leh during the first two weeks of September, is a spectacular collection of sporting displays and cultural exhibitions. Trekking, especially in Zanskar, is the best way to see the breathtaking valleys, mountains and rivers, and some of the more remote gompas.

The people of this region are particularly warm and hospitable. ∎

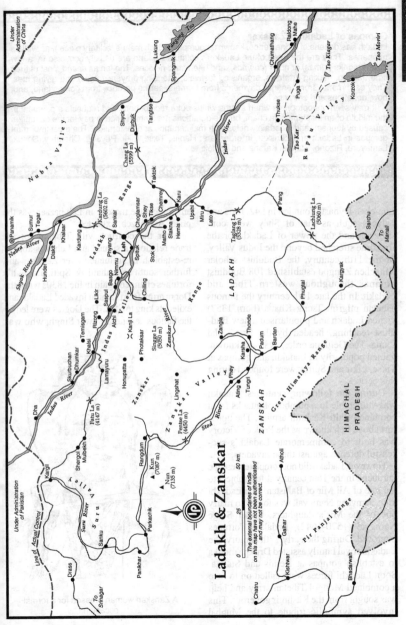

Ladakh & Zanskar

0   25   50 km

The external boundaries of India
on this map have not been authenticated
and may not be correct.

Gompas of Ladakh & Zanskar

Ladakh has dozens of monasteries, known as gompas (which means 'solitary place'), as well as nunneries. They are the heart of the Ladakhi's spiritual life, and are usually occupied by a few dozen monks *(lamas)* or nuns *(chomos)*, and often child novices. The lamas spend most of their time training, making artefacts, organising festivals, attending prayers *(pujas)* and giving rites. They earn money from tenancy payments from farmers, selling produce from gompa land and, now, donations and entrance fees.

It may seem inappropriate when a lama whips out a receipt book and requests a payment in the middle of an inspiring puja chant, but the donations are a small price to pay for the disruption caused by tourism, and it certainly helps with maintenance and restoration. The most important gompas in Ladakh and Zanskar, in order, are: Hemis, Tikse, Likir, Phyang, Chemrey, Spituk, Lamayuru, Rizong, Stakna, Karsha and Taktok. ■

Lha-chen Dynasty founded in 842, forts and palaces such as that of Shey were constructed, and the power of Ladakh for the first time stretched beyond the Indus Valley. In the 11th century, the Buddhist scholar Ringchen Zangpo established 108 Buddhist gompas throughout western Tibet and Ladakh. In the late 14th century the famous Tibetan pilgrim Tsong Khapa (born 1357) visited Ladakh and popularised a new Buddhist teaching, headed by the first Dalai Lama. The Gelukpa order, as it was known, gained popularity in Ladakh, and gompas at Tikse, Likir and Spituk were founded during this period.

During the following centuries, Ladakh was vulnerable to a number of attacks from combined Balti-Kashmir armies. The upper fort above Leh known as the Peak of Victory was built to commemorate Ladakh's successful defence against these invaders.

However, Ladakh did not completely escape intruders. In the 16th century it fell subject to the rule of Ali Mir of Baltistan. The Ladakhi king, Jamyang Namgyal, was forced to marry one of the Mir's daughters. Under Singe Namgyal (1570-1642), Ladakh's fortunes improved. During the early 17th century, the Ladakhi royal family assisted Drukpa monks to establish gompas at Hemis and Stakna. Soon Ladakhi forces were called on to face a combined Mongol-Tibetan army and help was sought from the Kashmir governor. This involved symbolic tribute to the Mughal empire and the mosque in Leh bazaar was the price Aurangzeb extracted.

After the conflict with Tibetan forces, trade relations resumed and Leh was able to re-establish its influence over Zanskar and further south to Lahaul & Spiti. Ladakh's fortunes changed again in the 1830s when the Dogra army from Jammu invaded Ladakh and exiled its king to Stok. The Dogras were led by the famous general Zorawar Singh, who was

A Zanskari woman dressed for a formal occasion.

Festivals of Ladakh

Festivals are an integral part of Ladakhi religion and agriculture, usually coinciding with the commemoration of religious events, and the end of the harvest. These festivals often used to take place in winter, but many have now moved to the summer to coincide with another important part of the year: the tourist season. Major festivals are held each year at Spituk, Matho, Hemis, and most other gompas in the region. The annual dates for these gompa festivals, which are determined according to the Tibetan lunar calendar, are listed below.

Now that tourism is flourishing in the region, the annual Ladakh Festival has been extended and is now held in the first two weeks of September in a blatant attempt to prolong the tourist season. Nevertheless, the festival should not be missed. Regular large, colourful displays of dancing, sports, ceremonies and exhibitions are held throughout Ladakh, but mainly in Leh, which has the highest population and receives the most visitors.

The first day of the festival starts with a spectacular march through the main streets of Leh. People from all over Ladakh, monks in yellow and orange robes, polo and archery troupes and Tibetan refugees from Choglamsar, walk proudly in traditional costume, wearing the tall, bright *perak* hats and the curled *papu* shoes. The march culminates in a day long cultural display at the polo ground in Leh. (If you want the best view of the opening ceremonies, ignore the march and go early to the polo ground to get a good seat.)

Other activities during the two weeks include mask dances, which are serious and hypnotic when performed by monks, or cheeky and frivolous when performed by small children. There are also archery and polo competitions, concerts and other cultural programmes throughout Ladakh. From year to year, handicraft, food, wildlife and thangka exhibitions are held in Leh. The tourist offices in Leh hand out free programmes which list the locations and dates of the various activities.

Apart from Leh, other smaller, associated festivals are held in Changspa, Tangtse (near Pangong Tso), Shey, Basgo, Korzok (on the shore of Tso Moriri) and Biama (in the Dha-Hanu region). In the Nubra Valley, Diskit and Sumur hold the biggest festival outside Leh, with camel races, 'warfare demonstrations' (not quite as violent as they sound), ibex and peacock dances, traditional marriage ceremonies, some sword dancing from Baltistan, flower displays and archery competitions.

Following are the dates of festivals until 1999 celebrated at the gompas of Ladakh & Zanskar:

Gompa	1996	1997	1998	1999
Chemrey	Nov 9-10	Nov 27-28	Nov 17-18	Nov 5-6
Diskit	Feb 16-17	Feb 5-6	Feb 24-25	Feb 14-15
Hemis	June 26-27	July 15-16	July 4-5	June 23-24
Karsha	July 13-14	Aug 1-2	July 21-22	July 11-12
Leh	Feb 16-17	Feb 5-6	Feb 24-25	Feb 14-15
Likir	Feb 16-17	Feb 5-6	Feb 24-25	Feb 14-15
Matho	March 4-5	Feb 21-22	March 12-13	March 1-2
Phyang	July 17-18	Aug 5-6	July 25-26	July 14-15
Spituk	Jan 18-19	Jan 7-8	Jan 26-27	Jan 15-16
Stok	Feb 27-28	Feb 15-16	March 6-7	March 24-25
Taktok	July 25-26	Aug 13-14	Aug 3-4	July 23-24
Tikse	Oct 29-30	Nov 17-18	Nov 6-7	Oct 27-28
Losar	Dec 11	Dec 30	Dec 19	Dec 8

(New Year – The New Year festival is celebrated at all gompas.) ■

appointed by the first maharaja of Kashmir, GulabSingh.

Ladakh became an integral part of the maharaja's vast state in 1846 and remained under the control of Jammu & Kashmir after independence until some administrative autonomy was granted in 1995. Ladakh is still a sensitive area and its borders with both Pakistan and China have been disputed. India's war with China in 1962 exacerbated the problem and was one of the main reasons why Ladakh was closed to outsiders until 1974. While China and India are approaching accord on the border dispute, some heavy fighting continues between India and Pakistan (above 6000m in the eastern Karakoram region). This costly warfare – a million US dollars a day since 1988 – ensures a significant military presence in Ladakh. Travellers are forbidden to travel near the border area.

GEOGRAPHY

The region of Ladakh is part of the Trans-Himalaya, a vast and complex mountain region between the main Himalaya Range and the Tibetan Plateau. The region receives only a minimal rainfall each year, which is diverted along irrigation canals. Here barley fields and lines of poplar trees in the depths of the valleys contrast with the barren ridges and mountains that define the geographical character of the region.

Ladakh is bordered to the south by the main Himalaya Range which includes many impressive snow-capped peaks, including Nun (7135m) and Kun (7087m), the highest peak in the Kashmir Himalaya. North and parallel to the Himalaya is the Zanskar Range, which is the main range between the Himalaya and the Indus Valley. The region is drained by the Zanskar River which flows into the Indus River just below Leh, and the Suru River which flows into the Indus downstream of Kargil.

The Stok Range immediately south of Leh is an impressive outlier north of the Zanskar Range, while north of Leh is the snow-capped Ladakh Range. North of the Ladakh Range the Nubra and Shyok rivers drain the huge peaks of the eastern Karakoram including Rimo 1 (7385m) and Teram Kangri 1 (7464m) that define the northern border of Ladakh.

In the east of Ladakh are several scintillating lakes including the Pangong Tso (lake) forming the border with Tibet and the Tso Moriri set in a high altitude desert characteristic of the Tibetan Plateau.

TRAVEL TAX

As a result of the formation of the Ladakh Autonomous Hill Council, a tourist entry tax of US$10 per foreign tourist has been introduced. This will be collected at the various entry points into Ladakh (eg at Upshi – on the road from Manali). It will also be collected at the airport for tourists arriving by air. Also, an additional US$20 will be levied on tourists visiting the newly opened areas of the Nubra Valley, Pangong Tso, Tso Moriri, and the Dha-Hanu region.

TOURIST OFFICES

Jammu & Kashmir (J & K) tourist offices throughout India handle enquires for travel to Ladakh and Zanskar, and are worth a visit for some up-to-date maps and information before you arrive:

	Leh		Kargil	
Month	Max	Min	Max	Min
Jan	-3	-14	-4	-13
Feb	1	-12	-2	-12
March	6	-6	5	-5
April	12	-1	14	3
May	17	3	22	9
June	21	7	26	14
July	25	10	30	18
August	24	10	29	17
Sept	21	5	25	12
Oct	14	-1	19	5
Nov	8	-7	10	-1
Dec	2	-11	1	-8

Average Temperatures for Leh & Kargil

Delhi
  201-203 Kanishka Shopping Plaza, 19 Ashok Rd, New Delhi (☎ (011) 33-2537)
Calcutta
  12 Chowringee Rd (☎ (033) 70-0001)
Madras
  837 Anna Salai Rd (☎ (044) 83-0672)
Mumbai (Bombay)
  25 Chinar, World Trade Centre, Cuffe Pde (☎ (022) 218-9040)

LANGUAGE

Ladakhi is the main language used by most indigenous people. Once similar to Tibetan, Ladakhi has now changed considerably, and there are disparate dialects throughout the region. Like most countries, learning a little Ladakhi will add to your enjoyment, earn some respect from the locals, and, in some cases, is quite necessary if travelling out of Leh, or trekking, where little English is understood. If you only remember one word, it will be the all-purpose *jule* (pronounced 'JOO-Lay'), which means hello, goodbye, please and thank you.

Useful Words

yes	*kasa*
no	*man*
how much/many	*tsam*
good	*demo*
rupee	*kirmo*
milk	*oma*
rice	*dras*
meat	*sha*
water	*chhu*
sugar	*khara*
I don't understand	*hamago*

Geographical & Climatic Terms

In Ladakh, life is completely dominated by the weather and geography. Here are a few words which you may hear or see:

bridge	*zampa*
ice	*kang*
mountain	*ri*
river	*tsangspo*
stream	*tokpo*
wind	*lungspo*
cold	*tangmo*
lake	*tso*
mountain pass	*la*
snow	*ka*
summer	*yar*
winter	*rgun*

Numbers

1	*chig*
2	*nyis*
3	*sum*
4	*zhi*
5	*nga*
6	*truk*
7	*dun*
8	*gyet*
9	*gu*
10	*chu*

Spelling

Beware that every guidebook, map and tourist brochure can offer up to about six different ways of spelling a name. For example, there is a famous gompa (or *gonpa* or *gomba)* at Tikse (or Thikse, Thiksey or Tiksey). The basic rule is: if it sounds the same, it is the same place.

Leh

Population: 24,500
Telephone Area Code: 01982

Leh is located in a small valley just to the north of the Indus Valley. Until 1947 it had close trading relations with Central Asia, with yak trains setting off from the Leh bazaar to complete the stages over the Karakoram Pass to Yarkand and Kashgar. Today Leh is an important strategic centre for India. The large military presence is a reminder that the region of Ladakh is situated along India's sensitive borders with both Pakistan and China.

Leh's character also changed when Ladakh was opened up to foreign tourists in 1974. Since then, well over 100 hotels have been established and many of the shops in the main bazaar have been converted to sell Ladakhi arts and crafts.

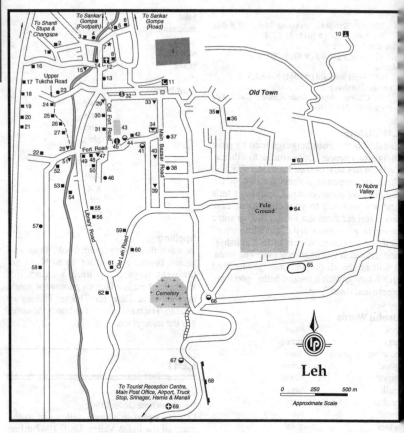

Leh

0   250   500 m

Approximate Scale

Leh is dominated by the dilapidated nine storey Leh Palace. Until the 1830s this was occupied by the Ladakhi royal family before they were exiled to Stok. Above the palace at the top of the Namgyal Hill is the Victory Fort, built to commemorate Ladakh's victory over the Balti-Kashmir armies in the early 16th century.

The old town of Leh is situated at the base of the Namgyal Hill, a labyrinth of alleyways and houses stacked with dry wood and dung which is collected for fuel to withstand the long winter months. To the south of the old town is the polo ground where weekly matches

are contested between Leh and the outlying villages of the Indus Valley. The mosque at the head of the Leh bazaar was commissioned by the Mughal Emperor Aurangzeb.

In Changspa, an outlying village of Leh, there are important Buddhist carvings dating back to the 8th and 9th centuries when Ladakh was converted to Buddhism. Close by is the village of Sankar, the site of a modern gompa which serves much of the Leh Valley. The gompa is attended by some 15 to 20 monks from the gompa at Spituk. It seems surprising that Leh does not have a more impressive gompa; even the Kings

PLACES TO STAY		42	Hotel Ibex & Druk Travels	47	Summer Harvest Restaurant
1	Rainbow Guest House	48	Dreamland Hotel & Restaurant	51	Tibetan Kitchen
2	Two-Star Guest House	49	Hotel Yak Tail & Restaurant	**OTHER**	
3	Tsemo-La Hotel	50	Khangri Hotel	4	LEDeG Centre
5	Himalayan Guest House	52	Hotel Rockland	7	Police Station
6	Antelope Guest House	53	Padma Guest House	9	Leh Palace
8	Khan Manzil Guest House	54	Hotel Choskor	10	Tsemo Gompa
14	Hotel Khang-la-Chhen Guest House	55	Pangong Hotel	11	Mosque
		56	Kang La	12	Morovian Church
16	Eagle Guest House	58	Mandala Hotel	13	Artou Bookshop
17	Tsavo Guest House	59	Singge Palace	23	SECMOL Centre
18	Hotel Omasila	60	Chospa Guest House	32	State Bank of India
19	Otsal Guest House			34	Post Office
20	Asia Guest House	61	Nezer View Guest House	37	Lost Horizon Books
21	Larchang Guest House			38	Tibetan Handicraft Emporium
22	Lung-Se-Jung Hotel	62	Hotel Hills View	41	Taxi Stand & Union Office
		63	Palace View Hotel	43	Vegetable Market
24	Indus Guest House			44	HPTDC Bus Office
25	Ti-sei Guest House	**PLACES TO EAT**		45	Tourist Office & Foreign Exchange
26	Dehlux Hotel	15	Mentokling Restaurant	46	Leh District Library
27	Bimla Guest House			57	Indian Airlines
30	Hotel Lingzi	28	Instyle German Bakery	64	District Magistrate's Office
31	Hotel Ga-Idan Continental	29	German Bakery	65	National Archery Stadium
35	Tak Guest House	33	Budshah Inn	66	Old Bus Stand
36	Old Ladakh Guest House	39	Mughal Darbar Restaurant	67	New Bus Stand
		40	La Montessori Restaurant	68	Mani Wall
				69	SNM Hospital

Gompa at the palace is run down, and administered by a monk seconded from Hemis.

Orientation

Leh is small enough to find your way around easily. The road from the airport goes past the New and Old bus stands, then turns into the main street, Main Bazaar Rd, where there are plenty of shops and restaurants. South of the Leh Palace, around the area of Fort Rd, is the most popular area for places to eat, sleep and spend money. To the west of the town and about two km out of Leh is the village of Changspa, with its many guesthouses and long-term visitors.

Information

Tourist Offices The Tourist Reception Centre (☎ 2497) is a long three km walk from the town centre, on the road to the airport. For general enquires, the small counter in the same building as the Foreign Exchange, next to the Tourist Bungalow on Fort Rd, is far handier. Both tourist offices are open from 10 am to 4 pm every day except Sunday. There is a small tourist information counter at the airport, but this really just handles Foreigner's Registration Forms. The airport arrivals area has an informative video presentation about the region.

Permits Permits are not required for Leh. However, you will be required to fill out a Foreigners' Registration Form at the airport, and again at your hotel. For permits to the newly opened regions of Ladakh, you will have to go to a travel agency and then to the District Magistrate's Office (☎ 2210), open normal business hours, just above the polo ground. For more details on permits, refer to the Ladakh Regions section later in the chapter.

Money Changing money is really only possible at the Forex (Foreign Exchange) counter, next to the Tourist Bungalow – although some travellers have had some luck at the State Bank of India. The Forex is open from Monday to Friday, 10.30 am to 1.30 pm; and on Saturday from 10.30 am to noon. You must fill out two copies of a currency form, and wait.

Post & Communications The main post office – open Monday to Saturday from 10 am to 5 pm; lunch from 1 to 2 pm – is hopelessly inconvenient, over three km from the centre of Leh. The smaller post office on the corner of Fort and Main Bazaar roads is open from 10 am to 4 pm, closed on Sunday. The poste restante at the main post office is not particularly reliable, and too far out to go every day to check, so use your guesthouse or the tourist office on Fort Rd as a mailing address, but warn them first so they hold onto the letters.

All around Leh, there are small telephone booths which have long-distance facilities. Calls within India cost Rs 30 to Rs 40 per minute; to Australia/New Zealand, Rs 80; and to USA/Canada, Rs 98. Faxes are a far more expensive method of communication, but machines are available.

Travel Agencies In Leh, there are many travel agencies operating in the summer. Almost all agencies work on a commission basis, selling tickets for other agencies' buses and tours.

It is easy enough to organise your own tours to the newly opened areas of Ladakh, by just arranging a taxi or going by public bus. Travel agencies can organise tours, but they often do little more than arrange the taxis themselves, and then take a commission. As a general rule of thumb, if booking an organised tour, deal with an agency in an up-market hotel; while you may pay more, the quality and reliability is more likely to be there. Of course, one of the best ideas is to talk to other travellers.

Recommended travel agencies include: Druk Travels in the Hotel Ibex (although the manager is often absent); Kailash Expeditions (near the Instyle German Bakery) on Fort Rd; Yak Tail Travels (☎ 2318), in the hotel of the same name; Yungdung Tours & Travels, opposite the taxi stand; Rimo Expeditions (☎ 3693), near the Hotel Khang-la-Chhen; Yasmin Trek & Tour (☎ 3929; open 24 hours), which is near the Hotel Ibex; and Gypsys World (☎ 3935) near Hotel Yak Tail on Fort Rd.

Equipment Hire Several travel agencies also rent sleeping bags, tents and so on, but the gear can be of low quality and poorly maintained. Check the gear carefully before you take it; some travellers have been charged extra after returning the gear for pre-existing 'damages'. Some places which rent gear include: Snow Leopard, opposite the taxi stand; Royal Express, near the Hotel Ibex; and the Traveller Shop (☎ 2248) on Fort Rd, towards the Indian Airlines office. Approximate rental prices per day are: two person tent, Rs 60; sleeping bag, Rs 50; and gas stove, Rs 10.

Rafting Agencies Several agencies in Leh run white-water rafting trips on the Indus and Zanskar rivers. Rafting is not especially popular, as the rivers aren't particularly good or reliable, and the season only lasts from about early July to mid-September. A three hour, calm trip from Hemis to Choglamsar, or a slightly more exciting one from Phey to Nimmu, costs Rs 750 per person. Better rafting from Nimmu to Alchi or to Khalsi will cost Rs 1200 for the day. Longer, customised rafting trips for the adventurous cost about US$65 per day, including all transport, gear, food and a guide.

Two of the better travel agencies in Leh which handle rafting trips are Indus Himalaya, opposite the taxi stand; and Rimo Expeditions (see Travel Agencies above).

Bookshops & Libraries Both the Artou Bookshop and Lost Horizon Books have great selections of books on Ladakh and Tibet, as well as novels. The Tibetan Handicraft Emporium, on Main Bazaar Rd, is also good for Tibetan literature.

Next to the Hotel Bijou, the small Leh District Library is a good place to read (mainly old) books about Ladakh, and recent issues of English-language newspapers and magazines. It is open on normal workdays from Monday to Saturday from 10 am to 4 pm. The Ladakh Ecological Development Group (LeDEG) runs a very good library with books on local issues, and ecological matters. For books on Buddhism and Tibet, try the Tibetan library in Choglamsar.

Newspapers & Magazines Daily English-language Indian newspapers can be obtained at Parkash Booksellers, next to the German Bakery. The bi-lingual (English and Ladakhi) quarterly magazine *Ladags Melong* (Rs 20) is a great source of information on Ladakhi culture, education, history and so on. It is not easy to find in Leh, but try the library, or the major bookshops.

Film & Photography Several places along Fort and Main Bazaar roads sell print and slide film, but always check the expiry date. The Gemini Lab on Fort Rd, opposite the Yak Tail, does a pretty good job with developing print (not slide) film.

Courses Buddhist study centres have been set up in Leh, and in nearby Choglamsar. The Mahabodhi International Meditation Centre in Leh (look for the sign on the way to the Shanti Stupa) has summer meditation sessions from 5 to 7 am every Monday, Tuesday and Thursday, and at 4 pm on Saturday. The Centre also holds popular five to 10 day study camps near Temisgam, and at Dewachan, near Choglamsar.

Medical Services Leh is at an altitude of 3505m, so it is important to acclimatise to avoid Acute Mountain Sickness (AMS). If you suspect you are suffering from the symptoms of AMS, medical advice (☎ 212/213/214; ☎ 560, 24 hours) is available during working hours. For more information on AMS, see the Health section in the Facts for the Visitor

chapter. Leh has several clinics and pharmacies which can dispense advice and medicines for low-level complaints, but for anything serious the Sonam Narbu Memorial (SNM) Hospital (☎ 2560) is nearly three km south of Leh.

Leh Palace
Looking for all the world like a miniature version of the Potala in Lhasa, Tibet, Leh Palace was built in the 17th century, but is now deserted and dilapidated. Try to find a monk to unlock the preserved, but now unused, central prayer room. If you can't get in, don't despair; there is no shortage of other more interesting, spectacular gompas near Leh.

The palace is just an amble up any old laneway at the back of the mosque. Going by the road is longer if you are on foot, and, however close it looks, there is no way up to the palace from the road to the west, which leads to the Sankar Gompa.

Namgyal Tsemo Gompa
The Tsemo (Red) Gompa, built in 1430, contains a fine three storey high Buddha image and ancient manuscripts and frescoes. It's open from 7 to 9 am. Another gompa above the Tsemo Gompa is ruined, but the views of Leh from here are superb. The steep laneway starts from the road to the Leh Palace.

Sankar Gompa
It's an easy stroll to the Sankar Gompa, a couple of km north of the town centre. (A return taxi costs Rs 115.) This interesting little gompa, which belongs to the Gelukpa order, is only open from 7 to 10 am and from 5 to 7 pm. The gompa has electric lighting so an evening visit is worthwhile. Upstairs is an impressive representation of Avalokitesvara (Chenresig, the Buddhist deity of Compassion) complete with 1000 arms and 1000 heads, a library, and great views from the roof.

Shanti Stupa
Looming impressively, especially at night-time when it is well lit up, this *stupa* (Buddhist religious monument) was built by a Japanese, Indian-based man whose intention was to

spread Buddhism by building temples throughout the world. With some eventual financial assistance from the Japanese government, it was opened by the Dalai Lama in 1985.

From the top, there are great views. The stupa is located at the end of the road which goes through Changspa, about three km from Fort Rd. If on foot, there is a very, very steep set of steps – not to be attempted if you have just arrived in Leh. By taxi (Rs 120 return) or with your own transport, a longish, winding (but less steep) road goes straight to the top.

There are five rooms at the stupa which can be rented for Rs 100 per night. There is an empty looking restaurant. Staying here will offer the greatest views of Leh, but it is a long way down to your favourite eatery!

Ladakh Ecological Development Group

The Ladakh Ecological Development Group (LEDeG) (☎ 3746), founded in 1983, initiates and promotes 'ecological and sustainable development which harmonises with and builds on the traditional culture'. This includes environmental and health education, strengthening the traditional system of organic farming, and publishing books in the local language.

At 4.30 pm every day in summer, except Sunday, the video *Ancient Futures – Learning from Ladakh* is shown at the LEDeG Centre, next to the Tsemo-La Hotel. It's well worth seeing for an insight into Ladakh, and the problems associated with tourism. There are also study groups every Wednesday at 10.30 am at the centre. The library is popular; and their handicraft shop has a good, if a little pricey (but it is non-profit), selection of locally made goods. For further information about the LEDeG, contact: Ladakh Project, 21 Victoria Sq, Clifton, Bristol, BS8 4ES, UK; or the Ladakh Project, PO Box 9475, Berkeley, CA 94709, USA.

Students' Educational & Cultural Movement of Ladakh (SECMOL)

SECMOL (☎ 3676) was founded in the late 1980s to organise cultural shows, promote traditional art forms, and to organise youth activities. It also produces a local magazine,

Ladags Melong, and a Ladakhi phrasebook. The SECMOL centre is worth a visit, at the end of Upper Tukcha Rd; it is often only open in the afternoon.

Places to Stay

There's an amazing number of hotels and guesthouses in Leh, almost all of which are only open during the tourist season. Prices are technically set by the local tourist authorities, but what you pay depends more on tourist demand – prices can soar in the peak season, especially after the arrival of a full flight. In low season, even a day or two after the season ends, prices can drop dramatically, sometimes by up to 50%. Prices quoted here are for the high season, but, remember, the cost of a hotel will change from day to day. A lot of places will also charge an arbitrary 'service tax' of about 10%.

Electricity can be spasmodic, so torches (flashlights) and candles may be needed. Before paying extra for hot water, enquire how regular it is; often it may only run for one or two hours a day. If you're staying for some time in Leh, it is worth checking into one place for the first night, then spending your first day, while acclimatising, finding a place that really suits.

Budget accommodation can be found in three main areas: the old town, which is a little noisy and smelly, but has character; the 'newer', greener areas along, or not far from, Fort Rd; and in the village of Changspa. Most other accommodation is in the newer parts of Leh.

Places to Stay – bottom end

Old Town Under the Leh Palace, along a quiet road to the Sankar Gompa, are several good places: the *Himalayan Guest House* has good value rooms for Rs 200; and the *Antelope Guest House*, popular for its friendliness and garden setting, has singles/doubles for Rs 70/130. A little further up the road, the *Hotel Kailash*, surrounded by a walled garden and fields, has doubles from Rs 130, all with common bathroom.

The long-established *Old Ladakh Guest House* has rooms with common bathroom for Rs 70/100, and with attached bath from Rs 120/150. Other good places in this area, between the Old Ladakh Guest House and the polo ground, with similarly priced rooms and facilities include the *Shalimar Guest House*, a clean, friendly place; the *Tak Guest House*, which is also popular; and the larger *Palace View Hotel*. More central is the friendly *Khan Manzil Guest House* (☎ 3781). Beside the archery stadium, *Firdous Hotel* is a friendly little place with doubles for Rs 80, or Rs 120 with attached bath.

Changspa Changspa, about 15 minutes walk from the town centre, is a very popular place for budget travellers. Many of the older places are basic, with outside bathrooms, but are usually very friendly, and surrounded by gardens. Recommended among the dozens of places around, or on the way to, Changspa are the *Eagle Guest House*, with singles/doubles for Rs 70/100; the *Tsavo Guest House*, which is very basic but is an authentic Ladakhi home and has doubles from Rs 60; and the *Otsal*, *Asia* and *Larchang* guesthouses, which have reasonable singles/doubles for Rs 60/80.

Along the road to the Shanti Stupa, past Changspa, a bit of a walk from town, are dozens of other nice family-run guesthouses – just look for the signs on the road. The *Rinchens Guest House* has clean doubles for Rs 70, or Rs 170 with attached bath. The *Oriental Guest House* has doubles from Rs 70, and is run by a very friendly family. Some other good guesthouses on this road with singles/doubles for about Rs 80/100 are the *Lyon*, *Karzoo* and *Shanti*; the popular *Two-Star Guest House*, which also has some dorm beds for Rs 50; the *Mansoor Guest House* with a nice family atmosphere and rooms from Rs 60; and the friendly *Rainbow Guest House*. Some places are now trying to compete, and offer extras such as hot water, so are worth checking out.

Other Areas Down Old Leh Rd are old favourites within the range of Rs 70 to Rs 150, usually with a shared bathroom, such as the *Spic-n-Span* (☎ 2238) (which isn't that clean), the *Singge Palace* (☎ 2422) and the *Chospa Guest House*, which has its own in-house astrologer. Along the lane known as Library Rd (which the library isn't actually on) there are several good places: the *Pangong Hotel* is a little in the mid-range, but has airy, bright singles/doubles with hot water for Rs 200/300; next door, the popular *Kang La* has small, cosy rooms, with bathroom, for Rs 100; the *Hotel Hills View* (☎ 2258) has rooms for Rs 100/150 with common bath, or Rs 250 for a double with attached bath; and the *Nezer View Guest House* is recommended, with rooms from Rs 80/100.

Up the lane to the back of the Instyle German Bakery, the *Ti-sei Guest House* is one of the best. It has a nice garden and a traditional Ladakhi kitchen; rooms are about Rs 80/150. Hot water costs Rs 5 per bucket. There are other cheap places further along this lane.

Camping The only camping site is at *Zen*, in Changspa. For Rs 30, you can place your tent on a small piece of turf. If you have a tent, you may be able to put it up at the back of a guesthouse for about the same price.

Places to Stay – middle

A few of the places which used to be in the 'bottom end' range have become a bit too popular, and have done some improvements, but now are a little overpriced. These include several along the lane to the back of the Instyle German Bakery: the ever-popular *Bimla Guest House* (☎ 3854) which has singles/doubles for about Rs 180/240 without a bathroom, Rs 400/450 with hot water and great views; the *Indus Guest House* has doubles with hot water for Rs 300; and the *Dehlux Hotel* is similarly priced. The *Padma Guest House* (☎ 2332) is very clean and has a pleasant garden. Singles/doubles are Rs 150/200 or Rs 180/240 with attached bath.

The *Yasmin Guest House* (opposite the Hotel Rockland) has good doubles with attached bath for Rs 280. The *Hotel Choskor* (☎ 3626) has similar doubles for Rs 200. The *Hotel Rockland* (☎ 3689) charges Rs

250/450, and a lot more for meals and better rooms. The *Hotel Bijou* (☎ 2331), near the Hotel Choskor, costs Rs 300/400, all with attached bath. The *Dreamland Hotel* is quite good with doubles/triples at Rs 250/350.

The *Lung-Se-Jung Hotel* (☎ 2393), past the Instyle German Bakery, is popular and pretty good value. Singles/doubles, including hot water, cost Rs 200/300. The *Hotel Ibex* (☎ 2352) is priced at Rs 425/440, more for meals.

Places to Stay – top end

Prices for these places are high, and offer little value; a room may have some form of heating or air-conditioning, and hot water, but no other extras. Many places offer an 'American Plan', which includes three meals for an additional Rs 400 to Rs 500 per day. It may look a reasonable deal, but there are plenty of good cheap places to eat in Leh, and why always eat at the same place?

With singles/doubles for at least Rs 600/800, Leh's best top-end places are the *Tsemo-La Hotel* (☎ 2281), the central *Khangri Hotel* (☎ 2251), and the *Mandala Hotel* (☎ 2423). Centrally located around the Fort Rd area are the *Hotel Lingzi* (☎ 2220), and the *Hotel Yak Tail* (☎ 2318) at Rs 725/925. The *Hotel Omasila* (☎ 2319) has an attractive garden and is in a peaceful location. Without meals, doubles are Rs 650. Top of the lot is the *Hotel Ga-Idan Continental* (☎ 2373). Luxury singles/doubles, including breakfast, cost from Rs 1000/1200.

Places to Stay – winter

Almost every place in Leh closes in winter. Prices at those places which remain open in the off season are still high because of a charge for room heating, which is certainly needed as the temperature in winter can plummet to about -35 °C.

The only places which reliably open in winter are the first and original *Old Ladakh Guest House*, which has remained open every day since 1974; the *Hotel Ibex*; and the *Khangri Hotel* (where you will be put up for free if your Indian Airlines flight is can-

celled), which charges an extra Rs 200 for heating per room.

Places to Eat

There is no shortage of places to eat in Leh (although supplies are sometimes in short supply), and it's a joy to sample various types of food from a multitude of good places. Almost all places serve a range of cuisine, some better than others. If you particularly want to eat at a popular place in the peak season, get a table before 7 pm.

Western Cuisine For places that serve western food, as well as a predictable selection of Chinese and Indian cuisine, the *Yak Tail* is good, if a little pricey, and is one of the few places that serves beer. The *Centerpoint* on Fort Rd, above the Tsomo Hotel, has nice decor and a good selection, including Ladakhi dishes at reasonable prices. Opposite, the *Summer Harvest* is very popular, and deservedly so.

Bakeries The bakeries in Leh also serve good western food, such as pasta, hamburgers and large, hot breakfasts, as well as fresh cinnamon rolls, and other tasty things. *Instyle German Bakery* on Fort Rd is a great place for a cup of coffee, sandwiches and breakfast, including piping hot porridge. The *German Bakery* at the top of Old Fort Rd is a very popular place; specialities include a large, set-price breakfast (Rs 40) and lasagne. The *Mona Lisa Bakery*, close to the State Bank of India, is small but good for tea and freshly baked goodies.

Hot, fresh Indian and Tibetan bread can be bought in the early morning from several unmarked bakery stalls in the street behind the mosque – follow the sign to the Antelope Guest House towards Sanskar Gompa. Get there early to watch them make the bread. It is great with locally made jam.

Tibetan Cuisine Leh has a sizeable Tibetan refugee population, which naturally has influenced the cuisine and increased the number of Tibetan restaurants. Along Main

Bazaar Rd, mostly on the 2nd or 3rd floors, are several, good, cheap (and well signed) places to try Tibetan specialities, including the *Kokonor Tibetan Restaurant*, the *Wok Tibetan Kitchen* and the two *Amdo* cafes, which also serve reasonable western and Chinese food. The *Budshah Inn*, near the mosque, serves Kashmiri and Tibetan treats.

The *Tibetan Kitchen*, at the end of Fort Rd, has a pleasant decor, good service, and the varieties of Tibetan cuisine are explained on posters and menus for the uninitiated. It will do a famous gyarhcee (Tibetan hotpot) for at least four people with a day's notice. The centrally located *Dreamland Restaurant* remains incredibly popular for its Tibetan specialities, among other types of food. The unpretentious *Tibetan Restaurant Devi*, near the State Bank of India, has managed to maintain its reputation for cheap, nourishing food. *La Montessori* serves up big portions of very tasty Chinese, Tibetan and some western favourites, and is popular with local monks. The *Tibetan Friends Corner Restau-rant*, near the taxi stand, is another established favourite for locals also.

Indian Cuisine For Indian, particularly Kashmiri, food, the *Mughal Darbar* on Main Bazaar Rd, is recommended. Although the servings are small, a great meal will only set you back about Rs 70 per person. For no-frills, cheap Indian food, the *Poora Barba*, opposite the Hotel Yak Tail, on Fort Rd, serves filling plates of vegetable curries and rice.

Bars If you are desperate for a bottle of Turbo Extra Strong Lager, there are a couple of bars including the *Penguin Bar* at the back of the Instyle German Bakery, and the dark and seedy *Namra Bar*, opposite the Hotel Yak Tail. The open-air *Mentokling Restau-rant* and *Mona Lisa* are relaxing places for a meal, a drink and western popular music.

Entertainment

The Cultural & Traditional Society (CATS) puts on a cultural show each summer

---

Gur-Gur & Chang

A trip to Ladakh would be incomplete without sampling *gur-gur* tea and *chang*. Similar to Tibet and other Tibetan-influenced areas like Lahaul & Spiti in Himachal Pradesh, gur-gur tea, or *chai*, is made with yak butter (which is either rancid or fresh depending on the region of Ladakh). The butter is mixed with salt, milk, a prepared green leaf tea and hot water. The churning of the liquid in a wooden vessel makes a 'gur-gur' sound – hence the name of the tea. Gur-gur tea, which is often mixed with barley flour *(tsampa)*, is usually kept hot in a copper kettle and placed on a stove. Churners and kettles can be bought in Leh.

You will be offered gur-gur during the two traditional cultural shows put on for tourists in Leh. A monk may offer you a small cup from the gompa kitchen, or during a puja, a child novice will continually refill the monks' and visitors' cups. In a Ladakhi home, a family will sit around a small, low table known as a *chogtse* and drink dozens of cups in a few hours. If you are offered some Ladakhi tea, remember that you may offend if you don't finish your cup, and whenever you do finish it, the cup will be refilled immediately.

Chang, made from excess barley during the harvests, is a dominant part of many Ladakhi rituals and celebrations. Drunk by women and men, chang helps to loosen the body and mind during traditional dancing, is an integral part of the celebration of a birth, and is drunk in large quantities while negotiating a wedding, and at the marriage ceremony. Chang is enjoyed by most Ladakhis, including monks, but not by Muslims (who live mainly in western Ladakh) because of its alcohol content.

Chang has a sour taste which is a little easier to get used to than gur-gur chai. You may be offered some rough home-brewed chang in a Ladakhi home, or you can buy some in bottle shops and restaurants in non-Muslim regions of Ladakh. Chang is especially welcome during long, cold evenings, but be careful – its intoxicating effect will be made worse by the high altitude. ∎

evening opposite the Hotel Yak Tail at 6 pm (which is not particularly pleasant if you have a room nearby). In competition to this, the Ladakh Artists' Society of Leh also puts on a show of Ladakhi songs and dances every day at 5.30 pm outside the Leh Palace. It's an entertaining show, at a great location. (Bring a torch (flashlight) for the walk back.) Each show costs Rs 50.

While they *are* set up for tourists, these shows are likely to be the closest you'll get to see some traditional songs and dances, and to try (if you dare) some Ladakhi gur-gur. It's a good idea to avoid the front rows unless you want to become part of the spectacle at the end of the show (as one of the authors was!).

Things to Buy

Prices in Leh are generally quite high; you may find exactly the same Tibetan-inspired item on sale at lower prices in Kashmir, Dharamsala or Nepal. For Tibetan goods, try places around Choglamsar, the Tibetan Handicraft Shop near the entrance to the airport, or the Tibetan Handicrafts Emporium on Main Bazaar Rd. Other reasonable places for local goods are the Ladakh Art Palace in the old town, and the LEDeG Centre. If you are around Leh at the time of the Ladakh Festival, there are good exhibitions and stalls selling local handicrafts and clothes.

Getting There & Away

Air From June to September Indian Airlines (IA) has daily return flights between Leh and Delhi (US$86), sometimes via Chandigarh (US$54). There are also direct flights once a week from Leh to Srinagar (US$39), and three times a week to Jammu (US$44). They can be a useful, indirect, way of getting out of Leh if the Leh to Delhi flights are hopelessly overbooked.

From October to May IA generally still flies into Leh every day from Delhi, but this depends greatly on weather conditions. If/when flights from Leh are delayed, IA will pay for passengers' overnight accommodation in Leh.

At the time of writing, Archana Airways (AA), which normally concentrates on flying around Himachal Pradesh, plans to commence flights between Leh and Delhi, and between Leh and Kargil. Although the

---

Polo & Archery

In summer, polo games are often held in Leh. During the last century, games were played in the bazaar, and even in the main street, but nowadays games are held at the polo ground on Tuesday and Saturday (on Thursday, the ground becomes the venue for a serious football game). Matches and competitions are held regularly during the Ladakh Festival.

Historically, the game has always been more popular in the Muslim regions near Kargil, and in Dha-Hanu than in other Buddhist areas. In Leh, the two goals are placed about 100m apart, although in some villages over a dozen players in both teams may use fields over 350m long. Normally, a team consists of six men on horses (normally tired old Zanskari ponies), with one player defending the goal. One local rule stipulates that the team changes ends after each goal, so when a goal is scored defenders make an immediate dash to the opposite goals. The game is played frantically over two 20 minute halves. (Beware: it can be dangerous sitting in the first row at the Leh polo ground!)

Archery competitions are usually held between two teams in the villages, or more often at the National Archery Stadium in Leh. A team with the most arrows closest to the target – often just a lump of sand with a painted round symbol – wins. Archery is not particularly exciting to watch, but it's a great excuse for local people to dress up in their finest traditional clothing. During a match, there is plenty of dancing, singing and drinking of chang – and some archery in between it all. Not surprisingly, the standard of archery is a lot better in Kargil, where drinking and dancing is forbidden by Muslim law. ■

planes are likely to be small, these extra AA flights will certainly help alleviate the congestion and overbooking with IA. Also, flights to Kargil will make travel to Zanskar easier, although you would miss a truly spectacular (and a little scary) bus trip.

IA warns passengers it cannot depart Leh with more than 70 to 80 passengers because of the altitude, climatic conditions and short runway. So, at peak periods, flights can be heavily overbooked. To avoid this, book well ahead but be prepared for disappointment. If you can't get a booking in economy class, it's worth trying for 1st class, as it's only about 10% more expensive. Another answer is to get to the airport early on the day you want to go, because even if you are waitlisted up to number 100, there is still a good chance you will get on a flight, and a sudden improvement in conditions may result in a larger passenger load.

The Indian Airlines office (☎ 2276; airport ☎ 2455) is on the extension of Fort Rd, in a small, white building. The office is open from 10 am to 5 pm every day – 10 am to noon on Sunday – with a lunch break from 1 to 2 pm. It is worth getting to the office early to avoid the crowds of frantic people confirming their flights.

Bus There are only two overland routes to Leh: the road from Srinagar, and the road from Manali in Himachal Pradesh. A complication when trying to leave Leh for Srinagar or Manali is that you may not be able to buy tickets on the local buses (or private buses at the end of the season) until the evening before departure, because buses may not turn up from either of these places. Thus you can't be certain you will be leaving until the last moment. Try to book ahead, if possible, especially in peak season, at the New bus stand in Leh, from where the public buses leave.

Srinagar The Leh to Srinagar road is usually open from the beginning of June to October, but in practice the opening date can be variable. The trip takes two days, about 12 hours travel on each day, with an over-

night halt at Kargil. There are three classes of public buses, but you may not get the class you want on the day you want. J&KSTC buses to Kargil/Srinagar cost: 'Deluxe' Rs 176/333; 'A Class' Rs 111/222; and 'B Class' Rs 88/176. They leave Leh at 5.30 am every day, in season.

At the time of researching, the regular deluxe/tourist private buses, which used to connect Srinagar and Leh, were cancelled due to lack of demand.

Manali The Leh to Manali road is open for a shorter period, usually from July to mid-September, sometimes up to mid-October; again, the opening and closing dates can be variable depending on climatic conditions. There is a good selection of private and public buses for this route, indicating its popularity. (For more information on the buses, and the trip, refer to the Leh to Manali section later in this chapter.)

Jeep & Taxi Long-distance jeeps and taxis are expensive, but a useful alternative to the buses.

'Indian jeeps' take five passengers, and 'Japanese jeeps' and Ambassador taxis take four passengers, plus driver. Fares are are listed in the taxi stands in Leh and Kargil. Extra charges are Rs 250 if staying overnight; waiting for the second and third hours (the first is free) is set at Rs 105 per hour.

The two day trip from Leh to Manali (including an overnight stop) will cost about Rs 10,200. A trip from Leh, via Lahaul & Spiti, on to Shimla, and back to Leh, over five or six days would be fantastic, but very expensive at Rs 25,000. If hiring a jeep or taxi for a long trip, try to get a driver who speaks English and knows the area. This is not always possible because the next driver on the Taxi Union list gets the fare, regardless of his talents. Taxi drivers in Leh and Kargil are unionised; they must wear uniforms, and have to go through union checkpoints on all routes outside Leh.

While officially 'fixed', jeep and taxi fares for longer, more expensive trips are certainly negotiable.

Truck Trucks are a worthy, and acceptable, method of travelling to, or to places on the way to, Manali. Talk to the drivers at the truck stop on the way to the airport in Leh.

Getting Around

The Airport The bus service from Leh to the airport costs Rs 5 but it doesn't run regularly, if at all. Rates for jeeps and taxis are set at Rs 70 to Leh, or Rs 100 to Changspa.

Bus All public buses leave the New Bus stand, where it's difficult to secure information on schedules. Both tourist offices have an updated, but often incomplete, timetable for public buses. To get to the New bus stand, walk through the areas with the *chortens*, like everyone else; don't follow the long road.

Jeep & Taxi A taxi from the Old and New bus stands to Fort Rd for those tired from a long journey and/or with loads of gear will cost about Rs 20. Day trips to nearby gompas cost: to Sankar, Shanti and Spituk, Rs 450; to Shey, Tikse and Stok, Rs 588; or to just about every nearby gompa mentioned in the Around Leh section, Rs 1492.

Taxis in Leh congregate around three designated stands; they generally don't go around the streets looking for customers – you will have to approach them. Taxi drivers are unionised and accept only the union rate; fares are listed at the taxi stands. The biggest stand, taxi stand No 1 (☎ 3823) on Fort Rd, is open from 7 am to 7 pm, but there are taxis hanging around Fort Rd in the very early morning, waiting for fares to the airport or the New bus stand. Taxi stand No 2 is at the Old bus stand, where a few old taxis loiter; and No 3 is at the New bus stand, but you may find it hard to get a taxi here.

Motorcycle Motorcycles are just about the perfect way of travelling around the area near Leh. Rental is still in its infancy, with no established rental agencies – it's more a case of an enterprising local person renting out their own motorcycle. Indian-made Vespa scooters can be rented for about Rs 500 per day, plus petrol, from several places: Oasis

Travels on the way to the Indian Airlines office; Yati Travels, opposite the small post office on Main Bazaar Rd; and Yasmin Trek & Tour on Fort Rd. In coming seasons, motorcycle rental is likely to be more readily available, and, hopefully, cheaper, but there will be restrictions on how far you can travel away from Leh. Ensure that you have comprehensive insurance that covers you in the event of an accident in which either yourself or a local person is injured.

Bicycle Similarly, bicycle rental is just catching on. Mountain-bikes – a great way to visit the more accessible villages (but you may have to walk up to the gompas, anyway) – can be hired from the Lost Horizon travel agency opposite the Hotel Yak Tail. Rental is Rs 200 per day, but this price may be reduced as more competition comes along.

AROUND LEH

There are many beautiful gompas and villages which can be visited in day trips from Leh. Unless you have a taxi or your own transport, you will probably only be able to visit one or two in one day. Even though there is often no need to stay overnight, the villages are usually pretty and quiet, and sometimes a worthy alternative to Leh. Places are listed in alphabetical order for ease of reference.

Chemrey Gompa

Chemrey village has a well maintained and quiet gompa which sees few tourists because it is a little difficult to get to. Built to commemorate the death of King Singge Namgyal in 1645, the gompa belongs to the Drukpa order, and is where invading Dogras defeated a Tibetan army in the 1840s. The friendly monks can show you the impressive ancient library, and lovely Buddhist images on the wall of the prayer room. Nearby is a **cave gompa**.

To get to Chemrey, catch the bus to Taktok, get off at Chemrey village, and be prepared for a long (about an hour) and steep walk (it's steeper than to the Tikse Gompa). By car, there is a road to the top, but it is very narrow and windy. From Leh, return taxis

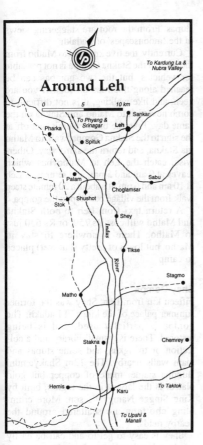

Around Leh

To Kardung La &
Nubra Valley

To Phyang &
Srinagar

Sankar

Pharka

Leh

Spituk

Palam

Sabu

Choglamsar

Stok

Shushot

Shey

Indus River

Tikse

Stagmo

Matho

Stakna

Chemrey

Hemis

Karu

To Taktok

To Upshi &
Manali

---

cost Rs 785, or you could try to arrange a side trip to Chemrey and Taktok if you're going on to Pangong Tso. There is nowhere to stay in Chemrey, but plenty of camping spots. However, before setting up your tent check with the villagers as to the correct places to camp.

Choglamsar

Choglamsar has become an important centre for the study of Tibetan culture and history, and Tibetan Buddhism. Around the Tibetan refugee camp, just off the main road from Leh, there is a Tibetan library, medical centre, handicraft shops, study centre, book-

shops, plenty of restaurants, and the Central Institute of Buddhist Studies.

Any of the buses heading south from Leh will drop you off at Choglamsar, or a one-way taxi will cost Rs 96. There are a couple of crummy guesthouses along the very noisy main road, but none worth recommending, especially as Choglamsar is so close to Leh.

Hemis Gompa

Also known as Chang-Chub-Sam-Ling (or the Lone Place of the Compassionate Person), Hemis Gompa, which belongs to the Drukpa order and was founded in the early 17th century, is 45 km from Leh. Now it is one of the most accessible, famous and, therefore, most popular and touristy gompas around. Cradled in a lovely valley, surrounded by streams and fronted by long *mani* walls, it is certainly worth a visit. The gompa is also important for Ladakhi Buddhists, who are meant to visit the gompa once in their lifetime.

The gompa has an excellent library, well preserved frescoes, showing some Kashmiri influence, and good Buddha figures. It is the sort of place where you may be invited to see a puja. The largest *thangka* in Ladakh, over 12m long, is at Hemis, but is only exhibited every 11 years. To commemorate the birth of the renowned Indian sage, Padmasambhava, the famous annual Hemis festival is held on the 9th to 11th days of the 5th Tibetan month. (See the Ladakh Festivals aside earlier in the chapter for details.)

There are no guesthouses near the gompa, but one or two in the village, a long walk away. Several places near the gompa allow camping: you can set up your own tent next to the gompa for Rs 35, or rent a pre-set two person tent for Rs 50. Book at the nice outdoor restaurant, next to the gompa entrance, which serves unexciting but welcome Chinese food, tea and beer. Hemis is worth staying over for a night to explore the **Kotsang Hermitage Gompa**, along a trail for an hour behind the gompa. There are also some **caves** nearby.

Daily buses leave Leh for Hemis at 9.30 am and 4 pm; and return to Leh at 6.30 am

The Hemis festival features chaams danced by monks in elaborate masks.

and 12.30 pm. The timings are not great, but allow you an hour or so to look around if you are on a day trip from Leh. Return taxis from Leh cost Rs 750.

Matho Gompa

Built in the early 16th century, but virtually destroyed in subsequent wars, the gompa at Matho belongs to the rare Sakyapa order. The festival here is famous for the incredible activities of the monks and the novices, who often go into trances, and inflict wounds on themselves which miraculously do not draw blood, or if they do, heal immediately.

Because tourists are not common at Matho, the monks have some time to really show you around, and explain the impressive thangkas in the very old library and the exhibits in the rather tacky museum (which includes a life-sized, stuffed yak!). It is a busy place, with a school for 30 children, and the 20 or so monks can be seen making intricate silver and gold decorations for

stupas. From the roof are staggering views of the 'moonscapes' of Ladakh.

Currently, the five km road to Matho from the back of the Stakna Gompa is not passable for vehicles, but the two gompas can be reached along this road on foot. If you are keen, and like walking, it is not difficult to combine a visit to Matho and Stakna on the same day. Take the bus to Hemis, get off at the sign to the Stakna Gompa, walk to Matho via Stakna, and return the same way. Otherwise, catch the Leh to Matho bus which leaves at 9 am and 5 pm, and returns to Leh at 10 am and 6 pm. It's about a 20 minute steep walk from the village bus stop to the gompa.

A return taxi from Leh to both Stakna and Matho will cost Rs 750, or Rs 630 just to Matho. There is nowhere to stay in Matho, but loads of pretty (but wet) places to camp.

Shey Gompa

Fifteen km from Leh, Shey was the former summer palace of the kings of Ladakh. The gompa is partially used, and is being restored. There is a small library and a collection of thangkas, and some stupas and mani walls nearby. The 12m Shakyamuni Buddha statue, made of copper but gold plated, is the largest in the region, built by King Singge Namgyal's son. More crumbling **chortens** are scattered around the nearby fields.

Shey is easy to get to and can be easily combined with a visit to Tikse by any form of transport. Catch any bus from Leh going to Tikse or Hemis and disembark at Shey; by taxi, it will cost Rs 230 return. The only place to stay is the pleasant and large *Shil Kar Hotel & Restaurant* near the road up to the gompa. Rooms with bathrooms cost Rs 150.

Spituk Gompa

On a hilltop above the Indus River and only eight km from Leh, the Spituk Gompa was built in the 15th century under the Gelukpa order. It is next to the airport, and so has an ugly view at the front, but the back looks onto the pretty local village. The two prayer rooms have some nice Buddha statues, only unveiled once a year during the annual festival held usually in January. Plenty of restoration was going on there at the time of researching.

Spituk has nowhere to stay or eat, as it is so close to Leh. From Leh to Spituk is a long, hot walk; a bike would be ideal. Alternatively, take one of the buses from Leh which go past Spituk every 15 minutes or so. Taxis from Leh cost Rs 185 return.

Stakna Gompa

The gompa at Stakna – which means 'tiger's nose' – is another set spectacularly on the Hemis side of the Indus River. Built by King Singge Namgyal's step-brother, as part of the Drukpa order, it is not difficult to get to, and can be combined with a trip to Matho on the same day (see the Matho section).

A brightly restored courtyard leads to several new and old prayer rooms, one of which has a lovely silver chorten. Thirty monks live here permanently. From the roof are the best 'moonscape' views to be had of Ladakh.

To get there, take the Leh-Hemis bus, and get off at the sign by the road to the gompa. Cross the bridge, and walk for 30 minutes across the shadeless fields and up the steep path. A return taxi from Leh costs Rs 550. There is no guesthouse in the village, but it should be possible to camp back near the Indus.

Stok Gompa & Museum

Over the bridge from Choglamsar, the Stok Gompa is where the last king of Ladakh died in 1974. Built in 1814, it is a popular place because it is so easy to get to. There are over 80 rooms, only a few of which are open to the public.

The museum has a unique display of rare ornaments from the royal family, thangkas, and traditional clothing and jewellery. Entry is Rs 20, and it's open in summer from 8 am to 7 pm. Photography is not permitted. The gompa, which has some fine masks and frescoes, is behind the museum, but don't wander near the Telecom plant.

The only nearby place to stay is the elegant *Hotel Highland,* just under the museum (there's no sign). There are other smaller places to stay towards the main road. Direct buses leave Leh at 7.30 am, and at 3 and 5 pm, or try to get there by mountain bike or motorcycle. A taxi will cost Rs 365 return from Leh.

Taktok Gompa

With at least five different spellings, Taktok is the only gompa belonging to the order of Nyingmapa in the upper Indus Valley. Built around a cave above the village of Sakti, the actual date of construction varies depending on who you talk to, but there have been some recent additions. The frescoes have been damaged over the years, but there are some intricate rugs and paintings to see.

Taktok is a little difficult to get to, and not on the usual 'gompa trail'. Tourists are not common, so you may have to find a monk to open the prayer rooms for you. Two festivals are held each year, from the 9th to 11th days of the sixth month (July/August), and from the 26th to 29th days of the ninth month (around November) of the Tibetan calendar.

There is nowhere to stay – the Tourist Bungalow opposite the gompa is closed – or to eat, but excellent camping sites are everywhere. One or two early morning daily buses go past Taktok from Leh, but departure times change regularly, so check at the tourist offices in Leh. There is at least one late afternoon bus back from Taktok to Leh every day. A return taxi from Leh costs Rs 946.

Tikse Gompa

About 17 km from Leh, this gompa is part of the Gelukpa order. It is a good example of how donations have been put to good use through extensive restoration work. It is a bit garish, but the setting is quite stupendous. Beside the car park is the small **Zan-La Temple**.

The Tikse Gompa has an important collection of Tibetan books in its library, some

TREKS IN LADAKH

Treks out of Leh and the Indus Valley can be organised by one of the local agents in Leh with prices between Rs 500 and Rs 1000 per day. You would, however, be advised to bring your own sleeping bag and tent with you. If making your own arrangements, it is possible to organise a horseman at one of the trekking-off points. However, this can take time and you should allow at least a day or two before setting off. Budget for Rs 200 and upwards per horse per day.

The trek from Spituk, just below Leh, to the Markha Valley and Hemis Gompa is the most popular trek in Ladakh. The trek from Lamayuru to Alchi is more demanding and requires a local guide on some sections where the trail is not well defined. Altitude is a very important consideration on these treks with many of the passes in the vicinity of 5000m. As an alternative, the trek from Likir Gompa to Temisgam is over relatively low passes and can be considered throughout the year.

Spituk-Hemis Trek

The trek from Spituk Gompa up the Jingchen Valley avoids crossing any passes on the first two stages. However, at least one rest day should be included before crossing the Ganda La (4920m). From the pass it is a steady descent to the Markha Valley and the village of Skiu. Trekking up the valley it is one stage to Markha village, a substantial place with a small gompa, before ascending to the yak grazing pastures at Nimaling. Above the camp is the impressive peak of Kangyaze (6400m). The Kongmaru La (5030m) is the highest pass on the trek and affords great views south to the Zanskar Range and north to the Ladakh Range. After crossing the pass there is one further campsite at the village of Chogdo before reaching Hemis Gompa and the bus back to Leh.

Stage 1	Spituk to Rumbak (6-7 hours)
Stage 2	Rumbak to Yurutse (3-4 hours)
Stage 3	Rest day
Stage 4	Yurutse to Skiu via Ganda La (7-8 hours)
Stage 5	Skiu to Markha (7-8 hours)
Stage 6	Markha to Nimaling (7-8 hours)
Stage 7	Nimaling to Chogdo via Kongmaru La (7-8 hours)
Stage 8	Chogdo to Hemis (4-5 hours)

Lamayuru-Alchi Trek

This trek is often undertaken by travellers coming from Srinagar or Kargil en route to Leh. At Lamayuru there are a number of lodges that can assist with horsemen before trekking over a small pass, the Prinkiti La, to the gompa at Wanlah.

From Wanlah allow a further two stages before crossing the Konze La (4950m) to the village at Sumdo. From here the trail to the village of Sumdo Choon at the base of the Stakspi La is not well defined. The views from the Stakspi La (4970m) are worth the effort, with a rewarding panorama of the Ladakh and Karakoram ranges, before a long descent to Alchi Gompa and transport to Leh.

Stage 1	Lamayuru to Wanlah (3 hours)
Stage 2	Wanlah to Phanjila (4 hours)
Stage 3	Phanjila to base of Konze La (5 hours)
Stage 4	Konze La base to Sumdo via Konze La (5-6 hours)
Stage 5	Sumdo to Sumdo Choon (5 hours)
Stage 6	Sumdo Choon to Alchi via Stakspi La (8 hours)

Likir-Temisgam Trek

This trek can be completed in a day if you are fit! From Likir Gompa the trail crosses a small pass to the village of Yantang, a short distance from Rizong Gompa. The next stage leads to the village of Hemis-Shukpachu. It is a further short stage over two minor passes to Temisgam, where there is a daily bus back to Leh.

Stage 1	Likir to Yantang (4-5 hours)
Stage 2	Yantang to Hemis-Shukpachu (3 hours)
Stage 3	Hemis-Shukpachu to Temisgam (3-4 hours)

excellent artwork and a new Maitreya temple. It's a busy place, with almost incessant chanting and music, and there is a good chance to witness a puja. Go to the roof for great views of the valleys and villages. There is even a small (and welcome) cafe and shop. The gompa is open daily from 7.30 am to 6 pm. Permission is required to use video or movie cameras.

The only place to stay in Tikse is the *Skalzang Chamba Hotel*, right at the start of the trail leading to the gompa. It is a well run and pleasant place with a small garden, and costs Rs 130 per room, including meals. Students (male only) of Buddhism, but not ordinary backpackers, may be able to stay at the gompa.

A bus from Leh to Tikse leaves about every hour or, alternatively, take the Hemis bus, which leaves Leh at 9.30 am and 4 pm. From the bus stop, it is a fair walk up to the gompa, as usual. A return taxi from Leh will cost Rs 350.

Ladakh Regions

This section deals with areas which have been recently opened up by the Indian authorities to allow travellers (with permits) to visit.

PERMITS

Permits are required for all foreigners (including non-Ladakhi and non-Zanskari Indians) for the four newly opened areas in Ladakh: the Nubra Valley, Pangong Tso, Tso Moriri and the Dha-Hanu region. In the past year, these permits and their enforcement have become less strict. Quite possibly (and hopefully) regulations for these new areas will be relaxed even further, or even abolished – although you are unlikely to ever get permission to go anywhere you want in the region, because it remains a sensitive part of India. Check the current regulations.

At the time of researching, permits were only valid for seven days, and although four people must *apply* for a permit together, checkpoints do not require that you actually need to *travel* together. Take your permits with you at all times – there are several checkpoints along most roads. If you need a group, leave messages around noticeboards in Leh, or get a travel agency to organise things

First, a 'letter of introduction' from a travel agency is necessary, even though you don't have to go on an organised tour. Travel agencies in Leh will charge about Rs 50 per person for the letter. Several travel agencies are willing to find some old photocopies of other passports to help 'fill up' the required numbers for your 'group'. Ask discreetly at agencies or check with other travellers.

Second, fill out the application form, which your travel agent will have. List every place you may go to, within the permitted regions. Then take a copy of the front page (ie with your personal details, and photo) of your passport, and Indian visa. Take it all to the District Magistrate's Office in Leh (open 10 am to 4 pm daily, except Sundays and public holidays), just above the polo ground. And wait. It is worth considering paying your travel agent another Rs 80 to Rs 100 per person, which includes a special 'fee' for speedy service at the Magistrate's Office, to let the agent organise the permit.

Take a photocopy of the permit for yourself. These permits must be shown at checkposts, and your hotels in the regions may also require details of your permit. You are allowed to travel to the regions by public or private transport, or by taxi; alone, or in a group of less than four. If any checkpost asks where the rest of your group is, make some excuse about them missing the bus, or being attacked by a vicious wild marmot, or something a bit more convincing!

Consider others if you are thinking of breaking your permit regulations and going to unpermitted areas, or overstaying your allotted seven days. If you do break the rules, you will be in trouble, your travel agency will be severely penalised, and regulations are likely to become stricter, affecting future travellers.

CLIMATE

The average summer (June to September) and winter (October to May) temperatures for the four regions are:

Region	Max	Min
Nubra Valley	28/15°C	-3/-15°C
Pangong Tso	18/5°C	-12/-25°C
Tso Moriri	17/6°C	-10/-22°C
Dha-Hanu region	29/15°C	-3/-15°C

WHAT TO BRING

For the two lake regions, Pangong Tso and Tso Moriri, there are currently no guest-houses, or shops to buy supplies (although this is likely to change soon). So, you must take all your own food, and sleeping and cooking equipment – which can be hired in Leh. In the more populated Dha-Hanu and Nubra Valley areas, there are a few guest-houses for accommodation and food, and small shops for basic supplies. To liven up a boring plate of *dhal* and rice or *thukpa*, or to please locals if you are willing to share, it's a good idea to bring some canned meat and fresh vegetables from Leh if visiting the remote villages in Dha-Hanu and Nubra.

Even in the height of summer, temperatures in some valleys in all regions can be extremely cold. A sleeping bag and warm clothes are vital in all areas. The days can be hot, causing dry skin and sunburn, so a good hat, sunscreen and so on are important. Other items worth considering are torches (flashlights) and candles, as electricity, if there is any, is unreliable in all regions; and binoculars to admire the wildlife, which are guaranteed to disappear when you get too close.

ORGANISED TOURS

Tours, organised by reputable travel agencies in Leh, are the easiest, most comfortable, but, naturally, most expensive way to go. If you want to pay more for a guide and some comfort, make sure the tour is not just a local taxi-driver-cum-guide, because you can organise one of them yourself at the taxi-stand in Leh for far less. The quality of jeep, tent accommodation, food, destination and guide, and the demand affects the price of organised tours, but a rough idea of the sort of costs per day per person for an up-market trip are: a five day package to the Nubra Valley for US$40 to US$60; three days at Pangong Tso, US$50 to US$65; and to Tso Moriri for four days US$55 to US$70.

NUBRA VALLEY

The Nubra Valley – *nubra* means 'green' – used to be on the trading route which connected Tibet with Turkistan, and was the envy of Turkistan, which invaded it several times. Also known as the Valley of Flowers, Ldomra, Nubra has always been well cultivated and fertile, with the best climate in Ladakh, so fruits, such as apples and apricots, and grains, have always been plentiful. The Nubra people are 90% Buddhist.

The valley is a wonderful area to visit, dominated by an incredible broad, empty valley between the Nubra and Shyok rivers. Camels are common near Hunder. There are pretty, small villages, dense forests and some wildlife, but, inevitably, the area is becoming slowly more affected by the increasing number of travellers who make the effort to visit. Remember that your permit only allows you to travel as far as Hunder along the southern valley, and to Panamik, in the northern valley.

Festivals

Nubra Valley isn't as crowded with gompas as the area around Leh, so festivals tend to be less religious and more sport-oriented. As part of the Ladakh Festival in the first two weeks of September each year, there are many activities in the Nubra Valley which should not be missed, including a camel safari between Diskit and Hunder. They are generally centred in the main villages of Diskit and Sumur.

Leh to Kardung

The road to the Nubra Valley goes through the highest motorable pass in the world at Kardung La (5602m). The pass is almost permanently covered in fog and snow, and is likely to be bitterly cold at the top regardless of the time of year. A free cup of hot chai, near the 'highest temple in the world' – Jai Kardungla Babe – is most welcome. In the summer, you may see the world's highest traffic jam of trucks and buses too.

The road between Leh and Khalsar is reasonable, except between the miserable road-building camps of South Pullu and North Pullu, just before and after Kardung La, where the road is atrocious. Near the pass, there are many places to stop for views, if you can, such as the intriguing-sounding Siachen Taggles' Gate.

The road then continues to Kardung village, which, most disappointingly, has no tea stall, one very basic shop, and an unused Government Rest House.

Khalsar

The Nubra Valley really starts at the village of Khalsar, where there *are* several tea houses and some hotels for about Rs 30 to Rs 50 per room. The better two are *L. Tonyot* which also serves good dhal and rice, and the *Wisnu Hotel*. The road then bisects just before the village of Lughzhun, to Hunder and beyond in the valley following the Shyok River, and, further north, to Panamik and beyond, following the Nubra River.

Diskit

To Diskit, the road suddenly turns left, along an awesome, wide and dry riverbed for about three km. Truck and bus drivers know where to turn off (there are no signs), so if you have your own transport, ask and follow the other vehicles. Diskit is about 10 km further up the hill.

The **Diskit Gompa**, with about 70 monks, is the oldest – over 350 years old – and the biggest of its kind in the Nubra Valley, and shouldn't be missed. It is particularly famous for its murals, and the scenery from the roof is wonderful. According to legend, there is a statue in the gompa which has the head and arm of an invader from over five centuries ago. There are three prayer rooms, on different levels, including a library, some very old frescoes, and a few nice thangkas. From the village, it is a 40 minute walk. The gompa is

slightly hidden, up the hill, and can be confusing to find, so, if in doubt, keep asking locals for directions.

Between Diskit and Hunder is an area of **sand dunes**, not unlike the Saharan regions (if you can ignore the snow-capped Alp-like mountains in the background!). There are a few herds of semi-wild and domesticated Bactrian (double-humped) camels. If you want to risk a ride, ask at your guesthouse or around the village. Sometimes, camel safari races are held between the two villages.

Places to Stay & Eat About 50m from the gompa is *Olthang Guest House and Camping*. It has a nice garden, and costs Rs 150 per room, with a bathroom. The *Shahen Hotel*, on the main street in the village, is very basic for about Rs 50 a room – you may have to find someone to open the hotel and take your money. The *Sand Dune Hotel* in the village has also been recommended. Your hotel will rustle up dhal and rice, or try one of the little tea houses along the main street.

Hunder

Hunder is a pretty village, set among lots of trees, and mingling streams. It is nicer than Diskit, but Diskit has slightly better facilities as it's the bigger village of the two. From Diskit, it is only about seven km to Hunder; some visitors enjoy the walk from one village to another, either along the main road, or across the sand dunes. (But watch out for wild camels!)

The **gompa** at Hunder is about a two km walk above the village, including a short, but steep, rocky climb. It is completely deserted, and quite eerie. There is only a small Buddha statue, and some damaged frescoes, but the climb is worth it for the views and atmosphere. Don't wander too far up the road because of the heavy military presence there.

Places to Stay & Eat Hunder is a spread out village, like many others, full of cobbled streets, with no centre and street signs. There is no way of finding out the name and location of a guesthouse – they are often just a few rooms at the back of someone's home; so it is a matter of constantly asking directions.

One of the better places, already set up (and the first of many more) is the *Nerchung Pa*, owned by the local headmaster. It is friendly, set in a nice garden, costs Rs 150 per person including three meals, and is impossible to find.

Camping sites are being developed, but their rumoured prices – over Rs 1000 for a pre-set two person tent with meals – are outrageous. Hopefully, prices will decrease with time and competition. Alternatively, find a spot near the village to camp for free. There is no electricity this far up the valley, so torches and candles are necessary, and should be brought from Leh.

Sumur
Sumur is the first major village along the Nubra River side of the valley. It is also a pretty place, and worth staying and exploring.

The **Samtanling Gompa** at Sumur, over 150 years old, is a large complex with seven temples. Inaugurated by the Dalai Lama in 1962, it is a busy, friendly place with about 45 children busy chanting, or cultivating apples and apricots. The prayer rooms open to the public house an impressive collection of thangkas and excellently restored frescoes.

By road, it is a fair distance from Sumur village to the gompa: about three km towards the village of Tegar, from where a three km road to the gompa starts. It's far quicker on foot, as you can go up the hill from the village and avoid the road, but you will have to ask directions. It can be confusing, because the gompa near the start of the road to the Samtanling Gompa is actually the Tegar Gompa. The Samtanling Gompa is the more colourful one, and is situated closer to Sumur.

Places to Stay & Eat Along the main road in Sumur is the pretty dingy *Hotel Sumur* for rock-bottom price and comfort. The *Tsering Angchok Hotel* is another no-frills place but cheapish at Rs 70 per person – just follow the signs from the main road. Further up – ask

for directions – is the *Stakrey Guest House* (also owned by the local headmaster). For about Rs 200 per person with three meals, you get good, friendly service and mountain views.

Just opposite the road leading to the Samtanling Gompa, near the village of Tegar, is the up-market *Hotel Yarab Tso*. For an overpriced Rs 975 per room, you get a large, clean room and immaculate bathroom with hot water. (This is the first of several, similarly priced places being built around the Nubra Valley.) You may be able to stay at the Samtanling Gompa if you are a serious (male) Buddhist student. There are some shops near the main road in Sumur with some limited supplies, and some tea stalls which serve basic food.

Panamik
Panamik is another small village, famous for centuries for its **hot springs**, and as the first or last stop along the ancient trade route between Ladakh and central Asia. While Panamik may be a long way to come for some hot springs, they are worth visiting if you're in the Nubra Valley.

The water, which is meant to cure rheumatism, among other ailments, is pumped in by pipe from the Nubra River, about two km from the village. It is usually easier for men to have a bath or shower; unfortunately, women will have to be a bit more modest and careful about their attire. There are also a couple of craft shops in the village, where you can buy some weaving and woodcarvings.

The 250 year old **Ensa Gompa** is a fair walk from the village – a couple of hours at least. It is further than it seems, and is not really worth the effort; relax and enjoy the hot springs instead. However, if you do want to get to the gompa, walk about five km to Hargam, then cross the bridge for some more walking. Some travellers have tried to cross the river by swimming or wading, and many have nearly come to a tragic end. Be sensible and take the bridge.

Places to Stay & Eat Currently, there is one guesthouse, which costs Rs 150 for a big double room; dhal, rice and tea will cost more. More guesthouses – and camping sites – are very likely to be built in the near future. There are one or two small shops for supplies, but they offer little. Panamik does not yet have electricity.

Getting There & Away

As with most of Ladakh, the road to the Nubra Valley (because of the very high Kardung La), and, therefore, the valley itself, is only open for three to four months of the year, from about June to September.

Air Indian Airlines (IA) reportedly wants to commence flights, probably from Delhi, direct to Hunder, where there is a military airfield which can be converted to accommodate civilian aircraft. At the time of researching, IA would not confirm its intentions. If flights to the Nubra Valley do start, there are serious implications for the infrastructure of the region which could not cope with a tourist influx yet, and it will presumably increase the availability of associated transport, such as taxis and local buses in the region.

Bus Buses travel to both sides of the Nubra Valley from Leh every few days. The time-tables are irregular, so check with local bus and tourist agencies. The buses are slow and crowded, as expected in this region, but are fun. Buses between Leh and Diskit travel on Monday and Friday (at least five hours, Rs 54); they leave Leh at 5.30 am. Buses from Diskit to Panamik and back go on Monday and Wednesday. The bus will drop you off in the main street of Diskit, a little way off the main road. A bus to Sumur, and Panamik (Rs 66), leaves Leh at 5.30 am on Monday and Wednesday.

Truck Lifts on trucks, even military ones – in fact, anything travelling along the roads to, and around, the Nubra Valley – is quite acceptable for tourists and locals alike. As usual, negotiate a fare (around the cost of the bus fare, ie Rs 60), and prepare yourself for a rough old ride.

Taxi Hiring jeeps or taxis may be the only alternative, and with a group it is often a good option. A one-way/return taxi to Diskit from Leh will cost Rs 2750/3630. A taxi from Leh to Panamik will cost Rs 3000, or Rs 4070 return. A return trip from Leh visiting Diskit, Hunder, Sumur and Panamik for three days will cost about Rs 7500 per taxi. If there are taxis around Diskit, they will offer full day tours around the area on that southern side of the valley for Rs 840; or Rs 1100 including both sides. From Diskit to Panamik, it will be Rs 1000/1290; from Diskit to Sumur, Rs 650/840.

PANGONG TSO

The salty Pangong Tso – Pangong means 'hollow' – is the highest lake in Ladakh at about 4300m, and is flanked by massive peaks over 6500m high. The lake is 150 km long, but is only four km at its widest, and extends almost in a straight line, way into Tibet; in fact, only a quarter of the lake is in India.

Pangong Tso is a good side trip from Leh: it involves less bone-crushing travel, transport is cheaper because it is closer to Leh, and less time is needed to see it than other regions. Permits allow travel from Leh to Pangong Tso via Karu, Chang La, Durbuk, Tangtse, Lukung and only as far as Spangmik, the first village on the north-western side of the lake.

The area around Tangtse, on the way to the lake, is of historical significance, as it was an important stop on ancient trade routes. There is a small **gompa**; and some **inscriptions** nearby, possibly 1000 years old, on the rocks around the area, but these are hard to locate.

Places to Stay & Eat

There are no guesthouses in the villages except a *Government Rest House* in Tangtse, which is not strictly for tourists, so you will have to bring your own tents and all your own supplies. Official camping sites are at Durbuk, Tangtse, Lukung and Spangmik; otherwise, just take your pick of any unofficial spot in the countryside. Lukung is about the best area for camping. There are several little villages along the lake, and on the way to it, but they offer little, if anything, in the way of supplies.

Getting There & Away

From Leh, the road is reasonable to the military town of Karu, goes through the Chang La (5599m), and then becomes terrible down to Tangtse, another military site. The road then alternates between very bad and barely adequate until Lukung, and then to Spangmik, which is as far as your permit will allow; a 4WD vehicle is necessary for this section.

By Indian or Japanese jeep from Leh the cost of a one-way/return fare to Tangtse is Rs 2500/3300. A more leisurely two day trip, which is about all you may need, will cost Rs 5000 per vehicle from Leh. You may be able to fit in a side trip to the gompas at Tikse and Chemrey along the way to Tangtse.

There are occasional buses from Leh to Tangtse, but taking a bus will severely limit your ability to explore the area, as there is no local public transport.

DHA-HANU

Dha-Hanu is an area along the road which starts north-west at Khalsi, while the main road continues to Kargil. It is a small region, and without the scenery of other newly opened areas, is not as popular. The definite pluses are its accessibility by bus, along a reasonable road, and the local people, who have different traditions and appearances to the rest of the population of Ladakh. Currently, permits will allow you to go only as far as the village of Dha.

People

The area is probably most famous for its nomadic inhabitants, known as Dards or Drukpas, 'people of the land'. Despite their proximity to Pakistan and other Islamic regions, they are traditionally not Muslims (though there are a few mosques in the area) but retain their own Buddhist traditions and beliefs. They belong to the whiter-skinned Aryan tribal group, who migrated to the area over 1000 years ago from the Karakoram area in far northern Pakistan. Two of their most unusual traits are their intense distaste for onions and cows, and anything bovine such as milk and beef.

The Drukpas often wear traditional clothes. Men wear coats similar to those worn in Leh, and some are made from goatskin. Women often wear caps (rather than the *gondas* found in Leh) adorned with jewellery, flowers and peacock feathers, have long, ornate chains, heavy earrings, and wear their hair long.

Places to Stay & Eat

There are a handful of cheap guesthouses in the villages of Dha, Biama and Skurbuchan, and many more will probably be built in the immediate future. It is also possible to stay at a home in one of the villages; just ask; someone will surely put you up for a small fee. There are recognised camping sites at the villages of Dhumkhar, Skurbuchan, Hanu, Biama and Dha, and plenty of other legal, but unofficial, places along the way. The one or two shops at Dha and Skurbuchan offer little in the way of food, otherwise your guesthouse will provide something basic to eat; or bring your own supplies.

Getting There & Away

Buses from Leh to Dha leave every day at 9 am; and from Leh to Skurbuchan daily at 10 am. A taxi to Dha from Leh will cost Rs 2150, and Rs 2850 return.

TSO MORIRI & TSO KAR

Known as 'mountain lake', Tso Moriri is located in the Rupsu Valley, only about 140 km, but a rough and tumble six or so hours by jeep, from Leh. The lake is about 28 km long and eight km at its widest, and at an elevation of over 4000m. Surrounded by barren hills, which are backed by snow-covered mountains, Tso Moriri is not in a really spectacular setting, but it's a good place to relax, visit the nearby **gompas** and walk around the lake area. On the way from Leh to Tso Moriri is another, brackish, lake the smaller Tso Kar, or 'white lake'.

This is an area of nomadic people, known as Khampas, who can often be seen taking advantage of the summer and moving herds of goats, cows and yaks from one grazing spot to another. Khampas live in large, movable, family tents, or in solid winter-proof brick huts.

Another great aspect of this region is the amount of wildlife – the best (accessible) place in Ladakh for it. Commonly seen are wild asses, known as kiangs, foxes, and cuddly marmots busy waking up from their last hibernation, or preparing for the next. On the lakes, you may see black-necked geese in large flocks.

Tso Moriri

The small collection of huts on the shore of Tso Moriri is simply called Tso Moriri also. Here you must register, and show your permit. You can pitch your tent here, but there is nothing stopping you from camping anywhere else. Tso Moriri village does have a toilet.

Korzok

A path at the back of the huts for a km or so leads to the delightful village of Korzok, inhabited by friendly people. The **gompa** there is quite unusual because it is inhabited predominantly by about 30 women, who often spend their days making beautiful garments for themselves, but which are not for sale (yet?). The gompa was built in about 1850, replacing one destroyed during a Dogra invasion.

Tso Kar

On Tso Kar, there is a small **gompa** at the village of Thukse, a collection of solid brick huts, set up for the dramatic winters. You will have to find the monk to let you in. On a slight – and legal – detour off the track linking Tso Kar and Tso Moriri is the smaller lake of **Tso Kiagar**.

Places to Stay & Eat

In short, there is nowhere to stay in the region at all – though this may change as the demand for guesthouses increases. You must bring your own tents and all equipment. There are pre-set tents at the astronomical price of Rs 800 per two person tent at Tso Moriri village; these are set up for up-market, organised tour groups. Some building was going on at Tso Moriri village at the time of writing, so small shops selling limited supplies may be set up soon.

There is no place to eat in the region, so, again, bring your own food, and cooking equipment. This is a very fragile environment, so take out, and back to Leh, everything that you bring in – cans, bottles, papers, *everything*.

Getting There & Away

There are two ways which your 4WD jeep is physically able, and permitted, to enter or leave the region. The first route is over the Mahe bridge (near Raldong, along the Indus Valley road) through Puga, and then to one or both lakes. The other route is the road south from Upshi, over the Taglang La, then a detour off the road – look out for the yellow sign. Once you get off any main road, there are no signs (or maps) at all.

There is no public transport that even remotely goes near the lakes. The area has no signposts, and quality maps of the area are nonexistent, so motorcycles or mountain-bikes are not recommended unless you have a guide. There will be very few people around to give you directions. (Marmots around here outnumber humans by about 50 to one!)

Taxi A round trip from Leh to Tso Moriri over three days will cost about Rs 8100 via Tso Kar and Taglang La, or the shorter, more direct way is Rs 6500. From Leh, a two day round trip just to Tso Kar will be Rs 4200. Travel agencies in Leh can organise a three day 'jeep safari' from Rs 7000 to Rs 9500 per vehicle, including meals and tent accommodation, depending which way you go.

Trekking With a guide, trekking is possible, and has been completed successfully by several travellers. On foot, you can enter the region from anywhere; the best starting point would be the Mahe bridge – it is easy to get a bus or truck there from Leh. But remember that suitable maps do not exist of the area.

CHUMATHANG

Not far from the Mahe bridge is the uninspiring village of Chumathang, set around a huge yard of rusting asphalt drums. Its claims to fame are its hot springs and rafting. You can organise yourself a private bath of hot sulphurous water, which is not worth the effort. There are a few tea stalls in the village, and one or two charmless guesthouses.

Leh to Manali

This road was opened to foreigners as recently as 1989. Since then, it has rapidly become a popular way into and out of Leh, especially because the only other road to/from Leh goes through the troublesome areas of Kashmir towards Srinagar, and there is often difficulty in getting flights into and out of Leh. There is nothing to see along the road in the way of villages or gompas; it is the scenery which will certainly impress, and is reason enough for travelling this way.

The road to Manali is the world's second-highest motorable road, reaching an elevation of 5328m at Taglang La. As only about half of the total distance of 485 km between Leh and Manali is paved, it can be a rough journey. Whatever form of transport, it will take at least two days, with an overnight stop at a tent camp, probably in Sarchu or Darcha.

It is not uncommon for there to be sudden changes in weather, even in the mid-summer month of August, causing delays of several days. While it may be sunny in Leh, it is worth having some cold and wet weather gear with you in the bus because the weather, especially around the very high passes, can be very cold and/or wet. The road is usually open between early June and mid-October.

LEH TO UPSHI

Leaving Leh, from the main road you will get your last glimpse (or your first, of course,

if coming from Manali) of the magnificent gompas at Tikse, Shey and Stok. For an hour or so before Upshi, along a paved, but dusty, road, there are plenty of ugly military sites, such as at Karu, where there is the turn-off to the Pangong Tso area, and to the gompas at Taktok and Chemrey.

UPSHI

The first checkpoint of Upshi is the turn-off south to Manali. Although permits are not needed for this trip, foreigners have to register at the police hut. If travelling on a bus with plenty of other foreigners, there is plenty of

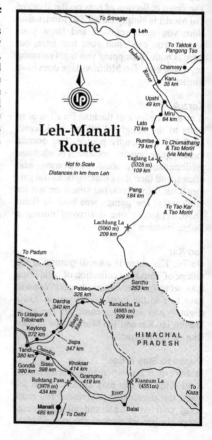

Leh-Manali Route

Not to Scale
Distances in km from Leh

To Srinagar
Leh
To Taktok & Pangong Tso
Indus River
Chemrey
Karu 35 km
Upshi 49 km
Miru 64 km
Lato 70 km
Rumtse 79 km — To Chumathang & Tso Moriri (via Mahe)
Taglang La (5328 m) 109 km
Pang 184 km
To Tso Kar & Tso Moriri
Lachlung La (5060 m) 209 km
To Padum
Patseo 326 km
Darcha 340 km
Sarchu 263 km
Baralacha La (4883 m) 299 km
To Udaipur & Triloknath
Keylong 372 km
Bhaga River
Jispa 347 km
Tandi 380 km
Chandra
Gondla 390 km
Sissu 398 km
Khoksar 414 km
Gramphu 419 km
Kunzum La (4551 m)
To Kaza
HIMACHAL PRADESH
Rohtang Pass (3978 m) 434 km
River
Manali 485 km
To Delhi
Batal

time for tea, an 'omlate', or to stock up on supplies of chocolate and other goodies. In Upshi, there are a couple of desperate-looking places to stay at the junction, at about Rs 50 per room, but there seems little point, as it is not far from Leh.

UPSHI TO TAGLANG LA

At Miru, there is a crumbling little **gompa**, worth a look, on the nearby hill, surrounded by chortens. There is nowhere to stay or eat, but plenty of camping sites. Lato has a huge **chorten** on the side of the road, but there is no village to speak of. Rumtse is another small village, with an empty Tourist Bunga-low, which may be open at another time, and some tent hotels which also serve food. From here the road starts to climb for about three hours to Taglang La (5328m), where there's a little shrine, and the world's highest 'Gents Urinal' and 'Ladies Urinal'. The bus will stop for a rest and a look around, but if coming from Manali and you haven't acclimatised to the altitude, take it easy.

TAGLANG LA TO LACHLUNG LA

Not long after Taglang La, the road surpris-ingly flattens out along a valley, and becomes paved. If going on to Tso Moriri or Tso Kar, you will have to look out for the sign. (Refer to the Ladakh Regions section.) The road to Pang is good, through a wind-swept valley, then becomes hopelessly potholed. Five km before Pang, the road descends through a dramatic **series of gorges** before reaching the tea house settlement.

Pang, at the bottom of these gorges, has several restaurants in tents set up by the river where most buses stop for lunch. A plate of rice, dhal and vegetables costs about Rs 20, and you may be able to stock up on mineral water and biscuits. Most tents have a mat-tress where you can unroll your sleeping bag for Rs 40 per night. There are hundreds of doorless toilet cubicles nearby which you can use.

At 5060m, Lachlung La is the second-highest pass on the Leh to Manali road. Nearby, there is an incredible 20 km of switchback roads, including a spine-tingling

21 'loops', or hairpin bends, on one side of one mountain.

SARCHU

Sarchu is just over the state line into Himachal Pradesh, and is where most buses will stop overnight. It is just a collection of tents, dotted over a length of 15 km or so, which all pack up for eight months of the year (ie October to May). Just opposite the striped Himachal Pradesh Tourist Develop-ment Corporation (HPTDC) tent camps, you must register, again, with the police. Your bus driver may collect passports and do it himself, but it still involves a lot of waiting.

HPTDC buses stop at HPTDC's own tent camps. They are the best of the lot: clean two person tents with camp beds and lots of blankets are Rs 115 per person. A tent kitchen does passable dhal and rice for dinner, and omelettes for breakfast, for about Rs 40.

Public and other private bus drivers seem to have some sort of 'arrangement' with other tent site owners, so you may have little choice but to stay in a tent camp not even remotely as good as the HPTDC site, but for around the same price. Although the driver will try to dissuade you, you can sleep on the bus for free, where it will be warmer. There are plenty of places to put your own tent.

Just over the bridge from the HPTDC camp are several tent restaurants which serve dhal and rice, tea, omelettes, curried noodles, and, for those long cold evenings, a shot (or bottle) of whisky or chang.

BARALACHA LA

It's only a short climb to this 4883m pass, which means 'crossroads pass' because it is a double pass linking both the upper Chandra and Bhaga valleys with the Lingti Valley and vast Lingti plains around Sarchu. About an hour further on is the **police checkpoint** at Patseo. Here the road begins to hug the Bhaga River to Tandi, where it meets the Chandra River.

DARCHA

Darcha is the other major tent site on this road. Faster buses from Leh, or slower ones from Manali, may stay here, depending on the time and the state of the road around Baralacha La, but Sarchu is more commonly used as a stopover. Like Sarchu, Darcha is just a temporary place, with some crummy tents for hire, and a few tent restaurants in the area. Shortly after Darcha, you pass through Jispa, where there is yet another large army camp.

Darcha is the start of a popular trekking option to get into Padum, and in winter it is the only way. From here, you can also trek into places such as Hemis (about 11 days). If you have your own transport, try to get to the little lake of **Deepak Tal** about 16 km from Darcha. It is a great spot for camping and exploring.

KEYLONG TO MANALI
Keylong is the first town of any size on the journey from Leh to Manali, and the administrative centre of Lahaul & Spiti. From Keylong, it isn't far to the T-junction at Tandi. From here there is a road that goes sharply to the north-west along the Chenab River to the little-visited parts of Himachal Pradesh towards Udaipur and the famous temple site of **Triloknath**.

The road to Manali heads south-east, and climbs steadily past Gondla, Sissu and Khoksar. There are PWD rest houses, which you may be able to use, in all three places, but nothing much else. At **Sissu**, there is a nice **waterfall** nearby, set under spectacular peaks. Further on, at Gramphu, the road continues to climb along Lahaul & Spiti – get off at Gramphu or at Keylong if you want to continue to Kaza – or heads south to Manali.

Rohtang Pass (3978m) – not high, but treacherous all the same – starts the descent to Manali.

Refer to the Himachal Pradesh chapter for more details on the towns of Keylong and Manali.

GETTING THERE & AWAY
Bus
As the road goes up to 5328m at its highest point, most people suffer the effects of altitude (eg headaches, nausea) from the rapid

ascent, as well as the high altitude, unless they have spent time acclimatising in Leh.

If you plan to fly one way, then fly into Leh and take the bus out because the effects of the altitude gain on the Leh-Manali journey will not be so great as doing the journey in the other direction.

All buses leave Leh at about 6 am to get an early start for the long haul to the overnight stop. Make sure you know your bus number because at this early hour, in darkness, it can be quite confusing finding your bus, among several others.

There are three types of buses which travel between Leh and Manali, all of which generally run daily during the season, more often if there is demand. Most bus services will not start until about early July and then cease in about mid-September, possibly later, if there is demand and the weather holds. Late in the season, the availability of buses from Leh depends on the demand for passengers travelling in the other direction, ie from Manali to Leh. From Manali, it is easy to get a connection on a deluxe bus almost straight away to Delhi for about Rs 400 or to many other places; less for the public bus.

HPTDC Bus The most comfortable bus is operated by the HPTDC. Bookings and departures are from the HPTDC office on Fort Rd in Leh, or the HPTDC Marketing Office (☎ 2116) on The Mall, Manali. Tickets cost Rs 700 (Rs 600 from Leh to Keylong), or Rs 1000 includes a tent, dinner and breakfast in Sarchu. This extra Rs 300 is not worth it, as you can stay in the same tent and order the same meals yourself in Sarchu for about half this. Try to book your bus ticket as far in advance as you can, especially if you intend travelling at the end of the season.

Private Bus Many other privately owned (by travel agencies in Manali) buses offer a slightly cheaper, and slightly less comfortable, alternative. All private buses cost around the same: about Rs 600, plus accommodation and food in Sarchu or Darcha – but the price can, and does, change according to the demand. In Leh, you must buy your tickets from any of the travel agencies, which means you probably won't know what bus you have a ticket for until you get on. In Manali, bookings can, and should be, made directly with the bus agencies themselves, or any of the travel agencies in Manali will sell you a ticket. Some of the bus companies in Manali servicing the Leh to Manali route on a regular basis are:

Enn Bee Tours & Travels, The Mall (opposite the bus station)(☎ 2650)
Ibex Tours, Hotel Ibex, The Mall (☎ 2480)
Swagtam's Tours, Mission Rd (☎ 2390)
Tarun Tours & Travels (just off The Mall) (☎ 2688)

Public Bus The third alternative is the far less comfortable, and generally slower, but certainly cheaper, public bus. They leave, according to demand, every one or two days from Leh and Manali at about 4 am. 'Super Deluxe' (a bit of a misnomer) costs Rs 490; 'A Class' is Rs 475; and 'B Class' is Rs 350. Subtract about Rs 70 from the fare if you plan to get off at Keylong.

Truck
Trucks can often be quicker than buses, and should be cheaper. They may not stop at Sarchu, but instead drive throughout the night, which is not a great idea; or they may stop overnight anywhere alongside the road – also not a great idea. Trucks can be more comfortable if there are only a couple of people in the cabin. Plenty of trucks travel this route, in season. It is just a matter of getting to the area where the trucks stop in Leh, and Manali, very, very early – or, better, organise a lift the day before. The cost should be about half the tourist bus price, and a little less than the cheapest bus – about Rs 300.

Taxi
An option – which is not outrageous if in a group – is a taxi between Leh and Manali for a 'fixed' (but in reality, negotiable at this price) Rs 10,000. This can be arranged at the Taxi Union on Fort Rd in Leh, or on The Mall, Manali. It will cost more for each day

you take, but it allows you to stop, take photos, visit villages, and, theoretically, have some control over your maniacal driver.

Motorcycle
Motorcycles are an increasingly popular means of travelling between Leh and Manali, and places beyond. (Refer to the Getting Around chapter for details.) This, of course, gives you the option of taking several days to admire the spectacular scenery.

It is worth remembering that there are no villages between Leh and Keylong, so you will have to take all your spare parts, particularly spare chains and tubes – and enough spare parts to get out of Leh, too, because Leh doesn't have much to offer either. Some tent sites may sell limited petrol at twice the Leh or Manali price; there are petrol stations at Tandi and Keylong, but nowhere else. At all times, it is advisable to wear cold and wet weather gear throughout the trip, including boots, because the road is always muddy, wet and dusty in places. It seems unnecessary to recommend that you take it easy. And look out for trucks and buses at all times!!

Leh to Kargil

This section refers to places on, or near, the main road from Leh to Kargil. The places below are listed in order of distance from Leh.

There are a number of buses which ply the 231 km to Kargil. Trucks are also a good way of getting a lift and for hitching between villages. Taxis may seem outrageous, but with a group sharing the cost, you can visit several gompas on the way to, say, Alchi or Lamayuru. For instance, a taxi from Leh to Alchi, stopping at Phyang, Basgo, Likir and Rizong, will cost about Rs 1200 – about US$10 each in a group of four.

PHYANG
Not far past Spituk (refer to the Around Leh section for further details on Spituk), a long,

roughish track off the main road leads to the pretty village of Phyang. **Mani walls** lead to the little-visited gompa which was built around the 15th century by King Tashi Namgyal, and now houses about 45 monks who belong to the Kagyupa order.

The gompa is in need of restoration, but it's a good place to scramble around and explore, if you can find a monk to show you around. There's a bronze Buddha statue reputedly almost 1000 years old, and some huge thangkas, one of which is unrolled once a year during the annual Phyang Festival held around July/August.

Direct buses from Leh leave daily at 8 am, 2 and 5 pm. Hitching is not really possible as very few vehicles make the detour to Phyang. Taxis from Leh cost Rs 335 or Rs 450 return. From Phyang, there is a trekking route which almost parallels the main road, passing through some lovely villages such as Likir and Temisgam, before returning to the main road near Khalsi.

NIMMU

Nimmu is a pleasant place to stop for tea. The only notable thing about Nimmu is that about eight km east, towards Leh, is the junction of the differently coloured Indus and Zanskar rivers. If you can, get out and admire this really spectacular sight. To Nimmu, take any bus going from Leh beyond Nimmu, or a one-way/return taxi from Leh will cost Rs 500/635.

BASGO

It's only six km further on to Basgo, which was the former capital of lower Ladakh, before the Ladakh kingdom was united at Leh. The 400 year old gompa is up some winding, steep tracks. It is often deserted, so ask around for one of the handful of monks in the village to open up. The prayer room in the Ser Zung Temple has great frescoes; another temple has an enormous gold and copper statue of the Maitreya Buddha (the coming Buddha), and some elaborate roof and wall frescoes. The views from the roof are wonderful.

The *Lagung Guest House*, next to the gompa, offers basic, but reasonable, accommodation. Daily buses from Leh go direct to Basgo at 1 and 4 pm (these times are changeable, so check at the tourist office in Leh for an update); or catch one of the daily buses to Alchi or beyond. A one-way/return taxi to Basgo from Leh will cost Rs 575/650.

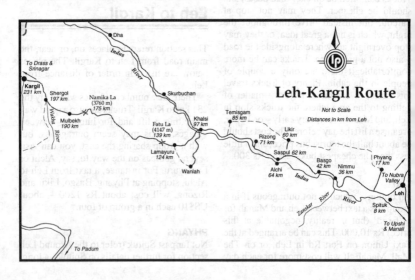

LIKIR

Located five km from the main road, just before Saspul, is another magnificent gompa, overlooking the village of Likir. Known as the Klu-kkhyil (water spirits) Gompa, it was founded in the 14th century, and was the first gompa in Ladakh known to have been built under the direction of Tibetan monks. The present gompa was rebuilt in the 18th century, re-dedicated to the Gelukpa order, and is now inhabited by almost 150 friendly monks, who offer free tea to visitors, and are happy to show you around.

There is a small museum upstairs, with an impressive collection of thangkas up to 500 years old, as well as some interesting Buddha figures. Unfortunately the wall paintings have suffered much water damage. There is no entrance fee, but there's a donation box for voluntary contributions. Among other things, the monks ask that visitors do not engage in '...smooching or hugging'.

To stay in Likir, return to the village, about 30 minutes walk across the fields. The *Lharjan Guest House* has a vicious dog, and a landlady who speaks no English at all. Far more hospitable is the pleasant *Norboo Guest House*, with a large, authentic Ladakhi kitchen. Rooms here, including all meals, are good value at Rs 100 per person. A bus to Likir village, which continues to the gompa, leaves Leh every day at 3 pm. A one-way/return taxi from Leh costs Rs 760/850.

ALCHI

Alchi is a busy village with several good places to stay and eat, and masses of stalls selling handicrafts. It is a pretty place, especially at the end of summer when villagers are harvesting, and is worth staying to break up the long haul between Leh and Kargil or Srinagar, or as a base for exploring other nearby places, such as Likir, Basgo and Rizong. But it has already become a little westernised: one monk now insists on wearing a pink LA Lakers cap with his robes.

One of the more enjoyable aspects of the Alchi Gompa is that it is the only one in the Ladakhi region on flat ground, so no knee-

breaking climbing is involved. The gompa was founded in the 11th century by The Great Translator, Ringchen Zangpo, on his return from India, which accounts for the Indian and, particularly, Kashmiri, influences.

The three storey **Dharma Wheel Gompa**, actually run by the gompa in Likir, is noted for its massive Buddha statues. Within the complex, there are other statues made out of clay, lavish woodcarvings, the only examples of Kashmiri-style wall paintings in the area, and many chortens around the village. Unfortunately, some of the frescoes showing the life of Buddha have been rather badly restored. But thanks to some help from German experts, all may not be lost or irrecoverable.

Places to Stay & Eat

In the village, a short walk from the gompa, is the best, and most popular (so, often full), place to stay. The family run *Choskpor* offers good, simple doubles/triples for Rs 70/80, and basic meals in a nice garden.

Near the gompa and car park, the *Zimskhang Guest House* offers poor value. *Pota La Guest House* has airy rooms with bathrooms for Rs 150. It also has a restaurant and camping site. At a similar price and standard is the nearby *Samdup Ling Guest House*. The cheapest here is the *Lotsau*: for Rs 50/80, it is simple, with share bathroom, but good value.

Getting There & Away

There is one direct bus to Alchi every day, leaving Leh at 3 pm. Otherwise, take any of the other daily buses to places beyond Alchi, get off at the blue sign to 'Alchi Chhoskor Gonpa', near the bridge (tee it up with the bus conductor or driver), then walk for an hour along the path to Alchi, or take the short cut, scrambling over the hills, near the first bend in the road. A one-way taxi from Leh, direct to Alchi, is Rs 805.

SASPUL

Saspul is a village on the main road, over the river from the turn-off to Alchi. Apparently there is a small **cave temple** nearby, but nobody seems to know much about it. While Saspul is nice enough, Alchi has far more to offer. The *Chakzoth Guest House*, on the main road in Saspul, has small rooms for Rs 30 to Rs 40.

RIZONG

About six km along a steepish, rocky track from the main road is the start of the area with the nunnery of Julichen and the gompa of Rizong. The gompa, belonging to the Gelukpa order, entails another very steep climb, so it is a long walk from the main road. Rebuilt in the last few hundred years, the gompa has less character than some of the others, but is known for its frescoes. The lamas and chomos follow a strict lifestyle.

There is no village at Rizong, so there is nowhere to stay or eat, but you may be able to stay at the gompa (for men only) or the nunnery (for women only) if you ask, and bring your own supplies. Alternatively, near the turn-off to Rizong, about 200m towards Alchi on the main road, is the pleasant *Uletokpo Camping Ground*, which is set among apricot trees.

There is no direct bus to Rizong from Leh, so it is a matter of getting a bus bound for beyond Lamayuru. If coming from Alchi, it is not difficult to hitch a ride on a truck or bus for 20 minutes between the turn-offs for Alchi and Rizong. As an alternative, a taxi one way from Leh to the bottom of the walk up to the gompa will set you back Rs 1050.

KHALSI

There has been some sort of bridge over the Indus River, and a turn-off to the Dha-Hanu region, at Khalsi for many centuries. Now it is a major military area, where your passport will be checked regardless of where you are going, and your permit checked if you're going to the Dha-Hanu region.

LAMAYURU

After exploring villages around the area, it comes as a surprise to find that Lamayuru is a scruffy little place. But it is completely overshadowed by one of the most famous and spectacularly set gompas in Ladakh.

The gompa, part of the Kagyupa order, is not as interesting as others; it's the location that makes it special. The oldest known gompa in Ladakh, dating back beyond the 10th century, it has been destroyed and restored several times over the centuries. There are renowned collections of carpets, thangkas and frescoes. Once criminals were granted asylum here (not any more, you'll be glad to know!) which explains one previous name for the gompa: Tharpa Ling or 'place of freedom'. Try to get there early to witness a mesmerising puja. Several km from Lamayuru is the small **Wanlah Gompa**, set on the popular trekking route to Padum in Zanskar.

Lamayuru Gompa is in a spectacular and isolated setting.

Places to Stay & Eat

Above the gompa, on the main road, are several places to stay, the better being the *Gompa Hotel*. But only stay up here if you are not going to explore Lamayuru village or the gompa – there are marginally better, quieter places to stay in the village. The *Shangrila Hotel*, near the main road, has nice views and rooms for Rs 50. Past the 'sheep & goat extension centre', above the post office, is the very basic *Tasigar*, but the price of Rs 20 per person can't be beaten just about anywhere in Ladakh. The best is the *Dragan* (just follow the ubiquitous signs) which offers large rooms, with share bathroom, for Rs 100 per room. Each hotel offers some food, but it's usually little more than dhal, rice or noodles.

Getting There & Away

There are no buses from Leh or Kargil directly to Lamayuru, so take the Leh to Kargil/Srinagar bus and get off at the truck stop at the top of the village. A better option is a ride on one of the many trucks that stop there. Trucks leave Lamayuru early morning; ask around at the truck stop for expected departure/arrival times. A one-way taxi in one long day from Leh costs Rs 1690. You can easily walk from the main road to the gompa, and to the village from a road which may be finished soon.

MULBEKH

From Lamayuru the road passes Fatu La (4147m), the highest pass on the route, then Namika La (3760m) before suddenly turning into a lovely green valley. Mulbekh is the last sign of Buddhism, as you shortly head into the Muslim-dominated regions near Kargil and beyond.

Mulbekh's main claim to fame is the impressive eight metre high **Chamba statue**, an image of a future Buddha, cut into the rock face, dating back to about 700 AD. Unfortunately, all buses stop for food and a rest at the village of Wakha, only two km from Mulbekh, so this gives you no opportunity to inspect the statue on the way, but you can see it from the bus window.

There are also two gompas: **Serdung** and **Gandentse**, which offer great views of the valley. As in other smaller villages, it is wise to enquire if the gompa is open before making the ascent. If it's not, somebody from the village may have keys and accompany you.

The only place worth staying at is the *Paradise Hotel and Restaurant* for Rs 50 per room, right opposite the Chamba statue. From Leh, take the Kargil/Srinagar bus. Mulbekh makes a decent day trip from Kargil. A couple of buses leave Kargil for Mulbekh every day. A return taxi from Kargil plus an hour or so in Mulbekh will cost Rs 700.

SHERGOL

About seven km further on towards Kargil, along a fertile valley, is the small village of Shergol. Meaning 'Lord of the Morning Star', Shergol is set on the opening of the Wakha River, and has a tiny **cave gompa** perched halfway up the steep, eastern slope of the mountain. It is almost deserted, and is really for those who can't get enough of gompas and stiff walks up mountains. The view, of course, is magnificent. Below the gompa is a **nunnery**, home to a dozen or so chomos.

Kargil & the Suru Valley

The valleys of Suru, Drass, Wakha and Bodkarbu lie midway between the alpine valleys of Kashmir, and the fertile reaches of the Indus Valley and Ladakh. The region is politically part of India, ethnically part of Baltistan, and geographically an integral part of Ladakh.

Geographically, there is little doubt that one has crossed the Himalayan watershed. The steep barren hills now stretch to the snow line. As the snows melt, the waters flow freely down into the heavily irrigated valleys. Here Tibetan-style settlements thrive. Whitewashed mud and stone houses contrast with deep-green barley fields. Mosques are the only sign that one has not yet entered Buddhist Ladakh.

The earliest settlers of these isolated tributaries of the Indus were the Dards. According to the noted historian AH Franke, the Dards were already acquainted with the Buddhist teachings prevalent in north-west India, and had absorbed them into their culture some time before 500 AD. Later, as the Tibetan forces invaded Ladakh, much of the Dardic culture was abandoned, although isolated pockets of their heritage remain significantly intact, notably at Drass.

The full cultural eclipse came far later, in the 15th century, shortly after the Kashmiris were converted to Islam. Most Dardic groups were also converted, including the people of Drass. What remain today are Dardic groups, distinct from the Baltis in both language and religion – the Dards are Sunni Muslims, and the Baltis are Shia. To complete this cultural patchwork, there are some isolated Dardic communities, in the main Indus Valley below Khalsi, which are still Buddhist.

In the Suru, Wakha and Bodkarbu valleys, the cultural similarities with Baltistan are more apparent. Trade links were also strong between Gilgit and Kargil, so the region's attention focused along the Indus Valley. Isolated Buddhist communities still remain at Mulbekh in the Wakha Valley, and in the tiny kingdom of Heniskot in the upper Bodkarbu Valley.

The regions of Dardistan and Baltistan maintained a degree of independence from both the Mughal armies that held Kashmir, and the Mongol-Tibetan armies intent on taking Ladakh. In the 1830s, however, the Suru Valley was invaded by the army of Jammu's Dogra leader Zorawar Singh, who was intent on invading Ladakh. As a result of the Dogra forays, Ladakh and Baltistan came under the influence of Jammu, and in 1846 became an integral part of the maharaja's state of Jammu & Kashmir. A century later the region was divided, and the cease-fire line between Pakistan and India was drawn across the state of Jammu & Kashmir a few km north of Kargil. As a consequence, the politically sensitive regions down valley from Kargil are strictly no-go areas for foreigners.

Kargil can be a little hotter than Leh. In summer (May-October), the average maximum/ minimum is 28/16°C, and in winter (November-April), it is -2/-12°C.

KARGIL
Telephone Area Code: 01985

The importance and influence of Kargil has changed dramatically over the past century. It was, until 1947, an important trading centre linking Ladakh with Gilgit and the lower Indus Valley. There were also important trading links between the villages of the Suru Valley and the Zanskar Valley, and even 20 years ago it was not uncommon to see yak trains making their way from Padum right the way into the Kargil bazaar.

Continuing political problems in Kashmir have seriously affected the number of visitors to Kargil and the hotels survive at present from the handful of visitors making their way from Leh to Padum and the Zanskar Valley.

The people of Kargil are mostly Shia Muslims: Arabic script is everywhere; women are rarely seen, and if so, are usually veiled; and mosques dominate the town.

Orientation & Information
Kargil, situated next to the roaring Suru River, is the second largest town in Ladakh but is really little more than one long main road called the Main Bazaar Rd, with lots of little lanes jutting off. (So watch out for wide trucks!) Along the Main Bazaar Rd, there are plenty of places with long-distance and international telephone facilities, as well as the post office and the State Bank of India, which changes money from 10 am to 2 pm weekdays.

There is no electricity during the day, but this should improve with the completion of a huge hydroelectric site nearby. If you have some time to kill, walk up Hospital Rd for some decent views of the area, or there are some nice fields and villages across the Qatilgah Bridge, at the end of Balti Bazaar Rd.

The Tourist Reception Centre, not to be confused with any similarly named government office, is now next to the taxi stand, just off the main road. Open from 10 am to 4 pm on normal working days, it has no great information on local areas, or on Zanskar. No permits are needed for the area; and there are no travel or trekking agencies in Kargil.

Places to Stay
Kargil used to be full of grotty places to stay overnight for those travelling between Srinagar and Leh, or onwards to Zanskar. There are still a couple of places on the Main Bazaar Rd, but they are really awful – it is not hard to get somewhere better. Near the bus stand area, but, thankfully, not affected too much by its noise, is the *Crown Hotel*

with reasonable singles/doubles for Rs 80/100, with dirty, common bathrooms. Next door, the large, rambling *Hotel International* is slightly nicer, with a bathroom, next to the roaring river (probably louder than the buses!) for Rs 100/150. *Hotel Greenland* (☎ 2324), near the taxi stand, has quiet rooms, with a verandah, some nice bathrooms (some with hot water) from Rs 100 per room. Next door, the *Hotel Evergreen* is the same standard and price.

The J&KTDC Tourist Bungalows in Kargil were deserted, but may be operational again if tourism picks up. Mid-range accommodation includes the *Hotel Siachen* (☎ 221), where singles/doubles cost Rs 300/450; it has a very nice garden, hot water and is good value. In upper Kargil, the *Caravan Sarai* is a nice place, catering for the up-market trekking crowd, with bed and breakfast, hot water and views, for Rs 700/1200. The *D'Zojila*, a little out of Kargil, is about the same price and standard.

Places to Eat

There is not much to recommend about the restaurants in Kargil – it really isn't set up for long-term visitors. Your hotel will probably do some bland Chinese dishes and some eggs and bread for breakfast. On and near the Main Bazaar Rd are some small restaurants – the *Naktul*, *Shashila* and *Popular Chacha* – all of which proudly display individual advertisements claiming they serve 'Chine's' food. Also worth a try is the *Ashi Yana*. The restaurant at Hotel Siachen serves a good breakfast and, discreetly, in the evenings, a bottle of beer, but watch for overcharging.

Getting There & Away

Air Indian Airlines and Archana Airways plan to launch regular flights to Kargil (which has India's second-highest airport) from Leh and Delhi, but at the time of researching, no details were available.

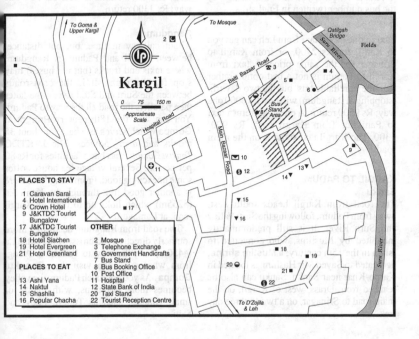

PLACES TO STAY
1 Caravan Sarai
4 Hotel International
5 Crown Hotel
9 J&KTDC Tourist Bungalow
17 J&KTDC Tourist Bungalow
18 Hotel Siachen
19 Hotel Evergreen
21 Hotel Greenland

PLACES TO EAT
13 Ashi Yana
14 Naktul
15 Shashila
16 Popular Chacha

OTHER
2 Mosque
3 Telephone Exchange
6 Government Handicrafts
7 Bus Stand
8 Bus Booking Office
10 Post Office
11 Hospital
12 State Bank of India
20 Taxi Stand
22 Tourist Reception Centre

Bus There are early morning daily buses from Kargil to Leh and Kargil to Srinagar, both costing Rs 88 in 'B Class'; Rs 111 in 'A Class'; and Rs 174 for 'Super Class' – but, in reality, there will probably be only one sort of public bus leaving each day. Towards Leh, there are also two daily buses to Mulbekh and one to Shergol; towards Srinagar, there are regular daily buses to nearby Drass.

There are at least two a day to nearby Panikhar and Parkachik. To Padum, in Zanskar, there is a 3 am bus on alternate days (check at the bus stand for up-to-date information).

The Kargil bus stand is divided into two adjoining lots, just off the main road. The office where you can book a bus ticket a day ahead for long trips, which is recommended, is in a burnt-out old building in the northern bus stand. There may be some more reliable and comfortable private buses between Kargil, Leh and Srinagar if/when the demand picks up. Buses often have their destinations in Arabic script. If you have a ticket, go by the bus number (written in English).

Taxi In one day, a taxi from Leh can get you to Kargil for Rs 2700, or from Kargil to Srinagar for the same price. A taxi from Kargil to Padum is not a bad option rather than the unreliable bus, but the two day trip (stopping at Rangdum) will cost Rs 6000 one way; Rs 9500 return. A one-way/return taxi to Panikhar from Kargil costs Rs 900/1300. The Kargil taxi stand is on the main road.

KARGIL TO PADUM
Sanku
The road from Kargil heads south-west, away from Padum, following the Suru Valley and Suru River. It is still predominantly inhabited by Muslims, who converted to Islam in the 15th century; a **Muslim shrine**, dedicated to Sayed Mir Hashim, is located in Karpo-Khar near Sanku. Sanku can also be reached from Drass, west of Kargil, on the main road to Srinagar, on a two to three day trek.

There is a bus from Kargil to Sanku every day at 3 pm (Rs 16). At Sanku, accommodation is limited to a *Government Rest House*, which may be rented, and a J&KTDC *Tourist Bungalow*, which was, at the time of researching, almost abandoned due to lack of tourist demand.

Panikhar
Further down the Suru Valley, Panikhar and Parkachik are the places to get off and admire, or even get closer to, the twin mountains of Nun (7135m) and Kun (7087m). It is a lovely area in summer, often full of flowers. In Panikhar, the best option is a room at the comfortable J&KTDC *Tourist Bungalow*. At the time of researching, with the lack of tourists in the area, it was a bargain Rs 80 per double.

Between Panikhar and Parkachik, and Kargil, buses cost Rs 30, and leave two or three times a day; or take the Kargil-Padum bus which leaves on alternate days. Taxis from Kargil to Panikhar cost Rs 900 one way; Rs 1300 return.

Rangdum
About halfway in time, but not distance, between Kargil and Padum, is Rangdum, where taxis and trucks (but not buses) may stop for the night. It is the crossroads between the Suru and Stod rivers; the latter then parallels the road all the way to Padum. You can visit the 18th century **Rangdum Gompa** which serves as a base for about 35 monks and many novices. The J&KTDC *Tourist Complex* has basic facilities for Rs 80 per person. Several village tea houses offer some unexciting food. From Rangdum, there is another good trek through the Kanji La (5255m) which links up to the Leh-Kargil road, at Lamayuru.

The road from Rangdum heads in a more southerly direction and crosses the Pentse La (4450m). On the way to Padum is Ating, from where you can visit the **Zongkul Gompa**. As you approach Padum, the valley becomes more populous, with plenty of small villages, such as Tungri, Phey and Sani.

GARRY WEARE

GARRY WEARE

adakh & Zanskar

Top: The Victory Fort in Leh commemorates Ladakh's victory over the invading Balti-Kashmir armies in the 16th century.

ottom: Above Wanlah village, near Lamayuru, Ladakh.

PAUL GREENWAY

GARRY WEARE

GARRY WEARE

Ladakh & Zanskar
Top Left: Lamayuru Gompa, Ladakh.
Top Right: Buddhist prayer flags, Ladakh.
Bottom: Around Rangdum, Zanskar.

Zanskar

The isolated region of Zanskar is composed of a number of small mountain-locked valleys to the south of Ladakh. The valleys are bounded to the north by the Zanskar Range, and to the south by the main Himalaya. To the east and west, high ridges linking the Himalaya and Zanskar mountains ensure that there is no easy link between Zanskar and the outside world.

Zanskar essentially comprises the Stod Valley in the west, and the Lunak Valley in the east, which converge at Padum, the administrative centre of the region. The fertile region of Padum and its outlying villages and gompas form the nucleus of Zanskar. It is a small Himalayan kingdom by any standards. The valley is no more than 20 km wide at the most, while 50 km north of Padum the Zanskar River enters the impressive gorges of the Zanskar Range as it flows down to the Indus Valley.

Zanskar's location on the lee side of the main Himalaya Range ensures that it attracts considerably more snow than any other region of Ladakh. Snow can fall for over seven months of each year. Passes are often snowbound for more than half the year, and the winter temperatures of -20°C make it one of the coldest inhabited places in the world. In the depths of winter, all the rivers freeze over. Even the fast flowing Zanskar River freezes on the surface, and the Zanskaris walk on the ice to reach the Indus Valley near Nimmu – an otherwise inaccessible route.

Until a generation ago it took villagers a week or more to reach the roadhead. However, in 1981 a jeep road linking Kargil and Padum was completed, creating direct access to Kashmir or the Indus Valley for three or four months a year. The Pentse La, the pass linking the valley from Kargil with Zanskar, is generally clear of snow by early July. The road lifeline has taken its toll on the traditional culture of Zanskar. Anyone searching for some long-lost Shangri La should look elsewhere. However, the yak and pony trains still make their way over the more remote passes to Lahaul, Kullu, Kashmir, and the Indus Valley.

Zanskar's uninterrupted Buddhist heritage has been principally due to its isolation. It can be traced back to a time when the Buddhist monks first made their way over the high passes from Kashmir. The gompa at Sani, founded in the 10th century, is an example of the earliest Buddhist influence. Indeed, legend has it that the sage Naropa meditated at the Sani chorten during his journeys through Ladakh. The original sites of such gompas as Phugtal, Karsha and Lingshat may also be attributed to this period. In many respects, the development of the Buddhist orders in Zanskar were the same as in other regions of Ladakh. The Dalai Lama's order – the Gelukpa – was established in the 15th century, and the well preserved gompas at Karsha, Lingshat and Mune date from this period. The King's order – the Drukpa – established its presence at Bardan and Zangla and 'colonised' the gompa at Sani in the 17th century.

Today, the Gelukpa gompas have established ties with Likir Gompa in the Indus Valley, while Bardan, Sani and Zangla have administrative and financial links with the gompa at Stakna, close to Leh.

The influence of Islam did not affect Zanskar until the 19th century. The presence of Muslim families in Padum dates from the 1840s, when the Dogras opened up the passes to Muslim traders from the Kishtwar area. The Dogra forces made their way over the passes from Kishtwar, and established their presence both here and in Ladakh. The fort at Pipiting below Padum was built as a fitting testimony to the Dogra times, when the powers of royal families in both Zangla and Padum were reduced to the same nominal status as the royal families in Ladakh.

In mid-1995, there was some political unrest in Zanskar, and foreign trekkers were discouraged from trekking in the region. However, a resolution of the issues seems to have been achieved and Zanskar leaders issued a statement in January 1996 that there will be no further impediment for foreign tourists who may 'come and go freely as before'.

PADUM

Padum is the administrative headquarters of the Zanskar region but was once an ancient capital. It is not a particularly attractive place, with incongruous government buildings that were constructed when the road from Kargil was completed in 1981. This has resulted in the town gaining a character similar to roadheads everywhere. Vehicles are repaired, diesel cans are discarded and much that is not used is disposed of here. The main campsite and the small hotel area is close by the newly constructed mosque (the only one in the Zanskar region) which serves the small Sunni Muslim community living here.

Padum is also the starting point for a number of difficult long-distance treks.

Places to Stay & Eat

There's a limited choice of just a few basic guesthouses. The *Hotel Shapodok-la*, in the centre of town, has cheap dorm beds. The *Hotel Haftal View* costs Rs 50 to Rs 80 per room, but the similarly priced *Hotel Chora-la*, nearby, is probably the better of the two. The *Tourist Bungalow* is more expensive but has fairly reasonable doubles with attached bath. The *Hotel Snowland* is one of the better choices, with a nice garden and singles/doubles for Rs 50/100. The *Hotel New Ibex* is newer, with better facilities than most. It is in the northern area of Padum, on the road from Kargil, and has rooms from Rs 150 upward. *Hotel Greenland* is not a bad option, near the mosque.

There isn't much to report about places to eat in Padum. The best choice is to eat at your (or any other) hotel. Better hotels such as the *New Ibex* serve adequate, though uninspiring, food.

Getting There & Away

Bus The road connecting Padum and Kargil – in fact, the only road in Zanskar – is only open from July to early October. It's com-

pletely impassable the rest of the year, effectively isolating the Zanskari people. In season, a bus runs between Padum and Kargil every alternate day (check with local bus stations for up-to-date information) departing very early, at about 4 am. The cost of the bus between Kargil and Padum is from Rs 87 to Rs 174, depending on what class of bus is leaving at the time.

The trip between Kargil and Padum is spectacular, even impressing those jaded travellers who thought that they had seen it all along the Srinagar to Leh road. But as usual in this area, the road is also narrow, windy, dangerous and very slow going. The trip should take 18 hours, but can take a lot longer, perhaps up to 24 hours. You can and should book your ticket the day before in Padum or Kargil. Naturally, you can get off anywhere you want (within the current political regulations, if there are any) on the road between Kargil and Padum, but you may have to then wait a day or so for another bus, or rely on hitching a lift on an infrequent truck.

Taxi By taxi, it costs a whopping Rs 6000 one way or Rs 9500 return from Kargil to Padum (no one with a vehicle in Padum will do the journey from Padum in reverse), but with a group to cut costs, this is a great way to really admire the amazing scenery. This trip would be done over two days, stopping about halfway at Rangdum.

Truck Trucks occasionally go along this route, but not nearly as often as the Srinagar-Leh road, because so few people live in and around Zanskar. Nevertheless, hitching rides on a truck, if you can find one, is normal practice, and most drivers will take you for a negotiable fee, maybe about the same as the cheapest bus fare.

AROUND PADUM

Padum itself has little to offer, but serves as a good base for exploring nearby villages, all of which need some trekking to get to, as local transport around Padum is virtually nonexistent.

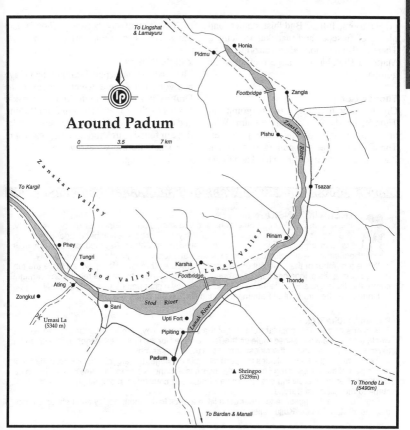

Bardan Gompa

The remote gompa at Bardan is about 12 km south of Padum, on the trekking route to Darcha. It belongs to the Drukpa order, and was built in the 17th century.

Karsha Gompa

This is one of the most important gompas in Zanskar, dating back to about the 11th century, and belonging to the Gelukpa order. A large white complex housing over 100 monks, the Karsha Gompa holds pujas, often different from those in Ladakh, which should be witnessed, if possible. The three day

Gustor Festival held in July or August each year is particularly spectacular. There is also a 500 year old **nunnery** nearby. It takes about three hours to walk to Karsha from Padum.

Sani Gompa

This is believed to be the oldest Ka-ni-ka (named after the former king of Kashmir) gompa in Zanskar. Unlike most in Ladakh and Zanskar, this gompa is built like a castle in the village on flat ground, and involves no steep climbs, and so is more welcoming than the average gompa. There is an impressive prayer room, full of Buddhist statues, and plenty of frescoes and thangkas to delight. There is also a famous **stone carving** of the Maitreya Buddha on a large rock near the gompa.

Thonde Gompa

On the way to Zangla is the gompa at Thonde, nearly 20 km from Padum. With about 50 monks of the Gelukpa order, Thonde is now the second largest gompa in Zanskar, after the one at Karsha. The village

of Tsazar, halfway between Thonde and Zangla, also has an impressive gompa.

Zangla Gompa

The road continues past Tsazar to the village and gompa at Zangla, which belongs to the Drukpa. It is also where the king of Zanskar has his castle. Zangla is 35 km from Padum, and can be included in one of a few popular three or four day treks around the area. There is a small **nunnery** nearby which is also worth exploring.

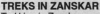

TREKS IN ZANSKAR

Trekking in Zanskar can be difficult and you should be equipped for every eventuality. You should bring most of your supplies with you. There are a number of agencies in Leh that can organise things for you for between Rs 500 to Rs 1000 per day but their equipment – sleeping bags, down jackets and tents – is not of a very high quality.

While a number of the treks out of Padum follow routes through villages where there are tea houses-cum-lodges, lodgings cannot be guaranteed and some of the stages require an overnight camp. It is therefore advisable that you bring all your own gear and be self-sufficient for the trek.

Horses can be hired out of Padum for around Rs 200 per day.

Padum-Darcha Trek

This is one of the most popular treks out of the Zanskar Valley. The trek can be completed in a week. It follows a well defined route up the Tsarap Valley for the first three stages before diverting to Phugtal Gompa, one of the oldest gompas in the Zanskar region.

From Phugtal the trek continues through a number of villages to Kargyak, the highest settlement in this part of the Zanskar region. From Kargyak it is a further stage to the base of the Shingo La (5090m). The pass crossing over the main Himalaya is completed in one stage before the final stage to the village of Darcha.

From Darcha it is possible to either get a lift in a truck to the Indus Valley and Leh, or to catch the bus to Manali in the Kullu Valley.

Stage 1	Padum to Mune (6 hours)
Stage 2	Mune to Purne (8 hours)
Stage 3	Purne to Phugtal Gompa & Testa (6 hours)
Stage 4	Testa to Kargyak (7 hours)
Stage 5	Kargyak to Lakong (6-7 hours)
Stage 6	Lakong to Rumjak via the Shingo La (6-7 hours)
Stage 7	Rumjak to Darcha (6-7 hours)

Padum-Lamayuru Trek

This trek crosses a number of high passes in the vicinity of 5000m in order to reach Lamayuru Gompa. As with the trek over the Shingo La, trekkers must be fully equipped as there are a number of stages where there is neither food nor overnight shelter.

The trek commences at Padum or at the nearby Karsha Gompa, the largest in the Zanskar region. The trek follows the true left bank of the Zanskar River for two stages before diverting towards the Hanuma La (4950m) and Lingshat Gompa. From here it is a single stage to the base of the Singge La (5050m), the highest pass of this trek. It is not a difficult pass crossing and the descent to the village of Photaksar can easily be completed in one stage.

From Photaksar the trail climbs to the summit of the Sisir La (4850m) to the village of Honupatta. Two further stages complete the trek to the Lamayuru Gompa and the Leh to Srinagar highway, where it is possible to get a lift by bus or truck to Leh.

Stage 1   Padum to Karsha (3 hours)
Stage 2   Karsha to Pishu (4-5 hours)
Stage 3   Pishu to Hanumil (4-5 hours)
Stage 4   Hanumil to Snertse (5 hours)
Stage 5   Snertse to Lingshat via the Hanuma La (5-6 hours)
Stage 6   Lingshat to base of Singge La (5-6 hours)
Stage 7   Singge La to Photaksar (5-6 hours)
Stage 8   Photaksar to Honupatta via the Sisir La (6 hours)
Stage 9   Honupatta to Wanlah (5 hours)
Stage 10   Wanlah to Lamayuru (3-4 hours)

Padum-Manali Trek

This challenging trek over the main Himalaya range at the Umasi La takes a minimum of nine days and should only be attempted by well prepared parties. Horses cannot cross the Umasi La, so porters from Sani Gompa close to Padum are often hired. The going rate is up to Rs 2000 per porter to the village of Suncham on the far side of the pass. Thereon the porters return to the Zanskar region and you are then left with hiring whatever horses or mules are available.

From Padum the main route heads up the Zanskar Valley past Tungri village to Zongkul Gompa. It is a further stage to the base of Umasi La. The actual route to the pass is not well defined and a local guide is essential. The climb to the pass crosses a series of glaciers and is very steep just below the summit. From the pass (5340m) there are panoramic views of the inner Himalaya. Beyond the pass there is a large rock overhang where the porters insist on sheltering overnight before a long descent to the village of Suncham. It is then recommended to allow two stages from here to the village of Atholi.

From Atholi you then head up the Chandra Valley by three trek stages through the Pangi region of Himachal Pradesh to the village of Kilar and the newly constructed road to the Kullu Valley and Manali.

Note Although this trek can be completed at Atholi from where there are buses to the town of Kishtwar, this is not recommended due to the current political disturbances in the area.

Stage 1   Padum to Zongkul Gompa (6-7 hours)
Stage 2   Zongkul to base of Umasi La (6-7 hours)
Stage 3   Umasi La to camp (7 hours)
Stage 4   Camp to Suncham (8 hours)
Stage 5   Suncham to Marchel (3 hours)
Stage 6   Marchel to Atholi (8 hours)
Stage 7   Atholi to Shoal (3 hours)
Stage 8   Shoal to Istahari (6 to 7 hours)

Jammu & Kashmir

Population: 8.5 million
Area: 125,535 sq km
Capital: Srinagar (summer); Jammu (winter)
People per sq km: 68
Main Languages: Kashmiri, Dogri, Urdu
Literacy Rate: 26.2%
Best Time to Go: May, September to November

Seasons: Jammu
Winter – December to March (snowfalls from end December to early February)
Spring – April to May (heavy rainfalls)
Monsoon – June to mid-September
Autumn –mid-September to November

Seasons: Kashmir
Winter – December to mid-March
Spring – mid-March to May
Summer – June to August (heavy rainfalls)
Autumn – September to November

Warning

Lonely Planet strongly advises against travelling to the regions of Jammu and Kashmir. While the Indian Government has not placed restrictions on visiting Jammu and Kashmir, it is still foolhardy to visit the regions particularly when it is possible that the Al-Faran or an associated organisation may attempt to take further hostages. The situation is exacerbated by the naive advice offered by members of the J&K Tourist Office in Delhi who even after July 1995 persist with the notion that the situation in Kashmir is under control. It is, therefore, essential to contact your embassy in Delhi for up-to-date information. ■

The regions of Jammu and Kashmir – including Srinagar, the summer capital, and the city of Jammu, the winter capital – form part of the vast state of Jammu & Kashmir, J&K for short. The state also incorporates the region of Ladakh. The regions of Jammu and Kashmir (as distinct from Ladakh) have been subject to political unrest since the late 1980s. The following information is included for background information only and travellers are advised to contact their embassy in Delhi before travelling to these regions.

The state of J&K is a region of wide cultural and geographical contrasts. The Kashmir Valley is a fertile, verdant region enclosed by the high snow-capped ridges of the Pir Panjal to the west and south, and the main Himalaya Range to the east. Its population is predominantly Muslim with a rich Islamic history that can be traced back to the 14th century. South of the Kashmir Valley is the region of Jammu. It includes the city of Jammu, situated on the North Indian plains, a short distance from the rolling Siwalik hills. North of the Siwaliks, the rest of the Jammu region is drained by the Chenab River whose vast catchment area includes several narrow valleys that extend deep into the high Himalaya. The region of Jammu is predominantly Hindu, although small Muslim communities are found in the vicinity of Banihal and Kishtwar immediately south of the Kashmir Valley.

Highlights

Before the troubles in this state, the Kashmir Valley was one of India's most popular tourist destinations. A stay on one of the magnificently appointed houseboats on Dal Lake in Srinagar and trekking were the main attractions. ■

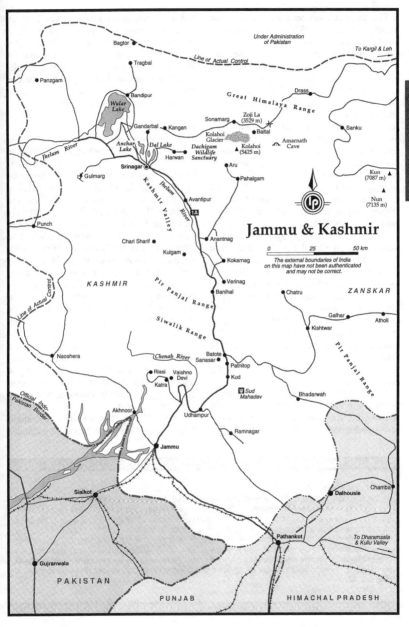

Jammu & Kashmir

| 0 | 25 | 50 km |

The external boundaries of India
on this map have not been authenticated
and may not be correct.

The political violence in the Kashmir Valley since the late 1980s has discouraged most travellers from visiting the region. Until 1989, a stay on the famous houseboats of Dal Lake close to the city centre of Srinagar was considered a must for anyone visiting northern India, while the treks out of Gulmarg, Sonamarg and Pahalgam were among some of the most popular in the Himalaya. Before the outbreak of violence, over 600,000 Indian tourists and 60,000 foreign tourists visited Kashmir throughout the summer season from early June until mid-October. Since 1990, this figure has been reduced to a handful of travellers and even these have now been 'warned off' the region following the tragic events that evolved in July 1995 when six foreign trekkers were taken hostage by a little-known guerilla group called the Al-Faran. One American managed to escape, but a Norwegian man was murdered the following month. The other four men remain captive.

In the region of Jammu, the situation is no better. There have been sporadic bomb blasts in the city of Jammu since 1992, as separatist groups have stepped up their campaigns. The town of Kishtwar has also been subject to separatist activity, and the Indian Army has actively discouraged foreigners from the area.

In spite of this, there are no special permits necessary to visit J&K. In July 1990, certain areas of the Kashmir Valley were declared 'disturbed areas'. That is to say, the Indian military and reserve police forces in Kashmir were given extraordinary powers of arrest, similar to the situation in the Punjab after 1984. However, there are no restrictions on movements in the state except the ones which were already in force, such as the ban on travel close to the India-Pakistan cease-fire line, or to areas under curfew.

HISTORY

J&K has always been a centre of conflict for independent India. When India and Pakistan became independent, there was much controversy over whether the region should be annexed to India or Pakistan. The population was predominantly Muslim but J&K was not a part of 'British India'. It was a 'princely state', ruled by a Hindu maharaja, in whose hands was left the decision of whether to merge with Muslim Pakistan or Hindu India. As told in *Freedom at Midnight*, by Larry Collins & Dominique Lapierre, the indecisive maharaja only made his decision when a Pathan group from North-West Pakistan was already crossing his borders, and the inevitable result was the first Indo-Pakistani conflict.

Since that first conflict, Kashmir has remained a flash point for relations between the two countries. A substantial part of the region is now Indian and the rest (Azad Kashmir) is claimed by Pakistan; both countries claim all of it.

Since 1987, militant activities in Kashmir have increased substantially and it's estimated

Shri Amarnath Yatra

At the full moon in the month of Sravana (July-August), thousands of Hindu pilgrims make the *yatra* (pilgrimage) to the Shri Amarnath Cave when a natural ice *lingam*, the symbol of Lord Shiva, reaches its greatest size. Although at this time the yatra is less a trek than a long queue, the spirit of this immense pilgrimage is amazing. In 1995, despite an escalation of tensions in J&K, over 60,000 pilgrims made the long trek to the cave, with the deployment of more than 20,000 security personnel along the Jammu-Pahalgam highway. The *Chari Mubarak* (holy mace) was installed in a bullet-proof vehicle under constant armed guard en route to the sacred cave. Despite these precautions, several bomb blasts along the route killed one security officer and injured several pilgrims. ■

that as many as 10,000 Kashmiris have died in the fighting. The main combatants are: the small Hizb-ul-Mujahedin, who are backed by Pakistan and want to be united with that country; the Jammu & Kashmir Liberation Front (JKLF) who are currently calling for nothing less than complete independence; and the Indian army which has moved into the area in large numbers, supposedly to keep the peace. There are continuing reports of horrific atrocities committed by all three of these groups and in spite of talks between India and Pakistan it is unlikely that the situation will improve in the near future.

In 1990 the J&K state government was dissolved and the state was placed under direct rule from Delhi (President's Rule). In November 1995, the independent Election Commission rejected the Indian Government's request for elections in the province because J&K was too unstable. The Kashmiri opposition parties (and the Pakistan Government, which assists the Muslim secessionists) planned to boycott the elections anyway, and have rejected the Indian Government's offer of limited autonomy. Elections are now scheduled for May 1996.

JAMMU REGION
Jammu
Population: 257,000
Telephone Area Code: 0191
Jammu is Kashmir's second-largest city, and is also its winter capital. It is situated on the plains, so in summer it is a sweltering, uncomfortable contrast to the cool heights of Kashmir. From October onwards it becomes much more pleasant. Jammu is actually two towns. The old town sits on a hilltop overlooking the river, and several km away across the river is the new town of Jammu Tawi.

Jammu to Srinagar
On the Jammu to Srinagar route are the hill resorts of Kud, Patnitop and Batote. The important Sudh Mahadev Shiva temple is situated 8 km from Kud and Patnitop. Also on this route is Sanasar, a beautiful valley which is a centre for the Gujar shepherds each summer.

During the winter months, Srinagar was often completely cut off from the rest of India before the Jawarhar Tunnel was completed. The 2½ km long tunnel is 200 km from Jammu and 93 km from Srinagar and has two separate passages. It's extremely rough and damp inside.

From Banihal, 17 km south of the tunnel, the Kashmiri region begins and people speak Kashmiri as well as Dogri. At the northern end of the tunnel is the green, lush Vale of Kashmir.

KASHMIR VALLEY
This is one of the most beautiful regions of India but over the last five years or so it has been racked by political violence.

The Mughal rulers of India were always happy to retreat from the heat of the plains to the cool green heights of Kashmir, and indeed Jehangir's last words, when he died en route to the 'happy valley', were a simple request for 'only Kashmir'. The Mughals developed their formal garden-style art to its greatest heights in Kashmir.

One of Kashmir's greatest attractions was undoubtedly the Dal Lake houseboats. During the Raj period Kashmir's ruler would not permit the British (who were as fond of Kashmir's cool climate as the Mughals) to own land here. So they adopted the solution of building houseboats – each one a little bit of England, afloat on Dal Lake. A visit to Kashmir, it was often said, was not complete until you had stayed on a houseboat.

Srinagar
Population: 725,000
Telephone Area Code: 0194
Srinagar, the summer capital of Kashmir, stands on Dal Lake and the Jhelum River.

It is a city with a distinctly Central Asian flavour. Indeed the people look different from those in the rest of India; and when you head south from Srinagar it is always referred to as 'returning to India'.

Srinagar now has the feel of an occupied city and there's often a curfew after dark.

There are roadblocks everywhere and soldiers in bunkers on all street corners. Most of the fighting takes place in the old city, usually during the night. This part of town looks like Beirut at the height of the war.

The old city is situated in the vicinity of the Hari Parbat Hill and the picturesque Jhelum River and includes the labyrinth of alleyways, mosques and houses that constitute the commercial heart of the city. The more modern part of the city is situated further up the Jhelum River (above its famous seven bridges) that sweeps through Srinagar.

East of the city is Dal Lake. Much of Dal Lake is a maze of intricate waterways. It comprises a series of lakes including Nagin Lake some eight km from the city centre. Most of the more modern houseboats are located on these lakes. The famous Mughal gardens including the Shalimar Bagh and Nishat Bagh are located on the far (east) side of Dal Lake.

Around Srinagar

There are a number of interesting places in the Kashmir Valley near Srinagar including Harwan, Sangam (a centre for the production of cricket bats!), and Verinag, where the Jhelum River has its source.

Pahalgam

Pahalgam is about 95 km from Srinagar, at an altitude of 2130m. Situated at the junction of the East and West Lidder rivers, Pahalgam was a popular base for trekking before the present troubles. The Shri Amarnath yatra still endures, however, and each year in July-August thousands of Hindu pilgrims approach the Amarnath Cave from this area.

Gulmarg

The large meadow of Gulmarg is 52 km south-west of Srinagar at 2730m. The name means Meadow of Flowers and in spring it's just that. This was also a popular trekking base. Before the terrorist activity, it used to be India's premier skiing resort. A number of fine day walks from Gulmarg are no longer

feasible in the current situation. In 1995, the hotels and ski-lifts here remained closed.

South of Srinagar

Interesting places in the south-west of the Kashmir Valley include Yusmarg, reputed to have the best **spring flowers** in Kashmir, which was, before the terrorist activity, a good base for treks further afield. **Chari Sharif** is on the road to Yusmarg. Its famous shrine (*ziarat*) of Kashmir's patron saint was destroyed in May 1995. Yusmarg (en route to Pakistan) is subject to separatist control. **Aharbal** was a popular resting place for the Mughal emperors when they made the long trip north from Delhi.

Srinagar to Kargil

Out of Srinagar is the **Dachigam Wildlife Reserve**, once a royal game park, and **Anchar Lake**, rarely visited but close to Srinagar, has a wide variety of water birds. The Jhelum River flows into **Wular Lake**, one of the largest freshwater lakes in India.

Sonamarg, at 2740m, is the last major town before Ladakh, and before the terrorist activity was an excellent base for trekking. Its name means Meadow of Gold, which could derive from the spring flowers or from the strategic trading position it once enjoyed.

Baltal, an army camp, is the last place in Kashmir, right at the foot of the Zoji La. The route from Baltal to **Amarnath Cave** is subject to landslides and extremely dangerous for this reason, as well as the political problems. The **Zoji La** is the watershed between Kashmir and Ladakh – on one side you have the green, lush scenery of Kashmir while on the other side everything is barren and dry.

The road up the pass is breathtaking, even more so than the road up the much higher Taglang La (5328m) on the Leh to Manali road. The road clings to the edge of sheer drops.

Drass is the first main village after the pass. From Drass, it is then another 56 km to Kargil.

For more information on the road from Kargil to Leh, refer to the Leh to Kargil section in the Ladakh & Zanskar chapter.

Himachal Pradesh

Population: 5.5 million
Area: 55,673 sq km
Capital: Shimla
Main Languages: Pahari, Hindi, Punjabi, various indigenous languages
People per sq km: 99
Literacy Rate: 64%
Best Time to Go: April to June & September to November (central, south & west); June to October (east and north-east)
Seasons: North, Centre & West
Winter (off season) – December to March
Spring – April to May
Monsoon (off season) – June to mid-September
Autumn – mid-September to November
Peak Tourist Season – April to mid-June
Seasons: Lahaul & Spiti, & Kinnaur
Winter (off season) – October to May
Summer – June to October
Monsoon (southern Kinnaur only) – July to August
Rafting Season – early May to mid-June, mid-September to mid-October (Beas River)

Himachal Pradesh – the land of the unmoving snow peaks – is a large amalgam of peoples, religions and contrasting geographical features. The Kullu Valley with its developed and tourist-oriented economy can be considered the backbone of the state. Off to the east is the Parbati Valley (popular with long-stay visitors). In the Chamba and Kangra regions can be found typical British hill stations. The residence of the Dalai Lama is in Upper Dharamsala, known as McLeod Ganj, which has become a centre for Buddhism, as well as the headquarters of the Tibetan Government in Exile. Shimla, the famous colonial hot-weather capital, remains Himachal's seat of government.

The northern and eastern areas of Lahaul & Spiti and Kinnaur (labelled officially as 'tribal districts') were opened up to tourists a few years ago. Permits, which are easy to obtain, are required for travel in some parts of these, and allow you to travel along the main roads and visit the main sights – but not to wander off to the Tibetan border. Lahaul & Spiti and Kinnaur are vast, barren regions (though Kinnaur also has some magnificent Alpine scenery) where traditional lifestyles are followed based on religion, agriculture and herding. These districts are dotted with *gompas* (monasteries) often in settings as spectacular as those found in Tibet and Ladakh. Thousand year old gompas in Lahaul & Spiti can be visited, as long as you are appropriately dressed and show proper respect. The typical pagoda style of Himachal is best viewed around Manali.

Highlights

In the old British hill station of Shimla, it's possible to experience the decrepit grandeur of the Raj, and the toy train journey there is delightful. For a bath in hot springs, Manikaran is well worth a visit.

Himachal has many ancient *gompas* (monasteries) and temples *(mandirs)*. The remote Shashur Gompa near Keylong in Lahaul & Spiti is one of the more spectacular. It has an annual festival in which the *lamas* perform mask dances. As well, a famous five metre *thangka* (Buddhist artwork) is housed here. Chamba, in the north-west, is a scenically beautiful town which has many ancient Hindu temples here, in the *shikhara* (spire) style. For those interested in Tibetan Buddhism, McLeod Ganj (home of the Dalai Lama and the headquarters of the Tibetan Government in Exile) is *the* place to head, and you can also do some beautiful walks in the area. The Kinnaur Kalachakra Celestial Palace, just behind Rekong Peo, is in a picturesque orchard setting and has wonderful views of the mighty Kinnaur Kailash. ∎

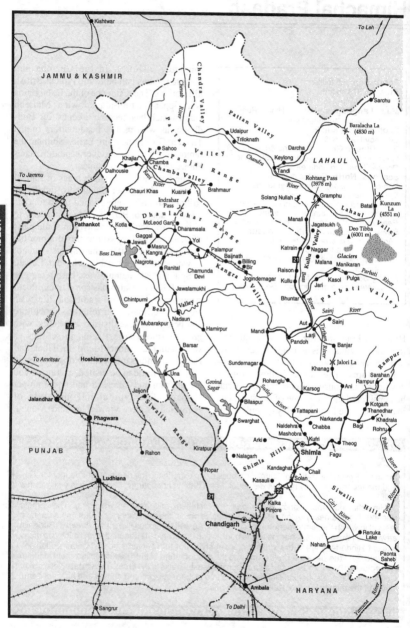

Himachal Pradesh

JAMMU &
KASHMIR

Spiti River

Lingti Valley

Kibber

Spiti Valley

Kaza

Dankar Tabo Sumdo CHINA
TIBET

SPITI

Nako
Leo Pargial
(6791 m)

Pin River

Pin Valley

KINNAUR

Puh

Sutlej River

Kalpa Rekong Peo Morang

Valley

Nichar Tapri Sutlej Kinnaur Kailash
(6050 m)

Wangtu

Sangla Valley

Sangla

UTTAR
PRADESH

To
Dehra Dun

0   30   60 km

The external boundaries of India
on this map have not been authenticated
and may not be correct.

Rajaji Wildlife
Sanctuary

There are equally fascinating Hindu temples
in Himachal. A classic example perched high
above the Sutlej at Sarahan shows the fortified style. The third religion of the state is
Sikhism and the *gurudwara* (Sikh temple) at
Paonta Saheb on the Yamuna River is most
scenic.

HISTORY

As with most other Himalayan states, the racial
intermix of Mongols and Aryans is evident in
Himachal and often you find interior villagers
with two names – Hindu and Buddhist – in an
attempt to straddle this dual inheritance. The
aboriginal hill people are a darker race associated with the Indus Valley civilisation.

Astride ancient trade routes to Tibet (over
the Shipki La) and Central Asia (via the
Baralacha La and Leh), as well as commanding the Sach Pass that led to Kashmir, the
regions that comprise Himachal had a proliferation of wealthy petty rulers. Some early
obscure references to republics suggest
social experimentation, but the feudal
warlord was the norm. Rajas, Ranas and
Thakurs ran their rival *rahuns* and *thakurais*,
the regions over which they presided,
making Himachal a patchwork quilt of tiny
states. Only Kangra and Kullu (and later
Chamba) had the power to break out of the
petty feuding system. Chandragupta Maurya
(enthroned 322 BC) suppressed some of the
supposed republics.

Chamba's distinguished history begins
under the Varman Dynasty in 680. It
extended its boundaries to include the town
of Chamba in 920. Several Himachal states
had kings from Bengal, the earliest founding
Suket in 1288. They were fleeing the Muslim
menace that had spread to the Bay of Bengal
in the centuries following Mahmud of
Ghazni's raid on Kangra in 1009. The best
known of these Bengali states is Mandi
founded as late as 1527. As befits its position
guarding entry both to the Kullu and Kangra
valleys Mandi means simply 'market'.
Bushahr, with its capital at Rampur on the
Sutlej River, controlled the Sutlej Valley
route to Tibet. Formerly it had been centred
in the Baspa Valley of Kinnaur, whose orig-

Festivals of Himachal Pradesh

Festivals, fairs and ceremonies play an integral part in the life of the people of Himachal Pradesh. They usually celebrate religious events, domestic occasions such as a birth, death or marriage, or the start or finish of the season or harvest. In the remote region of Lahaul & Spiti, festivals celebrate both Hindu and Buddhist religious events, agricultural events, to commemorate a birthday *(pingri)*, death or marriage *(paklen)* and often just to fill in the long winter months when this region is isolated from the rest of the world. Dancing, singing and drinking are a vital part of each festival. In most cases, dates of festivals in Lahaul & Spiti are determined according to the Tibetan calendar.

December-January

Halda – This is the name of the new year celebration held in January in the northern areas of Lahaul & Spiti. New year celebrations, are held throughout Himachal Pradesh in December.

Khojala – Celebrated in Lahaul & Spiti during the first full moon in January, huge fires are lit on nearby hills, and everyone throws snowballs at each other.

January-February

Phagul – Also known as *Suskar*, this Kinnauri festival lasts about two weeks in January. There are plenty of snowball fights.

Sazo – Held each January in Kinnaur, villagers bathe in natural springs, or if brave, in the freezing Sutlej River. This is eagerly followed by a large feast.

Dacchang – Called the 'festival of arrows', this is held over six days in many villages of Lahaul & Spiti. Men shoot arrows into the air to ensure that good prevails over evil.

Phagli – Held in the Pattan Valley (Lahaul & Spiti), Phagli is the new year celebration. Flowers are gathered and offered as greetings, especially to the elder members of the family.

February-March

Shivratri – Shivratri is celebrated throughout India in late February/early March, and is dedicated to Lord Shiva, who danced the *tandava* (the Dance of Destruction) on this day. In Himachal Pradesh, Mandi, at the gateway of the Kullu Valley, hosts the most interesting Shivratri. The celebrations continue for weeks and deities from all over Mandi district are carried into the town. Large numbers of people have *darshan* (viewing of a deity) at the 16th century Bhutnath Temple in the centre of the town. The Vaidyanath Temple at Baijnath, in the Kangra Valley, which is dedicated to Shiva and enshrines one of India's 12 *jyoti lingams* (Shiva shrines), or lingams of light, is also the centre of a good deal of devotional activity during Shivratri.

March-April

Sui Mata Festival – This four day festival is held at Chamba. Sui Mata, the daughter of an ancient raja, gave her life to save the inhabitants of her father's kingdom, and she is particularly revered by Chamba women, who carry her image from the old palace up to her small shrine, accompanied by singing and dancing.

Nalwari Fair – This cattle fair takes place at Bilaspur in the third week of March. Apart from bovine transactions, there are also wrestling bouts.

Opera Festival – Convened by the Tibetan Institute of Performing Arts (TIPA), at McLeod Ganj in April, this festival includes performances of the traditional *lhamo* opera as well as contemporary and historical plays.

Baisakhi – This popular agricultural festival is held in Kinnaur on 13 April, sometimes a little earlier. It celebrates the end of winter.

April-May

TIPA Anniversary Festival – On 27 May, a three day festival at McLeod Ganj celebrates the anniversary of the foundation of TIPA, with performances by students and artists from the school.

Hang-Gliding Rally – This international rally takes place in Billing, in the Kangra Valley, and attracts both national and international hang-gliders.

May-June

Summer Festival – Shimla's summer festival has a broad appeal with golf and other sporting tournaments, a flower show and cultural performances including folk dancing.

July-August

Dalai Lama's Birthday – His Holiness the Dalai Lama celebrates his birthday on 6 July, and this is a special time to visit McLeod Ganj, his home, as Tibetans pray for the long life of their leader.

Dakhrain – Held on 16 July, this festival celebrates the start of the rainy season in southern Kinnaur. Plenty of food, particularly dairy products, is enjoyed by everyone.

Shegtusm – Also held on 16 July, but in Lahaul & Spiti, this festival celebrates the start of the (limited) rainy season. Offerings are made to various gods.

Ladarch – This is a famous flower festival and trade fair held near Kaza (Lahaul & Spiti) in July.

Minjar Festival – This festival is celebrated in late July/early August in Chamba. The origins of the fair are said to date back to 935 AD when the founder of Chamba, Raja Sahil Varman, returned to the town after defeating the raja of Kangra. It more probably evolved from a harvest festival to celebrate the annual maize crop. *Minjars*, silk tassels worn by men and women, represent sheaves of maize, and are distributed during the festival. It culminates with a colourful procession and at this time there are busy crowds of Gaddi, Churachi, Bhatti and Gujar people. An image of Lord Raghuvira is carried aloft at the head of the procession and images of other gods and goddesses are borne in palanquins. The procession proceeds to the banks of the Ravi River, where the minjars are thrown into the water.

Manimahesh Yatra – Pilgrims from all over north India converge on the small village of Brahmaur, in the Chamba Valley, to commence the pilgrimage to the sacred lake of Manimahesh, below the peak of Manimahesh Kailash, at 5656m, and 28 km from Brahmaur. Parents blessed with a boy child take the child on the pilgrimage, during which time the boy's hair is ceremonially cut. Prior to the pilgrimage, a seven day fair is held at Brahmaur, followed by wrestling competitions and folk dances by pilgrims from distant villages. Fifteen days after the commencement of the festival, the pilgrims are led by priests to Manimahesh. Here there is an ancient and very beautiful temple dedicated to Lakshmi Devi in her form as slayer of the buffalo demon (Mahishasuramardini). The image of the goddess enshrined in the inner sanctum dates from the 7th century AD.

Chhishu – This festival held in Lahaul & Spiti celebrates the birth of the greatly revered Buddhist sage, Padmasambhava, in July.

August-September

Fulech – This festival is celebrated in Kinnauri villages from late August until mid-September, beginning in the village of Rupi and culminating at the village of Nesang, in upper Kinnaur. The festival heralds the end of summer, and is celebrated with the plucking of wildflowers, dancing and other festivities.

Ukhayang – Also known as the *Phulech* or *Flaich* Festival, this is celebrated in many villages throughout Kinnaur between August and November. All able villagers gather flowers and congregate on a nearby hill. A male goat is often sacrificed.

Pauri – This three day festival at Triloknath, near Udaipur (Lahaul & Spiti), attracts thousands of Hindu and Buddhist pilgrims every August.

September-October

Dussehra – Dussehra is celebrated India-wide as the victory of Rama over Ravana, the demon king of Lanka. In Kullu, Rama is worshipped in his form as Raghunath, whose image is borne through the streets on a wheeled *rath* (palanquin) pulled by pilgrims. Following the procession, villagers perform dances in traditional dress.

Namkan – This celebrates the new harvest in Lahaul & Spiti. Local people dress up in traditional clothing and participate in horse races.

November-December

Renuka Festival – This week-long festival, celebrated at Renuka Lake, in southern Himachal Pradesh, is held in honour of Renukaji. According to one of several local legends, Sahasarjuna killed Jamadagini and tried to take his wife, Renukaji. Preferring death to dishonour, Renukaji threw herself in the lake and drowned, but miraculously was brought back to life. Festivities include ritual bathing in the lake, dancing and general merrymaking.

Lavi Fair – This trade fair is held at Rampur, 140 km north-east of Shimla on the banks of the Sutlej River. At the time, the inhabitants of the remote regions of Lahaul & Spiti, and Kinnaur congregate at the town to trade locally made produce and horses. ■

inal inhabitants are said to be descendants of divine musicians. This tribe exemplifies the fusion of Aryan and Mongol cultures that characterises much of the Indian Himalaya. With the exception of the bigger states, most of the later hill states were founded by Rajput adventurers from the plains in the early medieval period.

The first westerners to the region were Jesuit missionaries in search of Prester John's legendary land. But both Hinduism and Buddhism were sufficiently colourful to retain their adherents. The British discovered Himachal after their wars with the Sikhs and the Gurkhas. Maharaja Ranjit Singh took Kangra fort as his price for helping Raja Sansar Chand expel the Gurkhas who had allied themselves with alienated local princes. Before the Sikh emperor annexed it, the fort at Kangra had attracted several other prominent rulers since the days of Mahmud of Ghazni, including the mad Tughlaq and Timur the Lame. Tughlaq's successor raided the nearby temple of Jawalamukhi to obtain Hindu texts he wished to translate. The emperor Akbar was fascinated by the eternal gas flame of Jawalamukhi, as was the Sikh emperor, who raised a gold canopy over it.

Following the supremacy of British arms against the Sikhs and Gurkhas, Himachal was discovered to be ideal apple growing country. An American missionary, the Reverend NS Stokes, developed the Kotgarh orchards (his family still runs them) and the apple industry quickly spread to Kullu. Little bits of England were created at Shimla, Dalhousie and Dharamsala during the late 19th century. The railway to Shimla with its 102 tunnels was built in 1902. Another railway line was laid through the Kangra Valley. In the interior, however, feudal conditions remained where men were forced to work without pay and women were regarded as chattels.

The new state of Himachal Pradesh comprising only 6 districts was formed in 1948. By 1966, the Pahari-speaking parts under Punjab administration, including Kangra, Kullu and Lahaul & Spiti, were added. Full statehood was achieved in 1971.

GEOGRAPHY

Himachal Pradesh is dominated by mountains, and associated rivers and valleys. The highest peaks, Shilla (7026m), Manerang (6597m) and Shipki (6608m), are in remote regions. Some of those you are more likely to see are Leo Pargial (6791m), near Nako, in Kinnaur; Deo Tibba (6001m), not far from Manali; and Kinnaur Kailash (6050m), which dominates the views from Rekong Peo and Kalpa in Kinnaur. The passes, such as the Baralacha La (4883m) and Kunzum La (4551m), are pivotal points along the northern roads. ('La' is a Tibetan word meaning pass.) In winter, Lahaul & Spiti is completely isolated when these and other passes are blocked by snow.

There are several major rivers running through the state. The unpredictable Beas River (pronounced 'bee-ahs') flows through the Kullu Valley, and then heads west below the Kangra Valley. (In September 1995, the Beas flooded and caused devastation along the Kullu Valley.) From the north, the Chenab River turns into the Chandra River in Lahaul & Spiti. The mighty Spiti River starts nearby before joining the Sutlej River in Kinnaur. The Sutlej flows all the way to the artificial Govind Sagar (lake), to the west of Bilaspur. In the west, the Ravi River flows through Chamba and on to Lahore in northern Pakistan. The wide Yamuna, Giri and Tons rivers congregate around Paonta Saheb in the south.

A lot of Himachal Pradesh can be easily segregated according to the various valleys. Lahaul & Spiti is a series of valleys stretching from the Chandra Valley in the northwest to the Lingti Valley along the Spiti River. The Kullu Valley, a populous area, stretches from Mandi to Manali. The Parbati Valley follows the Parbati River, which juts off the Beas River. In the west, the beautiful Kangra Valley stretches from Mandi to Shahpur, near Pathankot. To the north of the Kangra Valley, on the other side of the Dhauladhar Range, is the Chamba Valley, which is separated from the remote Pattan Valley (upper Chenab River Valley) by the Pir Panjal Range.

Temples & Gompas of Himachal Pradesh

The existence of numerous temples, castles and forts throughout every district of the state reflects the varied history and several different religions of Himachal Pradesh. Close to Manali, the Hadimba Devi and the Manu Maharishi temples are important for Hindus. Sarahan has the spectacular Hindu and Buddhist Bhimakali temple; in Rampur, the Padam Palace has some Islamic, Hindu and Buddhist links; Renuka Lake has several Hindu temples; and at Paonta Saheb, the Sikh temple, or gurudwara, is an important site.

The other former capital, Jagatsukh, also has a couple of famous Hindu temples. One of the most amazing religious sites, Rewalsar Lake (near Mandi, where there are 81 Hindu temples), has temples revered by Sikhs, Hindus and Buddhists. Near the town of Kullu, the Raghunath and Jagannathi Devi temples, and the stone temples of Bijli Mahadev and Basheshar Mahadev, are famous. Hindu and Sikh temples dominate Manikaran in the Parbati Valley.

In the Kangra Valley is the ancient Baidyanath temple at Baijnath, dedicated to Lord Shiva, which features fine stone carving and houses one of India's 12 jyoti lingams, or lingams of light. There are two important temple complexes in the Chamba Valley, at the town of Chamba, and the small village of Brahmaur. These were built during the Varman dynasty, and are a testament to the wealth of these rajas.

In the remote district of Lahaul & Spiti, Buddhist gompas dominate many villages. Some of the most spectacular and ancient gompas are at Dankar, Ki and Tabo which celebrated its 1000 year anniversary in 1996. In the north-west of the district, there is the 900 year old gompa at Khardong, other gompas at Guru Ghantal and Tayal, and the holy Buddhist and Hindu temple at Triloknath. At the capital of Kinnaur, Rekong Peo, the modern gompa overlooks the incredible Kinnaur Kailash mountain. ∎

TOURIST OFFICES

The Himachal Pradesh Tourist Development Corporation (HPTDC) provides some useful services. Every major town has a HPTDC tourist office which offers local information and maps, and sometimes handles bookings for Archana Airways.

The HPTDC manages about 40 hotels in Himachal Pradesh. These are usually luxurious log huts, modest guesthouses or expensive hotels. HPTDC hotels don't offer discounts nor are they great value in places like Manali or Shimla, where there is so much competition. The HPTDC has a central reservation office at Daizy Bank Estate in Shimla which can arrange bookings for HPTDC hotels.

In season, the HPTDC organises 'deluxe' buses for tourists between the major centres such as Shimla, Kullu, Dharamsala and Manali, and links these places with Delhi and Chandigarh. HPTDC buses are more expensive than public buses but are quicker and far more comfortable. The HPTDC also organises daily sightseeing tours out of Dharamsala, Shimla and Manali, which is a useful way of visiting local areas.

HPTDC offices elsewhere in India can also provide worthwhile information:

Calcutta
    25 Carmac St (☎ (033) 446-8477)
Chandigarh
    SCO: 1048-49, Sector 22-B (☎ (0172) 43-569)
Delhi
    Chandralok Bldg, 36 Janpath (☎ (011) 332-4764)
Madras
    28 Commander-in-Chief Rd (☎ (044) 47-2966)
Mumbai (Bombay)
    36 World Trade Centre, Cuffe Parade (☎ (022) 21-9191)

PERMITS

Inner Line Permits are usually required for some of Lahaul & Spiti, and Kinnaur. Regulations, and their implementation, have noticeably relaxed in the past year or so, and may relax further, and even be abolished entirely. Check the current regulations with the relevant authorities or other travellers.

Foreigners can travel between Leh and Manali without a permit. A permit is not usually required for travel between Leh or Manali and Kaza, the capital of the Spiti subdistrict (although some travellers have reported that they needed a permit). From Tabo to Rekong Peo, you need a permit, but from Rekong Peo to Shimla, no permit is required.

Permits can be obtained from the District and Sub-District Magistrates' offices in most regional centres. It is better to get them in Kaza or Rekong Peo so you don't waste any of your seven day permit just getting to these places.

Shimla

Population: 105,000
Telephone Area Code: 0177
Best Time to Go: mid-September to late November
Peak Season: early May to mid-July, mid-September to late October, mid-December to mid-January

Shimla was once part of the Nepalese kingdom, and called *Shyamala*, another name for the goddess Kali, but Shimla never gained any fame until it was first 'discovered' by the British in 1819. Three years later, the first 'British' house was erected, and by 1864 Shimla became the summer capital of India. After the construction of the Kalka to Shimla railway line in 1903, Shimla really boomed. Following independence, Shimla was initially the capital of the Punjab, then it became the capital of Himachal Pradesh.

Today, Shimla is a lovely, sprawling town, set among spectacular, cool hills, with plenty of crumbling colonial charm. It has very good facilities, although accommodation, particularly in the high season, is expensive. For reasons of cost and weather, it is important to time your visit well. (See the start of this chapter for information on seasons.)

Orientation

There are only two roads in the central part of Shimla. The Mall runs from the far west into the centre of town to the lower eastern side. In the centre it meets Scandal Corner – immortalised by Rudyard Kipling, and the

location of the ANZ Grindlays Bank. The mall area known as The Ridge runs from Scandal Corner to the Christ Church. Cart Rd circles the southern part of Shimla, and is where the bus and taxi stands and railway station are located. The rest of Shimla is connected by masses of unmarked, unnamed, steep lanes and steps. There is also a passenger lift connecting Cart Rd to The (eastern) Mall.

It seems that just about every hotel in Shimla lists its address as 'The Mall, Shimla', when many are not even close to The Mall. At Scandal Corner, The Mall heads east and west, and shop numbers start in both directions at number one – so '5 The Mall' can be at two places.

The main landmark is the Christ Church, which can be seen from many places in Shimla, especially at night. Some streets are havens for cute-looking monkeys, but be aware that they do bite, scratch and steal things – in early 1996 a monkey grabbed a bag containing money belonging to a Shimla trader and scattered the cash from a rooftop over the streets, which was quickly snatched by the delighted crowd!

Information

Tourist Office There is a confusing set of tourist offices in Shimla. Disregard the Directorate of Tourism which is way past the YMCA, and not worth the trek; the tourist booth at the railway station offers very basic information, but is only open when trains arrive; the Tourist Reception Centre on Cart Rd is run by an informative local guidebook author, but is really inconvenient.

The one to use is the HPTDC tourist office at Scandal Corner. It provides basic local information and maps, offers a taxi service, organises tourist buses and handles bookings for Archana Airways. It's open from 9 am to 9 pm every day in season; from 9.30 am to 5 pm in the off season.

Money There are several places to change money, but ask about encashment fees first. All banks are open from about 10 am to 2 pm, Monday to Friday; and from 10 am to noon on Saturday. The State Bank of India, along The (western) Mall, charges Rs 20 per transaction, plus Rs 3 for every travellers' cheque cashed. The UCO Bank, above the Central Telegraph Office, charges no fee, so is a good option. The ANZ Grindlays Bank, at Scandal Corner, charges an outrageous Rs 195 fee to change your travellers' cheques. They do allow advances on Visa Card and MasterCard for a comparatively reasonable Rs 75 per transaction. The two little, chaotic Punjab National Bank branches, either side of the Indian Coffee House, change money, with no fee, and offer friendly, albeit slow, service.

Post & Communications The main post office, not far from Scandal Corner, is open from 10 am to 6 pm, Monday to Saturday; 10 am to 4 pm on Sunday and public holidays. If you want your letter or postcard franked in front of you, take it to counter 13 in a building next door (to the right as you exit) to the post office. The poste restante here is reliable and worth using.

The Central Telegraph Office (CTO) (fax 20-4026), west of Scandal Corner is open 24 hours. Many travel agencies can arrange interstate and international calls, but the CTO is still the best place to make telephone calls, and to send and receive faxes. At the time of writing, a telephone call from the CTO cost Rs 85 per minute to Australia/New Zealand, Rs 90 to the USA/Canada, and Rs 85 to Europe.

Bookshops Maria Brothers, 78 The (eastern) Mall, has a fascinating, jumbled collection of antique local books – a great place to browse around. Minerva Bookshop, opposite the Gaiety Theatre, near Scandal Corner, has a fantastic selection of popular, and obscure (English-language only) novels (often cheap Indian-made books by popular western authors), and books on the history and culture of all parts of India. It also has a great range of maps, so buy any you may need here rather than other places which won't have the same selection. A few shops away, the Asia Book House is good for popular novels and magazines.

Maps & Books Maria Brothers publish the pocket-sized *Complete Guide to Shimla and Adjacent Country* (Rs 30). First published in 1959, it is a great little collection of historical stories. The Nest & Wings' *Tourist Guide to Shimla* (Rs 25) is also good for a history of Shimla, and information on places around Shimla. The best maps for Shimla and its surrounds are the yellow ones published by TT Maps & Publications, and the plastic map by Bharat Graphics (Rs 80), which is very handy if you're hiking to places in the vicinity of Shimla.

Medical Services The Indira Gandhi (or Snowdon) Medical College and Hospital (☎ 72-646) is not far from Lakkar Bazaar. Deen Dayal Upadhayay (or Ripon) Hospital (☎ 72-802) is near the centre of Shimla, close to Cart Rd. There are plenty of clinics and pharmacies around The Mall area. An ambulance service (☎ 3463 or 3464) is also available.

Film & Photography Shimla is well set up for the sale and developing of film, so if you're heading further north, especially to Lahaul & Spiti or Kinnaur, it may be a good idea to take advantage of what Shimla has to offer. Along The (eastern) Mall, the Kumar Studio Lab and Sohans Studio are good for developing print, but not slide film.

Himachal State Museum & Library
About 2½ km west of Scandal Corner, the State Museum has a good collection of statues, coins, photos and other items from around Himachal Pradesh. There is also a useful library, full of historical books, and the daily English-language newspapers. The museum is free, and is open daily from 10 am to 1.30 pm and from 2 to 5 pm; closed on Monday and public holidays.

Viceregal Lodge & Botanical Gardens
The Viceregal Lodge, also known as Rashtrapati Niwas, is based on Observatory

Hill. It was formerly the residence of the British viceroy Lord Dufferin, and is where many decisions affecting the destiny of the subcontinent were made. Incredibly, every brick of the six storey building was transported by mule (the train hadn't been built at that stage). The lodge was eventually finished in 1888.

Here there are magnificently kept lawns, botanical gardens, and a small cafe. The lodge now houses the Indian Institute of Advanced Study – look for this sign, rather than any other, as you approach. As you enter the institute complex, walk around the front building – the lodge is at the back.

The lodge is a pleasant two km walk further west from the museum – about 4½ km from Scandal Corner. It's open daily from 9 am to 8.30 pm in summer, and closes a little earlier during the rest of the year. It costs Rs 6 for a guided tour of the lodge (which is closed between 1 and 2 pm), or Rs 3 to look around the gardens only.

Himalayan Aviary

Right next to the entrance of the institute complex is the Himalayan Bird Park or Aviary. As expected, it has a collection of species found around Himachal Pradesh, such as the Himalayan monal (the state bird

of Himachal Pradesh), various types of pheasants, and the national bird of India, the Indian peafowl. The aviary is open daily (closed on Monday) from 10 am to 5 pm. Entrance is Rs 5, but a still camera costs an extra Rs 25, and a video camera, Rs 100. It's worth a wander around if you are going out to the lodge anyway.

Christ Church & St Michael's Cathedral

The second oldest church in northern India (the oldest is in Ambala), the Christ Church, overlooking The Ridge, was built between 1846 and 1857. The clocks were added three years later, but none of them now work. One of Shimla's major landmarks, the church is also renowned for its stained glass windows. You can discreetly have a look inside the church, or attend English-language services every Sunday during the tourist season. The other main church in Shimla is St Michael's Cathedral, just below the Central Telegraph Office.

Jakhu Temple

Dedicated to the monkey god, Hanuman, Jakhu Temple is at an altitude of 2455m near the highest point of the Shimla ridge. It offers a fine view over the surrounding valleys, out to the snow-capped peaks, and over Shimla

---

Colonial Shimla

From 1822, when the first 'British' home (Kennedy House at The Glen) was built in Shimla, it took only 40 years before the town became the official summer capital of the British Raj. By the end of the 19th century, Shimla had opulent colonial mansions (together with hundreds of local staff) such as the Viceregal Lodge and Wildflower Hall, grand hotels, including the famous Cecil Hotel at The Glen, and hotels (still operating) at Kasauli and Fagu, and huge churches. With the advent of the toy train in 1903, Shimla could be easily accessed by the rich and famous based in hot and crowded Delhi.

Until the end of WWII, and Independence shortly afterwards, the British continued to enjoy gymkhanas, polo and horse racing at Annandale, cricket at Chail, and golf at Naldehra. In Shimla, there were endless games of bridge, ballroom dancing, cocktail parties and promenades down The Mall and The Ridge where exclusive boutiques sold the latest fashions from London.

Shimla boasted exclusive boys' and girls' colleges (many are still used today), a Fine Arts Society, and regular productions of plays by Shakespeare, Agatha Christie and Noel Coward at its many theatres. Performances are still held at the Gaiety Theatre, modelled after the Garrick Theatre in London. Rudyard Kipling spent many years living and working in Shimla, and eminent colonialists such as Lord Curzon and Lord Kitchener managed to find time while here to govern India. ■

itself. Appropriately, there are many monkeys around the temple. It's a steep 45 minute walk from Scandal Corner. Take the footpath which goes past the Hotel Dreamland to the south. Sunrise is a good time to be there.

Bazaars
There are two main bazaar, or *mandi*, areas in Shimla. Just below the western end of The (eastern) Mall, the frantic Sabzi Mandi, also known as Lower Bazaar, is a maze of twisting, steep lanes full of stalls selling food and just about everything imaginable. Prices here for meals, and other things, are generally cheaper than places along The Mall. Beyond The Ridge, the small, busy Lakkar Bazaar is the place to buy souvenirs, although most shops seem to sell fairly tacky wooden stuff.

Walks
Apart from a promenade along The Mall and the walk to the Jakhu Temple, there are a great number of interesting walks around Shimla. For more information on places further afield, refer to the Around Shimla section.

The Glen, about four km west of Scandal Corner, is one of the former playgrounds of rich British colonialists. The turn-off is on the way to the State Museum, and goes through the other lovely area of **Annandale**. This was the site of a famous racecourse, where cricket and polo are still played.

Summer Hill is five km away, on the Shimla-Kalka railway line, and has pleasant, shady walks. It's also famous because Mahatma Gandhi stayed at the Raj Kumari Amrit Kaur mansion on Summer Hill.

Chadwick Falls are 67m high, but are only really worth visiting during or just after the monsoons – from July to October. The falls are seven km from Shimla and can be reached via Summer Hill.

Prospect Hill is about five km west of Shimla, and a 15 minute climb from Boileauganj. The hill is a popular picnic spot with fine views over the surrounding country. The **Kamna Devi Temple** is nearby.

Sankat Mochan, seven km from Shimla,

on the road to Chandigarh, has a Hanuman temple, and fine views of Shimla. It can also be reached by taxi.

Tara Devi Temple is 10 km from Shimla. It is dedicated to Tara Devi, Goddess of the Stars. It is situated on top of a hill, and another, dedicated to Lord Shiva, is nearby. It's about three km up a path from the Tara Devi station on the Shimla-Kalka railway, or you can take a taxi there.

Organised Tours
For a look around the areas near Shimla, an organised tour is not a bad idea. The HPTDC (book at the office on The Mall) organises daily sightseeing tours in season. There are tours to Kufri, Fagu and Naldehra (Rs 115), and to Narkanda via Fagu and Theog (Rs 125), for great views; to the lovely, historic Chail region (Rs 115); and to the hot springs at Tattapani, via Naldehra (Rs 115).

Places to Stay
Accommodation in Shimla is expensive, particularly during the peak seasons. During these times, if you don't want to pay more than Rs 80 for a room, forget Shimla, and go to the Kullu Valley instead. But in the off season, or when business is quiet, you can find some good value places in Shimla. The prices below are for the peak season – but, remember, they will drop dramatically, even halve, in the off season.

Many places offer 'hot water', but only in geysers, which are only taps and no substitute for a proper shower. If travelling in a group, a 'family room', usually with at least two double beds, is often better value.

Places to Stay – bottom end
If you're on a low budget, the cheapest areas are around the bus station, and along Cart Rd, heading east from the bus station.

The *YMCA* (☎ 72-375) (for men and women) has singles with temporary membership for Rs 190, and doubles, excluding temporary membership, for Rs 180. Both prices include breakfast, and share bathrooms with hot water. The YMCA is often booked out when it *does* offer a cheap alter-

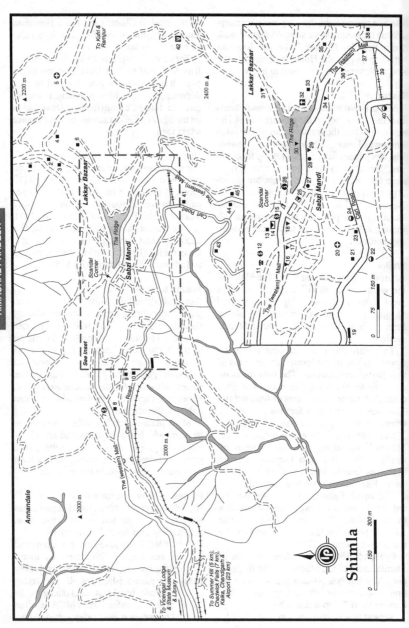

Shimla

native in the high season, but in the off season it doesn't drop its prices, so no longer represents good value. It's not far behind the Christ Church, up a laneway from The Ridge.

The *YWCA* (☎ 20-3081) (also for men and women), above the main post office, is better value. It's a convenient, friendly old place, with great views. Large rooms range from Rs 100 to Rs 150, plus Rs 10 with temporary membership. Meals are an extra Rs 15, and a bucket of hot water is available for Rs 3.

Near the bus station, there are several very plain and very noisy places. The *Hotel Himachal* (☎ 5466), a little south of the railway station (look for the hotel sign), has ordinary singles/doubles, often windowless, for Rs 125/150. The *Vikrant Hotel* (☎ 3602), off the laneway that goes to the Himachal, has rooms for about Rs 150, and the big *Thakur Hotel* (☎ 77-545) is a little better, with large rooms for Rs 100/180.

Along the busy Cart Rd, east from the bus station, are several cheap places. The best, and most popular for value, is the *Hotel Basant* (☎ 78-381) – a well run, friendly

place. Singles with common bath cost Rs 75; with attached bath, from Rs 95. Hot water comes by the bucket, at Rs 5. Right in front is the more expensive *Hotel High Way Lodge* (☎ 20-008). Rooms with attached bath and running hot water cost about Rs 200.

Around the Lakkar Bazaar area, a steep climb past The Ridge, there are several places which are reasonably priced. The *Hotel Snow View* (☎ 3244) has pretty good singles/doubles from Rs 150/250. The *Hotel Ridge View* (☎ 4859), where rooms cost from Rs 160 to Rs 400, with TV and hot water, offers 50% discounts in the off season – like many other places. To find it, just follow the signs from the Christ Church. The *Hotel Uphar* (☎ 77-670) is clean and friendly. Rooms with attached bath and hot water cost Rs 150/200, and Rs 260 with a view. The *Hotel Ashoka* (☎ 78-166), with rooms for Rs 175/275, is a similar standard. The *Hotel Shimla View* (☎ 20-3244) has rooms with a common bath for Rs 125.

Actually on The Mall, a short distance from Scandal Corner, are one or two noisy but handy places. The *Hotel Loveena* (☎ 20-2035),

HIMACHAL PRADESH

PLACES TO STAY		43	HPTDC Hotel Holiday Home	OTHER	
1	Hotel Auckland	44	Oberoi Clarke's Hotel	5	Indira Gandhi Hospital
2	Hotels Chanakya & White	45	Hotels Shingar & Sangeet	7	State Bank of India
3	Hotels Ashoka & Shimla View			11	Central Telegraph Office
4	Hotels Diplomat & Snow View	**PLACES TO EAT**		12	UCO Bank
6	Hotels Uphar & Dreamland			14	Main Post Office
8	Hotels Gulmarg & Fontaine Bleau	16	Indian Coffee House	15	ANZ Grindlays Bank
9	Hotel Prakash	17	The Devicos Restaurant	19	Railway Station & Reservation Office
10	Hotels Dalziel & Classic	18	Alfa Restaurant	20	Deen Dayal Upadhayay (Ripon) Hospital
13	YWCA	25	Baljee's & Fascination Restaurants	22	Bus Station
21	Thakur Hotel	29	Himani's	24	Kalka-Shimla Taxi Union Stand
23	Hotels Basant & High Way Lodge	30	Ashiana, Goofa & Quick Bite Restaurants	26	HPTDC Tourist Office
33	YMCA	31	Toran & Tripti's Restaurants	27	Gaiety Theatre
35	Hotel Bridge View & Doegar Hotel	34	Park Cafe	28	Maria Brothers
38	Hotel Samrat	36	Shere-e-Punjab	32	Christ Church
41	Hotel Crystal Palace	37	Embassy Restaurant	39	Passenger Lift
				40	Vishal Himachal Taxi Operators' Union Stand
				42	Jakhu Temple

above the Indian Coffee House on The (western) Mall, has rooms for Rs 400 with views and TV, which cost half that in the off season. The *Hotel Minerva* (☎ 72-043), 90 The (eastern) Mall, has nice, but small, singles/doubles for Rs 125/195 with bath and TV.

Across the road from the State Bank of India, the *Hotel Gulmarg* (☎ 3168) has a TV and hot water in each of its rooms. In the huge rambling hotel complex, there are charmless and windowless economy rooms from Rs 150, and 'Honey Moon' rooms up to Rs 850. Next door, the quaint, family-run *Hotel Fontaine Bleau* (☎ 3549) has a nice landlady who speaks English well, and rooms from Rs 175 to Rs 300, with a share bathroom.

If you're getting an early or late train, the *retiring rooms* at the Shimla railway station are standard Indian Railways issue. Comfortable but noisy rooms costs Rs 150 – with a 50% discount in the off season.

Places to Stay – middle

The majority in this range will usually include TV (often cable), and a bathroom with hot water. They are particularly good value in the off season, when a nice double room with cable TV and hot water costs about Rs 200.

Just off The (western) Mall, a short walk up from the railway station, there are three reasonable places: the *Hotel Prakash* (☎ 21-3321) has singles/doubles from Rs 200/375; the *Hotel Classic* (☎ 5463), friendly and comfortable, has rooms for Rs 250/400 with good views; and the *Hotel Dalziel* (☎ 2691) has rooms starting at the very negotiable price of Rs 280.

North of The Ridge, and around the Lakkar Bazaar area, are several good places, but it is a little inconvenient, and a steep climb up there. One of the best is the *Hotel Chanakya* (☎ 21-1232), which is clean and comfortable, with rooms from Rs 220. Just a few doors away, the *Hotel Diplomat* (☎ 72-001) has rooms from Rs 275, or a little more with a view. Near the Chanakya, *Hotel White* (☎ 5276) singles/doubles cost from Rs

330/380. The *Hotel Dreamland* (☎ 5057) is good value, and is popular, with rooms at about the same price. The *Hotel Auckland* (☎ 72-621) is a very pleasant place, with rooms from about Rs 350.

Around the lower end of The (eastern) Mall, near the passenger lift, is a gaggle of newish places. The large *Hotel Bridge View* (☎ 78-537) has great views and rooms from Rs 300. Above the Bridge View is the better *Doegar Hotel* (☎ 21-1927), with rooms from Rs 250.

The *Hotel Samrat* (☎ 78-572) has a range of rooms, many of them small. These are still about the best of the bunch at Rs 280, while bigger rooms with a view cost Rs 380. Nearby, the newer *Hotel Kwality* offers the same sort of standard and price as the others. At the bottom of the lift, the *Hotel Crystal Palace* (☎ 75-588) is better value at Rs 275 for rooms at the back, more for a view.

There are two good places across from the Oberoi Clarke's Hotel, at the bottom end of The (eastern) Mall. The *Hotel Shingar* (☎ 72-881) has rooms for Rs 300, Rs 400 with a view. It's well run and good value. Nearby, the *Hotel Sangeet* (☎ 20-2506) is another good place. Standard rooms are Rs 250; better rooms with views cost Rs 360.

The HPTDC's *Hotel Holiday Home* (☎ 21-2890) is on Cart Rd. It's friendly, well set up with a bar and coffee shop, but it's inconveniently located, and doesn't give off-season discounts. Rates start at Rs 400 for the cheapest rooms, and up to Rs 2000, including meals, for a deluxe room.

Places to Stay – top end

For some luxury and old colonial charm, try the *Woodville Palace Resort* (☎ 72-763), two km south past the Oberoi Clarke's on The (eastern) Mall. This ivy-covered building was constructed in 1938 by Raja Rana Sir Bhagat Chandra, the ruler of the former princely state of Jubbal. It's a small place, set among very pleasant gardens. Double rooms are Rs 1400, and suites cost Rs 2300 – bookings are recommended.

Down the far end of The (eastern) Mall, past the lift, is the Tudor-style *Oberoi*

Clarke's Hotel (☎ 21-2991), one of Shimla's earliest hotels. The luxurious rooms cost US$55/US$115 (no discounts, here, thank you) including the compulsory three meal 'American Plan'.

Places to Eat

If you have been in the wilds of India for a while, or have a sweet tooth, you'll be delighted to find several parlours selling (safe) ice cream, plenty of bakeries, and sweet and chocolate shops in Shimla. Just about every place serves hot, western breakfasts, but many don't open until about 9 am – Shimla is not a place for early starters. Most places serve a range of cuisines.

Western Cuisine One of the newer, better places, and worth the stroll, is the *Embassy Restaurant*, not far from the top of the lift on The (eastern) Mall. It's self-serve and no-nonsense, and has great individual pizzas and hamburgers, as well as Indian and Chinese food. *The Devicos Restaurant*, on The (western) Mall, near Scandal Corner, is a clean, trendy place that does good, but a little overpriced, fast food. Just down The (eastern) Mall and up some stairs, the *Park Cafe* also does great western treats, and Indian food. It's recommended for milkshakes, breakfasts, and laid-back late-evening music listening.

The HPTDC has a building on The Ridge with three places to eat. The *Ashiana* is about the best (and most expensive) place around the area for decor and service. The *Goofa* downstairs is nowhere near as classy or good, but serves a reasonable (and early) breakfast. In the same complex, the *Quick Bite* has cheap pizzas, and Indian food – or, for a combination of both, try their 'keema pizza'. At the other end of the scale, for a splurge in some luxurious surroundings, the *Oberoi Clarke's Hotel* has a buffet for Rs 189.

Indian Shimla has a lot of places serving Indian food, primarily southern Indian. Along The (eastern) Mall, one of the more popular restaurants is *Baljee's*. It has a delicious range of Indian and western food, and

the service is good. Prices can be a little high (but the seats are very comfortable). Upstairs, the associated restaurant, *Fascination*, is similarly priced and just as popular. Also near Scandal Corner, the *Alfa Restaurant* is about the same standard, price and popularity as Baljee's.

At 49 The (eastern) Mall, *Himani's* does tasty southern Indian snacks and meals, and has a bar. For Indian and Thai food, the *Rendezvous*, right on Scandal Corner, has moderate prices but slow service. Good cheap Indian food is available from many restaurants and *dhabas* around the Sabzi Mandi. In the Lakkar Bazaar area, *Toran* and *Tripti's* are great for thalis and samosas. One of the better places, the *Shere-e-Punjab*, along The (eastern) Mall, remains popular.

Bakeries There are many bakeries along The Mall. They sell an amazing selection of sweet pastries, with icing and cream, rather than the strudels and cinnamon rolls often found in other western-oriented bakeries in India. *Trishool's*, next to the Gaiety Theatre, is recommended; *Baljee's* has a bakery counter at the front, and is a great place for morning or afternoon teas; and *Krishna Bakers*, along The (eastern) Mall, does good burgers, cakes and pastries.

Drinks The *Indian Coffee House*, along The (western) Mall, is where traditionally dressed waiters serve great coffee (but no tea) and southern Indian snacks. *Himani's* has a bar, and so does the *Rendezvous*, on Scandal Corner, but it is dingy and unwelcoming. There are several small bars on the 1st floors of buildings along The Mall. The expensive hotels usually serve alcohol.

Entertainment

Probably the most popular, and best, entertainment is to stroll along The Mall and The Ridge (vehicle-free!) and watch everyone else watch everyone else. This is especially pleasant in the evenings when the views and lights are wonderful. An ice-skating rink is open in winter – follow the signs from Scandal Corner.

The lovely old Gaiety Theatre often has some shows or recitals, particularly in the tourist season, which are worth checking out. There are several cinemas, but they usually play the inevitable Hindi love epic or a dubbed Chinese kung-fu classic. The local daily newspaper *The Himachal Times* (Rs 1) has information on local things to do, particularly in the high season.

Getting There & Away
Air Shimla is not as well connected by air as the Kullu Valley or Leh, because Shimla is reasonably accessible by train and bus to Delhi and other major cities. Small aircraft, with up to 20 seats, link Shimla with Delhi and the other two airports in Himachal Pradesh.

Jagson Airlines flies to/from Delhi (US$82) every Tuesday, Thursday and Saturday as part of a milk run which also connects Shimla with Kullu (US$49) and Dharamsala (US$72). Archana Airways flies to/from Delhi (US$113) every Monday, Wednesday, Friday and Sunday.

Archana Airways bookings are possible at the HPTDC office at Scandal Corner. But beware that staff there will tell you, wrongly, that Archana is the only airline which flies to/from Shimla. Jagson Airlines is represented by Span Tour & Travels (☎ 52-220), 4 The (western) Mall. Airline bookings can be made at travel agencies along The Mall. The Jubbarhatti airport is 23 km south of Shimla.

Bus The large Shimla public bus station on Cart Rd is set up on the reasonable assumption that most foreigners take the train or a tourist bus; the chaotic station has no information booth, no timetables are displayed in English and most of the destinations listed on the buses are in Hindi.

However, there is a very handy private computer booking booth at the station, where the employees speak English, and you can book a ticket up to one month ahead on any public bus. This is often useful in the high season.

Public Bus There are public buses to Narkanda every 30 minutes (Rs 26); to Rampur every 30 minutes (Rs 56) – change buses in Rampur for Sarahan; and to Paonta Saheb/Nahan (Rs 72/55) – take the daily Dehra Dun bus. For other local places, such as Tattapani, Kasauli, places on the way to Kalka, and places on the way to Narkanda such as Kufri and Theog, catch one of the regular local buses along Cart Rd.

Buses go every day to other more distant places in Himachal Pradesh: to Manali (11 hours), there are two ordinary (Rs 106) and two deluxe buses (Rs 133); three semideluxe buses go to Dharamsala (10 hours, Rs 120); 10 go to Bilaspur/Mandi (Rs 34/63); one overnight bus goes to Dalhousie (Rs 160); five or six a day go to Kullu (Rs 91), via Mandi; and three buses leave every day for Chamba (Rs 155).

There is one overnight, and one early-morning deluxe bus to Delhi (10 hours, Rs 209) and ordinary buses every hour (Rs 110); to Chandigarh (Rs 43), ordinary buses leave about every 30 minutes; one bus a day goes to Dehra Dun (nine hours, Rs 86); two buses, one ordinary and one express, go to Jammu (Rs 161/180); and three early-morning buses go to Rekong Peo/Kalpa (Rs 120).

Private Bus Travel agencies along The Mall offer private 'deluxe' buses to Manali (Rs 225) and Delhi (Rs 225). These are neither regular nor reliable, and run almost always in the peak season when there is high demand, and after the bus from Manali or Delhi arrives with passengers. Prices change according to demand and the season.

HPTDC Bus The HPTDC offers daily buses, in season, to Manali (Rs 225); to Dharamsala (Rs 170; overnight); and overnight/day buses to Delhi (Rs 225/350) via Chandigarh (Rs 80). It also promises deluxe buses for the two day trip to Kaza, the capital of Lahaul & Spiti, for Rs 400, but these buses only leave when there is enough demand (which is not often). All HPTDC buses should be booked at the tourist office at Scandal Corner.

Train The railway reservation office (☎ 3021) at the station can arrange bookings for the Shimla-Kalka railway, and for other trips in northern India. The booking office is open from 10 am to 5 pm, Monday to Saturday; 10 am to 2 pm on Sunday.

The train journey to Shimla involves a change from broad gauge to narrow gauge at Kalka, a little north of Chandigarh. The narrow-gauge trip to Shimla takes about five hours (less by rail car). It's great fun as the little train winds its way around the mountains, although in the tourist season it can get uncomfortably hot and crowded. If you're travelling from Shimla to Chandigarh, you can catch the train to Solan (3 hours), then take a bus to Chandigarh from there. As you approach Shimla, don't make the mistake of getting off at the Summer Hill train station, which you may confuse with the Shimla station.

There are three classes: 2nd class (Rs 14) uses old coaches with wooden seats, and can be crowded; chair car (Rs 97) is modern and comfortable; but 1st class (Rs 134; Rs 159 by rail car) is definitely the way to travel, if you can afford it. Normally, there are four daily trains each way between Shimla and Kalka, and usually three more in season. Trains from Kalka to Shimla or vice versa can be cancelled if there is not enough demand.

To travel from Delhi to Shimla by train in one trip, the best and most reliable way is to catch the *Himalayan Queen* from New Delhi station at 6 am. It arrives in Kalka at about 11.40 am. Then cross to another platform from where the 12.20 pm toy train leaves, arriving in Shimla at 5.05 pm. In the opposite direction, the only way to do the Shimla-Delhi trip in one day is to catch the 10.15 am train from Shimla, which connects with the *Himalayan Queen* at Kalka and arrives into New Delhi station at 9.40 pm.

Taxi There are three agencies with fixed-price taxis – which are almost impossible to bargain down, even in the off season. They are the Kalka-Shimla Taxi Union (☎ 78-225) on Cart Rd, right opposite the Tourist Reception Centre; the Pre-Paid Taxi Service, which can be booked at the HPTDC office at Scandal Corner; and the Vishal Himachal Taxi Operators' Union (☎ 77-136), at the bottom of the lift on Cart Rd. All are about the same price, although the HPTDC taxis often cost a little more. Taxis are either 'gypsy jeeps' or 'multivans' which take three passengers, plus driver; or the Ambassador taxi, which can take four passengers, plus driver.

Examples of taxi fares from Shimla, which may include an extra charge for fuel,

Shimla's Toy Train

A 95½ km narrow-gauge track (69 cm wide) was constructed in 1903 at a cost of about 20 million rupees to link Shimla (2206m), the flourishing resort and summer capital of India, with Kalka (656m), only 25 km north of Chandigarh.

The tiny trains travel at speeds of between 15 and 25 km/h, so the trip can take up to five hours, and sometimes longer. The 102 tunnels total over eight km. The second longest tunnel, at Koti, takes about three minutes to pass through; the longest tunnel, near Barog, is 1143m long, and it takes five minutes before you emerge at the other end. Some carriages have no lights, so it's completely dark in the tunnels. There are 845 bridges, which, like the tunnels, are all numbered.

At least four toy trains travel each way between Shimla and Kalka every day. Barog, about 37 km from Kalka, has always been regarded as the suitable halfway stop for food and drink. ∎

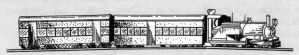

are: one day sightseeing tours to Naldehra, Fagu and other places, Rs 300 to Rs 500; one way to Chandigarh, Rs 800; to Kalka, Rs 600; to Rampur, Rs 700; to Manali, Rs 1800; to Kullu, Rs 1600; to Dharamsala, Rs 1800; to Rekong Peo/Kalpa, Rs 1200; to Dehra Dun, Rs 1500; and to Delhi, Rs 2400.

Getting Around

The Airport A fixed-price taxi costs Rs 300 from the airport to Shimla, but if you are staying anywhere along or near The Mall, you may have to walk the last bit yourself anyway. In season, the HPTDC normally runs a bus service (Rs 50) to/from the airport to connect with flights to/from Delhi.

Passenger Lift Around five hundred metres from Scandal Corner, along The (eastern) Mall, there is a lift which goes down to Cart Rd, finishing next to the Vishal Himachal taxi stand. In fact, it is two lifts, connected by a walkway – the Rs 3 ticket is good for a one-way trip on either lift. It certainly does save a steep climb. (There should be more of them in Shimla!)

Porters At the bus or railway stations you will be besieged by porters who will offer to carry your luggage for Rs 4 to Rs 20, depending on weight and distance. A porter is not a bad idea, especially when you arrive. From the railway station, for instance, it's a long, steep climb to The Mall, and, particularly, to somewhere like the Hotel Dreamland. Porters naturally double as hotel touts – ignore their comments about the hotel you want being 'full', except in the high season, when they may be telling the truth.

Around Shimla

There are a number of points of interest in the environs of Shimla which can be visited on day trips from the hill station, including Kasauli to the south-west, where it's possible to take some fine short walks; the village of Kufri, to the east, where you can hire horses

for rides to surrounding areas; and Naldehra, en route to the hot springs at Tattapani (see under Sutlej River Valley), which has a fine golf course.

SHIMLA TO KALKA

The road from Shimla to Kalka is windy but good, and lined with cafes and restaurants offering gorgeous views. Buses ply the road regularly, but visitors usually take the famous Shimla-Kalka train. You can get off and on the train at most stations along the way. If the train doesn't actually stop, it certainly goes slow enough to allow passengers to get off or on easily. Refer to Getting There & Away in the Shimla section for more information.

Solan
Telephone Area Code: 01792

Solan is known as the home of the Mohan Meakan brewery, built in 1835, and is the capital of the Solan district. It pretends to be another hill station but doesn't have the scenery, facilities or charm of nearby Shimla.

Places to Stay & Eat Most of the places in Solan are in the mid-price range. Some of the better places are: the *Flora Holiday Resort* (☎ 3492), near the bus stand, with a range of rooms from Rs 125 to Rs 450, with hot water, views and a restaurant; the *Hotel Utsav* (☎ 2874) on The Mall, with singles/doubles from Rs 200/250; and the *Mayur Hotel* (☎ 3870), near The Mall, from Rs 110/225. The *Kumar Hotel* (☎ 3847) is better value at Rs 100 a room. The *Tourist Bungalow* (☎ 3733), run by the HPTDC, provides typical HPTDC comfort. Rooms cost Rs 100 to Rs 350, which is cheaper than most HPTDC places.

Getting There & Away Solan is a major stop on the Shimla-Kalka railway line. Regular buses connect Solan with Shimla and with Chandigarh. A taxi between Solan and Shimla costs about Rs 200.

Barog
Barog is not a bad place for a day trip by train from Shimla. There are nice walks nearby,

including to the Churdhar mountain (3650m). The HPTDC's *Hotel Pinewood* (☎ 6125) has rooms (some with great views) from Rs 350 to Rs 1000 with hot water and TV. There are several other mid-range places from about Rs 200, and the railway *retiring rooms* cost from Rs 50 to Rs 100.

Kasauli
Telephone Area Code: 01793

About 12 km from the main road between Shimla and Kalka, Kasauli is a charming place. It's a good detour between Shimla and Kalka, a popular side trip from Shimla, or an alternative to staying in Shimla.

There are numerous lovely walks around Kasauli, including to **Sanawar**, another picturesque hill town, and the location of a famous colonial college. Only about four km away, **Monkey Point** has no monkeys (unlike Shimla) but it's a nice walk there, with great views. These days, the area is owned by the Indian Airforce, so you'll have to get their permission (at the gates) as you walk to Monkey Point.

Places to Stay & Eat Most places to stay are in the mid-price range. The *Alasia Hotel* (☎ 2008) costs from Rs 300; the *Maurice Hotel* (☎ 2074) has good value singles/doubles from Rs 150/250; and the *Anchal Guest House* (☎ 2052) is OK at Rs 200 a room. The HPTDC's *Hotel Ros Common* (☎ 2005) has rooms with TV from Rs 400 to Rs 750, and is set in a nice location. The restaurant is OK.

Getting There & Away Regular local buses connect Shimla with Kasauli. By train, get off at the Dharampur station, and catch a local bus, or hitch a ride to get the 12 km to Kasauli. A one-way taxi from Shimla to Kasauli costs about Rs 250.

Kalka
Past the unexciting industrial town of Parwanoo, and just over the border into Haryana, Kalka is the start/finish for the toy train trip to/from Shimla. There is nothing to see or do, and nowhere to stay in Kalka, so get on the train to somewhere else. About five km south-west of Kalka, on the Chandigarh road, is the attractive Yadavindra (or Mughal) gardens at **Pinjore**. A one-way taxi from Shimla to Kalka costs Rs 600.

WILDFLOWER HALL
Wildflower Hall, at **Chharabra**, 13 km from Shimla, is the former residence of the British commander-in-chief, Lord Kitchener. Before it was severely damaged by fire in 1994, the HPTDC ran the place as the *Wildflower Hall Hotel* (☎ 28-0239). At that time rooms cost from Rs 975 to Rs 2000. Local tourist authorities can't decide if or when it will reopen for visits or accommodation, but if you're interested, check with the HPTDC office in Shimla for the latest information.

CHAIL
Telephone Area Code: 01792

Chail was created as the summer capital of the princely state of Patiala by the maharaja after he was expelled from Shimla. The town is built on three hills – one is topped by the Chail Palace, one by the village itself, and the other by the SnowView mansion.

Three km from the village is the world's highest **cricket ground** (2444m), built in 1893. There is also a **wildlife sanctuary** three km from Chail with a limited number of deer and birds. This is also great hiking country.

Places to Stay & Eat
Built in 1891, the palace is pure colonial luxury. It's now the HPTDC's *Palace Hotel* (☎ 8337) with a range of suites, cottages, log huts, and rooms set among 70 acres of lawns. Modest luxury starts at Rs 600 for a double, and moves up to Rs 2375 for the 'Maharaja suite'. There is a top-class restaurant, cafe and bar.

Getting There & Away
For more modest accommodation, try the HPTDC's *Hotel Himneel* for Rs 400 a room. The *Hotel Deodar* has rooms from Rs 100, and the *Monal Tourist Lodge* (☎ 8359) has reasonable rooms from Rs 250.

Chail can be reached from the Shimla-

Kalka road via Kandaghat, or more commonly via the turn-off at Kufri. A return taxi from Shimla, via Kufri, costs Rs 550. There are irregular local buses (more in the high season) to Chail from Shimla and Chandigarh.

EAST OF SHIMLA
Kufri
Kufri is a nondescript little village, but there are a few things to do and see. The nearby countryside offers some great hiking, including to nearby Mahasu peak. Horses can be hired for Rs 30 to Rs 160 for trips around the valleys and hills.

The **Himalayan Nature Park** has a collection of animals and birds unique to Himachal Pradesh, but you won't see much unless you have your own vehicle or you're on a tour. There is a Rs 10 entrance fee, plus extra charges for cameras, and it's open from 10 am to 5 pm every day. Nearby, the **Indira Tourist Park** has great views, the HPTDC's *Cafe Lalit*, horse riding and a chance to have your photo taken standing next to a yak.

Kufri is promoted for its skiing (from December to February) but the snow isn't reliable and the location isn't particularly good. Enquire at the Kufri Holiday Resorts or the HPTDC office in Shimla for details of current costs and package deals. In winter, tobogganing is a popular and cheaper alternative.

Places to Stay & Eat The *Hotel Snow Shelter*, on the main road in the village, has cosy rooms, great views, and hot water at a reasonable Rs 250 for a double. This is the only alternative to the very up-market *Kufri Holiday Resorts* (☎ 28-341) where rooms cost from Rs 2250. On the main road, the *Atri Food Center* and *Deluxe Food Corner* may have inappropriate names for dhabas, but they serve reasonable food.

Getting There & Away Kufri is one of the stops for the regular buses which travel between Shimla and Narkanda and Rampur. A one-way taxi from Shimla to Kufri costs about Rs 200.

Fagu
Fagu is another unexciting village, but it serves as a good base for exploring the fantastic nearby countryside. The only hotel is the HPTDC's *Hotel Peach Blossom* (☎ 28-5522 – bookings recommended, and vital in season). This place is really recommended if you want some solitude and views in a colonial setting. The six rooms are enormous, and have old fireplaces. They cost from Rs 275 to Rs 350 a double. Taxis and buses can drop you off at Fagu easily.

Theog
The road either side of Theog is often prone to landslides, and is usually heavy going. A run-down little village, Theog is the junction for the road east to Hatkoti, about 85 km away, and to the north along the main road towards Narkanda. For Rs 220 to Rs 300, the large concrete *Hotel Apple Quest* (☎ 22-370), above Theog, has large rooms with hot water, TV and views.

Hatkoti Area
Along the Pabar River, the villages of Hatkoti, Rohru and Seema are rarely visited because the roads in the area are undeveloped, and most travellers follow the main road towards Narkanda instead. It is a very pretty area of orchards and hillside villages, and good for trout fishing. There is a famous **temple** at Hatkoti dedicated to Durga and Shiva, who fought each other there. Nearby, the ancient village of Jubbal is also pretty. Rohru has a famous festival at the **temple of Devta Shikru,** and there are several guesthouses in the village.

Irregular local buses link the area with Shimla and Narkanda.

NARKANDA
Halfway between Shimla and Rampur, Narkanda is basically a truck stop town, but it is a popular place for hiking (Hattu Peak is only six km away) and for skiing, in season.

Skiing
The ski season here lasts from January to mid-April. The road to Shimla usually

emains open in winter, which makes Narkanda accessible and popular. But Narkanda 's not as well set up for skiing as the other major site in the region, Solang Nullah, north of Manali.

The HPTDC office in Shimla or the HPTDC's Tourist Bungalow in Narkanda can provide details of current skiing courses. All inclusive seven day packages cost from about Rs 2000, which is a lot cheaper than at Solang Nullah. There are good opportunities for cross-country skiing around Narkanda if you have the equipment and experience.

Places to Stay & Eat

The HPTDC's *Tourist Bungalow* is 250m up a lane from the main road (look for the sign). It was being completed at the time of researching, and should be nice, but expensive, when finished. The *Hotel Mahamaya* (☎ 8448) has lovely, large rooms with hot water, balcony and views for the up-market price of Rs 550. It will possibly offer discounts in the off season.

Better value (but an unoriginal name) can be found at the *Hotel Snow View*. Dorms cost Rs 39, or a private room, with bathroom, costs Rs 220; amazing views and friendly staff are added attractions. Look for the sign from the village centre. Nearby, the *Cafe Vasant*, set in a large, old room, is the best place to eat. Otherwise, truck stop cafes are all around Narkanda.

Getting There & Away

Local buses travel in either direction along the main road at least every 30 minutes. A return taxi from Shimla will cost about Rs 600.

NORTH OF SHIMLA

Mashobra

About 11 km from Shimla is Mashobra, a small village where donkeys rule the streets. There are pleasant walks around the place, including to Sipi, where there is a fair every May and a wooden **temple** dedicated to Lord Shiva.

Places to Stay & Eat About three km from Mashobra, along a lovely trail, is the resort of **Craignano**. You can book a room at the *rest house* in Craignano through the Forest Department (☎ 72-911) in Shimla. The only other place to stay in or around Mashobra is the *Gables Resorts*, (☎ 28-376), which offers rural luxury from Rs 850 upwards. The village has one or two dhabas.

Naldehra

Fifteen km further north, Naldehra is a pleasant little village. It is mostly famous for having one of the oldest, highest (and certainly one of the most spectacular) golf courses in India. There is even a temple – the **Mahunag Temple** – in the middle of the course.

If you feel like a spot of golf on an incredible course, the charges are Rs 50 green fees for 18 holes (twice around the course); Rs 15 to hire golf clubs; and Rs 40 for a caddy; and a wad of rupees for replacing lost golf balls. (It's very hilly.)

Places to Stay & Eat The *Hotel Golf Glade & Restaurant* (☎ 28-7739) has six luxurious log cabins from Rs 950 to Rs 3000, and better value rooms from Rs 450 to Rs 600. The only place to eat outside the hotel is the reasonably good *Paradise Restaurant* on the main road.

BILASPUR

Telephone Area Code: 01978

About 80 km north-west of Shimla, on the road to the Kullu Valley, is the district headquarters of Bilaspur, the former capital of a fiercely independent state during British rule. Bilaspur was once planned as a hill station to rival Shimla, but never fulfilled expectations because Bilaspur is not particularly high (673m), and is often very hot!

Much of the historical part of the town was submerged when the **Govind Sagar**, the largest artificial lake in Himachal Pradesh, was created. Bilaspur is now a modern, soulless, transport hub, famous for its wrestling competitions and its annual cattle show in March. If you want to break the journey between Shimla and the Kullu Valley, try Mandi instead.

HIMACHAL PRADESH

Apparently the HPTDC may develop the Govind Sagar for boat rides and fishing, but at the moment there is nothing to do but admire it. To get to the lake, walk past the Kwality Hotel, continue left through the market, and opposite the sports stadium there are a couple of lanes down to the shore. Most of the shops – there is no real centre to the town – are behind the Kwality Hotel. A **Hindu temple**, next to the bus station, is interesting to wander around.

Places to Stay & Eat

The best places to stay are a five minute walk towards Mandi from the bus station. The *Kwality Hotel* (☎ 2291) has rooms from Rs 150 to Rs 200. Next door, the better *Neelam Hotel* (☎ 2474) costs from Rs 125 to Rs 350, and has a bar. Further up the road, the *Akashra Gang Guest House* has rooms from Rs 100, and a good restaurant (if you can find the cook). About 500m south of the bus stand, the *Raj Lodge* is dingy but cheap. Doubles cost Rs 60, and dorms, Rs 25.

The *Hotel Sagar View* (☎ 2620) has views and luxury from Rs 350 to Rs 900.

The best places to eat are in the hotels. The *Lake View Cafe*, about two km from the bus station on the main road to Shimla, is worth the walk for views and a good selection. Around the bus station, there are plenty of dhabas, and stalls selling welcome cold drinks.

Getting There & Away

There are at least 10 buses every day between Bilaspur and Shimla for Rs 34. To Mandi and further on to the Kullu Valley, buses leave every hour or so. Bilaspur is a transport centre, so you won't need to wait long for a bus to most places in the region. A return taxi from Shimla to Bilaspur costs Rs 800.

AROUND BILASPUR

Elsewhere in the Bilaspur district, and not far from the capital, there are several places worth a detour or a side trip, although transport to these places is not particularly regular. About 42 km south of Bilaspur, on the road to Chandigarh, Swarghat has a ruined **fort**. Another fort, the **Malaon Fort** is on the way from Bilaspur to Swarghat.

About 27 km to the north-west from Swarghat, near Govind Sagar, is the famous **Shri Naina Devi Temple**, revered by Hindus and Sikhs, and the site of the Navrata Festival held every August. Not far away, the huge **Bhakra Dam** can be visited if you get a permit (which is not difficult) at the nearby town of Nangal.

SUTLEJ RIVER VALLEY
Tattapani

Tattapani is famous only for its hot sulphurous springs. They are not as well developed or as nice as the ones in Vashisht, near Manali, or Manikaran, along the Parbati Valley. Tattapani is probably not worth visiting just for the springs, but the setting is great, and the village is small and relaxed. The hot water is piped from a section of the Sutlej River to the two guesthouses on the bank.

Places to Stay & Eat The HPTDC's *Tourist Bungalow* (☎ 28-6649) has four clean, sparse rooms from Rs 175 to Rs 250. You may be lucky with some dorms (20 beds in a room) for Rs 30, but they are often booked out in the high season. At the back of the hotel, the hot water 'deluxe' individual baths cost Rs 20 with soap and towel, or Rs 10 in a common, dirty pool.

The other place with access to the hot springs is the *Spring View Paying Guest House*. It is very basic, but friendly and relaxed, and rooms cost Rs 80. A soak in the pool costs Rs 10. The *Tourist Inn* offers old-world style, and great views, but nothing much else for an unbeatable Rs 15 – bring everything: sleeping bags, pillows etc. It's not easy to find: head up a lane about 100m to the left from the bridge before the other guesthouses, and turn sharp left again. You can also stay in the nearby village of Sunni, about five km away, where the cheap *Hotel Springdale* is located.

There are several reasonable places to eat by the bridge to Tattapani. Both guesthouses

Jammu & Kashmir
Top: A fishing boat on Wular Lake, one of the largest freshwater lakes in India.
Bottom: Shikaras, or water taxis, were once in demand on Dal Lake, Srinagar.

GARRY WEARE

PAUL GREENWAY

Himachal Pradesh
Top: Chandra Tal (moon lake), Lahaul.
Bottom: Ki Gompa, north of Kaza in Spiti.

near the river have restaurants, and there are one or two shops in the village.

Getting There & Away Get off the bus just after the bridge which is about 10 minutes past Sunni. The guesthouses and springs are about 200m further up alongside the river. The village is up a laneway on the left before the guesthouses. A local bus leaves Shimla every hour or so from Cart Rd to Tattapani and then visits other villages further north before heading back on the main Bilaspur-Mandi road. A return taxi from Shimla to Tattapani costs Rs 575, which includes some waiting time while you soak your weary limbs.

Nirath

About 20 km west of Rampur, the small, revered **Sun Hindu Temple** at Nirath, sits invitingly across the other side of the wide Sutlej. A small footbridge leads to the temple, which is worth a look if you have your own transport.

Rampur

Rampur was once on ancient trade routes between India and Tibet, and is a former centre of the mighty Bushahr Empire which spread into Kinnaur. The Lavi Fair is held in Rampur every November. It's a fascinating occasion when people from nearby regions sell and buy their goods. Rampur is not a particularly exciting place to stay overnight, but there are one or two things to see if you do stop.

The major attraction is the **Padam Palace** built in 1925, located on the side of the main road. You cannot go inside, but there are lovely gardens, flanked by a **Hindu temple**, which you can wander around. The older part of town, by the river and below the palace, is the most interesting place to explore, and to stay. It's a maze of tiny lanes, full of shops and Hindu and Buddhist temples, such as the (Buddhist) **Sri Sat Nahan Temple**, built in 1926.

Places to Stay & Eat The *Narindra* (☎ 33-155), not far from the bus station, is not bad value for Rs 80 a double. The *Hotel Bhagwati*

(☎ 33-117) – look for the huge sign on its roof – remains popular. Doubles start at Rs 100. The *Highway Home Guest House*, on the main road as you come from Shimla, is the same price and standard.

The cheapest is the *Himgiri Hotel & Restaurant* (☎ 33-176), in the old part of Rampur. It has ordinary singles/doubles for Rs 30/45. There are one or two other cheap places around the old town, but it's better to get on the next bus out of Rampur and stay in Sarahan, Narkanda or Shimla.

The *Cafe Sutlej* is worth the one km walk from the palace towards Shimla for views and good food. The old town has plenty of dhabas, and several pretty good bakeries.

Getting There & Away Rampur is a major transport hub, so is well connected by buses. There are buses every 30 minutes between 5.30 am and 4 pm from Rampur to Narkanda, and then on to Shimla. To Rekong Peo and Kalpa, there are three buses a day; one bus goes each day to Kaza, leaving at 1.30 am; and to Kullu, a 6.30 am bus leaves every day. A return taxi from Shimla to Rampur will cost Rs 700.

Sarahan
Telephone Area Code: 01702

Former summer capital of the Bushahr Empire, Sarahan (1920m) is a wonderful little village in a beautiful region of deodar forests. It is definitely worth a visit – there are spectacular views and trekking opportunities to nearby villages such as Ranwin, and Bashal peak.

The main attraction is the **Bhimakali Temple**, which dominates Sarahan village. In the Indo-Tibetan architectural style, Bhimakali has smaller temples inside dedicated to Lord Narsingh and Lord Raghunath, some silver decorations, other images from the Hindu and Buddhist religions, and a small **museum**. There are some entry rules. You must wear a cap (which can be borrowed from inside the temple); no cameras or leather goods (belts, wallets etc) are allowed (they can be left with the guards); and shoes must be removed.

Places to Stay & Eat Inside the temple complex are a handful of clean, quiet *rooms* for Rs 100 with bathroom. Others are being built nearby, which, thankfully, should blend in with the temple. Next to the temple entrance, the *Bushair Guest House* has clean, large rooms, with bathroom, for Rs 100.

The HPTDC's *Hotel Shrikhand* (☎ 7434), set over the edge of a cliff, dominates the view as you come up the hill. Large, quiet, comfortable rooms, with TV and hot water, are good value. They start at Rs 300, and cost Rs 600 in the modern wing. The dorms (Rs 45) were being 'repaired' at the time of writing. This may be a ruse to force you to pay for the more expensive rooms, so it's worth checking to see when the 'repairs' will finish. The restaurant here is good, and there are a few dhabas in the village.

Getting There & Away From Shimla, buses go every 30 minutes to Rampur, from where there are several daily buses to Sarahan. Alternatively, take any other bus going along the main road, get off at the dismal little junction of Jeori, where the road up to Sarahan starts, and wait for a local bus (every hour or two) up the steep 17 km road. A taxi from Jeori to Sarahan will cost about Rs 100.

To get from Sarahan to Shimla in one day, take the 6.30 or 7.30 am daily bus. To Rekong Peo or Kalpa in one day, take the early bus to Shimla, get off at Jeori, and wait for one of the hopelessly crowded buses heading east from Rampur or Shimla. A taxi from Rampur to Sarahan costs about Rs 200 and will save a lot of time.

Kangra Valley

The beautiful Kangra Valley starts near Mandi, runs north, then bends west and extends to Shahpur near Pathankot. To the north the valley is flanked by the Dhauladhar Range, to the side of which Dharamsala/ McLeod Ganj clings. There are a number of places of interest along the valley, including McLeod Ganj, home of the Dalai Lama and

the headquarters of the Tibetan Government in Exile.

The main Pathankot to Mandi road runs through the valley, and there is a narrow-gauge railway line from Pathankot as far as Jogindernagar. The Kangra school of painting developed in this valley.

JOGINDERNAGAR

The township of Jogindernagar lies 58 km north-west of Mandi, strung along a ridge. There is little of note here, but the town is worth visiting to pick up the narrow-gauge train which serves the Kangra Valley, terminating at Pathankot.

The *Tourist Hotel* at the bus and taxi stand has small but comfortable rooms with attached bath for Rs 100, or with common bath for Rs 50. However, the nicest place to stay is the *retiring rooms* at what could well be the quaintest railway station in India (with the friendliest stationmaster!). Singles/ doubles are Rs 25/50.

There are two daily train services from Jogindernagar to Pathankot at 7.50 am and 12.20 pm, passing en route Baijnath (1½ hours, Rs 4), Palampur (3½ hours, Rs 7), Nagrota (for Dharamsala, 4½ hours, Rs 9), Kangra (5½ hours, Rs 13) and Pathankot (nine hours, Rs 24).

BIR & BILLING

Fifteen km from Jogindernagar, along a track four km to the north off the main road to Baijnath, is the settlement of Bir, at 2080m. Just below the village, a road to the west leads, in several hundred metres, to a tiny Tibetan settlement with a fine gompa which belongs to the Nyingmapa order of Tibetan Buddhism. It's a beautiful peaceful location, and the monks, who are unused to visitors, are very friendly. There are several *chai* stalls here, but little else.

Fourteen km north of Bir is Billing, known for the international hang-gliding competition which is held here annually. For information about hang-gliding, contact the tourist office in Shimla.

There is one bus daily from Jogindernagar

to Bir, leaving at 9 am (45 minutes), and returning at 1 pm (Rs 8).

BAIJNATH

The small town of Baijnath, 46 km to the south-east of Dharamsala, is an important pilgrimage place due to its ancient stone **Baidyanath Temple**, sacred to Shiva as Lord of the Physicians. It is said to date from 804 AD, although according to tradition it was built by the Pandavas, the heroes of the *Mahabharata*, when they were in exile following the slaying of their kin, the Kauravas.

The temple features intricate carvings on the exterior walls, including those of Surya, the sun god, at the rear of the temple, and the marriage of Shiva and Parvati. The ceiling of the *mandapa*, or forechamber, is supported by four stone columns which were carved, along with their capitals, from single blocks. On either side of the inner sanctum are carvings of the Ganges and Yamuna rivers personified as goddesses, to the left and right respectively. Beneath the windowsills are two crouching Garudas supporting the sill with their raised arms, while on the opposite side, the sill is supported by two stone lions. The inner sanctum enshrines one of India's 12 jyoti lingams – lingams of light.

Baijnath itself is a chaotic and ramshackle town, although the Dhauladhar provides a fine backdrop. If you should find yourself stuck here, the PWD *Rest House*, 10 minutes walk from the temple on the Palampur side of town, has doubles with good views for Rs 104. As you enter Baijnath from Palampur, on the right is the *Cafe Bharva*, with fine views out over the valley, and a range of Indian cuisine.

The narrow-gauge railway line passes through Baijnath. To Pathankot it's Rs 24 (six hours), and to the end of the line, at Jogindernagar, it's Rs 7 (three hours). The station is at Paprola, one km from the main bus stand.

TARAGARH & TASHIJONG GOMPA

Taragarh lies five km north-west of Baijnath on the Palampur road. There is no settlement here as such, but it's possible to stay at the extraordinary *Palace Hotel* (☎ (018946) 3034), the summer palace of Dr Karan Singh, the son of the last maharaja of Jammu & Kashmir. The hotel is set in beautiful gardens complete with tennis court, aviary, swimming pool and brass statues of deer. Portraits of the royal family are displayed throughout the hotel, which has the usual assortment of tiger skins and colonial furnishings. Doubles range from Rs 600; the suites, which are beautifully furnished with old bureaus and dressers, cost up to Rs 1500.

You can hire mountain bikes (Rs 25 per hour) from the hotel to tour the environs, including the **Tashijong Gompa**, visible in the distance, two km to the north of the hotel. The gompa is the focus of a small Tibetan community who hail from Kham province in Tibet. They still engage in their traditional crafts of carpet making and woodcarving. A *chaam* (dance performed by lamas wearing masks) is held here on the 10th day of the second month of the Tibetan lunar calendar (usually mid-March).

PALAMPUR
Telephone Area Code: 01894

A pleasant little town surrounded by tea plantations, Palampur is 30 km south-east of Dharamsala and stands at 1260m. The main road runs right through Palampur and there are some fine walks around the town. A four day trek takes you from Palampur to **Holi** via the Waru La, or in a shorter walk you can visit the **Bundla chasm**, from which a waterfall drops into the Bundla Stream.

Places to Stay & Eat

There are numerous places to stay, including HPTDC's *Hotel T-Bud* (☎ 4031), one km north of Main Bazaar. It has doubles with attached bath for Rs 400 and Rs 500, and a four bed suite for Rs 700. The *Baghla Guest House*, opposite the bus stand, has very basic rooms for Rs 40. There's no hot water here. In Main Bazaar is the *Hotel Sawhney* (☎ 30-888), with basic doubles for Rs 150, or with TV, Rs 200.

The *Joy Restaurant* in Main Bazaar has cheap fare, including a very good egg chicken dosa for Rs 30. Nearby is the *Aahaar Real Value Foods*, which has a variety of ice cream. Opposite the main post office in Main Bazaar is the *Sapan Restaurant*, with Indian and Chinese cuisine.

Getting There & Away

The new bus stand is one km south of Main Bazaar; a taxi will charge Rs 15. Buses to Dharamsala take two hours and cost Rs 15. To Mandi, it's four hours and Rs 36, and to Pathankot, four hours and Rs 45. Palampur is on the narrow-gauge line between Pathankot and Jogindernagar. There are several trains daily between Palampur and either Nagrota to the west (for Dharamsala), or the end of the line at Jogindernagar, to the east.

CHAMUNDA DEVI TEMPLE

From Palampur the road leaves the wide green valley, passing through tea plantations and a pleasant wooded area, before descending to the settlement around the colourful Chamunda Devi temple complex on the bank of the Baner River, 10 km to the west. Chamunda is a particularly wrathful form of Durga; the idol in the main temple is considered so sacred that it is completely concealed beneath a red cloth.

The gateway to the complex is surmounted by brightly painted images of Rama, Krishna and Chamunda, and the road to the temple is flanked by stalls selling an incongruous assortment of items, with *prasaad* (food offerings for the gods) alongside electronic goods such as personal stereos. Mendicant *sadhus* recline in the shade after paying homage at the temple to attain *shiv shakti* – the power of Lord Shiva. More colourful statue groups along with two squatting stone ganja-smokers can be seen around a pool in which young children splash and swim.

Nearby are several places to stay , including the *Shaksi Restaurant*, on the right before the car park. Doubles with attached bath are Rs 220, and there's 24 hour hot water.

Buses between Dharamsala and Palampur will drop you at the Chamunda Devi Temple on request.

DHARAMSALA

Telephone Area Code: 01892
Peak Season: mid-April to mid-June, mid-September to mid-November

While Dharamsala is synonymous with the Tibetan Government in Exile, the actual headquarters is about four km above Dharamsala at Gangchen Kyishong, and most travellers head up to McLeod Ganj (see below), strung along a high ridge 10 km above Dharamsala. Dharamsala itself is a busy bazaar town, and few travellers base themselves here, although Kotwali Bazaar, at the foot of the roads leading up to McLeod Ganj, is an interesting and colourful market, and you can visit the Kangra Art Museum, which has examples of the miniature paintings for which the Kangra Valley was once renowned.

Orientation & Information

Tourist Office The HPTDC's tourist office (☎ 23-107) is in Kotwali Bazaar. It's open Monday to Saturday from 10 am to 5 pm. Jagson Airlines (☎ 24-928) is beneath the tourist office.

Money The main branch of the State Bank of India is near the tourist office in Kotwali Bazaar. American Express and Thomas Cook travellers' cheques in US dollars and pounds sterling only are accepted. Further down the main road is the Punjab National Bank, which also accepts other major travellers' cheques in various currencies. The Bank of Baroda, nearby, doesn't accept travellers' cheques, but can give cash advances on Visa cards within 24 hours.

Foreigners' Registration Office Fifteen day extensions of visas are granted at this office (☎ 22-244) in exceptional circumstances (ie, for medical problems). The office is open weekdays and every second Saturday from 10 am to 5 pm.

Kangra Art Museum

This museum is a few minutes walk down from the tourist office. In addition to the miniature paintings from the famous Kangra

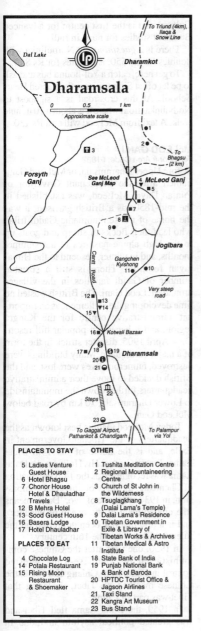

Dharamsala

To Triund (4km),
llaqa &
Snow Line

Dal Lake

Dharamkot

0   0.5   1 km
Approximate scale

To
Bhagsu
(2 km)

Forsyth
Ganj

See McLeod
Ganj Map

McLeod Ganj

Jogibara

Gangchen
Kyishong

Very steep
road

Cantt Road

Kotwali Bazaar

Dharamsala

Steps

To Gaggal Airport,
Pathankot & Chandigarh

To Palampur
via Yol

PLACES TO STAY	OTHER
5 Ladies Venture Guest House	1 Tushita Meditation Centre
6 Hotel Bhagsu	2 Regional Mountaineering Centre
7 Chonor House Hotel & Dhauladhar Travels	3 Church of St John in the Wilderness
12 B Mehra Hotel	8 Tsuglagkhang (Dalai Lama's Temple)
13 Sood Guest House	9 Dalai Lama's Residence
16 Basera Lodge	10 Tibetan Government in Exile & Library of Tibetan Works & Archives
17 Hotel Dhauladhar	11 Tibetan Medical & Astro Institute
PLACES TO EAT	18 State Bank of India
4 Chocolate Log	19 Punjab National Bank & Bank of Baroda
14 Potala Restaurant	20 HPTDC Tourist Office & Jagson Airlines
15 Rising Moon Restaurant & Shoemaker	21 Taxi Stand
	22 Kangra Art Museum
	23 Bus Stand

HIMACHAL PRADESH

school of art, which flourished in the Kangra Valley in the 17th century, the museum has elaborately embroidered costumes of Kangra tribal people, woodcarvings and tribal jewellery. It's open Tuesday to Sunday from 10 am to 5 pm. Entry is free.

Places to Stay & Eat

On Cantt Rd, Kotwali Bazaar, is the *Sood Guest House*. Doubles/triples cost Rs 220 with attached bath (hot water available in buckets for Rs 5). A 50% discount is offered during the monsoon. Less salubrious rooms can be found at the *B Mehra Hotel*, a few doors up on the opposite side of the road. Grimy doubles (with brilliant views!) are Rs 100 with attached bath. Singles with common bath are Rs 75.

HPTDC's *Hotel Dhauladhar* (☎ 24-926) has standard rooms for Rs 400/500, and deluxe rooms for Rs 562/750. There's a restaurant and bar here, as well as a billiard room for guests. Just before the Hotel Dhauladhar is the *Basera Lodge* (☎ 22-234), with basic double rooms with attached bath and hot water for Rs 250.

Opposite the Sood Guest House on Cantt Rd is the *Rising Moon Restaurant*, which has continental breakfasts, and Tibetan cuisine. It's run by a very friendly Tibetan man. The *Potala Restaurant*, up a narrow flight of stairs opposite, has good veg and nonveg Tibetan and Chinese cuisine.

Things to Buy

The shoemaker Chhotu Ram, in the store bearing the sign 'Specialist in Dingo Shoes', on Cantt Rd, close to the Rising Moon Restaurant, makes fine men's leather shoes to order from Rs 450.

Getting There & Away

Buses for the 30 minute trip up to McLeod Ganj depart every 30 minutes throughout the day. There are buses every hour to Pathankot between 5.45 am and 5 pm (3½ hours, Rs 35); to Mandi at 4, 5 and 11 am and 6 pm (six hours, Rs 50) which continue to Kullu (10 hours, Rs 85) and Manali (12½ hours, Rs 100).

Note: Beware of low-hanging power lines if you are riding on the roof of the bus between Manali and Dharamsala.

Buses to Shimla leave at 5.30, 6 and 8.30 am, and 5, 5.10, 7 and 7.45 pm. It takes 10½ hours, and costs Rs 119 on ordinary services, and Rs 170 for the deluxe service. There are numerous services to Chandigarh between 5.30 am and 9.30 pm (nine hours, Rs 77). To Delhi, there are ordinary services at 2, 5 and 9.30 pm, and a deluxe service at 6 pm (13 hours, Rs 130 ordinary, Rs 284 deluxe). There's an 8.30 am service to Dalhousie (six hours, Rs 55) which continues to Chamba (eight hours, Rs 68). To Dehra Dun there's one service at 9 pm (14 hours, Rs 153).

To the right of the bus terminal building is a steep staircase which leads up to the vegetable market at Kotwali Bazaar. If you walk through the market and turn left at the main road, after about five minutes you'll come to the taxi stand on your left. Here you can hire a Maruti van up to McLeod Ganj for Rs 80.

AROUND DHARAMSALA
Norbulinka Institute
This beautiful complex lies about 14 km from McLeod Ganj, and four km from Dharamsala, set amid Japanese-influenced gardens with shady paths, wooden bridges across small streams and tiny waterfalls. Norbulinka has been established to teach and preserve traditional Tibetan art, such as woodcarving, *thangka* painting, goldsmithing and fine embroidery. Presently, new arrivals from Tibet are learning these skills here, but Norbulinka will eventually become a Centre for Higher Studies, where laypeople can study all aspects of Tibetan Buddhism, and study traditional crafts under Tibetan masters.

Nearby is the **Dolmaling Nunnery**, where the Women's Higher Studies Institute is shortly to be opened, offering nuns courses at advanced levels in Buddhist philosophy. The institute evolved from the need to educate newly arrived nuns from Tibet in basic reading and writing skills. It is a joint initiative of the Tibetan Women's Association and the Department of Religion and Culture, and is the first centre for advanced Buddhist studies for nuns in India.

There is a *guesthouse* at Norbulinka with doubles for Rs 550, and suites for Rs 850.

To get here, catch a Yol-bound bus and ask to be let off at Sidhpur, near the Sacred Heart School. At this crossroad is a signpost to Norbulinka, from where it is about a 20 minute walk. A taxi from McLeod will cost Rs 130.

McLEOD GANJ
Telephone Area Code: 01892
Before Upper Dharamsala, or McLeod Ganj, named after the Lieutenant Governor of Punjab David McLeod, was established in the mid-1850s as a British garrison, it was the home of the seminomadic Gaddi tribe, who lead their flocks of sheep and goats up to the high alpine pastures in the summer months, and in winter, descend to the Himalayan foothills. There is still a sizeable number of Gaddi families in the villages around McLeod Ganj. The British wasted no time developing the settlement as an important administrative centre for the Kangra region, and it became a popular hill resort. On 4 April 1905, disaster struck in the form of a major earthquake. Many buildings were destroyed, numerous lives were lost, and the British decided to move their administrative headquarters further down the mountainside to Lower Dharamsala, 10 km by road below McLeod Ganj.

Today McLeod Ganj is best known as the headquarters of the Tibetan Government in Exile, and is the home of the 14th Dalai Lama, Tenzin Gyatso. His Holiness the Dalai Lama was recognised as the 14th incarnation of Chenresig, the deity of universal compassion, in 1937 at the age of two. 'Dalai' means 'the embodiment of the ocean of wisdom', and is a title that has been conferred on the rulers of Tibet since the 16th century.

In 1950, one year after the Chinese communists led by Mao Tse-Tung wrested control in China from Chiang Kai-Shek, the Chinese marched on Tibet, declaring that Tibet was part of China.

In 1959, the Dalai Lama fled Tibet and was granted political asylum in India. In

1960, Nehru offered the exiled leader and the thousands of devotees who followed him into exile the virtually abandoned settlement of McLeod Ganj. It is from here that the Tibetans continue their struggle to regain their homeland. In 1989, the Dalai Lama was awarded the Nobel Peace Prize, presented to him primarily for his endeavours to find a peaceful solution in his struggles for the liberation of Tibet.

Orientation & Information

The heart of McLeod Ganj is the bus stand. From here roads radiate to various points

around the township, including that back down to Dharamsala, which passes en route the church of St John in the Wilderness and

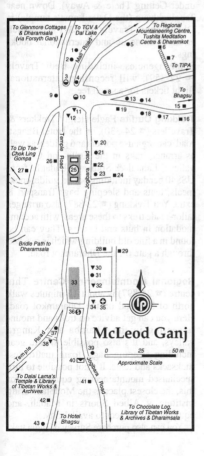

PLACES TO STAY

6 Paljor Gakyil Guest House
7 Kalsang Guest House
15 Tashi Khansar Guest House
16 Green Hotel & Tibetan Women's Association
19 Hotel Tibet & Take Out
22 Shangrila Guest House
24 Hotel Snow Palace
26 Kailash Hotel & Bhakto Restaurant
27 Om Guest House
28 Drepung Loseling Guest House
29 Tibetan Ashoka Guest House
41 International Guest House
42 Surya Resorts, Hotel Natraj & Hotel Him Queen

PLACES TO EAT

11 McLlo Restaurant
12 Friend's Corner & Bombay Studios
20 Cafe Shambhala & Malabar
30 Gakyi Restaurant
32 Aroma Restaurant
34 Ashoka Restaurant & Tibetan Handicrafts Society
38 Dreamland Restaurant

OTHER

1 Occidental Bookshop & Bedi Travels
2 Dharamsala Bookshop & Himachal Travels
3 Taxi Stand
4 Telecom Office
5 Yeti Trekking
8 Tara Herbal Gift Shop
9 Nowrogee Store
10 Bus Stand
13 Potala Tours & Travels
14 Tibetan Youth Congress
17 Green Shop
18 Branch Security & Tibetan Welfare Offices
21 Video Hall
23 Tibetan Bookshop & Information Centre
25 Chorten & Prayer Wheels
31 Video Hall
33 Office of Tibetan Handicrafts
35 Dr Yeshi Dhonden's Clinic
36 State Bank of India
37 Bookworm
39 Pema Youdon
40 Post Office
43 Eagle Height Trekkers & Travellers

McLeod Ganj

0   25   50 m
Approximate Scale

HIMACHAL PRADESH

the cantonment area of Forsyth Ganj. Other roads lead to the villages of Dharamkot and Bhagsu. To the south of the bus stand is the main bazaar area, along the sides of two parallel roads. Temple Rd proceeds to the Dalai Lama's temple, about 800m to the south, from where it's possible to take a shortcut down to the administrative area of Gangchen Kyishong, where you'll find the Library of Tibetan Works & Archives, a walk of some 20 minutes. The other road through the bazaar, Jogibara Rd, wends its way down to Gangchen Kyishong in about three km via the village of Jogibara.

Money The State Bank of India is near the post office. It's open Monday to Friday from 10.30 am to 12.30 pm and Saturday from 10.30 to 11.30 am. It changes American Express and Thomas Cook travellers' cheques in US dollars and pounds sterling only.

Post & Communications The post office is on Jogibara Rd, just past the State Bank of India. To post parcels you need to complete a customs form (in triplicate!), which you can get at the Office of Tibetan Handicrafts, opposite the State Bank of India (Rs 3). This form is not required for bookpost. There are several places which offer a parcel packing service, including a couple on Jogibara Rd. Pema Youdon, opposite the post office, also offers a parcel packing service. Letters sent c/- poste restante are held for one month.

The telecom office is up a flight of stairs behind the bus stand, and has a fax facility (Rs 116 per page). The fax number is 24-528, and in theory you can receive faxes here, although it seems to be a bit of a hit and miss affair. The office is open Monday to Saturday from 8 am to 8 pm, and the fax is turned off on the weekends, so ask your correspondents to send faxes on weekdays only. Faxes can also be sent and received at Bombay Studios, behind the McLlo Restaurant. The fax number is 23-002, and this place also has e-mail facilities.

Down at Gangchen Kyishong in the library compound is the Computer Resource Centre, above the Department of Information & International Relations (the building with the circular glass windows). You can send a one page e-mail message here for Rs 60, and receive messages for Rs 15. The address is tcrc@cta.unv.ernet.in. The centre also has computers for hire (Rs 50 per hour).

Travel Agencies There are numerous travel agencies in McLeod Ganj. A reliable outfit is Potala Tours & Travels (☎ 22-587; fax 24-327), opposite the Hotel Tibet. Potala can book domestic air tickets throughout India, and also books train and bus tickets (see under Getting There & Away). Down near Tsuglagkhang (the Dalai Lama's temple) is Dhauladhar Travels (☎ 23-158), which arranges domestic and international bookings.

Some agencies, including Bedi Travels (☎ 22-359), will reconfirm international flight tickets for a small fee.

Trekking Outfits Eagle Height Trekkers & Travellers (☎ 24-330), on the Hotel Bhagsu road, can organise porters and guides, as well as arrange treks in the Kullu and Chamba valleys, Lahaul & Spiti and Ladakh, from US$40 per day including porter, guide, cook, meals, tents and sleeping bag. Transport is extra. Yeti Trekking (☎ 22-887) also arranges tailor-made treks to these areas, with accommodation in huts and houses. They can be found in a fine old building which is reached through a gate off the Dharamkot road.

Regional Mountaineering Centre This centre (☎ 24-897) is about 15 minutes walk north of McLeod on the Dharamkot road. Here you can get advice on treks and mountaineering in the Chamba and Kangra valleys, and it's also possible to hire gear including sleeping bags, foam mattresses, rucksacks and tents. It's not possible to hire specialised mountaineering equipment; for this, the closest place is the Mountaineering Institute & Allied Sports in Manali, and equipment is subject to availability.

You can also purchase Survey of India trekking maps (Rs 15); it's a good idea to advise the centre if you are planning a trek in the region.

Bookshops & Newsagencies There's an excellent selection of new books at the Bookworm, up the road to the right of the State Bank of India. The Occidental Bookshop, on the Dal Lake road, has a very good selection of second-hand books. The Tibetan Bookshop & Information Centre on Jogibara Rd has a comprehensive selection of books on the Tibetan struggle for independence and Tibetan Buddhism. National English-language dailies arrive after 12.30 pm at the Nowrogee Store, at the bus stand.

Tibetan Publications *Chö-Yang* is a glossy journal published by the Department of Religion & Culture. There are currently seven volumes, which include scholarly essays on Buddhism and Tibetan culture. Other journals published in McLeod include the *Tibetan Bulletin*, which is published in Tibetan, Hindi, French and English, and *Rangzen* (Freedom), published by the Tibetan Youth Congress.

Emergency Police: ☎ 24-893; Ambulance & Zonal Hospital: ☎ 22-189/23-118.

Voluntary Work
If you're interested in teaching English to newly arrived refugees, check at the Library of Tibetan Works & Archives.

Organised Tours
Taxi operators have devised fixed-rate taxi tours to points of interest around McLeod Ganj and in the Kangra Valley. A local sightseeing tour taking in the Bhagsunag Temple, Tsuglagkhang (the Dalai Lama's temple) and Dal Lake is Rs 180. A tour to the colourful Hindu temple at Chamunda, the Hindu ashram at Tapovan, and to Palampur and Baijnath is Rs 650. To Kangra Fort and the Shakti Temple at Jawalamukhi, it's Rs 1000.

Activities
The Occidental Bookshop on Mall Rd, just beyond the bus stand, hires out horses for Rs 550 per day. A guide is an additional Rs 200 per day. You can also hire horses at the Dharamsala Bookshop, nearby.

Buddhist Philosophy Courses
About 20 minutes walk above McLeod, on a path off the road to Dharamkot (passing en route a colony of monkeys), is the Tushita Meditation Centre (☎ 24-966; fax 23-374). The path heads off to the right near a small white temple just beyond the Regional Mountaineering Centre. Tushita has facilities for retreats, as well as offering courses in Buddhist philosophy led by western and Tibetan teachers. There is a small library here (books cannot be borrowed), which is open to students and nonstudents, and there are also books on Buddhism for sale. The office at Tushita is open Monday to Saturday from 9.30 to 11.30 am and 1 to 4.30 pm.

Behind Tushita is the new Dhamma Sikhara Vipassana Meditation Centre, which offers courses in Indian Hinayana Buddhism.

Down at the library, in Gangchen Kyishong, classes in aspects of Buddhist philosophy are led by Tibetan lamas and translated into English. They take place on weekdays, and cost Rs 100 per month. If you're not sure you want to commit yourself to extended studies, it's possible to attend the first class free.

Other Courses
Pema Youdon is a friendly Tibetan woman who teaches Tibetan language from her home opposite the post office. It costs Rs 40 per hour, and there is a discount for two-hour sessions. It's also possible to study the Tibetan language at the Library of Tibetan Works & Archives. Classes are held on weekdays for both beginners and advanced students, and it costs Rs 200 per month.

It's possible to receive private tuition in the Tibetan performing arts at the Tibetan Institute of Performing Arts (TIPA), about 15 minutes walk from McLeod along the TIPA road. The cost is Rs 50 per hour, with instructors providing tuition for one to two hours per day up to 15 days.

Public Audiences with His Holiness the Dalai Lama

When the Dalai Lama is not touring around the world to raise awareness of the fate of Tibet at the hands of the Chinese, he resides in Dharamsala, and according to his schedule, gives 10 to 12 public audiences each year. To find out when the next audience is, check at the Branch Security Office, upstairs opposite the Kokonor Hotel on the Bhagsu road. You need to register your name two to three days before a scheduled audience, and your passport details are required.

On the day of the audience, it's best to get to the temple about one hour in advance to get through the security checks. Cameras, bags and rucksacks are strictly prohibited, and you should wear respectable dress and carry your passport. As you join the hundreds of other devotees, you file past the Dalai Lama, who will shake your hand, and probably grin broadly and, if you're lucky, utter a few words. His monk attendant will give you a red *jyendue* (sacred thread). ∎

Tibetan Offices & Institutions

As the headquarters of the Tibetan Government in Exile are in McLeod Ganj there are numerous offices and organisations concerned with Tibetan affairs and the welfare of the refugee community. These include the Tibetan Welfare Office, the Planning Council, Tibetan Youth Congress, Tibetan Children's Village (TCV), Yongling Creche & Kindergarten and the Tibetan Women's Association. Interested visitors are welcome at many of these, and it's possible here to learn more about the Tibetan struggle for independence from China.

All offices and institutions are open from 9 am to 5 pm on weekdays (closed for lunch between 1 and 2 pm in summer, and noon to 1 pm in winter), other than on Tibetan holidays and three Indian national holidays (26 January, 15 August and 2 October).

Tibetan Institute of Performing Arts (TIPA)

This institute promotes the study and performance of the Tibetan performing arts to ensure the preservation of these rich manifestations of Tibetan culture. Together with education, the establishment of this institute was given the highest priority by the Dalai Lama following his exile from Tibet. The institute served a role not only in perpetuating Tibet's traditional cultural heritage, but performances raised the morale of newly escaped refugees. Today TIPA performances instil a sense of pride and a shared heritage among the exile community. The most important of the arts taught and practised at the institute is the traditional *lhamo* opera. Performance of the lhamo incorporates dance, mime and singing, with performers, most of whom wear masks, and in richly coloured costumes, accompanied by drums and cymbals. The lhamo draws on both Tibetan historical events and adaptations of plays from India.

In April each year TIPA convenes an opera festival, which also includes folk dancing and contemporary and historical plays. There is also a three day festival from 27 May, the anniversary of the foundation of TIPA. Details of these and other performances at TIPA are posted around McLeod Ganj.

Tsuglagkhang (Dalai Lama's Temple)

This is the most important Buddhist monument in McLeod Ganj. Although a relatively modest structure, it enshrines three magnificent images, including an enormous (three metre high) gilt statue of Shakyamuni (Buddha), and to the left (facing Tibet), statues of Avalokitesvara (Chenresig, the Tibetan deity of compassion, of whom the Dalai Lama is considered an incarnation), and Padmasambhava, or Guru Rinpoche, the Indian scholar who introduced Buddhism and Tantric teachings to Tibet in the 8th century.

Also housed in the temple are a collection of sacred texts known as the *Khagyur*, which are based on the teachings of the Buddha, and have been translated from the original Sanskrit, as well as the *Tangyur*, which are translations of commentaries based on the Buddha's teachings and recorded by Indian scholars. They include works on Buddhist philosophy, art, literature, astrology and medicine.

The 14th Dalai Lama is the spiritual leader of the Gelukpa Buddhist order.

Dip Tse-Chok Ling Gompa

This beautiful little gompa lies at the bottom of a steep track which leads off the laneway past the Om Guest House. The main prayer hall houses an image of Shakyamuni, as well as two enormous drums covered in goat skin and painted around the rim, which were made by monks at the gompa. Also here are some superb butter sculptures. The butter is mixed with wax and sculpted into various forms. They are made during Losar (Tibetan New Year), and destroyed during Losar the following year.

Also made here are extraordinarily fine and detailed sand mandalas. A complete mandala can take up to a week, with seven or eight monks working in relays. First, coarse stones are crushed into a fine powder which is then coloured. The sand is poured into a ridged metal pipe which is tapped with a metal implement permitting the flow of a few grains of sand at a time onto a board on which the mandala design has been drawn. It is an extraordinarily painstaking and precise process, and monks take many years to learn their craft.

Library of Tibetan Works & Archives

The library, down at Gangchen Kyishong, halfway between Kotwali Bazaar and McLeod (take the shortcut down past the Dalai Lama's temple), is the repository of Tibet's rich literary heritage, containing about 40% of Tibet's original manuscripts, as well as an excellent general reference library on the Himalayan regions and a photographic archive.

Tibetan Medical & Astrological Institute

This institute is at Gangchen Kyishong, about five minutes walk below the main entrance to the library area. There's a museum, library, research unit, and a college at which is taught Tibetan medicine and astrology. There are two forms of astrological consultation. *Kartsi* considers aspects of astronomy and cosmic influences on human beings according to the configurations of the stars, moon and planets. *Nagtsi* is a system of astrology based on the elements of fire, water, earth, iron and wood. Calculations are made according to the year in which you are born. It's possible to have a life horoscope prepared for US$30.

The museum (opened on request) has a well displayed exhibition of materials used in Tibetan medicines, including herbs, cowrie shells, precious and semiprecious stones, fossils and metals. Exhibits are well labelled in both Tibetan and English, giving their scientific name and medicinal uses.

St John in the Wilderness

Dharamsala was originally a British hill resort, and one of the most poignant memories of that era is the pretty church of St John in the Wilderness. It's only a short distance below McLeod on the main road towards Dharamsala.

HIMACHAL PRADESH

Traditional Tibetan Medicine

The origins of Tibetan medicine date back some 2500 years. It is based on a holistic approach, which considers both the psychological and physiological bases of disease, known as Sowa Rigpa. The Buddha in his manifestation as Sangsrgyas Smangbla is attributed with the original medicinal teachings, which found their way into Sanskrit texts in the 4th century AD and were later translated into Tibetan where they were received at the Tibetan royal court in the 8th century AD. They were known as the Four Secret Oral Tantras on the Eight Branches of the Essence of Nectar. Later Tibetan scholars contributed to the body of medicinal knowledge encompassed within the texts, and they were recorded in the form of a dialectic between two scholars dealing with eight branches of medicine: the body, including anatomy and embryology; paediatrics; gynaecology; disorders related to the impact of harmful influences; disorders caused by wounds; toxicology; geriatrics; and fertility.

Suffering, according to Buddhist philosophy, is a result of delusion and ignorance, which in turn give rise to attachment in the form of greed and desire; the physiological bases of disease are attributed to the fact that we are all composed of five cosmo-physical elements: earth, water, fire, air and ether. A disequilibrium between these energies results in disease, and can be attributed to factors such as an unbalanced diet, emotional disturbance and other external influences.

However, the real essence of traditional Tibetan medicine lies in diagnosis, and three diagnostic techniques are employed: visual diagnosis, particularly of the tongue and urine; sphygmology, which determines the nature of the disorder through an examination of the pulse; and interrogation.

Even if you're not sick, it's worth visiting Dr Yeshi Dhonden's clinic on Jogibara Rd in McLeod Ganj. The doctor determines the nature of an ailment by taking the patient's pulse, and appropriate pills are prescribed. There are six different types of pills: those for migraines, for nervous disorders, for digestion, for blood purification, for food poisoning and as a general tonic. The herbs from which the pills are made are collected mostly from those regions bordering Tibet, including Ladakh, Lahaul & Spiti, Bhutan and Nepal. They are first dried and then ground into powder, which is then mixed with hot water. A pill-making machine forms them into round balls, and they are left to dry in the sun, and then polished. The most precious of these pills are individually wrapped in silk, and tied with a coloured thread secured with a wax seal.

Dr Yeshi's clinic is open from 8 am to noon, and 1 to 4 pm on weekdays. Medicines can be sent overseas (US$25 including postage and packing), which is enough for one month's supply. (Check the Customs laws of the country of destination.) Consultations are free, and one month's supply of pills costs from Rs 90 to Rs 300. ■

Walks

There are many fine walks and even finer views around McLeod Ganj. The sheer rock wall of Dhauladhar rises behind the township. Interesting walks include the two km stroll to **Bhagsu**, where there is an old temple sacred to Shiva, a spring, slate quarries and a small waterfall. It's a popular picnic spot and you can continue on beyond here on the ascent to the snow line. Dal Lake is now polluted, and it's not one of the most attractive spots in the region. About three km from McLeod Ganj brings you to the little village of **Dharamkot**, where you'll enjoy a fine view. From Dharamkot, you can continue to Bhagsu and walk back to McLeod along the main Bhagsu road.

An eight km trek from McLeod Ganj will bring you to **Triund** (2827m) at the foot of Dhauladhar. It's a steep but straightforward ascent, with the path veering off to the right across scree just beyond Dharamkot. The views of Dhauladhar from here are stunning. It's another five km to the snow line at **Ilaqa**. There's a *Forest Rest House* here for overnight accommodation. From Ilaqa, it's possible to continue over the Indrahar Pass to the Chamba Valley. See under Treks out of Dharamsala later in this chapter.

From the village of **Jogibara**, which lies between McLeod Ganj and Gangchen Kyishong, a village path leads down into the valley and up the opposite side, from where you can walk along a path to the end of the ridge, affording fine views down over Dharamsala. A shorter walk is around **Tsuglagkhang**. Take the road to the left past the entrance to the temple, and after a few minutes, where the road veers around to the left (towards Gangchen Kyishong), a small path leads off to the right, eventually looping all the way around the Dalai Lama's residence back to the entrance to the temple. The path is flanked by colourful mani stones and prayer flags, and at one section there is a series of small prayer wheels. As you are effectively circumambulating the sacred temple, this walk should be made in a clockwise direction only.

Places to Stay – bottom end

Two minutes walk down past the post office on Jogibara Rd is the *International Guest House* (☎ 22-476). Singles/doubles with common bath are Rs 80/130, or with attached bath with geyser, Rs 200/250. Further down Jogibara Rd past the Chocolate Log (see under Places to Eat), is the *Ladies Venture* (☎ 22-559). This is a very quiet place with a pleasant garden. Rooms with attached bath are Rs 150/250, or sharing a bathroom with one other room, Rs 125/175. Hot water can be provided with 30 minutes advance notice.

Very centrally located, opposite the chorten, the *Kailash Hotel* (☎ 22-344) has doubles/triples for Rs 70/80, all with common bath (with 24 hour hot water). Rooms at the back have great views, but are pretty rustic.

On a path leading down from the bus stand behind the Kailash is the popular *Om Guest House* (☎ 24-313). Singles/doubles with common bath are Rs 25/50, all with valley views. Hot water in buckets is Rs 8, and there's a good restaurant here.

On the other side of the chorten is the *Shangrila*, with doubles with common bath for Rs 60, and hot water available in buckets for Rs 10. Behind the Shangrila is the *Hotel Snow Palace* (☎ 22-291), with budget singles for Rs 35, and doubles for Rs 50 to Rs 70, all with common bath, or singles/doubles with attached bath and hot shower

for Rs 125/170. There are also deluxe rooms with valley views for Rs 200/300.

Further down Jogibara Rd, and down an alley beside the Drepung Loseling Guest House is the *Tibetan Ashoka Guest House* (☎ 22-763). There's a range of rooms, with doubles with common bath for Rs 54, with attached bath on the ground floor for Rs 162, and on the top floor, some with their own balconies, Rs 193 and Rs 204. The cheaper rooms are quite small and dark, but not bad value.

Very popular with travellers is the *Kalsang Guest House* (☎ 22-609), on the TIPA Rd. There's a range of rooms, including tiny singles with common bath for Rs 45, and doubles with common bath for Rs 75 and Rs 85. Doubles with hot showers but no external windows are Rs 180, or there are rooms with great views upstairs for Rs 200 and Rs 275. You can get a hot shower in the common bathroom for Rs 10, but 30 minutes advance notice is required. Taxes are extra.

Above the Kalsang is the *Paljor Gakyil Guest House* (☎ 23-143). There are dorm beds for Rs 25, singles/doubles with common bath for Rs 45/70, doubles with attached bath (cold water) from Rs 80 to Rs 100, or with hot water, Rs 120 to Rs 200.

A long-time favourite with travellers is the large *Green Hotel*, at the end of McLeod on the Bhagsu road. Small spartan rooms with common bath are Rs 45/60, and with attached bath, Rs 110/125, or Rs 200 for deluxe rooms. Some rooms have great valley views, and there's a good restaurant here. Opposite the Green is the *Tashi Khansar Guest House*. Single rooms with common bath (with hot water) are Rs 70, and singles/doubles with attached bath are Rs 120/135, some with excellent views.

There are several rooms at the guesthouse at the *Dip Tse-Chok Ling Gompa*, about 300m down a path which leads off the laneway beyond the Om Guest House. It's a beautiful peaceful place, although the precipitous staircase down to the gompa would make it difficult to approach after dark. Rooms are Rs 80, and have fine views down over the valley.

It's also possible to stay at the Zilnon Kagyeling Nyingmapa Gompa, about one km from McLeod on the Bhagsu road (below TIPA). Rooms are Rs 60, and a hot shower is Rs 10. There is a rooftop cafe here.

For genuine research scholars and students attending classes at the Library of Tibetan Works & Archives, there are a limited number of rooms, some with attached kitchens. Rents range from Rs 400 to Rs 1200 per month.

Places to Stay & Eat – middle & top end

Drepung Loseling Guest House (☎ 23-187) is popular with long-term volunteers. It has doubles with attached bath and cold shower for Rs 125, or with a hot shower for Rs 165 and Rs 220. The more expensive rooms have their own balcony and great valley views. There's also a dorm with beds for Rs 25, and breakfast is served in the dining hall downstairs.

The *Hotel Tibet*, a few steps from the bus stand on the Bhagsu road, has standard doubles for Rs 350, semideluxe doubles for Rs 450, and deluxe rooms for Rs 500. All rooms are carpeted and have cable TV and attached bath. There's a very good restaurant and bar here.

There are a couple of large Indian-run hotels on the road past Bookworm. The *Hotel Natraj* (☎ 22-529) has doubles on the ground floor for Rs 400, and semideluxe rooms for Rs 600; neither of these have views. Deluxe rooms with good views are Rs 800. There's 24 hour hot water, a roof terrace and a restaurant and bar.

Further along is the *Hotel Him Queen* (☎ 24-961), which has ordinary doubles for Rs 750, and super-deluxe and VIP rooms for Rs 1000 and Rs 1250 respectively. There's a roof terrace restaurant here. Nearby is the large *Surya Resorts* (☎ 22-678), which has standard deluxe rooms for Rs 1440/1600, or deluxe rooms for Rs 2500. A 50% discount is offered in the off season. All rooms have good valley views.

At the end of this road is HPTDC's *Hotel Bhagsu* (☎ 3191), which has a range of doubles from Rs 450 to Rs 1000. There's a good restaurant here, and the hotel has it's own roller-skating rink.

Close to the Dalai Lama's temple, behind Dhauladhar Travels, is the beautifully appointed *Chonor House Hotel* (☎ 22-006; fax 22-010). Rooms are from Rs 400 to Rs 700, and are decorated with traditional Tibetan artefacts.

About two km above McLeod along a track which branches off the main Dharamsala road is *Glenmore Cottages* (☎ 25-010), which has comfortable accommodation in five peacefully located cottages. Rates are Rs 700, Rs 990 and Rs 1500, and all rooms have heaters and geysers.

Places to Eat

The *Chocolate Log*, a few minutes walk down past the post office on Jogibara Rd, is an old favourite, serving western dishes such as pizza (Rs 15 per slice), various types of cakes (chocolate, black forest, banana), and cheese macaroni.

Friend's Corner serves good food and prices are reasonable. Right above the bus stand is *McLlo Restaurant*, which has an extensive menu, good food and a bar.

The restaurant at the *Hotel Tibet* has an extensive menu featuring Tibetan and Indian cuisine. There's also a convivial bar here. *Take Out* is a new place beneath the Hotel Tibet where you can buy freshly baked bread, cakes and doughnuts.

Beneath the Kailash is the *Bhakto Restaurant*, which has traditional mutton momos for Rs 14, and filling noodle soup for Rs 12. It's popular with local Tibetans, and is usually only open around lunch time. On the opposite side of the chorten, on Jogibara Rd, is the *Malabar*, a pleasant little place serving good Indian, Chinese and continental cuisine. Also popular is the nearby *Cafe Shambhala*.

Serving the best special muesli in town is the *Gakyi Restaurant*, on Jogibara Rd. In the morning you can also get freshly baked brown bread here for Rs 20.

The restaurant at the *Green Hotel* is very

popular, and has a range of home-made cakes, as well as good Indian and Chinese cuisine. The potato salad is very good (especially if you like loads of garlic). Another popular place is the restaurant at the *Om Guest House*. The vegie burger here is served with salad, a banana and chips, and is quite good, and there's a good sound system.

The best food in town is at the *Ashoka Restaurant*, on Jogibara Rd. The chicken korma is one of the best you'll get anywhere, and there's also good tandoori chicken (Rs 45 for a half serve); chicken Mughlai (Rs 60), and a very good malai kofta. There are also continental dishes such as pizza and spaghetti. Nearby is the *Aroma Restaurant* which has Israeli cuisine.

For the best salads (chicken, gado gado), try the *Dreamland Restaurant*, down a staircase to the right, just beyond Bookworm. The chef is from Delhi, and also dishes up very good, and very reasonably priced, veg and nonveg Tibetan and Chinese cuisine.

The restaurant at the *Hotel Bhagsu* has very good food and cold beers. However, it's a dark, gloomy and cavernous place. On sunny days, tables are set up in the gardens, and you can eat out here, a much more pleasant proposition. Nonguests are welcome.

Things to Buy

Tibetan textiles such as bags, *chubas* (the dress worn by Tibetan women), hats and trousers can be found at the Office of Tibetan Handicrafts, opposite the State Bank of India. Here you can have a chuba made to order with your own fabric (Rs 70), or with fabric supplied by the centre (from Rs 350 to Rs 450). Opposite is the Tibetan Handicrafts Society. The society employs about 145 people, many of them newly arrived refugees, in the weaving of Tibetan carpets which incorporate traditional Tibetan designs. Fine New Zealand wool carpets, with some 90,000 to 95,000 knots per sq m, cost Rs 1681 per sq m, while those of Indian wool are Rs 1477 per sq m. The society can pack and post purchases home, and visitors are welcome to watch the carpet makers at work on traditional looms.

Tara Herbal Gift Shop, near the bus stand, has traditional Tibetan herbal incense and books on Tibetan medicine. At the Green Shop, on the Bhagsu road, you can buy hand-painted T-shirts and recycled handmade paper.

HIMACHAL PRADESH

Cleaning Upper Dharamsala Project

This new project is an innovation of the Welfare Office and a young Dutch man who helped raise money for the project. It consists of four 'green workers' – generally new arrivals from Tibet – who collect about 40 to 50 kg of recyclable goods from homes and businesses around McLeod each day, including paper, glass, bottles, metals and plastic, which are then sold. At Nechung and Namgyal gompas, the Dialectic School and Gaden Chuling Nunnery are special baskets with separate receptacles for different materials. These are emptied once a week and the materials are then separated. So far the amount received from selling recyclables covers little more than the salary of one green worker, but profits are secondary to the goal of raising environmental awareness and promoting a cleaner township.

Another initiative under the Welfare Office is the Green Shop, on the Bhagsu road. This shop sells rechargeable batteries, hand-painted T-shirts, natural cosmetics and boiled and filtered water. In the off season, 25 to 30 bottles of water are sold each day. In the season, this increases to 100 to 120 bottles per day. Posters on environmental issues, in Hindi, have been posted in the Indian villages in the environs of McLeod, and the project officers plan to work in future in cooperation with the Indian community.

Tourists can support the project and help promote a cleaner McLeod by having their mineral water bottles refilled at the Green Shop, and encouraging hotel owners to separate garbage and give it to the green workers, rather than throwing it on dumps. ■

Entertainment

There are two video halls in the town centre on Jogibara Rd. They show new releases each evening, with the programme posted out the front. Tickets are Rs 5 to Rs 10. The Hotel Bhagsu, at the end of the Bookworm road, has it's own roller-skating rink, and hires out skates for Rs 20 per hour.

Getting There & Away

Air The closest airport to McLeod Ganj and Dharamsala is at Gaggal, 15 km south of Dharamsala. Jagson Airlines has flights to Delhi (US$100) leaving at 9.30 am via Kullu (US$49) and Shimla (US$72), on Tuesday, Thursday and Saturday. On the same days, flights leave the capital at 6.30 am, arriving into Shimla at 7.50 am, Kullu at 8.45 am, and Gaggal at 9.10 am. Potala Tours & Travels and Dhauladhar Travels can book tickets on these flights. Jagson's office (☎ 24-928) in Dharamsala is below the tourist office.

Bus The HRTC (Himachal Roadways Transport Corporation) booking office is at the bus stand. There's a daily bus to Manali at 6 pm (11 hours, Rs 125) and a direct bus to Dehra Dun at 7.30 pm (12 hours, Rs 164). There's also a direct service to Manali at 5.30 am (Rs 100). The deluxe (2x2) service to Delhi leaves at 5 pm (12 hours, Rs 300), and there's a semideluxe (3x2) service at 8.30 pm (Rs 225).

Potala Tours & Travels, opposite the Hotel Tibet, has a deluxe service to Delhi which arrives at Connaught Place at 6 am (Rs 325). Numerous other agencies book deluxe bus trips. Quoted prices at Himachal Travels (☎ 22-723), on Mall Rd, just above the bus stand, were: Shimla (ex Dharamsala at 7 pm; 11 hours, Rs 195); Manali 12 hours, Rs 250; Leh (via Manali), departing McLeod at 9 pm, arriving Manali at 6 am; then departing Manali at 7 am, arriving Leh the following evening (with an overnight stop en route) at 5 pm. Cost is Rs 950.

Bedi Travels (☎ 22-359), also on Mall Rd, can book ordinary bus tickets to Dalhousie and on to Chamba. It departs at 5 am, arriving Dalhousie (Rs 55) at 10.30 am, and Chamba (Rs 73) at 1.30 pm.

Train Many travel agencies will book train tickets for services out of Pathankot, down on the plains in the Punjab. Generally a Rs 25 booking fee is levied. There's a railway booking office at the bus stand in Dharamsala, but it has only a very tiny quota of tickets. It's open only between 10 and 11 am, and is closed on Sunday.

The closest railway station to McLeod is at the small village of Nagrota, 20 km south of Dharamsala. Nagrota is on the small narrow-gauge line which serves the Kangra Valley, connecting Pathankot with the small settlement of Jogindernagar, 58 km north-west of Mandi. It's a slow, five hour haul between Nagrota and Pathankot – the bus is much faster – but if you have the time, it's worthwhile taking the four hour trip between Nagrota and Jogindernagar, which wends through the Kangra Valley affording fine views of the Dhauladhar Range to the north. To Jogindernagar, trains from Nagrota leave at 7.02 am and 2.08 pm (Rs 9), passing through Palampur (one hour) and Baijnath (two hours).

Getting Around

Progress has hit McLeod Ganj with the arrival of its first (and hopefully only) autorickshaw. To Bhagsu, the charge is Rs 30. A taxi is Rs 35. To hire a taxi for the day, covering less than 80 km, costs Rs 500.

There are buses for the 40 minute trip down to Dharamsala from the bus stand every 30 minutes between 4.15 am and 8.30 pm.

AROUND McLEOD GANJ
Dusallan & Bhagsu

Many travellers planning to stay long-term rent rooms from villagers in the settlements around McLeod Ganj. Between McLeod and Bhagsu, below the Bhagsu road (take the path beside the Green Hotel) is the tiny village of **Dusallan**. The first place you come to on your right as you enter the village has several rooms for rent. Rates are around Rs 30 per day, including a bucket of hot water, and some have magnificent views down over the terraced fields. A few steps away is a large yellow house which has some very good rooms for rent, and there's a hot shower here. Enquire with the friendly fellow at the *Rajpal Cafe* on the Dharamkot road in McLeod.

Two km from McLeod is the village of **Bhagsu**, which has a small temple sacred to Lord Shiva which was built by the Raja of Kangra, Dharam Chand, in the 16th century.

The brand new *Hotel Triund* is on the left as you enter Bhagsu. Deluxe rooms are Rs 700, super deluxe rooms are Rs 800, and the VIP suites are Rs 1000. All rooms are carpeted and have TV and hot water.

The *Trimurti* has good and very cheap vegetarian food. Down near the temple is the *Bhagsu Cafe*, which is the best place in town for a cappuccino, and you can also get cakes here from the German bakery. The bakery itself is above the primary school. Here you can get freshly baked bread and croissants. The *Paradise Cafe* has an extensive menu and good food. The *Shiva Cafe* is a good spot for a chai, above the waterfall in Bhagsu.

From Bhagsu it is possible to continue to the little village of **Dharamkot**. The *Om Tara Bakery* in Dharamkot is run by a German woman, and you can get fresh home-cooked goods here, and very good German bread. She's also a hairdresser, and you can get your hair cut here!

SOUTH & EAST OF DHARAMSALA
Kangra
Telephone Area Code: 01892

There is little to see in this ancient town, once the seat of the Chand Dynasty who ruled over the princely state of Kangra. It lies 18 km almost directly south of Dharamsala, but at one time it was a place of considerable importance. The famous **temple of Bajreshwari Devi** was of such legendary wealth that every invader worth their salt took time to sack it. Mahmud of Ghazni carted off a fabulous fortune in gold, silver and jewels in 1009. In 1360 it was plundered once again by Tughlaq but it was still able to recover and, in Jehangir's reign, was paved in plates of pure silver. The temple is in the bazaar, at the end of a labyrinthine series of alleyways flanked with stalls selling *prasaad*.

The British took possession of the ancient

TREKKING OUT OF DHARAMSALA
McLeod Ganj-Chamba Trek (via Indrahar Pass)

Crossing the Dhauladhar – the snow-capped range immediately north of Dharamsala – does not lend itself to easy trekking. The most popular trek over the Indrahar Pass (4350m) to the Ravi Valley, Chamba and Brahmaur involves some strenuous stages that will prove problematic for the ill prepared. While the trails are regularly followed by the Gaddi shepherds they are not always well defined, and the very steep descent from the top of the pass needs to be taken with care.

Porters are available from the local agencies in McLeod Ganj. Budget for Rs 200 per day. Each porter will carry around 15 kg on account of the difficult pass crossing. There is heavy snow on most of the passes over the Dhauladhar until the middle of July and this must be taken into account if trekking in the pre-monsoon season. The post-monsoon period from mid-September to mid-October is the ideal time to undertake the trek with the likely prospect of gaining clear views north towards the Manimahesh Kailash Range while the birds-eye view south across the Indian plains is remarkable.

Stage 1	McLeod Ganj to Triund (3 to 4 hours)
Stage 2	Triund to Lahesh Cave (4 to 5 hours)
Stage 3	Lahesh Cave to Indrahar Pass & Chatru Parao (6 to 7 hours)
Stage 4	Chatru Parao to Kuarsi (5 to 6 hours)
Stage 5	Kuarsi to Machetar (6 hours)

fort of Kangra, 2½ km south of modern Kangra, according to the terms of the Jawalamukhi Treaty in 1846, and established a garrison here. The disastrous earthquake which shook the valley in 1905 destroyed the fort and the temple, the latter of which has since been rebuilt.

Nagar Kot, the ancient fort, is an evocative and beautiful place, perched high on a windswept ridge overlooking the confluence of the Manjhi and Baner rivers. It can be reached from Kangra by autorickshaw (Rs 25).

The State Bank of Patiala, next to the post office on Dharamsala Rd, has foreign exchange facilities.

Places to Stay There's a PWD *guesthouse* at Purana (old) Kangra, near the fort. There are also several places to stay in Kangra, including the *Hotel Maurya* (☎ 65-875), near the post office, which has singles for Rs 100 and Rs 125, and doubles for Rs 150, all with attached bath and hot water. The *Hotel Jai* (☎ 5568) is further down Dharamsala Rd, and has rooms at the same rate.

Getting There & Away Kangra's bus stand is on Dharamsala Rd. From here it is 1½ km to the temple. There are buses to Dharamsala every 15 minutes throughout the day (45 minutes, Rs 7). Kangra has two railway stations: Kangra station is accessible by road, but Kangra Mandir station lies 500m from the nearest road, where autorickshaws lie in wait to ferry you around the city. A taxi from McLeod Ganj to Kangra will cost Rs 375.

Masrur

South-west of Dharamsala via Gaggal is the small settlement of Masrur, which has 15 richly carved rock-cut temples in the Indo-Aryan style which were hewn from the sandstone cliffs in the 10th century AD. They are partly ruined but still show their relationship to the better known and much larger temples at Ellora in Maharashtra. This is a beautiful, peaceful place, fronted by a small artificial lake and a pleasant lawn compound. The sculptures are badly eroded, but three crude statues of Sita, Rama and Lakshmi can

still be made out in the dimly lit sanctum of the central temple. Several more badly damaged sculptures can be seen leaning against the low wall by the lake in front of the temples.

Getting There & Away A taxi from McLeod Ganj will charge around Rs 550 to get to Masrur, and the road affords some magnificent views, particularly on the section between Gaggal and Masrur.

Jawalamukhi

Lying in the south of the Kangra Valley, 34 km south of Kangra, is the temple of Jawalamukhi, the goddess of light. Pilgrims descend into a tiny square chamber where a priest, while intoning a blessing on their behalf, ignites natural gas emanating from a copper pipe, from which a blue flame, worshipped as the manifestation of the goddess, briefly flares. The temple is one of the most sacred sites in the Kangra Valley, and is topped by a golden spire, the legacy of a wealthy devotee.

Places to Stay The *Hotel Jawalaji* (☎ (01970) 2280) has doubles from Rs 300 to Rs 650, all with attached bath. Dorm beds here are Rs 45.

Getting There & Away Buses to Dharamsala (Rs 25) leave throughout the day from the stand below the road leading up to the temple.

Nurpur

Only 24 km from Pathankot on the Dharamsala road, this town was named by Jehangir, after his wife, Nurjahan. Nurpur Fort is now in ruins, but still has some finely carved reliefs. A ruined temple dedicated to Krishna, also finely carved, stands within the fort, which looms over the main road. There's a PWD *rest house* (☎ (01893) 2009), with large, very clean double rooms for Rs 105.

Pathankot
Population: 147,000

The town of Pathankot, in the extreme north of the Punjab, is important to travellers purely as a crossroad. It's the gateway to Jammu in the state of Jammu & Kashmir.

Pathankot is also the bus centre for departures to the HP hill stations, particularly Dalhousie and Dharamsala. It is a chaotic and uninspiring city, and you probably won't want to stay here for a moment longer than necessary.

Places to Stay There are a number of fairly unsavoury lodgings to the right as you exit the main city railway station. The *Green Hotel* has grimy air-cooled rooms for Rs 125. In the same building, above a gloomy dhaba, is the *Hotel Darshan*, with rooms with attached bath with cold water for Rs 80 to Rs 100. Further down the road is the *Tourist Hotel*, a slightly better choice with singles/doubles for Rs 75/150.

Close to Chowkibank station is the more salubrious *Sheetal Hotel* (☎ 22-334), with rooms for Rs 350/450, or with air-con, Rs 450/550.

Getting There & Away The dusty bus stand and the City railway station are only a hundred or so metres apart; Chowkibank railway station is about three km from the City station.

The superfast *Malwa Express* departs Chowkibank for Delhi at 10.10 am, arriving into the capital at 8.50 pm. There are several overnight services from the City station: one service leaves at 6.25 pm, arriving into the capital at 5.20 am; the second departs at 11 pm, arriving in Delhi at 11.05 am (Rs 127/421 in 2nd/1st class).

There are several services between Pathankot and Jammu, including the *Jammu Tawi Mail*, which departs at 7.20 am, arriving into Jammu at 10.25 am, and the *Jammu Tawi Express*, which leaves at 1.08 pm, arriving into Jammu at 3.10 pm (Rs 19/116 in 2nd/1st class).

There are buses to Dalhousie at 6.10, 8, 10.30, 11.20 and 11.35 am, and 12.30 and 1.20 pm (3½ hours, Rs 34). There are numerous buses to Dharamsala (3½ hours, Rs 35).

From Chowkibank to the City railway and bus stations by cycle-rickshaw will cost Rs 20. There is a 24 hour taxi stand at the City station; to McLeod Ganj the fare is Rs 660; to Dalhousie, Rs 660; and to Chamba, Rs 900.

Chamba Valley

Separated from the Kangra Valley to the south by the high Dhauladhar Range and the remote Pattan Valley to the north by the Pir Panjal Range is the beautiful Chamba Valley, through which flows the Ravi River. For over 1000 years this region formed the princely state of Chamba, the most ancient state in northern India. Few travellers find their way here, and of those that do, few continue down the valley beyond the hill station of Dalhousie. The valley is renowned for its fine *shikhara* temples, with excellent examples in the beautiful town of Chamba, 56 km from Dalhousie, and at the ancient capital of Brahmaur, a further 65 km down the valley to the south-east. Brahmaur is also the starting point for some fine treks, including that to the sacred lake of Manimahesh, and across the high Kugti Pass to the Chandra Valley and Lahaul.

DALHOUSIE
Telephone Area Code: 018982
Peak Season: mid-April to mid-July, mid-September to mid-November, mid-December to early January

Sprawling over and around five hills at around 2000m, Dalhousie was, in the British era, a sort of 'second string' hill station, mainly used by people who lived in Lahore. It was acquired from the raja of the princely state of Chamba by the British, and was a place frequented by those who could not aspire to Shimla. The settlement was named after Lord Dalhousie, then viceroy of India, by David McLeod (after whom McLeod Ganj was named). Today Dalhousie's population includes around 1100 Tibetan refugees.

Orientation
Dalhousie is very spread out; most of the shops are clustered around Gandhi Chowk, about a 15 minute walk up from the bus stand. Gandhi Chowk is connected to Subhash Chowk, also with a high concentration of hotels and restaurants, by The Mall – actually two roads, the highest of which is a pedestrian-only road locally known as

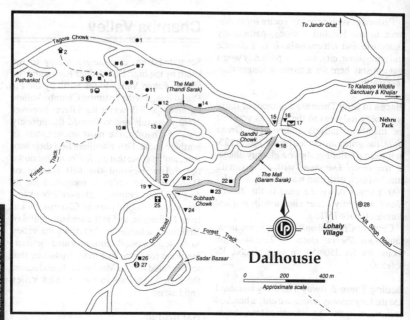

Dalhousie

0   200   400 m

Approximate scale

PLACES TO STAY		PLACES TO EAT			
2	Youth Hostel	15	Kwality Restaurant	8	Tibetan Market & Span Tours & Travels
4	Glory Hotel & Restaurant	16	Lovely Restaurant	9	Bus & Tax Stands
6	Hotel Mount View	19	Moti Mahal Restaurant	11	Cinema
7	Hotel Grand View	20	Restaurant Preet Palace	13	Himachal Handloom Industry Emporium
10	Hotel Satpushp	24	Shere-e-Punjab & Amritsari Dhabas	17	Post Office
12	HPTDC Hotel Geetanjali			18	Tibetan Handicrafts Showroom & Bengali Sweet Shop
14	Hotel Shangrila	**OTHER**		25	St Francis Catholic Church
21	Hotel Goher			27	Punjab National Bank
22	Hotel Green's	1	English Cemetery	28	Satdhana Spring
23	Hotel Craigs	3	Tourist Office		
26	Aroma-n-Claire Hotel	5	Dalhousie Club		

Garam Sarak (Hot Road) as it receives more sunshine than the other road, known as Thandi Sarak (Cold Road). A road also connects the bus stand with Subhash Chowk, about a 15 minute walk uphill.

Be careful if you are walking along Garam Sarak between Gandhi and Subhash chowks at night. It's badly illuminated, and some sections are in pitch darkness. Bring a flashlight.

There are many registered porters around the bus stand. In the off season, they charge Rs 15 between the bus stand and Gandhi Chowk, and Rs 10 to Subhash Chowk. Expect to pay double in the season.

Information
Tourist Office The tourist office (☎ 2136) is on the top floor of the building by the bus stand. It's open Monday to Saturday from 10 am to 5 pm, and during the tourist season on Sunday until 1 pm. During the season it runs full day tours to points of interest around Dalhousie including Khajiar and Chamba, for Rs 80.

Money The Punjab National Bank is about five minutes walk from Subhash Chowk, next to the Aroma-n-Claire Hotel. It's the only bank that exchanges travellers' cheques, but there are no foreign transactions on Wednesday.

Post Office The post office is on Gandhi Chowk.

Travel Agencies Span Tours & Travels (☎ 5341; fax 2841) can book luxury coaches during the season to Delhi, Manali and Dharamsala, and can also make train and air reservations.

Newsagencies You can get English-language newspapers at Neelam Studio photographic store at the bus stand, and at Dayal News Agency on Gandhi Chowk.

Emergency Police: ☎ 2126; Civil Hospital: ☎ 2125.

Things to See & Do
With its dense forest, old British houses and colourful Tibetan community, Dalhousie can be a good place to spend a few days.

About midway along Garam Sarak, between Gandhi and Subhash chowks, you'll pass brightly painted low-relief pictures of Tibetan deities, including Padmasambhava and Avalokitesvara (Chenresig), as well as script bearing the sacred mantra 'Om Mani Padmi Hum'. Close to Gandhi Chowk is a rock painting of Tara Devi, and a little shrine has been constructed here. There's a **Tibetan market** just above the bus stand.

Kalatope Wildlife Sanctuary is 8½ km from the main post office. To take a vehicle into the sanctuary, you require a permit from the District Forest Officer in Chamba. There's a checkpost at **Lakkar Mandi**, on the perimeter of the sanctuary, which has stupendous mountain views. It's possible to get a taxi here (Rs 150 return), and walk three km into the sanctuary. The sanctuary is home to a variety of species including the black bear and barking deer, as well as an abundant variety of birdlife. There's a *Forest Rest House* here, but to reserve a room, you'll need to contact the District Forest Officer (DFO) in Chamba (☎ 2639; dial the area code 85 if you're ringing from Dalhousie, 018992 from elsewhere).

From April until November, Lakkar Mandi is home to an itinerant group of villagers who originally hail from Mandi, in the Kangra Valley. Their main source of income is derived from preparing charcoal which they sell to the hotels in Dalhousie.

On the way to Panch Pulla (Five Bridges) along Ajit Singh Rd, there's a small, and easily missed, freshwater spring known as **Satdhana**.

Places to Stay
Dalhousie has plenty of hotels, although a fair number of them have a run-down, left-by-the-Raj feel to them. Prices fluctuate with the seasons. It's fairly congested during the peak Indian holiday periods, and getting accommodation at this time can be extremely difficult.

The friendly *youth hostel* (☎ 2189) is about a five minute walk from the bus stand. Rates remain constant all year and are Rs 10 in the dorm for members (Rs 20 for nonmembers), or there are doubles with attached bath for Rs 60 (Rs 80 for nonmembers). The hostel is closed between 10 am and 5 pm.

Right on the bus stand is the *Glory Hotel & Restaurant* (☎ 2533). Singles/doubles are Rs 75/150, both with attached bath and free hot water in buckets. Rooms are clean, if a little musty, but OK. Cheap rooms can also be found at the *Hotel Satpushp* (☎ 2346), near the bus stand. Doubles range from Rs 100 to Rs 400, with good discounts in the off season.

In the Subhash Chowk area, *Hotel Goher*

(☎ 2253) has singles with common bath for Rs 75, and doubles with attached bath from Rs 110 (with cold water) to Rs 350 (with hot water and TV). Some rooms are being renovated, so prices may increase.

About five minutes walk to the south of Subhash Chowk is the atmospheric *Aroma-n-Claire Hotel*, on Court Rd. Construction on this large rambling hotel commenced in 1925, with materials especially shipped from Belgium. Rates range from Rs 450 to Rs 1200. It's slightly ramshackle, but has wonderful eclectic decorations and rooms of all shapes and sizes. There's a small borrowing library for guests.

HPTDC's *Hotel Geetanjali* (☎ 2155) is just off Thandi Sarak, on the hill just above the bus stand. It's a lovely, if slightly run-down, old building. Rooms are enormous, and all have attached baths with hot water. The dining hall here has magnificent views. Doubles range from Rs 300 to Rs 500.

Nearby is the *Hotel Shangrila* (☎ 2134), which has a range of doubles from Rs 450 to Rs 800. All rooms have views of the Pir Panjal, and the more expensive ones have a separate sitting area. The staff here are friendly and helpful.

About five minutes walk from Gandhi Chowk on Garam Sarak is the *Hotel Green's* (☎ 2167). Doubles are Rs 400, Rs 500 and Rs 600, and a 30% discount is offered in the off season. All rooms have attached bath and colour TV. Further along this road is the *Hotel Craigs* (☎ 2124), which has one single for Rs 100, and doubles for Rs 250, Rs 350 and Rs 400. It's a somewhat dilapidated place, but it's in a quiet location with fine views out over the valley.

Just above the bus stand is the *Hotel Grand View* (☎ 2623), which has doubles for Rs 800, and double suites for Rs 1000. This is a beautifully maintained place, and better value than other hotels in the same price category. A 30% discount is offered in the off season. Nearby, and with less character, is the *Hotel Mount View* (☎ 2120), which has singles for Rs 275, and doubles for Rs 500, Rs 700 and Rs 900, including breakfast and one other meal.

Places to Eat

There are numerous places to eat, but many are high on price and low on quality. The dhabas are the best value, and Dalhousie's dhabas are a cut above the usual Indian dhaba.

Right on Subhash Chowk is the *Restaurant Preet Palace*. It features Mughlai, Kashmiri and Chinese cuisine, and prices are reasonable. Nearby is the *Moti Mahal Restaurant*, which also has a bar. On Court Rd, just off Subhash Chowk, is the *Royal Dhaba*. It's certainly not the Ritz, but it's cheap, and portions are generous. Also worth checking out are the *Amritsari* and *Sher-e-Punjab* dhabas, nearby.

The *Lovely Restaurant*, at Gandhi Chowk, is open all year, and there's a sun terrace with outdoor seating. The menu features South Indian and Chinese cuisine. Also at Gandhi Chowk is the *Kwality Restaurant*. There's an extensive menu, and this place is very popular. In the season, you might have to wait for a table. Near the Tibetan Handicrafts Showroom at Gandhi Chowk is the *Bengali Sweet Shop*, with a range of sticky favourites such as ras malai and gulaab jamun.

In the Tibetan Market, above the bus stand, there's a tiny *Tibetan restaurant* serving fried momos for Rs 10, and very cheap chow mein.

Things to Buy

Dalhousie is a good place to pick up a woollen shawl. Himachal Handloom Industry Emporium on Thandi Sarak has a good selection. At the Tibetan Handicraft Centre (☎ 2119), three km from Gandhi Chowk along the Khajiar road, you can have Tibetan carpets made to order. There are over 180 traditional designs to choose from. The Tibetan Handicraft Centre Showroom is on a road leading away from Gandhi Chowk which runs parallel to Garam Sarak. Here you can buy carpets, bags and purses. The shops nearby sell a range of goods, including Kashmiri shawls.

Getting There & Away

The booking office at the bus stand is open daily from 9 am to 5 pm (closed between 2 and 3 pm). There is one bus to Jammu at 10.10 am (seven hours, Rs 66), and one to Dharamsala at 8.30 am (six hours, Rs 55). There are several buses daily to Pathankot (3½ hours, Rs 34), and one daily service to Shimla (12 hours, Rs 120). Buses to Khajiar leave at 9.30 and 10.30 am, and 4 pm (1½ hours, Rs 10), and to Chamba at 6.45, 8.45 and 10.30 am, and 3 and 4 pm (three hours, Rs 30).

Quoted rates at the taxi stand were: Pathankot, Rs 700; Chamba, Rs 600; Khajiar, Rs 360; Brahmaur, Rs 1600; and Kalatope, Rs 275.

Getting Around
From the bus stand to Gandhi Chowk, taxis charge Rs 30, and to Subhash Chowk, Rs 36.

KHAJIAR
Telephone Area Code: 018992

This grassy *marg*, or meadow, is 22 km from Dalhousie towards Chamba, and you can get here by bus or on foot, a day's walk. Over a km long and nearly a km wide, it is ringed by pine trees with a lake in the middle. There's a **golf course** here and the 12th century **Khajjinag Temple**, with fine wood-carving on the cornices, and some crude carvings of the five Pandavas, the heroes of the *Mahabharata*, which were installed in the temple by Raja Balbhadra Varman in the 16th century.

It's possible to do a circuit of the marg by horseback (Rs 40 for 15 minutes).

Places to Stay & Eat
There are several places to stay, including the HPTDC's *Hotel Devdar* (☎ 233), which has cottages right on the edge of the marg for Rs 450, and doubles for Rs 550. There's also a dorm with beds for Rs 50.

Behind the temple is the *Parul Guest House* (☎ 244), which has pleasant rooms overlooking the marg for Rs 500, and a good off-season discount. On the east side of the marg is the PWD *Guest House* which has very pleasant rooms with attached bath for Rs 106. Bookings should be made through the Executive Engineer in Dalhousie (☎ (018982) 2145).

The *Sharma Confectionary Store*, near the temple, has a variety of meals, and is very busy during the season.

Getting There & Away
Buses from Dalhousie to Khajiar leave at 9.30 and 10.30 am and 4 pm (1½ hours, Rs 10). From Khajiar, they return at 8.30 am and 4 pm. To Chamba, they depart at 12.15 and 5.30 pm (1½ hours, Rs 10). If the 9.30 am bus from Dalhousie is running, you could spend the day at Khajiar, and proceed on to Chamba that evening at 5.30 pm. A taxi from Khajiar to Chamba is Rs 400.

CHAMBA
Telephone Area Code: 018992

It's a beautiful, if somewhat hair-raising 56 km trip from Dalhousie to Chamba. The views down over the terraced fields are spectacular, with tiny villages clinging to the sheer slopes of the valley. Chamba lies in a valley at an altitude of 926m – quite a bit lower than Dalhousie, so it's warmer in the summer. Perched on a ledge flanking the Ravi River, it has often been compared to a medieval Italian village and is famed for its ancient temples.

For 1000 years prior to Independence, Chamba was the headquarters of a district of the same name, and was ruled by a single dynasty of maharajas. The town was founded by Raja Sahil Varman, who shifted the capital here from Brahmaur.

Unlike Dalhousie, Chamba has a conspicuous absence of buildings dating from the Raj era, although a few can be seen on the right as you enter the town. Apparently, the raja of Chamba negotiated a deal with the British resident whereby he would pay an annual stipend of Rs 12,000 to maintain autonomy over Chamba. However, the wily raja then deducted Rs 3000 as compensation for the British settlement at Dalhousie, and Rs 2000 for the military quarters at Baklo Cantt (near Dalhousie). A further Rs 2000 was levied for 'electricity charges' (Chamba was one of the first places in India to receive electricity). So the shrewd raja ended up paying the British only Rs 5000!

HIMACHAL PRADESH

Chamba has a grassy promenade known as the Chowgan. The town is a busy trading centre for villagers from the surrounding hills. The **Minjar Festival** is held each year in late July/early August. See the festival list at the start of this chapter for more information.

The **Sui Mata Festival** is held in March/April. The legend of Sui Mata is described later in this section.

Orientation & Information

The tourist office (☎ 2671) is in the Hotel Iravati on Court Rd, and there's a divisional tourism development office (☎ 4002) in the white building adjacent to the Iravati.

You can arrange porters and guides at the Mani Mahesh Travel Agency, close to the Lakshmi Narayan temple complex. Porters are Rs 150 per day, guides are Rs 200, and the friendly people here can also tailor treks in the environs of Chamba, as well as rock climbing and snow trekking. You can also arrange a guide here who can provide a commentary on Chamba's beautiful temples (Rs 100).

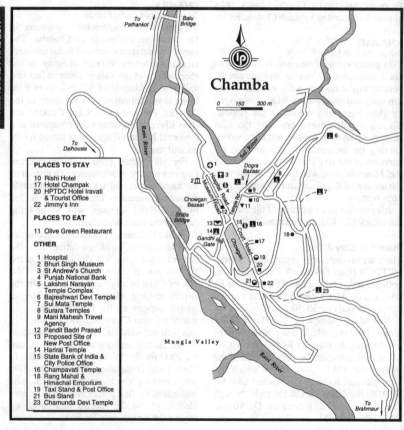

Chamba

0   150   300 m

PLACES TO STAY

10 Rishi Hotel
17 Hotel Champak
20 HPTDC Hotel Iravati
    & Tourist Office
22 Jimmy's Inn

PLACES TO EAT

11 Olive Green Restaurant

OTHER

1   Hospital
2   Bhuri Singh Museum
3   St Andrew's Church
4   Punjab National Bank
5   Lakshmi Narayan
    Temple Complex
6   Bajreshwari Devi Temple
7   Sui Mata Temple
8   Surara Temples
9   Mani Mahesh Travel
    Agency
12 Pandit Badri Prasad
13 Proposed Site of
    New Post Office
14 Harirai Temple
15 State Bank of India &
    City Police Office
16 Champavati Temple
18 Rang Mahal &
    Himachal Emporium
19 Taxi Stand & Post Office
21 Bus Stand
23 Chamunda Devi Temple

To Pathankot
Balu Bridge
To Dalhousie
Ravi River
Sal River
Dogra Bazaar
Hospital Road
Temple Rd
Chowgan Bazaar
Museum Road
Shitla Bridge
Court Road
Gandhi Gate
Chowgan
Mungla Valley
To Brahmaur

HIMACHAL PRADESH

You can get English-language newspapers at Pandit Badri Prasad, Museum Rd, Chowgan Bazaar.

Emergency Police: ☎ 2736; Ambulance: ☎ 2392.

Lakshmi Narayan Temple Complex

The six temples in this complex, all featuring exquisite sculpture, are representative of the shikhara style, although have distinctive characteristics which are found only in the temple architecture of the Chamba Valley. Three of the temples are dedicated to Vishnu, and three to Shiva. The largest (and oldest) temple in the group is that of Lakshmi Narayan (Vishnu), which is directly opposite the entrance to the complex. According to tradition it was built during the reign of the founder of Chamba, Raja Sahil Varman, in the 10th century AD. It was extensively renovated in the 16th century by Raja Partap Singh Varna. The image of Lakshmi Narayan enshrined in the temple dates from the temple's foundation. Some of the fine sculptures around the temple include those of Vishnu and Lakshmi, Narsingh (Vishnu in his lion form), and Krishna with the *gopis* (milkmaids). A small niche at the back harbours a beautiful sculpture of a goddess churning the ocean with Sheshnag, the snake of Vishnu, to bring the poison up from the bottom.

The fourth temple from the right, the Gourishankar Temple, is dedicated to Shiva. Its stone carving of the Ganges and Yamuna rivers personified as goddesses on either side of the door frame is renowned.

The complex is open from 6 am to 12.30 pm and 2.30 to 8.30 pm.

Chamunda Devi Temple

A terrace before this hilltop temple gives an excellent view of Chamba with its slate-roof houses (some of them up to 300 years old), the River Ravi and the surrounding countryside. It's a steep 30 minute climb along a path which begins above the bus stand, passing en route a small rock outcrop smeared with

saffron which is revered as an image of the goddess of the forest, Banasti. When you reach the road, you can either proceed up the steep staircase, or follow the road to the left.

The temple is dedicated to Durga in her wrathful aspect as Chamunda Devi. Before the temple is her vehicle, a lion. Almost the entire wooden ceiling of the *mandapa* (forechamber) is richly carved, featuring animal and floral motifs, and depictions of various deities. From it are suspended numerous brass bells, offered to the goddess by devotees.

Just before ascending the steps to the temple is a small pillar bearing the footprints of the goddess. Behind the temple is a very old, small shikhara-style temple dedicated to Lord Shiva.

Harirai Temple

This fine stone shikhara-style temple, at the north-west side of the Chowgan, near the fire station, dates from the 11th century. It is dedicated to Vishnu, and enshrines a fine triple-headed image of Vaikuntha Vishnu reputedly made from eight different materials. In April 1971, the statue was stolen from the inner sanctum. It was discovered by Interpol on a ship destined for the USA seconds before the boat was to sail, and was returned to Chamba. At the rear of the temple is a fine sculpture of Lord Vishnu astride six horses.

Sui Mata Temple

About 10 minutes walk from the Chamunda Devi Temple is a small modern temple dedicated to Sui Mata. Colourful paintings around the interior walls of the temple tell the story of Sui, a Chamba princess who gave her life for the inhabitants of Chamba. Women and children can be seen here laying wildflowers before the temple in devotion to Sui Mata.

About 10 minutes walk from Sui Mata (take the little path to the right just before passing the last few houses of Chamba) is the ancient **Bajreshwari Devi Temple**. The temple conforms to the shikhara style, and is topped by a wooden *amalaka* (fluted medal-

The Sacrifice of Sui Mata
Sui is an abbreviated form of Sunana, a royal Chamba princess who also went by the name of Rani Champavati (from whom the name of the town is derived). In bygone ages, Chamba was plagued by a dreadful drought. The princess received a message from the gods during a dream that in order to bring an end to the drought, she would either have to sacrifice her son, her broom, or herself. If she sacrificed her son, the princess feared that there would be no one to inherit the kingdom and care for the people of Chamba. Nor was she willing to sacrifice her broom, symbol of domestic harmony and peace. So the princess gave her own life, and was buried alive at the site of the current temple. From the place of her incarceration, a steam miraculously appeared, and the drought was broken. During the month of Chaitra (March-April), a fair is held in Sui Mata's honour. A golden image of the princess is carried on a palanquin by villagers from the maharaja's palace to the site of the temple, accompanied by women and children, with songs sung by the women of Chamba. ■

lion-shaped flourish). The sanctum enshrines an image of Bajreshwari (a form of Durga), although it is difficult to make out beneath its garlands of flowers. The entire surface of the temple is elaborately carved, featuring two friezes of rosettes at the lower levels. It is fronted by two stone columns with richly carved capitals and bases. A form of ancient script called *takri* can be seen crudely incised on the right column, and on other spots around the temple. In the niche on the west side of the temple is an image of Undavi, the goddess of food, with a bowl and a ladle. At the rear of the temple, Durga can be seen slaying the giant Mahisasur and his buffalo vehicle. The giant is dwarfed by Durga, who is standing astride him with her foot on the buffalo. On either side of the door jambs, the rivers Yamuna and Ganges are personified as goddesses holding pitchers of water.

The diminutive **Surara temples** are found down a series of alleyways in the area called Muhala, back down in Chamba, about 10 minutes walk from the Bajreshwari Temple.

Behind the City Police Office is the **Champavati Temple**, dedicated to the daughter of Raja Sahil Varman. The dimly lit mandapa features four solid wooden carved pillars featuring floral and bird motifs.

Rang Mahal
The Rang Mahal, or Old Palace, now houses

the **Himachal Emporium**. Here you can purchase *rumals* – small cloths featuring very fine embroidery in silk, a traditional craft executed by the women of Chamba which dates back almost 1000 years. The stitching is very fine, and the reverse side of the cloth features a mirror image of the design – there is no evidence of knots or loose threads. Popular images portrayed on the cloths include Krishna and Radha, and those of Gaddi shepherds. A finely stitched rumal can take up to a month to complete, and costs from Rs 200 to Rs 300.

You can also purchase from the showroom here repoussé brass plates and Chamba shawls, and above the showroom is a workshop where you can see the shawls being made. An elaborately decorated shawl can take up to 45 days to make on a traditional wooden loom.

The emporium is open Monday to Saturday from 10 am to 1 pm and 2 to 5 pm.

Bhuri Singh Museum
This museum has an interesting collection representing the art and culture of this region – particularly the miniature paintings of the Basohli and Kangra schools. Also here are some of the murals which were recovered from the Rang Mahal after it was damaged by fire. The museum is open Tuesday to Friday, Sunday and every second Saturday from 10 am to 5 pm. Entry is free.

Gandhi Gate

This bright orange gateway at the south-west side of the Chowgan was built in 1900 to welcome Viceroy Lord Curzon to the city. This was the main entrance into the city before the new road was built.

Places to Stay & Eat

The HPTDC's *Hotel Iravati* (☎ 2671), only a few minutes walk from the bus stand on Court Rd, has doubles with attached bath for Rs 400, Rs 500 and Rs 600. There's 24 hour room service, and rooms are spotless. There's also a good restaurant here (non-guests welcome). There's a second HPTDC place, the *Hotel Champak* (☎ 2774), behind the post office. Large doubles with common bath are Rs 100, and with attached bath with hot water, they're Rs 150. There's also a dorm here with beds for Rs 45.

Right opposite the bus stand is the friendly, family-run *Jimmy's Inn* (☎ 4748). Rooms are very comfortable, and range from Rs 100 to Rs 200, all with attached bath. Hot water is available in buckets for Rs 5.

Many travellers head for the *Rishi Hotel* (☎ 4343), on Temple Rd, right opposite the Lakshmi Narayan temple complex. Doubles for Rs 100 have attached baths with cold water; doubles for Rs 150 and Rs 200 have geysers, and some rooms have good views out over the temples. The cheaper rooms are at the back, and are a little gloomy. There's also a three bed dorm with beds for Rs 40. There's also a good dining hall here where you can sample the local dish Chamba madhra – kidney beans with curd and ghee – for Rs 18.

The *Orchard Hut* is in a lovely tranquil spot 12 km from Chamba. There are tents for Rs 50 per person, or very basic lodging for Rs 30. With all meals, it's Rs 175. Check at the Mani Mahesh Travel Agency.

The *Olive Green Restaurant* is upstairs on Temple Rd, in Dogra Bazaar. It's a very quiet and clean place, with good, reasonably priced veg and nonveg dishes.

Chamba is known for its *chukh* – a chilli sauce consisting of red and green peppers, lemon juice, mustard oil and salt. You'll find it in most of the provision stores in Dogra Bazaar for around Rs 22 a jar.

Getting There & Away

There are several buses daily for the (somewhat nerve-shattering) trip to Brahmaur (3½ hours, Rs 24). To Dharamsala there are buses at 6 am, 1.30 and 9.45 pm (10 hours, Rs 70). To Khajiar, buses leave at 7 am and 1.30 and 5.10 pm (1½ hours, Rs 10). To Dalhousie, they depart at 6 am and 6 pm (three hours, Rs 30). There are several buses daily to Pathankot (five to six hours, Rs 48).

To Khajiar, a reserve taxi will cost Rs 300; to Brahmaur, it's Rs 400.

Getting Around

A taxi from the town up to Chamunda Temple costs Rs 50 return.

BRAHMAUR

Telephone Area Code: 01090

Sixty-four km south-east of Chamba is the ancient slate-roofed village of Brahmaur, at 2195m. It's a spectacular trip along a fairly precarious road up the Ravi River valley, passing through the village of Holi, which is surrounded by apple orchards.

Before Raja Sahil Varman founded the new capital at Chamba in 920 AD, Brahmaur was the ancient capital of the princely state of Chamba for over 400 years, and the well preserved temples are a testament to its wealth.

Brahmaur is a centre for the seminomadic Gaddis, pastoralists who move their flocks up to the alpine pastures during the summer, and descend to Kangra, Mandi and Bilaspur in the winter.

There are some fine treks which commence from Brahmaur; see under Treks out of Brahmaur at the end of this section. The Mountaineering & Allied Sports Sub-Centre (☎ 236) can arrange guides and porters from Rs 200 to Rs 250 per day, and you can also hire two-person tents here (Rs 100 per day).

Manimahesh Yatra

The important *yatra*, or pilgrimage, to the sacred lake of Manimahesh commences from Brahmaur in the month of August. See

HIMACHAL PRADESH

the festival list at the start of this chapter for more information.

Chaurasi

In the heart of the village is a magnificent group of well preserved ancient temples – the site is called the Chaurasi, as there are 84 temples here, although some are tiny shrines, less than a metre high. The oldest temple in the group, dedicated to Lakhna Devi, the mother of the gods, was built in the 7th century AD during the reign of Raja Meru Varman. It's made of wood, and features fine carvings, such as beautiful rosettes on the ceiling of the mandapa and intricate carving on the capitals of the pillars. The entrance to the mandapa is also elaborately carved. In the inner sanctum is enshrined a brass image of the goddess who is seen standing.

Dominating the group is the large shikhara-style **Manimahesh Temple**, which is dedicated to Shiva. The temple's lingam is protected by a massive brass cobra which is coiled around it. Opposite is a smaller shikhara-style temple dedicated to Vishnu in his lion form as **Narsingh**. It enshrines a fine 1½m high statue of the god in its inner sanctum. To its left is the **Dharmeshvar Temple**, sacred to Shiva. It was originally built in the 14th century, but has been renovated over subsequent years.

Brahmani Mata Temple

From Brahmaur it's possible to walk to the small temple of Brahmani Mata. Follow the road up past the Chaurasi which leads in about five minutes to a small village. Beyond here a path leads in 20 minutes to the larger settlement of Makotta, from where it takes about 1½ to two hours to reach the temple. There are no houses between Makotta and the temple, so carry water with you. There's a small chai stall at the temple, and a pool in the freezing waters of which devout pilgrims bathe.

Places to Stay

The *Chamunda Guest House* (☎ 256) is a brand new place about five minutes walk up from the bus stand. Singles/doubles are Rs 50/100, and there are very pleasant doubles also at Rs 150.

On the bus stand is the *Krishna Lodge*, which has very basic rooms that open onto a balcony with superb views. Doubles are Rs 50. Nearby is the *Jamuna Lodge*, which has doubles with common bath and good views for Rs 75, and hot water free in buckets. There are also doubles with attached bath for Rs 100, but they don't have a valley view.

There are dorm beds (Rs 15) at the Mountaineering & Allied Sports Sub-Centre (☎ 236).

Getting There & Away

There are a number of buses to Chamba between 6.30 am and 5.30 pm (3½ hours, Rs 24).

Brahmani Devi

According to legend, the only son of a pious woman of Brahmaur died of shock when his pet partridge was killed by a farmer. The boy's mother was overwhelmed with grief and threw herself on her son's funeral pyre. The villagers were so moved by this act of love that they accorded the woman the status of a deity and built a temple in her honour, at which she was worshipped as Brahmani Devi.

En route to Mt Kailash in Tibet, Lord Shiva passed through Brahmaur with 84 holy saints. Unimpressed by her celestial guest, Brahmani Devi appeared before Shiva and asked him and his entourage to vacate the village immediately. Asserting his divine prerogative, Shiva refused to budge, and Brahmani Devi retreated to her temple. However, the next morning the 84 saints had vanished, and in their place stood 84 stone lingams, today encompassed within the temple complex of the Chaurasi. ■

TREKKING OUT OF BRAHMAUR

Only a handful of trekkers cross the passes over the Pir Panjal Range between Brahmaur and the Chandra Valley. The trek over the Kugti Pass (5040m) is the one most favoured by the Gaddi shepherds on their annual migration to the verdant grazing pastures of Lahaul. The Gaddi commence their migration through the village of Hardsar before selecting a series of alpine camps below the Kugti pass. They cross the pass as soon as the spring snows begin to melt in late June. The pass involves crossing a small crevasse before a short steep ascent up a narrow rock gully to the summit of the pass. Views south include the Manimahesh Range and the Dhauladhar, while to the north the high snow-capped peaks of the main Himalayan Range complete a spectacular panorama. The descent from the pass across a rock band should be undertaken with care before the long descent to the Chandra Valley and the grazing meadows in the Miyah Nullah north of the town of Udaipur.

This trek can also be combined with a visit to the sacred Manimahesh Lake (3950m) at the base of Manimahesh Kailash (5656m). The trek can be completed in two stages from the village of Hardsar and is undertaken by many Hindu pilgrims from Brahmaur, Chamba and beyond, particularly during the time of the July/August full moon. The pilgrims spend their first night camping at the meadow at Dancho before reaching the lake and returning direct to Dancho the following day.

Porters are available from Brahmaur and charge Rs 100 per day plus return. Loads are limited to around 15 kg per porter.

Stage 1	Hardsar to Kugti (5 hours)
Stage 2	Kugti village to Duggi Cave (4 to 5 hours)
Stage 3	Dudhil Nullah to Alyas (4 hours)
Stage 4	Alyas to high camp via Kugti Pass (6 hours)
Stage 5	High camp to Rape (4 hours)

Kullu & Parbati Valleys

Peak Season: mid-April to mid-June, mid-September to early November, Christmas and New Year

The Kullu Valley, and to a lesser extent the Parbati Valley, were always popular places, which managed to retain a very peaceful and

Warning

The Kullu Valley area and especially villages along the Parbati Valley are famous for marijuana, sometimes known as *bhang*. It is esteemed by connoisseurs, and grows wild in the valleys. Don't be fooled by the fact that you see it growing everywhere, or that everyone else is smoking the stuff – like anywhere, it's still very much illegal – the police can and will bust you and you'll find yourself in trouble you could do without. ■

unhurried atmosphere. With the troubles in Kashmir, however, the valleys, including Manali, have largely replaced the Kashmir Valley, as they are safer places to experience some outdoor activities, see the countryside, and hang out.

Originally known as Kulanthapitha, meaning the 'End of the Habitable World', the first recorded inhabitants of the Kullu Valley date back to the first century. The first capital was at Jagatsukh, then moved to Naggar, before the British moved it to Kullu town. The Kullu Valley, about 80 km long and often less than two km wide, rises northward from Mandi at 760m to the Rohtang Pass at 3980m, the gateway to Lahaul & Spiti.

In the south, the valley is little more than a narrow, precipitous gorge, with the Beas River sometimes a sheer 300m below the narrow road. The Beas is fed by melting snow through its northern and eastern tributaries, and further south by the monsoons,

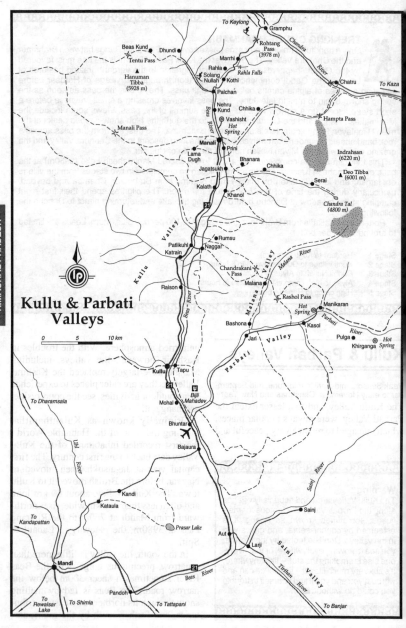

Kullu & Parbati Valleys

which often result in floods. The Parbati Valley joins the Kullu Valley at Bhuntar, and heads north-east, following the smaller, but pretty, Parbati River.

The entire Kullu and Parbati valleys, from Mandi to Manali and Manikaran, are serviced by the airport at Bhuntar, about 10 km south of Kullu town.

Things to Buy
The road along the Kullu Valley, particularly from the Bhuntar Airport to Kullu town, is lined with shops selling Kullu shawls and other locally produced handicrafts. Once an important part of household and village life, the manufacture and sale of Kullu shawls and other goods is now a thriving local industry. It's worth having a look at some of the shops to see the weaving, or to visit a farm of pashmina goats or angora rabbits – although there will be some real pressure to buy.

Pattoos are thick woollen shawls worn by local women, and fastened with a *gachi*. Kullu caps are always colourful, and worth buying if trekking in cold climates. Other items include a *gudma*, often used as a sort of blanket, or a *pullan*, which is a type of slipper worn in the home.

The shops between Bhuntar and Kullu cater more for the touristy crowds, and despite an obvious overabundance of places, they don't offer particularly competitive prices. The best places to buy Kullu gear are the market stalls and cooperatives along The Mall in Manali; and, in Kullu town, the best place is the Akhara Bazaar, one km north of the Kullu bus station.

MANDI
Population: 25,000
Telephone Area Code: 01905

Formerly an important junction on the salt route to Tibet, Mandi is the gateway to the Kullu Valley, and the junction where the road branches off along the Kangra Valley towards Dharamsala. Mandi, which means 'market', is quite a good place to break the journey between Shimla and the Kullu Valley – a far better option to stay than Bilaspur. In Mandi, there are some cheap

hotels, you will stumble across some of the 81 Hindu temples in the area, and can take a day trip to a nearby lake or two. At less than 800m above sea level, Mandi is considerably hotter than other regional areas.

Orientation
The centre of Mandi is the town square, dominated by a huge collection of shops called the Indira Market Square. A lot of hotels and places to eat are around or very near the square. Over the river, to the east, is the newer area, where the bus station is located. Mandi is easy to walk around; from the bus station to the town square, across the large bridge, only takes about 15 minutes on foot.

Tarna Hill
For a cool respite from the town, take an autorickshaw (about Rs 30 return) up the very steep four or five km to Tarna Hill – it's too far and steep to walk, unless you enjoy that sort of thing. At the top of the hill, the Rani Amrit Kaur Park (opened by the Dalai Lama in 1957) has superb views of the area, and there's a nice cafe for lunch or a snack. In the park, the 17th century Hindu **Syamakali Temple**, also called the Tarna Devi Temple, is worth a look.

Temples
Mandi's **Shivrati Festival**, held in February/March, is one of the most interesting festivals in Himachal Pradesh. Much of the activity takes place at the 16th century **Bhutnath Temple**, which is in the middle of the town surrounded by the incongruous concrete Indira Market Square. See the list of festivals at the start of this chapter for details. It's not hard to stumble across many other new and old, restored and decaying, Hindu temples around Mandi, such as the **Magru Mahadev Temple**, which features fine woodcarving.

Places to Stay
The HPTDC *Hotel Mandav* (☎ 22-123) is just up a laneway behind the bus station. Comfortable, quiet doubles with great views in the old part of the hotel cost Rs 200. The

more modern rooms have the same sort of facilities, but at Rs 750 are overpriced. There are no dorms. About 300m east of the bus station is the *Vipasha Guest House* (☎ 25-116), which is handy, and good value with singles/doubles for Rs 75/100. Also near the station, and about the same price, is the *Vyas Guest House* – just follow the signs from the station.

Along the road across the bridge from the bus station, there are a number of cheap, although noisy, places for about Rs 40/60. The better ones are: the *Hotel Anand* (☎ 22-515), which is cramped but reasonably clean; the *Hotel Koyal* (☎ 22-248); and the *Sangam Hotel* (☎ 22-009), which offers some views.

Around the town square, there are places of all types and prices. The popular *Hotel Standard* (☎ 22-948) charges Rs 65 for a double with attached bath. The *Hotel Shiva* (☎ 24-211) has rooms from Rs 90 to Rs 225 – it is good value with TV and hot water, but is a little noisy. Just behind the square, in areas known as Gandhi Chowk and Moti Bazaar, several mid-range places like the *Hotel Parth* (☎ 22-003) and the *Evening Palace* (☎ 3318) charge about Rs 300 a room.

For something rather different, try the rambling *Raj Mahal* (☎ 22-401). It's located at the back of a decrepit building (which has a modern gym nearby) at the town centre, next to the district library. Set around large gardens, comfortable rooms cost Rs 90/125, while the rooms for Rs 200/275 are considerably better.

Also on the square, and one of the top hotels in town, is the modern *Hotel Mayfair* (☎ 22-570). Doubles cost from Rs 330 to Rs 550, with TV, attached bath and constant hot water.

Places to Eat

The outdoor *Copacabana Bar & Restaurant* at the Raj Mahal is a popular place where good food is served. The *Hotel Mandav* is worth the walk up for a good selection, breakfasts, and the bar in the next room. The HPTDC *Cafe Shiraz*, just behind the square, serves so-so food, although their curried 'finger chips' (French fries) are not bad.

Most of the hotels around the Indira Market Square serve pretty good food, including the *Hotel Mayfair* for something a bit classier, with views; the *Hotel Standard* for good, cheap food; and the *Hotel Shiva*. Plenty of dhabas and stalls selling just about everything are scattered around the market.

Getting There & Away

Bus As the junction for the Kangra and Kullu valleys, Mandi is well served by local public buses. The bus station – where you can make advanced bookings – is across the river in the eastern part of the town.

There are buses every hour or so to Shimla via Bilaspur; approximately every hour up the Kullu Valley road to Pandoh, Bhuntar (for the airport and Manikaran), Kullu and Manali; and along the Kangra Valley road, to Dharamsala and any place on the way, such as Jogindernagar, at least 10 times a day.

Taxi Taxis congregate outside the bus station, and at a stand on the eastern side of the Indira Market Square. A one-way trip by taxi from Mandi to Kullu costs Rs 550.

Getting Around

If you need a lift around town, or up to Tarna Hill, an autorickshaw is the best value.

AROUND MANDI
Rewalsar Lake
Telephone Area Code: 01905

Rewalsar Lake is high up in the hills, 24 km south-west of Mandi and set beside the village of Rewalsar. It's a lovely area, with some pretty scenery, and is worth a day trip out, or an overnight stay.

The small lake is revered by Buddhists because it is where Padmasambhava departed for Tibet. Every year, shortly after the Tibetan New Year (February or March), many Buddhists make a pilgrimage here, especially from Dharamsala.

Hindus also revere the lake because it was where Rishi Lomas did his penance as a dedication to Lord Shiva, who, in return, gave Rishi the seven lakes in the vicinity, including Rewalsar.

Things to See & Do As you enter the lake area, the **Drikung Kagyud Gompa**, immediately on the right, is full of friendly monks who will show you around. The **Tso-Pema Ogyen Heru-kai Nyingmapa Gompa & Institute** may be a bit of a mouthful, but it's worth a visit. Built in the 19th century, it has a little museum, some friendly monks and colourful murals.

Around the lake, there are also three **Hindu temples** dedicated to Rishi Lomas, Lord Shiva and Lord Krishna. Outside one of the Hindu temples, hundreds of feverish fish in the lake, and menacing monkeys beside the lake, eagerly wait to be fed.

The Sikhs have the huge **Guru Govind Singh Gurudwara**. It was built in 1930 by Raja Joginder Sen, and dedicated to Govind Singh, who stayed at the Rewalsar Lake for a month.

Places to Stay & Eat The HPTDC *Hotel Rewalsar* (☎ 80-252) has dorm beds for Rs 45, and nice doubles from Rs 200 to Rs 400, all with a balcony (although most do not actually overlook the lake). The Drikung Kagyud Gompa offers cosy little rooms in its *Peace Memorial Inn* for Rs 30; more rooms will be finished soon. The *Lomosh Hotel & Restaurant* (☎ 80-238) looked decidedly empty at the time of researching, but may be open again soon. Surprisingly, there is nowhere to stay in the village on the main road.

As well as the *Hotel Rewalsar*, the only places to eat are a few good Tibetan cafes around the Tso-Pema Gompa, and the several Indian dhabas along the main road.

Getting There & Away Rewalsar isn't actually on the way to anywhere, so you will have to travel to and from Mandi, whether you stay overnight in Rewalsar or not. Buses from Mandi go to Rewalsar village, adjacent to the lake, every 30 or 40 minutes, so it is any easy day trip along a pretty, but fairly rough, road. A return autorickshaw from Mandi costs about Rs 150; a taxi is quicker and more comfortable but more expensive at Rs 250 return.

Prasar Lake
Prasar is another lovely little lake in a great area for camping and hiking. It's more difficult and expensive to get to than Rewalsar, so it's probably not worth the effort until it is better serviced by a road. The small lake is located at 2730m – about 2000m higher than Mandi. Alongside the lake, there is a small, pretty, deserted **temple** dedicated to Prasar.

There are no buses directly to the lake, so there are two alternatives. One is an irregular local bus from Mandi to the nearest accessible village, Kataula, and then a tough, steep 14 km walk to the lake, or a 16 km trek to the lake from the Kandi-Bajaura road. The other option is a return taxi from Mandi or Kullu (both cost a hefty Rs 1000 because the road is so rough). There is nowhere to stay, but the setting is perfect for camping. Of course you would need to carry in your gear, including drinking water.

Bijli Mahadev Temple
South of Kullu, across the river and high on a bluff, is the Bijli Mahadev Temple, surmounted by a 20m high rod said to attract blessings in the form of lightning. At least once a year the image of Shiva in the temple is supposed to be shattered by lightning, then miraculously repaired by the temple *pujari*.

The road to the temple is rough, which explains the high cost of transport there. A return taxi from Kullu will cost Rs 550 for the full day, including waiting time. Alternatively, take one of the few daily buses to Tambli. They normally leave from Tapu, which is connected by a footbridge from Akhara Bazaar in Kullu town. Ask the driver to let you off as close as he can to the temple, and then it's a steep walk a few km further on.

MANDI TO KULLU
Pandoh
About two km north of Pandoh, the impressive **Pandoh Dam** diverts water from the Beas River along two 12 km tunnels to Baggi. The water then joins the Sutlej River near Bilaspur, eventually feeding into the

huge artificial Govind Sagar. Pandoh Dam would be a nice place to visit and look around except for the gun-toting guards everywhere – this is a place where fun and photos are banned! The area around the dam looks great for hiking. There are defined trails leading south towards Bajahi, but don't risk it. Despite the guards, it's still worth a quick stop if travelling by taxi.

There is nowhere to stay at Pandoh or at the dam. The HPTDC's *Jai Tarang* cafe serves reasonable food – if it's open. A one-way/return taxi from Mandi costs Rs 150/200; a return taxi from Kullu costs Rs 450. On the main road, eight km past Pandoh towards Kullu, is the revered **Hongi Hindu Temple**, set among dramatic cliffs. Your bus or taxi driver will probably stop here to give a small prayer.

Sainj Valley

The Kullu Valley road passes the dismal little village of Aut, about 20 km past Pandoh. Aut functions as a turn-off to the Sainj Valley, and as the true start of the Kullu Valley. Only a few km along the road through the Sainj Valley is the pretty village of Larji, from where there is a turn-off to the village of Sainj. Larji, set at the spectacular junction of the Sainj and Tirthan rivers, is a centre for trout fishing, but you will need a licence from Kullu. The road along the Sainj Valley continues as far as Banjar.

Bajaura

Back on the main road, 15 km south of Kullu, is the village of Bajaura. It's the home of **Basheshar Mahadev**, the largest stone temple in the Kullu Valley. Built in the 8th century from carved stone blocks, the temple has fine carvings and sculptures. Outside, there is a sign with explanations in English, which is very handy. A new temple is being built in the village centre.

The Basheshar Mahadev Temple is at the end of a 200m trail leading from the main road currently with the sign overhead reading 'Indo Italian Fruit Dev'. The only place to stay in Bajaura, the *Raj Guest*

House, about 500m north of the village, is quite good value for about Rs 50 a room.

Bhuntar

Bhuntar's claim to fame is its airport, which serves all of the Kullu and Parbati valleys, and the bridge across the Beas River leading to the Parbati Valley. Otherwise, Bhuntar is not a particularly pleasant place, and not worth a stop or stay. Several of the airlines have offices in or near Bhuntar. (Refer to Getting There & Away in the Kullu section for details.) A tourist office will open soon, about 50m west of the airport entrance. There are plenty of travel agencies around the village.

Places to Stay & Eat Bhuntar is only 10 km from Kullu, but if you have an early or late departure or arrival, staying at Bhuntar may be handy. Just north of the airport gate, there are several very basic places such as the *Ratan Guest House*, the *Beas Valley Guest House* and the *Airlines Hotel* for about Rs 70 a room. Near the bridge to the Parbati Valley, about 500m towards Kullu, there are some places in the middle range with TV, hot water, and modern rooms: the *Hotel Sunbeam* (☎ 5190) has singles/doubles for Rs 150/250; the *Hotel Trans Shiva* (☎ 65-623) has rooms from Rs 300; and in the *Hotel Amit* (☎ 65-123), rooms cost from Rs 200 to Rs 500. One of the better places for value and location is the *Hotel Airport-End*, opposite the airport entrance. It has clean but noisy rooms for a negotiable Rs 250.

Around the airport entrance, and around the village streets, several dhabas serve basic food, and some stalls have fantastic, fresh fruit juices. Otherwise, any of the reasonable hotels have fairly good restaurants.

Getting There & Away As the regional airport and the junction for the Parbati Valley, Bhuntar is well served by buses which leave from outside the airport entrance. Most buses go to Kullu, where you may have to change for another bus for places further north. Some direct buses do go as far north as Manali, and as far south as Chandigarh. All buses between Manali and any place south of Kullu stop at, or very near, Bhuntar.

From the bus/taxi stand outside the airport entrance, taxis can take you to just about anywhere. To Kullu, it costs Rs 80; to Mandi, Rs 480; and to Manali, Rs 425.

KULLU
Population: 15,500
Telephone Area Code: 01902

At an altitude of 1200m, Kullu is the district headquarters of the valley but it is not the main tourist centre – that honour goes to Manali. Kullu is reasonably set up with hotels and other facilities, and is not a bad place, especially around Dhalpur, but many visitors do not bother to stay long in Kullu because there are nicer places around the valleys.

Orientation
Kullu is small enough to walk around. The *maidan* (field) area at Dhalpur, where Kullu's festivals are held, is the nicest part of town. The 'centre' of town is probably the area around the taxi stand. From there a busy footpath heads towards the large bus station area (don't take the road if walking; it's longer) called Sarwari, full of shops and cheap guest-houses. The road from the bus station then heads towards Manali through Akhara Bazaar, which is a good place to buy Kullu shawls and other handicrafts.

Information
The helpful HPTDC tourist office (☎ 2349) is by the maidan at Dhalpur. It's open daily from 9 am to 7 pm in summer, and from 10 am to 5 pm in winter. HPTDC buses leave from outside the office.

The only place that changes money is the State Bank of India, is on the maidan in Dhalpur. It's open from 10 am to 1.30 pm, Monday to Friday; on Saturday, from 10 to 11.30 am. This branch won't accept Citicorp or Visa travellers' cheques. The main post office, up from the taxi stand, is open from 10 am to 5 pm, Monday to Saturday, but is a bit slow.

Kullu

0   150   300 m

PLACES TO STAY

1	Vimay & Sangam Guesthouses
3	Central Hotel
5	Alankar Guest House
6	Beas View Hotel
7	Luxmi Guest House
9	The Nest
11	Aadikya Guest House
13	Bhaga Sidh Guest House
16	Hotel Bijleshwar View
17	Hotel Shobla & Restaurant
20	Hotel Rohtang & Restaurant
21	Sa-Ba Tourist Home
22	Fancy Guest House
24	Hotel Sarvari & Restaurant

OTHER

2	Palace
4	Naggar Bus Stop
8	Raghunath Temple
10	Main Bus Station
12	Main Post Office
14	Taxi Stand
15	Tourist Office & Monal Cafe
18	Dhalpur Bus Stand
19	District Magistrate's Office
23	State Bank of India

HIMACHAL PRADESH

If you want a permit for Lahaul & Spiti or Kinnaur, the District Magistrate's Office is located at the Dhalpur maidan, to the back of the small Dhalpur bus stand, however, it's better to get your permit in Keylong, Kaza or Rekong Peo. (Refer to the Lahaul & Spiti or Kinnaur sections for more information.)

Temples

In the north of the town, the **Raghunath Temple** is dedicated to the principal god in the valley. Although it's the most important temple in the area, it's not terribly interesting and is only open from 5 pm. Three km from Kullu, in the village of Bhekhli, is the **Jagannathi Devi Temple**. It's a stiff climb, but from the temple there are great views over Kullu. Take the path off the main road to Akhara Bazaar after crossing the bridge. Alternatively, take a return taxi for Rs 250, or an autorickshaw for far less. The temple area is now also used as a jumping off point for the very occasional irreverent hang-glider.

Places to Stay

Like Manali, and most places along the Kullu Valley, prices for hotels and guesthouses in the town of Kullu vary according to the season, and, more commonly, the current tourist demand. Prices aren't too bad, as you can shop around and get a good, discounted place. Below are prices for the high season – but they vary considerably from one week to another.

Accommodation can be divided into three areas: the nice, and more convenient, at Dhalpur maidan; the noisy but cheapest, at Akhara Bazaar, which is on the road from the bus station towards Manali; and around the busy bus station itself.

Places to Stay – bottom end & middle

Dhalpur The *Hotel Bijleshwar View* (☎ 2677), right behind the tourist office, remains incredibly popular, and good value. The cheaper rooms cost Rs 125; the larger, newer ones, with a balcony, are Rs 175. All rooms have hot water. The Jagson Airlines office is at the hotel. Only a little south of the maidan, and a short walk off the main road,

is the HPTDC *Hotel Sarvari* (☎ 2471). It's a well run place with doubles from Rs 400 to Rs 500, and dorm beds at Rs 50.

Around the maidan are several other good places: the *Hotel Rohtang* (☎ 2303) is good value at Rs 200 a room, and Rs 450 for a room with four beds, but some rooms are dark; the *Hotel Daulat* (☎ 2358) has rooms with a balcony for Rs 200 and more; and the nearby *Hotel Aroma Classic* (☎ 3075) has economy rooms for Rs 300, and full facilities for up to Rs 500. Up a lane at the back of the tourist office, the *Bhaga Sidh Guest House* has cheap singles/doubles in a family home for Rs 80/100, but the little yapping dog wasn't welcoming.

Across the other (eastern) side of the maidan, towards the river, is the *Fancy Guest House* (☎ 2681). There's nothing fancy about the place, but it's not bad value at Rs 100 to Rs 150 for a room with attached bath and constant hot water. Just a little further north, better value can be found at the clean, friendly *Sa-Ba Tourist Home*. It actually offers genuine single rooms for Rs 75, and doubles for Rs 150.

Akhara Bazaar The *Beas View Hotel* (☎ 4271) is popular, so is often full. The *Alankar Guest House* (☎ 2785) is about the best choice. Rooms cost Rs 100/150, and dorms are Rs 35, in a nice and friendly atmosphere. The *Hotel Naman* (☎ 2667), with rooms for Rs 100/150, and a good restaurant, is opposite the bus stop to Naggar and what used to be a bridge (before the floods) across the Beas River (on the east of National Highway 21). The *Central Hotel* (☎ 2482) at Rs 50/100 is another possibility. Any further out than the Naman is not convenient to facilities in Kullu.

Bus Station Area On the path which connects the central taxi stand area with the main bus station is the *Aadikya Guest House*, right by the bridge. The roar of the river can be amazingly loud at times. Rooms for Rs 100/180 have TV, attached bath and hot water. It's the best of several similar ones around the bridge area. Further back, along the main road, the *Vimay* and *Sangam* (☎ 4147) guesthouses are OK, but offer nothing much in the way of facilities or convenience.

Near the bus station, *The Nest* (☎ 2685) has enormous double rooms for Rs 250; Rs 400 with two double beds in the one room. The *Luxmi Guest House* (☎ 2851) and, nearby, the *Naravan Guest House*, are just a couple of the convenient but unavoidably noisy places around the bus station for up to Rs 100 a double.

Places to Stay – top end

In the centre of town, the *Hotel Shobla* (☎ 2800), a new place by the river, has some luxury rooms from Rs 550 to Rs 935, plus about Rs 345 for three meals. A few places south of Kullu, on the way to the airport, are in the top-end range but inconvenient unless you have your own transport. One of the best is the *Hotel Vaishali* (☎ 4225) with doubles from Rs 650. It also handles Archana Airways bookings, and is more convenient and easier to find than the Archana Airways office near Bhuntar.

Places to Eat

By the tourist office, the HPTDC's *Monal Cafe* serves good meals (particularly recommended is the puri bhajee), and snacks. Just opposite, *Hotstuff* is a great place for pizzas, soup and just about everything else. Plenty of other cheap places around the bus stand, or the central taxi stand, serve basic Tibetan and Indian food.

Of the hotels, the *Hotel Rohtang* has nice views of Dhalpur maidan, with a good selection and prices; it's very good for breakfast. The *Hotel Aroma Classic* looks expensive, but isn't – the setting, service and selection make it a good option. The top place is the *Hotel Shobla* which has the best views, all the service you would expect, and good food at prices which aren't outrageous (individual pizzas are Rs 30; omelettes, Rs 15).

Getting There & Away

Air UP Airways flies daily to/from Delhi for US$110. On Monday, Wednesday and Friday, KCV Airways has return flights between Delhi and Bhuntar for US$113, and then on to Amritsar; or just between Delhi and Bhuntar for US$123 on Tuesday, Thursday and Saturday. Jagson Airlines goes to/from Delhi every day for US$113; and also links Bhuntar with Shimla (US$49) and Dharamsala (US$49) every Tuesday, Thursday and Saturday. Archana Airways flies daily between Delhi and Bhuntar (US$113). Flights are in small aircraft, mainly 15 to 20 seaters.

The airline offices in the Kullu Valley are:

Archana Airways
  Mohal, about two km north of Bhuntar (☎ 65-630); or book at Hotel Vaishali, about one km south of Kullu (☎ 4225)
Jagson Airlines
  Hotel Bijleshwar View, Kullu (☎ 4830)
KCV Airways
  Aggarwarl Travels, opposite the airport, Bhuntar (☎ 65-774)
UP Airways
  Spectrum Travels, Hotel Amit (700m towards Kullu, and on the right), Bhuntar (☎ 65-634)

Bus Kullu has a large, busy bus station, with timetables displayed in English, and an advance booking system. The bus stop at the Dhalpur maidan is only good if you're going to nearby places to the south, such as Bhuntar, and, maybe, the Parbati Valley, but these buses may be full by the time they get to Dhalpur from the main Kullu bus station. For any bus out of Kullu, it is better to go to the large station, and get a seat or ticket as soon as you can.

Along the Kullu and Parbati valleys, there are several daily public buses to Mandi – or take any bus going to Shimla or Delhi; to Shimla, there are four buses each day; to Manikaran, a bus leaves every 30 minutes or so, or take a bus to Bhuntar and change there; and there is a bus every 15 or 20 minutes along the main road on the western side of the Beas River between Kullu and Manali. To Naggar, there is a bus stop in Akhara Bazaar, about two km north of the main bus station. Buses to Naggar leave there every few hours.

HIMACHAL PRADESH

There are three public buses every day (one overnight) to Dharamsala; and to Bajaura, Aut and the Sainj Valley, as far as Banjar, buses leave every hour or so. Regular daily express public buses go to Delhi (14 hours) and cost Rs 180. These go via Chandigarh. Direct daily buses to Chandigarh also leave several times a day.

The HPTDC runs daily buses in season from its office in Dhalpur to Dharamsala (Rs 200), Manali (Rs 75), Shimla (Rs 200), Delhi (Rs 375) and Chandigarh (Rs 250). Bookings can be made in advance at the tourist office.

Travel agencies in Kullu sell tickets for deluxe private buses 'from Kullu', but these are just really part of the trips from Manali organised by bus companies in Manali. In season, daily private buses to Delhi cost Rs 350; to Chandigarh, Rs 250; to Dharamsala, Rs 250; to Leh, with an overnight connection in Manali, Rs 800; and to Shimla, Rs 250.

Taxi Taxis from Kullu to Manali cost Rs 350 via the normal quicker National Highway 21 (on the western side of the river), or Rs 425 if you take the slower, but more scenic, route via Naggar. For a few extra rupees, you should be able to stop at Naggar for a quick look around. With a group, a taxi is not a bad option, because it gives you more time to visit a few places along the way. An example of long-distance taxis: to Mandi for Rs 550; to Bilaspur, Rs 1100; to Chandigarh, Rs 2200; to Ambala, Rs 2600; to Delhi, Rs 3700; to Dharamsala, Rs 1700; and to Shimla, Rs 1700.

The Kullu Taxi Operators' Union (☎ 2332) is just north of the Dhalpur maidan. It also offers three hour local sightseeing tours (Rs 450) to nearby temples and the inevitable Kullu shawl factory. The minimum charge is Rs 35; the charge for waiting is Rs 40 per hour; and prices are fixed. To the airport, the set price is Rs 80.

Getting Around
An autorickshaw is handy to get around, particularly if you have some heavy gear, or want to visit the nearby temples. From

Dhalpur to the bus station should cost about Rs 10, or to the airport at Bhuntar, Rs 40.

PARBATI VALLEY
Jari
Jari is halfway along the Parbati Valley – about 19 km from Bhuntar. It has recently been developed to cater for the hippy crowd who have spilled over from Manikaran, or who prefer Jari's peace and cheap rooms.

There are several cheap, friendly, basic places to stay. The *Om Shiun Guest House* (☎ 73-202) has double/triples, but some have no windows, for Rs 50/100. At about the same price, the *Roman Guest House* is OK. The *Krishna Guest House* is a little cheaper with singles/doubles for Rs 30/40. Other converted family homes, like the *Ratna* and *Village* guesthouses are further back from the main road, far quieter, more relaxed and cost about Rs 50 per person.

The best, and most popular, place for food is the *Deepak Restaurant* on the main road. The *Rooftop Cafe* on top of the Om Shiun Guest House has great views. At the Krishna, the mediocre *Freedom Restaurant* is downstairs. Parbati Valley buses will stop in Jari if required. A one-way taxi from Kullu to Jari is Rs 325.

Kasol
Kasol is another tiny village along the Parbati Valley road which has become a hangout. It's very pretty, in a lovely setting among pines and streams with some trout. The village is actually divided into 'Old Kasol', on the Bhuntar side of the bridge, and 'New Kasol', on the Manikaran side.

Most foreigners congregate around the *Rainbow Cafe and Guest House* in New Kasol (☎ 214). It has a few rooms for Rs 60 a double, and serves western food and eastern 'herbs' all day. Others stay in rooms at the back of village shops and homes.

The HPTDC has the *Tourist Hut* (☎ 74-8471), near the Rainbow Cafe, but it seemed to be abandoned at the time of researching. Perhaps it will reopen when the demand increases. It is worth checking out – a nice hut along the river normally costs Rs 150 a double.

Manikaran
Telephone Area Code: 01902

Famous for its hot springs, which apparently cure anything from rheumatism to bronchitis, and are hot enough to boil rice, Manikaran is another place where many foreigners have forgotten to leave. Manikaran means 'jewel from the ear' in Sanskrit. According to the local legend, a giant snake took earrings from Parvati while she was bathing and then snorted them through its nose to create spaces where the hot springs spewed forth.

The town is split into two, over both sides of the very loud Parbati River. Almost all of the guesthouses, places to eat and temples are on the northern side, where no vehicles are allowed. The first bridge you see as you approach from Bhuntar is a footbridge which leads to the hot springs under the enormous Sikh temple, and then out into the village. The second bridge is at the end of the Parbati Valley road, where there is a taxi and bus stand. There is no place to change money in Manikaran; the nearest bank is in Kullu town.

Temples The town is revered by followers of the Hindu and Sikh religions. The Hindu temple **Shri Ramchander** dominates the centre of the town. It's a quiet place where you can discreetly have a look around. Indian sadhus and western freaks huddle around outside the temple trying to get some sunshine. As you enter Manikaran, you cannot escape the extraordinary sight of the **Shri Guru Nanak Dev Ji** Sikh gurudwara.

Baths It's a good idea to have a hot bath while you're in Manikaran, if only to warm up. There are three alternatives: the hot baths (separate for men and women) under the Sikh temple; for a 20 minute bath, the Hotel Parvati charges Rs 15 for one person or Rs 20 for two; or there are baths in most local guesthouses.

Places to Stay Like the rest of the region, prices vary according to demand. The large, rambling HPTDC *Hotel Parvati* (☎ 73-838) has clean doubles at Rs 330, which is not good value around here. Of the cheaper places, the *Sharma Guest House* has good value doubles for Rs 50. It is close to the first footbridge – follow the signs around the village. Nearby, and of similar standard, the *Padha Guest House* (☎ 74-8228) charges Rs 60 a double, and has a balcony overlooking the loud river. There are one or two more good places around this area to choose from. Opposite the gurudwara, the *Goutam Guest House* is pretty good, but suffers from a distinct lack of sunshine, because of the towering Sikh temple.

Places to Eat Manikaran is now set up for short and long-term foreigners – there are several good places serving mostly western food. The unimaginatively named *Hot Spring* serves delicious pizzas; the *O-Rest* does similar food, and is popular. The *Holy Palace* has reasonable Italian and Israeli food. Nearer the gurudwara is the *SSMP* and *Shiva Restaurant*. Around the village, several dhabas serve cheap Indian food.

Getting There & Away Buses between Kullu and Manikaran leave every 30 minutes or so, or, alternatively, take a regular bus going to Bhuntar, and catch another on to Manikaran. Buses link Manikaran with Manali six times a day (Rs 35). Another option is a day trip from Manali on a tourist bus for Rs 140, which stops off at Kasol for a quick look, on the way.

A return taxi from Manali to Manikaran will cost Rs 900. A fixed-price taxi from the taxi stand at the end of the road into Manikaran will cost Rs 350 to Bhuntar (one way), and Rs 400 to Kullu (one way). A six hour sightseeing return taxi trip from Kullu along the Parbati Valley road costs Rs 550.

Around the Parbati Valley
From Manikaran, a well defined trail leads to the village of **Pulga** (four to five hours). The next stage continues on up the Parbati Valley to the hot springs at **Khirganga**, where Shiva sat and meditated for 2000 years. Here there are a number of tea houses

to spend the night before returning directly to Manikaran in one long stage. Porters and guides can be hired in Manikaran.

On the other side of the river from Jari, is the interesting Malana Valley. **Malana** (2652m) can be reached in a full day trek from Jari. There are about 500 people in Malana and they speak a peculiar dialect with strong Tibetan elements. It's an isolated village with its own system of government and a caste structure so rigid that it's forbidden for visitors to touch either the people or any of their possessions. It's very important to respect this custom; wait at the edge of the village for an invitation to enter.

Legends of Malana Valley
Local legends have it that when Jamlu, the main deity of Malana, first came here, he bore a casket containing all the other Kullu gods. At the top of the pass he opened the casket and the breeze carried the gods to their present homes all over the valley.

At the time of the Dussehra Festival in Kullu, Jamlu plays a special part. He is a very powerful god with some demonic qualities. He does not have a temple image so, unlike other Kullu gods, has no temple car to be carried in. Nor does he openly show his allegiance to Raghunathji, the paramount Kullu god, as do the other Kullu gods. At the time of the festival, Jamlu goes down to Kullu but stays on the east side of the river from where he watches the proceedings.

Every few years a major festival is held in honour of Jamlu in the month of Bhadon. In the temple at Malana, there is a silver elephant with a gold figure on its back which is said to have been a gift from Emperor Akbar. ■

KULLU TO MANALI
There are a number of interesting things to see along both sides of the 42 km valley between Kullu and Manali. There are two Kullu-Manali roads: the main highway runs along the west bank of the Beas, while the rougher, but more scenic, road goes along the eastern bank, through Naggar.

Vaishno Devi Temple
Four km along the Kullu to Manali road is the Vaishno Devi Temple – a small cave with an image of the goddess Vaishno. You may have to crawl in, and it's not really worth that much effort. There are several **temples** nearby dedicated to Lord Rama, Lord Shiva and Lord Krishna.

Raison
Thirteen km from Kullu, Raison is placed at a particularly wide and low part of the Kullu Valley. The HPTDC *Camping Site* (☎ 83-516) is right on the river. A hut with two bedrooms costs Rs 300, and a pretty camping spot is Rs 50. Above the river, in the village, is the *Saga Guest House*.

Katrain
Katrain is on one of the widest points in the Kullu Valley. The HPTDC's *Hotel Apple Blossom* (☎ 83-136) has doubles from Rs 200 to Rs 250, and a five bed dorm for Rs 45 per bed. The hotel has great views, but is looking a bit old and tired these days. The only other place in the village worth staying at is the cheap, family-run *Nangdraj Guest House*. A one-way taxi from Kullu to Katrain costs Rs 170.

Patlikuhl
Patlikuhl is the largest village between Kullu and Manali, and almost exactly halfway between the two towns. One of the few places to stay is the *Beas River Guest House*, near the bridge, with doubles for Rs 50. The *Avtar Guest House* (☎ 83-271) has similar basic facilities for Rs 75 a room. Being so close to the lovely village of Naggar, just across the river, there seems little or no need to stay at Patlikuhl.

Travellers have reported that the State Bank of Potalia at Patlikuhl is a good place to change travellers' cheques. In fact, if you have anything but Thomas Cook and American Express, this bank may be the only place in the Kullu Valley, including Manali, that will change your travellers' cheques.

Naggar
Telephone Area Code: 01902

Naggar is a lovely little village, set on a hill and surrounded by forests. There are good facilities and quite a few interesting things to see and do. Naggar can be visited in a day trip from Manali or Kullu, but if you have time Naggar is worth stopping over for a night or two.

Naggar Castle Naggar was capital of the Kullu Valley for nearly 1500 years. The castle, built about 500 years ago as the raja's headquarters, was converted to a hotel in 1978. The quaint old castle is built around a courtyard with verandahs right around the outside, providing stupendous views over the valley. Inside the courtyard is a small **temple** containing a slab of stone with an intriguing legend about how it was carried there by wild bees, and a small **museum**.

Temples There are a number of interesting temples around the castle and the village surrounds. The grey sandstone Shiva **temple of Gauri Shankar** is at the foot of the small bazaar below the castle and dates from the 11th or 12th century. Almost opposite the front of the castle is the curious little **Chatar Bhuj Temple** dedicated to Vishnu. Higher up the hill is the pagoda-like **Tripura Sundri Devi Temple** and higher still, on the ridge above Naggar, the **Murlidhar Krishna Temple**.

Roerich Gallery One km past the castle is the Roerich Gallery, a fine old house displaying the artwork of both the eccentric Professor Nicholas Roerich, who died in Naggar in 1947, and his son, Svetoslav Roerich, who died in Bangalore in 1993. Its location is delightful and the views over the valley are great. It's open daily from 9 am to 1 pm, and from 2 to 5 pm.

Places to Stay The reputedly haunted HPTDC *Castle Hotel* (☎ 83-116) has a good range of accommodation. The more basic rooms cost Rs 125, and others cost from Rs 300 and Rs 500. Dorm beds (10 in a room) for Rs 45 are often booked out. This is *the* place to stay in. (How often do you stay in a real castle?) Try to book in advance – it is very popular.

The *Poonam Mountain Lodge & Restaurant* (☎ 83-447) is near the castle. The owner is helpful and rents trekking gear. Good singles/doubles with hot water, overlooking the temple, cost Rs 100/120. The new *Hotel Ragini* (☎ 83-193) is in the middle range. It costs Rs 300 a room, with balcony, hot water and nice wooden decor in the rooms. The *Sheetal Guest House* (☎ 83-319) has older rooms with share bath for Rs 75/125, and up to Rs 400 for more luxury.

Of the many cheap guesthouses around the village (just follow the signs up the road to Naggar and around the village), two have been recommended: the *Snow View Guest House* (☎ 83-325), where good rooms cost Rs 100/120 with bath; cheaper singles from Rs 60; and the *Alliance Guest House* with similar prices and standard. Like anywhere in the Kullu Valley, these prices can drop significantly if business is quiet.

Nicholas Roerich, originally from Russia, settled in India and made a living from painting, and from the spiritual guidance he gave to followers in the USA.

Places to Eat The castle provides the best views, certainly the best atmosphere in the village, and the food is pretty good, too. Of the other hotels, the *Hotel Ragini* has a good, clean restaurant and the *Cinderella Restaurant* at the Sheetal Guest House is also worth a try. There are plenty of other places catering for the backpacker market, such as the *Poonam Restaurant*. Many have balconies, views, and good western food. Also, in the village on the main road, at the start of the road up to the castle, are plenty of cheap places to eat.

Getting There & Away Naggar Castle and the guesthouses are at the top of a steep two km path off the eastern Kullu-Manali road. To the castle, get off the bus at the village on the main road, and walk up, or take one of the autorickshaws milling around. Buses go directly between the village of Naggar (on the main road) and Manali six times a day (Rs 9). Alternatively, just wait by the road for a reasonably regular Kullu-Manali bus.

A return taxi from Manali to Naggar Castle will cost Rs 350; a return taxi from Kullu is Rs 450. A Kullu-Manali taxi, with a quick stopover in Naggar (if you smile nicely at the driver; or pay him extra – the latter is more likely to be successful) will cost Rs 425. Another way is to get the bus to Patlikuhl (there are more buses along the western side of the river) from either Manali or Kullu. Then take a taxi from Patlikuhl to Naggar Castle – or even walk, but it's steep, and about five km. From the Bhuntar airport, a taxi to Naggar Castle is Rs 400.

Jagatsukh

Between Naggar and Manali, Jagatsukh was another ancient capital of Kullu state until it was supplanted by Naggar. There are some very old temples in the village, notably the **Shiva Temple**. Shooru village nearby has the old and historically interesting **Devi Sharvali Temple**.

The *Rishi Guest House* is fairly ordinary, but still costs about Rs 140 a room. Because Jagatsukh is so close to Manali, it's an easy half day trip, or even a lovely walk along the road. From Jagatsukh, a steep trail leads to the Deo Tibba mountain (6001m) and to Chandra Tal (lake) (4800m), both of which are not far from the main road along Lahaul & Spiti.

Manali

Telephone Area Code: 01901
Peak Season: mid-April to mid-June, mid-September to early November, Christmas and New Year

At the northern end of the Kullu Valley and the Beas River sits the ancient site, but the modern town, of Manali. It doesn't have the colonial history or charm of Shimla, nor the culture and spectacular setting common in Lahaul & Spiti and Kinnaur. But it is a pleasant, if overdeveloped, town with lovely nearby countryside of forests and orchards for hiking, and there are good facilities for visitors.

In the 70s and 80s, Manali was very much a 'scene'. In the summer, the town would attract numerous western hippies and travellers drawn by the high quality marijuana that grows in the area. A lot of these people have moved to the nearby villages of Dhungri and Vashisht, or to Manikaran and Pulga, along the Parbati Valley. Now, the character of Manali has changed considerably; with literally hundreds of hotels and guesthouses, it's one of the most popular places in the country for honeymooning Indian couples.

Legend has it that Manu stepped off a boat in Manali to recreate human life after floods had devastated the world – Manali means 'home of Manu'.

Orientation

Manali is based around one street – The Mall. National Highway 21 on the left side of the Beas coming from the Kullu Valley becomes the busy, noisy Mall, which is not nearly as charming as its namesake in Shimla. The Mall splits at Nehru Park, which has a statue of the great man, and heads left (north-west) towards Old Manali, and right (east) to the main bridge. Across the bridge, the Naggar Highway, which runs along the right side of the Beas coming from the Kullu Valley, leads north past the nearby village of Vashisht and beyond, all the way to Leh.

From the bridge, the Naggar Highway also heads south along an area called Aleo, 'New Manali' or the Left Bank. (It's a bit confusing: it is the left bank as you travel from Manali to Kullu town). Aleo is an area with unexciting new hotels and little to offer the visitor.

Manali can be divided into an area known as Model Town, a charmless 'suburb' of new concrete hotels, one block west, halfway along The Mall; and the area unofficially known as the 'Tibetan area'. The Tibetan area is the start of Manali proper, and runs to the back of the Hotel Ibex. It is dominated by a Tibetan market, a gompa and more guesthouses.

Information

Tourist Office For tourist information go to the HPTDC Tourist Reception Centre (☎ 2175), which is the small, white hut, under the Hotel Kunzam. Open from 10 am to 5 pm in summer (fewer hours in winter), the Tourist Reception Centre should not be confused with the far larger HPTDC Tourism Marketing Office (☎ 2116) next door. This office sells bus tickets for HPTDC buses and makes reservations for HPTDC skiing courses, and hotels. The Marketing Office also has a useful noticeboard for the use of visitors.

Money The State Bank of India (SBI), just past the end of The Mall, on the way to Old Manali, will only change Thomas Cook and American Express travellers' cheques. Some travellers have been badly caught out by this, and have had to travel all the way to Mandi, or to Patlikuhl (between Kullu and Manali) to change other types of travellers' cheques.

The UCO Bank, opposite the HPTDC tourist offices, charges Rs 60 per transaction, and follows the same SBI restriction regarding travellers' cheques.

Post & Communications The post office is conveniently located in Model Town, and is open from 9 am to 5 pm every day; Sunday

and public holidays from 9 to 10 am, and 2 to 3 pm. The poste restante is more reliable and convenient than the ones in Leh or Kullu town. There are plenty of places in Model Town or along The Mall (but not in Vashisht, Dhungri or Old Manali) where you can make long-distance telephone calls, and send or receive faxes. Alternatively, you can make calls from the post office.

Travel Agencies Of the many travel agencies in Manali, the following places, run by locals, are reliable, have been long established, and organise their own tours:

Antrek Tours
  Manu Market (☎ 2292), which specialises in rock climbing and skiing
Chandra Trekkers & Expeditions
  The Mall (near UCO Bank) (☎ 85269), for trekking
Druk Expeditions
  Model Town (a little west of the Gozy Restaurant) (☎ 3135), for trekking and mountaineering
Himalayan Adventurers
  The Mall (next to the UCO Bank) (☎ 2750), for trekking and rafting
Himalayan Journeys
  The Mall (near the State Bank of India) (☎ 2365), for just about anything
North Face Adventure Tours
  The Mall (near the Mount View Restaurant) (☎ 2441), for paragliding and skiing
Snowbird Adventures
  Manu Market (☎ 2586), for trekking, mountain-bike trekking and skiing

Bookshops & Newsagencies The only bookshop in Manali is Bookworm at shop 16, in the NAC Markets, at the back of the bus station. A good range of English-language (only) novels can be bought or swapped. Daily English-language newspapers from Delhi and Chandigarh are available in the afternoon from the Verma Newsagency, under the Hotel Renuka, on The Mall.

Books & Maps Nest & Wings (India) put out a reasonable little booklet called the *Tourist Guide Map to Manali* (Rs 30), together with a large, fairly complete (but out of scale) map of Manali. *Tourist Paradise: Himachal* (International Publishers) (Rs 50) has some historical information, and plenty of advertisements. Although both can be bought in Manali, they are more readily available in the bookshops along The Mall in Shimla.

Film & Photography Several places along The Mall sell slide and print film, although it is a little expensive, and could be out of date. Both on The Mall, Parkash Studio, next to the UCO Bank, and Tibet Colour Lab, next to the Hotel Ibex, are good places to develop your prints (but not slides).

Medical Services Some travellers have reported that the Mission Hospital (☎ 2379) down School Rd, just off The Mall, provides good facilities and care. There are plenty of clinics and pharmacies around The Mall.

Dhungri Temple
The Dhungri or Hadimba Temple is a nice four storey wooden building in the middle of a lovely forested parkland, known as the Dhungri Van Vihar. Erected in 1553, the temple is dedicated to the goddess Hadimba. According to a local legend, Bhima killed the evil Hadimb, and married his sister Hadimba. She then became a goddess, who is worshipped at times of disaster. The temple has intricate carvings of dancers and characters from various Hindu stories, and horns of bulls and other animals decorate the walls. It is a very popular picnic spot for Indian tourists. Every May, there is a major festival at the temple.

Another legend says that Maharaja Bahadur Singh, who built the temple, arranged for the hand of the architect who designed it to be amputated so he couldn't design the same temple at any other place. But the cunning architect learned to draw with his left hand, and designed the temple at Triloknath, near Udaipur, in upper Lahaul & Spiti. Not to be outdone, the people of Manali, agreeing that such beautiful designs should never be replicated, then decided to cut off the architect's head!

On foot, follow the sign to the temple from the road out to the HPTDC Log Huts. Alternatively, walk past the Hotel Hilltop towards the Hotel Shrinagar Regency or the monstrous Hadimba Palace, through the apple orchards and past dozens of empty concrete guesthouses. It is an easy 20 minute walk; if you need directions, ask a local. A new road now goes all the way to the entrance of the park, near the temple, so a taxi or auto-rickshaw is another option.

Gadhan Thekchokling Gompa
Photos are permitted (for a small donation) in this small modern gompa – there are no priceless frescoes likely to be damaged by camera flashes.

Built by Tibetan refugees in the late 1960s, the gompa has some brightly coloured frescoes and a mid-size Buddhist statue. On the outside wall there is a list of Tibetan martyrs killed during the Chinese occupation from 1987 to 1989. The gompa, open from 6 am to 7 pm, dominates the 'Tibetan area' around the bottom of The Mall. There is a small Hindu temple nearby, but it is nothing special.

Old Manali
The original settlement of Manali is situated about three km north-west of the current 'new' Manali. Old Manali is a lovely area of old guesthouses and orchards, where livestock walk around aimlessly. It is worth a stroll around, even if you're not staying there. Past most guesthouses, the small **Manu Maharishi Temple** is where Manu meditated after he arrived in the area. To get to Old Manali, follow the road to the left at the top of The Mall and follow the signs – the village is across the bridge, and up the left hand road.

Markets
The Tibetan market, spread around the back of the Hotel Ibex, is a bit lifeless, but has many stalls selling shawls and other woollen clothes, and souvenirs – and it offers more choice and better prices than in Leh. Around the bus station, there are a few more stalls, and the NAC Markets, at the back of the bus station, has souvenir stalls and some travel agencies. The older Manu Market, along the eastern side of The Mall, has plenty of travel

agencies, hairdressers, dhabas with cheap food, and a good vegetable market for do-it-yourself meals, and to stock up if trekking.

Activities

Rafting Some basic rafting is available along the Beas River, depending on the weather and the state of the unpredictable Beas. Trips generally start at Mohal, halfway between the Bhuntar airport and Kullu town, and go onto Bajaura, a few km south of Kullu town – a total distance of about 10 km. For more adventurous rafting trips you will have to try the Indus or Zanskar rivers to the north, or maybe the Sutlej River, near Shimla.

The rafting season on the Beas generally lasts from May to mid-June, and, depending on the monsoon, from mid-September to mid-October. Himalayan Adventurers offer one day trips for about Rs 1250 per person, and Snowbird Adventures charges Rs 700. These prices, which depend on the number of passengers and your bargaining power, include transport, equipment, lunch and an 'experienced' guide (although the guide's 'experience' may be debatable).

Paragliding In summer, paragliding can be organised on the slopes of Solang Nullah, north of Manali, by the Himalayan Eagle Paragliding School (run by North Face Adventure Tours), Himalayan Adventurers, and Snowbird Adventures. Snowbird runs a one day course for Rs 650 per person; a week-long beginners' course, which costs Rs 4200; and a two week course for US$420. These prices include accommodation (if applicable), food, equipment and a guide, but not transport.

Skiing Skiing for beginners is possible at Solang Nullah from January to March; the later the better, because January is very cold. Refer to the section on Solang Nullah, in Around Manali, for details of courses there. Courses and tours can be arranged there, or through Manali-based agencies listed earlier in this section. Skiing in summer, between April and June, is possible at Rohtang Pass, north of Manali. This has not been developed

yet, and involves camping and skiing in generally rugged conditions. Ski gear can be rented from Snowbird Adventures, the Mountaineering Institute (see below), and North Face Adventure Tours. All the gear you'll need for a day's skiing will cost about Rs 250.

Helicopter skiing is a relatively new sport. For about US$600 a day, you can be dropped onto any deep snow fields around the region. Himalayan Journeys can organise this if you have the money, experience and courage.

Mountaineering Institute & Allied Sports

The institute (☎ 2342) is located about three km south of The Mall, not far from the Hotel Manali Ashok. It offers all sorts of tours and courses, which are outlined in a prospectus available from the institute for Rs 5. Established in 1961, the institute is an impressive complex with a library, museum and offices, and plenty of helpful experts if you want to try something adventurous around the region.

The institute runs a range of basic and advanced courses in mountaineering, rock climbing, skiing (refer to the Solang Nullah section for more details on its skiing courses), trekking and water sports. Class sizes are large (about 20 to 30 students). The cost is reasonable, even if foreigners have to pay about six times more than a Himachali (but the institute is subsidised by the local government). It offers mid-year three week basic and advanced mountaineering courses for US$220 per person, and two weeks of kayaking on the Beas River in October/November for US$140. Prices include food, gear, training and (dormitory) accommodation, but not transport.

Organised Tours

Tours are organised by the HPTDC Tourism Marketing Office, where you buy tickets, and by local private bus companies. They may be touristy, but are often the cheapest and easiest way to visit some local places, especially if you're on your own and you can't share the cost of a taxi.

Each bus agency offers four identical

trips. One is to Rohtang Pass (3978m) to feel some snow, via Nehru Kund (lake), Kothi and Marrhi for views, for Rs 125 per person. The second is to the fabulous village of Naggar, to visit the castle and art gallery, stopping at the Jagatsukh temples, with a side trip to Solang Nullah, for Rs 115. The third is along Parbati Valley, as far as Manikaran, stopping at Vaishno Temple, and maybe even to an angora rabbit farm, for Rs 140. The fourth is a local trip to the Dhungri Temple, and Vashisht, and not much else – all of which you can walk to easily.

Places to Stay

In Manali, prices are generally quite high, and vary considerably according to the season.

Prices are listed in hotel receptions, and are fixed by the government. This is the authorised maximum price, but there is nothing to stop a hotel or guesthouse offering an 'off-season discount'. In fact, if the season is quiet, you won't have to bargain too much, if at all, for the price to drop by up to a half. Prices below are for the high season, but, remember, prices will vary, almost from day to day. Some places will offer hot water; make sure it really does exist, and that the water supply is regular. A place with a generator is useful because blackouts are not uncommon. Many places add on an arbitrary 10% luxury tax.

Places to Stay – bottom end

Budget accommodation can be easily found in the nearby villages of Old Manali, Vashisht (see Around Manali section) and Dhungri – there are few cheap places in Manali itself.

Manali At the back of The Mall, the *Sukhiran Guest House* (☎ 2178) remains one of the best value places in Manali, at Rs 150 a double, with some dorm beds (eight in a room) available for Rs 30. A bucket of hot water is available for a little more. At the top of The Mall, the *Hotel Greenland* (☎ 2122) is popular, clean and convenient for about Rs 200 to Rs 250 a room. You can't beat the

Hotel Renuka (☎ 2309) for its central location, which makes it noisy, but there are good singles/doubles for Rs 200/300, with hot water and balcony. The *Samrat Hotel* (☎ 2356), a little further down past the Hotel Ibex, is pretty good value with doubles from Rs 350.

In the Tibetan area, crowded around the gompa, there are many basic, but comfortable, family-run and friendly guesthouses with appropriate names such as the *Potala* and the *Kathmandu*. These, and other romantic-sounding places like the *Sunflower* (☎ 2419) and the *Snow Drop*, offer clean, airy rooms in the range of Rs 100 to Rs 150, depending on the season, and the extra facilities they may offer. It's a convenient area, and worth looking around for a good place at a discounted price.

Old Manali Many travellers opt for the peace and quiet of Old Manali, a collection of old guesthouses, sometimes set among orchards. It is a three km walk from The Mall, which can be a drag if you're going in and out of Manali a lot. A trip on a three-wheeler, the local autorickshaw, is a good idea, especially if you have a lot of gear. The road to Old Manali starts to the left of the fork at the top of The Mall. At the bridge, just follow the signs advertising the places to stay. Almost everywhere is on or near the main road, and is not hard to find.

Over the bridge, and to the right, there are a few places, which are a little more expensive than in Old Manali proper but are in a great location. Some of the popular cheaper long-stays are the *Rising Moon*, *Apple View* and *Riverside* guesthouses which have doubles for about Rs 100. Crowding around the HPTDC Club House are: the *Hotel Riverbank* at about Rs 300 a double; *Hotel Him View*, with good value rooms from Rs 75; and the *Hema Guest House* (☎ 2285) for up to Rs 350 a double.

Over the bridge and up the hill to the left is the village itself. The basic *Hotel New Bridge View* has rooms for Rs 50/60, and larger rooms for a little more. The *Veer Paying Guest House*, and the *Kishoor Guest*

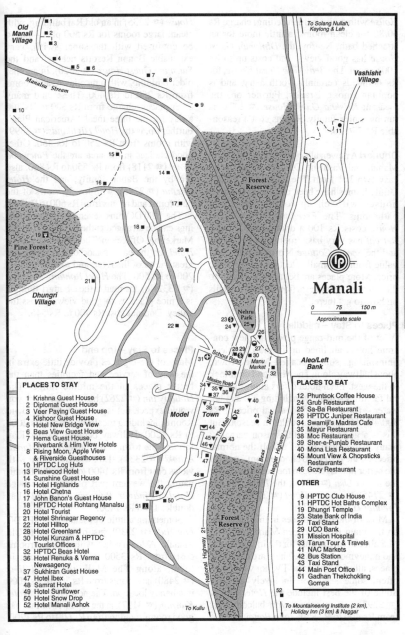

Manali

0   75   150 m

Approximate scale

*To Solang Nullah,
Keylong & Leh*

Old
Manali
Village

Manalsu Stream

Vashisht
Village

Forest
Reserve

Pine Forest

Dhungri
Village

Nehru
Park

Aleo/Left
Bank

School Road

Manu
Market

Mission Road

Model
Town

The Mall

Beas River

Naggar Highway

National Highway 21

Forest
Reserve

To Kullu

*To Mountaineering Institute (2 km),
Holiday Inn (3 km) & Naggar*

PLACES TO STAY

1   Krishna Guest House
2   Diplomat Guest House
3   Veer Paying Guest House
4   Kishoor Guest House
5   Hotel New Bridge View
6   Beas View Guest House
7   Hema Guest House,
    Riverbank & Him View Hotels
8   Rising Moon, Apple View
    & Riverside Guesthouses
10 HPTDC Log Huts
13 Pinewood Hotel
14 Sunshine Guest House
15 Hotel Highlands
16 Hotel Chetna
17 John Banon's Guest House
18 HPTDC Hotel Rohtang Manalsu
20 Hotel Tourist
21 Hotel Shrinagar Regency
22 Hotel Hilltop
28 Hotel Greenland
30 Hotel Kunzam & HPTDC
    Tourist Offices
32 HPTDC Beas Hotel
36 Hotel Renuka & Verma
    Newsagency
37 Sukhiran Guest House
47 Hotel Ibex
48 Samrat Hotel
49 Hotel Sunflower
50 Hotel Snow Drop
52 Hotel Manali Ashok

PLACES TO EAT

12 Phuntsok Coffee House
24 Grub Restaurant
25 Sa-Ba Restaurant
26 HPTDC Juniper Restaurant
34 Swamiji's Madras Cafe
35 Mayur Restaurant
38 Moc Restaurant
39 Sher-e-Punjab Restaurant
40 Mona Lisa Restaurant
45 Mount View & Chopsticks
    Restaurants
46 Gozy Restaurant

OTHER

9   HPTDC Club House
11 HPTDC Hot Baths Complex
19 Dhungri Temple
23 State Bank of India
27 Taxi Stand
29 UCO Bank
31 Mission Hospital
33 Tarun Tour & Travels
41 NAC Markets
42 Bus Station
43 Taxi Stand
44 Main Post Office
51 Gadhan Thekchokling
    Gompa

House with a nice garden setting, charge Rs 60/80 for clean rooms, a little more for an attached bath. Nearby, the *Diplomat Guest House* has good views, and costs up to Rs 100 a room. The *Beas View Guest House*, for Rs 60/80, is certainly worth a try, and is popular among Israelis. Further on, the pleasant *Krishna Guest House* (☎ 2271) is run by a nice family. Rooms cost a reasonable Rs 75/120.

Dhungri A newer, alternative hangout to Old Manali and Vashisht, Dhungri village is an easy two km from The Mall. Old village family homes have been converted to guesthouses with cheap rooms and share bathrooms. The *Freedom Paying Guest House* costs Rs 100 a double; the *Deodar Retreat* has very basic rooms for Rs 40/60; and the *Scenic Cottage* is probably the best value from the small selection for the same price. More places are being built. (Refer to the Dhungri Temple section for more details on how to get there.)

Places to Stay – middle

A lot of the mid-range places are new concrete hotels all lined up in the charmless, uninspiring 'suburb' called Model Town, about halfway along The Mall, and one block to the west. Each hotel offers almost identical facilities – usually including TV and hot water – for an almost identical price of Rs 300/400 for a single/double, in season. But this is a good area for off-season bargains; many places offer rooms at half the normal price. Of the dozens to choose from, some of the better hotels (close to the post office) are: the *Mona Lisa* (☎ 2447), the *Hotel Shishar* (☎ 2745), the *Lhasa Hotel* (☎ 2134) and the *Premier Hotel* (☎ 2473).

Most of the other places in this range are on the main road between Manali and Old Manali, catering mainly for the Indian family and honeymoon market. There are dozens of places, all of which offer TV, hot water and, often, some seclusion in lovely gardens. Some of the best include the *Hotel Tourist* (☎ 2297), where rooms with balcony cost from Rs 400 to Rs 850; *John Banon's Guest*

House (☎ 2335) in an old Raj building, with clean, large rooms for Rs 500 plus – not to be confused with the super swish, very expensive Banon Resorts nearby; and the *Sunshine Guest House* (☎ 2320), in another older building, with a nice lawn, and rooms from Rs 250 to Rs 400. These, and many other places, charge from Rs 300 to Rs 400 a day for the three meal 'American Plan'. Further up, is the *Hotel Highlands* (☎ 2399) with rooms from Rs 250 to Rs 450. Other good choices in the area are the *Pinewood Hotel* (☎ 2118) from Rs 550 to Rs 800, also run by the Banon family; and the *Hotel Chetna* (☎ 2245), with lovely views of the pine forest and rooms from Rs 500 to Rs 700.

The HPTDC runs several places – bookings can be arranged at the HPTDC Tourism Marketing Office on The Mall. The *Beas Hotel*, on the eastern side of The Mall, has great views of the river, and rooms from Rs 200 to Rs 500. The *Hotel Rohtang Manalsu* (☎ 2332), on the road to the Dhungri Temple, is a nice place, with good views across the valley. Doubles cost Rs 400 to Rs 545.

Places to Stay – top end

Many of these places provide little extra in the way of service and facilities than the better places in the middle range. The *Holiday Inn* (☎ 2262) has all the luxury you would expect, but is several km from town. Rooms, including meals, cost from Rs 2000 to Rs 4200. Halfway between the Holiday Inn and the town is the huge *Hotel Manali Ashok* (☎ 2331). Luxurious rooms with views cost from Rs 1400 to Rs 2000. Dominating the western part of town, the huge *Hotel Shrinagar Regency* (☎ 2252) has doubles from Rs 1400.

Something a little unusual is the HPTDC *Log Huts* (☎ 2330), just off the road to Old Manali. A luxury hut with two bedrooms costs from Rs 3500 to Rs 4000. Back in town, along The Mall, the *Hotel Ibex* (☎ 2480) has rooms from Rs 700 to Rs 1000 in a handy location. The new HPTDC *Hotel Kunzam* (☎ 3197), at the top of The Mall, has good rooms ranging from Rs 600 to Rs 1200.

Places to Eat

There is no shortage of great places to eat in the area. While Manali caters for all visitors, including Indian tourists, Old Manali, Vashisht (see Around Manali section) and Dhungri cater primarily for the budget backpacker crowd.

Manali For western food, such as hamburgers, pizzas and milkshakes, the *Sa-Ba* in Nehru Park, at the top of The Mall, is good, and in a nice location. Opposite, just past the start of the road to Old Manali, *Grub* has an awful name but serves good pancakes. The HPTDC's *Juniper Restaurant*, right near the bridge, offers a vast selection, in a good setting, but with higher prices. Just about every restaurant, regardless of what sort of food it may serve during the day, opens from about 8 am to serve good, hot western breakfasts.

The *Sher-e-Punjab*, on The Mall, has a sterile setting, but its Indian food (as well as pizza and pasta) is recommended, and is popular with Indian visitors. For good service and a great selection of authentic Punjabi and Gujarati food at a reasonable price, try *Gozy Restaurant* at the bottom of The Mall.

Down a little alley called Mission Rd, just off The Mall, is a group of cheap little places, all serving great vegetarian food. The *Mayur Restaurant* is very popular, and has a cosy decor; *Swamiji's Madras Cafe* has large thalis for Rs 35; and *Sangam*, *Meehak* and *Neel Kamal*, in the hotel of the same name, are also worth a try.

Halfway along The Mall are two highly recommended places for a great selection of Chinese, Tibetan and Japanese food. The *Mount View Restaurant* and, next door, *Chopsticks*, are cosy, friendly places where you can order genuine Chinese food – and not just chop suey – as well as momos or sukiyaki. They also have handy noticeboards for messages. *Moc Restaurant*, near the Sukhiran Guest House, also serves similar, but slightly lower-priced, Asian food.

Opposite the bus station, the *Mona Lisa* is another busy place, popular for its Indian and western food at good prices. Along The Mall, there are several dhabas, serving cheap, authentic Indian food – great places for a cup of chai and a couple of samosas. The *Kamal* and *Himalaya* are the best two around. In the Manu Market, there are also a couple of even cheaper dhabas.

The best place in the area is the Tibetan-run *Phuntsok Coffee House*, at the junction of the Naggar Highway and the road to Vashisht. It's worth coming from Vashisht, Manali (or just about anywhere in India) for, among other delights, its apple, banana or walnut cakes/pies with custard. (All three are highly recommended!)

Old Manali The best places are over the bridge, and up the road towards the village. They are easy to find. There are several outdoor places with great settings along the river, and it's worth a stroll out there even if you're staying elsewhere. They all cater for westerners, so you'll be lucky to find any real Indian cuisine.

Just over the bridge, and towards Old Manali, the *Ish Cafe* is deservedly popular. Nearby, the *Shiva Cafe* has good Italian food, and serves Israeli cuisine. The *German Bakery*, near the bridge, offers fresh goodies, but even better is the *Beas View Guest House* which serves great breakfasts, as well as freshly baked rolls and strudels. Nearby, the *Little Tibetan Cafe* serves wholesome, cheap Tibetan food. Opposite, the *Moondance Garden* is another laid-back, outdoor place.

Dhungri Near the guesthouses, *Our Freedom Cafe* serves some basic meals, as well as cooked breakfasts.

Entertainment

The HPTDC *Club House*, near the bridge on the way to Old Manali, offers some activities. For a Rs 5 one day temporary membership, you have access to the nice, but pricey, bar and restaurant, and a library where you can read (but not borrow) English-language books. Some indoor games, such as table tennis and snooker, can be played for a few extra rupees. The HPTDC Vashisht Hot Bath

HIMACHAL PRADESH

Complex is worth visiting to bathe in the hot sulphur water. (See the Around Manali section for details.)

The only place to find a drink is a very dingy bar in the Manu Market, or the expensive HPTDC hotels, which seem to have a monopoly on serving alcohol. There is a movie house on The Mall (if you want to see the latest Hindi love epic).

Things to Buy

There are plenty of places to buy clothes and souvenirs in Manali, particularly along The Mall. These places often claim to have 'fixed prices' but this is not strictly true. Some of the better places are the Tibet Emporium, near the post office, or any of the cooperatives run by local women, such as the Kullu-Kashmir Shawl Emporium, on The Mall.

Cheaper items, but probably of a lesser quality, can be bought at the many little roadside stalls. Many of these are set up in the evenings, especially around the Gozy Restaurant and the bus station. The Tibetan Market is another place to shop around. Manali has a better selection, and, for some reason, better prices than Leh for woollen clothes.

For an indulgence, try some of the locally made pickles, jams and juices, made from apples and apricots and other fruits and nuts. Natural oils for massages and shampoos are also available from the prominent shop on The Mall which sells nothing else.

Getting There & Away

Air Manali is connected by air with the rest of India through the Bhuntar airport, south of Kullu town, an inconvenient 50 km from Manali. Unfortunately, there are no flights between Manali/Kullu (Bhuntar) and Leh. Refer to Getting There & Away in the Kullu town section for details on flights which serve the Kullu region.

Bus The bus station is normally well organised. There are two booths – open from 9 am to noon, and from 2 to 5 pm – which provide computerised booking services. You can book a ticket up to a month in advance, which is very useful in the peak season.

The companies which do long-distance trips from Manali (and local sightseeing tours – refer to the earlier Organised Tours section) are listed below. Tickets for the long-distance bus trips can be bought from the respective bus companies, or from any other travel agency in Manali.

Enn Bee Tours & Travels, The Mall (opposite the bus station) (☎ 2650)
Ibex Travels, Hotel Ibex, The Mall (☎ 2480)
Swagtam Tours, Mission Rd (☎ 2390)
Tarun Tour & Travels, just off The Mall (☎ 2688)

Leh Several daily deluxe and public buses connect Manali with Leh from about June to late-September – a little later according to the weather and the demand. This is a long, but truly spectacular, ride over two days, with a stopover at a tent site. Manali is not high (2050m), so if you're not used to higher altitudes, take care along the way, especially at Baralacha La (4883m) and Taglang La (5328m). For details on the buses between Manali and Leh, and about the trip itself, refer to the Leh to Manali section in the Ladakh & Zanskar chapter.

Kullu & Parbati Valleys Public buses regularly go between Manali and Kullu town (two hours, Rs 17). They travel along both sides of the Beas River, but mostly via the quicker, western bank (if the road has been repaired since the devastating flood of 1995). To Naggar (one hour, Rs 9), there are six daily buses from Manali, leaving every hour or so from 9.30 am.

Along the Parbati Valley, six public buses leave Manali from 6.30 am to 1.30 pm every day to Manikaran (Rs 35).

Other Places To Delhi (16 hours), every day in summer, there is one public 'deluxe' bus (Rs 345), two overnight HPTDC buses (Rs 400 non-air-con; Rs 600 with air-con), and usually several private buses (about Rs 400). Private companies and the HPTDC (both for the same price) also run daily buses, in season, to Shimla (10 hours, Rs 225), Dharamsala (10 hours, Rs 170), and Chandigarh (10 hours, Rs

250). With demand, there may be private buses to Jammu and Dalhousie.

There are three daily public buses to Dharamsala (Rs 85); two to Keylong (seven hours, Rs 60); five to Delhi (Rs 168); six to Chandigarh (Rs 105), leaving in the early morning; four to Shimla (Rs 85); and five to Mandi (five hours, Rs 45).

Note: Beware of low-hanging power lines on the trip between Manali and Dharamsala if you're riding on the roof of the bus.

Taxi Long-distance taxis are available from the taxi union stands on The Mall. Taxis are not a bad option if travelling in a group. To Leh, a taxi costs a hefty Rs 10,000. A one-way/return taxi from Manali to Kullu is Rs 350/500, or from Rs 650 to Rs 750 return for a bit of sightseeing along the way. To other destinations, taxis from Manali cost about Rs 4000 to Kaza, Rs 1500 to Dharamsala, Rs 2500 to Udaipur and Rs 2000 to Keylong.

Truck Trucks are a good alternative for travel between Manali and Leh. In Manali, there is no particular truck station; trucks congregate along the two roads into Manali, usually just on the outskirts. It's a matter of getting out there, finding a truck, and asking around for a lift. To Leh, a lift should cost about Rs 300. Trucks are not a real option between Manali and Kullu or Manikaran because buses are so regular and cheap.

Motorcycle Refer to the Leh to Manali section in the Ladakh & Zanskar chapter for details on this mode of travel.

Getting Around
The Airport For buses between Bhuntar airport and Manali, take a regular Bhuntar-Kullu and a regular Kullu-Manali bus, or there may be a less regular one that goes directly between the airport and Manali. A taxi from Manali to Bhuntar or vice versa costs Rs 425.

The official office for Archana Airways is Ambassador Travels (☎ 2110), next to the State Bank of India. Jagson Airlines (☎ 2476) has an office at shop 24, NAC Markets. For other airlines, use any reputable travel agent in Manali, or ring the airline offices in Kullu town or Bhuntar yourself.

Taxi There are two taxi stands, both on The Mall, run by the HPTDC: Aanchal Taxi Operator's Union (☎ 2120/2135; 24 hours). Taxis are not really needed for trips around Manali, because you can walk or take a far cheaper three-wheeler. Taxis offer sightseeing trips to Vashisht, Old Manali and a couple of local temples for Rs 300, but this trip can be done on foot. Taxi prices are fixed; the minimum charge is Rs 35; and waiting costs Rs 40 per hour.

Three-Wheelers Autorickshaws, known locally as three-wheelers, can take you, and your heavy luggage, to Dhungri, Old Manali and Vashisht, but not much further, for very negotiable prices.

Bicycles Mountain-bikes are an excellent way to see the nearby countryside and to commute from Old Manali or, if you're fit, Vashisht. Himalayan Journeys rents mountain-bikes for Rs 125 per day. Snowbird Adventures will organise mountain-bike treks, if there is enough demand – to as far as Lahaul & Spiti, and even Leh! – for about US$40 per person per day.

AROUND MANALI
Vashisht
Vashisht is a lovely little village, high up the mountainside, about four km from The Mall by road. Its hot springs are a great way to relax after the long trip from Leh, and a good place to go if your hotel has no hot water, or if it does but the electricity has stopped. There is a decaying temple in the village dedicated to Vashisht Muni and Lord Rama.

The footpath and road to Vashisht go straight past the HPTDC Vashisht Hot Bath Complex, open every day from 7 am to 7 pm. It is a large area, full of little Turkish-style sauna rooms, where you can bathe in the hot sulphur water. A 30 minute soak costs Rs 30 a single, Rs 40 a double, and Rs 10 for every extra person. A towel costs an extra Rs 2.

TREKKING OUT OF THE KULLU VALLEY

There are a number of interesting treks that can be undertaken out of the Kullu Valley. These include treks out of Manali or from the nearby villages of Jagatsukh or Naggar or from Manikaran in the Parbati Valley.

There are several trekking agencies in Manali who can assist with trekking arrangements, including the hiring of guides and porters. Allow Rs 250 per day for guides and Rs 150 for porters. Pack horses are also available on some of the treks and cost around Rs 150 per day per pony. It is advisable to bring your sleeping bag and tent with you, as most of the good quality gear in Manali is only for hire to those on organised treks. A tent is also a necessity on most of the treks as there are no tea houses or PWD huts on most sections of these treks.

A trek out of the Kullu Valley can be completed from the end of June until the end of October. The residual winter snowfalls are always a consideration if planning to trek early on in the season, while the region is subject to the monsoon with heavy rains from the end of July until mid-September. Thereafter the weather pattern becomes clear and settled until the first of the winter snows fall on the high passes from mid to late October.

Manali-Chandra Valley Trek (via the Hampta Pass)

The trek over the Hampta Pass to the Chandra Valley in Lahaul is one of the most popular in Himachal Pradesh. The trek commences from Prini village which is four km down the Kullu Valley from Manali. The initial stage of the trek is up through pine forest to the village of Sythen. From here the trail enters the Hampta Valley with its verdant meadows that are occupied by Gujar and Gaddi shepherds throughout the summer months. There are many ideal campsites to choose from and a leisurely pace is recommended to assist with acclimatisation before reaching the Hampta Pass (4270m). From the pass, the peaks of Deo Tibba (6001m) and Indrashan (6221m) can be appreciated. The descent to the Chandra Valley is steep and care should be exercised when crossing the fast flowing Indrashan River en route to the roadhead and settlement at Chatru.

From Chatru there are a number of options including extending the trek up the Chandra Valley to the idyllic Chandra Tal (4250m) before ascending to the Baralacha La. From here the trail meets the Leh to Manali road and transport can be organised for the drive to Leh and the Indus Valley. Alternatively there is a daily bus from Chatru to Manali or to Kaza in the Spiti Valley.

Stage 1	Prini to Sythen & camp (3 to 4 hours)
Stage 2	Sythen to Chhikha (3 to 4 hours)
Stage 3	Chhikha to Bhalu ka kera (3 hours)
Stage 4	Bhalu ka kera to Siliguri via Hampta Pass (7 hours)
Stage 5	Siliguri to Chatru (3 hours)
Stage 6	Chatru to Batal (5 to 6 hours)
Stage 7	Batal to Chandra Tal (6 to 7 hours)
Stage 8	Chandra Tal to Tokpo Yongma (6 hours)
Stage 9	Tokpo Yongma to Tokpo Gongma (6 to 7 hours)
Stage 10	Tokpo Gongma to Baralacha La (4 hours)

Jagatsukh-Deo Tibba Trek

This delightful trek to the base of Deo Tibba commences from the village of Jagatsukh. The trek winds through a series of small villages to the grazing pastures at Khanol. From here it is a steady ascent up the forested gorge (steep in places) to the Gujar encampment at Chhikha. The alpine trail then crosses the extensive meadows where Gaddi shepherds graze their flocks. The meadows are carpeted with wildflowers in July and August while the hanging glaciers beneath Deo Tibba form an impressive backdrop at the head of the valley.

Stage 1	Jagatsukh to camp (2 hours)
Stage 2	Khanol to Chhikha (4 to 5 hours)
Stage 3	Chhikha to Serai (4 to 5 hours)
Stage 4	Serai to Deo Tibba base & return (7 hours)

Naggar-Parbati Valley Trek (via the Chandrakani Pass)

The trek over the Chandrakani Pass (3650m) commences from the village of Naggar. The trail to the pass goes via the village of Rumsu before winding up through conifer forest to the alpine meadows that afford magnificent views of the Kullu Valley, the Pir Panjal Range and many of the 6000m plus peaks that form the crest of the main Himalaya. The pass crossing is not difficult but the descent to Malana village is very steep, even for the sure-footed.

The isolated village of Malana supports its own system of government and a caste system so rigid that it's forbidden for visitors to touch either the people or any of their possessions. The rules for entering the village have been relaxed over the last decade or so. However, it is best to camp well away from the village and not to intrude too closely on the daily lifestyle.

From Malana it is a further stage down the valley to the roadhead at Jari. From here there are buses back to the Kullu Valley and Manali.

Stage 1	Naggar to Rumsu & camp (2 to 3 hours)
Stage 2	Rumsu to camp below Chandrakani Pass (5 hours)
Stage 3	Across the Chandrakani Pass to Malana (6 hours)
Stage 4	Malana to Jari (4 to 5 hours)

Manikaran-Spiti Valley Trek (via the Pin Parbati Pass)

The Parbati Valley provides a number of trekking options including the challenging trek over the Pin Parbati Pass to Spiti. There is also a shorter trek from the roadhead at Manikaran to the hot springs at Khirganga (2850m).

From Manikaran the well defined trail leads to the village of Pulga before continuing along a forest trail to the hot springs at Khirganga. Here there are a number of tea houses where you can spend the night before returning directly to Manikaran on one long stage.

The trail up the Parbati Valley continues through mixed forest to a series of alpine pastures to the famous Pandu Bridge, a natural rock bridge over the Parbati River. It is a further stage to Mantakal Lake before crossing extensive moraine and boulder fields to the base of the Pin Parbati Pass (4730m). The pass is located at the head of a small glacier and there are magnificent views of the main Himalaya Range.

From the pass the trail descends through a series of small settlements to the roadhead at Sangam where there is a daily bus service to Kaza, the headquarters of Spiti.

Stage 1	Manikaran to Pulga (4 to 5 hours)
Stage 2	Pulga to Khirganga (4 to 5 hours)
Stage 3	Khirganga to Bhojtunda (5 hours)
Stage 4	Bhojtunda to Thakur Khan (4 to 5 hours)
Stage 5	Thakur Khan to Mantakal Lake (6 to 7 hours)
Stage 6	Mantakal Lake to high camp (7 hours)
Stage 7	High camp to Pin Valley camp via Pin Parbati Pass (5 hours)
Stage 8	Pin Valley camp to Mud (8 to 9 hours)
Stage 9	Mud to Sangam (4 to 5 hours)

The common public baths (separate areas for men and women) in the Vashisht village are free, but do not look very hygienic. These baths are open from 5 am to 9 pm every day.

Places to Stay Vashisht remains a very popular place for long-term budget travellers, who are attracted by its cheap facilities, great setting, and the availability of some locally grown 'horticultural products'. Most places to stay are located along the road up to the village, or crowded around the village centre and the temple. Vashisht is about a four km walk north of Manali, or you can get a three-wheeler there.

The *Dharma* (☎ 8241), a bit of a walk

behind the temple, and the *Amrit, Dolnath* and *Kalptaru* guesthouses all offer very similar, no-frills, older-style accommodation, usually with share bathroom, for about Rs 60 a room. Newer, clinical, but reasonable value, is the *Prachi Hotel & Restaurant*, which also serves fresh trout. Just down the road from the village centre, the cheaper *Sanam* and *Janata* guesthouses also have basic rooms from Rs 60.

More expensive, but still good value, is the *New Surabhi* with nice rooms and a *real* bath with hot water for Rs 350 – about half that in the off season. The *Hotel Bhrigu* (☎ 8240), and the *Hotel Valley View* next door, offer good rooms, and great views, for Rs 200 to Rs 425 a room.

Places to Eat The cafe at the HPTDC Hot Baths Complex serves hot and cold drinks, and a selection of pretty good Chinese and Indian food. Next door, the *Rose Garden Inn*, with great views, has pricey, but delicious, Italian and other 'continental' food. In the village, the *Hari Om Cafe Bijurah* is popular for its snacks; the *Super Bake*, next to the temple, serves wonderful baked goodies; and one or two places, such as the *Kathmandu Cafe*, provide cheap, authentic food. Good places to hang out are the *Ranu* or the *Zodiac Cafe*, next to the Sanam Guest House.

Just down the road a bit, the *Freedom Cafe* has a great outdoor setting, and serves pretty good western food and cold drinks, although it's a little more expensive than it used to be. The *Hotel Bhrigu* and nearby *Hotel Valley View* offer something a bit more up-market, with views. The Bhrigu serves a great vegetarian thali for Rs 35.

Getting There & Away Vashisht is connected by a good road, so a three-wheeler can take you there – which is a good idea if you have loads of gear. On foot, it's quicker not to take the road. About 200m past the turn-off by road to Vashisht, take an unmarked trail up, which starts opposite a small dhaba. If in doubt, ask a local; it is a commonly used trail, which goes all the way to the Hotel Valley View, via the HPTDC Hot Baths.

Vashisht to Solang Nullah

The main northern road from Manali to Rohtang Pass is dotted with little villages, and some hotels. At Bahang, there are one or two places to stay, such as the *Laxmi Guest House*. From Bahang you can explore and admire the nearby, dramatic **Jogni waterfalls**. Nehru Kund is famous as the place where former Prime Minister Nehru relaxed in 1958 and 1960 after sorting out India's problems, and tasted the delights of a nearby spring. There is nothing much there now but a big hotel – the *Hotel Ekant*, which has rooms from Rs 450 to Rs 500.

Solang Nullah

Some of Himachal Pradesh's best ski slopes are at Solang Nullah, about 14 km north-west of Manali. There are 2½ km of runs, with black, red and blue routes mainly for beginners, and one 300m ski lift. February and March are the best months to ski; January is bitterly cold, and Christmas time can be busy with Indian tourists. But don't disregard Solang if it isn't snowing; the area is very pretty in spring and summer. If you want some seclusion, Solang Nullah is worth a stay for a few days. This is outstanding hiking country and a perfect place to day trip out to when there's no snow.

There are several options for skiing courses. (Refer to the Travel Agencies section under Manali for details of agencies there involved in skiing.) Firstly, the HPTDC organises seven day skiing packages. These include accommodation in Manali (which is not the least bit convenient if the road between Manali and Solang is snowed under), food, lessons and some sightseeing for Rs 3200 per person, excluding transport to Solang.

As it's better to stay in Solang, the second option is better – take a course based at a hotel in Solang. The Raju Paying Guest House, through Antrek Tours in Manali, offers seven to 10 day packages, including accommodation, all meals, porters and instruction, for Rs 600 per day; Rs 200 extra per day for ski-gear hire. The Friendship Hotel in Solang offers similar week-long packages. Manali-based agencies North

Face Adventure Tours and the Hotel Ibex offersimilarpackages,withaccommodation inSolang.

Snowbird Adventures (also Manali-based) seems to have more to offer. A five day basic or intermediate course costs Rs 5000, including transport, accommodation, food, gear and an instructor. Five day all-inclusive advanced courses are Rs 10,000. A one day all-inclusive trip with some skiing and horse riding costs Rs 1000. Cross-country skiing/trekking costs Rs 1200 per person per day, all inclusive.

The third option is the Mountaineering Institute & Allied Sports. It runs basic, intermediate and advanced all-inclusive 16 day courses for US$170, which includes rental of gear, food and dormitory accommodation near the slopes – but not transport.

Places to Stay & Eat All places are in the tiny, picturesque village, only a few hundred metres below the ski slopes. Prices listed are for the high season, but they will probably halve in the off season. The small *Friendship Hotel* has large rooms for Rs 300, and Rs 150 for smaller rooms with a common bathroom. The *Raju Paying Guest House* has large doubles with nice wood panelling for Rs 200, or Rs 300 for a room with up to four beds. The *North Face*, which offers a more basic, but still comfortable, alternative place to stay caters mainly for prearranged skiing packages.

Each hotel serves large plates of simple, hot vegetarian food, accompanied by loads of tea. There are several other good restaurants around the village catering for the tourist crowd, but these are usually closed in the off season.

Getting There & Away A bus leaves Manali at noon and 1 pm every day to Solang Nullah (Rs 5). A nicer way is to take the bus to Palchan, the turn-off to Solang Nullah from the main road, and then walk for about an hour to Solang through gorgeous countryside. If you're fit you can head north along the western side of the Beas River along any trail starting from Old Manali. It's about a 12 km hike.

Lahaul & Spiti

Lahaul & Spiti, the largest district in Himachal Pradesh, is a vast area of high mountains and narrow valleys bounded by Ladakh and Tibet to the north, Kinnaur to the east and the Kullu Valley to the south. Lahaul is often regarded as a midway point en route to Leh and the Indus Valley. It does, however, have much to offer. Spiti has only recently been opened to foreign tourists attracted to the isolated Buddhist gompas and villages.

Lahaul consists of two regions – upper Lahaul which includes the Chandra and Bhaga valleys and lower Lahaul which comprises the region of the Chenab Valley below the confluence of the Chandra and Bhaga rivers. Spiti is located to the east of Lahaul and comprises the populous Spiti Valley.

Both Lahaul and Spiti are cut off from the Kullu Valley for many months of the year. The Rohtang Pass linking the Kullu Valley and Lahaul was completed in the 1960s, and it is only relatively recently that a motorable road was constructed from Lahaul to Spiti over the Kunzum La. However, both road passes are closed due to heavy snows for much of the year. To combat Lahaul's winter isolation, a tunnel under the Pir Panjal is being constructed to provide year round access to the Kullu Valley; for Spiti the road down valley to the Sutlej Valley and the Hindustan-Tibet highway is being upgraded to ensure better links with other parts of Himachal Pradesh.

The climate of Lahaul & Spiti is similar to that of Ladakh. Lahaul is wedged between the main Himalaya Range to the north, and the peaks of the Pir Panjal Range to the south. It is the Pir Panjal that effectively blocks out most of the rain, particularly during the monsoon. The region of Spiti is situated between the Himalaya and the Zanskar ranges. Like Lahaul, the air is rarefied and clear on account of its elevation, which on average is well over 3000m. Cultivation is therefore restricted to the depths of the valleys, where irrigation schemes have

HIMACHAL PRADESH

been developed over the centuries. Like the Zanskar region of Ladakh, Lahaul & Spiti is subject to heavy snowstorms in the early winter, which close the passes for many months of the year.

The area is very pleasant in summer (from June to September) when it is warm during the day and the nights are cool. In winter, there is plenty of snow, which cuts off Lahaul, north Spiti and upper Kinnaur for six or seven months a year, and temperatures can drop to -30°C. But a daily bus usually manages to run – except during periods of heavy snowfall in January and February. Beware of the burning power of the sun in this region – you can get burnt very easily even on cold days.

HISTORY

In many ways Lahaul & Spiti's historical background runs parallel with that of Ladakh. Accounts recall how sages crossed the Rohtang Pass and the Baralacha La en route to Ladakh. In the 10th century, upper Lahaul was united with Spiti and Zanskar as part of the vast Lahaul-West Tibet kingdom sometimes referred to as Guge. Ladakhi influence at this time stretched to the upper limits of the Kullu Valley, and for centuries the Kullu rajas paid tribute to Leh.

Although political allegiances changed over the centuries, it was Ladakh's defeat by the Mongol-Tibetan armies in the 18th century that led to Lahaul being split into two regions. Upper Lahaul came under the influence of the Kullu raja, while lower Lahaul, across to the district of Pangi, came under the influence of the courts of Chamba. Trade agreements evolved between Kullu and Ladakh, and Lahaul was considered neutral territory. Records have it that trade was conducted during the summer months in a series of camps on the vast Lingti Valley just beyond the Baralacha La.

Spiti was more geographically isolated than Lahaul. It did not command any major trading crossroads and paid tribute to Ladakh until the Dogra army under Zorawar Singh installed a governor for a brief period between 1834 and 1839.

After the annexation of Kullu in 1841, the Sikhs extended their power north across Lahaul and for a time the entire region came under the influence of Ranjit Singh. However, the Sikhs did not establish their influence over Spiti. A small army made a token invasion but the region remained part of Ladakh until 1846.

In 1847, Kullu and Lahaul came under the British administration as a division of the Kangra state. Spiti was linked to Ladakh at the time and became part of the newly formed maharaja's state of Jammu & Kashmir. However, in 1849 it was exchanged for other territories and came under the Kangra administration.

Under British administration, the region's trails were upgraded, and bridges were constructed along the main trading highways that linked Kullu, Lahaul and Spiti. Records recount how huge logs were hauled over the Rohtang Pass by upwards of 200 porters, while the system of *begar*, or forced labour, was the only means that contractors had for improving the roads.

While the Nonos, or rulers, of Spiti tended to confine their trading activities to the Tibetan borderlands, the Hakurs of Lahaul secured many valuable trade agreements with Kullu and the towns to the south. To maintain these agreements many of the Hakurs set up bases in the Kullu Valley – a situation that has continued to the present day.

PEOPLE & CULTURE

In Spiti, most people are Buddhists, and colourful gompas dominate the villages and village life. In Lahaul, about half of the population is Buddhist, while the other half is Hindu. In some Lahauli temples and homes, it is not unusual to see idols from both religions side by side.

The people of Lahaul & Spiti congregate into communal groups (*kotchis*), which are then divided into smaller groups (*puttees*). Farms, which are usually inherited by the eldest son, rely on natural springs or complicated irrigation systems, to grow their crops. Barley (*no*), wheat (*do*), potatoes (*aalu*) and feed for their goats, sheep and yaks, or an animal which is a cross between a cow and a yak, called a *zo*, are grown. Lahaul & Spiti is the only area in India where hops are grown, mainly for the manufacture of beer, as well as coffee and chocolate. *Kuth*, a famous herb with apparent medicinal powers, is exported to Europe.

Food and drink in the region is similar to Tibet and Ladakh – noodles called *thukpa*; fried or steamed dumplings called *momos*; *tsampa*, which is cooked or raw barley flour; barley wine called *chang*; yak butter tea; and a bread made from buckwheat called *kalhu*.

During ceremonies and festivals, men and women sometimes decorate themselves with jewellery called *murki* and *kyanti*; women sometimes wear similar items called a *kirkistsi*. The men in the region often wear a long thick coat called a *cholu*, fastened at the waist by a *gachi* – but this sort of traditional dress is slowly being replaced by modern clothes. You may see the men play a high-spirited Tibetan dice game called *cholo*.

The main indigenous language of the area is Bhoti, which is very similar to Tibetan. There are several distinct, but mutually comprehensible, dialects in the region, such as Machat (spoken around Udaipur) and Gaheri (found near Keylong). If you have travelled to Ladakh, you'll be glad to know that the very handy word *jule*, which means hello, goodbye, please and thank you, is also used in Lahaul & Spiti.

PERMITS
Inner Line Permits are not necessary for travel to Spiti and you are now permitted to go as far down valley as Tabo. A permit is only necessary if you're travelling between Tabo and Rekong Peo, the capital of Kinnaur.

Seven day permits are available from the Senior District Magistrate (SDM) in Kaza, Keylong and Rekong Peo, from the Deputy Commissioner in Kullu or Shimla, and from the Ministry of Home Affairs in Delhi. They are best obtained in Kaza or Rekong Peo. In Kaza, you will need a group of four people to apply (but this has been relaxed, as it is often difficult to get a group together); three

passport-sized photos (but this has also often been waived – there is nowhere in Kaza to get any photos done); an application form from the Magistrate's office; and a lot of patience – the whole process could take up to a day.

Despite what may be written on the permit, you can stay in any village and camp anywhere along the main road between Kaza and Rekong Peo; you can travel on any form of public or private transport; and you can travel alone or in a group of any size.

KAZA
Telephone Area Code: 01906

Kaza is the major transport hub along the vast eastern part of Himachal Pradesh, and is the administrative centre of the subdistrict of Spiti. It is an easy-going place to spend a few days – to rest from the arduous bus trips, or to wait for your permit if you're going on to Kinnaur.

Orientation & Information
Kaza can be easily divided into two areas. The 'old town', south of the current bus stand, is a maze of little shops, hotels and houses. The 'new town', a collection of government buildings, including the District Magistrate's office (look for the Indian flag), is over the creek. The State Bank of India doesn't change travellers' cheques, but may be able to exchange small US dollar notes. There is a small gompa, not particularly old or interesting, of the Sakyapa order, at the back of Sakya's Abode hotel – there are better gompas not too far away.

Places to Stay & Eat
In the new town, the best place to stay is *Sakya's Abode* (☎ 254), run by a helpful family and set in a lovely garden. Good rooms cost Rs 200; a bucket of hot water, Rs 5. Next door, *Milarepa's Guest House* is good value, but a bit scruffy – rooms cost Rs 100. About one km from Milarepa's, on the main road to the north, the new *Khangsar Hotel & Restaurant*, above the government offices, is a bit far out to be of use. Rooms cost about Rs 200.

HIMACHAL PRADESH

In the old town, there are a few ordinary places from Rs 50 to Rs 80 a room, such as the *Hotel Sharma* and the *Hotel City*, both near the current bus stand, and the *Ladakhi Hotel* next to the large chorten, further down into the old town. Slightly up-market is the *Zambala Hotel & Restaurant* (☎ 250), next to the State Bank, where large rooms cost Rs 150.

Sakya's Abode does good Spitian food, basic Indian meals, and breakfast. In the old town, several places, such as the *Lyul Cafe* and *Flax*, serve thukpa and momos. Better is the restaurant in the *Zambala*. The *Whispering Willows* in the old town has a restaurant which is more inviting than the very small, rocky camping site of the same name next door.

Getting There & Away

The Taxi Operators' Union in Kaza has no stand or office; if you want to hire a taxi, your guesthouse will find a local with a car. Taxi fares are high because of the lack of competition and petrol transportation costs. The first hour of waiting is free, then it's Rs 50 per hour.

The bus stand is in the top end of the old town, near the creek, but a new bus station will be built soon. Get to the bus early to make sure that you get a seat, or a ticket. A bus to Rekong Peo (12 hours, Rs 77) leaves Kaza at 6 am. There is a bus between Kaza and Shimla on alternate days (two days, Rs 195) via Rekong Peo; and one or two daily buses to/from Manali (12 hours, Rs 115). There are also irregular buses between Kaza and Keylong (eight hours).

AROUND KAZA

Dankar Gompa

Built nearly 1000 years ago, Dankar Gompa has a spectacular rocky setting. Once the site of the capital of Spiti, and then a jail, the gompa has over 150 monks, some outstanding thangkas (usually locked away), sculptures, frescoes and a statue of Dhyan Buddha (Thinking Buddha). Some of the gompa was destroyed during a particularly harsh winter in 1989.

The gompa is also popular for the medicinal herbs grown there, which cure lung and heart complaints. Some lamas come from as far as Dharamsala to collect these herbs.

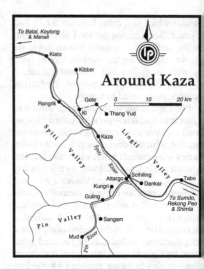

There is a small **lake** about three km to the back of the Dankar village. Fifteen km from Dankar is the **Lhalung Gompa**, which is not located on most maps (so you will have to ask directions to get there). Lhalung Gompa is over 1000 years old – reputedly older than the one at Tabo – and famous for its woodcarvings and isolation.

Getting There & Away From Kaza to Dankar, take one of the irregular local buses directly there, or any other bus going in that direction. Get off at the village of Scihiling, from where there is a steep eight km walk (including an altitude increase of about 600m), or, if you are lucky, there might be a daily bus between Scihiling and Dankar. A return taxi from Kaza to the Dankar Gompa costs Rs 700; or just to Scihiling, Rs 500 return.

Ki Gompa & Kibber

Ki, the oldest and largest gompa in Spiti, about 14 km from Kaza, was built by Ringchen Zangpo and belongs to the Gelukpa order. The gompa was invaded three times in the 19th century by Ladakhis, Dogras and Sikhs. It was damaged by fire, and was partially destroyed by an earthquake n 1975. A modernised head lama (he often wears jeans) leads the hundred or so monks, who spend their days training, painting or playing music.

Although being restored (donations are welcome), the gompa is still famous for its priceless collection of ancient thangkas, including Tibetan silk thangkas up to 800 years old, and frescoes depicting the life of Padmasambhava. No photos are allowed. There are a few trinkets for sale.

About 11 km from Ki village is the small village of Kibber, also known as Khyipur. It claims to be the highest village in the world, at 4205m, although Gete (4270m), another village about seven km east of Ki, has a better claim to this honour. Kibber was a part of the overland salt trade centuries ago, and is a pretty little place. The Ladarch Festival in Kibber each July attracts Buddhists from all over the region.

Places to Stay & Eat Kibber has three small guesthouses. The *Sargaung Guest House*, *Parang La Guest House* and *Sargong Hotel*, offer no-frills rooms for about Rs 50, and are easy to find. They also offer some very basic food. It may be possible to stay at the Ki Gompa if you ask.

Getting There & Away Some travellers have attempted to walk to both Ki and Kibber from Kaza in one day, but it is a very long walk (about 22 km from Kaza to Kibber). From Kaza, head along the northern road for about four km, cross the bridge (there are signs) and then the steep road starts. The Ki Gompa is actually about three km by road above the Ki village. There is an unmarked turn-off to the gompa, but you will see the gompa clearly from the road.

In summer, a bus leaves Kaza every day to Ki and Kibber at 8 am. This will allow you time to see Ki village or Ki Gompa while the bus goes to, and comes back from, Kibber, but you won't be able to see both Ki and Kibber in one day. A return taxi from Kaza to both the Ki Gompa and Kibber costs Rs 500; to only Ki and back, Rs 300; or to only Kibber and back, Rs 450.

Along the way up, check out some of the flying foxes – small wooden boxes operated by pulleys and wire strung across the enormous valley. These flying foxes are still used as the only way to cross some more remote valleys in the region.

Pin Valley

Pin Valley starts just south of Dankar, along the Pin River. The valley is reputedly famous for its wildlife – tourist agencies refer to it as the 'Land of Ibex and Snow Leopard', but you are likely to see little else but marmots. Along the valley there are several gompas following different forms of Buddhism to that normally found in Lahaul & Spiti. The village of **Guling** has a gompa, which belongs to the Nyingmapa order, where you can stay. The most important gompa in the valley is the 600 year old gompa at **Kungri**, a few km from the main road down the valley.

This is trekking and camping country. Public transport is scarce, and guesthouses nonexistent, although there is a government rest house at **Sangam**. Buses from Kaza go about 25 km along the valley road as far as the village of Mud. Alternatively, get off the bus on the main Lahaul & Spiti road, walk to Attargo, the gateway to the valley, and wait for a lift.

Tabo Gompa

Tabo Gompa is one of the most important in all of the Tibetan Buddhist world, and is planned as the place where the current Dalai Lama will retire. It was built in 996 AD by The Great Translator, Ringchen Zangpo, who brought artists from Kashmir to decorate the gompa. Designed in a western Tibetan style, the gompa houses impressive murals, and sculptures. There are eight temples in the complex, all at ground level and some dating from the 10th century. A new **painting school** founded by the Dalai Lama is also there.

On the other side of the road, opposite Tabo village, there are some **caves**, known locally as *duwang*, with some famous ancient murals. The caves have been damaged over the years, but are being gradually restored.

HIMACHAL PRADESH

You will have to ask for directions to find them. The 1000 year anniversary of the Tabo Gompa was held in June 1996.

A few rooms may be available at the gompa, for a donation, or at the Forest Department and PWD *rest houses* in the village. The *Himgiri Restaurant*, near the bus stop, serves very ordinary food, but you will have little or no other choice. Tabo is two hours one way by bus from Kaza. It's a time-consuming day trip, but it may be the only option until some places to stay are built at Tabo village. From Kaza to Tabo, take the 6 am bus, which goes on to Rekong Peo, and catch any afternoon bus back.

Thang Yud Gompa

About 13 km north of Kaza, and seven km from Gete, the 14th century Thang Yud Gompa, also known as Hikim, belongs to the rare Sakyapa order. There are no roads or public transport to this secluded gompa. It involves a steep trek, and you'll need reliable directions from local people.

KAZA TO KEYLONG

From Kaza, the main road through Lahaul & Spiti continues towards Udaipur and beyond, turns north at Tandi towards Leh via Keylong, or goes south at Gramphu towards Manali. The first main village along the road is Losar, about 60 km from Kaza. It is pleasant enough, but has little to recommend a stopover. A little further on is the **Kunzum La** (4551m). From the pass, a 12 km trail goes to the lovely **Chandra Tal** ('moon lake'), at about 4250m, and continues to Baralacha La, on the road to Leh.

Batal is the starting point for treks to nearby **Bara Shigri** ('big glacier'), up to 10 km long and one km wide, and one of the longest glaciers in the Himalaya. Get off at Gramphu (or Keylong) if you want to continue on to Manali. Khoksar is desolate and regarded as the coldest place in Himachal Pradesh. Sissu, which has a rest house where you may be able to stay, is the location of the revered **Lord Geypan Temple** – not currently open for tourists.

The road continues on to Gondla, the start-

ing point for a visit to the **Guru Ghantal Gompa** at the village of Tupchiling, a steep four km away. Founded about 800 years ago, but repaired extensively about 30 years ago, the gompa is linked to the one at Stakna, near Leh in Ladakh, and belongs to the Drukpa order. Guru Ghantal is built from wood, and renowned for its carvings and idols of Padmasambhava.

KEYLONG

Telephone Area Code: 019002

Located on a fertile plain, Keylong, the capital of Lahaul & Spiti, is a reasonable place to break up the journey from Leh to Manali (although you're almost at Manali anyway), to base yourself for day trips to nearby gompas.

Places to Stay & Eat

The *Tourist Bungalow*, run by the HPTDC, has a few doubles at Rs 200, and some dorm beds (10 in a room) for Rs 45. During the summer (June to late September), they also set up tents which cost Rs 125 for two people. Other reasonable places with singles/doubles for about Rs 80/120 are the *Lamayuru*, although some rooms can be dark and dirty, the *Geypa Hotel* and the *Hotel Gang Steng*. In the higher range, the *Hotel Snowland* has good, but overpriced, rooms from about Rs 300.

All hotels will serve something reasonable to eat, or try one of the tea houses around the town. The restaurant at the *Lamayuru* is one of the better places. It has good food and music and a pleasant atmosphere.

Getting There & Away

Two daily buses travel directly between Keylong and Manali (Rs 60). To Kaza, there are irregular buses in season. The main way in and out of Keylong is to catch one of the regular buses which travel between Leh and Manali in summer. The comfortable HPTDC bus costs Rs 100 from Keylong to Manali, or Rs 600 from Keylong to Leh (plus tent accommodation and food); private buses cost slightly less; and the public bus will cost about half the HPTDC price depending on which class you choose, or which is available. Plenty of trucks ply the busy road and are a great alternative. (Refer to the Leh to Manali section in the Ladakh & Zanskar chapter for more details on travel to and from Keylong.)

AROUND KEYLONG
Khardong Gompa
The 900 year old gompa at Khardong, formerly a capital of Lahaul, is only four km from Keylong. Of the Gelukpa order, this is the largest gompa in the area with about 30 lamas and *chomos* (nuns). There are good frescoes, some old prayer drums, a large Buddha statue and a famous library of ancient scriptures. The trail to the gompa starts across the other side of the Bhaga River.

Shashur Gompa
Three km from Keylong is the Shashur Gompa. Dedicated to a Zanskari lama, it was built in the 16th century and is of the Gelukpa order. The five metre thangka is famous in the region. An annual festival, held every June or July (depending on the Tibetan calendar), is renowned for the mask dances performed by the lamas.

Tayal Gompa
Six km from Keylong, in the village of Satingri, is a gompa called Tayal, which means 'chosen place' in Tibetan. The 300 year old gompa has a library, a fine collection of thangkas and a four metre high statue of Padmasambhava.

PATTAN VALLEY
The upper Chenab Valley is sometimes known as the Pattan Valley. This is the section of the Chenab Valley between the village of Tandi down to the village of Udaipur. Tandi rests at the confluence of the Chandra and Bhaga rivers. It is a little-visited area, regularly bypassed by tourists travelling between Manali, Keylong, Leh and Kaza, but not by the thousands of pilgrims who flock to the Triloknath Temple every August for the three day Pauri festival.

The main town in the valley, Udaipur, has its own finely carved wooden temple, built in the 15th century and dedicated to the goddess Markula Devi. About 16 km from Udaipur is the ancient **Triloknath Temple**, near the village of Tunde. Once a Hindu temple, then rededicated to Buddhism with a white marble six armed image of Avalokitesvara, it is now sacred to followers of both religions. There are also some Kashmiri influences in the temple's design.

Udaipur has a couple of government rest houses and some basic guesthouses. Buses to this valley start from Keylong, and are irregular. There are also direct daily buses from Manali.

Kinnaur

Telephone Area Code: 017852
Kinnaur is a district of Himachal Pradesh situated between the Shimla district and the Tibetan border. The region was derestricted and opened up to tourism in 1991. Travel to and around Kinnaur is now possible with easy-to-obtain permits.

The early history of Kinnaur is sparsely recorded. Perhaps the most remarkable fact is that the region was (unlike nearby Lahaul & Spiti and Ladakh) not invaded by the forces of West Tibet (Guge).

In the 19th century the region, as with the Shimla Hill states, paid tribute to the Gurkha rulers and thereafter to the British colonialists. A tribute was exacted by the Superintendent of the Shimla Hill states that included terms of military support should it be needed and the provision of a system of *begar* (forced labour) to work on the construction of roads in the area. The agreement also included the leasing of forests to the British which resulted in the establishment of forest rest houses for local forest officers on their tours of duty. Following local protests, the system of begar was abolished in 1920-21. In 1960, Kinnaur became a district of Himachal Pradesh, with the capital at Kalpa. The

Kinnaur

Not to Scale

The external boundaries of India on this map have not been authenticated and may not be correct.

capital was transferred to nearby Rekong Peo a few years ago.

Kinnaur is bounded to the north by the formidable Zanskar Range that provides the border with Tibet. To the south, the main Himalaya Range forms the backdrop of the region including the impressive Kinnaur Kailash Range, with the peaks Kinnaur Kailash (6050m), Jorkanden (6473m) and Phawarang (6349m), that provides an effective barrier to the monsoon rains. South of Kinnaur Kailash Range is the popular Sangla Valley, which has been described as one of the most scenic in the entire Himalaya.

Kinnaur is drained by the Sutlej River, which flows from close to Mt Kailash in Tibet through the Zanskar Range before joining the headwaters of the Spiti River. Thereon the region is characterised by deep gorges as the waters surge through the main Himalaya Range and flow south to Rampur.

The road up the Sutlej Valley – the Hindustan Highway – remains open for most of the year. The ideal time to visit the popular Sangla Valley is either in the springtime from April to the end of May or in the autumn in September and October.

PEOPLE & CULTURE

Because of regular mentions in ancient Hindu texts, including the *Ramayana*, Kinnauris have always regarded themselves as a distinct people of the Aryan group. Nearer the Tibetan border, Tibetan and Mongol features are also obvious. Most Kinnauris follow a mixture of Hinduism, which they gained from the area's ancient links with the rest of India, and Tibetan Buddhism. Especially near the borders of Tibet, villagers often have a Hindu and Buddhist name, and lamas continue to influence village life. Attempts by missionaries to introduce Christianity to the areas of Kinnaur in the 19th century never succeeded.

Probably the most distinctive part of the Kinnauris' dress is the grey, square woollen cap worn by men and women. It is curled up at one side, edged with red and green strips, and is called a *thepang*. On men, the thepang is often accompanied by a woollen shirt called a *chamu-kurti* and a coat. Women wear dresses called a *sari dhori* covered by the all-purpose *choli* or *bergi* (shawl), fastened by a *digra*.

Most Kinnauris live in two storey houses, with one storey used as a workshop or for the storage of animals, and the other for living. These houses, which usually have a *togang*, or balcony, always face the sun, and can be seen in small villages dotted along the mountain sides. Kinnauris are mostly involved in subsistence agriculture and breed sheep, goats (*chigu*) and yaks. The climate and altitude is perfect for apples, apricots and walnuts (*akrot*).

Barley and wheat are the dominant crops, and peas and potatoes are often grown. Kinnauris like to eat meat; tradition forbids them to consume chicken; and there is a burgeoning fishing industry around the Baspa and Spiti rivers. They enjoy alcohol (*ghanti*), such as *angoori* grape wine and *arak* made from fermented barley.

Kinnauri (often called Homskad) is the major indigenous language which has about 2 different dialects. One of these is called Sangnaur, and is only spoken in the village of the same name, near Puh.

PERMITS

From the Shimla region, you can travel as far as Rekong Peo, Kalpa and the Sangla Valley without a permit. For travel to northern Kinnaur and as far as Tabo in Spiti, you currently need a permit. These can be obtained from the Senior District Magistrate's office in Shimla, Keylong, Kullu and Chamba, or the Sub-District Magistrate's office in Rampur and Nichar. However, they are easier to get in Rekong Peo, Keylong or Kaza. (Refer to the Lahaul & Spiti section for further details on permits from Kaza.)

The only place to obtain a permit in Kinnaur is the district capital, Rekong Peo. The permit is valid for seven days but can be easily extended in Rekong Peo or Kaza. The permit allows you to travel from Rekong Peo to Kaza and back; from Kaza onwards you do not usually need to get another permit (although some travellers have required one, so check for the current situation). In Rekong Peo, you must apply for the permit in a group of at least four, which may be difficult if there are not a lot of travellers around. You can travel alone, however, or in a group of less than four, and by any available public or personal transport.

Firstly, you will need three passport-size photos – there are photo booths in Rekong Peo if you don't have any. Secondly, get a 'letter of introduction' from a travel agency. About the only place in Rekong Peo is the Mandala travel agency (next to the Mayur Guest House) which will charge a pricey Rs 100 per person. Ask the manager of Mandala to earn his fee and help you hurry up the magistrate.

Thirdly, complete an application form, available at the travel agent or the magistrate's office. Fourthly, take a photocopy of the front pages of your passport (with your personal details and photo) – there are several places which will do this in Rekong Peo. And lastly, take it all to the magistrate's office, a three-storey building, just below the bus stop. The whole process may take an entire day, so start early.

You can ignore the rules on the old forms. For instance, they state that: a) you are not allowed 'any night halt' – you *are* allowed to stay anywhere along the main road, but there is little choice anyway, and you can camp; b) you 'shall not resort to photography' – there is no restriction, but be careful around any sensitive or military areas; and c) you cannot carry any 'maps' – you are allowed to do this, but the maps aren't very good anyway. But you should never venture too close to the Tibetan border or too far from the main roads. The checkpoints between Rekong Peo and Kaza are at Jangi, Chango and Sumdo.

REKONG PEO

Up a side road from the main thoroughfare through Kinnaur are the two main towns of Kalpa, the former capital, and Rekong Peo, the current capital of Kinnaur. Both places have the most stupendous settings in probably all of Himachal Pradesh – anywhere up the road will give you incredible views of the mighty Kinnaur Kailash mountain, among several others, at around 6000m. While it may lack the charm of nearby Kalpa, Rekong Peo is probably a better place to stay because it has better facilities and transport connections, and it is where you will have to apply and wait for your permit anyway, if going on further to Kinnaur or Lahaul & Spiti.

Orientation & Information

Rekong Peo is very small; everything is within a yak's spit of the bus stop in the centre of the village. The banks here do not change foreign currencies. There are plenty of little shops around the bus stop, and up a lane to the north of the bus stop. At these shops, you can take photocopies of permits and passports, and stock up on some necessities (mineral water is not sold around here) for the trip to Lahaul & Spiti, where village shops have very, very limited supplies.

A lovely, brightly coloured gompa, the **Kinnaur Kalachakra Celestial Palace**, is about a 20 minute steep walk above the village, just behind the radio station. Inaugurated by the Dalai Lama in 1992, the gompa itself is not the major attraction – there is a huge outdoor Buddha statue, in an area

overrun by apple orchards, and facing the mighty Kinnaur Kailash mountain. The setting alone is probably worth the trip to Kinnaur.

Places to Stay & Eat

There are a couple of reasonable places in Rekong Peo, but nothing of particularly good value. The *Hotel Snow View* is opposite the bus stand and, therefore, noisy. It has clean rooms and hot water for Rs 200 a double, and gets no prizes for the originality of its name. Better is the *Hotel Fairyland*, 200m from the bus stop. For Rs 200 a room it has hot water, and the views from some of the rooms would cost an absolute fortune in Europe. The only budget option is the *Mayur Guest House*, next to the Fairyland. The Mayur's dingy rooms offer little or no privacy and cost about Rs 80. Very ordinary dorm beds, which cater for the bus crowd stopping overnight, cost Rs 30.

There are a few tea shops along the main street, but the best bet for food is the *Snow View* or the *Fairyland*. The latter has a good selection of Indian food, and serves very cold drinks (when the electricity is working).

Getting There & Away

The chaotic little ticket booth, about 80m from where the buses actually stop, sells tickets for all buses, but most people just get on the bus and pay the conductor. There are occasional buses to Powari, at the turn-off to Rekong Peo on the main road, and to Kalpa – but it is certainly quicker to get a taxi to these places. A daily bus from Rekong Peo goes to Kaza (12 hours, Rs 77) at 7 am; several buses each day, starting from 4.30 am, go to Shimla (10 hours); and there's one bus a day to Rampur. Unfortunately, some of these buses do not originate in Rekong Peo or Kalpa, so they are often hopelessly full by the time they arrive.

A curiously apathetic bunch of taxi drivers lounge around the village centre. If you plead, they may give you a one-way/return ride to Kalpa for Rs 100/150; or a one-way ride to Powari for Rs 100.

GARRY WEARE

PAUL GREENWAY

MICHELLE COXALL

GARRY WEARE

A		
	C	
B	D	

Himachal Pradesh
A: Atop Kunzum La, the pass between the regions of Lahaul and Spiti.
B: The view from behind Kinnaur Kalachakra Celestial Palace.
C: Mani stones, Dalhousie.
D: Chorten, Kinnaur.

MICHELLE COXALL

PAUL GREENWAY

MICHELLE COXALL

PAUL GREENWAY

MICHELLE COXALL

A	
B	C	D
E	

Himachal Pradesh

A: Rural scene en route to Brahmani Mata Temple.
B: Basheshar Mahadev Temple, Bajaura.
C: Buddha, Dalai Lama's Temple, McLeod Ganj.

D: Viceregal Lodge, Shimla.
E: A break in the weather.

KALPA

Known as Chini when it was the main town in Kinnaur, Kalpa is the legendary winter home of Shiva; during the winter, the god is said to retire to his Himalayan home here and indulge his passion for hashish. In the month of Magha (January/February), the gods of Kinnaur supposedly meet here for an annual conference with Shiva. Kalpa was also a favourite resting place for several high-level British colonialists.

Kalpa is a tiny collection of narrow lanes, seven km and 600m higher in altitude up a windy road from Rekong Peo. What it lacks in facilities, Kalpa makes up with atmosphere, charm and history. The road between Rekong Peo and Kalpa takes you through a pretty area of forests, overshadowed by peaks. The walk can be shorter, but still steep, if you go straight up the hill rather than follow the road.

Places to Stay & Eat

There are only two places to stay in Kalpa – both are relatively expensive. The *Timber Lane Trekking Camps* is 600m from the village centre. It's in a great location, and has some luxuries like hot water, but they only have glorified tents, for which they charge Rs 650 per person. The whole place packs up and goes back to Delhi from October to May.

Far better value, and well worth the effort of getting there, is the *Circuit Rest House* – now renovated for tourists. A huge double room, with bathroom and fireplace, with spine-tingling views of Kinnaur Kailash just outside, costs Rs 250. It is about a two km walk from Kalpa. It is best to take a one-way taxi there (Rs 100) from the bus stop at Rekong Peo.

Getting There & Away

There are irregular buses between Kalpa and Rekong Peo. Long-distance buses to/from Rekong Peo often do not go through Kalpa, so for bus transport out of Kalpa, you will probably have to get to Rekong Peo first. If you can find one, a taxi may take you from Kalpa to Rekong Peo for Rs 100; or Rs 150, return.

SANGLA VALLEY

The Sangla Valley is also called the Baspa Valley because it follows the 95 km long Baspa River. The valley is a remote area, full of wildlife and dominated by spectacular mountains.

Sangla village, has a **temple** dedicated to Nagesh. From the village, you can trek about two km to Kamru which has a five storey, wooden **fort**. Kamru is a former capital of the Bushahr Empire which once ruled Kinnaur. The valley road continues to Rakchham, which means 'rock bridge'. The 44 km valley road finishes at Chitkul, where there are three **temples**, dedicated to the goddess Mathi, built about 500 years ago.

REKONG PEO TO SUMDO

From Rekong Peo to Kaza in Lahaul & Spiti, there is no official accommodation. If you make arrangements in Shimla, Kaza or Rekong Peo, you may be able to stay at the rest houses owned by the Public Works Department (PWD) at Puh, Jangi, Yangthang and Morang. Alternatively, there are plenty of suitable camping sites along the way.

About 20 km north of Powari is **Ribba**. This pleasant little place is famous for its 1000 year old gompa and angoori grape wine. **Morang** also has a gompa, with renowned sculptures and carvings. The village of Puh is the usual place for buses to stop and for passengers to eagerly devour large serves of dhal, rice and vegetables. At Khabo, the mighty Spiti River fades out and is replaced by the dominant Sutlej River. About 10 km further on, Kah is the starting point for a one km walk to the **Tilasangh Gompa**.

From the Yangthang checkpoint, it's about a seven km walk to Nako, close to the Tibetan border. Dominated by Leo Pargial, Nako is famous because of the legend that Padmasambhava created the village by throwing a rock there. His footprints on a rock in the village are still worshipped. Nako village is set around a lovely, small lake which freezes in winter. The 11th century **gompa**, of the Drukpa order, has four temples. Destroyed badly by an earthquake in 1975, there are still some *mandalas*, murals and damaged masks to see. There is nowhere to stay in Nako, but camping is allowed.

TREKKING OUT OF KINNAUR

The trek over the Charang La (5260m) commences from the village of Thangi. While the initial stages of the trek are at present being upgraded into a jeepable road, the fascinating gorge country and the villages en route make the trek worthwhile. The highest village at Charang is situated at the base of the pass. Here trekkers should spend time acclimatising before crossing the pass and a number of intermediary camps are recommended in addition to the stages outlined below.

The pass is located at the head of a small snow field and offers outstanding views of the Kinnaur Kailash Range and south to the Himalayan divide between the Sangla Valley and the Har ki Dun Valley in Uttar Pradesh. There is a very steep descent from the pass to the roadhead at the village of Chitkul where there is a bus service down valley to Sangla village.

Porters are available from Thangi; budget for Rs 150 per day.

Note: Do not consider doing the trek in reverse. The trek from Chitkul to the pass is very steep and does not allow sufficient intermediary camps for acclimatisation before crossing the pass.

Stage 1	Thangi to Lambar (4 to 5 hours)
Stage 2	Lambar to Charang (5 to 6 hours)
Stage 3	Charang to Lalanti (4 hours)
Stage 4	Lalanti to Chitkul via the Charang La (7 to 9 hours)

Southern Himachal Pradesh

Telephone Area Code: 01702

There are several areas of interest in the southern regions of the state, including the old settlement of Nahan, and the picturesque Renuka Lake. If you're heading for the hill station of Mussoorie in northern Uttar Pradesh, you'll find you'll need to travel via Paonta Saheb, on the border, which has an ancient Sikh gurudwara.

NAHAN

The historical town of Nahan was founded in the early 17th century by Raja Karan Prakash. Now the headquarters of the Sirmour district, Nahan is set in a pretty area of southern Himachal Pradesh, on a good road linking Shimla with Dehra Dun. Nahan hosts a festival called Sawan Dwadshi at the end of the monsoon season, when over 50 idols of Hindu gods are placed in a pool of water at a nearby temple. Nahan is a good place to break a journey, to use as a base for a day trip to the nearby Renuka Lake, and to enjoy some hiking in the countryside.

Nahan is actually built on two levels above each other on a hill side and linked by the steep main road. One level is dominated by the football ground, next to the Lytton Memorial building – this is the best place to base yourself. The other level is around the bus stand.

Places to Stay & Eat

Opposite the football ground, the *Hotel Renuka* has singles/doubles for Rs 75/100, with attached bath, but the rooms downstairs are windowless and uninspiring. At the back of the Lytton Memorial, on Hindu Ahram Rd, the *Keshav Guest House* (☎ 2459) has good, quiet doubles for Rs 100.

There are also a couple of places to stay near the bus station, but they are fairly ordinary. The *Hotel Renuka* has a reasonable, small restaurant, and, nearby, the *New Mehek Restaurant* is OK.

Getting There & Away

The daily Shimla-Dehra Dun bus goes through Nahan (Rs 55), and other regular local buses also go to Dehra Dun from Nahan. About every hour, crowded buses leave Nahan for Dadahu, near Renuka Lake, and others go to Paonta Saheb. You can get off or on the bus at the Nahan bus station or outside the Hotel Renuka. A one-way taxi from Shimla to Nahan (or to Renuka Lake) costs Rs 1200.

RENUKA LAKE

About an hour by bus from Nahan is Renuka Lake or Renukaji, which is fed by underground springs. It's a lovely place to visit from Nahan, or, even better, to stay and relax for a day or two. A week-long festival is celebrated here in November.

To enjoy the lake, walk along the three km circular track, or walk seven km up a path to the **Jamu Peak** for great views. You can also hire a small rowboat from the Hotel Renuka for Rs 30 per half-hour; a tour in a motorboat, in season, costs Rs 100. The lake has plenty of large (protected) fish. Around the lake there are thousands of gorgeous butterflies, a small **aviary** with local birds, a **wildlife park** (open in the tourist season) with some deer, and several Hindu **temples**, including the Parashuruma.

Places to Stay & Eat

The only place to stay around the lake area is the HPTDC's *Hotel Renuka* (☎ 8339). Comfortable rooms in secluded gardens, with a children's playground, range from Rs 300 to Rs 500, with TV and hot water. It is worth booking ahead before you make the trip to Renuka Lake. Surprisingly, there is nowhere to stay in the village of Dadahu, four km away, but this may change if there is some future demand.

The *Hotel Renuka* has a good restaurant. Near the entrance to the wildlife park, several stalls have hot and cold drinks and serve some basic meals.

Getting There & Away

About every hour, a bus from Nahan goes to Dadahu, from where you can walk (40 minutes) to the lake, but some buses do continue on to the lake. A one-way taxi from Shimla to the lake will cost Rs 1200.

PAONTA SAHEB

On the Uttar Pradesh Border is the uninteresting town of Paonta Saheb. Dedicated to the 10th Sikh guru, Govind Singh, who lived there between the age of 16 and 20, the town's gurudwara is an impressive place, situated right on the river. During the Holi festival in March, the temple overflows with pilgrims.

Inside the temple, there's a small **museum** dedicated to Govind Singh. Below the gurudwara is the **Yamuna Temple**. Rules for entry are the same for all Sikh temples: bring a head covering (or borrow one from a counter on the right at the temple entrance); take off your shoes (and if you value them, leave them at a counter on the left at the temple entrance); and then wash your feet.

Places to Stay & Eat

The HPTDC's *Hotel Yamuna* (☎ 2341) is about 100m from the entrance to the temple. It is the best option. Doubles cost Rs 200 to Rs 600. The very few budget options are awful. *Omjee's Hotel* on the main street, north of the temple, is about the best – rooms cost Rs 80, and there's a downstairs restaurant. Cycle-rickshaws can take you around, which is not a bad idea – at an altitude of only 350m, Paonta Saheb is hot.

Getting There & Away

The daily Shimla-Dehra Dun bus goes through Paonta Saheb (Rs 72). There are other regular local buses to Shimla, via Nahan, and to Dehra Dun. Two daily buses directly connect Paonta Saheb with Delhi. A taxi from Shimla to Paonta Saheb costs Rs 1500 one way.

HIMACHAL PRADESH

Uttarakhand

Population: 5,932,146
Area: 51,100 sq km
People per sq km: 58
Language: Hindi, Garhwali, Kumaoni, English
Literacy Rate: 58%
Best Time to Go: mid-May to mid-July; mid-September to mid-November
Seasons:
Winter (off season) – December to February
Spring – March to May
Summer – June to August
Monsoon (off season) – July to August
Autumn (mid-season) – September to November
Peak Tourist Season – May to June, Dussehra (September), Diwali (November)
Pilgrim Season – late April to mid-November
Rafting Season – September to March

Traditionally the hills of Uttar Pradesh (UP) stretching between Himachal and the eastern border of Nepal are known as Uttarakhand – the 'northern parts'. Historically this is a spiritually evocative term for Hindus. They dream of making a pilgrimage at least once in this lifetime to attain *moksha* (release) at the feet of their gods. Today Uttarakhand refers to eight hill districts of northern Uttar Pradesh which make up the culturally distinct provinces of Garhwal and Kumaon. The pilgrimage sites of the Char Dham – four sacred shrines marked by the sources of the Yamuna and Ganges and the temples of Kedarnath and Badrinath – are located in Garhwal.

HISTORY

Stone age implements found in Garhwal date back to 8000 BC. Waves of Aryan invaders and settlers in the millennia between 1500 BC and 1500 AD pushed the aboriginal population and the Mongol highlanders to the periphery of society.

An Ashokan edict near Kalsi, west of Mussoorie, indicates effective penetration of Buddhism into the hills. The fact that the Chinese pilgrim Hsuan Tsang spent time in the area in the 7th century, probably at Uttarkashi, is further evidence of this. The Hindu reformer Shankaracharya is credited in the 9th century with restoring the Brahmanical faith.

Between the 8th and 14th century the Katyuri Dynasty, who ruled from central Kumaon, held sway in Uttarakhand leaving a legacy of beautiful temples in Josimath, Baijnath (Garur) and Jageshwar. The Katyuri Dynasty was succeeded by Kumaon's Chand rajas whose first capital was at Champawat but was later moved to Almora.

In Garhwal, the Panwar Dynasty, claiming descent from the famous Raja Bhoj of Dhar (in Madhya Pradesh), united Garhwal's 52 warring fiefdoms to make their capital in

Highlights

Uttarakhand features some of the finest mountain scenery in the Indian Himalaya, and this can be enjoyed on some of the region's excellent treks, such as that to the beautiful Valley of Flowers, or to Har ki Dun Valley, both in Garhwal, or while dining at a Raj-era hotel in, for example, the hill station of Mussoorie. The hill station of Nainital may not have the awe-inspiring mountain vistas of Mussoorie or even of the smaller hill station of Kausani, but it is a beautiful place, set around an emerald-green lake, affording an assortment of boating and leisure activities.

For those interested in learning more about Hinduism, a visit to one of the region's holy places, such as Rishikesh, Haridwar, or the Char Dham (four shrines) of Yamunotri, Gangotri, Kedarnath and Badrinath, is essential.

Uttarakhand also has some stunning ancient temple groups – the three most notable are the beautiful temple complexes of Jageshwar, Bageshwar and Baijnath, all in Kumaon. ■

the 14th century at Chandpur. It was moved to Devalgarh in 1512 and then to Srinagar in 1517 (the latter a bad choice in view of the periodic flooding by the Ganges).

The Gurkhas took over Kumaon and Garhwal in 1803 and were not evicted until 1815 when British arms proved stronger. Kumaon was declared British territory as was Pauri Garhwal, the land east of the Ganges including Srinagar. Only Tehri Garhwal survived as a native state with a new sweltering capital at Tehri.

With the founding of hill university campuses in Nainital (*tal* means lake) and Srinagar after independence, the agitation for a separate hill state of Uttarakhand has grown. Matters came to a head in September 1994 when the police opened fire on demonstrators in the usually sedate hill station of Mussoorie, killing seven. Soon after, a convoy of buses taking hill demonstrators to a rally in Delhi were stopped by the police in Muzaffarnager and several women raped. (Action has since been taken against the guilty policemen.) On the anniversary of these atrocities, massive and prolonged strikes kept all government functioning at a standstill. However, the popular feeling aroused by the

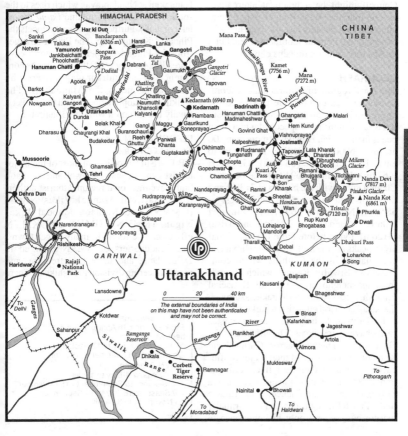

agitation was not matched by the quality of leadership that emerged. There is some disenchantment with the leadership, but not enough to quell the universal demand for a hill state. In terms of size and population Uttarakhand is comparable to Himachal Pradesh, though that state is more economically viable in view of its climate and terrain. Uttarakhand is fast approaching desert status which is why the Chipko movement caught the public imagination.

Uttarakhand as a separate state seems unlikely since Delhi would be reluctant to set a precedent. A separate administrative hill council similar to the Darjeeling Gorkha Hill Council might be a practical alternative, except that the West Bengal experiment, after almost a decade, has not lived up to its expectations. Popular sentiment is real but a satisfactory solution remains elusive.

GEOGRAPHY

The vast region of Uttarakhand encompasses an area comparable in size to the entire adjacent state of Himachal Pradesh. It has some of the most spectacular mountain peaks in the Indian Himalaya (more than 100 are over 6000m), including, from west to east, Bandarpanch (6316m), Gangotri (6672m), Kedarnath (6940m), the peaks of Chaukhamba, with the highest at 7138m and those of Badrinath, with the highest at 6853m, Nhilkanth (6957m), Dunagiri (7066m), Nanda Devi (7817m) and Trisul (7120m). Lying before these Greater Himalayan peaks are the mid and lesser Himalaya, culminating in the foothills which comprise the Siwalik Range, which extends from the neighbouring state of Himachal Pradesh, across southern Uttarakhand through the Rajaji and Corbett national parks.

In Garhwal, the holy Yamuna and Ganges rivers have their sources. The affluents of the Ganges form a network across Garhwal and Kumaon, and the sites of their major confluences, of which there are five, form the Panch Prayag (*panch* means five, and a *prayag* is a sacred confluence). A pilgrimage to the Panch Prayag is deemed as spiritually meritorious, second only in importance to

that to the confluence of the Yamuna and Ganges at Allahabad. The most sacred of the prayags is at Deoprayag, 68 km east of Rishikesh. Here the Bhagirathi, which emerges from the snout of the Gangotri Glacier at Gaumukh, meets the Alaknanda, which rises near Badrinath. It is here that the river is officially bestowed with the title Ganga. Before reaching the Bhagirathi, the Alaknanda, flowing south-west, is joined by four other rivers, and the site of their confluences are revered as the remaining four of the Panch Prayag. The Alaknanda meets the Dhauliganga at Vishnuprayag, 10 km to the north of Josimath. It is joined by the Nandakini at Nandaprayag which rises to the south of the sacred Homkund (*kund* means lake or tank). Further south-west it meets the Pindar at Karanprayag. The Pindar emerges from the Pindari Glacier, to the north-east. Threading its way west, the next major confluence is at Rudraprayag, where the Alaknanda meets the Mandakini. The Alaknanda, supplemented by all these rivers, finally has its union with the Bhagirathi.

INFORMATION
Tourist Offices

UP Tourism has offices in most of the major tourist centres, and Garhwal and Kumaon both have their own regional tourist authorities: Garhwal Mandal Vikas Nigam (GMVN), and Kumaon Mandal Vikas Nigam (KMVN). GMVN and KMVN offices can be found in many larger towns. The headquarters of GMVN is based in Dehra Dun, and there is a trekking and mountaineering division in Rishikesh. There

---

GMVN Seasons
Peak Seasons: 16 April to 30 June, 16 September to 31 October
Mid-Season: 1 July to 15 September
Off Season: 1 November to 15 April
KMVN Seasons
Peak Season: 1 May to 15 July
Mid-Season: 15 September to 15 November
Off Seasons: 16 July to 14 September,
16 November to 30 April

is a network of GMVN and KMVN tourist bungalows throughout Uttarakhand, with discounts offered in the off season. GMVN and KMVN rates vary according to the season, as defined by them (see table following). These seasons are not necessarily followed by privately run establishments, who define their own seasons.

UP Tourism also has offices in most of the major Indian cities:

Ahmedabad
    303 Ashwamedh House, 5 Smriti Kunj, Navrangpura (☎ (0121) 40-0752)
Calcutta
    12A Netaji Subashi Rd (☎ (033) 220-7855)
Chandigarh
    SCO 1046-47, 1st floor, Sector 22B (☎ (0172) 70-7649)
Delhi
    Chandralok Bldg, 36 Janpath, New Delhi (☎ (011) 332-2251; fax 371-1296)
Lucknow
    Chitrahar Bldg, 3 Naval Kishor Rd (☎ (0522) 223-3632)
Madras
    28 Commander-in-Chief Rd (☎ (044) 828-3276)
Mumbai (Bombay)
    World Trade Centre, Cuffe Parade, Colaba (☎ (022) 218-5458)

UP Tourism offers five day mountain cycling tours from Nainital and six day tours from Chaukori, both in Kumaon. Contact the office in New Delhi for details.

UP Tourism operates package tours during the yatra season (April to November) to the Char Dham temples of Garhwal. Packages ex Delhi including luxury 2x2 bus and accommodation include a seven day tour to Badrinath and Kedarnath (Rs 2255); and a 13 day tour to the four temples (Rs 3680).

In addition to its coach tours to the Char Dham during the yatra season, UP Tourism also offers taxi packages. A seven day package departing from Delhi to Kedarnath and Badrinath is Rs 4005 per person for twin accommodation. Seven day taxi packages to Kedarnath and Badrinath from Delhi are Rs 5445 per person.

Jet & Helicopter Charters

Amber Tours (☎ 331-2773; fax 331-2984), Flat 2, Dwarka Sadan, C-42 Connaught Place, New Delhi, can arrange jet and helicopter flights (maximum four people) to the High Himalaya. Amber Tours can also arrange yoga study tours. Prices are available on application.

Festivals of Uttarakhand

January
Uttarkashi Fair – On the day of Makar Sakranti, images of various Hindu deities are carried into Uttarkashi on palanquins by pilgrims from outlying centres.

February
International Yoga Festival – Every year from 2 to 7 February, Rishikesh hosts this festival, which attracts yoga masters and practitioners from around the world. See under Rishikesh, later in this chapter, for more details.

February-March
Tapkeshwar Mahadev Mela – This large fair is held in honour of Shiva at the Tapkeshwar Mahadev Temple (near Dehra Dun). It generally corresponds with the nationwide celebration of Shivratri.

July-August
Jayanty Festival – This festival celebrates the birth of the god Shiva in Uttarkashi. At this time, pilgrims throng to the Vishwanatha Temple at Uttarkashi to pay homage to the god. ■

Garhwal

Population: 2,982,947
Area: 30,029 sq km
People per sq km: 99
Main Languages: Garhwali & Hindi
Literacy Rate: 58%

For many people the Garhwal region epito-
mises the essential spirit of the Himalaya;
this is a land steeped in history, mythology
and religious lore. It is the source of the
sacred Ganges and Yamuna rivers, and is
scored by dramatic gorges, studded with
glacial lakes and vast cascading waterfalls,
traversed by valleys which, during the
monsoon, are carpeted with wildflowers, and
dotted with green *bugyals*, high-altitude pas-
turelands. Garhwal is also the home of the
Char Dham, the holy pilgrimage sites of
Yamunotri, Gangotri, Kedarnath and Badrinath.

Garhwal is a stronghold of the Shaivites,
or worshippers of the god Shiva. Shiva fled
to the high Himalaya here hotly pursued by
the heroes of the *Mahabharata*, the five
Pandavas, who sought atonement from the
god after they slew their kinsfolk, the Kauravas.
The Panch Kedar is the most important
yatra (pilgrimage) for Shaivites, representing the five parts of Shiva which emerged
after he dived earthwards to escape the
Pandavas at Kedarnath. The temple at
Kedarnath is the most sacred site, but after
they have had *darshan* (presentation to the
deity) here, devout pilgrims proceed to the
remaining four of the five Panch Kedars, at
Tunganath, Rudranath, Madmaheshwar
and Kalpeshwar.

Many villages have their own local
deities; worship of the goddess Nanda Devi
predominates in many of those regions
which are within sight of the magnificent
mountain, revered as a manifestation of the
goddess. The Devi's marriage as Parvati to
Shiva is commemorated annually in the
Nandashthami Festival. In the remote Har ki
Dun Valley, Duryodhana, the eldest Kaurava
brother, is revered. The snow-melt lake of
Hem Kund, near the Valley of Flowers

National Park, is held sacred by Sikhs, as it
was on the shores of this lake that the Sikh guru
Govind Singh is believed to have meditated.

Five of the hill districts of northern Uttar
Pradesh are in Garhwal: Dehra Dun, Chamoli,
Uttarkashi, Pauri Garhwal and Tehri Garhwal.
The remaining three hill districts lie in
neighbouring Kumaon, to the west. Garhwal
is bordered by Himachal Pradesh to the east,
and the Greater Himalaya forms the Indo-
Tibetan border to the north.

One form of Nanda Devi, the presiding
goddess of Uttarakhand.

DEHRA DUN
Population: 515,480
Telephone Area Code: 0135

Many visitors rush straight through Dehra
Dun en route to Mussoorie, which is a shame,
as this city exudes its own peculiar charm,
being blessed with a moderate year-round
climate, several points of interest in the
immediate environs, and a colourful bazaar.
The city is sited at 701 m; to the north extends
the Himalaya, with the hill station of
Mussoorie visible 34 km distant above
Dehra Dun. To the south lie the Siwalik hills,
named after Lord Shiva, and to the east and
west are the Ganges and Yamuna respectively.

In the late 17th century, Guru Ram Rai,
one of a succession of gurus who propagated
the teachings of the 15th century reformer,
Guru Nanak, the founder of the Sikh religion, fled to the fertile valley from the
Punjab following controversy over his legitimate right to succeed his father. With the
patronage of Aurangzeb and a warm reception from the Maharaja of Tehri Garhwal in

whose kingdom the valley was sited, he settled in the valley and founded a *guru-dwara* (Sikh temple). Over the next few decades a township began to grow around the gurudwara, which today is the busy administrative centre of Dehra Dun *(dun* or *doon* means valley).

Dehra Dun was occupied in 1757 by the Governor of Saharanpur, Nazib-ud-Daula, the first of a succession of invaders, the last of whom were the Gurkhas, who, not content with simply invading the city, annexed the entire region. The British managed to prise Dehra Dun from the Gurkhas in 1815 according to the terms of the Treaty of Sugauli, and with its pleasant climate, easy accessibility and Himalayan vistas, it became an important research and academic centre.

The Indian Military Academy and the Survey of India are both based here. There are also several prestigious boarding schools including Doon School, India's most exclusive private school, which numbers Rajiv Gandhi among its former pupils. The extensive forests which once covered the valley have suffered widespread denudation, but an endeavour is being made to reverse this trend.

Orientation
The clock tower is the hub of the town and many of the budget hotels are near it or close to the railway station and the Mussoorie and Delhi bus stands. The middle and top-end hotels are clustered around the area known as Astley Hall, about one km north of the clock tower, and further north along Rajpur Rd, the main road to Mussoorie. (Astley Hall comprises an entire city block on the east side of Rajpur Rd, but the hall itself remains mysteriously elusive.) The main market is Paltan Bazaar, and one of the most important items sold here is high quality *basmati* (long-grain) rice, for which the region is famous. The Delhi bus stand is about one km from both the railway station and the clock tower, on Gandhi Rd. The Mussoorie bus stand is adjacent to the railway station, about two km south of the clock tower. The main post office is just a few steps north of the clock

tower. Just to the south of Astley Hall, extending for a city block along the east side of busy Rajpur Rd, is Gandhi Park, a pleasant shady place to while away an hour or two.

Information
Tourist Offices For information on Dehra Dun itself, head for the Tourist Information Bureau (☎ 23-400), at 9-B Astley Hall, Raipur Rd. It's open from 10 am to 5 pm daily except Sunday, and has money exchange facilities. The bureau can arrange cultural/anthropological study tours which are tailored to suit visitors' requirements. Costs start at Rs 1000 per day, including accommodation in dorms, guides and meals. Transport is extra. UP Tourism (☎ 65-3217) and GMVN (☎ 65-4371) both have offices at the Hotel Drona, near the Delhi bus stand at 45 Gandhi Rd. They're both open Monday to Saturday from 10 am to 5 pm (closed for lunch between 1 and 2 pm). GMVN operates day tours during May and June, and September and October around Dehra Dun (Rs 50), to Mussoorie (Rs 100), Rishikesh and Haridwar (Rs 120), Haridwar and the Chilla Wildlife Sanctuary (Rs 120), and to the waterfalls at Assan Bairoj, and Dakpathar, at the extreme west end of the Dehra Dun Valley (Rs 100). It also arranges luxury coach trips to the Char Dham during the pilgrimage season. The main office for GMVN is at 74/1 Rajpur Rd (☎ 65-6817; fax 24-408), just south of the Hotel Great Value.

Money The State Bank of India is close to the clock tower, at 11-A Rajpur Rd, in the Windlass Shopping Complex, beneath the Hotel Ambassador. Most travellers' cheques are accepted, but *not* Visa. The Tourist Information Bureau at Astley Hall will exchange all major travellers' cheques, and can also arrange cash advances on Visa and American Express credit cards – it takes about three days for the money to come through. The Central Bank, Astley Hall area, on Rajpur Rd near the Hotel President, is one of the few banks that will exchange Visa travellers' cheques.

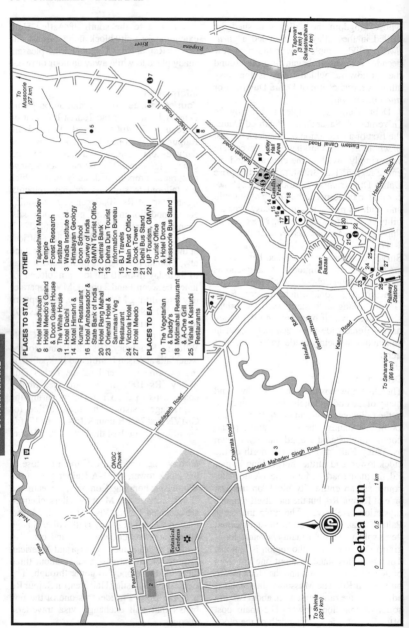

PLACES TO STAY

6   Hotel Madhuban
8   Hotel Meedo's Grand
    & Doon Guest House
9   The White House
11 Hotel Daichi
14 Motel Himshri &
    Kumar Restaurant
16 Hotel Ambassador &
    State Bank of India
20 Hotel Rang Mahal
23 Oriental Hotel &
    Sammaan Veg
    Restaurant
24 Victoria Hotel
27 Hotel Meedo

PLACES TO EAT

10 The Vegetarian
    & Daddy's
18 Motimahal Restaurant
    & A-One Grill
25 Vishal & Kasturbi
    Restaurants

OTHER

1   Tapkeshwar Mahadev
    Temple
2   Forest Research
    Institute
3   Wadia Institute of
    Himalayan Geology
4   Doon School
5   Survey of India
7   GMVN Tourist Office
12 Central Bank
13 Dehra Dun Tourist
    Information Bureau
15 BJ Travels
17 Main Post Office
19 Clock Tower
21 Delhi Bus Stand
22 UP Tourism, GMVN
    Tourist Office
    & Hotel Drona
26 Mussoorie Bus Stand

Dehra Dun

Travel Agencies BJ Travels (☎ 65-7888), about 200m north of the main post office at 15-B Rajpur Rd, has a computerised reservation system and can provide instant confirmation on domestic and international flights. To arrange treks, contact Bajaj Tours and Trekking (☎ 62-4425), S Gurcharan Singh, 14A National Rd, Luxman Chowk, or Trek Himalaya Tours (☎ 65-3005). For enquiries in person, call into the Bengali Sweet Shop at the clock tower.

Bookshops Natraj Booksellers (☎ 23-382), at 17 Rajpur Rd, next to the Motel Himshri, has an extensive selection of books on environmental issues, with particular emphasis on the Indian Himalaya. There's also a hefty selection of Penguin titles. Around the corner at 15 Rajpur Rd, the English Book Depot also has an excellent range.

Film & Photography For photographic requirements, advice and excellent service, Harish Studio, in the Motel Himshri complex, is a good place to head.

Forest Research Institute
Established by the British earlier this century the FRI, five km north west of the heart of the city, is now reputedly one of the finest institutes of forest sciences in the world. It's set in large botanical gardens, with the Himalaya providing a spectacular backdrop.

In the six galleries of the extensive museum, exhibits are laid out in glass cases with Victorian attention to detail. They include examples of wood types, before and after models for social forestry programmes, a furniture gallery, stuffed examples of forest dwellers (from bugs and pests to tigers), and a cross section of a deodar (Himalayan cedar) which was over 700 years old. There's also a bookshop and library.

The institute is open Monday to Friday from 10 am to 5 pm and there's no admission charge. To get there take a tempo (Vikram) from the clock tower out Kaulagarh Rd along route No 8 (Rs 3).

Tapkeshwar Mahadev Temple
This pretty cave temple, sacred to Lord Shiva, is six km north of the city centre, two km beyond the FRI, at the village of Ghari. The temple derives its name from the perpetually dripping water which falls on a sacred *lingam* (phallic symbol): *tapke* is the sound made by the water, and *Ishwar* is a collective name for the Hindu gods. After passing beneath a natural arch formed by the branches of a peepal and banyan tree, steps lead down to a stream, beside which a path leads to the rock cave which houses the sacred lingam, images of Lord Krishna and his consort Radha, Hanuman and Kal Bharo, the latter a disturbing black image of evident antiquity with startling rhinestone eyes. The dank interior of the cave is the home of the resident *pujari* (priest).

A large *mela* (fair) is held here on Shivratri day. It's a colourful event, with carnival rides for children, and food stalls catering to the thousands of pilgrims. To get to the temple, take a Vikram along Kaulagarh Rd (route No 8) to ONGC Chowk and ask the driver to continue to the temple; if there are other passengers, it costs Rs 3. To charter the whole Vikram from ONGC Chowk costs Rs 15. An autorickshaw from the clock tower will cost Rs 60 return.

Other Things to See
At the **Wadia Institute of Himalayan Geology** there's a museum containing rock samples, semiprecious stones and fossils. The museum is on General Mahadev Singh Rd, and is open Monday to Friday from 10 am to 5 pm. Eight km west of Dehra Dun is the **Robbers' Cave**, a popular picnic spot just beyond Anarwala village. Local buses run to Anarwala, from where it is a 1½ km walk to the caves.

Four km from the clock tower, just off Rajpur Rd, is the headquarters of the **Survey of India**, in the Hathibarkala Estate. The selection of maps in the map shop on the premises is a rather motley collection. The Survey of India is open from 10 am to 5 pm from Monday to Friday (closed for lunch between 1 and 2 pm).

UTTARAKHAND

Everest or Chomolungma?

It was at the headquarters of the Survey of India that the height of the unnamed Peak XV was calculated and discovered to be the highest mountain in the world. Survey officials allegedly spent a decade trying to determine whether Peak XV had a local name, oddly coming up empty handed, despite the great reverence in which the mountain was held in Tibet, where it was known as Chomolungma, abode of the goddess Tashi Tsering-ma. Breaking with the conventionally accepted practice of adopting local names wherever possible, the peak was named after the former Surveyor-General of India, disregarding Everest's own reservations about the difficulties of rendering his name (which incidentally he pronounced 'Eve Rest') in local script. ■

There are cold sulphur springs at the village of **Sahastradhara**, 14 km from Dehra Dun. Take the Mussoorie road, and after five km a turn-off to the right leads in nine km to the springs. GMVN has a *Tourist Rest House* here; double cabin-style accommodation is Rs 150, and bookings can be made through GMVN in Dehra Dun.

Places to Stay – bottom end

There are two *railway retiring rooms*, with doubles for Rs 100; the eight bed dorm costs Rs 30. A popular budget option is the *The White House* (☎ 62-765), in a quiet location at 15/7 Subhash Rd (formerly Lytton Rd). It's a stylish old building, if a little run down, with singles at Rs 115, and doubles on the ground and first floors at Rs 160 and Rs 190 respectively. Air-coolers and heaters are available for Rs 30 per day. There's no restaurant here. This place is a bit of a hike from the bus and railway stations – an autorickshaw will cost about Rs 15, or you could hail down a Vikram for Rs 2 (ask to get off at Kanak Cinema).

Only two minutes walk from the bus and railway stations is the salubrious *Oriental Hotel* (☎ 62-7059), run by a friendly Sikh family. Singles/doubles with common bath are Rs 65/110, or with attached bath, Rs 75/120. You'll be roused at an indecent hour with a boy bearing bed tea (Rs 3).

In a handy location close to the Mussoorie bus stand and the railway station, on Haridwar Rd, is the *Victoria Hotel* (☎ 62-3486). All rooms have attached bath (cold water only; bucket hot water is Rs 3).

Doubles are Rs 60, Rs 100 and Rs 150. Opposite is the *Hotel Meedo* (not to be confused with the more up-market Hotel Meedo's Grand, on Rajpur Rd), which has singles with attached bath for Rs 100, doubles at the back (with no TV) for Rs 180, and at the front, with B&W TV, for Rs 190. Unusually for Dehra Dun, the Meedo has a generous 24 hour checkout. There's running cold water year round, and running hot water is provided in winter. Rooms are spotless, if spartan, but those at the front are a bit noisy. This is a great budget option, and the staff are friendly. There's a sleazy bar next door, but the beers (Rs 45) are cold.

The *Hotel Daichi* (☎ 28-107) is handy to Rajpur Rd, although set off the main drag at 6 Mahant Laxman Dass Rd. This is a relatively new place, with loads of marble trimmings, and comfortable singles/doubles are very good value at Rs 150/250, or Rs 225/350 with air-cooling. All rooms have hot water and B&W TV, but there's no restaurant.

The *Hotel Rang Mahal* (☎ 65-5924) by the Delhi bus stand is a handy place if you've got an early morning Delhi-bound departure planned. Poky and dark singles/doubles are Rs 125/175, or there are doubles at Rs 250, Rs 300 and Rs 400, all with air-cooling. The front rooms are noisy. All rooms have attached bathrooms with cold water; hot water by the bucket is free.

Next door to the Hotel Meedo's Grand at 28 Rajpur Rd, and run by the same people, is the budget-option *Doon Guest House* (☎ 65-7171). Large, high-ceilinged singles/doubles in this charming (if somewhat run-down) old edifice are Rs 150/200. Bathrooms are attached, and free hot water in buckets is delivered to rooms by the creaky but gallant old caretaker.

Places to Stay – middle & top end

Dehra Dun has an excellent selection of mid-range hotels, the majority strung out along the main road (Rajpur Rd) to Mussoorie. The *Hotel Ambassador* (☎ 65-5831) is centrally located at 11-A Rajpur Rd, in the Windlass Shopping Complex. Singles/doubles start from Rs 225/325 with air-cooling, and more expensive rooms are available with air-con. All rooms have colour TV. Staff are friendly and there's 24 hour room service.

A short distance north is the *Motel Himshri* (☎ 65-3880), at 17 Rajpur Rd. Smallish ordinary singles/doubles are Rs 250/350, or Rs 275/374 with air-cooling. The deluxe rooms with air-con are spacious and airy, and cost Rs 450/550.

About three km from the railway station at 28 Rajpur Rd is *Hotel Meedo's Grand* (☎ 65-7171). Despite its modern ugly grey exterior, rooms are comfortable, although pricey at Rs 350/455, or with air-con, Rs 500/700. There's a restaurant and bar, all rooms have wall-to-wall carpet and piped music, and credit cards are accepted.

Further north along Rajpur Rd is the up-market *Hotel Madhuban* (☎ 65-6041). All rooms are doubles, but single occupancy rates are offered. This enormous concrete edifice is set on two hectares, with amenities including a mini-golf course and a multicuisine restaurant. Singles/doubles are pricey at Rs 1150/1700.

The *Hotel Ajanta Continental* (☎ 29-595) is just a few hundred metres north on Rajpur Rd. Rooms aren't large, but are tastefully appointed and comfortable, and aren't bad value in this range at Rs 750/1000 for singles/doubles, with suites at Rs 1400.

Right by the Delhi bus stand is GMVN's *Hotel Drona* (☎ 24-371), at 45 Gandhi Rd. There are dorms (men only) for Rs 60, standard singles/doubles for Rs 225/300, and air-con rooms for Rs 450/600. A 10% discount is offered in the GMVN mid and off

seasons. All rooms have running hot and cold water, there's 24 hour room service and a good restaurant and bar.

Places to Eat

Close to the English Book Depot is the superlative *Kumar* on Rajrur Rd, with some of the best vegetarian dishes you'll get anywhere. No alcohol is served here, but the lassis are great, and in winter they have the sweet gajar ka halwa, made from carrot, spices and milk. The Rs 40 house special – makki ki roti saron ka saag with lassi (corn roti with mustard-leaf spinach, and lassi) – is worth a postcard home – it's delicious. There's a second *Kumar* about 100m south of the original, which also offers nonveg and Chinese cuisine. The restaurants are open from 11 am to 4 pm and 7 to 10.30 pm.

On the opposite side of Rajpur Rd are a string of eateries. The *Motimahal* is the pick of the bunch, with a pleasant atmosphere, low lighting and good food – the cheese pulao (Rs 25) is excellent. Next door is the *A-One Grill*, a hole-in-the-wall type eatery with tandoori chicken and kebabs to take away. It's open each evening from 8 pm until late. Also right by the Motimahal is the *Punjab Restaurant*, with cheap Punjabi favourites such as aalu gobi and mattar panir (both Rs 18).

Further north, but also on the east side of Rajpur Rd, is the *Vegetarian*, next to the Hotel President, at Astley Plaza. The spartan dining hall does not have the most convivial of atmospheres, but meals are cheap (most dishes are under Rs 30) and good. Above the Vegetarian is *Daddy's*, which features Mughlai, South Indian and Chinese cuisine. It specialises in 'birthdays and kitty parties', so bring the cat.

Only two doors down from the Oriental Hotel, right in the middle of the Paltan bazaar, is the *Sammaan Veg Restaurant*. It's popular with locals, and has a very filling thali for Rs 30. Two other popular thali restaurants in the bazaar are the *Vishal* and the *Kasturbi*, but they're rather more basic. At all these places you can follow your thali with kheer (rice pudding).

Dehra Dun has several good bakeries and sweet shops. The *Standard Confectioners* near the Vegetarian restaurant has delicious home-made toffees, as well as fresh breads, pastries and cakes. The *Grand Bakers* in Paltan Bazaar has a large selection of bread, snacks and excellent macaroons. There are several good sweet shops by the clock tower.

Getting There & Away

Air Jolly Grant airport is 24 km distant from Dehra Dun. Currently there are no scheduled flights to Jolly Grant, but at the time of writing, daily flights to and from Delhi (50 minutes, US$75) and thrice weekly flights to Lucknow (70 minutes, US$90), were slated with UP Airways (Delhi: ☎ (011) 463-8201). A taxi for the 45 minute trip to or from the airport and Dehra Dun should cost around Rs 250, or BJ Travels may offer a bus service from their office which will cost about Rs 50.

Bus The Mussoorie bus stand, by the railway station on Haridwar Rd, is for destinations in the hills. Buses to Mussoorie (1½ hours, Rs 13), leave regularly between 6.30 am and 8.30 pm. To Uttarkashi (for Gangotri), the 209 km trip takes eight hours via Tehri, and buses leave at 6, 8.30 and 10 am (Rs 74); to Tehri it's 130 km and five hours (Rs 44). It takes six hours to cover the 152 km to Srinagar (en route to Kedarnath). There are several departures between 4.30 and 10 am via Rishikesh (note that there are many more buses to Rishikesh from the Delhi bus stand – see below). The 11 hour, 288 km trip to Nainital costs Rs 106. There's one bus daily to Hanuman Chatti (for Yamunotri) via Mussoorie, which departs at 8.30 am (nine hours, Rs 94).

Buses for Delhi and destinations on the plains depart from the Delhi bus stand (☎ 65-3797), next to the Hotel Drona on Gandhi Rd. There are deluxe (2x2) services for the seven hour, 255 km trip to the capital every hour from 5.15 am until 10.30 pm (Rs 114, or Rs 121 with video), and ordinary services every 15 to 30 minutes (Rs 66). Other destinations include: Haridwar (1½ hours, Rs 14); Rishikesh (1½ hours, Rs 10.50);

Lucknow (1.30 and 6 pm; 16 hours, Rs 141); Shimla, via Paonta Saheb, Solan and Kumar Hatti (ie via the hills – seven hours, departures at 5.30, 6.30, 8.30 10.30 and 11.30 am; Rs 82); or via Saharanpur, Ambala and Chandigarh (ie via the plains – nine hours, 7.25 and 9.15 am; Rs 100); Dharamsala (15 hours, 12.30 pm, Rs 155); and Kullu (14 hours, Rs 176) and Manali (16 hours, Rs 191), departing at 3.15 pm.

Train Services to Dehra Dun, the terminus of the Northern Railway, include the speedy *Shatabdi Express*, leaving New Delhi at 6 am daily and reaching Haridwar at 10.45 am and Dehra Dun at 11.45 am. Chair car/1st class costs Rs 270/540 to Haridwar, and Rs 300/600 to Dehra Dun.

The *Mussoorie Express* is an excellent overnight train service from Delhi to Dehra Dun (Rs 98/411 in 2nd/1st class to Haridwar; slightly more to Dehra Dun). It leaves Old Delhi station at 10.25 pm, arriving into Haridwar at 6 am and Dehra Dun at 7.50 am. On the return journey, it leaves Dehra Dun at 9.30 pm, Haridwar at 11.20 pm, arriving into Old Delhi at 7 am.

The *Doon Express* operates between Lucknow and Dehra Dun. Cost for the 545 km journey is Rs 109/408 in 2nd/1st class. There are also services from Dehra Dun to Calcutta, Varanasi and Mumbai (Bombay).

Taxi There's a share taxi stand in front of the Mussoorie bus stand on Haridwar Rd. Taxis leave for Mussoorie when full (five passengers required), and depart every hour or so between 6 am and 6 pm (1¼ hours, Rs 40). You'll have more luck if you hang around the taxi stand when trains disgorge their passengers from Delhi. A second share-taxi stand is by the Hotel Prince, on Rishikesh Rd. Taxis and jeeps (called 'trekkers' by locals) depart when full for Rishikesh (Rs 12); Haridwar (Rs 14); and Paonta Saheb (just over the border in eastern Himachal Pradesh – Rs 18; the vehicle stops one km before the border, from where you can catch a rickshaw into Himachal Pradesh).

To reserve a whole taxi to Mussoorie will

cost Rs 200; to other destinations expect to pay the following during the off season: Rishikesh (Rs 200); Haridwar (Rs 300); Uttarkashi (Rs 1000); Shimla (Rs 1600); and Nainital (Rs 1800). During the peak seasons, you'll be stung for at least Rs 100 more.

Getting Around
Tempo & Autorickshaw Six seater tempos (Vikrams) belch diesel fumes all over the city, but are a cheap way to get around. They run on fixed routes charging, for example, Rs 2 from the station to the clock tower (route No 5). For this distance an autorickshaw would charge about Rs 10. Route No 1 extends from the clock tower along Rajpur Rd.

Car Hire cars can be booked through GMVN at either its Rajpur Rd or Hotel Drona offices. You will probably be able to negotiate more competitive rates through Ventures Rent a Car (☎ 22-724), at 87 Rajpur Rd.

MUSSOORIE
Population: 29,000
Telephone Area Code: 0135
Peak Season – May to early July
Mid-Season – April, October
Off Season – Mid-November to late March, late July to September

At an altitude of 1921m and only 34 km beyond Dehra Dun, Mussoorie was founded by an Irishman, Captain Young, who stumbled upon the 15 km long ridge on which the town was later sited in 1827 while out enjoying a spot of hunting. He immediately recognised the potential of the site, with its salubrious climate and magnificent mountain vistas, as a hill station, and in under 10 years a thriving town had emerged. Indian maharajas, British officers and their entourages were borne up to Mussoorie on ponies or carried up on *jhampanies* (chairs) by labouring bearers, essential accoutrements such as crystal chandeliers, billiard tables and grand pianos being hauled up on bullock carts. As the settlement developed, Mussoorie, the closest hill station to New Delhi, became a favourite summer retreat of the British.

Today the once-glorious Victorian relics are in a sad state of dilapidation, jostled on all sides by ugly modern concrete edifices catering to the thousands of holiday makers who converge on the hill station during the summer months. Outside the peak summer months of May and June, Mussoorie is a far more pleasant proposition, with good walks along the mountain ridges and fine views of the Himalayan massifs of western Garhwal from Gun Hill, rising 609m just above the town.

Orientation
Despite initial impressions, the lay out of Mussoorie is relatively straightforward: The Mall extends two km across the face of a long mountain ridge, oddly oriented to the south failing to take advantage of the stunning Himalayan panorama. It connects the library area, at the west end of The Mall, with Kulri Bazaar to the east. East of Kulri Bazaar is the Masonic Lodge bus stand (also known as the Picture Palace bus stand).

Buses or taxis will drop you at either the Library bus stand at Gandhi Chowk or the Masonic Lodge stands. If you arrive at the Library bus stand, walk west about 100m and you'll pass beneath a brightly coloured archway, announcing your arrival at the library area, which is riddled with hotels in all price categories (see under Places to Stay). Hotels are strung out along the length of The Mall, with some a short distance off The Mall up steep roads and paths. A 600m walk west of the Masonic Lodge bus stand will bring you into the thick of the Kulri Bazaar, similarly full of places to stay. Looping north above the Kulri Bazaar end of The Mall rejoining The Mall further west is the Camel's Back Rd, which was built as a promenade and passes a rock formation that looks like a recumbent camel. It also has its fair share of hotels strung along its length. The main post office, State Bank of India and Bank of Baroda are all in the Kulri Bazaar area; there's nowhere to change money at the library end of The Mall.

UTTARAKHAND

Information

Tourist Offices There's a very helpful UP tourist office (☎ 63-2863) towards the Kulri Bazaar end of The Mall, near the ropeway station, and a GMVN office (☎ 63-2984) at the Hotel Garhwal Terrace, about 500m further west along The Mall. There's a small GMVN booth (☎ 63-1281) at the Library bus stand at Gandhi Chowk, which runs tours to Kempty Falls (three hours, Rs 25); Mussoorie Lake (Rs 15, season only); and full-day tours (October and November only – Rs 100) which include the picnic site of Dhanolti, set amid deodar forests and with excellent Himalayan views, and the Surkhanda Devi Temple, perched at 3050m and also affording magnificent views of a 300 km long stretch of the Himalaya.

Money The State Bank of India at Kulri Bazaar will exchange American Express travellers' cheques in US dollars only, and Thomas Cook and MasterCard cheques in US dollars and pounds sterling only. There's an encashment fee of Rs 25. The Bank of Baroda, Kulri Bazaar (beneath the Tavern Restaurant), exchanges most travellers' cheques, including Visa and Citicorp.

Travel Agencies Ambica Travels (☎ 63-2238) at the Hotel Hill Queen, Upper Mall Rd, The Mall (west) can book deluxe buses to Delhi (10.30 am and 10.30 pm, non air-con, and 11 am and 10 pm, air-con). They also book air and train tickets. Hire cars can be arranged through Kulwant Travels (☎ 63-2717), at the Masonic Lodge bus stand, or Harry Tours & Travels (☎ 63-2507), also at this bus stand.

Trekking Outfits & Tour Operators A respected trek operator is Trek Himalaya Tours (☎ 63-1366; fax 63-1302), at Powy's Cottage, Hakman's Compound (take the path down beside the UP tourist office). Neelamber Badoni here can arrange treks in the Garhwal area, and jeep safaris to Kinnaur, Spiti and Ladakh, as well as sorting out the paperwork and necessary permits for these areas. It is also possible to hire tents (Rs 50 to Rs 80 per day), sleeping bags (Rs 25 to Rs 30), mats (Rs 5) and rucksacks here. Harry Tours & Travels (see Travel Agencies above) is another outfit who can organise treks.

Bookshops There's a good selection of books, including Penguins and regional guide books, and maps at Cambridge Booksellers and Chander Book Depot, both opposite the State Bank of India, Kulri Bazaar.

Medical Services James Chemist is a well stocked dispensary near the Picture Palace. Similarly well provisioned is A Kumar & Co, beneath the library at the west end of The Mall.

Emergency Police: ☎ 63-2013; Fire: ☎ 63-2100; St Mary's Hospital: ☎ 63-2845.

Things to See & Do

A 400m long **ropeway cable car** (Rs 25 return; open 9 am to 7 pm daily; until 10 pm from 15 May to 15 July) runs up to the 609m high **Gun Hill**, so named, as in bygone days precisely at noon the surrounding hills and vales resounded with the sound of a gun fired by the British. For the early-morning views of the Himalaya, including Bandarpanch (6316m), Kedarnath (6940m), Badrinath (6853m) and Nanda Devi (7817m), you have to walk up. At the top, photo agencies will dress you up in Garhwal national dress in which you can have your photo taken for Rs 30.

The **Camel's Back Rd** loops for three km above Kulri Bazaar, and also affords good mountain views. If you're feeling lazy, you can plod around at walking pace on a pony, or be alternately pushed and pulled by rickshaw-wallahs. Both cost around Rs 60. Another good walk takes you down to **Happy Valley** and the **Tibetan Refugee Centre**, where there's the diminutive Tchechen Choling Gompa, and a small shop selling hand-knitted sweaters. You can sample the local *chang* here in one of the small wooden eateries nearby. An enjoyable longer walk (five km) takes you through the colourful **Landour Bazaar** (two km from the UP tourist office) to **Childers Lodge** (Lal Tabba), the highest point in Mussoorie, and

Sisters' Bazaar. There is an old **cemetery** on the Camel's Back Rd and at Landour Bazaar with tombstones erected during the days of the Raj.

Fifteen km north-west of Mussoorie are the **Kempty Falls**, a series of five falls which terminate in a pool in which hot day trippers converge in rented togs (towels can also be hired here). Frankly it's a bit of a tourist trap, but if you're in need of a refreshing dip, GMVN runs tours here during the summer.

There's a small **Tibetan market** which extends along the path leading from the Hotel Padmini Niwas towards Kulri Bazaar, but the merchandise is mostly cheap electronic junk.

Other suggestions to while away the time include having your senses assailed by an Indian blockbuster at the **Picture Palace** (Rs 10 in the stalls, Rs 15 in the gallery); playing billiards in the fine old **billiard hall** at Hotel Clarks, Kulri Bazaar (Rs 50); or roller skating (Rs 30) on the wooden floor of **The Rink**, which was until recently the largest in the country.

If you're still at a loose end, you could sit in the reading room at the **Tilak Memorial Library**, to the east of Kulri Bazaar, and peruse the English-language dailies or tackle the *Collected Works of Lenin* (temporary membership Rs 25; security deposit of Rs 100 required to borrow books; open 9 am to noon and 4 to 8 pm). The main library, at Gandhi Chowk, is less hospitable, and you'll probably get short shrift there.

If you simply don't know what to do next, consult one of the astrologers. Mr Jai Krishan Shah has a small booth opposite the Hotel Ratan in the library area and promises to make 'a sincere attempt to probe your future'. Mr GA Baig makes similar claims, and can be found in the shop called Jewellers – Astrologer, 5 The Mall. Consultations cost Rs 150 for 30 minutes.

Language Courses

The Landour Language School (☎ 63-1467) in the Sisters' Bazaar area has introductory courses in Hindi which get very good reports. Private lessons are Rs 50 per hour, or for two people, Rs 30 each per hour. Group lessons are Rs 25 per hour. Forty hours per week are recommended, and the standard introduction course is held over four weeks. Advanced classes are also available. Write to the principal, Mr Chitranjan Datt, Landour Language School, Landour Cantt, Mussoorie, 248179. Many students stay at the nearby Hotel Dev Dar Woods.

Places to Stay

The sheer number of hotels in Mussoorie can be bewildering for the first-time visitor: the brochure published by UP Tourism lists over 130! There's something to suit all budgets, although bear in mind that during the peak season, bargains are hard to come by, and prices can rise by up to 300%, and you will probably pay slightly more in the mid-season. Finding anything during the Hindu festivals of Dussehra or Diwali can be a nightmare.

Most places only have double rooms, but some will offer single occupancy reductions in the off season. Checkout time is generally 10 am. Porters from either bus stand to most hotels will expect about Rs 20.

Places to Stay – bottom end

Kulri Bazaar & The Mall (East End) The deservedly popular *Hotel Broadway* (☎ 63-2243), about five minutes walk from The Mall on the Camel's Back Rd, is one of the best budget places in the Kulri Bazaar area. Singles are Rs 75, doubles are Rs 100 and Rs 150, and triples are Rs 150 in the off season (Rs 150, Rs 250 and Rs 300, and Rs 350 in the season). The rates include bed tea, and the charming atmosphere is enhanced with potted geraniums on the window sills, a lovely tiled sunroom and friendly courteous service from Mr Malik and his family. Food is available on request.

Another good choice, right on The Mall, is the *Hotel Valley View* (☎ 63-2324). Spotless singles/doubles are Rs 100/150, with deluxe doubles for Rs 350 (Rs 400/600 and Rs 800 in the season). Mid-season deductions are also offered from April until 14 May and 16 to 30 July. Fresh towels are provided, and the staff are friendly and helpful. There's a nonveg dining hall here.

Right in the thick of things is the evidently once-grand *Hotel Clarks*. The enormous staircase leads up to somewhat shabby rooms, from Rs 150 to Rs 550 in the off season (Rs 550 to Rs 1500 in the season). Still, the place has loads of character, and is complete with a billiard room with full-size table and tiered spectator seats.

The *Hotel Vikram* (☎ 63-2551) is in a quiet location about five minutes from the bazaar (take the path leading past the Tilak Memorial Library). Doubles are Rs 75 (no geyser), Rs 150 and Rs 200, or in the season, Rs 200, Rs 250 and Rs 600. Bucket hot water is provided free to guests in the cheaper rooms. Some rooms have Doon Valley views. Also in this area is the friendly *New Bharat Hotel*. It's a creaky old building run by an equally creaky old caretaker who's very helpful. Rooms start from Rs 75. This place is usually closed in the off season.

Library Area & The Mall (West End)
Unquestionably the best budget option in the library area, in the off season at least, is the *Hotel Laxmi Palace* (☎ 63-2774), only five

minutes walk from the bus and taxi stands. This brand new place has small but beautifully appointed rooms, with fresh towels and soap in the spotless bathrooms, attentive staff and a handy location. Singles/doubles cost Rs 100/250 in the off season, Rs 500/800 during the season. If you're approaching from the bus stand, take the path to the left just before the entrance to the library area.

The *Whispering Windows* (☎ 63-2020), also known as the Hotel Upstairs & Downstairs, is a popular choice, close to the library and right on The Mall. Large rooms (double rates only) are Rs 175 and Rs 275 in the off season, Rs 225 and Rs 375 in the mid-season, and Rs 375 and Rs 675 in the peak season. The rather tatty 60s furnishings seem eminently appropriate, but the cheaper rooms (at the back) are a trifle dark.

A short distance above The Mall is the *Hotel India* (☎ 63-2359), run by a friendly Sikh family (take the path up from The Mall beside the Sriram General Store). The rooms facing north have breathtaking views of the Nagtibba Range. In the off season, double rates are Rs 100, Rs 200 and Rs 300; in the peak season they're Rs 600, Rs 800 and Rs

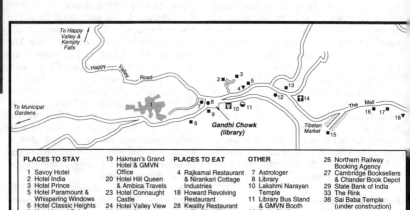

PLACES TO STAY	19 Hakman's Grand Hotel & GMVN Office	PLACES TO EAT	OTHER	26 Northern Railway Booking Agency
1 Savoy Hotel	20 Hotel Hill Queen & Ambica Travels	4 Rajkamal Restaurant & Nirankari Cottage Industries	7 Astrologer	27 Cambridge Booksellers & Chander Book Depot
2 Hotel India	23 Hotel Connaught Castle	18 Howard Revolving Restaurant	8 Library	33 The Rink
3 Hotel Prince	24 Hotel Valley View	28 Kwality Restaurant & The Rice Bowl	10 Lakshmi Narayan Temple	36 Sai Baba Temple (under construction)
5 Hotel Paramount & Whispering Windows	30 Hotel Clarks	34 Green Restaurant	11 Library Bus Stand & GMVN Booth	38 James Chemist
6 Hotel Classic Heights	31 New Bharat Hotel	35 Madras Cafe & Alki Restaurant	12 Doon Studio	39 Bertz Bikes
9 Hotel Laxmi Palace	32 Hotel Broadway	37 The Tavern & Bank of Baroda	14 Christ Church	41 Tilak Memorial Library
13 Hotel Roselynn Estate	40 Hotel Shipra		16 Astrologer	44 Masonic Lodge
15 Hotel Padmini Niwas	42 Hotel Horizon		21 Trek Himalaya Tours	Bus Stand
17 GMVN Hotel Garhwal Terrace & Tourist Office	43 Hotel Vikram		22 UP Tourist Office	45 Tehri Bus Stand
			25 Main Post Office	

1000. Some rooms in all price ranges provide great views; the more expensive rooms have private balconies and carpet. Hot water is not a problem here.

Economy rooms at the *Hotel Prince* (☎ 63-2674) are Rs 100 and Rs 150 in the off season, and you may be able to negotiate a single occupancy rate at this time of the year. In the peak season you'll pay Rs 300 and Rs 350. Frankly they're a bit a grim. Bucket hot water is available for Rs 5. Larger, more salubrious but still fairly tatty rooms with geysers are Rs 200 and Rs 400 in the off season. This is another lovely old building which is sadly in need of timely maintenance before the entire glorious edifice collapses in an untidy heap. The views from the terrace are great, and here you can endlessly ponder how the gentlefolk of yore got the grand piano up the mountainside into the drawing room (the fire is lit in winter).

Landour Bazaar If you want to escape the decaying vestiges of the Raj and immerse yourself in the busy Indian market area of Landour Bazaar, cheap rooms (doubles for Rs 60) can be found at the *Hotel Nishima* (☎ 63-2227), beyond the clock tower.

Places to Stay – middle & top end
Kulri Bazaar & The Mall (East End) If you're a nostalgia buff, there's a treat in store at *Hakman's Grand Hotel* (☎ 63-2959). The lobby is replete with a sky blue grand piano and a cash register still calibrated in annas. The cavernous ballroom is a delight with pressed-tin ceiling and old prints on the walls. But the rooms have to be seen to be believed: cushioned vinyl bed heads, multi-coloured polka dots on the walls, 1920s club arm chairs, and claw-feet baths in the enormous bathrooms, which open onto a dilapidated balcony – walk on it at your peril! If sheer bad taste doesn't offend your tender sensibilities, you'll love this place. In the peak season, rooms are Rs 400, or in the off season, Rs 200.

At the other extreme is the *Hotel Shipra* (☎ 63-2662), on the left just before the Masonic Lodge bus stand. You'll be spirited up to the luxuriously appointed rooms in a high-tech glass lift which gives the odd sensation of levitating over the Doon Valley. For deluxe doubles you'll pay Rs 1050 in the peak season, or Rs 1250 in the super-deluxe doubles with enormous beds and valley views. A 40% to 50% discount is offered in the off season. There's a restaurant and bar here.

UTTARAKHAND

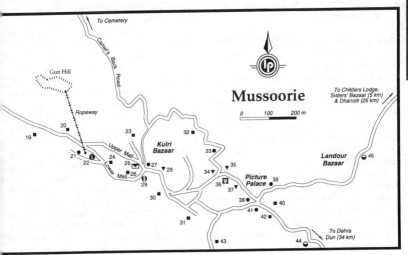

Opposite the Shipra is the brand new *Hotel Horizon* (☎ 63-2899). Rooms are beautifully appointed, with Scarlet O'Hara bottle green wedding dress curtains and thick pile carpets. There's cable TV, and glimpses out over the Doon Valley through the branches of the shady trees outside the windows. In the season, doubles are Rs 900, or Rs 1000 for the deluxe suites. A 40% discount is offered in the off season. There's no restaurant, but room service is available.

A good (but expensive) top-end option is the *Hotel Connaught Castle* (☎ 63-2210; fax 63-2538, up a long driveway leading off the Upper Mall Rd. It has luxuriously appointed rooms and marble corridors. In the season, standard doubles are Rs 1650, and deluxe doubles are Rs 2250. A 50% discount is offered in August and September. There's a generous noon checkout.

About midway between the Kulri Bazaar and the library area, right on The Mall, is GMVN's *Hotel Garhwal Terrace* (☎ 63-2682). An attempt has been made at modern luxury, but the decor is a bit pink and frilly. All rooms have Star TV, and cost Rs 495 in the off season, Rs 695 from July to October, and Rs 995 in May and June. Four bed dorms cost Rs 60, Rs 80 and Rs 100 respectively. All rooms have Doon Valley views. There are two restaurants here.

Library Area & The Mall (West End) Two doors down from the Whispering Windows is the *Hotel Paramount* (☎ 63-2352), right on The Mall. Rooms are smallish, but nicely furnished, with plenty of natural light. The more expensive rooms have views. In the off season, double rates range from Rs 200 to Rs 500, and during the season, Rs 500 to Rs 1200. There's no restaurant here, but room service is available, and the hotel is run by a very friendly Sikh man.

About 250m east along The Mall is the *Hotel Roselynn Estate* (☎ 63-2201). Double rooms are Rs 400 in the off season, and a four bed suite is Rs 500. Add 50% to these rates during the season. Rooms are a little shabby, but OK, and some open onto a small sunroom with good views out over the library area. There's a nonvegetarian restaurant here.

The *Hotel Padmini Niwas* (☎ 63-2793), about 600m east of the library, is an excellent choice. This lovely gracious old hotel has doubles in the off season for Rs 450, Rs 550 and Rs 750 (Rs 850, Rs 1100 and Rs 1500 in the season). Most rooms have Doon Valley views, and the deluxe suites at Rs 750 are beautifully appointed. The hotel once belonged to the Maharaja of Rajpipla, and the old-world charm has been maintained with features such as a delightful rose garden, and a pleasant patio with wicker chairs. With advance notice, staff can arrange a yoga instructor for guests, and there's also a mini library, comfortable drawing room and laundry facilities. There's also a pure Gujarati vegetarian restaurant here.

Just a short distance to the south of the library is the *Hotel Classic Heights* (☎ 63-2514). During the season, regular singles/doubles are Rs 495/795, or there are better doubles from Rs 995 to Rs 1495. A 40% discount is offered in the off season. The more expensive doubles have enormous stadium-sized beds on two-stepped platforms, royal red carpet and Doon Valley views. The travel counter can arrange trekking, angling and horse riding.

The *Savoy Hotel* (☎ 63-2010) is an extraordinary complex which, with its ivy-covered buildings and turrets, seems to have leapt straight from the pages of a Grimm brothers' fairy tale. According to legend there's a resident ghost, apparently that of Lady Gore Ormsby, whose mysterious death at the hotel baffled the best sleuths of the day. Agatha Christie allegedly based her first novel, *The Mysterious Affair at Styles* (1920), on the dastardly deed. Moth-eaten deer heads complete the somewhat decayed period ambience. There are also tennis and squash courts, a beer garden and an enormous billiard room. Frankly it's a bit overpriced, at Rs 995/1695 for singles/doubles, and Rs 1795 up to Rs 2495 for larger rooms with extra period trimmings. You may be able to negotiate a discount in the off season.

Sisters' Bazaar Beyond Landour Bazaar, and four km from Mussoorie, the *Hotel Dev Dar Woods* (☎ 63-2544) is in a lofty wooded location by Sisters' Bazaar. It's popular with foreigners working at the Landour Language School, only 250m away. Year-round rates are Rs 250 per person in either single or twin rooms, and include breakfast. For stays of more than 15 days, this rate includes all meals.

Places to Eat

You won't go short of a bite to eat in Mussoorie – most of the middle and top-end hotels have their own restaurants, and there is a high concentration of very good (and reasonably priced) restaurants in the Kulri Bazaar area. Due to a steep hike in the licensing fees, many restaurants no longer have bars. During the off season, restaurants close generally around 10 to 10.30 pm.

Kulri Bazaar & The Mall (East End) The
Madras Cafe specialises in South Indian food, with the menu featuring 24 different types of dosa (Rs 10 to Rs 30). There are also idlis (steamed rice rissoles in dhal gravy) and vadas (dhal rissoles).

A few doors down is the *Alki Restaurant*, with South Indian and Chinese dishes. Here a sweet kulfi faluda (kulfi ice cream with faluda: long cornflour noodles) costs Rs 15. The nearby *Green Restaurant* has the best vegetarian food in town, with an excellent cheese korma (Rs 28).

Nearby, near the Bank of Baroda, is *The Tavern*, which specialises in Mughlai and Chinese cuisine. There's live and recorded music here in the season, and this place is one of the few that remains open late throughout the year. The reshmi kabab – tender chicken kebabs cooked in the tandoor, is excellent (Rs 75).

In the heart of Kulri Bazaar is the *Kwality Restaurant*; the food's OK, but the spartan canteen atmosphere doesn't entice you to linger. Nonveg dishes are between Rs 35 to Rs 50, with most veg dishes under Rs 30. Next door to the Kwality is a fruit juice stand, where fresh juice is squeezed while you wait. The mango shakes are very good. Upstairs

nearby is *The Rice Bowl*, featuring Tibetan and Chinese cuisine, including good steamed mutton momos (Rs 14) and special thukpa (Rs 18). A few steps further along The Mall is *Clarks Restaurant* at the hotel of the same name. The cappuccinos are excellent, but the period ambience is somewhat spoilt by the masonite tables.

Heading towards the library area, about 600m along The Mall, west of Kulri Bazaar, is *Howard Revolving Restaurant*. Aesthetically it's a bit of a blight on the landscape, but you can admire the Doon Valley at one revolution every nine minutes. It's not too expensive, with veg dishes between Rs 25 and Rs 40, and nonveg dishes mostly under Rs 60. Try the excellent murg Mughlai (chicken in a gravy sauce with dry fruits and eggs – Rs 55). If you're hanging out for a hearty continental breakfast (served between 9.30 and 11 am), juice, toast and coffee costs Rs 45, with eggs and cereal extra.

Nearby are the *Hot Spot* and *China Room* restaurants at the Hotel Garhwal Terrace. The food's nothing special, but the views out over the valley are superb.

Library Area & The Mall (West End) A
popular spot for watching the holiday makers promenading along The Mall is the restaurant at the *Whispering Windows*. During the season there's dancing to recorded music on the red and black tiled floor (the live band was exiled after the enthusiastic patrons got too rowdy!). Next door is the *Rajkamal Restaurant*, with good cheap veg and nonveg food, and a dignified and ancient old waiter resplendent in brass-buttoned livery.

Next door at the Hotel Paramount is the *Swiss Cafe*, which has Chinese and Indian food, as well as a selection of muffins and Danish pastries during the season.

You can relive the halcyon days of yore by spending an evening in the dining room at the *Savoy Hotel*. Meals are not cheap, with nonveg dishes around Rs 90, but perhaps you'll be rewarded with a glimpse of the ghost of Lady Gore Ormsby (perhaps the esteemed Lady Ormsby expired at the sight of the bill). If you're feeling really magnan-

UTTARAKHAND

imous, you can shout your dining companions to a bottle of Moët et Chandon champagne (Rs 1500), or a 25 ml shot of Johnnie Walker Blue Label (Rs 395). Beers are Rs 80. Several hours notice is required if you plan to dine here.

Sisters' Bazaar A Prakash & Co is a long-established grocery store that produces superb cheddar cheese (Rs 150 to Rs 175 per kg; not made during the monsoon), as well as home-made peanut butter, jams and chutneys.

Things to Buy
There is a swag of curio shops in Mussoorie. You'll find a good range of artefacts at Nirankari Cottage Industries, at the library end of The Mall, which has carved wooden boxes, brass statues of Hindu deities and Buddhas, Tibetan prayer wheels, ceramic Chinese vases and hand-carved wooden walking sticks made from oak, the latter of which Queen Mary, then the Princess of Wales, took away with her as a souvenir of her visit to Mussoorie.

At the top of Gun Hill or at the Doon Studio, at the library end of The Mall, you can dress in traditional Garhwali garb and have your photo taken against a painted Himalayan backdrop (Rs 30 for three postcard-sized prints; pictures ready in three to four days).

If you're heading for the chilly climes further north, Mussoorie is a good place to pick up a woollen shawl. Pure Ladakhi *pashmina* wool shawls can be purchased at Jewellers – Astrologer, 5 The Mall (near the GMVN Hotel Garhwal Terrace), but they're not cheap, with prices starting at Rs 7000, up to Rs 60,000 for antique Jamawar shawls, produced on wooden looms, and employing a method now lost.

Getting There & Away
Bus There are numerous buses from the Mussoorie bus stand (next to the railway station) in Dehra Dun to Mussoorie between 6.30 am and 8.30 pm (1½ hours, Rs 13). These go either to the library bus stand (Gandhi Chowk) or Kulri Bazaar (Masonic

Lodge bus stand). When travelling to Mussoorie from the west or north (ie Jammu) by train, it is best to get off at Saharanpur and catch a bus from there to Dehra Dun or Mussoorie, if there's no convenient train connection.

Library Bus Stand Buses from the Library bus stand for Dehra Dun leave every hour between 8 am and 6 pm (1½ hours, Rs 13). There's a deluxe (2x2, but not pushback seats) overnight service to Delhi, departing at 8.30 pm and arriving at the Interstate terminal at 4.30 am (Rs 135). Advance booking is required during the season. You'd do better to find your way to Dehra Dun and get a luxury, pushback seat service to Delhi from there, or reserve a seat through the travel desks found at most mid and top-end hotels. Buses to Hanuman Chatti (for Yamunotri), which originate in Dehra Dun, pick up passengers at the Library bus stand around 10 am (six to seven hours, Rs 80).

Masonic Lodge Bus Stand Also known as the Picture Palace bus stand, deluxe (not pushback) services depart at 9.15 am for Delhi, take eight hours and cost Rs 135. There's an ordinary express overnight service which departs at 8.30 pm (Rs 86.50). Buses for Dehra Dun (1½ hours, Rs 13) leave every 30 minutes from 6 am until 7 pm.

Tehri Bus Stand Buses to Tehri (four to five hours, Rs 30) with connections to Uttarkashi (for Gangotri) leave from this bus stand, just east of the Landour Bazaar at 7, 9 and 10.30 am (year round) and 2 pm (season only). It's a pretty rough trip, but this is compensated for by the marvellous mountain scenery.

Train With at least 24 hours notice, train tickets can be arranged through the Northern Railway booking agency (☎ 63-2846), at the Kulri Bazaar end of The Mall. The office is open Monday to Saturday from 10 am to 4 pm, and Sunday from 8 am to 2 pm.

Taxi – Library Bus Stand Fares of reserve taxis (☎ 63-2115) from the Library bus stand are as follows: Rishikesh: 2½ hours, Rs 500; Haridwar: three hours, Rs 600; Delhi: seven hours, Rs 1500; Sisters' Bazaar: 30 minutes, Rs 120 one way, Rs 180 return (with a half-hour wait); Tehri: three hours, Rs 800; Uttarkashi (for Gangotri): 5½ hours, Rs 1400; Tehri bus stand: 30 minutes, Rs 90. Share taxis depart when they've got five passengers between 6 am and 6 pm (6 am and 8 pm during the season – 1¼ hours, Rs 40).

Taxi – Masonic Lodge Bus Stand Reserve taxi prices from this stand (☎ 63-1407) are identical to those from the library bus stand other than for the following destinations: Rishikesh (Rs 600); Sisters' Bazaar (Rs 80 one way, Rs 100 return); and Tehri bus stand (15 minutes; Rs 50).

Getting Around

The Mall is closed to traffic at most times of the year, so to traverse the two km between Kulri Bazaar and the library area, you can either walk, rent a pony (officially Rs 15 per km), or take a hand-drawn rickshaw (pulled by two rickshaw-wallahs and often pushed by a third). Expect to pay Rs 30 from the Picture Palace and Kulri Bazaar to the UP tourist office, and about Rs 15 to Rs 20 from the tourist office to the library (ie Rs 45 from Kulri Bazaar to the library).

At the time of writing, Bertz Bikes, from where it used to be possible to rent 100cc motorcycles from their shop on the road heading towards Landour Bazaar, was closed, but they may reopen in the near future.

HARIDWAR

Population: 189,000
Telephone Area Code: 0133

Haridwar's propitious location at the point where the Ganges emerges from the high Himalaya, threading its way through the Siwalik foothills to begin its slow progress across the northern plains, makes it a particularly holy place. It serves as a gateway to the holy pilgrimage sites of Badrinath, Kedarnath, Gangotri and Yamunotri further north: in fact Haridwar (or Hardwar) means 'gateway *(dwar)* of the gods (Hari)'. With such a distinguished spiritual pedigree, it is not surprising that it is a favourite pilgrimage site of tens of thousands of Hindus, many of whom can be found at any one time bathing

Sankri-Ruinsara Lake Trek

The trek up the Har ki Dun Valley commences from Sankri, a small village a full day's drive from Mussoorie. The trek follows the well defined trails past a number of settlements before reaching the highest village at Osla. It is a further stage to the alpine meadows at Har ki Dun. From Har ki Dun there are views of Swargarohini (6252m) while the snow-capped range at the head of the valley is the main divide between the Har ki Dun Valley and the Sangla Valley in Kinnaur. A recommended option after visiting Har ki Dun is to backtrack part of the way down the valley to Osla and then head up the trail leading to Ruinsara Lake. The valley is particularly attractive in the springtime when the rhododendrons are in full bloom. For well prepared trekkers there are two further stages (one to the base and one over the Yamunotri Pass) to Yamunotri and Hanuman Chatti.

The trek to Har ki Dun can be completed from April through to the end of October, although the valley is subject to the monsoon rains in July and August. Accommodation is available at GMVN hotels, and porters can be hired from Sankri for around Rs 100 per porter per day.

Stage 1	Sankri to Taluka (3 hours)
Stage 2	Taluka to Osla (5 to 6 hours)
Stage 3	Osla to Har ki Dun (4 to 5 hours)
Stage 4	Har ki Dun to Dev Thach (3 hours)
Stage 5	Dev Thach to Ruinsara Lake & return (7 hours)
Stage 6	Dev Thach or Seema to Sankri (6 hours)

off the Har ki Pairi *ghat* (landing), revered as the precise spot where the Ganges completes its mountain descent and meets the plains. The Ganges is actually diverted just to the north of the town by a barrage, with the city extending along the west bank of the Upper Ganges Canal.

Every 12 years, the Kumbh Mela attracts (literally) millions of pilgrims. Kumbh Mela takes place every three years, consecutively at Allahabad, Nasik, Ujjain and then Haridwar (see below). It is next due to take place in Haridwar in 1998. At the 1986 Kumbh Mela, despite extensive safety precautions, at least 50 people were killed in a stampede to the river, as the pious jostled each other in their race to reach the waters at the most auspicious time (determined astrologically) to have their sins washed away. Dozens more were drowned when they lost their footing in the swift-moving water.

There are dozens of ashrams at Haridwar, but most westerners interested in studying Hinduism head for Rishikesh, 24 km north. It is difficult to imagine how anyone could

possibly hope to attain tranquillity and peace of mind in Haridwar's chaotic milieu. Nevertheless, if you've just arrived from Delhi and want to immerse yourself in the colour and pageant of a thriving Hindu *dham* (holy place) – or simply want to see some of the most extraordinary examples of modern temple architecture you'll find anywhere – Haridwar is not a bad place to spend a few days. Haridwar is also a good point of access for the little visited Rajaji National Park, just to the east of the city.

Orientation

Buses pull into the bus stand at the south-west end of town, on Railway Rd, the long road which runs parallel to the Upper Ganges Canal, connecting this end of town with Har ki Pairi, about 2½ km north-east. The railway station is opposite the UP Roadways bus stand. The canal is traversed by the Laltarao Bridge, which you'll cross if you're coming from Rishikesh. The road over the bridge meets Railway Rd; the north-eastern section of Railway Rd (ie from Laltarao Bridge to Har ki Pairi) is known locally as Upper Rd. There are places to stay and eat scattered along the length of Railway Rd, with a high concentration of budget options in the area known as Shiv Murti, just to the north-east of the bus stand. Behind Har ki Pairi, running parallel to the canal, is the busy market area known as Bara Bazaar.

Information

Tourist Offices The GMVN tourist office (☎ 42-4240) is on Upper Rd, directly opposite the Laltarao Bridge. It's open Monday to Saturday from 10 am to 5 pm. You can book Char Dham packages here, but the office is a bit short on local information. The best source for the low down on Haridwar and the surrounding district, including the Rajaji National Park, to the east of the city, is Sanjeev Mehta at Mohan's Fast Food, Railway Rd (see the Places to Eat section). Sanjeev is a keen photographer, and spends most of his free time stalking through the jungle endeavouring to capture its inhabitants on film. UP Tourism's regional office

Kumbh Mela

Aeons ago the gods and demons, who were constantly at odds, fought a great battle for a *kumbh* or pitcher. Apparently whoever drunk the contents of this pitcher would be ensured immortality. They had combined forces to raise the pitcher from the bottom of the ocean, but once it was safely in their hands, Jayant, the son of Indra, grabbed it on behalf of the gods and ran. After a struggle lasting 12 days the gods eventually defeated the demons and drank the nectar – it's a favourite scene in illustrations of Hindu mythology. During the fight for possession of the pitcher, four drops of *amrita* (nectar) spilt on the earth, at Allahabad, Haridwar, Nasik and Ujjain. The mela is held every three years, rotating among the four cities. Thus each has its own mela every 12 years (for a god's day is a human's year).

Holiest of these four sacred sites is Prayag in Allahabad where the Kumbh Mela returns in 2001. ∎

(☎ 42-7370; open daily from 10 am to 5 pm) is based at the Rahi Motel, further west down Railway Rd, past the bus stand.

Money The Bank of Baroda, next door to the Hotel Mansarovar International, exchanges American Express and Thomas Cook travellers' cheques in US dollars and pounds sterling only. The State Bank of India, on Sadhu Bela Marg, also has foreign exchange facilities.

Post & Communications The main post office is on Upper Rd (Railway Rd), about 200m north-west of Laltarao Bridge. The Foreigners' Registration Office is next door.

Trekking Outfits & Tour Operators Ashvani Travels (☎ 42-4581), at 3 Railway Rd, can organise trekking, white-water rafting (September to March) and ski packages to Auli (January and February). They can also provide guides and porters, or local guides

to take visitors around the salient spots of Haridwar, and hire trekking equipment.

Emergency Police: ☎ 42-6200; Fire: ☎ 42-6000; Hospital: ☎ 42-6060.

Things to See
Although Haridwar is a very old town, mentioned by the Chinese scholar/traveller Hsuan-tsang in the 7th century AD, its many temples were constructed comparatively recently, and are of little historical interest, although they do have many idols and illustrated scenes from the Hindi epics.

The main ghat, **Har ki Pairi** ('the footstep of God'), is supposed to be at the precise spot where the Ganges leaves the mountains and enters the plains. Consequently the river's power to wash away sins at this spot is superlative and the seal of sanctity is a footprint Vishnu left in a stone here. The ghat is on the west bank of a canal through which the Ganges is diverted just to the north. Each

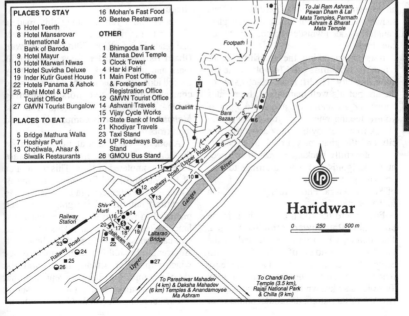

PLACES TO STAY
6 Hotel Teerth
8 Hotel Mansarovar International & Bank of Baroda
9 Hotel Mayur
10 Hotel Marwari Niwas
18 Hotel Suvidha Deluxe
19 Inder Kutir Guest House
22 Hotels Panama & Ashok
25 Rahi Motel & UP Tourist Office
27 GMVN Tourist Bungalow

PLACES TO EAT
5 Bridge Mathura Walla
7 Hoshiyar Puri
13 Chotiwala, Ahaar & Siwalik Restaurants

16 Mohan's Fast Food
20 Bestee Restaurant

OTHER
1 Bhimgoda Tank
2 Mansa Devi Temple
3 Clock Tower
4 Har ki Pairi
11 Main Post Office & Foreigners' Registration Office
12 GMVN Tourist Office
14 Ashvani Travels
15 Vijay Cycle Works
17 State Bank of India
21 Khodiyar Travels
23 Taxi Stand
24 UP Roadways Bus Stand
26 GMOU Bus Stand

Haridwar

0   250   500 m

To Jai Ram Ashram, Pawan Dham & Lal Mata Temples, Parmath Ashram & Bharat Mata Temple

To Pareshwar Mahadev (4 km) & Daksha Mahadev (6 km) Temples & Anandamoyee Ma Ashram

To Chandi Devi Temple (3.5 km), Rajaji National Park & Chilla (9 km)

evening at sunset priests perform the Ganga Aarti, or river worship, ceremony here, when lights which are set on the water drift downstream and the priests engage in their elaborate rituals. Previously non-Hindus were forbidden from stepping on the ghat, but in a new spirit of rapprochement, foreign visitors are now welcome to join the throngs of Hindu pilgrims. The glare from the sun's rays reflecting off the water and marble paved bridges is phenomenal – if you're here at noon, bring sunglasses.

In addition to the main ghat, a series of smaller ghats extends along the canal bank, with large orange and white life-guard towers at intervals – strangely reminiscent of Brighton Beach – to ensure that bathing pilgrims don't get swept away.

On the north side of the canal, between Har ki Pairi and the Upper Rd, is the colourful **Bara Bazaar**. Along with the usual religious paraphernalia (*prasaad* – food offered to the gods, images of the deities, religious pamphlets, etc) are scores of tiny stalls crammed along both sides of the bazaar selling an assortment of goods including tiffins, shawls, ayurvedic medicines, brassware, glass bangles, wooden whistles, bamboo canes and cane baskets.

It is worth taking the chairlift (Rs 13 return) to the **Mansa Devi Temple** on the hill above the city. The lift is not exactly state of the art, but it's well maintained. It operates between 8 am and noon, and 2 and 5 pm. If you're feeling energetic, you can walk up (1½ km) and enjoy the view down over the city and the ghats at your leisure. Vendors sell colourfully packaged prasaad of coconuts, marigolds and other offerings to take up to the goddess. Mansa is one of the forms of Shakti Durga. Photography is forbidden in the temple.

Four km to the south of Haridwar is the brand new **Pareshwar Mahadev Temple**. The temple, which was inaugurated by the late former president of India, Gyani Zail Singh, houses a sacred lingam reputedly made of mercury. The **Daksha Mahadev Temple** (also known as Shri Dakheswar), is two km further along this route, on the river

bank at Khankhal, six km to the south of Haridwar. Daksha, the father of Sati (Shiva's first wife), performed a sacrifice here but neglected to invite Shiva. Sati was so angry at this unforgivable indiscretion that she managed to spontaneously self-immolate! Opposite this temple is the **Anandamoyee Ma Ashram**, which, since the death of this Bengali guru who counted among her devotees Indira Gandhi, has become an enormous mausoleum.

Other temples and buildings of note in the environs of Haridwar include the **Bhimgoda Tank**, about one km to the north of Har ki Pairi. The tank is said to have been formed by a blow of Bhima's knee – Bhima is the brother of Hanuman. About 150m further north, on the Rishikesh road, is the **Jai Ram Ashram**. Here the usual multicoloured deities characteristic of Hindu temples are strangely absent. Sculptures are in pristine white, and depict the gods and the demons battling for the waters of humanity. Also here are electronically animated images of the deities which depict various scenes from the Hindu epics.

About 500m further along this road, a turn-off to the right at a (usually) dry river bed leads in a further 500m to the **Pawan Dham Temple**. This temple is famed for its glass and mirror work, and its elaborately garbed idols. There is an enormous life-sized chariot drawn by two horses depicting Arjuna and Krishna in a scene from the *Mahabharata* which is completely covered in mirrors.

About one km further along this road, on the left, is the extraordinary **Lal Mata Temple**, completed in 1994. This is a replica of the Vaishno Devi Temple in Jammu & Kashmir. The engineers, in an endeavour to be entirely faithful to the original, have even managed to recreate the hill on which the latter is sited. The artificial hill is surmounted by a cave housing an image of Vaishno Devi. Adjacent to the hill is a lingam made of ice which remains perpetually frozen with the aid of a compressor. This is a replica of that in the Amarnath Cave in Jammu & Kashmir.

Further along this road, which eventually

rejoins the main Rishikesh road, is the **Parmath Ashram**, which has fine images of the goddess Durga. The road proceeds past the recently constructed **Bharat Mata Temple**, looking like an apartment block with a central dome. It's eight storeys high and there's a lift to the top for lazy pilgrims. On the top floor is an image of Lord Shankar (Shiva). Just before this route rejoins the main Rishikesh road is the **Sapt Rishi Ashram**, about five km from Haridwar, named after the seven *rishis* (Hindu saints) who prayed here for the good of humanity. According to tradition, in order to please the seven rishis who were meditating in seven different locations, the Ganges split into seven streams here. Tempos (Vikrams) ply this route.

Chandi Devi, erected on Nhil Hill by a Kashmiri raja, Suchet Singh, in 1929, and a number of other temples in the hills are reached by an approximately four km walk to the south-east. Municipal approval has been granted for the construction of a ropeway cable car from Haridwar to Chandi Devi.

You may see large **river turtles** on the banks of the Nildhara River, near Haridwar, which is over two km broad during the monsoon.

Places to Stay

The *Hotel Mayur* (☎ 42-7586), Upper Rd (near the ropeway), has very basic singles/doubles for Rs 110/165 in the off season, and Rs 165/265 in the peak season (May & June). Rooms have attached baths, air-coolers and geysers, and those at the front are larger. The laneway beside the Mayur will bring you to the *Hotel Marwari Niwas* (☎ 42-7759), in the area known as Subzi Mandi. Air-cooled doubles (no single rates) are Rs 220, and rooms with air-con are Rs 500. Rooms are set around a well, and all have running hot water and Star TV. Room service is available.

Back on the Upper Rd, about 200m north, is the *Hotel Mansarovar International* (☎ 42-6501). This is a relatively new place, with comfortable but drab singles/doubles with fans for Rs 250/300, with air-coolers,

Rs 350/400, and with air-con, Rs 550/600. A 15% to 20% discount is offered in the off season, and there's a good restaurant here (the Swagat). Credit cards are accepted.

The *Hotel Teerth* (☎ 42-7111), in the heart of Bara Bazaar, is set right on the river, with great views over Har ki Pairi. Air-cooled doubles are Rs 575, or with air-con, Rs 800. All rooms face the river and have balconies, and the staff are friendly and helpful. There's a restaurant here.

There's a cluster of budget and mid-range hotels in the area called Shiv Murti, just to the north-east of the bus stand and railway station. The *Hotel Kailash* (☎ 42-7789), Railway Rd (the western extension of Upper Rd), has air-cooled doubles for Rs 250, and air-con doubles for Rs 550. Some of the rooms have balconies, and there's a restaurant here.

The *Hotel Panama* (☎ 42-7506), just down the road from the Bestee Restaurant on Jasharam Rd, has cheap singles/doubles at Rs 45/90 with attached bath (bucket hot water available). Rooms are small and a little dark, but clean, and tea, toast and cold drinks are available through room service.

A few doors down, also in the Shiv Murti area, is the *Hotel Ashok* (☎ 42-7328). Basic singles with attached bath (cold water only) are Rs 75. Doubles with common bath are Rs 150, or with attached bath (running hot water), Rs 225. Air-cooled deluxe doubles are Rs 425, and air-con doubles are Rs 825. Rooms are spotless, and there's a travel desk and dining hall.

About five minutes walk away, in a quiet location at Sharwan Nath Nagar, is the relatively new *Hotel Suvidha Deluxe* (☎ 42-7423). Pleasant comfortable singles/doubles, all with colour TV, are Rs 450/550 with air-cooler, Rs 700/800 with air-con. There's a restaurant here.

Handy to the bus stand, but in a quiet location about 150m east of the terminal, is the *Rahi Motel* (☎ 42-6430), which is also the home of UP Tourism's regional tourist office. Air-cooled singles/doubles are Rs 250/300, or with air-con, they're Rs 400/450. These rates include breakfast, and there is also a six bed dorm (Rs 50). All rooms have colour TV, and there's a restaurant here.

The friendly family-run *Inder Kutir Guest House* (☎ 42-6336) is recommended. It is a clean place close to the Upper Ganges Canal, at Sharwan Nath Nagar. Air-cooled singles/doubles are Rs 150/200, and there's a dining hall here.

GMVN's *Tourist Bungalow* (☎ 42-6379) is in a peaceful location right on the river, outside the main part of town in Belwala. Singles/doubles are Rs 300/350, or Rs 550/650 with air-con. Dorm beds are Rs 50. There's no restaurant, but nonveg meals can be brought to your room.

Places to Eat

As a holy pilgrimage place, alcohol and meat are strictly prohibited; in fact, imbibing the one or consuming the other is a prosecutable offence. There is, however, a good selection of vegetarian restaurants. In the Shiv Murti area, close to the Hotel Panama, is the *Bestee Restaurant*, which has good shakes (in season, try the delicious cheiku shake – cheiku is a small brown fruit similar in appearance to a potato, but sweet). There are also snacks such as vegie rolls (Rs 14) and cutlets (Rs 13), and for breakfast you can wash down your porich (!) with a chocolate lassi (Rs 16).

The *Hoshiyar Puri* has been serving thalis for over 50 years, and they're still good value. The special thali features cheese korma, mattar panir, dhal and kheer (rice pud).

The *Bridge Mathura Walla* sweet shop in the heart of the Bara Bazaar has a range of sticky temptations including ras malai (Rs 5) – a milk and sugar based sweet served in a banana leaf plate, floating in sugar syrup and sprinkled with pistachio nuts; rabri, a similar milky confection; and wedges of cashew-nut-studded halwa. Bhaturas (whopping big puris served with aalu and mattar) are also a cheap eat in the bazaar.

Close to Shiv Murti, in the Chitra Cinema Compound, Railway Rd, is the deservedly popular *Mohan's Fast Food*. There are the usual offerings such as pizza and vegie burgers, with a few special Gujarati dishes thrown in for good measure, such as batata vada – four pakhoras, green mint chutney and chilli (Rs 15), and pao bhaji – two buns with minced vegetables served in a thali with salad (Rs 15). There's also an astonishing range of ice creams and sundaes, and the friendly owner, Sanjeev Mehta, has a wealth of knowledge on sights around Haridwar, and on the Rajaji National Park.

Opposite the GMVN tourist office are three good up-market dining places. The pick of the bunch is the *Ahaar Restaurant*, specialising in Punjabi, South Indian and Chinese cuisine. It's down a flight of stairs next door to the Ahaar ice-cream parlour. There's also good Punjabi food at the long-running *Chotiwala*, a few doors down, and the *Siwalik*, on the corner, is a multicuisine restaurant which also specialises in Gujarati dishes.

Getting There & Away

Air Jolly Grant is the closest airport to Haridwar, 35 km to the north, but there are currently no scheduled flights. UP Airways may commence a daily service to Delhi in the near future. See the Dehra Dun section above.

Bus The UP Roadways bus stand (☎ 42-7037) is at the south-west end of Station Rd. Buses leave every 30 minutes for Rishikesh (one hour, Rs 7) and Dehra Dun (1½ to two hours, Rs 14). For Mussoorie, you'll need to change at Dehra Dun. There are ordinary bus services every 30 minutes up to 11.30 pm to Delhi (eight hours, Rs 53.50), and early morning and late afternoon and evening services to Agra (12 hours, Rs 100). Buses for Shimla leave at 8 and 9.30 am (14 hours, Rs 95); to Nainital, at 5.30, 8.45, 9.15, 9.30 and 10.30 am (seven hours, Rs 80); to Almora at 5, 5.30 and 7 am (10 hours, Rs 107); to Ranikhet at 6.30 am and 4.30 pm (nine hours, Rs 89); and to Tehri (five hours, Rs 40) and Uttarkashi (10 hours, Rs 80) at 5.30, 6.30, 8.30 and 9.30 am.

For the Char Dham (Yamunotri, Gangotri, Badrinath and Kedarnath), you'll need to find your way to Rishikesh. As many of the buses to these pilgrimage sites leave in the wee hours, you'd do better to stay overnight in Rishikesh at one of the hotels opposite the Yatra bus stand.

To get to Chilla (for Rajaji National Park), catch a Kandi-bound bus from the Garhwal Motor Owners' Union (GMOU) stand near the Rahi Motel. Buses leave at 7 and 9 am, and return at noon and 4 pm (Rs 7).

Train See the Dehra Dun section for details of trains between Haridwar and Delhi. Other direct trains connect Haridwar with Calcutta (1472 km, 35 hours), Mumbai (Bombay) (1649 km, 40 hours), Varanasi (894 km, 20 hours) and Lucknow (493 km, 11 hours).

Taxi The Taxi Drivers & Owners Association (☎ 42-7338) is directly opposite the bus stand. Posted rates are as follows: Rishikesh (Rs 200), Dehra Dun (Rs 300), Mussoorie (Rs 500), Tehri (Rs 700), Uttarkashi (Rs 1000); Hanuman Chatti (for Yamunotri – Rs 2800), Gangotri (Rs 2800), Delhi (Rs 900), Chilla (for Rajaji National Park – Rs 200 one way, Rs 300 return), Ranikhet (Rs 1700), Almora (Rs 1800), Nainital (Rs 1500) and Shimla (Rs 2500). A nine day tour to the Char Dham is Rs 8000 (transport only). The taxi office is open 24 hours. You might be able to get more competitive rates from the travel agents on Jasharam Rd in the Shiv Murti area such as Shakti Wahini Travels (☎ 42-7002) or Khodiyar Travels (☎ 42-3560).

During May and June, share taxis ply between the taxi stand and Rishikesh, Dehra Dun and Mussoorie, and possibly Chilla.

Getting Around
You can get from the railway station or UP state bus stand to Har ki Pairi by cycle-rickshaw for Rs 7 or Vikram for Rs 3.

Low-tech rattle-you-senseless bicycles can be hired from Vijay Cycle Works, Railway Rd (near the Hotel Aarti), but for Rs 1.50 per hour, or Rs 10 per day, who's complaining?

RAJAJI NATIONAL PARK
This beautiful park, covering 820 sq km in the forested foothills east of Haridwar, is best known for its wild elephants, numbering around 150 in all. Unfortunately their future is in question since human competition for land has severed their traditional migration route, which once stretched from here to the area which is now part of Corbett National Park, 170 km to the east. Plans for a 'migration corridor' would involve moving several villages and have become bogged down in the usual bureaucracy. Nevertheless, increasing ecological awareness has brought about some advances, with large ducts having been constructed under the Chilla-Rishikesh road to enable the migrating animals to pass beneath.

As well as elephants, the park contains some rarely seen tigers and leopards, chital (spotted deer), which can be seen in herds of up to 250 at one time, sambar (India's largest species of deer), wild boars, sloth bears, barking deer, porcupines, jungle fowls, hornbills and pythons.

Open from mid-November to mid-June, the entry fee is Rs 100 for up to three days, and Rs 50 for each additional day. Entry into the park is not permitted between sunset and sunrise. Photography fees are Rs 50 for a still camera, Rs 500 for a video camera.

The (rather unattractive) village of Chilla, 13 km east of Haridwar, is the only area which currently has an infrastructure in place for visitors. From Chilla it is possible to take elephant rides (Rs 50 per person, up to four people; Rs 200 for solitary would-be *mahouts*, or masters) into the park. Official hire rates for jeeps (available from Chilla) are Rs 20 per km. The Forest Ranger's office is close to the tourist bungalow at Chilla; entry fees are paid here, and you can also book elephant rides here. Chilla has become the adoptive home of Raja, a baby elephant, who became an orphan when his mother, and several other elephants, were struck and killed by a train on the Rishikesh Rd.

One km beyond the entry gate is a *machaan* (hide), previously used by hunters, but now a vantage point from where visitors can unobtrusively view the park's inhabitants.

It may be possible to visit tribal villages in the park, where Gujars, who still live in their traditional clay huts and tend buffaloes, greet visitors with bowls of fresh, warm buffalo milk. Check at the Forest Ranger's bungalow in Chilla, or contact Sanjeev at Mohan's Fast Food, Railway Rd, Haridwar.

Places to Stay

There is a GMVN *Tourist Rest House* at Chilla. Here it's Rs 265 in a standard double, Rs 400 in an air-cooled double, and there's dorm beds for Rs 65; you may also be able to camp in the grounds here.

Accommodation is available at the nine *Forest Rest Houses* dotted around the park. Double rates at Beribara, Ranipur, Kansrao, Kunnao, Phandowala, Satyanarain and Asarodi are all Rs 150; at Motichur and Chilla, rates are Rs 300. At these places, other than at Chilla, you'll need to bring your own food. For bookings contact the Chief Forest Officer, Tilak Rd, Dehra Dun, or write to the Director, Rajaji National Park office, 5/1 Ansari Marg, Dehra Dun (☎ 62-1669).

Getting There & Away

Buses to Chilla leave from the Garhwal Motor Owners' Union (GMOU), Haridwar, close to the Rahi Motel, en route to Kandi. They depart at 7 and 9 am, and return at noon and 4 pm (Rs 7). If there are enough passengers, share taxis leave from the taxi stand opposite the UP state bus stand or from Chandi Ghat, opposite Har ki Pairi (Rs 10). The official rate for a reserve taxi to Chilla from Haridwar is Rs 200 one way, Rs 300 return (although ensure that the driver knows how much time you plan to spend at the park). You could also cycle to Chilla; bikes are available for hire in Haridwar (see under Haridwar's Getting Around section).

To walk to Chilla from Haridwar, cross the Laltarao Bridge and walk to the roundabout, then turn left onto the Rishikesh road. Just before the cable bridge over the Ganges canal, turn right. After 100m you'll reach a

dam; cross the dam and turn left, where a short walk will bring you to a small artificial lake. Here you'll see migratory birds, including Siberian cranes, ducks and other water fowl, and in the evening, wild animals, including elephants, come here to drink (although you should beware of wild elephants at dusk). The road flanking the lake leads to Chilla, a further five km distant.

AROUND CHILLA

Fourteen km north-east of Chilla, two km off the Chilla-Rishikesh road, is the small village of **Bindevasani**. Local buses ply between the village and both Chilla and Haridwar, with the section between Chilla and the turn-off to Bindevasani at a high elevation, affording good views out over the national park. There's a small temple sacred to Durga (Shiva's consort in her fierce form) a steep 15 to 20 minute walk above the village. The temple itself is not of great interest, but it commands an excellent position, overlooking the *sangam* (confluence) of the Bindedhara and Nildhara rivers.

There are a number of walking trails in the environs of the village, including one to **Nhilkantha**, 14 km north. Here there is a Shiva temple, Nhilkantha Mahadev. 'Nhilkantha' is derived from *nhil* (blue) and *kantha* (throat), alluding to the time when Shiva saved the world by swallowing the poison which rose during the churning of the oceans at the beginning of creation; the toxic beverage caused his throat to turn blue. In July, pilgrims converge on the village to commemorate this event.

From Nhilkantha, it is possible to continue to **Lakshman Jhula** (see the Rishikesh section), the suspension bridge which traverses the Ganges to the north-east of Rishikesh. The trail follows the original pilgrim trail, which affords magnificent forest scenery – beware of wild elephants, especially at dusk.

There are *dharamsalas* (pilgrims' rest houses) at Nhilkantha, but you'll need to be prepared to camp out, and will require provisions, at Bindevasani.

RISHIKESH
Population: 71,000
Telephone Area Code: 01364

Rishikesh has been a holy place of pilgrimage since time immemorial, with sages and ascetics making their way here to pay homage to the great Mother Ganga en route to the pilgrim sites further north in the Himalaya. According to tradition, Lord Rama and his brother Lakshman stopped over here after slaying the demon Ravana. The town grew around the Bharat Mandir (*mandir* means temple), which was erected on the site at which Lord Vishnu appeared to two rishis – a father and son – who had impressed the god with their intense veneration. The town lies at 356m, only 24 km north of Haridwar, and is surrounded by forested hills on three sides. It is dissected by the holy Ganges flanked by ashrams and dharamsalas. This is an excellent place to stay and study yoga, meditation and other aspects of Hinduism.

Rishikesh is where the Beatles came to be with their guru, the Maharishi Mahesh Yogi.

Swami Alert
While many of Rishikesh's ashrams have charitable dispensaries and hospitals, providing invaluable service to India's sick and destitute, the sheer opulence of some suggests concerns with matters more earthly than spiritual, and the behaviour of some of their gurus leaves much to be desired. In 1995, one of these 'holy' men, Swami Rameshwarand Giriji Maharaj, fell from grace when he murdered the husband of a female devotee with whom he had enjoyed a less than spiritual alliance. He allegedly told the woman that she could attain spiritual salvation only through sexual relations with a person close to God like him! ■

Orientation
The city comprises loosely designated districts which tend to merge into each other. The main administrative and commercial sector is to the south of the (usually dry)

Chandrabhaga River, and it is here that you'll find both the main and Yatra bus stands, the main post office, banks and hotels.

If you arrive by share jeep, you'll probably be dropped on Haridwar Rd in this commercial area. The northern extension of Haridwar Rd is called Lakshman Jhula Rd. It proceeds over the Chandrabhaga River, passing the GMVN tourist office, about 1½ km north of the main post office in the area known as Muni ki Reti, and continuing to Shivanand Jhula (*jhula* means bridge), a further 1½ km north. (This bridge is also known as Ram Jhula.) Here, on both the east and west sides of the Ganges (the east side here is known as Swarg Ashram, and there is no vehicular traffic) are the bulk of the temples and ashrams.

A further two km north is Lakshman Jhula, the second suspension bridge over the Ganges, where there is another concentration of temples and ashrams. There are several guesthouses at Shivanand Jhula and Lakshman Jhula, and many travellers prefer to stay here than in the busy town centre.

Information
Tourist Offices The helpful UP tourist office (☎ 30-209) is on Railway Station Rd. It's open Monday to Saturday from 10 am to 5 pm (lunch from 1.30 to 2 pm). The GMVN tourist office (☎ 30-372) is in the area known as Muni ki Reti (open Monday to Saturday from 10 am to 5 pm; closed for lunch between 2 and 3 pm). It's set a little back from Lakshman Jhula Rd, near Kailash Gate.

Money The State Bank of India is next to the Inderlok Hotel on Railway Station Rd. It exchanges most major travellers' cheques, but *not* Visa or MasterCard. If you're carrying either of these, try the Bank of Baroda.

Travel Agencies Ajay Travels (☎ 32-897), beneath the Hotel Neelkanth on Ghat Rd in the commercial district, can arrange taxis and bus travel to the Char Dham and elsewhere. Similar services are offered by Blue Hills Travels (☎ 31-865), in the Swarg Ashram area.

Trekking Outfits & Tour Operators At the GMVN tourist office (☎ 30-372) you can book Char Dham packages, and there's also a Trekking & Mountaineering division (☎ 32-648) where you can hire tents, rucksacks, sleeping bags and mountaineering equipment, as well as book treks. Rates for treks start at Rs 1325 per day (minimum of three people required), including transport by deluxe coach or taxi, all meals, porters, guides and accommodation in tourist rest houses or tents. Treks include a nine day Har ki Dun trek, a 10 day trek to the lake of Rup Kund, eight day treks to the Valley of Flowers, and a 14 day trek to the Khatling Glacier (all during the summer months only).

Triveni Travels (☎ 32-989; fax 32-881), on Railway Station Rd, can arrange whitewater rafting at Brahmpuri, 10 km from Rishikesh, or the more exhilarating rapids at Shivpuri, 18 km from Rishikesh. Cost is Rs 550 and includes transport, lunch, life jackets and helmets with two to three hours racing the rapids down the Ganges. A minimum of five people is required. They also have caving expeditions through the 200m long Vishitha *gufa* (cave), 16 km from Rishikesh near Shivpuri (Rs 500), and half-day elephant safaris in the Rajaji National Park (Rs 800), as well as offering trekking and Char Dham packages.

Apex Adventure Tours (☎ 32-804), at Muni ki Reti, next door to the GMVN office, offers rafting and trekking packages at comparable rates, and also has rock-climbing expeditions (for beginners and more experienced climbers).

Himalayan River Runners (☎ 61-5736), 188-A Jor Bagh, New Delhi, offers whitewater rafting expeditions ex Delhi on the Alaknanda and Ganges rivers between Rudraprayag and Rishikesh, or shorter expeditions on the Ganges between Deoprayag and Rishikesh.

UP Tourism also offers rafting packages from their camp at Kaudiyala, near Rishikesh. Prices start at Rs 350 per day for rafting, Rs 150 for meals, and Rs 65 for share lodging (or Rs 100 for single occupancy).

UP Tourism offers coach tours to the Char Dham from Rishikesh. A four day bus tour to Badrinath is Rs 1320, including share accommodation. To Yamunotri and Gangotri, a seven day tour departs each Friday during the yatra season (Rs 2050).

UP Tourism offers taxi package tours to the Char Dham ex Rishikesh. A 10 day package to the Char Dham is Rs 5610 per person. The six day taxi package ex Rishikesh to Kedarnath and Badrinath is Rs 3400 per person.

Meditation & Yoga Courses

There is a plethora of ashrams offering courses in mediation, yoga and Hindu philosophy. It's worth first talking to other travellers and going to a few lectures (free) at different ashrams to find your guru, if you're looking for one.

Many westerners attend the Hatha yoga and pranayama meditation classes at **Sri Ved Niketan Ashram**, Swarg Ashram, founded by Shri Vishwaguruji Maharaj Yogasamrat. Lectures on various aspects of Hindu philosophy are also given here (in English). Classes are Rs 50 each, and are held between 6.30 and 8 am, and 6 and 7.30 pm. If you attend for one month, you'll receive a certificate. It is also possible to stay here (see the Places to Stay section).

The **Mahesh Yogi Ashram**, on the east side of the river above Ved Niketan, has courses in transcendental meditation. The term 'Maharishi' has been dropped from the title, as the master who moved the hearts and minds of the Beatles was not technically a maharishi. Six month courses are Rs 5000, including lectures, meditation and yoga classes, and meals. You will need to write in advance to reserve a spot. Write to Mahesh Yogi Ashram, Shankaracharya Nagar, Rishikesh, 249201 (☎ 30-121).

Shivanand Ashram (☎ 30-040) was founded by Swami Shivananda and is under the auspices of the Divine Life Society. The ashram is on the west side of Lakshman Jhula Rd, directly opposite the Shivanand Jhula. There are lectures, discussions and meditation and yoga classes daily, with courses from three days to two months (all free). It is

GARRY WEARE

GARRY WEARE

Uttarakhand
    Top: Shepherds in the Josimath area.
Bottom: A village in the remote Har ki Dun Valley, north-west Uttarakhand.

MICHELLE COXALL

MICHELLE COXALL

MICHELLE COXALL

MICHELLE COXALL

A	B	C
D

Uttarakhand
A: A prasaad vendor at Triveni Ghat, Rishikesh.
B: An ashram in holy Rishikesh.
C: Mother and child paying homage to Durga during the Dussehra festival, Almora.
D: The Savoy Hotel in Mussoorie, a grand relic of the British Raj.

Swami Shivananda & the Divine Life Society

Swami Shivananda was born on 8 September 1887 in the village of Pattamadai, in South India, and named Kuppuswamy. As a young man, Kuppuswamy studied medicine, excelling in his final examinations. After practising as a doctor for several years, he made his way to Rishikesh in 1924, where he met Sri Swami Visvananda Saraswati. This encounter was to change the direction of his life. He was initiated into the Sannyasa order, discarded the trappings of wealth, undertook various privations including long fasts and immersing himself for hours in the freezing waters of the Ganges, and pledged to serve humanity.

Among the thousands of pilgrims who came to the holy town of Rishikesh were many suffering terrible afflictions, and there was no shortage of patients upon whom the doctor-turned-swami could practise his healing craft, including those afflicted with diseases such as cholera and smallpox. In 1927 he founded a charitable dispensary at Lakshman Jhula.

During the course of his life, Swami Shivananda visited all of the most important places of pilgrimage in India, and in 1936, returned to Rishikesh where he founded the Divine Life Society, whose primary aims were the dissemination of spiritual knowledge and service to humanity. The society now continues to propagate the ideals formulated by Swami Shivananda, with over 500 branches around the world. Swami Shivananda died on 14 July 1963. ∎

possible to stay at the ashram (for a limited period, by donation), but one month's advance notice is required; write to the Divine Life Society, PO Shivanandanagar, 249192, District Tehri, Garhwal, UP.

Close by, reached along a path leading up from Lakshman Jhula Rd, and set in lovely gardens high above the Ganges, is the **Yoga Niketan Ashram** (☎ 30-227). The ashram was founded by Swami Yogeshwarananda, who died in 1984. Classes on meditation and the pranayama form of Hatha yoga are held throughout the year, and you can join classes at any time. It's possible to stay if you're attending classes (by donation), and meals are available.

Above Yoga Niketan is the **Omkarananda Ashram** (☎ 30-763; fax 31-531), also known as Durga Mandir, which runs courses (by donation) in a separate building called the Omkarananda Ganga Sadan, back down on Lakshman Jhula Rd, near the Shivananda Arch. If there are enough students (minimum of 20 required), beginner courses are run in Hatha yoga. Regular Hatha yoga classes are held daily (except Sunday) from 5.30 to 7 pm. Meditation is lead by Acharya Surya Prakash Prabhuji, who spent seven years in the Himalaya on a solitary retreat. Instruction in various forms of Indian classical dance is also given.

The **Yoga Study Centre** (☎ 31-196), about 1½ km south of the main post office just off Haridwar Rd at Ganga Vihar, offers three week courses in the Iyengar form of Hatha yoga during February, April and September for beginners and more advanced students. According to the centre's prospectus, the aim is to 'propagate yoga and spiritual knowledge' and to 'promote the ideal of universal Brotherhood and Service among Mankind irrespective of Caste, Creed, Community & Nationality'. Fees are by donation only, and reservation should be secured at least two weeks in advance. There's no accommodation here.

In the Lakshman Jhula area, on the right when approaching the bridge from the west side of the river, is the **Vanmali Gita Yogashram** (☎ 31-316). The ashram was founded by Sri Swami Jayendra Saraswati Maharaj Jagadguru Sankaracharya; two hour classes in yoga and meditation are held at 4 and at 6.30 pm respectively.

International Yoga Festival

This festival, organised by UP Tourism, is held annually from 2 to 7 February (the dates remain constant each year). Yoga and meditation masters from around India converge on Rishikesh at this time to impart their

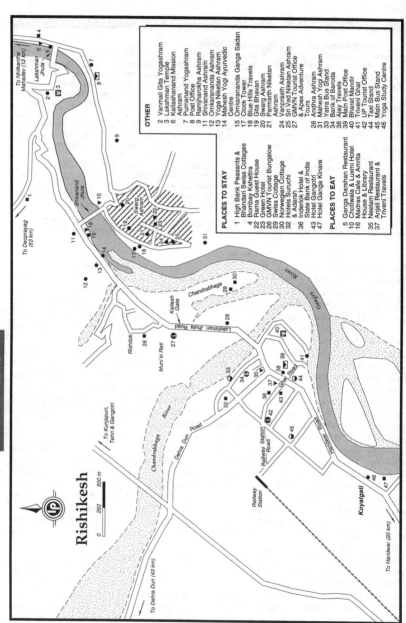

Rishikesh

0   250   500 m

OTHER
2   Vanmali Gita Yogashram
3   Lakshman Temple
6   Kailashanand Mission
     Ashram
7   Purnanand Yogashram
8   Post Office
9   Ramjharokha Ashram
11   Shivanand Ashram
12   Omkarananda Ashram
13   Yoga Niketan Ashram
14   Maesh Yogi Ayurvedic
     Centre
15   Omkarananda Ganga Sadan
17   Clock Tower
18   Blue Hills Travels
19   Gita Bhavan
20   Swarg Ashram
21   Parmarth Niketan
     Ashram
24   Vanprasth Ashram
25   Sivananda Niketan Ashram
27   GMVN Tourist Office
     & Apex Adventure
     Tours
28   Andhra Ashram
31   Mahesh Yogi Ashram
33   Yatra Bus Stand
34   Bank of Baroda
38   Ajay Travels
39   Main Post Office
40   Bharat Mandir
41   Triveni Ghat
42   UP Tourist Office
44   Taxi Stand
45   Main Bus Stand
46   Yoga Study Centre

PLACES TO STAY
1   High Bank Peasants &
     Bhandari Swiss Cottages
4   Bombay Kshettra
22   Rama Guest House
23   Green Hotel
26   GMVN Tourist Bungalow
29   Swiss Cottage
30   Norwegian Cottage
32   Hotels Suruchi
     & Adarsh
36   Inderlok Hotel &
     State Bank of India
43   Hotel Gangotri
47   Hotel Ganga Kinare

PLACES TO EAT
5   Ganga Darshan Restaurant
10   Chotiwala & Luxmi Hotel
16   Madras Cafe & Amrita
     House & Library
35   Neelam Restaurant
37   Anjali Restaurant &
     Triveni Travels

knowledge. Seven day packages inclusive of meals, hotel accommodation, transportation from your hotel to venues, lectures, and air-con deluxe coach transfer between Delhi and Rishikesh are US$470/500/940 for singles/doubles/triples. Bookings should be made at least two months in advance by writing to the Director, UP Tourism, Chitrahar Building, 3 Naval Kishor Rd, Lucknow (☎ (0522) 223-3632).

As the festival is held during the off season, you shouldn't have too much trouble organising your own accommodation at this time. Costs to attend lectures are around Rs 1200 for the week.

Things to See

Triveni Ghat, at the east end of Ghat Rd, the extension of Railway Station Rd, is an interesting place to be at dawn, when offerings of milk are made to the river and pilgrims feed the surprisingly large fish. After sunset, priests wave *diya* (lamps) on the water in the Ganga Aarti (river worship) ceremony.

Nearby is the **Bharat Mandir**, the oldest temple in Rishikesh. The temple is sacred to Bharat Ji Maharaj, an incarnation of Lord Vishnu. The black image of the deity housed in the temple, formed from a single stone, is believed to have been installed by Shankaracharya in the 9th century AD. There are some large and unusual carvings around the exterior walls, including carvings of Narsingh and other incarnations of Vishnu. The temple is open from 5 to 11 am and 1 to 9 pm.

Swarg Ashram, on the east side of the river over the Shivanand (or Ram) Jhula, is the spiritual heartland of Rishikesh, full of multicoloured ashrams, dharamsalas and bathing ghats, set against a beautiful backdrop of wooded hills. Two km further north along the Lakshman Jhula Rd is the **Lakshman Jhula** itself, a suspension bridge built in 1939 to replace a rope bridge. This is where Rama's brother Lakshman is said to have crossed the Ganges on a jute rope after he and his brother killed the demon Ravana. The old Lakshman Temple, where Lakshman undertook penance for *brahmahatya* (Brahmin slaughter), is on the west bank.

Across the river are some turreted architectural edifices, including the 13 storey **Kailashanand Mission Ashram**, also known as Swarga Niwas – Heavenly Abode – founded by Sri 108 Swami Kailashanand Ji Maharaj. A fair swag of the Hindu pantheon is represented by colourful statues on almost every floor, and there's a good view from the top. It's a pleasant two km walk from here along the east bank of the Ganges back to Shivanand Jhula.

Pilgrims take Ganga water to offer at **Nhilkantha Mahadev** at Nhilkantha (see the Around Chilla section), 11 km from Rishikesh and a four hour walk from Lakshman Jhula starting from the east bank. There are fine views on the way up to the temple at 1700m, but take something to drink and start early, as it can get very hot. It's possible to get a Kandi-bound bus to Maongaon, from where it is a three km walk to the village.

There are also good views from **Kunjapuri**, in the hills north of Rishikesh. It's a three km walk from Hindola Khal (45 minutes by bus from Rishikesh), which all buses to Tehri pass through.

Places to Stay

Chandrabhaga & Rishilok In a good location on Railway Station Rd is the *Hotel Gangotri* (☎ 31-139), which has ordinary singles/doubles for Rs 150/225, air-cooled rooms for Rs 275/350, and air-con rooms for Rs 450/550. All rooms have attached bath (cold water only; hot water in buckets free). The air-con rooms at the front of the hotel have private balconies and a *joola* (bamboo chair) suspended from the ceiling! The restaurant here is open in the season only.

Diagonally opposite is the *Inderlok Hotel* (☎ 30-555), which has standard singles/doubles for Rs 300/400, air-cooled rooms for Rs 400/450, or with air-con, Rs 500/600. Rooms are cool and comfortable, all with colour TV, and there's a resident yoga teacher who gives free lessons on the pleasant rooftop garden terrace. There is also a travel desk here.

There are a couple of good choices right beside the Yatra bus stand. The *Hotel Suruchi*

(☎ 30-356), built around a spacious atrium, has standard singles/doubles for Rs 175/250, or air-cooled rooms for Rs 250/350. Attached baths have cold water only, but hot water is free in buckets. The restaurant here is very reasonably priced.

Nearby is the cheaper *Hotel Adarsh* (☎ 31-301). Rooms are pretty ordinary, and cost Rs 100 for singles and doubles. Some have attached baths. There are also dorm beds for Rs 35, and there's a dining hall here.

The *Hotel Ganga Kinare* (☎ 30-566) is a bit of a hike from the centre, about two km south of Railway Station Rd at 16 Virbhadra Rd. However, it's in a lovely peaceful spot on the west bank of the Ganges, and rooms are very well appointed, some (the more expensive ones!) having beautiful river views. All rooms are centrally air-conditioned, and singles/doubles cost Rs 990/1090, or Rs 1090/1190 with better views. Free meditation classes are held on the terrace, and guests can use the hotel's rowing boats. There's also a reference library on yoga, a travel desk which can arrange trekking, rafting, skiing, cycling and wildlife and cultural tours, and a reasonably priced restaurant. Evening prayers take place on the hotel's private ghat.

On the north side of the Chandrabhaga River is the very popular *Swiss Cottage* (no phone). It's run by Swami Brahmananda, a disciple of Swami Shivananda, and is a lovely tranquil place, with rooms set around a shady courtyard. Singles, doubles and triples are all Rs 50, some with attached bath. No meals are provided, but self-catering is OK. If this place is booked up, ask here for directions to the nearby *Norwegian Cottage*. It's equally as friendly, if not quite as atmospheric.

Further towards Shivanand Jhula, on a road which leads to the left off Lakshman Jhula Rd just past the GMVN office, is GMVN's *Tourist Bungalow* (☎ 30-373), in the area known as Rishilok. It's set in lovely grounds, but it's a little pricey, with ordinary singles/doubles with common bath for Rs 100/130, with attached bath, Rs 200/265, or with air-cooler and geyser for Rs 357/450.

Hot water is available in buckets for Rs 2, and there's a restaurant here.

Swarg Ashram Area There are a couple of guesthouses and a choice of two ashrams on this east side of the river, over the Shivanand Jhula. A deservedly popular choice is the *Green Hotel* (☎ 31-242). It's down a quiet lane, and has clean, if spartan, rooms at Rs 75/125 for singles/doubles. Larger doubles with air-coolers are Rs 250, and hot water is free by the bucket. There's a good restaurant here.

Behind the Green is the *Rama Guest House* (no phone). Clean doubles with common bath are Rs 60 (there's one *tiny* single for Rs 40). The guesthouse is run by a very friendly Madrasi man. There's no restaurant here.

Right on the Ganges, at the south end of Swarg Ashram about a 10 minute walk from the Shivanand Jhula, is the *Vanprasth Ashram*. There's a resident yoga teacher, but you don't have to attend classes if you don't want to. Doubles and triples are Rs 75 with attached bath (cold water only), and there's a room which can accommodate up to six people (Rs 300). There's a canteen in the ashram, or it's OK to self-cater using the ashram's kitchen facilities (free). You can hire a gas cylinder for Rs 15 per day. This place has lovely flower gardens, and the double rooms face the Ganges. Foreign visitors can only stay between 1 November and 31 March.

Next door is the *Sri Ved Niketan Ashram*, an unmissable orange and turquoise edifice. There are daily yoga and meditation classes (see under Yoga & Meditation, above), but no pressure to attend. Large but spartan singles/doubles are Rs 50/70 with attached bath (cold water only; bucket hot water free). The upstairs rooms at the front have good views over the Ganges.

Lakshman Jhula Area The most popular budget option is the *Bombay Kshettra* (no phone), on the east side of the river. It's an atmospheric old building with rooms ranging from Rs 40 to Rs 70, depending on the size, all with common bath, and set around a pleasant courtyard.

An excellent choice is the lovely *High Bank Peasants Cottage* (☎ 31-167), set in beautiful flower gardens high above the Ganges. Take the road to the left, one km before Lakshman Jhula; the cottage is about 200m up this road. Rooms are Rs 190/290 for singles/doubles with attached bath (hot water free in buckets), and the balcony has wicker chairs were you can sit and contemplate the Ganges. Discounts are offered for stays of over a week. Each morning Lisa, the family dog, brings the newspaper up from the front gate. Good homely Indian meals (not too spicy!) using vegies from the garden are available, and you can arrange treks and river rafting here.

Just above the cottage is the *Bhandari Swiss Cottage* (no phone). Rooms are plain but OK, and cost Rs 100 for singles or doubles with common bath. Meals are available, and there are great views from the balcony.

Places to Eat

Rishikesh is a holy pilgrimage town, and is therefore strictly vegetarian. In the town centre, the *Indrani* restaurant at the Inderlok Hotel has a good range of Chinese cuisine (Cantonese and Manchurian), as well as specials such as rajmah – seasoned kidney beans (Rs 25) and gajjar halwa in season (Rs 15). The *Anjali Restaurant*, further down Railway Station Rd towards Triveni Ghat, has very cheap dishes (most under Rs 10) in its *dhaba*-cum-mirrored-dining hall. The *Neelam Restaurant*, run by the helpful Mr Singh, is a low-key place in a small lane just off Haridwar Rd. It's popular with westerners, who are tempted here with dishes such as macaroni (Rs 15) and minestrone (Rs 12), as well as the standard Indian fare. The rice pud is very good.

In the Shivanand Jhula area, on the west side of the bridge near the boat landing, is the *Madras Cafe*. There's a good range of dosas, and if you don't like it hot, you can ask the cook to exercise restraint with the spices. There are also good lassis and cold coffee here. A few steps further towards the

bridge will bring you to the tiny *Amrita House & Library*, a groovy little eatery with books for perusing while you tuck into your banana, raisin and curd pancakes. Neem honey is for sale here at Rs 125 for 500 gm, yellow cheese is Rs 40 for 100g, and there's also soft and garlic cheese (both Rs 30 for 100g).

Across the Shivanand Jhula, in Swarg Ashram, is the long running *Chotiwala*. The filling special thali is Rs 30, and there's a good variety of Kwality ice cream. Next door is the equally salubrious and far less frenetic *Luxmi Hotel*, with comparable fare and prices.

If you're staying in the Yatra bus stand area, the *Tripti Restaurant* at the Hotel Suruchi has excellent fare, including dhal makhani – black lentils and red kidney beans with cream and butter – Rs 15, and the sublime Suruchi sundae with hot chocolate sauce and nuts (Rs 12).

In the Lakshman Jhula area, on the east side of the river, opposite the Bombay Kshettra, is the *Ganga Darshan Restaurant*. It's set right on the river, and has cheap, filling thalis for Rs 15, as well as South Indian food (dosa, idlis, etc).

Things to Buy

Rishikesh is a good place to pick up a *rudraksh mela*, the strings of beads used in *pujas* (offerings) made from the nuts of the rudraksh tree. Prices start from around Rs 80, with beads of the smaller nuts commanding higher prices. Flanking the waterfront on the east side of the river, in the Swarg Ashram area, are dozens of stalls selling devotional accoutrements such as prasaad, scriptural booklets and cassettes, as well as shawls and ayurvedic medicines. There's also a good range of ayurvedic medicines made from herbs collected from the Himalaya at the Mahesh Yogi Ayurvedic Centre, on Lakshman Jhula Rd, opposite the pathway up to Yoga Niketan Ashram.

It may seem a strange sort of purchase in the spiritual heartland of Rishikesh, but Mukesh at Jungle Vibes (next to the Inderlok Hotel on Railway Station Rd) sells handmade didgeridoos.

Getting There & Away
Air There are currently no scheduled flights to Jolly Grant airport, 18 km west of Rishikesh. See under Dehra Dun for more information.

Bus From the main bus stand (☎ 30-066), there are buses to Haridwar every 30 minutes from 4.30 am to 10.30 pm (one hour, Rs 7), and numerous buses to Dehra Dun between 6.30 am and 8 pm (1½ hours, Rs 10.50). Between 4.30 am and 10.30 pm there are hourly buses to Delhi. The trip takes around six hours and costs Rs 60 (ordinary), Rs 175 (semideluxe) or Rs 212 (super deluxe).

There's one bus at 8.15 am to Ramnagar (six hours, Rs 57.50) which continues to Nainital (8½ hours, Rs 88). To Shimla, you'll need to find your way to Dehra Dun, from where there are several services between 5.30 and 11.30 am (seven hours, Rs 82).

From the Yatra bus stand, during the pilgrimage season buses leave regularly for Badrinath between 3.30 am and 4 pm (14 hours, Rs 117); Kedarnath at 3.45, 4.15 and 5 am, and 12.30 and 1 pm (12 hours, Rs 85); Uttarkashi at 3.45, 5.30, 8, 10 and 11.30 am and 12.30 pm (seven hours, Rs 60); the 5.30 am bus to Uttarkashi continues to Gangotri (12 hours, Rs 102). There's one bus to Hanuman Chatti, the roadhead for Yamunotri, at 7 am (10 hours, Rs 94).

Train Bookings can be made at the railway station (☎ 131) from 10 am to 4 pm (closed for lunch from 1.30 to 2 pm). The station has a small allocation of seats for Haridwar. There are trains to Haridwar at 6.40 and 9.15 am, 2.10, 3.15 and 6.40 pm (Rs 4). The 6.40 am service arrives into Delhi at 5.20 pm. The 6.40 pm train connects with the *Mussoorie Express* for Delhi and with overnight trains to Lucknow and Agra. The 2.10 pm train connects with the *Jammu Tawi* express to Pathankot and Jammu.

Taxi & Jeep Official (off-season) reserve taxi rates are: Delhi, Rs 1000; Dehra Dun, Rs 250; Mussoorie, Rs 500; Uttarkashi (for Gangotri), Rs 900; Tehri, Rs 550; Haridwar,

Rs 180; and Ranikhet, Rs 1800. Expect to pay 20% to 50% more during summer. The main office for the Taxi Operators' Union (☎ 30-413) is on Haridwar Rd, just over Ghat Rd. Official rates for the Char Dham are Rs 7500, or for Badrinath and Kedarnath only, Rs 4200.

You can flag down share jeeps (called trekkers) for Dehra Dun anywhere along the Dehra Dun Rd. Cost to Dehra Dun is Rs 12. You may be able to get a share taxi to Haridwar from the main bus stand (Rs 20). An alternative (and grubbier) proposition is to pick up a shared Vikram anywhere along the Haridwar Rd (Rs 10).

Getting Around
Vikrams run from Ghat Rd junction up to Shivanand Jhula (Rs 3) and Lakshman Jhula (Rs 5). Shivanand Jhula is a pedestrian-only bridge, so you'll have to lump your backpack across if you're planning to stay on the east side of the Ganges (ie in the Swarg Ashram area). On the east bank of the river, a seat in a jeep between Lakshman Jhula and Shivanand Jhula costs Rs 3.

For Rs 3 you can cross the river to Swarg Ashram between 8 am and 7 pm by boat (particularly auspicious).

YAMUNOTRI
At a height of 3291m the Yamunotri Temple, one of the four holy dham, or Himalayan pilgrimage sites, is near the source of the Yamuna River, second-most sacred river in India after the Ganges. Hanuman Chatti, a small village 14 km short of Yamunotri, is as close as you can get to the pilgrimage site by vehicle. From here it's a fine 14 km trek to the holy settlement.

Trail to Yamunotri
The 14 km (five to six hour) trek up to the small settlement from the roadhead at Hanuman Chatti following the course of the Yamuna offers a good taste of high Himalaya scenery. There are dharamsalas and several budget hotels near the bus stand at Hanuman Chatti, or the GMVN *Tourist Bungalow* has

expensive dorm beds for Rs 80 or deluxe doubles for Rs 350.

From Hanuman Chatti the trail passes through Phoolchatti, six km from Hanuman Chatti with several basic chai stalls, to the pleasantly sited hamlet of Jankibaichatti, three km distant. There are several guesthouses here, as well as an expensive GMVN *Tourist Bungalow*, with dorm beds for Rs 80, ordinary doubles for Rs 150, or better doubles for Rs 250. This is also a good place to arrange a guide if you are planning to undertake more serious treks in this region.

The last leg of the trek is certainly the most rigorous, and frequently nerve racking, as the path at sections is literally carved out of the walls of precipitous gorges. Nevertheless, it affords fine mountain views and a variety of Himalayan vegetation.

Yamunotri Village & Temple

The village itself has a somewhat ramshackle appearance, but this is more than compensated for by the setting, with huge waterfalls behind Yamunotri falling dramatically like a curtained backdrop into the valley below Bandarpanch, and stunning views back down the valley before the village.

The small image of the goddess Yamuna is virtually indiscernible beneath garlands of flowers. The temple itself is little more than a shelter over the spring revered as the source of the Yamuna. According to tradition, the temple is built on the site of the hermitage of a holy man, Asit, a devout sage who received the blessings of both goddesses Yamuna and Ganga by regularly bathing in their waters. However, as he succumbed to old age and infirmity, he was unable to make the arduous pilgrimage to Gangotri, and the Ganga, in her benevolence, sprung from a rock at Yamunotri. The old sage was thus able to ritually bathe in both rivers daily, and continued to do so until his death, when the Ganges mysteriously disappeared.

Yamunotri remains the least developed of the Char Dham, receiving fewer pilgrims than Gangotri, Badrinath and Kedarnath: apart from the temple, there are only a smattering of dharamsalas, ashrams and chai stalls. The *Ramananda Ashram* welcomes foreign visitors (donation only), and the GMVN *Tourist Bungalow* has dorm beds only (Rs 60).

The Yamunotri Temple opens on the holy day of Akshaya-Tritiya (end of April or early May), and closes on Diwali (November), at which time the entire village is vacated and the village is obscured beneath the heavy winter snows.

Getting There & Away

GMVN operates seven day luxury coach tours to Yamunotri and Gangotri during the pilgrim season. Cost is Rs 2015 from Dehra Dun. There's a daily bus service during the pilgrim season from Rishikesh's Yatra bus stand to Hanuman Chatti (10 hours, Rs 94), which passes through Dehra Dun at 8.30 am (Rs 87) and Mussoorie at 10 am (Rs 75).

TEHRI
Population: 32,895

Buses from either Mussoorie or Rishikesh en route to Uttarkashi (and on to Gangotri) will inevitably make the short detour off the main route to the town of Tehri for a chai halt. Strangely, despite its rich history, Tehri fails to find its way into many guide books. The town is idyllically sited above the east side of the Bhagirathi River, but a pall of gloom hangs over the inhabitants, as their town will, probably within the next decade, be submerged following the completion of the partly Russian-funded Tehri Dam, being constructed upstream. The vast river valley project has received extreme criticism from environmentalists, and the critical findings of reports on the hazardous nature of the project in this seismically active area have been ignored. Construction continues apace.

Tehri was founded in 1815 by Maharaja Sudarshan Shah. The maharaja was compelled to cede his former capital at Srinagar and half of the entire region of Garhwal to the British, who had helped him drive out the Gurkhas of Nepal. From Tehri, a succession of four maharajas ruled, until in 1924, Narendra Shah, the fifth in line, moved the

UTTARAKHAND

capital to a new spot and modestly named it after himself – Narendranagar.

There is virtually no infrastructure in place for tourists – why bother, when in the not-too-distant future the entire town will be under hundreds of metres of water? Nevertheless, there are a few interesting relics of the days of the maharajas, including the **Rajmahal** (palace), a one km walk above the old town overlooking the confluence of the Bhagirathi and Bhilanganga rivers, and an old temple in a beautiful position on a shelf above the Bhagirathi, with stone steps leading down to the water's edge.

New Tehri is to be built high above the old town, on the opposite side of the river, and already dam works have disfigured the landscape.

Places to Stay

There are two budget hotels close to the bus stand. The *New Krisna Hotel* has basic rooms with common bath at Rs 45/80 for singles/doubles. Directly above it and, as its name suggests, with good views over the Bhagirathi River, is the *Hotel River View*, with rooms with common bath for Rs 55/70, or with attached bath, Rs 70/100.

Getting There & Away

Buses from Tehri's busy bus stand leave for Uttarkashi (three hours, Rs 29), continuing to Gangotri (seven hours, Rs 80). The interesting (but arduous) journey across to Mussoorie takes around three hours (Rs 29). There are also numerous services south to Rishikesh and Haridwar, and services west to Srinagar and Rudraprayag, with connections north to Kedarnath. Taxi rates are Rs 500 to Uttarkashi, Rs 700 to Mussoorie and Rs 550 to Rishikesh.

UTTARKASHI
Population: 17,261
Telephone Area Code: 01374

Uttarkashi, 155 km from Rishikesh, is the administrative headquarters of the district. Several trekking companies operate from here and the town is also the base for the Nehru Institute of Mountaineering, where Bachhendri Pal, the first Indian woman to climb to the summit of Mt Everest, was trained. The town is pleasantly sited on the banks of the Bhagirathi River, drawing pilgrims to its Vishwanatha Temple, sacred to Lord Shiva. It's possible that you'll wind up here looking for a bed before proceeding further north to Gangotri. You can stock up on supplies here if you're planning a trek further north, although the town has more to offer. On the day of Makar Sakranti, which usually falls in January, the town hosts a

Reeh-Khatling Glacier Trek

The Khatling Glacier is a lateral glacier from the centre of which the Bhilanganga River emerges. The summer rains turn the flat land on the glacial moraines into excellent pasture, which makes for ideal camping sites. Around Khatling Glacier are the snow-capped peaks of Jogin Ground (6466m), spectacular Sphetic Prishtwan (6905m), Kirti Stambh (6402m) and Barte Kanta (6579m).

Ghuttu, the main village, is three hours by bus from Tehri which is five hours from Rishikesh. From Ghuttu, there is a local bus to the village of Reeh where the trek commences. There are hotels at Ghuttu, a *Forest Rest House* at Buranschauri (above Reeh) and at Gangi you can stay in the school shelter.

Stage 1	Reeh to Gangi (4 hours)
Stage 2	Gangi to Kharsoli (6 hours)
Stage 3	Kharsoli to Khatling (5 hours)
Stage 4	Khatling to Kharsoli (4 hours)
Stage 5	Kharsoli to Reeh (7 to 8 hours)

colourful fair, when deities are borne aloft into the town on palanquins from outlying villages.

Orientation & Information

UP Tourism (☎ 2290) can be found in an office upstairs behind the GMVN Tourist Bungalow at the bus stand. None of the banks in Uttarkashi exchanges travellers' cheques. The post office is down a laneway off Hanuman Chowk. The District Forest Officer (☎ 2444) is in a densely forested region called Kot Bangla, 2½ km south-east of the main market. (Rooms are available in the *Forest Rest House* here – about Rs 40 per night.)

Trekking Outfits & Tour Operators As the headquarters of the Nehru Institute of Mountaineering, it is not surprising that Uttarkashi has several reputable trekking-cum-mountaineering agencies. A good first point of contact is Mount Support (☎ 2419; fax 2459), about 10 minutes walk north of the bus stand on the Gangotri road. Attar Singh here can tailor treks to visitors' requirements, and offers packages including all meals, guides, porters, cook, tent and sleeping mat from Rs 850 per day. High-altitude porters are Rs 300 per day; a cook is Rs 250 per day; and a mountain guide (a graduate from the Institute) is Rs 450. Regular porters and trekking guides (ie nongraduates) are Rs 85 and Rs 275 respectively per day. You can also hire gear here including sleeping bags (Rs 15 per day); two person tents (Rs 100); four person tents (Rs 125); kitchen tents (Rs 150); rucksacks (Rs 15); sleeping mats (Rs 5); and cooking gear (pots, pans, kerosene stove, etc – Rs 100). It's best to write in advance and specify your proposed itinerary and requirements, but Attar will definitely be able to help you out if you turn up with no advance notice. Write to Mount Support, PO Box 2, BD Nautial Bhawan, Bhatwari Rd, Uttarkashi, Garhwal, UP.

Things to See & Do

The **Vishwanatha Temple** is sacred to Shiva, and during the Jayanty Festival, around July/August, villagers from outlying regions throng to Uttarkashi to celebrate the god's birthday. Remarkably, this temple, and the **Kuteti Devi Temple**, two km to the south of Uttarkashi on the opposite side of the river, both escaped damage during the devastating earthquake which shook the region in 1991. The Kuteti Devi Temple houses a simple statue of the mother goddess, and can be reached via a path which leads up from the vehicular bridge over the river. There are very good views back over Uttarkashi from the temple.

Eleven km before Uttarkashi, if coming from the south, is the Bhotiya village of **Dunda**, where it's possible to buy woollen shawls, sweaters and blankets made by the villagers. Twenty-nine km south of Uttarkashi is Chaurangi Khal, from where a three km trek through dense forest leads to the **Nachiketa Tal** (*tal* means lake). There is a small temple on the lakeshore.

It's possible to take a pleasant two day excursion/trek to **Dodital**. The trek is described below.

Places to Stay

Strangely, virtually none of the hotels in Uttarkashi take advantage of the excellent river and mountain views. A good choice is GMVN's *Travellers' Lodge* (☎ 2222), at the bus stand. Spacious singles/doubles with common bath are Rs 90/120. Hot water in buckets is Rs 5. There's a canteen here.

Also at the bus stand is the *Hotel Bhandari* (☎ 2203). Doubles with common bath are Rs 50, and singles/doubles with attached bath are Rs 70/150. Hot water in buckets is Rs 5. Rooms are small and a bit dark, but OK.

Another budget option at the bus stand is the *Hotel Kashmira* (no phone). Rooms are tiny but clean, and cost Rs 75/150 with common bath.

There are a couple of good places in the main market, including the friendly *Hotel Amba* (☎ 2646). Doubles are good value in the off season, at Rs 75 with attached bath (Rs 200 during May and June). Bucket hot water is free. Nearby is the *Hotel Meghdoot* (☎ 2278), with double, triple and four-bedded rooms for Rs 150/250/350, all with attached baths and geysers. Run by the same people is the *Hotel Ganga Palace* (☎ 2567), in Hanuman Chowk. Doubles range from Rs 250 to Rs 450, all with attached bath, geysers, showers and colour TV (its rates remain constant all year).

Places to Eat

One of the best cheap eats is fresh Bhagirathi river trout, smothered in red chilli sauce, and dished up from trolleys at the bus stand. It's Rs 20 per 250g. Other fare to tempt you on the trolleys is chunks of fresh liver, and goats' legs, complete with trotters. In the main market is the *Sonali Restaurant*, next door to the Hotel Meghdoot, featuring South Indian and Chinese cuisine.

Getting There & Away

Buses depart for Gangotri at 5, 6, 7, 10 and 11 am, noon and 2 pm (five hours, Rs 42). There are two services to Gaurikund (for Kedarnath) at 4.30 am and 2 pm (10 hours, Rs 94; the afternoon service requires an overnight halt in Srinagar). The 6 am service to Tehri connects with a bus through to Mussoorie (seven hours, Rs 58 to Mussoorie). To Rishikesh there are buses at 5, 7.30, 8, 8.45 and 11 am, and 12.15 and 1.45 pm (six hours Rs 60). The taxi union office is at the bus stand. Quoted rates are: Gangotri, Rs 800 one way, Rs 1200 return; Rishikesh, Rs 1000; and Mussoorie, Rs 1200. If there are enough passengers, a share taxi to Rishikesh will cost Rs 125 per person.

GANGOTRI

The long (and frequently nerve-racking) journey from Uttarkashi to Gangotri affords spectacular forest and mountain scenery. On the final approach, the road steeply ascends from the valley floor to an elevation hundreds of metres above the river, with glimpses at intervals of the snow-clad peak of Sudarshan (6151m), standing like a sentinel at the valley head. About 20 km before Gangotri is the small village of **Darali**, where bus passengers are assailed by villagers selling large juicy Garhwal apples. Fourteen km before Gangotri, the road crosses high above the Jadganga River on a 100m long bridge just before the village of **Lanka**. At 3000m above sea level, and 123m above the gorge floor, this is reputedly one of the highest bridges in the world.

Despite the numbers of pilgrims who con-

Uttarkashi-Hanuman Chatti Trek

From Uttarkashi there are three buses a day for the short drive to the roadhead at Sangam Chatti, from where it is a short stage up the hillside to the village of Agoda. The following day the climb continues through pine forest and past the occasional Gujar shepherd encampment to Dodital (3310m) where there is a Forest Rest House. The lake (stocked with trout) is set amid a forest of oak, pine, deodar and rhododendron.

From Dodital it is possible to extend the trek over the Darwa Pass (4150m) for grand views of Bandarpanch (6316m). An overnight camp in one of the many meadows is necessary before completing the long descent to the Hanuman Ganga and the town of Hanuman Chatti and the onward buses to Mussoorie.

The trek can be completed from May until the end of October. The profusion of wildflowers can also compensate for the monsoon rains that continue throughout August until mid-September. Porters and guides can be organised from one of the agencies in Uttarkashi. Budget for Rs 120 per day.

Stage 1	Sangam Chatti to Agoda (2 to 3 hours)
Stage 2	Agoda to Dodital (6 hours)
Stage 3	Dodital to Seema via Darwa Pass (6 to 7 hours)
Stage 4	Seema to Hanuman Chatti (4 hours)

verge on the holy town, venerated as the spot where the Ganges first tumbled to earth, Gangotri, at 3140m, has managed to retain the ambience of a small Himalayan village. Sudarshan is always within sight, and the reflected light which bounces off its snow-clad flanks at sunset is truly soul stirring.

As Gangotri is snow-bound for at least half the year, during the winter months the inhabitants retreat further down the mountainside and the village is completely vacated. On the day of Akshaya-Tritiya (end of April or the beginning of May), elaborate pujas announce the opening of both this and the temple at Yamunotri. On the day of Diwali, celebrated on the 15th day of Kartika (in November), closing ceremonies are performed, and the idol of the Goddess Ganga is removed to Haridwar, Prayagraj and Varanasi.

Orientation & Information

The town straddles both sides of the river, technically the Bhagirathi, but venerated as the Ganges. The bus stand, several guesthouses and the temple are on the north side of the river; a number of ashrams and more guesthouses, the GMVN Tourist Rest House, and a tiny postal agent, beneath the Bhagirathisadan Ashram, are on the south side of the river. The two sides are connected by bridges, one near the temple, and one which crosses the river about 200m to the west.

There is an ayurvedic clinic at the Kailash Ashram (above the right bank of the river near the Yoga Niketan ashram) but you can't stay here.

Gangotri Temple

The object of veneration of the thousands of pilgrims to Gangotri, the temple, is a relatively modest structure. The facade is painted silver and topped by four gilded spires on each corner and a large central spire, each surmounted by a golden acroterion. The silver image of the Goddess Ganga in the inner sanctum is surprisingly small. Before it lies an assortment of conch shells, *chattris* (silver umbrellas), bells and tridents. The idol is surrounded by a silver frame featuring floral and bird motifs. A few steps from the temple is a stone known as **Bhagirath Shila**, upon which King Bhagirath sat while endeavouring to cause the Ganges to fall to earth through the powers of intense medita-

The Divine Descent of the Ganges

The event which caused the Ganges to fall at Gangotri has its origins in a tussle for supremacy between King Sagar, who slayed the demons which were troubling the earth, and Indra, the ruler of the abode of the gods. Having dispatched the demons, the king prepared to embark on an *aswamedh yagya*, an elaborate religious ritual to proclaim his supremacy. This posed a threat to Indra, who feared that his own power would be usurped. Indra set out to thwart the king by stealing his horse and tethering it to the ashram of the sage Kapil, who was himself engaged in a deep meditative retreat. The 60,000 sons of the prolific king, and their half brother, Asamanjas, traced the horse to the ashram, but their noisy entrance disturbed the meditating sage from his deep trance, and when he opened his eyes, all those upon whom his gaze fell were turned to ashes. The only survivor was Asamanjas. The now fully cognisant sage advised the king's grandson Anshuman that the 60,000 brothers could only enter heaven if the Ganges was brought down to earth so that the ashes of the immolated brothers could be cleansed in its divine waters.

The task of enticing Ganga down to earth proved too much for Anshuman, but his grandson Bhagirath resolved not to move from the spot until the deed had been accomplished and his ancestors could enter the heavenly abode. He entered a state of deep meditation, and after several years was partially rewarded when the Ganga fell earthward but became entangled in the locks of Lord Shiva's hair. Further intensive meditation on the greatness of Shiva was required before the god released the waters of Ganga, which fell in seven distinct streams, including the Bhagirathi which fell at Gangotri, and the 60,000 brothers finally attained entrance to heaven. ■

tion. According to tradition, it originally fell from heaven at Gangotri.

The path leading to the temple is flanked by stalls selling prasaad, and sadhus sit before aromatic fires of burning deodar branches. Close to the temple, steps descend to the main bathing ghat, and hardy pilgrims brave the freezing waters.

Places to Stay & Eat

Most of the guesthouses do not have electricity, and generators are generally only run for a few hours in the evening. This is a holy town, and meat is therefore forbidden. The *Bhagirathi Motel*, right by the bus stand, has double rooms with attached bath (cold water only; hot water in buckets Rs 8) for Rs 75 and triples for Rs 100 (from May to July, Rs 150 and Rs 200 respectively).

Opposite the bus stand is the *Jahanvi Guest House*, with singles/doubles for Rs 80/100, all with attached bath; hot water in buckets is Rs 8. This is one of the few places which has electricity. Basic meals are available downstairs (dhal bhat, roti, sabzi, aalu paratha, etc).

On the south side of the river, just over the footbridge near the temple, to the right is the *Ganga Niketan*, with tables set up right on the riverbank. There are no double rooms here; singles with common bath are Rs 50, and four bed rooms are Rs 100. Hot water in buckets costs Rs 8. There's a restaurant here.

A path up behind the Ganga Niketan to the right leads to the *Yoga Niketan Ashram*, affiliated to the ashram of the same name in Rishikesh. Several of the rooms here are in lovely little wooden cabins made of fragrant deodar. It costs Rs 100 per day to stay here, which includes Hatha yoga classes, meals and accommodation. *Sadaks* (students of yoga and meditation) are accommodated in individual rooms, and hot water is available free in buckets. Classes are held from May to July; when there are no classes, the cost to stay here is Rs 75. If you want to stay here and attend classes (although there's no pressure to attend), write in advance to Yoga Niketan Ashram in Rishikesh (see the Rishikesh section for details).

Also on this side of the river, but to the left after you cross the main bridge, is the *Bhagirathisadan Ashram*. Rooms accommodate from one to five people, all with attached

Gangotri-Gaumukh & Tapovan Trek

The popular pilgrimage destination of Gangotri is connected by road to Uttarkashi and Haridwar; allow two days by bus to reach Gangotri with an overnight at Uttarkashi. The trek to the source of the holy Ganges starts from Gangotri and continues along the bank of the Bhagirathi River. It takes two stages to reach Gaumukh (3890m) with the actual source of the river emanating from a huge glacier below the Bhagirathi Range. En route to Gaumukh there are plenty of tea houses, and a GMVN *Tourist Bungalow* at Bhujbasa (3790m). Doubles are Rs 200, dorm beds are Rs 75, and tent huts are Rs 60. You can get meals here. Most pilgrims try to reach Bhujbasa in one day and leave early to reach Gaumukh with time to return to Gangotri on the same day.

Beyond Gaumukh there are possibilities to trek across the large terminal moraine fields to the alpine camp at Tapovan (4450m). This is a magnificent camp with clear views to Shivling (6543m) and Bhagirathi 1 (6856m) across the valley. However, to complete this stage additional time must be spent trekking to Gaumukh in order to acclimatise

Porters are available from Gangotri for around Rs 80 per day while guides are available from the tea houses below Gaumukh to head you in the right direction across the moraine to Tapovan.

Stage 1	Gangotri to Bhujbasa (6 to 7 hours)
Stage 2	Bhujbasa to Gaumukh & Gangotri (2 hours & 6 hours return to Gangotri)
Optional Stage	Gaumukh to Tapovan (5 to 6 hours return)

bath, and open onto a balcony which catches the morning sun. The canteen below the ashram will provide hot water in buckets for Rs 5. The manager of the ashram is both a pujari (along with his father and brother) at the temple, as well as the local postmaster (the post office is downstairs).

GMVN's *Tourist Rest House* is the top of the range, with doubles/triples with common bath for Rs 250/300, and deluxe doubles with attached bath for Rs 447. There are also two dorms, both with nine beds; beds in the ordinary dorm cost Rs 75, or in the deluxe dorm, Rs 100. Hot water is available in buckets for Rs 7, and there's electricity to all rooms from 7 to 10 pm, and to deluxe rooms, in the morning also.

Getting There & Away

Buses depart at 5, 6 and 7 am for Uttarkashi (five hours, Rs 42) with connections to Rishikesh (Rs 102) and Haridwar (Rs 111). The 8 am bus to Uttarkashi connects with a service to Gaurikund and Kedarnath (15 hours, Rs 136) with an overnight halt in Srinagar (11 hours). If you don't wake up in time, there are additional services to Uttarkashi at 9 and 11 am, and 1, 2 and 3 pm, but you'll need to spend the night in Uttarkashi before proceeding further.

SRINAGAR
Population: 22,000
Telephone Area Code: 01388

If you're travelling from the east (ie Rishikesh or Uttarkashi) to the pilgrimage town of Kedarnath, or to the snow fields at Auli, you may find that you'll need to spend a night in this busy transit town on the banks of the Alaknanda River, 60 km south-east of Tehri, and 118 km short of Kedarnath. Srinagar was the capital of Garhwal from the 14th century, when it was founded by Raja Ajai Pal, until 1815, when it was ceded to the British by Maharaja Sudarshan Shah as part payment for the former's help in the fight to expel the Gurkhas. Once the cultural capital of Garhwal, successive floods and the invasion by the Gurkhas have sadly erased vestiges of the city's former grandeur, and

it's not a particularly interesting place to linger. It you do have a few hours to fill in, the ancient temple of **Kamleshwar Mahadev**, sacred to Shiva, has an interesting history, having miraculously survived floods in 1893 and 1970.

UP Tourism (☎ 2110) can be found in the same building as the GMVN Tourist Complex in Upper Bazaar, on the Rishikesh road. The post office is about 200m east (ie towards Rudraprayag) of the bus stand.

Places to Stay & Eat

The *Hotel Himalaya*, on the Rishikesh road, right opposite the bus stand, has tiny single rooms for Rs 100, and doubles for Rs 175, all with attached bath. GMVN's *Tourist Complex* (☎ 2199) is also on the Rishikesh road in Upper Bazaar, about 100m from the bus stand. There are dorm beds available for Rs 40 or Rs 60, executive single/doubles for Rs 135/180, and deluxe rooms with air-coolers for Rs 268/355. There's a dining hall here. Opposite is *Rajhans Hotel* (☎ 2192) with small doubles with attached bath for Rs 125.

Getting There & Away

Buses to Gaurikund (for Kedarnath) may require a change at Rudraprayag, 34 km to the north-east. There's a railway booking agency (☎ 2199) in the same building as the GMVN Tourist Complex. It has a small allocation of seats on trains from Haridwar only to Delhi, Lucknow, Varanasi, Calcutta and Mumbai (Bombay). Bookings need to be made 72 hours in advance.

TO KEDARNATH VIA GAURIKUND

Rudraprayag is 34 km north-east of Srinagar. Here the road divides, the route to the north proceeding to Gaurikund, roadhead for Kedarnath, and that to the east continuing to another important junction, Karanprayag, and from there, north to Badrinath. Rudraprayag is revered as the site where the Mandakini River meets the Alaknanda, forming one of five holy confluences, or Panch Prayag. Here in 1926 Jim Corbett shot a killer tiger, responsible for the death of about 300 villagers.

The route to Kedarnath passes through **Guptakashi** *(Gupta* means hidden), where Shiva dwelt temporarily incognito in an endeavour to elude the pursuing Pandavas who sought redemption for the slaying of the Kauravas, the great battle which forms the basis of the ancient Sanskrit epic, the *Mahabharata*. From Guptakashi it is possible to undertake a 30 km trek to Madmaheshwar, where a shrine marks the site where Shiva's naval appeared after he plunged into the earth at Kedarnath to escape the Pandavas.

Just over a km from Rudraprayag is the tiny settlement of **Nala**, which is notable as the only place in Uttarakhand where a Buddhist shrine may be found, a vestige of the period prior to the sweeping reforms of the 9th century Hindu philosopher Shankaracharya who heralded the revival of Hinduism. The road proceeds through **Rampur** and **Soneprayag**. From Soneprayag it is possible to walk (or drive, if the road hasn't been washed out by the monsoon rains) three km to the village of **Trijuginarayan**. A temple dedicated to Narayan (Vishnu) marks the site where, according to Hindu tradition, the wedding between Shiva and Parvati took place. Before the temple is a sacred fire, believed by devotees to have burned continually from the time of the divine union.

Gaurikund

Gaurikund is the last village accessible by motor vehicle before Kedarnath. Daily during the pilgrimage seasons, busloads of dusty pilgrims are disgorged at its small bus stand and assailed by pony keepers and *dholi* (litter) bearers all vying for their custom. The small town, despite its important role catering to the pilgrim trade, retains a certain charm. The path towards Kedarnath leading up behind the bus stand is flanked by stalls in which the relatively well looked after ponies breathe their steamy sweet breath over the passing throngs of pilgrims, some on horseback, others borne aloft on the labouring shoulders of doolie bearers, and the majority briskly walking towards the

object of their devotion, 14 km distant and 1600m closer to the heavens.

At Gaurikund, Parvati engaged in a protracted (several hundred years) meditation to impress Shiva with her devotion, finally being rewarded for her labours when Shiva took her as his consort. She is worshipped in the form of Gauri, along with Shiva as Mahedev, in an ancient temple at Gaurikund.

There are numerous stalls where you can store your excess luggage before beginning the straightforward but gruelling trek to the Kedarnath Temple (Rs 5 per piece per day).

Places to Stay & Eat On the right at the beginning of the pilgrim trail is the *Rajmahal Guest House*, with tiny doubles with attached bath for Rs 50, and hot water available in buckets for Rs 5. The yellow building on the right just beyond the Rajmahal is the *Annapurna Lodge*, which has singles/doubles for Rs 50/75 with attached bath (hot water Rs 5). Prices jump to Rs 300 (double rates only) during May and June. Above the trail to the left is the GMVN *Tourist Lodge* which is a bit overpriced with fairly ordinary rooms for Rs 350, or Rs 250 between 15 July and 15 September. Dorm beds are Rs 75. Hot water in buckets is Rs 8, and there's a restaurant here. The staff can help organise guides and porters.

There are numerous dhabas of similar standard flanking both sides of the path. The *Hariom Restaurant* on the left has the usual fare: aalu paratha is Rs 5 and dhal and sabzi is Rs 15.

Getting There & Away The dhaba-wallahs near the bus stand will help with information regarding bus schedules. There is a direct service daily to Badrinath which leaves at 5 am (13 hours, Rs 92), which passes through Josimath (10 hours, Rs 90). If you don't wake up in time, there are later buses to the road junction at Rudraprayag at 7, 8 and 10 am, noon and 2 pm (four hours, Rs 32) from where there are frequent services south-west to Rishikesh, south-east towards Almora and Nainital or north-east to Josimath (for Auli) and on to Badrinath.

Trail to Kedarnath

You certainly don't require the services of a guide on the straightforward but steep ascent to the temple – just follow the throngs of other pilgrims along the wide bridle path. The most pleasant way to tackle the ascent is on the broad back of a mountain pony. You'll need to engage in some heavy bargaining to negotiate a fair rate for the pony and its owner, who'll accompany you on foot.

Make sure you know what you're paying for before you set out, or you might find you're forking out for the pony-wallah's meals and even for the pony's lunch of sugar and water, as well as for the hire of a horse blanket. In May and June, expect to pay either Rs 350 one way or Rs 700 return; at other times you shouldn't pay more than Rs 200 up, Rs 100 down, or Rs 300 return.

The pony-wallahs set a blistering pace, covering the 14 km in about 4½ hours up, and 3½ hours down. Lesser mortals on foot will probably take about seven hours up and five to six hours down. If you require the services of a porter, he'll charge upwards of Rs 150 each way or Rs 300 return (double these rates during May and June).

There is a great sense of camaraderie between the toiling pilgrims on the arduous hike, who greet each other with a hearty 'Jai Kedar'! as they meet on the trail. The path affords beautiful views down over the Mandakini River, with waterfalls plummeting down the sides of the valley and colourful alpine flowers bordering the trail. The path is flanked by chai stalls at regular intervals, with the largest settlement, **Rambara**, at the halfway point, seven km from Gaurikund. There's a GMVN *Tourist Rest House* here, to the right behind the chai stalls which flank the trail, set above the river. Spotless deluxe doubles with attached bath are Rs 350 and dorm beds are Rs 50.

The landscape becomes more barren as the trail ascends above the tree line beyond Rambara. Six km beyond Rambara, after a series of switchbacks and a particularly steep ascent, the extraordinary vision of the south flank of Kedarnath (6940m) looms into view, and the village is visible one km distant.

KEDARNATH VILLAGE & TEMPLE

The object of devotion which lures pilgrims to these chilly heights (Kedarnath village is at 3584m above sea level) is housed in a relatively plain grey stone temple. Here in the dim inner sanctum pilgrims, in paroxysms of religious fervour, pay homage to a large black rock protruding from the ground, which is worshipped as the hindquarters of the god Shiva. This is one of the 12 *jyoti lingams*, lingams believed to derive currents of power *(shakti)* from within themselves as opposed to lingams ritually invested with *mantra-shakti* by the priests.

The myth of the jyoti lingam (the lingam of light) stems from a long dispute for primacy between Brahma and Vishnu. During this dispute, according to legend, the earth split apart to reveal an incandescent column of light. To find the source of this column, Vishnu became a boar and burrowed underground, while Brahma took to the skies in the form of an eagle. After 1000 years of fruitless searching, Shiva emerged from the lingam of light and both Brahma and Vishnu acknowledged that it was he who was the greatest god.

Shiva the Bull

According to Hindu scriptures, Shiva, while seeking to elude the pursuing Pandavas who sought atonement for the slaying of their kinsfolk, the Kauravas (the epic battle described in the *Mahabharata)*, espied a herd of grazing cattle and, taking the form of a bull, hid himself among them. The giant Pandava Bhim stood astride the head of the Kedarnath Valley, with a foot on each mountain, and all the cattle, other than Shiva, passed beneath his legs as they wended their way homewards. Bhim reached down to grasp Shiva, who he recognised as his Lord despite his bovine disguise, but Shiva sank into the ground, and Bhim was left holding only his rump. Shiva, impressed at the great lengths to which the Pandavas had gone to secure exoneration, finally appeared before them, granting the long-awaited *darshan* and atonement, and requesting that his rump be worshipped at Kedarnath. ■

On the walls of the *mandapa*, or outer chamber, are relief sculptures of the five Pandavas and their wife, Draupadi, and in the centre of the chamber is a small recumbent Nandi bull, the vehicle of Shiva, reputedly made from eight different materials. Between the mandapa and the inner sanctum is a small vestibule with a sculpture of Ganesh engaged in a passionate tryst with his consort.

In the dark inner sanctum, priests anoint the sacred lingam with holy water from copper libation vessels, and pilgrims, for most of whom this pilgrimage represents the realisation a life-long quest, smear prasaad in the form of rice, ghee and flower petals on its surface. In times past, some pilgrims ascended a path known as Mahapanth behind the temple and threw themselves from a cliff top to gain immediate access to the heavenly abode.

In the centre of the courtyard before the temple is a large stone Nandi bull, and on either side of the entrance are stone images of Jai and Vijay, the gatekeepers, or *dwarpal*, of Lord Shiva.

Up on a ridge 500m to the east of the temple, coloured flags mark the site of a shrine to **Bhairava**, who, according to tradition, guards over the holy pilgrimage site during the winter months when the temple is closed. At the rear of the temple is the somewhat surreal sculpture of a giant fist holding an enormous staff, which marks the *samadhi* (final resting place) of the philosopher **Shankaracharya**, who revived the Hindu religion in the 9th century AD.

From the bridge before the village, a four km path leads to the **Chorabari Tal**, also known as the Gandhi Sarovar, a glacial lake over whose waters the ashes of the mahatma were scattered. Nearby, emerging from the vast glacier behind Kedarnath, three streams mark the source of the Mandakini, joined further down by a fourth which falls from the mountainside. The ice surrounding the source of the river is treacherous and brittle, and should not be approached.

Places to Stay & Eat

Just past the temple to the left is the *Bharat Sevasram Sangha*, an ashram founded by a

Bengali man revered as a saint, Acharya Sreemat Swamy Pranavanandaji Maharaj. There are dorm beds or private rooms (by donation), and hot water by the bucket is available for Rs 10. About 50m before the temple on the right is the *Punjab Sindh*, which has dorm beds for Rs 50, and doubles with common bath for Rs 50, or Rs 100 with attached bath. There are also VIP rooms for Rs 200. Rooms are very clean, and those at the back have views of the temple and the peaks. Close by is the *Baba Kali Kamli Wala Ashram*, founded by a Punjabi saint, Baba Vishudhanandji Maharaji.

This is a rather drab building, with rooms with common bath (mattresses on the floor) for Rs 50, or slightly better rooms with jute matting and attached bath for Rs 75. Hot water in buckets is Rs 10. The large yellow building with the bright red roof to the right of the path into the village is GMVN's new *Tourist Bungalow*. Dorm beds are Rs 50 and double rooms with attached bath are Rs 400. The old GMVN *Tourist Bungalow*, about 300m before the village on the left side of the path, has four bed rooms with common bath for Rs 180.

The final approach to the temple through the village is lined with chai stalls and dhabas, all serving pretty basic (and of course, vegetarian) fare. On the left as you approach the temple is *Tiwari Hotel & Sweets*, with good fresh samosas.

PANCH KEDAR

According to the Puranic texts, after Shiva plunged into the netherworld to escape the Pandavas, five *(panch)* parts of his body appeared in five different locations: the most holy site is Kedarnath, where his hindquarters are worshipped; his arms *(bahu)* emerged at Tunganath; his face *(mukh)* at Rudranath; his navel *(nabhi)* at Madmaheshwar; and his hair *(jata)* at Kalpeshwar. Shrines erected at these sites are worshipped as the Panch Kedar, or five parts of Shiva, and all lie within Garhwal. They can be reached either on a long (10 to 12 day) trek from Kedarnath, or by utilising bus services to various access points and hiking from there.

Madmaheshwar

Madmaheshwar, where the naval of Shiva reappeared, can be reached on a 30 km trek from Guptkashi, following the Madmaheshwar Ganga via Kalimath, set at 1463m, and six km to the north-east. A temple at Kalimath is dedicated to Kali, here worshipped as the destroyer of evil forces. The trail then ascends seven km to Ransi and a further six km to Gaundhar. From here it is a steep 11 km ascent to Madmaheshwar, at an elevation of 3289m.

Legend tells that a dog belonging to the hunter Shambhuk fell in a pool here. When it emerged, it shook itself dry, covering Shambhuk in the holy water. This unwitting act of piety resulted in both master and dog attaining moksha, or salvation from this life, and both gained immediate admission to the heavenly abode. There is basic accommodation in dharamsalas and simple fare is available at chai stalls.

An alternative route to the small stone temple here is via the Deoria Tal, eight km north of Okhimath (see below). From the lake, a 15 km path branches to the north-west, crossing the Madmaheshwar Ganga and joining up with the trail from Ransi.

Tunganath

To get to Tunganath, during the pilgrim season, and contingent on road conditions, take the daily bus from Kedarnath at 5 am for Badrinath. Heading due east from the settlement of Kund, six km to the south of Guptkashi, the bus proceeds through Okhimath, where you can pick up the trail for Madmaheshwar (see above). Murli Singhnegi (☎ (0137286) 6741), a graduate of Uttarkashi's Nehru Institute of Mountaineering, is based at the tiny village of Sari, 10 km from Okhimath towards Deoria Tal, and offers his services for treks in this region.

The main Badrinath road proceeds to the beautifully sited hamlet of Chopta, 21 km further east. It wends through dense forests of deodar, emerging at intervals at vast green bugyals, or high-altitude meadows, affording spectacular vistas of snow-covered peaks which can be enjoyed without the usual concomitant terror which is standard on Garhwal's frequently more precipitous roads. Chopta is generally the first halt on the long gruelling bus trip to Badrinath, and you can thaw out with a cup of chai at one of the several stalls and enjoy unrestricted mountain views from the grassy meadows which surround the settlement.

From Chopta it is an arduous but relatively straightforward five km trek, ascending above the tree line, to Tunganath, where the stone temple, considered to be the highest Hindu shrine in India, is fronted by a Nandi bull. The temple commemorates the appearance of the arms of Shiva. A further one km climb brings you to Chandrashila Peak, at 3930m, affording magnificent and unobstructed views of the entire face of Chaukhamba (7138m). Basic accommodation in a dharamsala is available at Tunganath, or there's a *Tourist Rest House* at Chopta (Rs 300 or Rs 400 in a double, Rs 90 for a dorm bed). You can also camp here.

Rudranath & Kalpeshwar

The two pilgrimage sites Rudranath and Kalpeshwar, where temples commemorate respectively the appearance of Shiva's face and hair, can be accessed either from Helang, 13 km south of Josimath, or from Mandal, beyond Chopta, 10 km west of Gopeshwar on the Kedarnath-Badrinath route. The trails are somewhat confusing, so you should avail yourself of the services of a guide.

From Mandal, a six km trail ascends to the temple of **Anasuya Devi**, from where it is a further 16 km to the settlement of Rudranath, set in a densely forested region. There is a dharamsala here, but inhabitants usually decamp during the heavy winter snows, so be prepared to camp out. From Rudranath the trail passes through Panar, a good well watered spot handy for a night halt. Beyond Panar is the tiny village of Dumak, 12 km from Rudranath, where you should be able to rustle up dhal bhat and negotiate to spend the night in a chai stall. The next village is Urgam, at 2134m, from where it is a two km hike to Kalpeshwar. You'll need to backtrack to Urgam, from where it is nine km to

Helang, with the trail crossing to the east side of the Alaknanda River. From Helang you can pick up a local bus for the 13 km trip north to Josimath.

JOSIMATH
Telephone Area Code: 01389

Josimath is the place where the 9th century philosopher Shankaracharya meditated before embarking on his quest to revive Hinduism and establish the four *maths* (seats of learning) and *dhams* (religious centres) in the four cardinal points of the country. Josimath was designated the first of the maths (named Jyotiramath), and Badrinath was established as the first dham, with the installation in the temple there of an image of Vishnu.

The most important of Josimath's many temples is that dedicated to Narsingh (Vishnu in his lion form). When the winter snows enshroud Badrinath, making pilgrimage to the holy site impossible, pilgrims pay homage to Vishnu, worshipped at Badrinath in the summer months, at Josimath, and the temple administrators of Badrinath Temple descend to live in the city.

Vaishnavites believe that one arm on the idol of Vishnu enshrined in the temple is becoming thinner, and that the age of Kali-Yuga, or Evil Times, will be heralded by the shattering of the arm. At this time, a great flood will cause the collapse of the mountains of Jay and Vijay at Vishnuprayag, effectively blocking passage through to Badrinath, and a new temple will appear at Bhavishyabadri (Furture Badri), in the Tapovan Valley.

Josimath has a busy market which is a good place to stock up on supplies if you are planning to trek in this region, and you can also arrange guides and porters here (see the Information section below). The city is also within short distance of the access points for some of Garhwal's most stunning treks, including those to the outer Nanda Devi Sanctuary; and north to the Valley of Flowers. The Curzon Trail, over the Kuari Pass, begins at Tapovan (15 km to the east of Josimath) or Auli. The ski fields at Auli lie

only 15 km (by road) to the south, or a more direct 3½ km by ropeway.

Information

UP Tourism (☎ 2181) can be found at the Jyotir Tourist Complex, above the bus stand. The office is open Monday to Saturday from 10 am to 5 pm, and you can hire trekking gear and organise porters and guides here. Treks can also be arranged at the Garhwal Adventure Sport School & Mountain Service (GASSMS), Nanda Devi Hotel, Josimath, District Chamoli 246443 (☎ 2288). Popular treks include that to the outer Nanda Devi Sanctuary, taking in Lata Kharak, Sena Kharak, with possibly the best views of Nanda Devi available outside the sanctuary, and a number of tribal villages. GASSMS also arranges skiing packages to Auli, as well as ecological and environmental awareness trips.

None of the banks has foreign exchange facilities, but the manager at the Shailja Guest House may be able to help you out. The post office is on the Badrinath road, about 250m north of the bus stand. Note that after 6 pm, the power supply is reduced and you might need a torch (flashlight) to find your way around.

Ropeway to Auli

A 3½ km ropeway carries a cable car between Josimath and the ski fields at Auli. The terminus is near the police station at Upper Bazaar in Josimath. Cars hold 25 people and leave when full between 9 am and 5 pm. The 30 minute trip costs Rs 150 for both adults and children, and there is a generator in case of power failure. The ropeway is supported by 10 towers between Josimath and Auli, and it is possible to get off at the eighth tower and take the chairlift from there. During the ski season, 24 to 48 hours advance booking is preferable. Bookings can be secured through UP Tourism.

Places to Stay & Eat

Close to the bus stand, in Main Bazaar, is the *Hotel Nanda Devi* (☎ 2170), with singles/doubles with common bath for Rs 50/100, or with attached bath, Rs 80/150. Rooms are basic but clean, although those with common bath are on the small side. Hot water in buckets is Rs 5. There are two tourist complexes run by GMVN, both near the bus stand; the lower *Tourist Complex* (☎ 2118) and, about 50m above it, and with UP Tourism on the premises, the *Jyotir Tourist Complex*. The first has doubles for Rs 200 and Rs 300, and the second for Rs 300 and Rs 400. Both have dorm beds for Rs 60, and both offer discounts in the off season.

Between the two GMVN places is the popular *Shailja Guest House* (☎ 2208). Off-season double rates range from Rs 60 to Rs 180. In May and June, you'll pay between Rs 80 and Rs 240. More expensive rooms have better furnishings and are larger. You can exchange foreign currency here, and the helpful manager can also arrange guides and porters.

The *Hotel Marwari* (☎ 2277), about 500m south of the bus stand, has doubles with attached bath for Rs 100. There's a very good veg restaurant downstairs (filling thalis for Rs 15, and a range of sticky sweets). About 50m further south is the *Hotel Neelkanth* (☎ 2131), which has very pleasant, large rooms with valley views for Rs 150 with attached bath, or four bed rooms with attached bath for Rs 250. Prices increase to Rs 200 and Rs 300 in the peak season.

The *Paradise Cafe*, close to the bus stand, is a popular cheap eatery serving Chinese, South Indian and Punjabi cuisine.

Things to Buy

Carpets and woollen shawls can be purchased at the showroom at the Garhwal Wool and Craft House, directly opposite the

---

Govind Ghat-Valley of Flowers/Hem Kund Trek

Ten km north of Josimath on the road to Badrinath is the small settlement of Govind Ghat, from where it is possible to trek to the beautiful Valley of Flowers National Park and the important Sikh pilgrimage site of Hem Kund.

According to Hindu lore, Hanuman searched the length and breadth of the valley to find the Sanjivini butti, a herb possessing medicinal properties, which Lord Rama knew would save the life of his brother Lakshman. Bewildered by the vast array of floral specimens, and fearing that he would pluck the wrong herb, Hanuman simply lifted the entire valley on his shoulders and brought it back to Rama.

The flowers can be seen in their full glory from mid-July to mid-August, but are in bloom from mid-June until the end of the monsoon in mid-September. Some of the hundreds of varieties of flowers which can be seen in the valley include rare specimens such as the white androsace; other varieties include anemones, cypripediums, forget-me-nots, pansies, geraniums, blue poppies, and primulas in shades of pinks and blues, among many others.

The valley has suffered from large numbers of trekkers in the past and was recently designated as a national park. The current stipulation allows trekkers to camp or stay at one of the several gurudwaras or at the *Tourist Rest House* at Ghangaria (seven hours from Govind Ghat – doubles are Rs 300 and Rs 450, or there are dorm beds for Rs 90) and take day walks into the valley. No overnight camping is permitted in the valley and there is a daily entrance fee of Rs 100 for foreigners and Rs 20 for Indian trekkers.

From Ghangaria, you can follow the Lakshmanganga to the lake of Hem Kund – quite a steep climb. In the Sikh holy book, the *Granth Sahib*, the Sikh guru Govind Singh recounts that in a previous life he had meditated on the shores of a lake, surrounded by seven snow-capped mountains. Hem Kund, set at a height of 4329m, was earlier this century identified as that lake.

From Govind Ghat it is possible to hire a pony for the trek to Ghangaria (Rs 200 to Rs 250 one way).

Stage 1	Govind Ghat to Ghangaria (7 hours)
Stage 2	Ghangaria to the Valley of Flowers & return (5 to 6 hours)
Stage 3	Ghangaria to Hem Kund & return (8 hours)
Stage 4	Ghangaria to Govind Ghat (5 hours)

UTTARAKHAND

Garhwal Motor Owners' Union (GMOU) office.

Getting There & Away

The office of the GMOU is open from 5 am to 6.30 pm. There are regular buses from Josimath to Badrinath between 6.40 am and 4 pm (2½ hours, Rs 17). Same-day buses to Rishikesh leave at 4 and 6 am (10 hours, Rs 99), with the 4 am service continuing to Haridwar (11 hours, Rs 106). Later services depart at 8.30 and 9 am, but require an overnight stop in Karanprayag, Rudraprayag or Srinagar. For Kausani, you'll need to change at Karanprayag (3½ hours to Karanprayag, Rs 32). To Gaurikund (for Kedarnath), a service departs at 10 am, passing through Gopeshwar and Chopta (12 hours, Rs 68.50).

You may be able to get a seat on the mail taxi to Rishikesh which departs at approximately 5.30 am. Ask at Bhatt News Agency,

a few doors north of the GMOU office. There are often two seats available, for which you'll be charged Rs 150 each. A reserve taxi to Badrinath will cost between Rs 600 and Rs 700 one way. Share jeeps for Tapovan leave when full from near the bus stand (Rs 15). Depending on road conditions, local buses ply between Josimath and Malari, following the Dhauliganga River and passing through Tapovan and Lata. In the past, a permit was required to visit Malari, but with restrictions easing, it would be worth checking this out at the UP tourist office.

SKIING AT AULI

The ski season extends from the beginning of January to the end of March. India's premier ski resort, at Auli, can be reached along a 15 km road from Josimath, or more speedily, by cable car suspended from the 3½ km ropeway which extends from Josimath to Auli (see the Josimath section

---

Josimath-Kuari Pass Trek

The route from Josimath to the Kuari Pass is also known as the **Curzon Trail** – Lord Curzon was an enthusiastic Himalayan hiker. There is a bit of a misnomer here for the Curzon party did not cross the Kuari Pass, abandoning their attempt after being attacked by wild bees a few stages before the crossing.

There are two approaches to the pass. The most established trail comes direct from the village of Tapovan while the other meanders through the meadows from Auli, a small village above Josimath. Nonetheless, the Auli route is preferable for the birds-eye views up the Rishi Ganga into the Nanda Devi Sanctuary.

On the approach to Kuari Pass, the summit of Dunagiri (7066m) features prominently on the north rim of the Nanda Devi Sanctuary while Chaukhamba (7138m) and the rest of the impressive Chaukhamba Range can be seen above Josimath. To gain the best views of Nanda Devi (7817m) requires a day walk along the ridge above the pass.

The Kuari Pass (3640m) is by no means demanding although there is a short steep descent to the meadow at Dakwani before continuing to the shepherd camp at Sutoli. It is a further two stages across the forested ridges and past small villages high above the Birthi Ganga to the village of Ramni. From here it is a further stage down to the roadhead at Ghat where jeeps and buses complete the 30 km to Nandaprayag on the Josimath to Rishikesh road.

The trek can be completed from early June till the end of October. However, the trail is subject to heavy monsoon rains from mid-July to mid-September. Porters can be hired from one of the local agencies in Josimath. Budget for Rs 120 per day plus return.

Stage 1	Auli to Chitraganta meadow (6 to 7 hours)
Stage 2	Chitraganta to Dakwani via Kuari Pass (4 to 5 hours)
Stage 3	Dakwani to Ghangri (7 hours)
Stage 4	Ghangri to Ramni (5 to 6 hours)
Stage 5	Ramni to Ghat (3 hours)

above for details). Cross-country skiing has yet to take off here, but it is possible to hire alpine (downhill) equipment for Rs 100 per day. There is one 500m long ski lift which costs Rs 50 per person, and several rope tows which cost Rs 15 per person. Seven and 15 day packages are available for beginners, at Rs 1600 and Rs 2600 respectively, including all meals, lodging, equipment hire and lessons. To secure a reservation, write in advance to the General Manager, GMVN, 74/1 Rajpur Rd, Dehra Dun, UP (☎ (0135) 65-6817; fax 24-408).

There is no privately run accommodation; the GMVN *Tourist Centre* has dorm beds for Rs 75 to Rs 90, and doubles for Rs 500 and Rs 550. Meals are available here.

If you don't fancy the 3½ km cable car trip, there is one bus daily during the ski season from Josimath, which departs at 8 am (one hour, Rs 7), leaving Auli for Josimath at 11.30 am.

BADRINATH
Telephone Area Code: 01381

Badrinath receives more pilgrims than Yamunotri, Gangotri or Kedarnath, and as a consequence, is the largest of the four dham villages. It is not a particularly attractive town, with its busy bus stand and numerous sturdy grey dharamsalas and ashrams built to withstand the heavy winter snows, but the setting is superlative, lying beneath the snow-capped peak of Nhilkanth (6957m), known as the Shining Peak. Below Nhilkanth is the black bulk of Urvashi, connected by a saddle with the slopes of Narayan. To the north is the snow-capped Mukat Peak, also known as Mana Peak, and behind Urvashi is Sunarsuli Peak. Above the Badrinath Temple and to the right, the peculiar pyramid-shaped mounds at regular intervals slow the descent of the winter snows.

The settlement flanks both sides of the Alaknanda River; the temple, several ashrams and the interesting bazaar area of Old Badrinath are on the west side of the river. Numerous guesthouses, restaurants,

the post office and the bus stand are on the east side of the river. Here the Alaknanda is a small mountain stream, but as it flows south-west, it is joined by the Mandakini at Rudraprayag, before finally merging with the Ganges at Rishikesh, 298 km to the south-west.

The temple is built above the west bank of the Alaknanda, and is reached by a small footbridge. At either end of the bridge, moneychangers sit before pyramids of coins, converting pilgrims' rupees into handfuls of paisa which are distributed to the beggars and mendicant sadhus who line the bridge (who then return their takings to the moneychangers and exchange them for rupees, the moneychangers making a tiny commission on each transaction).

The history of the temple is somewhat obscure. It is believed that Badrinath may have been an important place of pilgrimage in the Vedic Age (c1500-1200 BC), but was converted into a Buddhist shrine during the time of Ashoka (3rd century BC). After attaining enlightenment at Josimath, the Hindu theologian and philosopher Shankaracharya made his way to Badrinath, where he was instructed during a dream to retrieve the *shaligram* (black-stone) idol from the temple which had been thrown into the Narad Kund – either by iconoclasts or by those endeavouring to protect the idol from their ravages – and reinstate it as the idol of Vishnu. The Buddhist legacy is apparent in the posture of the idol, which is seated in the *padmasana*, or lotus position.

As the winter snows begin to thaw, temple officials, in consultation with astrologers and the former maharaja of Tehri Garhwal, determine an auspicious day for the opening of the temple, which usually falls towards the end of April or the beginning of May. The temple is closed generally during the second week of November following an elaborate ceremony during which the statue of Vishnu is draped with a *choli* woven by *kanyas* (maidens) – from a chosen family by the name of Molapa who reside in the nearby village of Mana.

Vishnu at Badrinath

The presiding deity at Badrinath is Lord Vishnu. According to the Hindu scriptures, while Vishnu was reclining by the shores of the Celestial Lake as the Goddess Lakshmi massaged his feet, a sage by the name of Narad passed by and rebuked him for indulging in worldly pleasures. Abashed, Vishnu sent Lakshmi away and himself retreated to the fastness of the high Himalaya where he fed himself on the berries *(badri)* growing wild in the region and, adopting the Yogdhyani posture, proceeded to meditate for several years.

Lakshmi eventually traced Vishnu to his mountain retreat, and implored the god to resume his original Sringaric form. This Vishnu agreed to do, on the condition that the valley remain a place of meditation, and not of worldly pleasures, and that he be worshipped in both his Yogdhyani and Sringaric forms, the former by gods and sages, and the latter by pilgrims.

Lakshmi, as the consort of Vishnu, is usually placed on the left-hand side of the idol. However, during the summer, when pilgrims throng to Badrinath to pay homage to the god, the statue of Lakshmi can be seen on the right-hand side of the idol of Vishnu – the deities are worshipped as individual entities, not as a couple. During the winter months, when Badrinath is blanketed under deep snow and the temple is closed to pilgrims, leaving the valley to the gods and sages, Vishnu adopts his Yogdhyani form, with Lakshmi, as his consort, seated on his left-hand side. ■

Badrinath Temple

The temple of Badri Narayan is an imposing hive-shaped edifice, reminiscent of the temples constructed during the reign of the Katyuri rajas, who had their seat in Kumaon. Before the main entrance is a stone Garuda, the vehicle of Vishnu. Six large carved pillars of shaligram support the ceiling of the mandapa, each formed from single blocks of stone which were brought to Dehra Dun by train and shifted to their present site with the assistance of the Indian army. The double doors before the inner sanctum are of silver and feature finely wrought repoussé work. On either side are the celestial bodyguards, Jai (to the right) and Vijay (to the left). In the top panel of each door are raised images of Surya, the sun god.

The small shaligram idol of Vishnu is almost impossible to make out, being heavily garlanded with flowers.

Other Things to See

Just below the temple are the **Tapt Kund** hot springs, in whose sulphurous waters pilgrims bathe before visiting the temple. Three km to the north of the village is the small Bhotiya settlement of Mana, the final village before the Tibetan border, just over 30 km distant. From here, according to Hindu lore, a path leads directly to Mt Kailash, the abode of Lord Shiva. Certainly Mana was once an important trading village on the trade route between India and Tibet which proceeded over the Mana Pass, but with the escalation of border tensions between India and China, the villagers have lost their traditional livelihood and many of the seminomadic inhabitants are now engaged in weaving pure wool carpets called *duns*, using traditional Indian and Tibetan designs, and tending sheep, goats and yaks on the meadows in the environs of the village. During the winter months, the villagers retreat from the heavy snows to Josimath and Chamoli.

About 200m north-west of Mana is the **Vyas Gufa** (cave). Locals believe that the *Mahabharata* was dictated to Lord Ganesh here by the saint Vyasji. A path leads across the **Bhim Pul** (*pul* means bridge), believed to have been constructed by the giant Pandava Bhim to enable his brothers to cross the Sarasvati River to the base of the **Vasudhara Falls**, four km from Mana. The falls are believed to be the source of the Alaknanda as it falls from heaven. If the weather is clear, there are excellent views of Neelkanth to the west. Special permission is required from the District Magistrate in

Chamoli to walk beyond the waterfall and is unlikely to be granted.

Mana can be reached along a path which flanks the west bank of the Alaknanda River. The path commences just above and to the right of the temple. Alternatively you could hire a taxi (Rs 150 return) or there's one bus daily to the village, departing at 3.30 pm. Due to its proximity to the Tibetan border, foreigners have to report at the army checkpost in Mana before proceeding outside the village.

A short distance beyond Old Badrinath, which lies to the left of the temple, on the west bank of the Alaknanda, a path divides. The right-hand path mounts the foothills of Nhilkanth, ascending a saddle, where there are excellent views back over Badrinath, to Chandrapaduka, a walk of some 30 minutes. Here a boulder bears an impression which is believed to be the **footprint** of Lord Vishnu. The left-hand path at the fork just beyond Old Badrinath proceeds to the village of Bamni, crossing a small bridge over the Rishiganga. Above the village, which is less than one km from Badrinath, at the base of Urvashi, is a small **temple** dedicated to the beautiful nymph Urvashi, sent by Indra to distract the devout sage Arghya from his meditations.

Places to Stay & Eat

A few doors up from the Kwality Restaurant on Main Rd is the *Gujarat Bhavan* (☎ 2266). Here you'll find spotless singles/doubles with attached bath for Rs 50/150 (in May and June, doubles only from Rs 150 to Rs 200). The manager is very friendly and helpful, and there's a dhaba downstairs serving basic fare. Nearby, opposite the post office, is the *Modi Bhavan*, also with good rooms, at Rs 100 for doubles with attached bath. Hot water in buckets is Rs 10.

Close to the bus stand is the GMVN *Rest House*, with small double/triple rooms with common bath for Rs 120/150 (Rs 100/120 in July and August).

Top of the range is GMVN's *Hotel Devlok* (☎ 2212). Executive single/double/triple rooms in a separate annexe are Rs 265/325/390. Carpeted deluxe rooms in the main building are Rs 384/480/576, including tax. Rates are reduced in July and August. There's a restaurant here, as well as a pleasant lounge area where you can peruse the (day-old) English-language newspapers. The staff are friendly and informative.

If all of the above places are full, the *Temple Committee Reception Office*, Temple Rd, may be able to help. The committee has accommodation in triple and four bed rooms with attached bath for Rs 150/200. The office is open daily from 8 am to 8 pm.

There are three restaurants on Main Rd, at the corner where it meets Temple Rd. At the *Kwality*, a full meal will set you back about Rs 50. Next door is the *Saket Restaurant*, serving Punjabi, South Indian and Chinese cuisine. A good choice is the *Vijay Laxmi*, opposite, which has South Indian and Gujarati cuisine. The makki ki roti and saag is not bad (Rs 15), and during May and June, when fresh milk is brought up daily from Srinagar, there's kheer (Rs 6).

Things to Buy

Apart from the usual religious paraphernalia, of which there is no shortage, Badrinath is a good place to pick up a perky little woollen hat. They come in a variety of colours and cost only Rs 10 each.

Getting There & Away

Buses to Josimath depart at 6.30, 9 and 11.30 am, and 1.50 and 4 pm (2½ hours, Rs 17). The 6.30 am bus continues to Rishikesh (12 hours, Rs 117). The 9 am bus will get you as far as Srinagar (eight hours, Rs 76). The 11.30 am bus terminates at Rudraprayag (eight hours, Rs 60). The 1.50 pm bus will get you to Karanprayag on the same day (5½ hours, Rs 50). At 8 am daily there's a direct service to Gaurikund (the roadhead for Kedarnath; 13 hours, Rs 92). During the busy pilgrimage season of May and June, you may be able to get a share taxi (Rs 20) to Josimath. A full taxi will cost from Rs 500 to Rs 600 one way.

UTTARAKHAND

NANDA DEVI SANCTUARY

While not the highest of the snow-clad peaks of the Himalaya, Nanda Devi has been frequently described as the most beautiful, with mountaineers eulogising the splendour of her twin peaks, with the higher of the two at 7817m. They are surrounded by a virtually impenetrable curtain of lesser peaks, some of which have never been scaled, which form a bastion around the twin summits and encompass a vast wilderness area.

The mountain finds a special place in the hearts of many of the villagers of Garhwal and Kumaon; the cult worship of Nanda Devi, the bliss-giving goddess, forms an integral part of the religious life of those who live within sight of the magnificent peaks.

In 1934 the mountaineers Eric Shipton and Bill Tilman, accompanied by three Sherpas, pioneered a route through the Rishiganga gorge, accessed from Lata, 25 km from Josimath. Tilman was the first person to conquer the summit of Nanda Devi, but the goddess has exacted a heavy toll on subsequent attempts to violate her sanctity. In 1976, an American woman, 24 year old Nanda Devi Unsoeld, collapsed and died only 300m short of the summit after which she had been named by her mountaineering father, Willi Unsoeld. The first woman to reach the summit was the Indian Rekha Sharma, in 1981.

Unfortunately, this national park is currently closed to trekkers and it is not known when (or even if) it will reopen. Contact GMVN or KMVN for details.

GWALDAM

Easily accessible from Almora and Nainital, 78 km and 131 km respectively to the south, Gwaldam is ideally located as a base from which to embark on treks further north, including that to Rup Kund and the Curzon Trail. From this small market town, set amid apple orchards, can be obtained the best views of Trisul (considered to be the trident of Shiva). There are good bus connections to Tharali, 21 km to the north, from where there is a daily bus or jeep to Mandoli, roadhead for the trek to Rup Kund. Gwaldam has a very good GMVN *Tourist Rest House*, with doubles for Rs 150 and Rs 300, or dorm beds in the separate annexe for Rs 60.

Ghat-Rup Kund Trek

The trek can either be undertaken from the village of Ghat (or as an extension of the Kuari Pass trek) or if coming direct by road from Almora or Nainital can commence from the roadhead village of Mandoli. Whichever approach is selected, the route goes via the village of Wan before a steep climb up through mixed forest to the alpine meadow of Badni Bugyal. The views from the meadow are some of the finest in the western Himalaya. To the east are the peaks beyond Josimath, while to the south-east the main Himalaya Range extends as far as the eye can see to western Garhwal.

It's a further stage to the exposed camp at Bhogabasa and on the following day Rup Kund can be reached with time to return to Badni Bugyal the same day. From Badni Bugyal there is a short cut down to the trail between the villages of Wan and Lohajang and the trailhead at Mandoli.

The upper sections of the trek to Rup Kund are normally under snow until mid-July and from then to mid-September the area is subject to the monsoon. From then on till the middle of October is the best time to trek to Rup Kund before the first of the winter snows settle on the high ridges.

Porters can be hired out of Mandoli and Ghat. Budget for Rs 120 per porter per day.

Stage 1	Ghat to Ramni (5 hours)
Stage 2	Ramni to Sutol (6 to 7 hours)
Stage 3	Sutol to Wan (5 hours)
Stage 4	Wan to Badni Bugyal (5 hours)
Stage 5	Badni Bugyal to Bhogabasa (4 to 5 hours)
Stage 6	Bhogabasa to Rup Kund & return to Badni Bugyal (7 to 8 hours)

RUP KUND

At an altitude of 4778m and set beneath the towering summit of Trisul (7120m), Rup Kund is sometimes referred to as the 'mystery lake' on account of the large number of human skeletons (over 300) found here. The skeletons are over 500 years old, and various theories have been proposed as to the calamity which must have deposited them here. The most probable explanation is that they represent a party of pilgrims who were en route to Homkund to pay homage to the goddess Nanda Devi. While crossing the precipitous bank above the lake, the pilgrims evidently lost their footing, with those higher up falling on their brethren lower down, and the whole unfortunate party tumbling down into the icy depths of the lake.

The vision of these long-dead pilgrims presents a rather gruesome spectacle, the atmosphere enhanced by the desolate nature of the landscape. Nevertheless, trekkers with a penchant for the macabre continue to make the arduous trek to Rup Kund.

Kumaon

Population: 2,949,199
Area: 21,071 sq km
People per sq km: 140
Main Languages: Kumaoni & Hindi
Literacy Rate: 57.6%

Bordered by Garhwal to the west and north, and Nepal to the east, the district of Kumaon encompasses three of the eight Himalayan districts of Uttar Pradesh, those of Pithoragarh, Almora and Nainital. Kumaon is known for its hill stations, most well known of which are Almora and Nainital, the first perched along a five km ridge which affords a fine Himalayan panorama, and the second around an emerald green crater lake. However, it also has the less well known, and hence less developed and more tranquil, hill stations of Ranikhet and Kausani.

Mahatma Gandhi was particularly inspired by the forested slopes and stunning 350 km wide vistas at peaceful Kausani, which he believed were unsurpassed. It was here that he wrote the preface for his commentary on the *Bhagavadgita*. Ranikhet was the favourite of India's first prime minister, Jawaharlal Nehru, who, after visiting the hill station, advocated that more people from the plains should travel to the Himalaya where he was sure they would return home more invigorated and spiritually restored.

Other natural assets include the Corbett National Park and adjacent Sonanadi Wildlife Sanctuary, collectively known as the Corbett Tiger Reserve, and the beautiful alpine scenery on the way to the Pindari and Milam glaciers.

Apart from its superb natural assets, Kumaon also possesses a number of beautiful temple complexes which are sacred to Lord Shiva, legacies of the Katyuri (8th to 14th centuries) and Chand (15th to 18th centuries) dynasties. These can be found at Baijnath, Bhageshwar and Jageshwar. The main temple at Baijnath enshrines an exquisitely beautiful statue of Shiva's consort Parvati. The temple at Jageshwar is revered as the site of one of India's 12 jyoti lingams—lingams of light. All of these temples feature ornate sculpture, and some, such as those at Jageshwar, show a strong Buddhist influence. The patron goddess of Kumaon is Nanda Devi – although the mountain of Nanda Devi, perceived as a manifestation of the goddess, is located in Garhwal, her beautiful twin peaks are eminently visible from Kumaon, inspiring the reverence and awe of its inhabitants.

Kumaon forms an integral part of the important pilgrimage to Mt Kailash and Lake Mansarovar, in Tibet, with pilgrims crossing into Tibet via the 5334m high Lipu Pass. British interest in Kumaon's proximity to Tibet was inspired more by concerns of a commercial than spiritual nature: the British coveted the pure pashmina shawls from Tibet, for which they envisaged a lucrative market, and they were keen to exploit the traditional Indo-Tibetan trading routes. In 1815, Kumaon was relinquished to the East India Company, along with half of Garhwal, in payment for British assistance in routing the Nepali Gurkhas.

NAINITAL

Population: 34,000
Telephone Area Code: 05942
Peak Season: Mid-April to mid-July, mid-September to mid-November

At 1938m in the Kumaon Hills, this attractive hill station, 280 km north-east of Delhi, was once the summer capital of Uttar Pradesh. The hotels and villas of this popular resort are set around the emerald waters of the Nainital, or lake, hence the name.

Nainital is very much the green and pleasant land that immediately appealed to the homesick Brits, who were reminded of the Cumbrian Lake District. During a hunting expedition in 1839, an English businessman by the name of Barron came across the lake, built himself a small villa on its shores and had his yacht carried up here in 1840. Barron's claim to the area was contested by a local inhabitant by the name of Nur Singh. In a particularly unsporting act, Barron rowed his unwitting adversary out into the centre of the lake and strongly suggested that he relinquish his claims or make his own way back to the shore. Unable to swim, the unfortunate Nar Singh was compelled to comply.

While the lake itself is unquestionably beautiful, the hundreds of hotels and guesthouses which vie for attention along its eastern perimeters somewhat spoil the peaceful ambience, as do the throngs of holiday makers who come to Nainital during the busy summer months. Nevertheless, there are some very good walks through the forests to points with superb views of the Himalaya.

The peak season, when Nainital is packed and hotel prices double or triple, corresponds to school holidays. Also, Christmas and the New Year here is best avoided.

Orientation & Information

During the season, The Mall is closed to heavy vehicles for most of the day. Cycle-rickshaws take passengers along the 1½ km Mall between the bazaars at Tallital ('lake's foot'), at its south end, and Mallital ('lake's head'), to the north-west. The bus stand is in Tallital. Hotels and guesthouses can be found here, as well as along the entire length of The Mall and in the Mallital area. Most of the top-end hotels are about 10 to 15 minutes walk to the west of Mallital in the area known as Sukhatal.

There is a post office near the bus stand in Tallital and the main post office is in Mallital.

There are several banks in Mallital which exchange travellers' cheques, including the State Bank of India, the Bank of Baroda and the Allahabad Bank. The helpful UP tourist office (☎ 2337) is towards The Mallital end of The Mall. The Nainital Mountaineering Club (☎ 2051), CRST Inter College Building (take the road behind the Central Hotel), runs courses and can give advice on treks and expeditions in the area. Mr CL Sah at the club can help arrange guides and porters, or put you in touch with an English-speaking guide for nature walks in the environs of Nainital, and the club also hires out equipment. The District Forestry Officer can be contacted on ☎ 3145, or at his residence on ☎ 3230.

There's a good selection of English-language books, with a special section on the Kumaon region, at Narains, on The Mall near Naini Billiards. You can also get English-language newspapers here. Books (and just about everything else!) can be found at the Modern Book and General Store. English-language newspapers arrive after 11 am, and there's an excellent selection of the *Adventures of Tintin*.

Naini Lake

This attractive lake is said to be one of the emerald green eyes of Shiva's wife, Sati. (*Naina* is the Sanskrit word for 'eye'.) When Sati's father failed to invite Shiva to a family sacrifice, she self-immolated in protest. Shiva gathered the charred remains in his arms and proceeded to engage in a cosmic dance which threatened to destroy the world. To terminate the dance, Vishnu chopped up the body into pieces, and the remains were scattered across India. The modern Naina Devi Temple at the northern end of the lake is built over the precise spot where the eye is believed to have fallen. Nearby is a small Tibetan market.

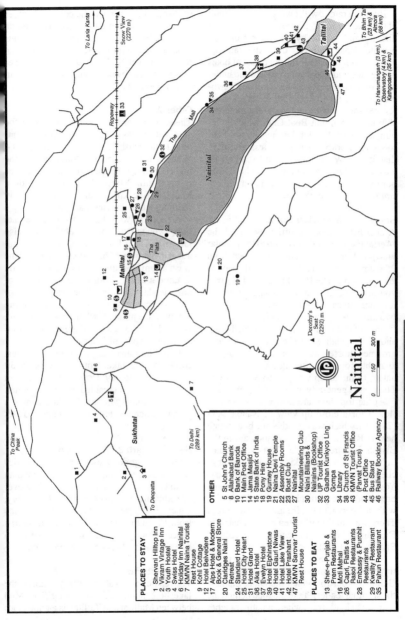

UTTARAKHAND

Nainital

0   150   300 m

PLACES TO STAY

1 Shervani Hilltop Inn
2 Vikram Vintage Inn
3 Youth Hostel
4 Swiss Hotel
6 Holiday Inn Nainital
7 KMVN Naina Tourist
   Rest House
9 Kohli Cottage
12 Hotel Belvedere
17 Alps Hotel & Modern
   Book & General Store
20 Claridges Naini
   Retreat
24 Standard Hotel
25 Hotel City Heart
31 Hotel Grand
36 Alka Hotel
37 Evelyn Hotel
39 Hotel Elphinstone
40 Hotel Gauri Niwas
41 Hotel Lake View
42 Hotel Prashant
47 KMVN Sarovar Tourist
   Rest House

PLACES TO EAT

13 Sher-e-Punjab &
   Prem Restaurants
16 Moti Mahal
26 Capri, Flattis &
   Rasoi Restaurants
28 Embassy & Purohit
   Restaurants
29 Kwality Restaurant
35 Pahun Restaurant

OTHER

5 St John's Church
8 Allahabad Bank
10 Bank of Baroda
11 Main Post Office
14 Jama Masjid
15 State Bank of India
18 Pony Hire
19 Gurney House
21 Naina Devi Temple
22 Assembly Rooms
23 Boat Club
27 Nainital
   Mountaineering Club
30 Naini Billiards &
   Nairains (Bookshop)
32 UP Tourist Office
33 Gadhan Kunkyop Ling
   Gompa
34 Library
38 Church of St Francis
43 KMVN Tourist Office
   (Parvat Tours)
44 Post Office
45 Bus Stand
46 Railway Booking Agency

Boat operators will take you on a circuit of the lake for Rs 45 in a row boat or you can hire a small yacht by the hour from the Nainital Boat Club (Rs 60). Alternatively, you can join the small flotilla of pedal boats on the lake and make your way around under your own steam (Rs 25 per hour for a two-seat boat, or Rs 45 for a four seater). It costs Rs 300 for a three day temporary membership to the Nainital Boat Club which gives you access to the club bar, restaurant, ballroom and library. The club is less exclusive than it was. When Jim Corbett lived here he was refused membership because he'd been born in India, and hence was not a *pukkah sahib* ('proper' gentleman).

Snow View & Tibetan Gompa
A chairlift (ropeway), officially called the 'Aerial Express', takes you up to the popular viewpoint at 2270m. The lift is open from 9.30 am to 1 pm and 2 to 5 pm and costs Rs 20 (one way). The Rs 30 return ticket gives you only one hour at the top and a set time for your return. Alternatively, it's a pleasant two km walk up past Gadhan Kunkyop Ling Gompa (Tibetan monastery). At The Mallital end of The Mall, near The Flats, beautifully groomed horses and mountain ponies are available for hire, offering a pleasant alternative to the steep walk up to Snow View. The cost is generally about Rs 40 per hour.

At the top there are powerful binoculars (Rs 2) for a close-up view of Nanda Devi (7817m) which was, as the old brass plate here tells you, 'the highest mountain in the British Empire'. Nanda Devi was India's highest peak until Sikkim (and thus Kangchenjunga) was absorbed into the country. You can be dressed in Kumaoni traditional dress and have your photo taken for Rs 15, with a spectacular Himalayan backdrop. There's a small marble temple dedicated to Dev Mundi housing images of Durga, Shiva, Sita, Rama, Lakshman and Hanuman.

A walk up to Snow Peak can take in the tiny **Gadhan Kunkyop Ling Gompa** of the Gelupka order (of which the Dalai Lama is the spiritual leader). Take the road behind the Standard Hotel, from where a path branches off towards the gompa (the colourful prayer flags are visible from the road). The gompa serves Nainital's small (and mostly itinerant) Tibetan community. Most of the Tibetan families travel to Nainital in the summer season to sell sweaters and shawls, and in winter descend to the plains.

Other Walks
There are several other good walks in the area, with views of the snow-capped mountains to the north. **China Peak** (pronounced 'Cheena'), also known as Naini Peak, is the highest point in the area (2610m) and can be reached either from Snow View or from Mallital (five km). Climb up in the early morning when the views are clearer.

A four km walk to the west of the lake brings you to **Dorothy's Seat** (2292m), also known as Tiffin Top, where a Mr Kellet built a seat in memory of his wife, killed in a plane crash. From Dorothy's Seat it's a lovely walk to **Land's End** (2118m) through a forest of oak, deodar and pine. The walk will take about 45 minutes, and in the early morning you may see jungle fowl or goral (mountain goats). From Land's End there are fine views out over the lake of Khurpa Tal.

From the Jama Masjid, at the north-west corner of the lake, you can walk in 30 minutes to **Gurney House**, the house in which Jim Corbett resided while in Nainital. This two storey wooden dwelling is now a private residence, but the caretaker may let you look inside.

Hanumangarh & Observatory
There are good views and spectacular sunsets over the plains from this Hanuman temple, three km south of Tallital. Just over one km further on is the state observatory, which should be open Monday to Saturday from 10 am to 5 pm, but check at the tourist office before you head out here. There is a free slide show between 1.30 and 3 pm.

Other Activities
The reading room at the **library**, right on the lakeshore about halfway along The Mall between Mallital and Tallital, is a good place

o escape the frenetic activity on The Mall, particularly in the late afternoon, when reflections from the lake create a lovely rippling effect on the walls and ceiling. Bibliophiles will appreciate the old wooden card files and hundreds of old volumes, and there are current newspapers for visitors' perusal. It's open in summer from 7.30 to 10.30 am and 5.30 to 8.30 pm, and in winter, from 8.30 to 10.30 am and 4 to 7 pm.

At The Mallital end of The Mall is **Naini Billiards**. It's open daily, and costs Rs 35 per hour. Coaching is available for Rs 10 per hour. Fishing gear can be hired at **Bhim Tal**, an overrated excursion spot 23 km to the east of Nainital. You will require a permit which is issued here by the Fisheries Officer.

Organised Tours

Package tours can be booked at either of the two KMVN rest houses. A two day tour to Kausani is Rs 200 by bus or Rs 1200 by taxi. To Jageshwar, a two day tour costs Rs 100 by bus or Rs 1200 by taxi. A six day tour to Badrinath and Kedarnath is Rs 600 by bus or Rs 6000 by taxi. Prices include dormitory accommodation, transfers and evening meals.

Parvat Tours (☎ 2656), run by KMVN, is at the Tallital end of The Mall. The office is run by helpful and efficient staff keen to promote their new range of adventure and recreational activities which include mountain cycling, river rafting and canoeing, hang-gliding and paragliding. They can also arrange high and low-altitude trekking, including winter trekking, and also run regular tours such as day trips to Corbett National Park (Rs 900 return by taxi, or Rs 150 by luxury bus). Luxury bus trips to Delhi can also be booked here (see the Getting There & Away section below).

Places to Stay

There are over 100 places to stay, from gloomy budget guesthouses to five-star hotels. During the peak season, school holidays and during the festivals of Dussehra and Diwali, prices can triple, and finding anywhere to stay can be a major hassle.

Places to Stay – bottom end
Tallital & The Mall (South End) There are several good budget choices at the Tallital end of the lake on the road which runs above and parallel to The Mall at its south end. The *Hotel Lake View* (☎ 2532), Ramji Rd, run by the gracious Mr and Mrs Shah, has doubles in the season from Rs 150 to Rs 450 (Rs 100 to Rs 200 in the off season). All rooms have attached bath and hot water is available in buckets for Rs 4. Views from the balcony extend from the plains, over Tallital, across the lake and to Mallital. The more expensive rooms are at the front of the building.

Nearby, also on Ramji Rd, is the *Hotel Gauri Niwas* (no phone). Double rooms with geysers and lake views range from Rs 200 to Rs 250; gloomy windowless rooms at the back (hot water available in buckets: Rs 3) are Rs 100 and Rs 150. A 50% to 60% discount is offered in the off season.

Also in this area is the *Hotel Prashant* (☎ 2347). Doubles range from Rs 150 to Rs 300, with the more expensive rooms having better views; the cheaper rooms are a bit shabbier. All rooms have attached baths, and there's running hot water in the morning. There's a dining hall here. A 50% discount is offered in the off season.

Mallital & Sukhatal An excellent budget choice in the heart of Mallital, opposite the Allahabad Bank, is *Kohli Cottage* (☎ 3368). In the season, doubles are Rs 200 and Rs 250, all with attached bath and hot water. Four bed rooms are Rs 300. In the off season, doubles are Rs 125 and Rs 150, and four bed rooms are Rs 200. Rooms are light and airy, and the manager is friendly and helpful. There are good views from the roof terrace.

The *Standard Hotel* (☎ 2602), in a good location at the end of The Mall just before you reach Mallital, has fairly ordinary rooms, but some have great views out over the lake. In the season, doubles with attached bath are Rs 150, or with common bath, Rs 100 (Rs 80 and Rs 50 in the off season). The rooms without windows are a bit grim.

The 100 year old, somewhat rickety *Alps Hotel* (☎ 2317) has enormous double rooms for Rs 200 with attached bathroom. A 50% to 60% discount is offered in the off season, and there's a lovely old broad balcony for watching the promenaders on The Mall.

Set in a peaceful wooded location, about 20 minutes walk west of Mallital in the area known as Sukhatal is the *Youth Hostel* (☎ 3353). Beds (with lockers) in the dorms cost Rs 12 for members, Rs 22 for nonmembers. There are also two double rooms with common bath for the same rates. Filling vegetarian thalis (Rs 12) are available in the dining hall, and you can enquire about the Pindari Glacier and other treks here.

Places to Stay – middle & top end
Tallital & The Mall (South End) Very handy to the bus stand is KMVN's *Sarovar Tourist Rest House* (☎ 2570). From 1 May to 15 July, doubles/four bed rooms are Rs 500/600, and beds in the spotless dorm (with terrific lake views) are Rs 40. Between 15 September and 15 November, rates are Rs 350/425, and Rs 35 in the dorm, and during the rest of the year, rates are Rs 200/250, or Rs 30 in the dorm. Rooms are comfortable, although nothing special, and some have very good views over the lake.

The *Hotel Elphinstone* (☎ 2534), right on The Mall, has doubles from Rs 200 to Rs 400. All rooms face the lake, other than rooms at Rs 200, and all have attached bathrooms. There's a pretty garden terrace here, complete with a bust of Queen Victoria bearing a plaque with the inscription 'Victoria the Good'. A 40% discount is offered in the off season.

Further north along The Mall is the enormous *Evelyn Hotel* (☎ 2457). Double rates range from Rs 400 to Rs 800, with a 50% discount offered in the off season. To get to the cheapest rooms entails a strenuous climb up a seemingly endless series of stairs, but the views from up here over the lake are excellent, and rooms are comfortable. There are several large sunny roof terraces.

Continuing towards Mallital, also right on The Mall, is the *Alka Hotel* (☎ 2220). Economy doubles are Rs 500, and standard doubles are Rs 800 (Rs 300 and Rs 500 in the off season). All rooms have running hot and cold water and piped music.

Mallital & Sukhatal At The Mallital end of The Mall is the large *Hotel Grand* (☎ 2406). Singles/doubles are Rs 450/600, or suites (with separate sitting area) are Rs 700. There's running hot water in the morning only. This place is open between 15 April and 15 November only. In the off season, a discount of Rs 100 is offered. There's a lovely wide shady balcony with potted geraniums from where there are good lake views.

The lovely old *Hotel Belvedere* (☎ 2082, fax 2493) was formerly the palace of the Raja of Awagarh. Take the road which leads up behind the Bank of Baroda. Doubles start from Rs 650, or with a separate sitting area Rs 800. Enormous double suites are Rs 1000. Some of the rooms have very good lake views, or you can look out over the lake from the wicker chairs on the shady verandah. Mr and Mrs Singh are the gracious hosts, and they offer a discount of 30% in the off season.

Directly opposite the Nainital Mountaineering Club on the road behind the Standard Hotel is the excellent *Hotel City Heart* (☎ 2228). Run by the effervescent Mr Pramod, a bass guitarist in an Indian heavy metal rock band, doubles are very good value, with prices ranging from Rs 450 to Rs 1100. The cheaper rooms have no views, but are large, comfortable and spotless. The more expensive rooms have superlative views of the lake. There's a good roof terrace, and the bright cheery atmosphere is enhanced by dozens of pretty potted plants. A discount of 50% to 60% is offered in the off season.

At Sukhatal, about one km from Mallital on the road towards New Delhi is the KMVN *Naina Tourist Rest House* (☎ 3374). Doubles from 1 May to 15 July range from Rs 450 to Rs 550; from 15 September to 15 November, rates are Rs 250 to Rs 350, and in the off season, Rs 150 to Rs 225. There is a dormitory here.

About 10 minutes walk west of Mallital, in a peaceful location, and set in pretty gardens, is the charming old *Swiss Hotel*

3013). Run by the Nanda family, this is a very good choice, with comfortable, airy rooms, some with views over the garden. Doubles are Rs 1200, suites are Rs 1500 and our bed rooms are Rs 1800. A 25% discount is offered in the off season. Rates include breakfast and dinner. Mr Nanda's son is a keen naturalist, and can arrange bird and butterfly-spotting excursions around Nainital.

Fifteen minutes walk from Mallital brings you to the *Shervani Hilltop Inn* (☎ 3128), formerly the residence of a maharaja. Rooms aren't that special, but are quite comfortable, and the flower garden is spectacular. In the off season this is a good mid-range choice. In the season, doubles are Rs 1225, Rs 1425 and Rs 1625, including breakfast and dinner. In the off season, room-only rates are Rs 500, Rs 700 and Rs 900.

The best value mid to top-end choice is the beautifully appointed *Vikram Vintage Inn* (☎ 3177), in a secluded location about 20 minutes walk west of Mallital, in Sukhatal. Singles/doubles are Rs 950/1800, and there are also triple rooms for Rs 1800. Rates include breakfast, and a 10% to 30% discount is offered in the off season. Checkout is a generous 11 am. There's billiards and table tennis here, and the staff at the reception desk can arrange a private consultation with a palmist/numerologist (Rs 200 for 30 minutes).

Claridges Naini Retreat (☎ 2105), in a quiet spot above Mallital, has doubles for Rs 2150 including breakfast and one other meal. You can hire golf sets here (guests only) for Rs 75. The *Holiday Inn Nainital* (☎ 2531), Grasmere Estate, about 10 minutes walk north-west of Mallital, has luxuriously appointed rooms, most with lake views, for Rs 2600, Rs 3100, Rs 3500 and Rs 4000. There's a disco here, two restaurants and Nainital's only bar. A 30% to 40% discount is offered in the off season.

Places to Eat

There's a wide range of eating establishments strung out along the length of The Mall, and all of the top-end hotels have their own restaurants (visitors welcome). There are a couple of places in a small cul-de-sac in Mallital's main bazaar, including the *Shere-Punjab*, featuring, as it's name suggests, Punjabi cuisine. Just around the corner is the *Prem Restaurant*, with Punjabi and South Indian cuisine. The friendly chef will whip you up a bhutara (large puri), served with channa (chick peas) and sliced onion, for only Rs 5. The *Moti Mahal*, opposite the north side of The Flats, specialises in Punjabi cuisine. There's a *fresh fruit juice stall* beneath the Standard Hotel, Mallital. You can also get shakes and lassis here. The *Capri Restaurant*, near the Standard Hotel at The Mallital end of The Mall, has Indian, Chinese and Continental cuisine. It's popular, and is often full at lunch time. Nonveg dishes are around Rs 50. Next door, the *Rasoi Vegetarian Restaurant*, has good thalis and pizza.

With prices comparable to the Capri, the *Flattis Restaurant* is another popular eatery which features mutton and chicken sizzlers. Also in this area is the *Embassy*, considered one of the best restaurants by locals. There is a conspicuous absence of ashtrays, and the menu features veg and nonveg cuisine, with main dishes between Rs 65 and Rs 90. Next door to the Embassy is *Purohit's*, with pure vegetarian South Indian cuisine. There's alfresco dining with views across the lake, and filling thalis for Rs 32.

Also at The Mallital end of The Mall is the *Kwality*, set right on the water's edge. It's a bit rowdy at lunch time, but prices are reasonable, with most main dishes under Rs 50. There is also an ice-cream parlour here.

Further down The Mall, about halfway between Tallital and Mallital, is the excellent *Pahun Restaurant (pahun* means 'guest'). This place, which proudly bears a sign declaring that it is 'A complete women's enterprise', features traditional Kumaoni cuisine such as aalu ke gutke (fried potato with masala), badeel (fried chickpea patties served with chutney or relish, and the sweet sooji ke pue (deep-fried semolina and curd balls). If you want to sample a variety of Kumaoni dishes, there's the special Kumaoni thali (Rs 60), but advance notice is required to prepare the thali – advise the

UTTARAKHAND

friendly staff in the morning if you plan to dine here in the evening. Prices are very reasonable, with most dishes under Rs 20. This place is closed on Mondays.

There are two restaurants at the Holiday Inn Nainital, Grasmere Estate: the multicuisine *Kumaon*, and the *Lotus Garden*, serving Chinese cuisine. This hotel also has Nainital's only bar, the *Viceroy*. Main dishes in the restaurants cost between Rs 75 and Rs 120, with sweets around Rs 40. If you're hanging out for a continental breakfast, the buffet breakfast bar has croissants, Danish pastries, cereals, scrambled eggs, etc, for Rs 100. Cocktails in the bar are Rs 100, and a beer will set you back Rs 90.

Getting There & Away
Air The nearest airport is Pantnagar, 71 km south, but it's not currently served by any scheduled flights.

Bus Buses leave from the bus stand at Tallital every 30 minutes for the railhead at Kathgodam (1½ hours, Rs 30). There's a deluxe 2x2 service to Delhi at 8.30 am (nine hours, Rs 148) and an ordinary service at 8.45 am (Rs 90). Many private agencies also book deluxe coach tickets to Delhi, and KMVN have their own luxury services; aircon coaches are Rs 230.

Buses to Bhim Tal leave at 8 and 8.30 am, 1.45, 3.15, 4, 4.30 and 6 pm (one hour, Rs 9). To Ramnagar buses leave at 8.45 am and 2, 3 and 3.45 pm (3½ hours, Rs 25). To Almora there are services at 7 and 10 am and noon (three hours, Rs 28). Buses for Ranikhet leave at 6.30 am, 12.30 and 2.30 pm (3½ hours, Rs 25). To Kausani there's one service at 10 am (five hours, Rs 48), and there's also only one daily service to Pithoragarh at 7 am (9½ hours, Rs 75). To Bareilly buses leave at 7.15 am, 1.30 and 2.30 pm (five hours, Rs 38). To Haridwar, buses depart at 5, 6 and 7 am, 4.30 and 8 pm (eight hours, Rs 96).

There's only one direct service to Rishikesh, which leaves at 5 am (nine hours, Rs 105). To Dehra Dun, ordinary buses leave at 6 and 7 am and 4.30 pm (10 hours, Rs 94),

and there's a deluxe service at 8 pm (Rs 170). A daily bus to Song (for the Pindari Glacier trek) leaves Bhowali, 11 km from Nainital at the junction of the main routes to Ranikhet and Almora, at 10 am (six hours).

Train Kathgodam (35 km south) is the nearest railway station, and the railway booking agency, near the bus stand, has a quota for trains to Delhi, Lucknow and Calcutta. The *Ranikhet Express* departs Old Delhi station at 11 pm, arriving into Kathgodam at 6.30 am. It departs Kathgodam at 8.45 pm arriving into Old Delhi station at 4.50 am (Rs 97/403 in 2nd/2nd air-con class). The office is open from 9.30 am to 4 pm.

Taxi & Jeep Share jeeps leave from the bus stand for the bazaar at Bhowali, 11 km below Nainital, when full (30 minutes, Rs 50). Share taxis depart when full for Kathgodam and Haldwani (Rs 30).

Getting Around
The official rate for a rickshaw from Tallital to Mallital is Rs 3; tickets can be purchased at the booths at either end of The Mall.

CORBETT TIGER RESERVE
Telephone Area Code: 05945
Established in 1936 as India's first national park, Corbett National Park is famous for its wide variety of wildlife and its beautiful location in the Siwalik foothills of the Himalaya. It is set in dense sal forest in the Patlidun Valley, traversed by the Ramganga River. With the recent inclusion of the Sonanadi Wildlife Sanctuary, which abuts the national park on its west side, Corbett has grown from 520 to 1318 sq km, and the national park and Sonanadi Wildlife Sanctuary are known collectively as the Corbett Tiger Reserve.

It may seem incongruous for a national park to be named after a famous British hunter – Jim Corbett is best known for his book *The Man-Eaters of Kumaon*, and was greatly revered by local people for shooting tigers that had developed a penchant for human flesh. Over 90 tigers had fallen at the

hands of Corbett before the hunter symboli-
cally buried his guns and turned
conservationist. He was instrumental in
setting up the reserve. The Project Tiger
programme, a joint initiative of the Indian
government and the World Wildlife Fund
(now the World Wide Fund for Nature), was
inaugurated at Corbett National Park, in
1973, and now 19 reserves across India have
been adopted into the programme.

Originally the Patlidun Valley was covered in dense forest and formed part of the
Tehri-Garhwal state. Disputes over territory
between the Garhwalis and the Rohillas
resulted in the clearing of vast tracts of land
in the valley, where the Garhwalis installed
themselves in encampments to fend off their
adversaries. No sooner had the Rohillas been
expelled than the Garhwalis faced a new
enemy in the form of the Gurkhas. With the
assistance of the British, these new invaders
were also dispatched, but as part of the war
costs, the Garhwalis were compelled to relin-

quish the valley to the British. The large
valley, cleared of its original forest cover,
remained uninhabited, and vast grasslands,
known locally as *chaur*, emerged – the
perfect habitat for the tiger, wild elephant
and other large animals.

Seeing a tiger here is dependent on
chance, since baiting has been discontinued
(unlike at Kanha in Madhya Pradesh).
However, your best chance is if you come
late in the season (April to mid-June) and
stay for several days.

More commonly seen wildlife includes
wild elephants, langur monkeys (black face,
long tail), rhesus macaques, peacock, and
several types of deer, including chital
(spotted deer), sambar, hog deer and barking
deer. There are also crocodiles, the odd-
looking gavial or gharial (a thin-snouted
fish-eating crocodile, often spotted from
High Bank, between the Dhangarhi Gate and
Dhikala), monitor lizards, wild boars and
jackals. Leopards (referred to as panthers in

UTTARAKHAND

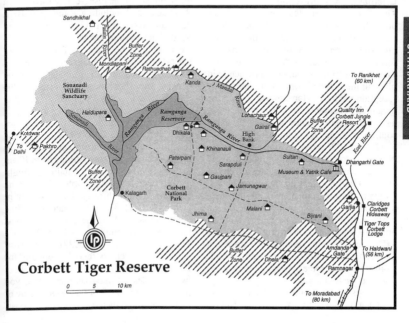

Corbett Tiger Reserve

India) are occasionally seen. Don't wear brightly coloured clothing, carry radios or engage in any boisterous or noisy activity which will frighten the animals away.

Corbett is also a bird-watcher's paradise, with over 500 species of indigenous or migratory birds, and since the creation of the Ramganga Reservoir, large numbers of waterfowl have been attracted here. Keen anglers can set their wits against the mahseer *(Tor putitora)*, a belligerent fighting fish which inhabits the waters of the Kosi River, which runs outside the eastern perimeter of the reserve. Fishing permits can be obtained from the reception centre in Ramnagar.

The Sonanadi Wildlife Sanctuary, unlike Corbett National Park, has no grasslands, and due to the dense forest cover, it is more difficult to spot wildlife here. This pristine forest has remained largely undisturbed over the centuries, apart from occasional Gujar settlements, and there is a rich variety of bird and animal life here.

Orientation & Information

The Corbett Tiger Reserve encompasses both the original Corbett National Park, comprising the eastern side of the reserve, and the Sonanadi Wildlife Sanctuary, forming the western side of the reserve. There is an elaborate tourist infrastructure in place in the national park itself, and a busy reception centre at **Ramnagar**, outside the park on its south-eastern perimeter. There is a second reception centre at Kotdwar, on the south-west perimeter of the park.

The Tiger Reserve is open from mid-November to mid-June but you should avoid the crowded weekends. The gates are closed at sunset and no night driving is permitted. **Dhikala**, in the national park, is the main accommodation centre in the reserve, 51 km north-west of Ramnagar, the nearest railhead, and is the headquarters of Project Tiger. Access to Dhikala is from the **Dhangarhi Gate**, about 20 km to the north of Ramnagar. Outside Corbett there are some expensive resorts and a few hotels in Ramnagar.

Day visitors are not allowed to enter from Dhangarhi Gate or to visit Dhikala. To visit Bijrani you must first get permits from Ramnagar. Only 100 visitors are permitted daily on a first come first serve basis.

At Dhikala there's a library and interesting wildlife films are shown here (free) in the evenings. The elephant rides at sunrise and sunset are not to be missed and cost Rs 50 each for four people for about two hours. During the day you can sit in one of the observation posts to unobtrusively watch for animals. When the park is closed, elephant rides are available at Dhangarhi Gate.

At Bijrani there's an interpretation centre and restaurant. It's sometimes possible to get elephant rides from here, although as there are only four elephants, priority is given to those staying overnight. There's a State Bank of India in Ramnagar which exchanges travellers' cheques.

Permits & Photographic Fees Two types of permits are available: day-visit permits and permits for overnight stays. The former can be obtained from access points around the perimeter of the reserve; clockwise from Ramnagar, and including Ramnagar itself, these are: Kalagarh, Pakhro, Kotdwar and Sendhikhal. Permits for an overnight stay in the park must be obtained from the park reception centre at Ramnagar (☎ 85-489; fax 85-376) where some accommodation can be booked. The office is near the bus stand on the Ranikhet road, and is open daily, including holidays, from 8 am to 1 pm and 3 to 5 pm.

Forest rest houses in the Sonanadi Wildlife Sanctuary can be booked at the new reception centre at Kotdwar (☎ (01382) 8235), open Monday to Saturday from 10 am to 5 pm. You can also obtain overnight permits here. It's also possible to book some accommodation through UP Tourism in Delhi (☎ (011) 332-2251), and the three double rooms at Khinanauli (Rs 600) must be booked through the Chief Wildlife Warden in Lucknow (☎ (0522) 28-3902).

Charges given in this section are for foreign nationals; Indians are charged about two-thirds less. At the reception centres you must pay an entry fee of Rs 100 for a stay of up to three days, then Rs 50 per day. It costs

Rs 50 for a camera permit, Rs 500 for a video or movie camera. To take a car into the park costs Rs 50, plus another Rs 100 (full day) or Rs 50 (half day) for a (compulsory) guide, available at Amdanda Gate, the closest gate to Ramnagar. At Dhangarhi Gate it's Rs 100 for the day, even if you will not be there for the duration.

Places to Stay & Eat

The highest concentration of accommodation is at Dhikala, but there are forest rest houses scattered around both the national park and the Sonanadi Wildlife Sanctuary. Elephant rides are available at Dhikala and Bijrani, but bear in mind that if you stay outside these areas, your chances of spotting wildlife are reduced to sightings from the rest houses themselves, as venturing into the reserve on foot is prohibited.

Dhikala There's a wide range of accommodation but the prices charged for foreigners mean that it's not good value. There's a very basic dormitory (like three-tier train sleepers!) for Rs 50 in the *Log Huts* but it's better to go for the triples (Rs 240) in the *Tourist Hutment*. An extra charge (Rs 25) is made for mattresses and sheets in all these places. All these can be booked at the reception centre at Ramnagar.

More comfortable doubles at Rs 450 are in the *cabins*, which must be booked through the Chief Wildlife Warden in Lucknow (see the Information section). Also bookable through Lucknow are the double rooms in the *Old Forest Rest House* (Rs 600) or the *New Forest Rest House* (Rs 450). There are two restaurants, one run by KMVN, and another place run by a private operator.

Other Forest Rest Houses With your own transport and food, you can also stay in the forest rest houses at **Sultan** and **Malani** (doubles for Rs 150), **Sarpduli** or **Gairal** (doubles at Rs 450), all in the Corbett National Park (ie the east end of the reserve). There is no electricity at any of these places, although the rest house at Sarpduli has its own generator. Bring a torch (flashlight). All

these places can be accessed from the Dhangarhi Gate. Bookings should be made with the Chief Wildlife Warden, Lucknow. Even if you have booked your accommodation in advance, you will still need to check in at the reception centre at Ramnagar to obtain overnight permits to enter the park. There is also a forest rest house at **Bijrani**, in the south-eastern corner of the reserve. Singles/doubles are Rs 250/450, and bookings must be made at the reception office in Ramnagar. Access to Bijrani is via the Amdanda Gate.

There are also forest rest houses in the reserve buffer areas of **Dhela**, **Jhirna** and **Kalagarh**, on the southern perimeter of the reserve, and at **Lohachaur**, in the buffer zone to the north of the national park. Doubles at all of these cost Rs 150. You should bring a flashlight and your own food. Bookings must be made at Ramnagar; the rest houses are not available between June and November.

There are a number of forest rest houses in the **Sonanadi Wildlife Sanctuary** at the western end of the reserve, including those at **Sendhikhal, Mondiapani, Rathuadhab, Haldupara** and **Kanda** (actually just over the boundary in the Corbett National Park). Again there is no electricity and you'll need to bring your own food. Double rates in all of these are Rs 150, and they must be booked through the reception office at Kotdwar. Write in advance to the Sub-Divisional Officer, Kotdwar Reception Centre, Sonanadi, Kotdwar, UP.

Ramnagar Note that if you use Ramnagar as a base you'll have to rent a jeep here and you won't be able to go out on elephant rides in the centre of the park, as day visits to Dhikala are not permitted.

There's a good KMVN *Tourist Bungalow* (☎ 85-225) next to the reception centre. It has ordinary doubles for Rs 100, deluxe doubles for Rs 200 and super-deluxe doubles for Rs 250. Dorm beds are Rs 30. The *Hotel Everest* (☎ 85-099) has clean and comfortable rooms for Rs 100 to Rs 200 between 15 November and 15 June, and Rs 70 to Rs 125 at other times. Hot water is available in buckets for Rs 4, and room service is available. The hotel is in a side street about two blocks up from the reception centre. Rooms with common bath are available at the *Hotel Govind* (☎ 85-615), near the bus stand. Doubles cost Rs 60, Rs 70 and Rs 80, and there's a good restaurant featuring Indian and Chinese cuisine downstairs.

Private Resorts There are several up-market resorts strung along the Ramnagar to Ranikhet road, all outside the reserve precincts. *Tiger Tops Corbett Lodge* (☎ 85-279; Delhi (011) 644-4016), seven km from Ramnagar, is a very luxurious place with prices to match: Rs 3600 per person per night; a single supplement is 40% extra. Prices include all meals and two day-visits to the reserve during the season. There are elephant rides, jeep trips and a swimming pool, and a wildlife slide show in the evenings. Between 16 June and 14 November, a 40% discount is offered. Despite the name, it's not part of the company that operates the famous resort in Chitwan (Nepal).

The *Claridges Corbett Hideaway* (☎ 85-959; Delhi (011) 301-0211) has accommodation in attractive ochre cottages set in an orchard of mango trees. Air-con double rooms cost Rs 3300, and rates include all meals. Staff can arrange bird-watching and nature-trail excursions, and mountain-bikes are available for hire for Rs 50 per hour. A 50% discount is offered when the reserve is closed.

The *Quality Inn Corbett Jungle Resort* (☎ /fax 85-230), in the Kumeria Forest Reserve, has attractive cottages high above the river for Rs 2600, including all meals. This place features its own in-house elephant (named Ramkali), so rides are assured. Jeep safaris are run in the morning and evening (Rs 350 per person), and include entrance fees, toll charges and guides. When the reserve is closed, double rates here are Rs 1800.

Getting There & Away
Buses for Delhi depart Ramnagar approximately every hour, with the first service leaving at 5.30 am and the last at 8 pm (seven hours, Rs 68). Tickets can be booked at the Delhi Transport Corporation, hidden in the back room of the Anand Mistham Bhandar sweet shop, in a side street two blocks up from the reception centre.

Services for other destinations in Kumaon are booked at the Kumaon Motor Owners' Union (KMOU) office, near the petrol pump on the Ranikhet road, on the opposite side to the reception centre. To Nainital, there are services at 6 am and 2.30 pm (3½ hours, Rs 25). The Ranikhet services depart at 4 and 9.30 am (4½ hours, Rs 39) and continue to Almora (6½ hours, Rs 60).

Ramnagar is connected by train with the busy railway junction of Moradabad. A nightly service leaves Ramnagar at 8.40 pm, arriving into Delhi at 5 am. The railway station is 1½ km south of the reception centre.

Getting Around
There is a local bus service from Ramnagar to Dhikala which leaves at 3 pm (2½ hours, Rs 10), and from Dhikala to Ramnagar at 9 am. None of the other places in the park are served by buses. Jeeps can usually only be rented at Ramnagar, and will cost about Rs 1000 per day. Book through the KMVN Tourist Bungalow. Safaris on foot are strictly prohibited. The only other mode of transport is the ubiquitous elephant.

RANIKHET
Telephone Area Code: 2447
Peak Season: Mid-April to mid-July, mid-September to mid-November
Fifty-eight km north of Nainital at an altitude of 1829m, the peaceful hill station of Ranikhet offers excellent views of the snow-capped Himalaya including Nanda Devi (7817m). The name is derived from *rani*, or queen, and *khet*, meaning field, an allusion to a legendary queen who visited the site and, overwhelmed by the green glades and snow-capped vistas, fell in love with the place and built herself a palace here. Ranikhet was founded by the British in 1869, and is now an important army town and the headquarters

of the Kumaon Regiment. It's a delightful and laid-back place to spend a few relaxing days.

Orientation & Information

Ranikhet essentially comprises two areas: the busy Sadar Bazaar, where the buses arrive, either at the UP Roadways stand, at its east end, or the Kumaon Motor Owners' Union (KMOU) stand about one km away at its west end; and the beautiful wooded area known as The Mall, which meanders along a ridge above the town, three km distant. Development hasn't yet taken its toll up here, and trees still outnumber the few hotels and administrative buildings strung along its shady length.

At the west end of Sadar Bazaar, the road divides; the KMOU office is about 20m down the lower road; the upper road proceeds up past the State Bank of India and the Nar Singh stadium to The Mall. A shortcut leads from up behind the stadium to The Mall

through the forest, emerging after 15 minutes near the military hospital.

There's a small UP tourist office (☎ 2227) above the UP Roadways stand. The main post office is on The Mall, about 200m before Hotel Meghdoot. There is a small postal agency in Sadar Bazaar, near the Hotel Raj Deep.

Golf Course

Despite the sign which says 'Defence Land; Trespassers Prosecuted', visitors are welcome to play a round of golf at this nine-hole golf course at Kalika, four km outside Ranikhet on the Almora Rd. Set at 1820m above sea level, there are fine 300 km panoramic views of the Himalaya. Green fees are Rs 400, and caddies are available. Club hire is Rs 100 for a half set. A taxi to the course from Ranikhet will cost Rs 70, or you could catch one of the numerous Almora-bound buses and get off at the golf course. The club house is open from 6 am to 6 pm.

Ananda Puri Ashram

Founded to propagate the teachings of Sri Sri 1008 Hairakhan Wale Baba, more commonly known as Babaji by his devotees among whom are many Europeans, this ashram is located at Chiliyanaula, three km from Ranikhet. There is a second Babaji ashram, called the Hairakhan Vishwa Madadham (☎ (05942) 1026) on the banks of the Gotamaganga, 27 km from Haldwani, near Surat. Babaji's devotees believe that he is a *mahavatar* (human manifestation of God, not born of woman) of Shiva Mahavatar Babaji, of whom Paramahansa Yogananda wrote in his *Autobiography of a Yogi*. He mysteriously appeared in a cave in the Nainital district as an 18 year old youth and exhibited an extraordinary knowledge of the scriptures and the Sanskrit language. During his short earthly incarnation (he left his earthly body in 1984), Babaji performed according to his many devotees several miracles. His teachings advocate a return to God and to spiritual values.

Things to See

One km to the south of the West View Hotel

To Ananda Puri Ashram (3 km) & Ramnagar (76 km)

Kalika Golf Course (4 km) & Almora (40 km)

Sadar Bazaar

Ranikhet

0   250   500 m

The Mall

UTTARAKHAND

PLACES TO STAY

2 Moon Hotel
3 Alka Hotel
5 Hotel Raj Deep & Postal Agency
8 Parwati Inn
14 Hotel Meghdoot
15 Norton's Hotel
16 KMVN Tourist Rest House
17 West View Hotel

OTHER

1 KMOU Bus Stand
4 State Bank of India
6 Nar Singh Stadium
7 Shawl & Tweed Factory
9 UP Roadways Bus Stand & Railway Booking Agency
10 UP Tourist Office
11 Catholic Church
12 Main Post Office
13 Kumaon Lodge (Officers' Mess)

To Jhula Devi Temple (1 km) & Chaubatia

Mahatma Gandhi Road

To Nainital (56 km)

is the Shakti temple of **Jhula Devi**, from where you can continue to the orchards of apples, apricots and peaches at **Chaubatia**, three km distant. From here you can continue along the ridge top to the artificial lake of **Bhaludam**, which supplies Ranikhet's water.

Places to Stay & Eat

Sadar Bazaar The *Hotel Raj Deep* (☎ 2447), on the second floor of a building in Sadar Bazaar, has singles/doubles with a separate sitting area for Rs 100/250 during the peak season and Rs 60/150 at other times. The rooms are very clean and well maintained, unlike the shabby Natraj on the first floor of the same building. There's a small dining area on the balcony overlooking the bazaar.

Diagonally opposite is the large *Moon Hotel* (☎ 2382). Triple rooms are Rs 550, and deluxe cottages with hot and cold running water are Rs 850. The cottages have good views and colour TV. There's a large cavernous restaurant here, with main dishes for around Rs 45. The garden features roaming chickens and white rabbits in a cage. Rooms are a little shabby, but OK.

A short distance to the west and on the opposite side of the road is the *Alka Hotel* (☎ 2269), with doubles in the summer for Rs 300 (hot water available in buckets), or four bed rooms for Rs 400 with geyser. A 50% discount is offered in the off season. Rooms conform to the usual Ranikhet style, with the bedroom behind the separate sitting room. Bedrooms have skylights, so are not too dark.

The three-star *Parwati Inn* (☎ 2325), Ratan Palace Compound, near the UP Roadways bus stand, has doubles from Rs 350 to Rs 850 between May and June, and September to October. At other times a 40% discount is offered. All rooms have running hot and cold water, and the more expensive rooms have good Himalaya views. However, although this is a relatively new place, rooms are already showing signs of wear and tear. The multicuisine *Host Restaurant* here is not cheap, with nonveg dishes from Rs 70.

The Mall In a quiet location on The Mall is the pleasant *Hotel Meghdoot* (☎ 2475).

Between 15 April and 15 July, and 15 September to 15 November, singles are Rs 250 and doubles are Rs 400 and Rs 500 (the more expensive rooms overlook The Mall). All rooms are carpeted and have attached baths with running hot and cold water; the double rooms have a separate sitting area. A 25% to 40% discount is offered in the off season. There's a very good multicuisine restaurant here, with fresh fish taken from streams near Rampur.

A little further down The Mall is *Norton's Hotel* (☎ 2377), which was established in 1880. It's set in a pretty, if somewhat unruly garden. During the season, doubles are Rs 250 and Rs 600, and there are cottages with tiled floors and wood panelling for Rs 350. There's a four bed room for Rs 400, and an eight bed dorm for Rs 50 per person. Hot water is free in buckets. This place closes over December and January. A 50% discount is offered outside the summer months.

Also in The Mall area, but about one km further out, just off Mahatma Gandhi Rd, is KMVN's *Tourist Rest House* (☎ 2893). Between 1 May and 15 July, doubles are Rs 400 and Rs 550, with discounts offered at other times of the year. Beds in the dorm cost Rs 40. The rest house is set in a quiet area amid forests of deodar, oak and eucalyptus. You can buy local Kumaon honey here for Rs 14.50 for 100g.

About 300m from the rest house, on Mahatma Gandhi Rd, is the *West View Hotel* (☎ 2261). This lovely old bluestone hotel was originally built for British officers on R & R. Singles are Rs 600, and doubles are Rs 850, Rs 1050 and Rs 1250. All rooms (other than singles) have balconies from where you can view stunning sunsets. There's a badminton court, and the hotel can provide golf sets (Rs 60) for guests only. Nonguests are welcome to dine in the restaurant, but two hours notice is required.

Things to Buy

The Shawl & Tweed Factory is above Sardar Bazaar adjacent to the Nar Singh Stadium parade ground. The factory is housed in an old deconsecrated church, and here you can buy shawls, lengths of tweed, woollen scarves and gents' shawls (known as *pankhis*). Ladies' shawls range from Rs 280 to Rs 300, and gents' from Rs 350 to Rs 400. Lengths of tweed will cost between Rs 200 and Rs 250 depending on quality. The factory is run by the Kumaon Regiment Centre, and employees are either war widows or dependents of deceased army personnel.

Getting There & Away

From the UP Roadways bus stand at the east end of Sadar Bazaar, buses can be booked for Nainital (3½ hours, Rs 25); Kausani (two hours, Rs 25); Ramnagar, one only at 8.30 am (four hours, Rs 37); Almora (two hours, Rs 23); Kathgodam (four hours, Rs 33); Delhi (12 hours, Rs 132); and Lucknow (3 pm only, 13 hours, Rs 134). There are additional services to Kausani, Nainital, Ramnagar, Almora and Kathgodam from the KMOU stand, at the west end of Sadar Bazaar.

The railway booking agency is at the UP Roadways stand. The office has a small allocation of seats on services from Kathgodam. Bookings should be made at least one day in advance. The office is open Monday to Saturday from 9.30 am to 2.30 pm.

Getting Around

Local buses leave from the UP Roadways stand for The Mall (outside the Hotel Meghdoot) at 8.30, 9.30 and 11 am, 1, 2.30, 4 and 5.30 pm (20 minutes, Rs 2). From The Mall, they return at 9, 10 and 11.30 am, 1.30, 3, 4.30 and 6 pm. A taxi from Sadar Bazaar to The Mall costs Rs 60 one way.

KAUSANI
Telephone Area Code: 059628

Kausani, 51 km from Almora and 76 km from Ranikhet, is set on a pine-covered ridge at 1890m. With its fine snow views, this peaceful settlement is ideal for quiet contemplation. Gandhi stayed at the Anasakti Ashram here in 1929, and was inspired by its beauty. The Hindi poet laureate Sumitranandan Pant grew up here.

Tourist information is available at the post office, near the bus stand. Most of the places to stay are about 10 to 15 minutes walk to the north-west of the bus stand.

Along a narrow path above the bus stand is the small **Sumitranandan Pant Gallery** (open Tuesday to Saturday from 10.30 am to 4.30 pm), which has a selection of photographs and memorabilia pertaining to the life of the poet, including his clothes and hat *(topi)* and his framed doctorate of letters. The enthusiastic curator will explain the various exhibits, which are, unfortunately, rather shabbily displayed.

Places to Stay & Eat

At the top of the stairs leading up from the bus stand is the *Uttarakhand Tourist Lodge* (☎ 84-112), with basic double rooms with attached bath on the ground floor for Rs 75, or on the first floor, for Rs 200. There are also four bed rooms for Rs 250. Good discounts are offered in the off season, and all rooms face the snows. There's a good restaurant here, serving continental and Indian cuisine.

Budget accommodation can be found at the *Hotel Prashant* (☎ 84-137), on Ashram Rd. There are a range of rooms, with singles from Rs 50, doubles from Rs 100 to Rs 300, and four bed rooms from Rs 200 to Rs 400. Cheaper rooms are a bit gloomy, but this is a popular place, and a 50% discount is offered in the off season.

Very simple rooms are available (by donation) at the Anasakti Ashram. Pure vegetarian food is served here, and hot water is available by the bucket.

An excellent choice is the *Amar Holiday Home* (☎ 84-115), on Ashram Rd, about 10 minutes walk from the bus stand. Rooms are set in a beautiful garden and there are fine panoramic views of the snows. Usha is the friendly manager, and she ensures that guests will be comfortable in the spacious rooms. Singles/doubles with attached bath (hot water in buckets) are Rs 150/450, and a 50% discount is offered in the off season.

The *Krishna Mount View* (☎ 84-108), near the Hotel Prashant on Ashram Rd, has doubles with Star TV and running hot water for Rs 600 to Rs 1200. A 40% discount is offered in the off season. All rooms face the snows. The *Vaibhav Restaurant* here features Mughlai and Gujarati cuisine. Main nonveg dishes are between Rs 55 and Rs 95, and there's a good range of sweets, including sooji halwa, a wheat and sugar-based dessert (Rs 20).

The KMVN *Tourist Rest House* (☎ 84-106) is a couple of km beyond the village. It's very good value and has doubles from Rs 200 with great views, balconies and hot water. There are also dorm beds for Rs 50. Good off-season discounts are offered.

The *Hill Queen Restaurant*, in SN Pant Marg, beyond the Hotel Sagar, is a popular eatery, but is closed in the off season. Good basic food in a more rustic setting is available at the nearby *Sunrise Restaurant*, run by friendly fellows.

Getting There & Away

Buses to Almora depart approximately every hour between 7 am and 3 pm (2½ hours, Rs 23), continuing to Nainital (six hours, Rs 45). There are a couple of services to Ranikhet between 7 am and 2 pm (four hours, Rs 23). To visit the beautiful stone temples at Baijnath, 19 km to the north, take a Bhageshwar-bound bus. They leave approximately every hour between 6 am and 6 pm. The trip to Baijnath takes 30 minutes (Rs 10), and to Bhageshwar, it's 1½ hours (Rs 16).

For Karanprayag and destinations further north, there's one direct bus at 7 am (three hours, Rs 42).

The town's one taxi will charge Rs 200 to Rs 250 one way to Baijnath (Rs 350 to Rs 400 return).

AROUND KAUSANI
Baijnath

Nineteen km north of Kausani, and easily reached by bus or on foot is the tiny settlement of Baijnath which has a stunning – if diminutive – temple complex on the west bank of the Gomati River. If walking from Kausani, don't follow the road, as it's six km further; ask for directions along the path through the forest. From the bus halt, a flower-flanked path follows the river for five minutes before reaching this group of fine temples which were constructed during the era of the Katyurs, who once ruled over much of Garhwal and Kumaon between the 8th and 14th centuries.

There are 18 temples in the complex. The main temple is in the centre, a square edifice sacred to Shiva, with numerous brass bells hanging from the eaves – donated, according to the Kumaoni tradition, by grateful petitioners to Lord Shiva and his consort Parvati on the birth of a boy child. It is surrounded by a series of temples. Carvings of various deities including Ganesh and Hanuman lie against the face of the main temple, but the most exquisite carving is in the inner sanctum – a beautiful and voluptuous stone image of Parvati, standing about 1½m high. She holds in her arms many smaller carved images including those of Ganesh and his vehicle, a rat, Shiva astride a Nandi bull, and at the top, on the left, a beautiful carving depicting the marriage of Shiva and Parvati.

The temple was badly damaged during the rampages of Aurangzeb, and only the first metre or so is original. It was rebuilt in the 19th century using the original blocks.

There is nowhere to stay in Baijnath, which is little more than a motley collection of chai stalls where you can get samosas and pakhoras, but not much else.

BHAGESHWAR
No Telephone Area Code; book calls through the operator

The important pilgrimage town of Bhageshwar, with its ancient stone temples sacred to Lord Shiva, lies 74 km to the north of Almora. The main road, known as Station Rd, is an unattractive strip of commercial chaos, but a labyrinth of windy alleyways leads down through the interesting bazaar to the Sarayu River, which bisects the town. Here there are pleasant views across to the eastern side of the town on the opposite side of the river, where the houses seem to tumble down upon each other to the waters' edge. Along the banks of the river are a number of ghats and the temple complex.

The town lies in a valley between two small mountains; on the west side is Mt

Nhileshwar, which is topped by a temple sacred to Lord Shiva, in his form as Nhileshwar, hence the west side of the town is known as Nhil Bhageshwar. A path leads up from the petrol pump on Station Rd to the temple; it takes about 30 minutes to reach the summit, from where there are good views out over the town and the confluence of the Gomti and Sarayu rivers. The bus stand, the hotels listed below, and the ancient temple complex are on the west side of the Sarayu River. Behind the settlement on the east side of the river is a small hill topped by the modern Chandika Temple, sacred to Durga.

Temple Complex

Approaching the Sarayu River, a path branches to the right from Station Rd, passing through the busy bazaar down to a small ghat at the waters' edge. Here is sited the Baghnath Temple, sacred to Lord Shiva. The ancient stone temple, topped by a fluted *amalaka* (disk-shaped flourish) which is protected with a square wooden lattice edifice, is in a sorry state of disrepair, but it appears that at least superficial attempts at restoration are being undertaken.

Before the temple are a number of small stone shrines, many of which still retain sculpted stone idols. Fragments of sculpture which have been retrieved from the temple complex are displayed behind an iron grille in the temple compound, but the identification labels are in Hindi only.

On the opposite side of the path is the smaller Baneshwar Mahadev Temple. (Mahadev is the form of Lord Shiva as Supreme Being, reflecting both his functions as creator and destroyer.) An impressive sculpture of a tiger with an elephant's head between its paws protrudes from the roof.

Places to Stay & Eat

The *Hotel Rajdoot* (☎ 3246), Station Rd, about 200m east of the bus stand, has very basic but clean and light singles/doubles for Rs 60/80 with cold water only. The *Hotel Siddhartha* (☎ 3214), diagonally opposite, has a range of rooms, including dorm beds from Rs 35 to Rs 60, doubles for Rs 150 and

triples for Rs 200 and Rs 250, all with attached baths. Hot water is available free in buckets, and off-season discounts are available. The doubles open onto a pleasant balcony with good views out over the river.

The *Hotel Mount Everest* is a restaurant on Station Rd near the junction where a lane branches off down through the bazaar. This place opens early, so is handy for breakfast.

Getting There & Away

There are two buses daily to Pithoragarh, at 6.30 and 7.30 am (eight hours, Rs 61), and hourly buses to Almora between 5.30 am and 2 pm (four hours via Takula, Rs 32.50; 4½ hours via Kausani, Rs 38.50). Buses to Ranikhet (via Kausani) leave at 7, 8 and 9.30 am and noon (4½ hours, Rs 45).

ALMORA

Population: 53,507
Telephone Area Code: 05962

This picturesque hill station, at an altitude of 1650m, and 68 km north-east of Nainital, is one of the few not created by the British. Some 400 years ago it was the capital of the Chand rajas of Kumaon, who moved their capital here in 1563 from Champawat. The Chands successfully repelled the invading Rohillas, and managed to later fend off the Gurkhas in 1815 with the help of the British. However, to compensate the British for their participation, Almora was ceded to the East India Company by the Chands. The British wasted no time on their quest to 'convert the infidels', with the arrival of the London Missionary Society, who found a captive audience at the leprosarium upon whom they imposed their proselytising energies.

Nehru spent an involuntary period in Almora when he was incarcerated here during the Quit India campaign. More recent visitors include Dr Timothy Leary, influential author during the psychedelic movement of the 1960s; he was followed by scores of readers, inspired more by the (accurate) reports of cannabis growing wild in the environs of the town than its fine snow views.

Almora has interesting vestiges of both the British and earlier Chand eras. The town

UTTARAKHAND

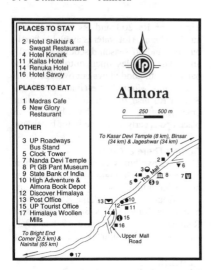

PLACES TO STAY
2 Hotel Shikhar &
   Swagat Restaurant
4 Hotel Konark
11 Kailas Hotel
14 Renuka Hotel
16 Hotel Savoy

PLACES TO EAT
1 Madras Cafe
6 New Glory
   Restaurant

OTHER
3 UP Roadways
   Bus Stand
5 Clock Tower
7 Nanda Devi Temple
8 Pt GB Pant Museum
9 State Bank of India
10 High Adventure &
   Almora Book Depot
12 Discover Himalaya
13 Post Office
15 UP Tourist Office
17 Himalaya Woollen
   Mills

Almora

0   250   500 m

To Kasar Devi Temple (8 km), Binsar
(34 km) & Jageshwar (34 km)

The Mall

Upper Mall
Road

To Bright End
Corner (2.5 km) &
Nainital (65 km)

extends along a five km ridge, affording fine views of distant snow peaks. Behind The Mall, along whose length are the majority of hotels and restaurants, is the busy and colourful bazaar.

Orientation & Information

The UP tourist office is on the Upper Mall Rd, just before the Hotel Savoy about 500m to the south of the bus stand. Take the road which runs above The Mall (away from the bus stand) opposite the post office. The District Forest Officer can be contacted on ☎ 22-229 or ☎ 22-065. The State Bank of India is on The Mall, opposite the bus stand.

Discover Himalaya (☎ 23-507), opposite the main post office, arranges porters and guides, organises high-altitude treks, rock climbing, photographic excursions, and meditation and yoga courses. You can book train tickets here. The office is open daily.

High Adventure, nearby on The Mall near the Almora Book Depot, also books treks, including a nine day trek to the Pindari Glacier. Cost is Rs 650 per day including meals, accommodation, guides and transport from Almora. High Adventure also books scooter tours, cultural and cave tours, and

day tours to local sights, including the stone temples at Bineshwar, near Binsar, and Jageshwar (Rs 125 per head, or Rs 1000 for a full taxi). There's also a two day coach tour to Kausani including meals and accommodation which terminates at Nainital for Rs 225, and a daily taxi service to Delhi via Nainital for Rs 175.

The Almora Book Depot (☎ 22-148), The Mall, has a good selection of books on the Himalaya with particular emphasis on the Kumaon Himalaya. English-language newspapers are available after 11.30 am from the news stand above the Swagat Restaurant, near Hotel Shikhar.

Things to See

The **clock tower** on The Mall was built in 1842 and carries the motto 'Work as if thou hadst to live for aye, Worship as if thou wert to die today'. There's a **Shiva shrine** in the room below it. Opposite the clock tower in a tiny flower garden is a gilded, cross-legged statue of **Gandhi** surmounted on a squat plinth. The **Pt GB Pant Museum**, opposite the UP Roadways office, is open Monday to Saturday from 10 am to 5 pm.

In the bazaar, about 10 minutes walk to the north-east of the bus stand, is a small group of **temples**. The Nanda Devi Temple is a relatively modern structure. It houses a very small image of the goddess flanked by images of Sarasvati (on her left) and a black image of Mahakali. Also in this compound are two stone temples dedicated to Shiva. On the ceiling of the smaller of the two temples is a rosette, and the walls feature carvings of Ganesh, Shiva and Parvati. The bottom courses of masonry feature sculptures of rampant lions, elephants and horses. The other, larger temple, is of a similar architectural style, but its amalaka is protected by a wooden pagoda, and its stone sculpture is more elaborate.

The eight km walk up to the **Kasar Devi Temple** is recommended – this is where Swami Vivekananda came to meditate. The area has the reputation of being something of a 'power centre' and some travellers rent houses and stay for months.

Two and a half km south-west of the town centre, good views of the distant snows can be had from a hilltop known as **Bright End Corner**. The name is a corruption of Brighton End, derived somewhat incongruously from Brighton Beach in England – you couldn't be further from the waves here!

Places to Stay
On the Upper Mall Rd, just beyond the tourist office, is the *Hotel Savoy* (☎ 22-329). Doubles downstairs are Rs 200, and those upstairs are Rs 200 and Rs 250. There's also a double suite with TV and geyser for Rs 300. The more expensive rooms open onto a sunny verandah. Hot water is available in buckets for Rs 4. Rooms are a little tatty, but quite clean, and a 25% discount is offered in the off season.

Directly opposite the main post office is the *Renuka Hotel* (☎ 22-860). Rooms aren't bad value with attached bath and geyser for Rs 200 and Rs 300 in summer (Rs 150 and Rs 250 in the off season). There's also a dormitory with beds for Rs 50. The restaurant is open in the season only.

A short distance along a path opposite the main post office is the extraordinary *Kailas Hotel*, run by the charming, if slightly eccentric, Mr and Mrs Shah (who celebrated 52 years of marriage in 1995). This may well be one of your more memorable accommodation experiences in India. Fairly rustic singles and doubles with attached bath are Rs 125 in the summer (Rs 75/95 in the off season), and there's a five-bed dorm for Rs 40 per bed. Singles with common bath are Rs 60 (Rs 40 in the off season). One room has a primitive water heater which looks like a reject from Dr Frankenstein's workshop – hot water in buckets is a safer bet. Mrs Shah is in charge of the kitchen, and rustles up western favourites such as banana pancakes.

If you'd prefer the comforts of a more modern establishment, the *Hotel Konark* (☎ 23-217) is a brand new hotel on The Mall near the State Bank of India and the bus stand. Singles are Rs 100, and doubles range from Rs 150 to Rs 250. All rooms have attached baths, and hot water is available

free by the bucket. Staff are very friendly, and rooms are spotless.

The *Hotel Shikhar* (☎ 22-395), The Mall, only a few minutes walk from the bus stand, has double rooms with common bath for Rs 100, and a range of doubles with attached bath from Rs 200 to Rs 800. Prices remain constant all year.

Places to Eat
Almora is a good place to sample bal mithai, a form of brown barfi which is covered in tiny white sugar balls. This sweet is found only in the foothills of Kumaon. Another local favourite is singauri, a milk-based sweet with a creamy consistency served in a leaf from the chyur tree. It comes in both brown and off-white varieties – the brown form is considered to be tastier.

There is a variety of places to eat in Almora, with the highest concentration just to the north of the bus stand. Most places close early, particularly in the off season. During summer, last orders are taken before 10.30 pm.

The *Madras Cafe*, The Mall, is a no-frills, very reasonably priced vegetarian restaurant, with main dishes under Rs 25. Opposite is the *New Glory Restaurant*, featuring Indian and Chinese cuisine. The navrattan korma is very good (Rs 28), and there's also a good selection of Indian sweets.

The cavernous *Mountview Restaurant* in the Hotel Shikhar has veg and nonveg cuisine. Just before the Hotel Shikhar, stairs lead down to the *Swagat Restaurant*. There's an extensive vegetarian menu which features the sweet milk-based rabri faluda. The brightly lit Sikh-run *Soni Restaurant*, just before the State Bank of India, is very popular with locals and has veg and nonveg cuisine. Chicken Malai is Rs 40, as are most main dishes. The menu is in Hindi.

Things to Buy
Inhabitants of Almora are renowned for their Gandhian loyalties, evident in the production of *khadi* – home-spun cloth, the production of which was strongly encouraged by the mahatma. Khadi can be purchased

at the Gandhi Ashram, near the UP Road-ways office. There are also several woollen mills where you can purchase shawls and jumpers, including the Himalaya Woollen Mills, upstairs on The Mall.

Getting There & Away

The UP Roadways office and bus stand is down a flight of stairs on The Mall, opposite the Pt GB Pant Museum. There are several buses to Ranikhet (two hours, Rs 21) and Pithoragarh (six hours, Rs 45). To Delhi, buses leave at 7 am, 4.30 and 5 pm. The 5 pm service is semideluxe and costs Rs 139. The ordinary services cost Rs 112 for the 12 hour journey. There's one service to Nainital at 8.30 am (three hours, Rs 28.50), and one to Song, for the Pindari Glacier trek, also at 8.30 am (3½ hours, Rs 42). The daily bus to Banbassa, the closest Indian village to the Nepalese border town of Mahendre-nagar, leaves at 7.30 am (seven hours, Rs 60).

Share taxis cost Rs 30 to Ranikhet, Rs 50 to Nainital and Rs 100 to Haldwani, the nearest railhead. Drivers charge Rs 350 for a reserve taxi to Ranikhet; Rs 250 one way to Jageshwar or Binsar (Rs 350 return); Rs 400 to Nainital.

AROUND ALMORA
Binsar

Unobstructed, and possibly unsurpassed, vistas of a 300 km stretch of the Himalaya are available from this hilltop, also known as Jhandi Dhar, 2412m above sea level, and 34 km north-east of Almora, accessible from Kafarkhan on the Almora-Bhageshwar road. The Chand Dynasty of Kumaon (15th to 18th centuries) based their summer capital here, but there are few legacies of this era, apart from the Bineshwar Temple, sacred to Lord Shiva, which was built by Raja Kalyan Chand. The stone temple lies three km below the hilltop. Apart from its stunning mountain vistas, Binsar is notable for its profusion of wildflowers and pleasant walks through forest glades of oak and rhododendron.

There is no private accommodation at Binsar. Double rooms at the KMVN *Tourist Bungalow* on the brow of the hill are Rs 250 between 1 May and 15 July, with discounts offered at other times of the year. The *Forest Rest House* here can be booked through the District Forest Officer in Almora (☎ 22-229 or 22-065).

There are several buses each day between Almora and Bhageshwar which will drop you off on request at Kafarkhan, but it's a steep 13 km walk from here to the summit of

---

Loharket-Pindari Glacier Trek

The Pindari Glacier flows from the impressive peaks of Nanda Kot (6861m) and Nanda Khat (6611m) on the southern rim of the Nanda Devi Sanctuary.

From Nainital it takes a full day by bus to reach the roadhead at Song, three km below the village of Loharket. The initial stage up and over the Dhakuri Pass (2835m) is long and tiring before continuing to the village of Khati and the confluence of the Pindari and Sunder rivers. The trail then follows the course of the Pindari River through mixed forest to the camp at Dwali – although most continue to the meadow at Phurkia where there are clear views of the glacier and its setting beneath the peaks of Nanda Kot and Nanda Khat at the head of the valley. The trek from Phurkia to the glacier and return can be completed in a day before completing the return trek to Loharket.

Stage 1	Loharket to Khati via Dhakuri Pass (7 hours)
Stage 2	Khati to Phurkia (6 hours)
Stage 3	Phurkia to Pindari Glacier & return (6 hours)
Stage 4	Phurkia to Khati (4 hours)
Stage 5	Khati to Loharket (5 hours)

the hill. A taxi will charge Rs 200 one way from Almora.

Jageshwar

This little-visited but lovely village is found 34 km east of Almora, three km north of the tiny settlement of Artola which is on the main Pithoragarh road. Most visitors make the detour to Jageshwar to visit the stone temple complexes of Dandesavra, 1½ km before the village, and the larger group at Jageshwar itself. However, Jageshwar can also be used as a starting point for walks to Old Jageshwar, four km from Jageshwar (or 12 km by road), or Binsar.

It is three km from Artola to Jageshwar along the road which follows the contours of the Dandesavra *nulla*, or stream, flanked by dense stands of deodar. Halfway to the village, 1½ km from the main road on the right, is the small **Dandesavra temples**. The largest (and most elaborately sculpted) of these temples dates from around the 10th century AD, and enshrines a naturally formed lingam.

There are several houses near the temple group, but nowhere to stay. You might be able to get very basic fare at the chai stalls by the roadside.

Between this group of temples and Jageshwar village, 1½ km further north down the wooded valley, are several more isolated roadside temples. Jageshwar is an important pilgrimage centre, being one of India's 12 jyoti lingams. The **Jageshwar temple complex** encompasses 124 temples. The earliest temples date from the 8th century AD and were constructed during the Katyuri Dynasty; the most recent temples in the group date from the closing period of the Chand Dynasty (18th century). The oldest temple in the group is probably the **Mrityunjaya Temple**, the large temple to the right as you enter the compound. The sides of the temple are elaborately carved. The round medallion which protrudes at the front of the temple represents Dattatreya – the three faces of one God. Below is a carving of Lord Shiva, the presiding deity of Jageshwar. He can be seen sitting in the padmasana, or lotus position, suggesting the pervasive influence of Buddhism. Shiva is flanked by his consort, Parvati, and his son Kartikiya.

The other large temple dominating the compound is to the left, behind numerous smaller temples. This is the **Jageshwar Temple** which enshrines the sacred jyoti lingam. On either side of the doorway are life-sized sculptures of the *dwarpals* – gate-keepers. On the right is the four armed Nandi, and on the left is Bhrangi, holding a three headed snake. These represent the bodyguards of Lord Shiva. In the inner sanctum, the lingam is concealed beneath a repoussé silver cover in the form of a snake, which is removed by the temple priest in the morning and evening only. Originally the lingam was protected by a large silver serpent, but this was stolen. As your eyes adjust to the dark interior, a small shrine to Lord Ganesh, Shiva's son, can be made out.

Walks

A path leads from near the Jageshwar temples through forest of deodar, pine and oak to **Old Jageshwar**, four km distant. Here there is a very old stone temple sacred to Shiva, and fine panoramic views of the Himalaya extending from the Garhwali peaks to the west, across to the snow-covered peaks of western Nepal.

From the bridge 200m before Jageshwar, a path to the west proceeds to Old Jageshwar and on to **Binsar**. It follows the Jataganga for about 500m then ascends to **Kunjakhali** village, about three km from the bridge. One km further is **Janubaj**, on the bus route to Old Jageshwar. A further six km takes you through pine forest to **Dholchina**, on the main Almora to Sheraghat route, a small settlement where basic food is available. Beyond Dholchina it is a steep six km climb through dense forest of oak and rhododendron to the temple of **Bineshwar**, one km before Binsar.

Places to Stay & Eat

The KMVN *Tourist Rest House* is on the left as you enter Jageshwar. It is set in pretty flower gardens. Dorm beds are Rs 30, ordi-

UTTARAKHAND

nary singles/doubles are both Rs 150, and deluxe doubles (with carpet) are Rs 250. Good discounts are available in the off season. All rooms have attached baths with geysers. There is a vegetarian dining hall here, but nonvegetarian meals are available with advance notice. There are two rooms at the *Forest Rest House*, set in dense forest behind the temple complex. Bookings need to be made with the District Forest Officer in Almora (☎ 22-229 or 22-065). There are several dharamsalas in the village where you may be able to get simple accommodation.

The small *Raj Mahel* restaurant is opposite the entrance to the temple compound. It is open from March to August only. The *Jageshwar Restaurant*, behind the temple group, is open all year, and serves very basic fare (chapattis and sabzi). There are several chai stalls in the village.

Getting There & Away
There is one bus daily from Almora to Jageshwar which leaves at noon (2½ hours, Rs 17). It returns to Almora at 8 pm. Alternatively, you could catch one of the many buses to Pithoragarh and disembark at Artola, from where it is a three km walk to Jageshwar. You may be able to hitch a lift on a motorcycle from Artola. A taxi from Almora will charge Rs 250 one way, or Rs 350 return.

PITHORAGARH
Population: 42,113
Telephone Area Code: 05964
Pithoragarh is a large and pleasantly clean city in the eastern district of Kumaon, and serves as an important halt on the long pilgrimage route to Mansarovar and Mt Kailash in Tibet (although the chances of foreign nationals being granted trekking permits to enter Tibet are negligible). Nevertheless, at an altitude of 1815m and with sweeping views down over the broad Sore Valley, and across to the peaks of Panchachuli and those of western Nepal, it is a pleasant place to while away a few days. You may find yourself needing to spend a night in Pithoragarh

if you're en route to Munsiyari for the Milam Glacier trek (described later in this section).

Information
The tourist bureau (☎ 22-527) is on Bank Rd at the Shiltham Station Bazaar, about 10 minutes north of the lower bus stands. It's open Monday to Saturday from 10 am to 5 pm. The post office is nearby. Between the lower bus stands and Shiltham station is the busy Naya Bazaar, and above it, Gandhi Chowk.

Things to See
The road to the village of Chandag, seven km north of Shiltham Station Bazaar, follows the ridge top and affords fine views across to the peaks of Panchachuli (five chimneys), to the north. Just before the KMVN Tourist Lodge is the modern **Ulka Devi Mandir**, the temple of the patron goddess of Sera village which lies below it. From a terrace here there are very good views of Pithoragarh to the south, across to Mt Thalkedar. From **Chandag**, the unobstructed view encompasses the Panchachuli and beyond to the western Nepal peaks of Saipal and Api.

Places to Stay & Eat
Directly opposite the UP Roadways office is the *Hotel Samrat* (☎ 22-450). Singles/doubles with attached bath are Rs 40/75, and hot water in buckets is Rs 5. The *Hotel Uttranchal Deep* (☎ 22-654) is about five minutes walk from UP Roadways. Doubles with attached bath are Rs 100 (hot water available in buckets: Rs 5). The staff are friendly and attentive, and there's an extensive room service menu.

In the Shiltham Station Bazaar is the *Hotel Ulkapriyadarshani* (☎ 22-596). Very basic singles are Rs 40, and doubles range from Rs 50 to Rs 95, all with attached bath. All the rooms are clean, but the cheaper ones are quite dark and shabby. Nearby, right by the bus stand, is the *Hotel Trishul* (no phone). Very spartan and somewhat tatty, but clean, singles/doubles are Rs 30/50, with hot water free in buckets.

About 1½ km from the upper bus stand is

the KMVN *Tourist Lodge* (☎ 22-434), on the Chandag road. Doubles with attached bath and geyser are Rs 200, and there are dorm beds for Rs 30. Rooms are basic but OK, and there are good views from the ridge on which the lodge is sited. There's a restaurant here serving veg and nonveg cuisine. There are numerous jeeps between the bazaar and Chandag which will drop you here (Rs 2).

On Bank Rd are the *Trishul* and *Rawat* hotels, which serve veg and nonveg cuisine. Meals at the Rawat are notoriously spicy.

Getting There & Away

Air At the time of writing, scheduled flights to Delhi and Lucknow were due to commence from Pithoragarh's airport. Check at the tourist office or phone Delhi (☎ (011) 461-7248).

Bus To really confuse things, there are three bus stands; at the bottom of the town is the UP Roadways office, opposite the Samrat Hotel, where buses leave for the plains. This is known locally as the Roadways Station. To Tanakpur (the closest railhead, 151 km to the south of Pithoragarh, near the Nepal border), there are buses every 30 minutes between 4.30 am and noon (seven hours, Rs 58). All these buses continue to the border town of Banbassa (eight hours, Rs 61). There's one service daily to Nainital at 6.30 am (nine hours, Rs 71), and several services to Almora between 5 and 10.30 am (five

hours, Rs 46). To Delhi, there are several services via Tanakpur (506 km), and one service (at 6 am) via Haldwani (507 km).

One hundred metres further west is the private bus stand, where you can book buses to Almora and Ranikhet – the 5.30 and 8 am services to Almora continue to Ranikhet (seven hours, Rs 65). UP Roadways has a second office about 10 minutes walk north through the bazaar in the area known as Shiltham Station. Here you can catch buses to the hills area, such as Munsiyari, and share jeeps to the nearby village of Chandag (Rs 6) and to Thal (Rs 30). From Thal you can get another share jeep, or bus, 61 km further north to Munsiyari.

Train There is a railway booking office at the Roadways (lower) Station, next to the UP Roadways office. It is open daily from 10 am to 4 pm and has a small allocation of seats on services departing from the nearest railhead at Tanakpur, 151 km south, near the Nepal border.

BANBASSA

Banbassa is the closest Indian village to the Nepalese border post of Mahendrenagar, and it is possible to enter Nepal at this point (see the Getting There & Away chapter for more details). There are daily buses from Delhi (12 hours) and Banbassa is also connected by rail to Bareilly. From Almora, there's a daily bus leaving at 7.30 am (seven hours, Rs 68).

UTTARAKHAND

Munsiyari-Milam Glacier Trek

The trail along the Gori Ganga is well defined through a series of villages which until a generation ago had traditional trading relations with Tibet. It takes four stages to reach the main village of Milam at the head which is situated below the impressive Milam Glacier.

Time should be allocated to explore this extensive glacier that is fed by the snows of Hardeol (7151m), Rishi Pahar (6992m) and Tirsuli (7074m) at the head of the valley. There are also many other possibilities for exploring the adjoining glaciers. The glacier immediately to the south-west of Milam affords uninterrupted views of the Nanda Devi East peak (7434m) while the Lwanl Glacier above the village of Martoli leads to the technical Traills Pass, an innovative route for trekkers with climbing experience to complete a challenging traverse into the upper Pindari Glacier.

The trek is possible in May and June and also in the post-monsoon season from mid-September till mid-October. Porters are available at Munsiyari and in the villages along the trail.

West Bengal Hills

The hills area of West Bengal encompasses an area of 3149 sq km, bordered by Sikkim to the north, Bhutan to the north-east, Nepal to the west, Assam to the east, and the Indian plains to the south.

Most travellers to this region will inevitably visit the large hill station of Darjeeling (2134m above sea level). Darjeeling, prised from Sikkim in the mid-19th century by the British and established as a sanatorium for officers of the Raj, affords spectacular panoramic vistas of the distant snow-clad peaks of the eastern Himalaya, including Kang-chenjunga, third highest mountain in the world (and the highest peak in the Indian Himalaya). The imperial legacy of the Raj lives on in wonderful (if somewhat rundown) colonial buildings and hotels, and a highlight of a visit to Darjeeling is a trip on the spectacular toy train, which ascends over 2000m in 90 km from Siliguri on the plains. Apart from Darjeeling, a trip to this region can also take in the less visited (and less frenetic!) hill towns of Kalimpong, once an important halting point on the trade route to Tibet, and Kurseong, both of which afford good opportunities for walking in their environs. Down on the plains, to the west of Siliguri, are the Jaldhapara Wildlife Sanctuary and the Buxa Tiger Reserve.

HISTORY

Until the beginning of the 18th century the whole of the area between the present borders of Sikkim and the plains of Bengal, including Darjeeling and Kalimpong, belonged to the rajas of Sikkim. In 1706 they lost Kalimpong to the Bhutanese, and control of the remainder was wrested from them by the Gurkhas who invaded Sikkim in 1780, following consolidation of the latter's rule in Nepal.

These annexations by the Gurkhas, however, brought them into conflict with the British East India Company. A series of wars

Highlights
The busy hill station of Darjeeling has some lovely old Raj buildings, and is fascinating for the insights it offers into the Raj era. The tea plantations are a feature of the area, and on clear days you can catch wonderful views of Kangchenjunga. The famous toy train journey to Darjeeling is not to be missed. Kalimpong, 74 km east of Darjeeling, offers some great walks and fine views of the surrounding countryside. It also has a number of orchid nurseries. At the Jaldhapara Wildlife Sanctuary you can see the endangered one-horned Indian rhinoceros, wild elephants, and various types of deer, including sambar, muntjac (barking deer), chital (spotted deer) and hog deer. Royal Bengal tigers are also here, but are rarely sighted. ■

were fought between the two parties, eventually leading to the defeat of the Gurkhas and the ceding of all the land they had taken from the Sikkimese to the East India Company. Part of this territory was restored to the rajas of Sikkim and the country's sovereignty guaranteed by the British in return for British control over any disputes which arose with neighbouring states.

One such dispute in 1828 led to the dispatching of two British officers to this area, and it was during their fact-finding tour that they spent some time at Darjeeling (then called Dorje Ling – Place of the Thunderbolt – after the lama who founded the *gompa*, or monastery, which once stood on Observatory Hill). The officers were quick to appreciate Darjeeling's value as a site for a sanatorium and hill station, and as the key to a pass into Nepal and Tibet. The officer's observations were reported to the authorities in Calcutta and a pretext was eventually found to pressure the raja into granting the site to the British. The raja was promised in return the territory of Debgong, but the British reneged on their side of the bargain, and in return for the loss of his territories, the unfortunate raja received one double-barrelled gun, one rifle,

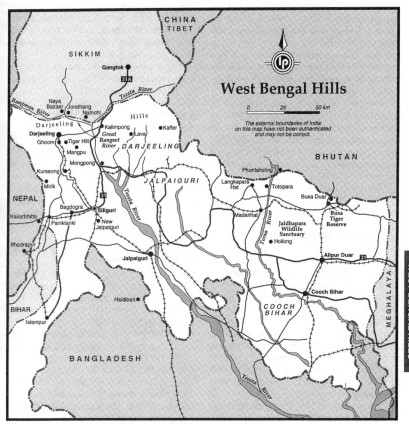

a 20 yard bale of red cloth and two shawls – one of superior, and one of inferior quality. Evidently unhappy with this bargain, the raja appealed to the British in 1841 and was granted an annual stipend of Rs 3000 (raised to Rs 6000 in 1846).

The transfer of Darjeeling to the British, however, rankled with the Tibetans who regarded Sikkim as a vassal state. Darjeeling's rapid development as a trading centre and tea-growing area in a key position along the trade route leading from Sikkim to the plains of India began to make a considerable impact on the fortunes of the lamas and leading merchants of Sikkim. Tensions arose, and in 1849 two British travellers, Sir Joseph Hooker and Dr Campbell, who were visiting Sikkim with the permission of the raja and the British government, were arrested. Various demands were made as a condition of their release, but the Sikkimese eventually released both prisoners unconditionally about a month later.

In reprisal for the arrests, however, the British annexed the whole of the land between the present borders of Sikkim and the Bengal plains, and withdrew the annual Rs 6000 stipend from the raja. (The latter was restored to his son, raised to Rs 9000 in 1868 and raised again to Rs 12,000 in 1874.)

The British annexations brought about a significant change in Darjeeling's status. Previously it had been an enclave within Sikkimese territory and to reach it the British had to pass through a country ruled by an independent raja. After the takeover, Darjeeling became contiguous with British territory further south and Sikkim was cut off from access to the plains except through British territory. This was eventually to lead to the invasion of Sikkim by the Tibetans and the British military expedition to Lhasa.

Still not content with their new possession, the British mounted a military expedition into neighbouring Bhutan in 1864, resulting in the Treaty of Sinchula in which the Bhutan Duars and the current district of Kalimpong were annexed to the region.

Development of Darjeeling was rapid and by 1857, it had a population of some 10,000.

Most of the population increase was due to the recruitment of Nepali labourers to work the tea plantations established in the early 1840s by the British. Even today, the vast majority of people in the environs of Darjeeling speak Nepali as a first language and the name Darjeeling continues to be synonymous with tea.

The immigration of Nepali-speaking peoples, mainly Gurkhas, into the mountainous areas of West Bengal eventually led to political problems in the mid-1980s. Resentment had been growing among the Gurkhas over what they felt was discrimination against them by the government of West Bengal. Their language was one of those not recognised by the Indian constitution and they were, therefore, denied government jobs, which were only open to those who could speak Bengali.

The tensions finally came to a head in widespread riots throughout the hill region in the 1980s, instigated by the Gurkha National Liberation Front (GNLF), led by Subhash Ghising, who demanded a separate state to be known as Gurkhaland.

A compromise was reached in late 1988 whereby the Darjeeling Gorkha Hill Council (DGHC) was to be given a large measure of autonomy from the state government and fresh elections to the council were held in December of that year. Darjeeling remains part of West Bengal but with greater control over its own affairs as a Nepali-language administrative unit within it.

Unfortunately, less than 10 years after the establishment of the Hill Council, which it was hoped would serve as a model for effective compromise for other statehood movements in India, trouble is again brewing in the hills. Dormant for many years, the Akhil Bharatiya Gorkha League (ABGL), which originally fought alongside the GNLF, has openly challenged the legitimacy of the GNLF and its chairperson, Subhash Ghising. The ABGL claims that the council, under the leadership of Ghising, had insufficient economic expertise, and was unable to effectively use the unprecedented funds being directed to it from the central and state governments. The result of almost a decade of what is seen as financial mismanagement is a string of half-completed projects and the deterioration of existing infrastructure.

The GNLF has also come into opposition with the central government over a dispute which centres around the *panchayat* system of village-level government, established by Rajiv Gandhi. Despite having constitutional legitimacy, the GNLF are opposed to the system, claiming that it undermines its autonomy. Unwilling to loosen his grasp on the purse strings, Mr Ghising has been instructed to release funds earmarked for the panchayat, but has been reluctant to do so. Claims not only of mismanagement but misappropriation of funds have further fuelled the fires.

Since mid-1995, the ABGL, led by a defector from the GNLF, Chetan Sherpa, has called public meetings throughout the Darjeeling region, and is beginning to garner popular support. Under attack on all sides, the GNLF has also had state and central government funds withheld until it submits a detailed account of expenditure.

A lack of faith in the mainstream parties and dissatisfaction with the Hill Council could result in widespread support for the ABGL, and possibly, the revival of separatist agitation.

GEOGRAPHY

The Teesta is the major river in the region. Rising in Sikkim, it flows south-west across the northern border of West Bengal, meeting the Great Rangeet River near Kalimpong and carving a dramatic valley down the centre of the three administrative subdivisions of Darjeeling region: Darjeeling, Kurseong and Kalimpong. The elevation profile commences at around 60m above sea level in Jalpaiguri district, on the plains, and 117m at Siliguri, rising through the Kurseong and Kalimpong ranges to over 3500m along the lesser heights of the Singalila Range, which rises near Darjeeling and culminates in the massive bulk of Kangchenjunga, in Sikkim.

TOURIST OFFICES

There are Government of West Bengal tourist offices in most major cities. Accommodation in the Jaldhapara Wildlife Sanctuary must be booked through the Government of West Bengal Tourist Bureau in Calcutta, or the Sub-Regional Tourist Office in Siliguri. West Bengal tourist offices can also book package

---

Festivals of the West Bengal Hills

The high concentration of Tibetan gompas in the West Bengal hills, particularly in Darjeeling and Kalimpong, ensures that there is a ready succession of colourful Tibetan festivals. Visitors are welcome at these gompa festivals. See the Facts for the Visitor chapter for details and dates of Tibetan and nationwide festivals.

April
Bengali New Year – This is celebrated on the first day of Vaishaka (mid-April).

August
Accord Day – This public holiday in Darjeeling commemorates the anniversary of the foundation of the Darjeeling Gorkha Hill Council.

September-October
Durga Puja – Celebrated as Dussehra in the rest of India, Durga Puja is the most important religious festival in West Bengal. It is celebrated with the construction of large images of Durga on her vehicle, the lion, which are then carried to nearby rivers and ceremonially immersed. ■

Carbon-Monoxide Poisoning

Lonely Planet recommends that travellers do not use fires as a means of heating in hotel rooms. The Indian police have confirmed that a number of deaths from carbon-monoxide poisoning occur each year. The tragic story below explains why you should especially avoid burning charcoal or other fuels which give off toxic fumes.

On 25 January this year (1996), we had the heart-breaking news our precious son John and his beautiful girlfriend Lisa had been found dead in their hotel room in Darjeeling. Apparently the weather was freezing, and on asking for some heating, they were brought a bucket of charcoal. Unfortunately, ventilation was almost nonexistent and they died from carbon-monoxide poisoning.

Diane Stevens

tours into the park. See the Jaldhapara Wildlife Sanctuary section for details.

Calcutta
  3/2 BBD Bagh East (☎ (033) 248-8271)
Darjeeling
  1 Nehru Rd (☎ (0354) 54-050)
Delhi
  A2 State Emporium Bldg, Baba Karak Singh Marg, New Delhi (☎ (011) 373-2840)
Madras
  Karim Mansions, 787 Anna Salai (☎ (044) 83-2346)
Siliguri
  Tenzing Norgay (Hill Cart) Rd (☎ (0353) 43-1974)

Northern Plains

Siliguri is not one of India's most salubrious cities, but if you're heading north to Darjeeling or Sikkim, you'll probably find that you'll need to spend at least a day or two here. Lying to the east of Siliguri, which falls in Darjeeling district, are the districts of Jalpaiguri and neighbouring Cooch Bihar, which borders Assam to the east. In Jalpaiguri are two little-visited wildlife sanctuaries, Jaldhapara Wildlife Sanctuary, with

a small population of the endangered Indian rhinoceros *(Rhinoceros unicornis)*, and the Buxa Tiger Reserve, which recently became a member of Project Tiger.

SILIGURI & NEW JALPAIGURI
Population: 249,000
Telephone Area Code: 0353

New Jalpaiguri (known throughout the district as NJP), the main railway junction, is eight km south of Siliguri, though there's effectively no break in the urban sprawl between the two places. This crowded sprawl is the departure point for visits to Darjeeling, Kalimpong, Sikkim and the North-East states. Siliguri is the major trade centre for the north-east, Darjeeling, Sikkim and eastern Nepal, so it's packed with trucks and buses and is not a pleasant place to stay for a moment more than necessary. It is one hour from Siliguri to Paniktanki – opposite the Nepal border town of Kakarbhitta.

Orientation
The towns of Siliguri and New Jalpaiguri comprise essentially just one north-south main road – Tenzing Norgay Rd, renamed in honour of the Everest conqueror (although it is still known locally as Hill Cart Rd). It's about five km from New Jalpaiguri railway station to Siliguri Town railway station, and a further three km from there on to Siliguri Junction railway station, behind the Tenzing Norgay Central bus terminal. You can catch the toy train (if it's running) from any of these railway stations. Twelve km west of Siliguri is Bagdogra, the airport serving this northern region.

Information
Tourist Offices The West Bengal Sub-Regional Tourist Office (☎ 43-1974) is up a flight of stairs on Tenzing Norgay Rd, on the south side of the river. It's open Monday to Friday from 10 am to 5 pm. The doorway is easy to miss, but there's a sign across the front of the building. Here, it's possible to book accommodation in the Jaldhapara Wildlife Sanctuary (see later), 135 km east of Siliguri,

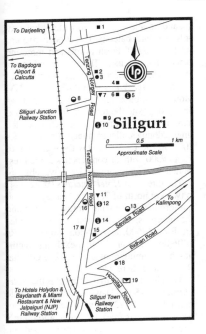

PLACES TO STAY

1   Hotel Sinclairs
2   Mainak Tourist Lodge & Indian Airlines
4   Hotel Hindustan
6   Tourist Services Agency Guest House
9   Siliguri Lodge
15 Hotel Chancellor & Rajesh Agarwal
    Newsstand
17 Hotel Vinayak & Jet Airways

PLACES TO EAT

7   Shere Punjab Restaurant
11 Anand Hotel Restaurant

OTHER

3   Mallagur Garage
5   Government of Assam Tourist
    Information Office
8   Tenzing Norgay Central Bus Terminal &
    Share Jeeps
10 Sikkim Tourism & Sikkim Nationalised
    Transport (SNT)
12 State Bank of India
13 Share Jeep Stand
14 West Bengal Sub-Regional Tourist Office
16 Taxi Stand
18 Railway Booking Office
19 Main Post Office

in Jalpaiguri district, which is open from 16 September until 14 June.

There are tourist information counters at the New Jalpaiguri and Siliguri Junction railway stations, and the West Bengal Tourist Office and Sikkim Tourism counters at Bagdogra Airport. The police information post is in front of Tenzing Norgay terminal.

Money The State Bank of India, on the 3rd floor of a building a few doors north of the Sub-Regional Tourist Office, exchanges American Express travellers' cheques in US dollars and pounds sterling only. An Rs 20 encashment fee is levied.

Post & Communications The main post office is on Hospital Rd, near the railway booking office.

Newsagency English-language newspapers (from Delhi and Calcutta) are available from Rajesh Agarwal newsstand beneath the Hotel Chancellor after 4 pm.

Fishing Permits To obtain fishing permits, check with the Sub-Regional Tourist Office in Siliguri. (The mahseer may be found at the confluence of the Teesta and Rangeet rivers, and near the Riang River junction.)

Permits for Assam There's a tiny Government of Assam Tourist Information Office (no phone) down the lane directly opposite the bus terminal, on the east side of Tenzing Norgay Rd. It's open Monday to Saturday from 10 am to 5 pm. Brochures are available here, but officers are a bit vague on current permit requirements. (According to the Assam Government Tourist Office in New Delhi, restricted area permits are no longer required by foreign visitors to enter Assam.)

Permits for Sikkim Permits for Sikkim are available from Sikkim Tourism (☎ 43-2646) at the Sikkim Nationalised Transport (SNT) office (☎ 43-2751) on the east side of Tenzing Norgay Rd, diagonally opposite Tenzing Norgay Central bus terminal. Sikkim Tourism is open Monday to Saturday from 10 am to 4 pm.

Emergency Police: ☎ 20-101; Fire: ☎ 22-222; Sadar Hospital: ☎ 20-150.

Places to Stay

There are dozens of hotels opposite the Tenzing Norgay Central bus terminal. Down a small lane directly opposite the terminal is the *Hotel Hindustan* (☎ 26-571). Singles/doubles with common bath are Rs 100/125. With attached bath and geyser, they range from Rs 120/150 to Rs 280/450. Mosquito nets are provided, and there's room service here. Directly opposite is the *Tourist Services Agency Guest House* (no phone). Singles/doubles are Rs 150/200, and hot water is available in buckets (Rs 5).

In a quiet spot next door to Sikkim Nationalised Transport is the *Siliguri Lodge* (no phone). There's a pleasant garden fronting the lodge, and rooms are very clean and airy. Doubles on the ground floor with attached bath are Rs 155, and in the four bed dorm, it's Rs 45. Decent-sized doubles upstairs with attached bath are Rs 165, or with common bath, Rs 120.

About 750m to the north on Tenzing Norgay Rd is West Bengal Tourism's *Mainak Tourist Lodge* (☎ 43-0986). Non air-con rooms are Rs 300/400/500, and with air-con, they're Rs 450/600/750. There are foreign exchange facilities here and a restaurant. Rooms are showing signs of wear and tear, but are clean. Next door is the *Hotel Sharda* (☎ 21-649). Singles/doubles are Rs 110/165 (hot water in buckets), or Rs 165/220 with running hot water. They're basic but neat, and mosquito nets are provided.

A good budget choice is the friendly, Tibetan-run *Hotel Chancellor* (☎ 43-2360), on the corner of Sevoke and Tenzing Norgay roads. Small but comfortable singles are Rs 80, and doubles are Rs 150 without balcony or Rs 165 with balcony. Three/four bed rooms are Rs 195/240. Fresh towels and mosquito zappers are provided. The front rooms are a little noisy. Hot water is provided in buckets.

The *Hotel Vinayak* (☎ 43-1130), LM Moulik Complex, Tenzing Norgay Rd (diagonally opposite the tourist office), is a good mid-range choice. Spotless and well appointed singles/doubles, all with attached bath, are Rs 200/250 and Rs 300/350 without air-con, or Rs 450/500 with air-con. There's a good restaurant here, and room service is available.

The three-star *Hotel Sinclairs* (☎ 22-674) is two km north of Tenzing Norgay Central bus terminal on Tenzing Norgay Rd, beyond the overpass. Non air-con singles/doubles are Rs 500/600, and air-con rooms are Rs 700/900. There are foreign-exchange facilities, a swimming pool, and bar. The Oriental Restaurant is here, also.

The closest place to the airport is the *Hotel Marina* (☎ 45-0371), which has comfortable rooms for Rs 150/200 with attached bath (hot water in buckets free). It's quiet, and there's a restaurant and bar, as well as free bed tea.

There are a couple of places within walking distance of New Jalpaiguri railway station. You're a bit isolated out here, but they're handy for early-morning departures. The *Hotel Holydon* (☎ 23-558) has singles with common bath for Rs 88 and doubles with attached bath (hot water) for Rs 154 and Rs 220. The more expensive rooms are at the front, and are bright and airy. There's a small restaurant here. Next door is the brand new *Hotel Baydanath* (no phone). Very good singles/doubles with attached bath and running hot and cold water are Rs 150/200.

Places to Eat

There's a good restaurant (the *Oriental Room)* at Hotel Sinclairs, serving Chinese and Mughlai cuisine, but service is excruciatingly slow. You can have a beer (Rs 36) with your 'tomator stuff with cream' (Rs 28) at the *Shere Punjab Hotel*, opposite the bus terminal. The very reasonably priced *Anand Hotel* restaurant, to the north of the tourist office, has great chicken rolls – minced chicken with cardamom in batter (Rs 12), and Quality ice cream is available here. The multicuisine air-con restaurant at the *Hotel Vinayak* is a good place to escape the heat. Handy to the railway station is the *Miami Restaurant*, next to the Hotel Holydon, featuring South Indian and Chinese cuisine.

Getting There & Away

Air The airport serving the hills region of West Bengal is at Bagdogra, 12 km west of Siliguri. Jet Airways and Indian Airlines have regular flights between New Delhi and Bagdogra, some via Gawahati, in Assam. Indian Airlines also has regular services to Calcutta. It's better to fly into Bagdogra with Indian Airlines from Delhi, and return to the capital with Jet Airways, as these flights are direct (ie not via Gawahati in Assam).

Jet Airways has a daily direct flight to Delhi (9W 602), leaving Bagdogra at 2.10 pm and arriving into Delhi at 4.05 pm (US$137). The Delhi-Bagdogra flight (9W 601) is via Gawahati. It leaves Delhi at 10 am and arrives into Bagdogra at 1.40 pm. Indian Airlines has a flight on Monday, Tuesday, Thursday and Sunday (IC 879) to Delhi via Gawahati (US$137). It leaves Bagdogra at 1.05 pm, arriving into Gawahati at 1.55 pm (US$36), and Delhi at 5 pm. On the same days, direct flights from the capital depart at 10.20 am, arriving into Bagdogra at 12.15 pm (IC 879). Flight IC 722 to Calcutta leaves on Monday, Wednesday, Friday, Saturday and Sunday at 11.55 am, arriving into Calcutta at 12.50 pm (US$55).

There's a direct bus to Darjeeling from the airport (3½ hours, Rs 55) which connects with flights. Ask at the West Bengal Tourist Office at the airport as taxi drivers try to convince you that it doesn't exist.

Indian Airlines (☎ 43-1509; airport 45-0666) has an office beside the Mainak Tourist Lodge, on Tenzing Norgay Rd. It's open daily from 9 am to 1 pm and 2 to 4.30 pm. Jet Airways (☎ 43-5876; airport 45-0589) has an office in the LM Moulik Complex, next door to the Hotel Vinayak on Tenzing Norgay Rd. It's open daily from 9 am to 6 pm.

Bus Most North Bengal State Transport Corporation (NBSTC) buses leave from the Tenzing Norgay Central bus terminal. Private buses, including the Hilly Region Mini Bus Owners' Association, with services to Darjeeling, Kurseong, Mirik and Kalimpong (WB hills), and Jorethang and Gangtok (Sikkim) also have counters at the terminal. Note that if you are travelling to Jorethang in West Sikkim, you will require a trekking permit. See the Permits section in the Sikkim chapter for details.

NBSTC buses to Madarihat (for Jaldhapara Wildlife Sanctuary) leave at 5.45, 8 and 10.15 am, 12.30, 1.30 and 2.30 pm (three hours, Rs 23). For Darjeeling, NBSTC buses leave from the Tenzing Norgay Central bus terminal at 6.30, 7.30, 8, 10.30 and 11.30 am (three hours, Rs 26). There's one service daily to Kalimpong at 7 am (three hours, Rs 23). For Mirik, buses leave at 7.30 am and 2.30 pm (2½ hours, Rs 20). There's no NBSTC service between Mirik and Darjeeling, but you can get private buses for this route in Mirik.

Rocket services (2x2 pushback seats) to Calcutta leave at 6, 7 and 8 pm (12 hours, Rs 147). There's an ordinary service at 5.30 pm (Rs 123). To Malda, ordinary services depart every 30 minutes between 5 am and noon (six hours, Rs 47). There's an overnight service at 5.30 pm (five hours, Rs 55), and a speedy day service at 5.30 pm (five hours, Rs 47).

To Berhampore, buses leave at 5, 6, 7 and 7.30 am (eight hours, Rs 71). A daily rocket service for Patna leaves from the NBSTC depot at Mallaguri Garage, a 10 minute walk north up Tenzing Norgay Rd (a rickshaw will cost Rs 2). Tickets for all destinations in Bihar must be booked here. The bus leaves at 4 pm (12 hours, Rs 120).

For Gawahati, in Assam, there's a NBSTC rocket service from Tenzing Norgay terminal at 5 pm (12 hours, Rs 146), and an ordinary service from Mallaguri Garage at 7.30 am (Rs 120).

Sikkim Nationalised Transport (SNT) buses leave from the SNT terminal on the east side of Tenzing Norgay Rd. Fares for the 114 km journey to Gangtok are Rs 38 in ordinary buses, and Rs 80 for the deluxe service.

Nepal Local buses leave from in front of the Tenzing Norgay Central bus terminal for Paniktanki, opposite the Nepal border town of Kakarbhitta. You can arrange a Nepalese visa (US$25; payment in cash only) at Paniktanki. The trip takes one hour, and costs Rs 6. A rickshaw across the border to Kakarbhitta costs Rs 5. Buses depart Kakarbhitta daily at 4 pm for Kathmandu (17 hours, Nepalese Rs 250). Buses between Darjeeling and Kathmandu also run through Siliguri and, regardless of which company you go with, you'll have to change buses here. See the Darjeeling section for more details.

Train The *Darjeeling Mail* departs Sealdah (Calcutta) at 7 pm (566 km, 12 hours). Tickets are Rs 175/562 in 2nd/1st class. The return trip leaves New Jalpaiguri railway station at 6.45 pm, arriving into Sealdah at 8.30 am. The *North East Express* is the fastest train to Delhi (1628 km, 33 hours). It departs at 5.25 pm and costs Rs 214/901 in 2nd/1st class, travelling via Patna (636 km, 16 hours, Rs 152/469).

For Gawahati (Assam), the *North East Express* leaves at 7 am, arriving at 6 pm (423 km). Second/1st class costs Rs 114/382. The *Abadh Assam Express* leaves New Jalpaiguri at 7.15 pm, arriving into Gawahati at 5.15 am. Second class sleeper tickets are available on the *Kanchenjunga Express*, which departs at 5 pm, arriving into Gawahati at 5 am (Rs 129).

There's a railway booking office on Bidhan Rd, just off Tenzing Norgay Rd. It's open Monday to Saturday from 8 am to 8 pm, and on Sunday and holidays, from 8 am to 2 pm.

Toy Train If the toy train from Siliguri/New Jalpaiguri to Darjeeling is running, tickets can be purchased from New Jalpaiguri, Siliguri Town or Siliguri Junction railway stations. As there are no advance reservations, it may be easier to pick up tickets at New Jalpaiguri, where the train originates, during the busy peak season (May to mid-July). When operating, there is a daily service at 9 am, and during the peak period, at 7.15 am. The journey takes an interminable nine hours to cover the 80 odd km up to the hill station, or four hours to Kurseong, 30 km short of Darjeeling. Tickets cost Rs 17/137 in 2nd/1st class. For more details on the toy train, see Getting There & Away in the Darjeeling section.

Bangladesh From New Jalpaiguri to Haldibari (the Indian border checkpost) takes two hours and costs Rs 9 by train. From here it's a seven km walk along the disused railway line to the Bangladesh border point at Chiliharti. From here you can travel by train into Bangladesh. See the Getting There & Away chapter for more details.

Taxi & Jeep The fastest and most comfortable way of getting around the hills is by share jeep. There are a number of taxi stands where you can get share jeeps to destinations in the WB hills, and to Sikkim, including one on Sevoke Rd, and one outside Tenzing Norgay terminal. Share rates are: Darjeeling (2½ hours, Rs 41); Kalimpong (2½ hours, Rs 41); Mirik (two hours, Rs 35); and Gangtok (4½ hours, Rs 80). Posted rates to reserve a taxi are: Darjeeling, Rs 450;

Smooth Ride

If you've just come from the hills region of west India, you'll be pleasantly surprised by the excellent condition of the roads here. Drivers are constantly assailed with noticeboards proudly proclaiming the virtues of northern West Bengal's roads, as well as signs imploring drivers to take it easy and 'enjoy the beautiful nature'. Some of the more compelling ones include: 'Hey! Speed lovers, this road leads to Hell!', or the even more evocative 'If you want to give blood, leave it at the blood bank, not on the road!' ■

Kalimpong, Rs 400; Mirik, Rs 400; and Gawahati, Rs 3500. From Bagdogra airport to Darjeeling, a taxi will cost Rs 500.

Getting Around

There are hundreds of cycle-rickshaws vying for your custom on Tenzing Norgay Rd (that's if they're not already burdened down with pyramids of pineapples). The official rate for cycle-rickshaws is Rs 1 per km. If you are flying out of Bagdogra airport, you may be able to get a lift from Siliguri to the airport with airline staff. Check at the Jet Airways or Indian Airlines offices in Siliguri. A taxi between the airport and Siliguri costs Rs 120. A less expensive option is to take a taxi to Bagdogra bazaar (three km, Rs 25), and get a local bus from there into Siliguri (nine km, Rs 2). From Tenzing Norgay Central bus terminal to New Jalpaiguri railway station, taxis will charge Rs 100, and autorickshaws, about Rs 35. A cycle-rickshaw will cost about Rs 15 for the 40 minute trip from New Jalpaiguri railway station to Siliguri Junction, or Rs 20 to Tenzing Norgay Central bus terminal. There are infrequent bus services along this route (Rs 2).

JALDHAPARA WILDLIFE SANCTUARY

Although most visitors are keen to make a hasty exit from the chaotic strip of mayhem which is Siliguri and head due north for Darjeeling and Sikkim, if you have the time, it's worth making the 135 km trip east to this little-visited sanctuary, established in 1941 for the protection of wildlife, particularly the Indian rhinoceros (*Rhinoceros unicornis*), which is threatened with extinction. The sanctuary has had some success in stabilising depleting rhino numbers, with an estimated population of 35 in the park precincts, although the highly coveted rhino horn has accounted for the brutal slaying of numbers of these magnificent beasts by poachers. Lying only 61m above sea level, the park encompasses an area of some 116 sq km, located in the east of Jalpaiguri district between the Torsa and Malangi rivers, with the mountains of Bhutan visible to the north.

The best season to visit Jaldhapara is from October to May, particularly in March and April, when the wild animals are attracted by the growth of new grasses. Apart from rhinos, other animals found in the park environs are (rarely seen) Royal Bengal tigers, wild elephants, and various types of deer, including sambar, muntjac (barking deer), chital (spotted deer) and hog deer.

It is possible to take elephant safaris from Hollong, inside the park. Cost is Rs 20 per person. The park entry fee is Rs 4 per person, and Rs 5 per light vehicle. Still camera charges are Rs 5 per day.

Places to Stay & Eat

Within the park itself is the *Hollong Forest Lodge*, with double rooms for Rs 200, plus Rs 95 per person (compulsory) for breakfast and dinner. Outside the park precincts is the *Jaldhapara Tourist Lodge*, at Madarihat. Doubles are Rs 475 and dorm beds are Rs 185, including all meals. Both of these places must be booked in advance through the Sub-Regional Tourist Office (☎ (0353) 43-1974) in Siliguri, or the Government of West Bengal Tourist Bureau (☎ (033) 248-8271), 3/2 BBD Bagh East, Calcutta, 700001. West Bengal Tourism has packages including accommodation, all meals, and a one-hour elephant safari.

Getting There & Away

From Tenzing Norgay Central bus terminal in Siliguri, buses ply to Madarihat, a small village 124 km to the east, and nine km from Jaldhapara. The trip takes three hours and costs Rs 23. From here, a taxi to Hollong, inside the park, will charge Rs 100. To hire a taxi from Siliguri to Jaldhapara will cost about Rs 850. In theory, there is a daily train to Madarihat from Siliguri, which departs at 11.30 am, arriving into Madarihat at 4 pm, but the service is erratic.

AROUND JALDHAPARA
Totopara

Lying on the banks of the Torsa River, 30 km from Madarihat, is the village of Totopara, close to the Bhutan border. This is the last remaining settlement of Totos, an indigenous tribal group whose numbers have dwindled to less than 100. A bus operates between Madarihat and Totopara in the winter months only (Rs 7). During the summer rains, it is impossible to cross the Titi River which lies between the two settlements.

Buxa Tiger Reserve

The Buxa Tiger Reserve encompasses an area of 761 sq km, of which 369 was designated as a wildlife sanctuary in 1987. The reserve is accessible from the settlement of Rajabhatkawa, a four hour bus trip from Siliguri, or 3½ hours from Madarihat. As a newly created reserve, there is little infrastructure in place for visitors, but the reserve does possess a wide variety of animal species, including over 230 species of birds and 60 species of mammals. These include a population of some 29 tigers, as well as numbers of wild elephant, deer, gaur (bison), barking, spotted and hog deer, and sambar. Intensive training programmes have been undertaken to educate field staff in the importance of conservation-based wildlife management, as opposed to revenue-based forestry.

There are dormitory facilities (Rs 10) at Buxa Duar, a five km trek from the ranger's office at Santrabari. Close by is an old fort which once protected the most important of the 11 routes into neighbouring Bhutan. During the independence movement, the fort was used by the British as a detention camp for freedom fighters. Triple rooms are available at Rajabhatkhawa, at Rs 30 per bed, or doubles with attached bath are Rs 175. For bookings, contact the Director, Buxa Tiger Project, PO Aliporedooar, District Jalpaiguri (☎ (03572) 2777).

There is one bus daily from Siliguri to Rajabhatkawa, departing at 10.15 am and arriving at 2 pm (Rs 25), and a daily train service from Siliguri Junction railway station, departing at 11.30 am. The bus is the better bet, as the train arrives after dark, at 7.30 pm (Rs 35). From Madarihat, it's 2½ hours by bus to Hashimara (Rs 25), from where you can get a local bus or taxi for the remaining 15 km to Rajabhatkawa.

Darjeeling District

Population: 1,335,600

Darjeeling district encompasses three administrative subdivisions: Darjeeling, Kalimpong and Kurseong. The hill station of Darjeeling is the main attraction in this region, but Kurseong and Kalimpong are also well worth visiting, with some interesting walks and treks, particularly from Kalimpong. Mirik is also being promoted as a hill resort. It's still a relatively laid back place, although rapid development is beginning to spoil the environment here.

DARJEELING
Population: 73,060
Telephone Area Code: 0354

Straddling a ridge in the Darjeeling-Sikkim Himalaya at 2134m and surrounded by tea plantations on all sides, Darjeeling has been a popular hill station since the British established it as an R&R centre for their troops in the mid-1800s. The industrious Brits, not averse to mixing a little business with pleasure, recognised that the quality of the soil and the mild climate were ideal for tea cultivation, and the forested hill slopes were soon denuded of their cover and planted with this most lucrative revenue earner. These days people come here to escape from the heat and humidity of the north Indian plain. You get an indication of how popular Darjeeling is from the 70 or so hotels recognised by the tourist office and the scores of others which don't come up to their requirements. Here you will find yourself surrounded by mountain people from all over the eastern Himalaya who have come to work, to trade or – in the case of the Tibetans – as refugees. Mother Teresa spent her early years as a nun here with the sisters at Loreto Convent, and Lawrence Durrell was educated at the prestigious St Joseph's College.

Outside the monsoon season, the views over the mountains to the snowy peaks of Kangchenjunga and down to the swollen rivers in the valleys are magnificent. Even when the peaks are enshrouded with mist (as they generally are during the monsoon) Darjeeling is an interesting place where you can visit Buddhist gompas and tea plantations, ride on the chairlift, spend days hunting for bargains in colourful markets and handicraft shops, or go trekking to high-altitude spots near the border with Sikkim.

While the fine old buildings which graced what was once affectionately referred to as the 'Queen of Hills' are for the most part still standing, most are in shocking states of dilapidation, with neither the will nor the resources to return them to their former glory. The former queen retains her charm, but she is looking distinctly shabby these days, her royal vestments sullied with fast-food joints, multilevel grey hotel complexes, and convoys of jeeps and tourist buses.

Like many places in the Himalaya, half the fun is getting there and Darjeeling has the unique attraction of its famous toy train. This miniature train loops and switchbacks its way up the steep mountainsides from New Jalpaiguri to Darjeeling.

Orientation

Darjeeling sprawls over a west-facing ridge, spilling down the hillside in a complicated series of interconnecting roads and flights of steps. Hill Cart Rd has been renamed Tenzing Norgay Rd (even though there's already another road by that name in Darjeeling; to eliminate confusion, the name Hill Cart Rd will be used in this section). It's the main road through the lower part of the town, and the railway station and the bus and main taxi stand are all on it. The most important route connecting this road with Chowrasta (the town square) at the top of the ridge is Laden La Rd and Nehru Rd. (Nehru Rd was recently renamed, and is still sometimes referred to as The Mall.)

Running more or less parallel to, and above, Laden La, and connected to it by staircases at intervals, is Gandhi Rd, with several mid-range places to stay along its length. Laden La and Gandhi roads converge at a major junction known as Clubside. Robertson Rd and Nehru Rd run off Clubside to the north. Nehru Rd (The Mall) meets Chowrasta at its north end. Along its length are a number of mid-range hotels, photographic supply shops, curio shops and restaurants.

The youth hostel and a number of budget guesthouses are on or near Dr Zakir Hussain Rd, which extends along the top of the ridge. It can be reached via Rockville Rd, above Gandhi Rd.

The bulk of the top-range hotels, including the Windamere, are clustered around Observatory Hill beyond Chowrasta.

Information

Tourist Offices The Government of West Bengal Tourist Office (☎ 54-050) is below the Bellevue Hotel, on Chowrasta. The staff are helpful and have free maps and brochures on Darjeeling. You can book here for the bus to Bagdogra airport (Rs 55). The bus leaves from the Police Traffic Point, Clubside, and stops to pick up passengers near the Hotel Windamere. The office is open Monday to Friday from 10 am to 4.30 pm. When this office is closed, tickets for the airport shuttle can be purchased from the Darjeeling Gorkha Hill Council Tourism office (☎ 54-214), in the Silver Fir building, opposite the Hotel Alice Villa, to the north of Chowrasta. The office is open daily from 10 am to 5 pm.

During the main tourist season, there are tourist assistance booths at the Darjeeling railway station and Clubside taxi stand.

Money ANZ Grindlays and the State Bank of India are both on Laden La Rd, to the north of the post office. Most major travellers' cheques are accepted.

Post & Communications The post office is centrally located on Laden La Rd. There's a handy parcel posting office next door. In the near future, all Darjeeling telephone numbers will have five digits.

Bookshops & Borrowing Libraries The Oxford Book & Stationery Company on Chowrasta is the best bookshop here. It has a comprehensive selection of books on the Himalayan zone. Books can be packed and shipped home here. There is a good selection of second-hand books which you can borrow at Greenland Tours & Travels (see the Trekking Outfits & Tour Operators section below). Many of the budget guesthouses have borrowing libraries for guests' use.

Photography Das Studios, on Nehru Rd, is a good place to head for advice regarding matters photographic, but they have no fast film, and there is no provision for slide processing in Darjeeling.

Medical Services Puri & Co has a well stocked dispensary on Nehru Rd, just up from Keventer's. If you need a doctor, enquire here. Opposite the post office at 7 Laden La Rd is the Economic Pharmacy. The Tibetan Medical & Astro Institute is beneath the Hotel Seven Seventeen, at 26 HD Lama Rd. It's open Monday to Friday from 9 am to noon and 2 to 4 pm.

Emergency Police: ☎ 2193; Ambulance: ☎ 2131; Fire: ☎ 2121; Darjeeling Hospital: ☎ 54-218.

Permits for Sikkim The Foreigners' Registration Office is on Laden La Rd. It's open daily from 10 am to 5 pm. To get a 15 day permit for Sikkim you must first visit the Deputy Commissioner's Office, otherwise known as the DM (District Magistrate), to the north of the town centre on Hill Cart Rd. Then get an endorsement from the Foreigners' Registration Office and return to the DM to collect your permit. The DM's office is open for permit applications on weekdays from 11 am to 1 pm and 2 to 4 pm. The whole process takes about an hour. If you want to enter West Sikkim direct from Darjeeling, rather than first going to Gangtok, make sure that Naya Bazaar is one of the places listed on your permit.

Trekking Outfits & Tour Operators Trek-Mate (☎ 54-074), at the Pineridge Hotel on Nehru Rd, is run by the enthusiastic Indra Gongba. Indra can tailor treks in the Sikkim and Darjeeling areas, as well as arrange guides and porters. For those interested in aspects of Buddhism and Hinduism, Indra can arrange special-interest tours including visits to temples and gompas, with detailed explanations of religious iconography, and introductions to Buddhist *rinpoches* (highly revered lamas) and Hindu priests.

Clubside Tours & Travels (☎ 54-646), JP Sharma Rd (off Laden La Rd), arranges treks and tours in North Bengal, Sikkim and Assam. They specialise in wildlife tours, and can arrange trips to Manas and Kaziranga wildlife reserves in Assam, and Jaldhapara Wildlife Sanctuary.

Himalayan Tours & Travels (☎ 54-544) has 20 years of experience booking treks in the regions of Darjeeling and Sikkim, and also leads mountaineering expeditions.

There are several good trekking agents in the Super Market complex, near the Bazaar bus stand on Hill Cart Rd. Himali Treks & Tours (☎ 2154) books treks and also hires equipment. They also have a half-day mountain-bike tour which leaves from Chowrasta, taking in the Aloobari Gompa and Senchal Lake (Rs 160); and rafting on the Teesta River. Diamond Tours & Travels (☎ 3180) has been operating for 11 years, and can arrange treks in Sikkim, make hotel reservations and book luxury bus trips. Kasturi Tours & Travels organises tours to Kathmandu, Gangtok and Bhutan.

Between mid-September and mid-December, the West Bengal Tourist Office offers a sunrise trip to Tiger Hill which leaves daily at 4 am. Tickets are Rs 40 and must be booked in advance. Most people go with the independent operators who charge a little less; some operators send a runner to your hotel to make sure you get up! Depending on demand, the tourist office also organises a local sightseeing tour, a trip to Mirik and a two day tour to Kalimpong and Gangtok.

Equipment Hire Trekking gear can be hired from the youth hostel, but you must leave a deposit to cover the value of the articles you borrow (deposits returnable, less hire charges, on return of the equipment). Typical charges per day are: sleeping bag Rs 25, rucksack Rs 15, and down jacket Rs 25. There is a good comment book here compiled by other travellers. Indra Gongba at Trek-Mate also hires out equipment at comparable rates. Two person dome tents (Rs 70) and other equipment can be hired at Himali Treks & Tours.

Tiger Hill

The highest spot in the area at 2590m, Tiger Hill, near Ghoom, is about 11 km from Darjeeling. The hill affords magnificent dawn views over Kangchenjunga and other eastern Himalayan peaks. On a clear day even Mt Everest is visible, looking strangely diminutive against the closer peaks which appear higher from this perspective.

Every day a large convoy of battered jeeps leaves Darjeeling for Tiger Hill at 4.30 am, which means that in the smaller lodges you get woken up at this time every day, whether you like it or not. The return trip costs Rs 40. It can be very cold and very crowded at the top, but coffee is available.

The early-morning start and discomfort are worthwhile for the spectacular vision of a 250 km long stretch of the Himalayan massifs, with, from left to right, Lhotse (8501m) flanked by Everest (8848m) and Makalu (8475m), then an apparent gap before the craggy Kokang (5505m), flanked by Janu (7710m), Rathong (6630m), the apparently flat-summited Kabru (7338m), Kangchenjunga (8598m), Pandim (6691m), Simvo (6811m) and the cone-like Siniolchu (5780m).

There's a view tower and entry costs Rs 2 for the top or Rs 7 for the warmer VIP lounge. Halfway down the hill a temple priest causes a massive traffic jam by anointing the steering wheel of each vehicle on the return trip!

Many take the jeep one way (Rs 30) and then walk back, a very pleasant two hour trip. Tickets can be purchased at the tourist office beneath the Bellevue Hotel.

Senchal Lake

Close to Tiger Hill is Senchal Lake, at 2448m, which supplies (somewhat erratically!) Darjeeling with its domestic water. It's a particularly scenic area and popular as a picnic spot with Indian holiday makers.

Kangchenjunga Views

At 8598m this is the world's third-highest mountain (and since India's annexation of Sikkim in 1975, the highest in India). From Darjeeling, the best uninterrupted views are to be had from Bhan Bhakta Sarani. From Chowrasta, take the road to the right-hand side of the Windamere Hotel and continue about 300m.

Yogachoeling Gompa

Also known as Ghoom Gompa, this is probably the most famous gompa in Darjeeling, and is about eight km south of town, just below Hill Cart Rd and the railway station near Ghoom. The gompa was built in 1875 by Lama Sherab Gyantso, and its monks belong to the Gelukpa order of Tibetan Buddhism. It enshrines an image of the Maitreya Buddha (the coming Buddha). The image of the Buddha has an unconventional western posture – seated, and with his hands on his knees, rather than in the traditional lotus position, and the eyes of the image are blue. Buddhists believe that the next Buddha will appear in the west, hence these western manifestations. The gompa also houses a very fine image of Mahakala (Shiva as Great Time, a personification of the dissipating power of time). Foreigners are allowed to enter the shrine and take photographs. A small donation is customary and the monks are very friendly.

Bhutia Busty Gompa

Not far from Chowrasta is this colourful gompa, with Kangchenjunga providing a spectacular backdrop. Originally a branch of the Nyingmapa order's Phodang Gompa in Sikkim, it was transferred to Darjeeling in 1879. The shrine here originally stood on Observatory Hill. There's an old library of Buddhist texts upstairs which houses the original copy of the *Tibetan Book of the Dead* – the *Bhardo Thüdol*. The manuscript was discovered here by the Swedish scholar, Dr

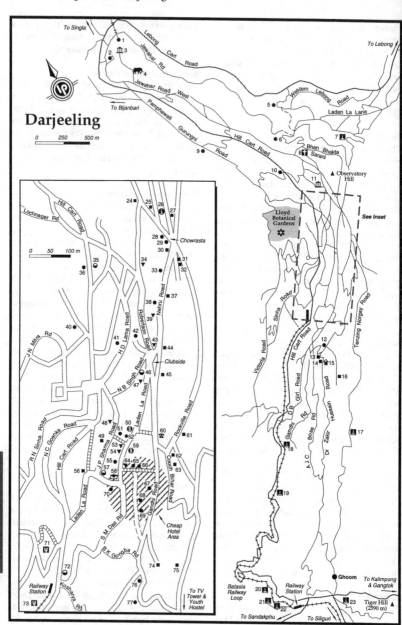

PLACES TO STAY

13 Ratna Restaurant
14 Triveni Guest House & Restaurant & Aliment Restaurant & Hotel
15 Youth Hostel
16 Hotel Tower View
24 New Elgin Hotel
25 Hotel Alice Villa
27 Windamere Hotel
30 Pineridge Hotel, Trek-Mate & Eastern Art
31 Bellevue Hotel, Tourist Office & Indian Airlines
32 Main Bellevue Hotel
37 Hotel Shangrila
44 Darjeeling Club
45 Hotel Dekeling & Dekevas Restaurant
49 Hotel Tshering Denzongpa
56 Hotel Apsara
61 Hotels Valentino, Continental, Dil & Daffodil
62 Rockville Hotel
63 Hotels Purnima & Broadway
66 Hotel Prestige
68 Hotel Pagoda
69 Hotel Shamrock
74 Hotel Sinclairs
75 Palace Mahakal

PLACES TO EAT

34 Great Punjab Restaurant
39 Glenary's
43 Kev's (Keventer's Snack Bar) & Puri & Co
47 Dafey Munal Restaurant & Bar
48 New Dish Restaurant

53 Jain Jaika & Park Restaurants & Hayden Hall
54 Golden Dragon Restaurant & Bar
64 Tibetan Restaurants

OTHER

1 Ropeway Station
2 Snow Leopard Enclosure
3 Himalayan Mountaineering Institute & Museums
4 Zoo
5 Tibetan Refugee Self-Help Centre
6 Raj Bhavan
7 Bhutia Busty Gompa
8 Gymkhana Club & St Andrew's Church
9 Happy Valley Tea Estate
10 Deputy Commissioner's Office
11 Bengal Natural History Museum
12 TV Tower
17 Aloobari Gompa
18 Sonada Gompa
19 Thupten Sangachoeling Gompa
20 Samdenchoeling Gompa
21 Yogachoeling (Ghoom) Gompa
22 Sakyachoeling Gompa
23 Phin Sotholing Gompa
26 Darjeeling Gorkha Hill Council Tourism Office

28 Oxford Book & Stationery Company
29 Habeeb Mullick & Sons
33 Nepal Curio House & Kalimpong Art Gallery
35 Buses, Jeeps & Taxis to Kalimpong, Siliguri & Sikkim
36 Super Market & Trek & Tour Operators
38 Das Studios
40 Market
41 Tibetan Medical & Astro Institute
42 Manjushree Centre of Tibetan Culture
46 Clubside Taxi Stand & Juniper Tours & Travels
50 ANZ Grindlays Bank
51 Clubside Tours & Travels
52 Foreigners' Registration Office
55 Nathmull's Tea Merchants
57 Darjeeling Motor Service Co (Sikkim Nationalised Transport)
58 Main Post Office
59 State Bank of India
60 Telegraph Office
65 Greenland Tours & Travels
67 Himalayan Tours & Travels
70 Economic Pharmacy
71 Maa Singha Temple
72 Taxis to Ghoom
73 Dhirdham Temple
76 Tibetan Refuge Self-Help Centre (Head Office)
77 Nepali Girls' Social Service Centre

WY Evans-Wentz, who translated the text. There is also a very fine mural depicting Mahakala. You will require permission from the caretaker monk to view the mural.

Other Gompas

Halfway between Ghoom and Darjeeling is the **Thupten Sangachoeling Gompa** at Dali. Westerners interested in Tibetan Bud-

dhism often study here. Behind the gompa, a keen gardener has planted over 40 species of rhododendron and yuille trees. Visitors are welcome. There are three other gompas in Ghoom: the large but relatively uninteresting **Samdenchoeling**, the nearby and smaller **Sakyachoeling**, and the **Phin Sotholing**.

Closer to Darjeeling, on Tenzing Norgay Rd, the **Aloobari Gompa** welcomes visitors.

The monks often sell Tibetan and Sikkimese handicrafts. If the gompa is closed, ask at the cottage next door and they'll let you in.

Beyond Ghoom in the settlement of Rongbul is the **Gonjan Gompa**, and adjacent to it, the **School of Tibetan Thangka Painting**. The school is run by the Tibetan lama Tsondu Sangpo, and his finely executed work is on display. On Hill Cart Rd, between Ghoom and Darjeeling, is the opulent **Sonada Gompa** over which the Kaloo Rinpoche presides. Kaloo Rinpoche is believed to be an incarnation of the previous Kaloo Rinpoche who founded the gompa, and established retreat centres in France and other parts of Europe and the USA.

Observatory Hill
Situated above the Windamere Hotel, this viewpoint is sacred to both Hindus and Buddhists. Observatory Hill was once the site of the gompa of Dorje Ling, from which the town takes its name. There's a shrine to Mahakala, for Hindus an incarnation of Shiva, and for Buddhists an incarnation of Padmasambhava (also known as Guru Rinpoche), who established Buddhism in Tibet and founded the Nyingmapa order. The multicoloured Tibetan prayer flags here double as trapezes for monkeys. Watch out for the monkeys as they can be aggressive.

Dhirdham & Maa Singha Temples
Built in 1939, the Dhirdham Temple is the most conspicuous Hindu temple in Darjeeling. It is just below the railway station and is modelled on the famous Pashupatinath Temple (sacred to Shiva as Lord of the Beasts) in Kathmandu.

Nearby is a tiny temple presided over by a female priest, or *mataji*, named Kumari Mataji. Her devotees, who include Hindus, Buddhists and westerners, believe she is a prophetess. Her temple is sacred to the goddess Durga, and devotees believe that Durga speaks through mataji.

Bengal Natural History Museum
Established in 1903, this interesting museum has a comprehensive but dusty collection of Himalayan and Bengali fauna. (However, there is something rather unsettling about walking between the cases beneath a triumphal arch formed by the heads of large, unfortunate Himalayan beasts.) The exhibits include over 56 species of mammals, 450 species of birds, 45 species of reptiles, 75 species of fish, and over 290 species of butterflies and moths, as well as a library containing over 2000 books and journals.

This magnificent collection is in a very sorry state. Some of the beetles have come off their pins and are lying in the bottom of their display cases with dismembered legs scattered about them. In a back room, generally not open to visitors, are hundreds of drawers, each full of birds lying on a bed of mothballs – an ornithological mortuary.

The museum is open daily except Thursday from 10 am to 4 pm. Entry is Rs 1.

Padmaja Naidu Himalayan Zoological Park
This zoo was established in 1958 with the objectives of study, conservation and preservation of Himalayan fauna. However, as with zoos anywhere, it is distressing to see magnificent wild animals kept in small enclosures in pseudo-natural habitats. The zoo houses India's only collection of Siberian tigers, and some rare species such as the red panda and the Tibetan wolf. While there has been some success in the breeding of the Tibetan wolf at the zoo, that of the red panda has been negligible, with the breeding of only one pup in captivity since the zoo's inception. Factors contributing to the poor rate of success include a nutrient-deficient diet and disturbance by visitors. To mitigate these problems, the diet of the pandas has been supplemented and the entry of visitors to the panda enclosure has been regulated. The snow leopards have been moved to a separate enclosure to enhance prospects of successful breeding (see below). The zoo can be reached in a 30 minute walk from Chowrasta. It is open daily except Thursday from 8 am to 4 pm. Entry is Rs 3.

CHRIS BEALL

RICHARD I'ANSON

RICHARD I'ANSON

West Bengal Hills
Top Left: Tea plantation, Darjeeling.
Top Right: Spinning, Tibetan Refugee Centre, Darjeeling.
Bottom: Darjeeling, the metropolis.

West Bengal Hills

Top: The awe inspiring Kangchenjunga, as it is seen from Darjeeling.
Bottom: Snow leopard, Snow Leopard Breeding Programme, Darjeeling.

Himalayan Mountaineering Institute (HMI) & Museums

India's most prestigious mountaineering institute, founded in 1954, lies about two km from the town centre on a hilltop known as Birch Hill Park. It is entered through the zoo, on Jawahar Rd West. There are a couple of interesting museums here. The **Mountaineering Museum** has a collection of historic mountaineering equipment, specimens of Himalayan flora and fauna and a relief model of the Himalaya showing the principal peaks. There is a display of badges and pins of mountaineering clubs around the world, and of the traditional dress of the hill tribes of the Himalaya. The **Everest Museum** next door traces the history of attempts on the great peak.

Sherpa Tenzing Norgay, who conquered Everest with Edmund Hillary in 1953, lived in Darjeeling and was the director of the institute for many years. He died in 1986 and his statue now stands beside his cremation spot just above the institute.

There are film shows at the institute and for Rs 1 you can view Kangchenjunga close up through a Zeiss telescope given to a Nepalese maharaja by Adolf Hitler.

The institute is open from 9 am to 1 pm and 2 to 5 pm (until 4 pm in winter), and entry costs Rs 3. There's a reasonable vegetarian restaurant by Sherpa Tenzing's statue.

Tea Plantations

Tea is, of course, Darjeeling's most famous export. From its 78 gardens, employing over 40,000 people, it produces the bulk of West Bengal's crop, which is almost a quarter of India's total. About 80% of Darjeeling tea is exported; the domestic market is quite small. Darjeeling tea is quite mild, and most Indians prefer the bracing jolt afforded by the stronger teas produced in Assam.

The most convenient plantation to visit is

Producing the World's Best Tea

Tea from some of the estates in the Darjeeling area is of very high quality, attracting the highest prices at auction. Although the climatic conditions are just right for producing fine tea bushes, the final result is dependent on a complex drying process.

After picking, the fresh green leaves are placed 15 to 25 cm deep in a 'withering trough' where the moisture content is reduced from 70% to 80% down to 30% to 40% using high-velocity fans. When this is completed, the withered leaves are rolled and pressed to break the cell walls and express their juices onto the surface of the leaves. Normally two rollings at different pressures are undertaken, and in between rolls the leaves are sifted to separate the coarse from the fine. The leaves, coated with their juices, are then allowed to ferment on racks in a high-humidity room, a process which develops their characteristic aroma and flavour. This fermentation must be controlled carefully since either over or under-fermentation will ruin the tea.

The fermenting process is stopped by passing the leaves through a dry air chamber at 115°C to 120°C on a conveyer belt to further reduce the moisture content to around 2% to 3%.

The last process is the sorting of the tea into grades. In their order of value they are: Golden Flowery Orange Pekoe (unbroken leaves), Golden Broken Orange Pekoe, Orange Fannings and Dust (the latter three consisting of broken leaves).

In the last few years modern agricultural practices have been brought to the tea estates to maintain and improve their viability. The tea plantations were one of the first agricultural enterprises to use clonal plants in their replanting schemes, though most of the tea trees are at least 100 years old and nearing the end of their useful or even natural lives. The ageing plants and deteriorating soil causes grave concern, since tea not only earns the country valuable export revenue, but also provides much employment in the area.

Although the auction prices for the lower qualities of tea are often disappointing for producers, the top qualities continue to achieve record prices. At an auction in 1991, tea from the Castleton Estate in Darjeeling went to a Japanese bidder for Rs 6010 (US$220) per kg – a world record! ■

the Happy Valley Tea Estate, only two km from the centre of town, where tea is still produced by the 'orthodox' method as opposed to the 'Curling, Tearing and Crushing' (CTC) technique adopted on the plains. However, it's only worth going when plucking is in progress (April to mid-November) because it's only then that the processing takes place. It's open daily from 8 am to noon and 1 to 4 pm (closed all day Monday and on Sunday afternoon). An employee might latch on to you, whisk you around the factory and then demand some outrageous sum for their trouble; Rs 10 per person is not inappropriate.

See the Things to Buy section for information about purchasing tea in Darjeeling.

Passenger Ropeway
At North Point, about three km north of the town, is India's oldest passenger ropeway (cable car). It is five km long and connects Darjeeling with Singla Bazaar on the Little Rangeet River at the bottom of the valley. Due to the power problems which have plagued Darjeeling over recent years, only the first two km of the route is currently operational. A return trip (including insurance and a very necessary standby generator!) is Rs 30 and takes about an hour. Cars leave every 30 minutes between 8 am and 3.30 pm (closed Sunday and holidays during the off season). You can phone to check if it's running (☎ 2731). It's a popular trip and you need to book one day in advance, but this can only be done in person at the Ropeway station.

Lloyd Botanical Gardens
Below the bus and taxi stands near the market, these gardens, which are over 100 years old, contain a representative collection of Himalayan plants, flowers and orchids. The hothouses, although in disrepair, are well worth a visit. The gardens are open between 6 am and 5 pm; entrance is free.

Tibetan Refugee Self-Help Centre
A 20 to 30 minute walk from Chowrasta brings you down to this Tibetan centre. It was established in October 1959 to help rehabil-itate Tibetan refugees who fled from Tibet with the Dalai Lama following the Chinese invasion. The centre produces carpets of pure Ladakhi wool (US$27 per sq m), woollens, woodcarvings and leatherwork, and has various Tibetan curios for sale (coins, banknotes, jewellery, etc).

You can wander at leisure through the workshops and watch the work in progress. The weaving and dyeing shops and the woodcarving shop are particularly interesting, and the people who work there are very friendly. Prices are on a par with those in the curio shops of Chowrasta and Nehru Rd. The views from here are excellent.

Snow Leopard Breeding Programme
The snow leopards (*Panthera uncia*) were originally housed in the main zoo complex. Due to the disturbance of visitors and the proximity of other animals, they were moved to a large separate enclosure on the way to the ropeway (about 15 minutes walk beyond the zoo). These rare and beautiful animals are reputedly less keen to breed in captivity than the panda (whose disinterest in sex is legendary), but they've had some success here.

Kiran Moktan at the centre talks at great length on and with great affection for his charges. He welcomes interested visitors between 9 and 11 am, and 2 to 3.30 pm; it's better to visit in the afternoon when the leopards are more active, but you should not make too much noise. During the mating season, entry of visitors to the enclosure is prohibited. The centre is open daily except Thursday. Entry is Rs 2.

Gymkhana Club
Membership of the Darjeeling Gymkhana Club costs just Rs 30 per day, but the activities here are not just equestrian. The word gymkhana is actually derived from the Hindi *gendkhana* (ball house). Games on offer include tennis, squash and badminton (court hire from 6 am to noon, Rs 25 per hour per person including balls or shuttlecocks, racquet and court hire); roller-skating (sorry, no blades here!) from 10 am to 1 pm and 3

Fight for Survival

The Snow Leopard Breeding Programme in Darjeeling commenced in 1986 with two leopards which were brought here from Switzerland. Female snow leopards have two breeding cycles per year, but are more likely to conceive in the winter cycle. The gestation period is from 97 to 104 days. There are normally two cubs per litter, although sometimes there can be up to five. The mortality rate is high. Two cubs have been born at the centre since the programme's inception, but sadly, only one has survived (and is currently thriving). This apparently low rate of success is actually something of a minor triumph; in China, it took 30 years to successfully breed snow leopards in captivity. While it is distressing to see these magnificent animals in wire enclosures, it's a sad fact that it is programmes such as this one at Darjeeling which may be the only means of enhancing the snow leopard's prospects for survival as a species, and the dedication of the staff here has to be applauded.

It is almost impossible to estimate the population of snow leopards in the wild, due to the inaccessibility of the terrain and the high altitudes at which they are found (over 3600m). Snow leopards are found across the entire Indian Himalaya chain, from Kashmir in the west to Bhutan beyond Sikkim's eastern borders. To the north they are found in Tibet, Central Asia and the Altais.

Although the snow leopard is a highly endangered and protected species, the smuggling of pelts continues, with pelts commanding high prices.

Much credit for the success of the programme in India must be given to Kiran Moktan at the centre in Darjeeling, who spends his days with the leopards. Ask to see his drawings, as he's an accomplished artist. ■

Illustration by Kiran Moktan

to 5 pm, Rs 5 per hour; table tennis, Rs 5 per hour; and billiards, Rs 10 per person per hour.

Pony Rides

Beware of the pony-wallahs who congregate on Chowrasta. They come along with you as a guide and at the end you'll find you're paying for a second pony and for their guiding time! The usual charge is around Rs 25 an hour, but establish the price before you set off.

Courses

Three month Tibetan-language courses for beginners are conducted at the Manjushree Centre of Tibetan Culture (☎ 54-159), 8 Burdwan Rd. There are also more advanced six and nine month courses. The centre can also arrange Buddhist study courses for groups of six or more, and organises talks and seminars on Tibetan culture. For details, contact Norbu at Devekas Restaurant, who has worked at the centre as a volunteer for the last seven years. You can learn traditional Tibetan woodcarving at the Tibetan Refugee Self-Help Centre (☎ 54-686; fax 54-237). Contact the head office (☎ 73-4101) at 65 Gandhi Rd.

Voluntary Work

The Nepali Girls' Social Service Centre (☎ 2985), Gandhi Rd, undertakes projects which promote the empowerment of women, child survival and development, and environmental protection. Volunteers would be welcome on an informal basis to teach English, art, or musical instruments. Contact the centre for details.

Volunteers may be welcome at the Tibetan Refugee Self-Help Centre teaching English and adult education, but you should write to the head office of the centre in advance. (For address and telephone details, see the Courses section above.)

Places to Stay

There is a bewildering number of places to stay in Darjeeling. Those that follow are only a limited selection. Prices vary widely with the season. The peak season extends roughly from 15 March to 15 July and 15 September to 15 November. It is well worth checking for discounts in the off season; sometimes rates are reduced by up to 75%.

Darjeeling suffers from chronic power and water shortages. Many hotels have backup (and noisy!) generators, but some don't, so bring a torch (flashlight). Many of the mid to top-range places provide a hot water bottle on request during the chilly winter months.

Places to Stay – bottom end

Just beyond the post office there's a whole cluster of cheap hotels either on Laden La Rd or on the alleys and steps running off it. Take the stone steps uphill just beyond the post office which connects Laden La Rd with Gandhi Rd. Halfway up, a laneway known as Upper Beechwood Rd branches to the right. Along here is the popular *Hotel Shamrock*, run by a no-nonsense Sherpa woman. Singles/doubles/triples cost Rs 65/150/165, some with attached bath. Hot water is available free in buckets. There are good views from the upstairs rooms which, with their wood panelling and sloping roofs, have a Swiss chalet ambience.

Next door is the *Hotel Pagoda* which has basic but pleasant doubles for Rs 150 with attached bath. There are cheaper doubles, but they're a bit gloomy. This is a good location, and the staff are friendly. There's a cosy TV room with a fireplace; the fire is lit in winter. Back on the stairway leading up from Laden La Rd is the *Hotel Prestige* (☎ 2699). All rooms have attached bath with geyser, and cost from Rs 200/300/450 to Rs 300/350/600. A 50% discount is offered in the off season. The upstairs rooms are bright and clean, but those downstairs are quite dark. There's a borrowing library here.

Many travellers head for the area around the youth hostel and TV tower, on or near Dr Zakir Hussain Rd. It's about a 20 minute (uphill!) walk from the railway station. If you're coming from Chowrasta, Dr Zakir Hussain Rd divides at the TV tower. A few steps along the road to the left is the *Hotel Tower View*, run by a friendly family. There are a range of rooms, from Rs 50 for a single with attached bath, Rs 60 for a double with great views and common bath (it's right next door), up to Rs 120 with views and attached bath. There's a convivial lounge area where tasty meals are dished up, and Krishna here is an excellent source of information on sights around Darjeeling. There's also a very good travellers' comment book here.

If you take the right-hand road from the TV tower, you'll come to a cluster of budget guesthouses. The *Youth Hostel* has seen better days, and dorm rooms are pretty shabby. For members, it's Rs 15, or for non-members, Rs 25. The hostel is open during the daytime, but there's a strict curfew of 10.30 pm. There's a good travellers' comment book here, and the staff are informative about treks in the area. Opposite the hostel is the *Triveni Guest House & Restaurant* (☎ 3114). Beds in the dorm are Rs 25, there are singles/doubles with common toilet for Rs 40/80, or with attached toilet and bath, Rs 50/80. Nearby is the *Aliment Restaurant & Hotel*, which has singles/doubles for Rs 50/70, and dorm beds for Rs 30. There's a good borrowing library here and a popular restaurant.

Near the Triveni is the *Ratna Restaurant*, which has four charming and cosy double rooms for Rs 60, and a comfortable sitting room. This is a great place and rooms are very good value.

An excellent place is the very friendly, Sherpa-run *Hotel Tshering Denzongpa* (☎ 3412), at 6 JP Sharma Rd. Doubles range from Rs 100 to Rs 400. The more expensive rooms have better views, but even the cheaper rooms are good value. Hot water is available free in buckets. A 40% discount is offered in the off season.

Places to Stay – middle
An old favourite in this price bracket is the two-star *Bellevue Hotel* (☎ 54-075), a charming old hotel right on Chowrasta. Fine old wood-panelled doubles range from Rs 550 to Rs 800, and all rooms have attached baths with hot water in the mornings. Room 49 has the best views, and also has a separate sitting room. There's a cafe here for guests only, which is a shame, as the views out over Chowrasta are excellent. Very good discounts are offered in the off season.

Behind the Bellevue is the *Main Bellevue Hotel* (☎ 54-178). This is a lovely old Raj-era building with doubles/triples for Rs 500/550, and a special double with Kangchenjunga views for Rs 650. The hotel is set in a lovely established garden. It has a slightly shabby, yesteryear atmosphere, and a gracious and attentive manager.

Opposite the Bellevue Hotel on Nehru Rd is the *Pineridge Hotel* (☎ 54-074). Singles/doubles/triples are Rs 350/500/650, and the deluxe rooms with polished wooden floors are Rs 450/650/850. All rooms have fireplaces and are simply but tastefully furnished. This hotel is currently undergoing extensive renovations, so it remains to be seen if the gracious old-world character is retained. Further down Nehru Rd is the *Hotel Shangrila* (☎ 54-149). Enormous light, airy rooms with polished wooden floors and pine ceilings are Rs 750 (Rs 400 in the off season). The restaurant downstairs is disappointing.

A short distance to the north of Chowrasta is the *Hotel Alice Villa* (☎ 54-181), at 41 HD Lama Rd. Doubles/triples are Rs 600/700 (Rs 300/350 in the off season). Rooms in the original building are charming, but those in the ugly new annexe are a bit disappointing. Rates include breakfast and one other meal.

The *Darjeeling Club* (☎ 54-349), above Nehru Rd, was the Tea Planters' Club in the days of the Raj. The downstairs doubles for Rs 500 are shabby and gloomy (and probably chilly). Large, comfortable doubles upstairs are Rs 1500, or there are identical rooms, which are cheaper simply on account of having been allowed to get shabbier, for Rs 700. There's a billiard room, a musty library, plenty of memorabilia and lots of nice sitting areas. There's a temporary membership charge of Rs 50 per day, and rates are discounted by up to 40% in the off season.

The *Hotel Dekeling* (☎ 54-159), 51 Gandhi Rd, above the Dekevas Restaurant and owned by the same Tibetan family, is a popular place with travellers. Doubles are Rs 300 and Rs 700, all with attached bath. A 50% discount is offered in the off season. Many students studying at the Manjushree Centre of Tibetan Culture stay here long-term in the pleasant wood-panelled attic rooms (Rs 125 to Rs 150 for singles with common bath), complete with desks, which open onto a friendly sitting area.

A good mid-range choice is the *Palace Mahakal* (☎ 2026), behind Hotel Sinclairs. This is a small, intimate and luxurious place, with singles/doubles/triples for

Rs 450/600/800, or super-deluxe rooms with great views for Rs 800/1050/1250. The better rooms are beautifully appointed with satin quilts, engravings and fine paintings.

The *Hotel Apsara* (☎ 54-444), Laden La Rd, about 300m west of the post office, has standard doubles for Rs 500 and luxury doubles for Rs 700. There are good views from all rooms, and the more expensive rooms have geysers. There's a travel desk here.

There's a collection of mid-range (and almost identical) hotels along Cooch Bihar and Rockville roads, including the *Hotel Purnima* (☎ 3110), *Hotel Broadway* (☎ 3248) and *Rockville Hotel* (☎ 2513), all with doubles from Rs 250; the *Hotel Daffodil* (☎ 2605) and *Continental* (3196), with doubles from Rs 300, and the *Hotel Dil* (☎ 2773), at 12A Rockville Rd, which has cosy and very clean doubles/triples for Rs 450/600. All these places offer good discounts in the off season.

At 6 Rockville Rd is the *Hotel Valentino* (☎ 2228), which has singles/doubles for Rs 700/850, and deluxe rooms for Rs 900/1050. Rates include breakfast, and heaters are provided free in winter. The hotel has an Oriental ambience with Chinese *objets d'art* and a fountain which falls into a pool full of fat goldfish. This place is a pleasant discovery among some less salubrious prospects. There's an excellent Chinese restaurant here.

Places to Stay – top end
The *New Elgin* (☎ 54-114; fax 54-267), off Robertson Rd, a short distance to the north of Chowrasta, is a fine choice in this category. Singles/doubles cost US$59/71, and double suites are US$81. Rooms are elegantly furnished, and hot-water bottles are provided. There's 24 hour room service, a fully stocked bar, a very good restaurant and laundry/valet service. The resident labrador Kaizer keeps a sleepy eye out over the lovely gardens. A 20% discount is offered in the off season.

The *Windamere Hotel* (☎ 54-041; fax 54-043) is a veritable institution among raj relic aficionados, with Tibetan maids in starched frilly aprons, high tea served in the drawing room to the strains of a string quartet, and a magnificent old bar where the silence is broken only by an old pendulum clock. The hotel has been owned since the 1920s by Mrs Tenduf-la, a Tibetan lady now in her 80s. A discreet notice in the lounge requests visitors not to 'lie supine on the hearth or sleep behind the settees, lest unintended offence be given to others'. Rooms are by no means luxurious, but are cosy and comfortable, and TVs are conspicuously (and deliberately) absent. Guests' comfort is assured with little touches like heaters and hot-water bottles in the bedrooms, and a torch (flashlight) in case of power failure. Single rates are from US$64 to US$75, and doubles are US$99, including all meals. There is also a double suite for US$110. Nonguests are welcome to dine here for lunch or dinner, but advance notice is required.

Tastefully appointed singles/doubles with polished wooden floors at *Hotel Sinclairs* (☎ 3432), 18/1 Gandhi Rd, are Rs 1085/1620, including breakfast and one meal. The front rooms have excellent views.

Places to Eat
There are good views and great chocolate pudding with rum sauce (Rs 20) at the *Dafey Munal Restaurant & Bar*, Laden La Rd, at the Clubside taxi stand. *Kev's* (Keventer's Snack Bar), on Nehru Rd, is still the best place to head for a bacon sandwich (Rs 10), and other porcine fare. The deli downstairs has sausages, cheeses, ham and other goods. On the opposite side of Nehru Rd is the popular *Devekas Restaurant*, with very good (but spicy!) Hong Kong chicken, as well as whopping big pizzas. Devekas' special pizza with the works costs Rs 35.

A short walk up the hill brings you to *Glenary's*, established in 1935. Tea time here is still an occasion that calls for freshly starched table linen. The bakery is downstairs, and if you arrive early enough, you can get excellent brown bread. They also have a range of cakes (cherry, Madeira, Dundee) from Rs 30, and some devilish-looking chocolate-coated rum balls, as well as sausage rolls and jam biscuits. The restaurant upstairs is open until 8.30 pm, and features continental dishes such as roast chicken (Rs 30), as well as tandoori and Chinese dishes. The tipsy pudding – sponge cake liberally sloshed with rum, served with jelly and cream – is Rs 25, and you can finish the evening with an Irish coffee (Rs 40).

The best Chinese food in Darjeeling can be found at the *Embassy* restaurant, at the Hotel Valentino, 6 Rockville Rd. It's not terribly expensive, with most main dishes under Rs 55. The Manchurian fish (Rs 49) is very good. This place is only open until 8 pm, and you probably won't be admitted after 7.30 pm.

The *Palace Mahakal* has a multicuisine restaurant in an extraordinary atrium-style setting with an enormous winged statue in the centre, and fine views out over Darjeeling.

The *Great Punjab Restaurant*, Robertson Rd, has excellent Punjabi cuisine including dhal makhani (black dhal with butter) – Rs 20, and rajma (kidney beans and masala) – Rs 15.

If you can't afford to stay at the Windamere, it's possible to enjoy the period ambience over lunch or dinner. Nonguests are welcome, but advance notice is required. Breakfast is US$5, and a set-menu lunch or dinner is US$9. High tea is served from 4 to 5.30 pm in the drawing room for US$3. Nonguests are also welcome at the *Silver Restaurant* at the New Elgin, where the set lunch or dinner costs Rs 175. Advance notice is required.

Opposite the State Bank of India on Laden La Rd is the brand new *Jain Jaika Restaurant* with pure vegetarian cuisine. Upstairs is the *Park* restaurant, with a pleasant outlook over Darjeeling. The speciality is the murg tikka – clay-oven roasted chicken kebabs with herbs (Rs 38). The minced chicken kebabs marinated in lemon yoghurt (Rs 30) are also very good.

A few doors away is the *Golden Dragon Restaurant & Bar*, with rainbow-painted walls and a seedy 20s ambience. It's a smoky little den with a very basic menu; the beer's the main attraction here (Rs 38). Further down Laden La Rd, close to the main post office, are a series of tiny eateries serving cheap fare – generally Tibetan cuisine – including the *Washington Restaurant*, the *Soaltee Restaurant*, the friendly family-run *Lhasa Restaurant*, and also the *Utsang* and the *Penang Restaurant*.

The *New Dish* restaurant and bar, on JP Sharma Rd, specialises in Chinese fare and sizzlers, including the mixed grill (Rs 65) and sizzling chicken (Rs 60). This is a large airy place with great sunset views.

Most of the guesthouses in the TV tower area have their own dining rooms and can rustle up traditional dishes as well as western favourites such as banana pancakes, jaffles, etc. Good choices are the *Tower View*, *Ratna* and the *Triveni* (which does a good fixed nonveg breakfast – Rs 38).

Things to Buy

Curio Shops There is a high concentration of curio shops on Chowrasta and along Nehru Rd, and another group on Laden La Rd in the post office area. All things Himalayan are sold here – *thangkas* (Buddhist religious art produced on cloth with vegetable dyes, generally with a brocade surround), brass statues, religious objects, jewellery, woodcarvings, woven fabrics, carpets etc – but if you're looking for bargains, shop judiciously and be prepared to spend plenty of time looking.

If you're looking for bronze statues, the real goodies are kept under the counter and cost in multiples of US$100! Woodcarvings tend to be excellent value for money. Most of the shops accept international credit cards.

There is also a market off Hill Cart Rd next to the bus and taxi stands. Here you can find excellent and relatively cheap patterned woollen sweaters and umbrellas.

Habeeb Mullick & Sons (☎ 54-109), on Chowrasta, was established in 1890, and has a veritable cornucopia of curios. Originally they specialised in furs. Distinguished patrons included Queen Sofia of Spain, and Rajiv and Sonia Gandhi. Today the merchandise is of a more environmentally friendly nature. There is an astonishing variety of hats: fur-lined Tibetan hats with amazing gold brocade; Lepcha hats covered in black felt with a colourful brim, the crown surmounted by a red knot; soft woollen Kullu and Nepali *topis*; Kumba (Tibetan warrior) hats; Afghan, Kashmiri, Sherpa and Sikkimese hats; and even gold lama's hats with red trimming, worn by the Gelukpa order. Prices start at Rs 250, but the *pièce de résistance* is a 90 year old Tantric Tibetan hat with carved human bone panels depicting Buddha, which will set you back Rs 7000 – about US$240! There are also tribal artefacts and locally made woollen jumpers (Rs 350 to Rs 550).

At 16 Nehru Rd is the Nepal Curio House (☎ 54-010), owned by the third generation of the family who established the business in 1891. The back room specialises in artefacts from the Himalayan region, including thangkas ranging in price from Rs 400 to Rs 5000, and statues up to Rs 6000. The informative owner is happy to explain the significance of the postures of the Buddha, as well as the iconography of the thangkas. You can also purchase Nepalese jackets or lengths of *yatha* – handloom coarse woollen Bhutanese cloth.

The Kalimpong Art Gallery, nearby, specialises in Nepalese pastel paintings (usually portraits), local jewellery and *khukuri* (traditional Gurkha knives). The tourist models feature brass filigree work and are studded with turquoise and coral, with a bone or wood handle (Rs 115). The more authentic (and more sinister!) models are plain and much larger, and can cost up to Rs 850.

Eastern Art, in the Ajit Mansion (Pineridge Hotel complex), has thangkas, brass, silver and gold statues, pure silver jewellery, woodcarvings and copper items, as well as chainstitch Kashmiri carpets (from Rs 700 to Rs 3500), papier mâché items, wooden masks and brass *aftaba* – elegant long-necked vessels for water or wine, from a few cm to half a metre in stature.

Tibetan Carpets For Tibetan carpets, the cheapest place in the area is at Hayden Hall, opposite the State Bank of India on Laden La Rd. This women's co-operative was established by the Jesuit priest Father EP Burns for the poor of Darjeeling, particularly mothers. It also runs adult literacy programmes, TB eradication programmes, and housing projects for low-income people. A 90 x 180 cm pure Indian wool carpet would cost from Rs 2100 to Rs 2400 depending on the intricacy of the design. The co-op also sells *casemillon* (wool/synthetic mix) shawls, woollen hats, socks and mufflers.

Darjeeling Tea If you're buying tea, First Flush Super Fine Tippy Golden Flowery Orange Pekoe I is the top quality. (First flush refers to the first picking, which takes place in spring.) The price varies enormously; you'll pay anything from Rs 150 to Rs 3000 per kg! The way to test the tea is to take a small handful in your closed fist, breathe firmly on it through your fingers and then open your hand and smell the aromas released from the tea by your warm breath. At least it will look like you know what you're doing even if you don't have a clue! Avoid the tea in fancy boxes or packaging as this is all blended and comes from Calcutta.

If you find that you become hooked on a particularly fragrant brew, most tea merchants in Darjeeling offer a mail order service. Airmail prices to the UK, for example, are Rs 109 for 250g, plus Rs 15 for packing. A good place to head is Nathmull's Tea Merchants (☎ 3437; fax 54-426), near the post office on Laden La Rd. Mr Vijay Sarda here will hold you in thrall as he waxes lyrical over the virtues of various teas.

Getting There & Away

Air The nearest airport is 90 km away at Bagdogra, down on the plains 12 km from Siliguri. See Getting There & Away in the Siliguri section earlier in this chapter. The agent for Jet Airways is Clubside Tours & Travels (☎ 54-646), on JP Sharma Rd (off Laden La Rd). The Indian Airlines office (☎ 54-230) is beneath the Bellevue Hotel on Chowrasta. The office is open daily from 10 am to 5 pm (closed between 1 and 2 pm). Tickets for the airport transfer to Bagdogra can be purchased at the tourist office, next door.

Kathmandu It is possible to fly from the border (the airstrip is Bhadrapur) to Kathmandu with Everest Air, Royal Nepal Airlines, or Necon Airways (US$99). A number of agents can book this flight, including Juniper Tours & Travels (☎ 2625), Clubside, and Himali Treks & Tours (☎ 2154), Super Market complex, above the Bazaar bus stand on Hill Cart Rd.

Bus The agent for Sikkim Nationalised Transport (SNT) is the Darjeeling Motor Service Co (☎ 2101), 32 Laden La Rd. The office is open daily from 10 am to 1 pm only. There is one bus daily which leaves from opposite the office to Gangtok at 1 pm (five hours, Rs 60). There are no bus services to Jorethang, in West Sikkim.

Most of the buses from Darjeeling leave from the Bazaar bus stand (Hill Cart Rd). To Gangtok, buses leave at 7.30 and 8 am, 1.15 and 1.30 pm (five hours, Rs 60). Buses for Siliguri leave every 20 minutes between 6.20 am and 5.30 pm (three hours, Rs 26). Every 40 minutes, buses depart for Mirik between 8.30 am and 3.15 pm (2½ hours, Rs 20). To Kalimpong, there's one bus at 8 am (3½ hours, Rs 30).

Numerous private agencies book luxury bus trips. Rates at Greenland Tours & Travels (☎ 3190), 21 Beechwood Rd (on the steps near the Hotel Prestige, above the main post office) are as follows: Kathmandu, 26 hours, Rs 275; Pokhara, 25 hours, Rs 285; Calcutta (disembark at Chowringhee, handy to Sudder St), 19 hours, Rs 210; Patna, 18 hours, Rs 190; Gawahati (with changes at Siliguri), 20 hours, Rs 210; Shillong (with changes at Siliguri and Gawahati), 26 hours, Rs 245; New Jalpaiguri, four hours, Rs 55; Gangtok, five hours, Rs 75; Kalimpong, 2½ hours, Rs 50; Mirik (day tour), Rs 90.

Kathmandu There are a number of companies which offer daily buses between Darjeeling and Kathmandu (26 hours, Rs 275), but none of them actually has a direct service; you have to change buses at Siliguri.

The usual arrangement is that the agents will sell you a ticket as far as Siliguri, but guarantee you a seat on the connecting bus with the same agency. You arrive at the border around 3 pm (Kakarbhitta is the name of the town on the Nepalese side), leave again round 4 pm and arrive in Kathmandu around 9 or 10 am the next day.

Most travellers prefer to do the trip independently, although it involves four changes – bus from Darjeeling to Siliguri (Rs 26), bus (Rs 6) or jeep (Rs 20) from Siliguri to Paniktanki on the border, rickshaw across the border to Kakarbhitta (Rs 5), and bus from Kakarbhitta to Kathmandu (17 hours, Nepalese Rs 250). This is cheaper than the package deal, and you get a choice of buses from the border, plus you have the option of travelling during the day and overnighting along the way. There are day buses from Kakarbhitta that go to a number of other towns on the terai (Nepalese plains), including Janakpur (Nepalese Rs 100), and night buses direct to Pokhara (Nepalese Rs 250). For more information on the trip from the border to Kathmandu, see the Getting There & Away chapter.

The nearest Nepalese consulate is in Calcutta, but visas are available at Paniktanki on the Indian side of the border for US$25 (which must be paid in cash), and these can be extended in Kathmandu.

Taxi & Jeep Most travel agencies book jeeps. Quoted rates are: Siliguri Rs 500; Kalimpong Rs 600; Gangtok Rs 1500 (Maruti van, Rs 1200; share jeep, 10 people required, Rs 120 per person); West Sikkim, ie Jorethang (2½ hours, Rs 800); Pemayangtse (4½ hours, Rs 2500); and Yuksom (five hours, Rs 2800). The section between Darjeeling and Naya Bazaar (21 km) is very steep, and during the monsoon it is subject to landslides. If the road is closed, a detour is taken via Teesta Bridge which costs an additional Rs 500.

There is a share jeep stand for destinations in Sikkim to the right of the bus ticket office at the bus stand on Hill Cart Rd.

Rates are Rs 5 cheaper in the back of the jeep. In the front and middle seats, rates are as follows: Gangtok (8.30 and 9.30 am, 1 and 2 pm, Rs 130); and Jorethang (leaves when full between 9 am and 3 pm, two to three hours, Rs 60). Buses from Jorethang to Yuksom, roadhead for the Dzongri trail (8 and 9.30 am, three hours, Rs 27). You will require a trekking permit to visit Yuksom. See the section on Permits in the Sikkim chapter for details.

The share jeep office for Kalimpong is at the south end of the taxi rank, beneath the staircase to the first level of the Super Market.

Train New Jalpaiguri/Siliguri is the railhead for all trains other than the narrow-gauge toy train. See under Getting There & Away in the Siliguri section earlier in this chapter for details to or from Calcutta, Assam and other centres. Reservations for major trains out of New Jalpaiguri can be made at the Darjeeling railway station (the toy train terminus) between 10 am and 4 pm daily (closed for lunch between 1 and 2 pm).

Toy Train The toy train runs daily, although services during the monsoon are often disrupted due to the track being washed away. It leaves Siliguri at 9 am, arriving into Darjeeling at 5.30 pm. An additional service leaves Siliguri at 7.15 am during the peak season. The cost is Rs 17/137 in 2nd/1st class, with the return journey from Darjeeling leaving at 7 and 10 am.

Mother Teresa claims that she was on her way to Darjeeling on the toy train when God inspired her to establish the Missionaries of Charity. It's difficult to imagine thoughts turning to anything heavenly on this slow but interesting trip, with the black soot belched out by the little steam engine soon enveloping passengers in a coat of grime. If divine inspiration remains elusive, you can disembark at Kurseong (Rs 9/33, four hours) and from there take a bus (Rs 14) or a seat in a jeep (Rs 30) for the 1½ hour run to Darjeeling. This also gets you into Darjeeling before dark. For an even shorter trip, it's a pleasant ride from Darjeeling to Ghoom (Rs 3, 45 minutes).

Heading for the Hills

The 90 km journey to Darjeeling from New Jalpaiguri or Siliguri on the famous miniature railway is an experience that shouldn't be missed. The construction of a railway line to Darjeeling formed part of the British campaign to link the major cities of India and its important agricultural regions with its ports. With the growth of the tea industry in the environs of Darjeeling, a more efficient means of transporting heavy agricultural equipment and building materials to the hill regions of West Bengal was required, as well as a method to ship the packaged tea down onto the plains. Construction of the railway line commenced in 1879, and the little steam train made its maiden trip in 1880, carrying the viceroy 20 km uphill to Tindharia. In 1881 the line was completed through to Darjeeling. The train crawls up to the hill station at a slow rate of knots, passing through dense jungle on the plains, and ascending through tea plantations and forests of sal and teak with brilliant splashes of colour afforded by poinsettia, bougainvillea and orchids. It navigates some tortuous gravity-defying loops, and steep grades, negotiating a complete circle at the last loop, known as the Batasia Loop, five km short of Darjeeling.

The engineer responsible for this extraordinary feat was apparently frustrated on a particularly steep grade on the Selim Hill at Tindharia. He wrote to his wife in England expressing his dismay at the possibility of a train negotiating the seemingly impossible grade. His inventive wife wrote back suggesting that the train could be reversed at intervals to enable it to ascend in a zig zag formation. She drew her inspiration from ballroom dancing, in which, as she astutely observed, reversing was a perfectly appropriate way of negotiating tricky manoeuvres on the dance floor. The engineer subsequently completed the job, and at certain stretches along the route, the train does indeed reverse before advancing in zig zag fashion on its ascent. ■

Getting Around

There are no local buses between Darjeeling and Ghoom. Share taxis leave from the market near the bus stand on Hill Cart Rd every five minutes (Rs 6). Having a taxi to yourself costs Rs 100. The centrally located Clubside taxi stand is at the intersection of Robertson and Laden La roads. A taxi from the bus stand to the Clubside taxi stand is about Rs 40.

AROUND DARJEELING

At **Mangpu**, 20 km from Darjeeling, is India's only cinchona plantation. Quinine is produced from the bark of this tree which is used in malaria medication. The name cinchona is derived from Countess Chinchon, the Spanish Vicerene of Peru, who was treated with the bark of this tree while suffering a life-threatening fever, and a remarkable cure was effected. The very humble Mongpu Gompa here is presided over by Drinchen Rinpoche. The rinpoche is a talented artist, and created the image of the Buddha and Guru Rinpoche enshrined in the prayer room. Rabindranath Tagore used to spend his summer holidays in a house at Mangpu with his friends, and used the setting as inspiration for some of his poems.

Darjeeling-Sandakphu/Phalut Trek

You don't need to bring much with you on this trek, as there's accommodation along the way. Most places have quilts, but in the high season it might be worth bringing your own sleeping bag (you can rent them in Darjeeling) in case there's not enough bedding to go round. Also, you'll need clothing for low, tropical climates and high mountain passes.

Although you can get basic meals along the way, bring some snacks such as nuts, biscuits, raisins and chocolate. You'll need a water bottle – even a plastic mineral water bottle will do – as there are some stretches where there's no water or places to eat.

Guides and porters are not necessary but can be arranged through numerous trekking agencies in Darjeeling. A porter costs about Rs 80 per day, a guide Rs 150 per day. If you don't take a guide, you should ask directions at every opportunity, as the path is not always clear.

Note Before leaving Darjeeling you're advised to browse through the travellers' comments books at the youth hostel or Hotel Tower View, in which trekkers have recorded notes about the routes.

This trek to the Himalayan viewpoint at Phalut (3600m) is the most popular trek in the area. It involves a short bus trip from Darjeeling to Manaybhanjang, from where you walk steadily towards the mountains via Sandakphu. Here you can turn back or continue to Phalut and walk down to Rimbik for a bus to Darjeeling. The trek can be done in the opposite direction but you'll spend more time walking with your back to the mountains.

There's a rough jeep track from Manaybhanjang through Sandakphu but it's not used much. If you prefer, Rs 2500 will get you a return trip from Darjeeling to Sandakphu by jeep.

Stage 1	Darjeeling to Jaubari (8 to 9 hours)
Stage 2	Jaubari to Sandakphu (5 to 6 hours)
Stage 3	Sandakphu to Molley (4 to 5 hours)
Stage 4	Molley to Gorkhey to Phalut to Ghorkey (5 to 6 hours)
Stage 5	Gorkhey to Rimbik (6 to 7 hours)
Stage 6	Rimbik to Darjeeling

Short Cut If you don't have time for a six day trek, you could take a short cut. You can go just as far as Sandakphu where there are also good views. Sandakphu is actually slightly higher than Phalut, although further back from the mountains. From here you can backtrack to Bikhay Bhanjang and cut straight across to Rimbik in five to six hours for a bus to Darjeeling. Bear in mind that there's no water or food on this stretch.

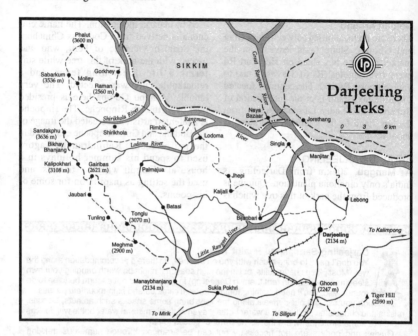

Darjeeling Treks

MIRIK
No Telephone Area Code; book calls through the exchange

Being promoted as a 'new' hill station, Mirik is about 50 km from both Siliguri and Darjeeling at an altitude of 1767m. The artificial lake is the main attraction here, and there's a 3½ km path around it. The main tourist area lies to the south of the lake, in the area known as Krishnanagar. While this is certainly a pretty spot, surrounded by tea estates, orange orchards and cardamom plantations, attempts to 'develop' the area for tourism are already threatening to spoil the tranquil ambience. Swimming in the lake is strongly advised against, as it is highly polluted – there is no sewage system in Mirik, and human and animal excreta is washed into its murky and turbid waters. A report has found that even the fish are coming out of the water to try to obtain oxygen from the air!

The post office is in the lane opposite the State Bank of India (which doesn't exchange travellers' cheques; there are currently no foreign exchange facilities here).

Things to See & Do
Perched high above the town is the **Bokar Gompa**, a small and brightly coloured gompa whose 70 monks are Mahayana Buddhists. It can be reached on a path leading up from the south end of the main road in about 10 minutes. On the west side of the lake, about 10 minutes walk from the taxi stand and set amid banana trees, are three small Hindu **temples** sacred to Hanuman, Kalamata (Durga as the Mother of Time) and Shiva.

Boats can be hired on the east side of the lake for Rs 30 per 30 minutes.

Places to Stay & Eat
Very basic, rustic rooms can be found at the *Wooden Lodge*, on the main Darjeeling road. Doubles with common bath are Rs 70, with

WEST BENGAL HILLS

hot water available free by the bucket. There's a restaurant here with a very tasty fish curry (Rs 12), and chicken korma (Rs 20).

Down a small lane opposite the State Bank of India is the *Lodge Ashirvad* (☎ 43-272). Doubles with common bath are Rs 100, or with attached bath, from Rs 130 to Rs 250. Singles with attached bath are Rs 110, and hot water in buckets is Rs 5. The downstairs rooms are cheaper than those upstairs, and are a little dark. There are separate kitchen facilities here for people who wish to self-cater.

Next door is the *Lodge Panchashil* (☎ 43-284). Tiny but light and airy singles with attached bath are Rs 100, or larger doubles/triples are Rs 120/150. The manager is friendly and helpful, and there's a pleasant rooftop terrace here. You may be able to negotiate a discount in the off season (August-April). If you continue down this lane to the end, and follow the path across the fields for three minutes, you'll arrive at the *Lodge Hitaishi* (☎ 43-278). Singles/doubles with common bath are Rs 80/100, and with attached bath, from Rs 100/120. Rooms at the front have pleasant views out across the school to the lake. Meals can be provided on request.

The flashy *Hotel Jagdeet* (☎ 43-231), on the main road, has doubles with attached bath for Rs 350, and with geyser, Rs 550 and Rs 1000. All rooms are carpeted, and room service is available. There is a popular restaurant-cum-bar next door.

The *Jay Durga* is a very basic eatery right on the lake's edge, with nonveg dishes under Rs 25. The *Restaurant Liberty* has a convivial atmosphere and a friendly manager. You can get Tibetan fare here, including momos and thukpa. On the left as you enter Mirik from Siliguri is the tiny *Trident Restaurant*, with Indian and Chinese cuisine.

Getting There & Away

Buses to Darjeeling leave at 11.30 am, 1.15, 1.45 and 2.15 pm (2½ hours, Rs 20). The journey to Kurseong takes three hours, and costs Rs 28. There are a number of buses to Siliguri between 6.30 am and 3 pm (2½ hours, Rs 20). Tickets can be purchased from

the wooden shack next to the Restaurant Liberty, near the lakeshore.

There are no share taxis to Darjeeling. To hire a taxi will cost Rs 500 to either Darjeeling or Siliguri.

KALIMPONG
Population: 45,000
Telephone Area Code: 03592

Kalimpong, 74 km east of Darjeeling and 72 km north of Siliguri, is a bustling and rapidly expanding, although still relatively small, bazaar town set among the rolling foothills and deep valleys of the Himalaya at an altitude of 1250m. It was once part of the lands belonging to the rajas of Sikkim, until the beginning of the 18th century when it was taken from them by the Bhutanese. In the 19th century it passed into the hands of the British and thus became part of West Bengal. It became a centre for Scottish missionary activity in the late 19th century.

Until the outbreak of the Sino-Indian war in 1962, Kalimpong was one of the most important centres of Indo-Tibetan commerce, with mule trains passing over the 3300m high Jalepla mountain pass. The Kalimpong-Jalepla road was the largest all-weather route between the two countries. With relations improving between India and China, Kalimpong will probably lose its transborder business to Gangtok, in Sikkim. The main crops grown locally are ginger and cardamom. Kalimpong division was once densely forested, but widespread tree felling has left large areas denuded. There are still some areas where tracts of forest still stand, including along the left bank of the Teesta River, and in the environs of Lava and Richila.

Kalimpong's attractions include three gompas, a couple of solidly built churches, a sericulture centre, orchid nurseries and the fine views over the surrounding countryside. Although not many travellers visit Kalimpong, there's enough here to keep you occupied for a couple of days, and for the energetic, there's some good trekking.

The most interesting part of the trip to Kalimpong is the journey there from Darjeeling via the Teesta River bridge.

Orientation & Information

Life centres around the sports ground and east through the market. The bus stand (known locally as the Motor Stand) and Dambar Chowk, at the north end of Main Rd, is also a busy area, and it's here that most of the cheap hotels are situated.

Rinkingpong Rd heads south from Main Rd, the central artery through the town. Dambar Chowk, at the head of Main Rd, was originally known as Maharani Chowk, as it was adorned with a huge bronze statue of Queen Victoria. After the removal of the queen, a statue of the local leader of the Gorkha League, Dambar Singh, was erected in her place, but the plaque declaring 'Queen Victoria, Empress of India' remained in place, no doubt to the confusion and consternation of visitors to the town!

Market days are Wednesday and Saturday, a colourful spectacle as villagers from outlying regions bring their produce into town.

The main post office is on Rinkingpong Rd. It's open Monday to Friday from 9 am to 4 pm and Saturday until 3 pm. Parcels can be posted between 9 am and 1 pm. The Central Bank of India, at the north end of Main Rd, has a very efficient and speedy foreign exchange service, and accepts most major travellers' cheques.

There's a reasonable selection of English-language books, including books on the Eastern Himalaya, at Kashi Nath & Sons, Rishi Rd. There are a couple of other bookshops at this Dambar Chowk end of Rishi Rd.

Rooms in WBTC forest rest houses at Lava, Kaffer, Rangpo and Mongpong (see the Around Kalimpong section) can be booked at the Forest Development Corporation (☎ 55-783), in the Forestry Compound off Rinkingpong Rd. The office is open Monday to Friday from 10 am to 4.30 pm.

Trekking Outfits & Tour Operators Gurudongma Travels (☎ 55-204), Hill Top Rd, runs some very interesting adventure and ecology trips out of Kalimpong. There's a three day trek to the Samthar Plateau, 80 km from Kalimpong, with magnificent mountain scenery, and taking in traditional Lepcha, Bhutia and Thamang tribal villages. From the plateau, it is possible to descend into the Teesta Valley and cross the river on the 1½ km long Samco Ropeway (see the Around Kalimpong section), from where you can continue under your own steam to Gangtok or Darjeeling. Cost is from US$40 to US$45 per day, including pick up from Bagdogra or Siliguri to Kalimpong. Gurudongma can also offer support services to cycling groups, such as backup vehicles, meals, guides, and accommodation in tents and guesthouses. They also have 10 and 18 speed Indian-made mountain bikes for touring. As well, they conduct rhododendron tours (May).

Himalayan Travels (☎ 55-023), at the bus stand, runs half-day tours to points of interest around Kalimpong (Rs 500 by jeep).

Emergency Police: ☎ 55-268; Sub-Divisional Hospital: ☎ 55-254.

Temples

There's a small temple complex behind Main Rd (walk down the lane beside the State Bank of India). The **Thakurbari Temple** here was built over 100 years ago, while the newer section was built in 1982. Presiding deities are Shiva, Vishnu and Lakshmi.

The most important temple in Kalimpong is the **Mangal Dham** temple complex, near the Thongsa Gompa to the north of the town centre. It is sacred to Lord Krishna, and was completed in 1993 as a memorial to Kalimpong's most revered guru, Shri 108 Mangal Dasji Maharaj, whose *samadhi* (resting place) is at the temple. The temple is notable for its contemporary temple architecture, employing tonnes of white marble. Its large central sanctum features colourful scenes from the life of Krishna. Some of these feature Nijanandacharya Shri Dev Chandraji (1581-1655), who founded the Krishna Pranami cult, and of whom Mangal Dasji is considered an incarnation. Krishna can be seen effortlessly holding up the earth with his little finger, and in one scene, the guru is seen bearing Krishna on his head in a basket.

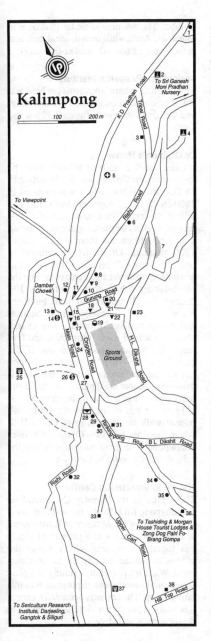

Kalimpong

0   100   200 m

To Sri Ganesh Moni Pradhan Nursery

To Viewpoint

Dambar Chowk

Sports Ground

To Tashiding & Morgan House Tourist Lodges & Zong Dog Palri Fo-Brang Gompa

To Sericulture Research Institute, Darjeeling, Gangtok & Siliguri

Gompas

Established in 1922, the **Tharpa Choeling Gompa** belongs to the Gelukpa order of Tibetan Buddhism, founded in Tibet in the 14th century, and of which the Dalai Lama is head. It's a 40 minute walk (uphill) from town; take the path to the right off KD Pradhan Rd, just before the Milk Collection and Extension Wing Building.

Lower down the hill, the Bhutanese

PLACES TO STAY

3	Deki Lodge
13	Gompu's Hotel & Restaurant
15	Lodge Himalshree
20	Classic Hotel
21	Janakee & Cozy Nook Lodges
23	Crown Lodge
31	Hotel Silver Oaks
33	Himalayan Hotel
36	Kalimpong Park Hotel
38	Gurudongma House & Travels

PLACES TO EAT

9	Lark's Provisions
16	New Restaurant
18	Mandarin Restaurant
22	Kalsang Restaurant

OTHER

1	Dr Graham's Home
2	Tharpa Choeling Gompa
4	Thongsa Gompa & Mangal Dham Temple
5	Hospital
6	Kanchan Cinema
7	Market
8	Railway Booking Office
10	Kashi Nath & Sons
11	Bhutia Shop
12	Kalimpong Arts & Crafts Co-Operative
14	Central Bank of India
17	Sikkim Nationalised Transport (SNT)
19	Bus & Jeep Stand
24	Mintri Transport
25	Thakurbari Temple
26	State Bank of India
27	Speedways
28	Main Post Office
29	Foreigners' Registration Office
30	Town Hall
32	Cinema
34	Forest Development Corporation & Nature Interpretation Centre
35	Rishi Bankim Park
37	Kali Mandir

WEST BENGAL HILLS

Thongsa Gompa is the oldest gompa in the area and was founded in 1692. The present building is a little more recent since the original was destroyed by the Gurkhas in their rampage across Sikkim before the arrival of the British. It's home to a small community of about 60 monks.

Zong Dog Palri Fo-Brang Gompa, five km south of the town centre at the end of the ridge, was founded in the mid-1970s by Dudjom Yeshi Dorje, the former head of the Nyingmapa order (he died in 1987), and was consecrated by the Dalai Lama. The walls of the prayer room are richly (and completely) covered in vibrant frescoes executed by a Tibetan artist residing in Darjeeling, and the ceiling is embellished with large *mandalas* (circular paintings depicting the universe). Close to the ceiling can be seen the 25 disciples of Padmasambhava, the founder of the Nyingmapa order, each inhabiting a stuccoed cave, and engaged in different miraculous feats, such as flying through the sun's rays and bringing the dead to life. Suspended from the ceiling are some magnificent thangkas.

In an upstairs room is an intricate wooden model of the palace of Guru Rinpoche, Zangdok Palri. It includes tiny figures of lamas blowing *radungs*, long-stemmed Tibetan horns, and statues of Padmasambhava and Chenresig, the Buddhist deity of compassion. (The Dalai Lama is believed by Buddhists to be an incarnation of Chenresig.) There is also a **three dimensional mandala**, one of only three in the world (the others are in Taiwan, and in Spiti in Himachal Pradesh). A larger statue of Chenresig is enshrined in this room. It is depicted with 1000 arms, each of which has an eye in the palm of the hand.

Flower Nurseries

Kalimpong is an important orchid-growing area and flowers are exported here to cities in India and overseas. All the nurseries belong to one family, and apart from orchids, also produce 80% of India's gladioli, as well as cacti. The Sri Ganesh Moni Pradhan Nursery and the Udai Mani Pradhan Nursery are among the most important in the area. There's a flower festival in Kalimpong in

October. The best time to see the gladioli is in March and April, while orchids are at their best in the winter months (December-February).

Sericulture Research Institute

This institute, where silkworms are bred and silk is produced, is on the road to Darjeeling, and welcomes visitors between 9.30 am and 4 pm.

Dr Graham's Home

It takes less than an hour to walk from the town centre up through stands of bamboo to Dr Graham's Home, which was founded in 1900 on the lower slopes of Deolo Hill. The school was established to educate the children of workers on the tea gardens. It started with six children, but there are now about 1300 students. Originally encompassing only 50 acres (20 hectares), the beautiful grounds, spread over an extensive area on the south-facing ridge, now encompass 193 hectares. Enrolment is open to all, but there is a reserve quota for children from economically deprived backgrounds. The chapel above the school dates from 1925, and features fine stained-glass windows. If the caretaker is around, he'll open it for visitors. Visitors are welcome to visit the fine turn-of-the-century school building, and many people bring a picnic lunch to eat in the grounds.

From the school itself, it is a further 40 minute walk to the summit of Deolo Hill, where there are fine views back down over Kalimpong. The three reservoirs below the school provide water to the town

Nature Interpretation Centre

This centre in the Forestry Compound on Rinkingpong Rd is run by the Soil Conservation Division of the Ministry of Environment & Forests. It consists of a number of nicely put together dioramas which depict the effects of human activity on the environment. While it's not wildly exciting, it's good to see public-awareness displays such as this being set up. The centre is open daily, except Thursday, from 10 am to 1.30 pm, and 2 to 4 pm; admission is free.

Places to Stay – bottom end

Gompu's Hotel (☎ 55-818), on Dambar Chowk, at the north end of Main Rd, has pleasantly rustic wooden singles/doubles/triples for Rs 100/200/300 with attached bath. Hot water is free in buckets.

The *Lodge Himalshree* (☎ 55-070) is a small place on the third floor of a building on Ongden Rd. It's run by a friendly family, and rooms are plain, but spotless. Doubles/triples are Rs 120/200 with common bath, or there's a triple with attached bath for Rs 250. There's no running water here, but hot and cold water is supplied in buckets.

One of the most popular places to stay with travellers is the *Deki Lodge* (☎ 55-095), on Tripai Rd (off Rishi Rd, about 10 minutes walk north of the bus stand). There is a range of singles/doubles, from Rs 70/150 with common bath, to Rs 90/250 with attached bath (cold water). There's also a triple room with attached bath and geyser for Rs 350. The common bathroom has hot showers. Rustic doubles in the wooden annexe behind the guesthouse are Rs 150 with attached bath. This place is run by a friendly family, and they're a good source of information on treks in the area. A 10% discount is offered in the off season.

There are a number of very basic places around the bus stand. *Janakee Lodge* (☎ 55-479) has spartan but clean rooms which vary in price according to which floor they are located on; those on the 1st floor are cheaper. Single/double/triple prices range from Rs 130/200/260 with common bath, to Rs 180/270/360 with attached bath. A 30% discount is offered in the off season. Hot water is free in buckets.

In a small cul-de-sac around the corner from the Janakee is the *Classic Hotel* (☎ 56-335), with singles/doubles for Rs 120/220 with attached bath (running cold water). Rooms are small, but some have good valley views. There's an extensive Chinese and Indian menu in the downstairs restaurant. The *Cosy Nook Lodge* (☎ 55-541) has singles/doubles for Rs 100/200. Rooms are fine, but there's no running hot or cold water, and privacy here is not what it could be.

The *Crown Lodge* (☎ 55-846) is on Murgihatta Rd, a few metres off HL Dikshit Rd. It's quiet, spacious and clean, and has singles/doubles for Rs 200/350 with attached bath with geysers (hot water in the morning only). A good discount is offered in the off season, and double rooms have B&W TV. Towels and soap are provided and there's free bed tea. Some of the rooms have pleasant views out over the playing ground.

Places to Stay – middle

The few mid-range places are all out of the town centre to the south, along Rinkingpong Rd. Pick of the bunch is the *Kalimpong Park Hotel* (☎ 55-304). Singles/doubles are Rs 450/550, or double deluxe rooms are Rs 600. There is also a double suite for Rs 900. All rooms have attached baths with hot showers. The double deluxe rooms are in the original building, which was once the summer residence of the Maharaja of Dinajpur; room 5 has beautiful views of Kangchenjunga and Deolo Hill. Most of the other rooms are in the 20 year old annexe behind the hotel, which is quite comfortable, although not sumptuous.

The Government of West Bengal Tourist Office has two places further out along the same road. They are also in old colonial bungalows, and have nice gardens and views, but can be a hassle to get to without your own transport. The nicer of the two is the *Morgan House Tourist Lodge* (☎ 55-384), about three km from the town centre. It's a beautiful old ivy-covered Victorian building with leaded windows and a sweeping driveway. Ordinary singles/doubles are Rs 450/825, and there are larger doubles for Rs 925 and Rs 1250. All rooms have attached baths and hot showers, and rates include meals and bed tea. The hotel is in a wonderful position on the top of a ridge with valleys falling away on either side. Above the hotel is Gouripur House, where Rabindranath Tagore lived and wrote a number of his poems. On his birthday in 1938, he recited his poem *Janmadin* from here over the telephone to a Calcutta radio station.

A cobblestone path through a magnificent

flower garden leads from Morgan House to the adjacent WBTC *Tashiding Tourist Lodge* (☎ 55-929). Singles are Rs 480 and Rs 510, and doubles are Rs 875, including all meals. The rooms have a lovely outlook but are fairly basically furnished. A discount is offered at both these places in the off season.

A lovely quiet place to stay is *Guru-dongma House* (☎ 55-204), on Hill Top Rd. It's about two km from the centre of Kalimpong, but General Jimmy Singh will pick up guests from the town centre. Singles/doubles are Rs 600/800, or three to four person tents are Rs 100. There's a lovely garden here, and rooms are in private cottages with pine trimmings and low Japanese futon-style beds. There are also rooms inside the main house. Meals are available here.

Places to Stay – top end

If you have the money, there's no better place to stay in Kalimpong than the beautiful old *Himalayan Hotel* (☎ 55-248; fax 55-122), on Upper Cart Rd, about 300m up the hill past the post office. The hotel is surrounded by superb gardens featuring camellias, azaleas, orchids and poinsettias, and there are views across to the snow-covered peaks of Kangchenjunga. It features old-world furnishings and is a great place to stay. Room-only rates are Rs 800/1100 plus 10% tax, and there are also full-board rates.

The modern *Hotel Silver Oaks* (☎ 55-296) is on Rinkingpong Rd, about 100m uphill from the post office. There's 24 hour room service and foreign-exchange facilities. All rooms have views, either of the valley or Kangchenjunga, and are furnished in an old-world style with heavy bureaus and dressers. Rates are US$59/71/97, and there's a good restaurant and a bar here.

Places to Eat

Kalimpong lollipops are a local speciality. They were originally produced at the Swiss dairy, which was established by Jesuit fathers, but the fathers have returned to Switzerland and the dairy is now closed. Nevertheless, the tradition continues with these sweet caramel confections, and you can buy them in most grocery shops. Cheese is still made by locals who trained under the priests. Kalimpong cheese is similar to cheddar, but a bit more tart. You can sample it at Lark's Provisions, Rishi Rd. Cost is Rs 100 per kg.

Most places to eat close early in Kalimpong, and you'll have trouble getting a bite to eat after 9 pm, particularly in the off season. *New Restaurant* is a tiny little eatery at the north end of Main Rd serving very good steamed momos (Rs 8). The *Kalsang Restaurant*, Link Rd (behind Cosy Nook Lodge), is a lovely rustic little place run by friendly Tibetans. Butter tea is Rs 3, and pork ghaytuk is Rs 14.

One of the best places to eat in town is the *Mandarin Restaurant*, at the bus stand. The speciality is Mandarin fish (Rs 35), but you'll need to order it two hours in advance. Other tasty dishes include fried chicken balls (Rs 52) and Chinese roast pork (Rs 40). A large pot of jasmine tea is Rs 25.

The dining hall at *Gompu's Hotel*, Dambar Chowk, has very good chicken wanton soup (Rs 30), and a beer here will set you back Rs 40.

Nonguests are welcome to dine at the *Himalayan Hotel*. Breakfast is Rs 70, and lunch and dinner are Rs 150. Advance notice is required.

Things to Buy

The Bhutia Shop, Dambar Chowk, is run by the friendly Mr K Shila Bhutia, and stocks traditional Bhutia crafts such as woodcarvings, as well as pastel paintings, embroidered bags and other items.

Kalimpong tapestry bags and purses, copperware, scrolls and paintings from Dr Graham's Home are sold at the Kalimpong Arts & Crafts Co-Operative, which was founded by Dr Graham's wife, Katherine Graham. The co-op is behind Dambar Chowk and is open Monday to Friday from 10 am to 3 pm, and until noon on Saturday. Shops selling Tibetan jewellery and artefacts can be found in the streets to the east of Dambar Chowk.

Getting There & Away

Air Bagdogra is the closest airport, 12 km from Siliguri on the plains. Mintri Transport (☎ 55-741), Main Rd, is the agent for Jet Airways, Indian Airlines and Royal Nepal Airlines (the last for flights to Kathmandu from Bhadrapur, over the border in Nepal). Speedways (☎ 55-074), further south down Main Rd, can book flights from Bhadrapur and Biratnagar to Kathmandu with Necon Air.

Bus Mintri Transport operates a daily bus to Bagdogra (three hours, Rs 100). There are numerous booking agents at the bus stand, including Sammy's Corner Bus Booking Office (☎ 55-861), with a daily bus at 12.30 pm to Darjeeling (3½ hours, Rs 30), and buses to Siliguri departing every 30 minutes between 6.30 am and 4 pm (three hours, Rs 23).

Purnima Tours & Travels (☎ 56-193) also has services to Siliguri, as well as to Gangtok (four hours, Rs 30). Himalayan Travels (☎ 55-023) has a service to Kaffer (4½ hours, Rs 25) at 1 pm daily; and Samco Ropeway (1½ hours, Rs 15).

Sikkim Nationalised Transport (SNT) is at the west end of the bus stand. The office is open daily between 8 am and 3 pm. If the road is clear, the journey to Gangtok will take about four hours. If a detour is required, it could take up to five hours. Tickets are Rs 30.

Bhutan From Kalimpong it is possible to visit Phuntsholing, just over the Bhutanese border, without a visa. There's a daily bus to Jaigaon, on the Indian side of the border, which leaves at 8.40 am (six hours, Rs 40). There are hotels and guesthouses at Phuntsholing, but not Jaigaon.

Train There's a railway booking agency (☎ 55-643) on Mani Rd, a tiny lane below Rishi Rd, behind the Lion's Reading Room. It's open for bookings daily from 10 am to 1 pm and 4 to 5 pm.

Jeep There are regular share-jeep departures for Gangtok. The trip takes 2½ hours, and costs Rs 55. They leave when full, generally between 7 am and 3 pm. A private jeep to

Gangtok will cost Rs 550, and to Siliguri, Rs 500. To reserve a jeep for Lava will cost Rs 500, and to Kaffer, Rs 1200.

AROUND KALIMPONG
Lava & Kaffer

At 2353m, about 30 km east of Kalimpong, Lava is a small village with a small **gompa**, which belongs to the Kagyupa order. Tuesday is market day, and a good time to visit. The tip of Kangchenjunga is visible from Kaffer, at 1555m, and is best viewed at sunrise. There are forest rest houses at both Lava and Kaffer (Rs 450 for doubles; hot water provided in buckets). Also at Kaffer is the *Yankee Resort*, with singles/doubles for Rs 150/250. Buses and jeeps ply regularly between Kalimpong and Lava.

Mongpong

Between Kalimpong and Siliguri, via a bypass off the main road near Coronation Bridge, is Mongpong. The *Forest Rest House* here is set beside a meandering length of the Teesta River. Doubles are Rs 450. It's possible to take elephant safaris here. All of these forest rest houses can be booked at the Forest Development Corporation (☎ (03592) 55-783) in Kalimpong. See under Orientation & Information in that section for details.

Rafting It's possible to tackle the rapids of the Teesta here on rafting expeditions, between 15 November and 15 February.

Samthar Plateau

About 80 km from Kalimpong is the Samthar Plateau, which can be used as a base to visit tribal villages in the environs. Gurudongma Travels (☎ (03592) 55-204) (see the Kalimpong section) has cabins here at the *Farm House Inn* for Rs 200 for singles, or Rs 400/500 in cottages, or deluxe singles/doubles for Rs 600/800. There are also three to four person alpine tents for Rs 100 per person.

Samco Ropeway

Thrill seekers should head for the Samco Ropeway, a chairlift installed by the Swedish as part of an aid programme to help villagers cross the Teesta River. If the idea of dangling from a piece of wire 30m above the water doesn't entice, then give this a miss – it's definitely not for vertigo sufferers! The ropeway is on the main Siliguri to Gangtok road, at a place known locally as 27th mile. A bus to the ropeway from Kalimpong will take 1½ hours and cost Rs 15.

KURSEONG
Population: 18,000
Telephone Area Code: 03554

Kurseong, at an elevation of 2458m, is 30 km south of Darjeeling. The name is probably derived from the Lepcha word, *kurson-rip*, a reference to the small white orchid prolific in this area. There are several good walks in the environs of the town, including that to Eagle's Crag, which affords fine views down over the Teesta and the southern plains. The toy train passes right through the heart of the town, and this is a good place to break the journey en route to or from Darjeeling.

A Canadian priest by the name of Father Abraham has set up an innovative programme here to teach villagers how to grow vegetables with the least disturbance to the environment using greenhouses. It is financed by a sponsorship programme whereby Canadians are foregoing their puddings and donating the equivalent amount of money to fund the project.

There are several places to stay including the *Tourist Lodge* (☎ 44-409), with doubles for Rs 450 in the new annexe, and Rs 250 and Rs 300 in the original building. There's a restaurant here, and discounts are offered in the off season. Doubles at the *Amarjeel Hotel*, on Hill Cart Rd, are Rs 200, and there's a bar here. The *Shyam Hotel*, on Dr Kumar Rd, has doubles/triples for Rs 80/130. At the *Luxury Hotel*, at 72 TN Rd, singles/doubles/triples are Rs 125/175/250, and there's a restaurant here.

Regular buses run to Darjeeling (1½ hours, Rs 14); Siliguri (2½ hours, Rs 18); and Mirik (three hours, Rs 28). The toy train from Siliguri to Kurseong takes four hours and 2nd/1st class costs Rs 9/33.

Sikkim

Until 1975, Sikkim, or New House, was an independent kingdom, albeit under a treaty which allowed the Indian government to control Sikkim's foreign affairs and defence. However, following a period of political crises and riots in the capital, Gangtok, India annexed the country and Sikkim became the 22nd Indian state by the 38th Amendment Act of the Indian constitution.

The move sparked widespread criticism, but tensions have now cooled. The central government has been spending relatively large sums of money to subsidise Sikkim's road building, electrification, water supply and agricultural and industrial development. Much of this activity was no doubt motivated by India's fear of Chinese military designs on the Himalayan region. Even today, there's still a lot of military activity along the route from Siliguri to Gangtok.

For many years, Sikkim was regarded as one of the last Himalayan 'Shangri-las' because of its remoteness, spectacular mountain terrain, varied flora and fauna and ancient Buddhist *gompas* (monasteries). It was never easy to visit, and, even now, you need a special permit to enter, although this is easy to obtain (see the Permits section later in this chapter). All the same, access to the eastern part of Sikkim along the Tibetan border remains highly restricted, and trekking to the base of Kangchenjunga revered throughout Sikkim as the guardian of the land, has to be organised through a recognised travel agency. Compared with other parts of the country, tourism in Sikkim is in its infancy.

The current population of Sikkim is approximately 18% Lepcha and 75% Nepali; the other 7% are Bhutias and Indians from various northern states. About 60% of the population is Hindu and 28% is Buddhist, although the two religions exist, as in many parts of Nepal, in a syncretic form. The ancient Buddhist gompas, of which there are a great many, are one of the principal attractions of a visit to Sikkim.

Highlights
The main attractions of Sikkim are undoubtedly its stunning gompas. These include Rumtek, the seat of the head of the Kagyupa order of Tibetan Buddhism, only 24 km from Gangtok, and the Enchey Gompa, in Gangtok itself. In West Sikkim is the extraordinarily ornate Pemayangtse Gompa, accessible from Pelling, and the less ostentatious but still beautiful gompas of Tashiding and Sangachoeling.

There are fine treks in the Dzongri region of West Sikkim from the roadhead at Yuksom, and Sikkim's rhododendrons and orchids are renowned among botanists and flower enthusiasts. Gangtok hosts an international flower festival annually, between March and May. ■

HISTORY

The country was originally home to the Lepchas, a tribal people thought to have migrated from the hills of Assam around the 13th century, although some scholars have suggested that they may have migrated from South-East Asia. The Lepchas were pacifist forest foragers and small-crop cultivators who worshipped nature spirits. They still constitute some 18% of the total population of Sikkim, though their ability to lead their traditional lifestyle has been severely limited by emigration from Tibet and Nepal.

The Tibetans started to immigrate into Sikkim during the 15th and 16th centuries to escape religious strife between various Buddhist orders. In Tibet itself, the Gelukpa order (of which the Dalai Lama is the head) gradually gained the upper hand. In Sikkim, the Nyingmapa order was introduced by three Tibetan lamas, Lhatsun Chempo, Kathok Rikzin Chempo and Ngadak Sempa Chempo. It was these lamas who consecrated the first *chogyal* or king, Phuntsog Namgyal, at Yuksom, which became the capital of the kingdom (it was later moved to Rabdentse, near Pelling). In the face of the waves of Tibetan immigrants, the Lepchas retreated to the more remote regions. A blood brotherhood was eventually forged between their leader, Thekong Tek, and the Bhutia leader, Khye-Bumsa, and spiritual and temporal authority was imposed on the anarchistic Lepchas.

When the kingdom of Sikkim was founded, the country included the area encompassed by the present state as well as part of Eastern Nepal, the Chumbi Valley (Tibet), Ha Valley (Bhutan) and the Terai foothills down to the plains of India, including Darjeeling and Kalimpong.

Between 1717 and 1734, during the reign of Sikkim's fourth chogyal, a series of wars fought with the Bhutanese resulted in the loss of much territory in the southern foothills, including Kalimpong, then a very important bazaar town on the trade route between Tibet and India. More territory was lost after 1780 following the Gurkha invasion from Nepal, though the invaders were eventually checked by a Chinese army with Bhutanese and Lepcha assistance. Unable to advance into Tibet, the Gurkhas turned south where they came into conflict with the British East India Company. The wars between the two parties ended in the treaty of 1817 which delineated the borders of Nepal. The Gurkhas also ceded to the British all the Sikkimese territory they had taken; a substantial part was returned to the chogyal of Sikkim in return for British control of all disputes between Sikkim and its neighbours. The country thus became a buffer state between Nepal, Tibet and Bhutan.

In 1835, the British, seeking a hill station as a rest and recreation centre for their troops and officials, persuaded the chogyal to cede the Darjeeling area in return for an annual stipend. The Tibetans objected to this transfer of territory. They continued to regard Sikkim as a vassal state, and Darjeeling's rapid growth as a trade centre had begun to

A man of Lepcha origin. The Lepchas were the original inhabitants of Sikkim.

make a considerable impact on the fortunes of Sikkim's leading lamas and merchants.

Tensions rose and, in 1849, a high-ranking British official and a botanist, who were exploring the Lachen regions with the permission of both the Sikkim chogyal and the British government, were arrested. Although the two prisoners were unconditionally released a month later following threats of intervention, the British annexed the entire area between the present Sikkimese border and the Indian plains and withdrew the chogyal's stipend (the stipend was eventually restored to his son).

Further British interference in the affairs of this area lead to the declaration of a protectorate over Sikkim in 1861 and the delineation of its borders. The Tibetans, however, continued to regard these actions as illegal and, in 1886, invaded Sikkim to reassert their authority. The attack was repulsed by the British, who sent a punitive military expedition to Lhasa in 1888 in retaliation. The powers of the Sikkimese chogyal were further reduced and high-handed treatment by British officials prompted him to flee to Lhasa in 1892, though he was eventually persuaded to return.

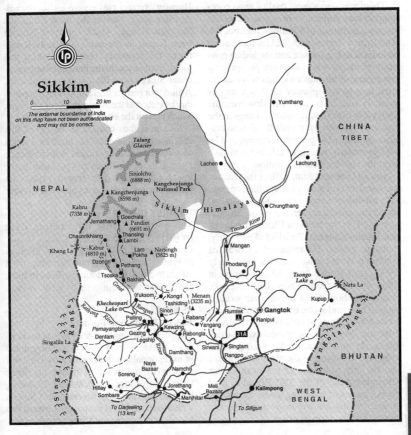

Keen to develop Sikkim, the British encouraged emigration from Nepal, as they had done in Darjeeling, and a considerable amount of land was brought under rice and cardamom cultivation. This influx of labour continued until the 1960s and, as a result, the Nepalese now make up approximately 75% of the population of Sikkim. The subject of immigration became a topic of heated debate in the late 60s and the chogyal was constrained to prohibit further immigration. New laws regarding the rights of citizenship were designed to placate those of non-Nepalese origin, but they served to inflame the opposition parties.

There was also a great deal of grass-roots support for a popular form of government as opposed to the rule of Sikkim by the chogyal. The British treaties with Sikkim had passed to India at independence and the Indian government had no wish to be seen propping up the regime of an autocratic raja while doing their best to sweep away the last traces of princely rule in India itself. However, the chogyal resisted demands for a change in the method of government until the demonstrations threatened to get out of control and he was eventually forced to ask India to take over the country's administration.

In a 1975 referendum, 97% of the electorate voted for union with India, with Congress (I)'s candidate, Lendup Dorje Kazi, installed as the first chief minister. Following an election in 1979, Nar Bahadur Bhandari, head of the Sikkim Sangram Parishad (SSP) party, came to power. He remained as head of Sikkim's democratic congress until early 1994 (apart from a brief, 13-day period in 1984 when BB Gurung was chief minister), when allegations of corruption were levelled against him, and a vote of no confidence was passed. For a brief interim period, an ally of Bhandari, Sancha Man, crossed over to Congress (I) and became the acting chief minister. However, in the state election six months later, he lost the job to Pawan Kumar Chamling, head of the SSP. Bhandari now faces charges of acquiring assets disproportionate to his known sources of income during his first term of office.

GEOGRAPHY

Wedged between Tibet to the north and north-east, West Bengal and Bhutan to the south and south-east respectively, and Nepal to the west is the tiny state of Sikkim. In the north lies the Greater Himalayan peaks, including the third-highest mountain in the world, Kangchenjunga (8598m). From this northern region the snow-fed waters of the Lachen and Lachung wend their way southwards, before meeting with the Teesta, which, together with the Rangeet, forms the southern boundary, separating Sikkim from northern West Bengal to the south.

From the formidable massifs of the Greater Himalaya project two enormous southward-thrusting spurs: that to the west forms the Singalila Range, which separates Sikkim from Nepal; to the east, the Chola Range forms the boundary between Sikkim and Tibet. Further south, the Pangola Range separates Sikkim from Bhutan to the south-east. A third spur pierces the heart of Tibet, separating the valleys of the Teesta and Rangeet rivers, which meet at the southern end of the ridge.

Sikkim is thus cradled in the lap of this enormous amphitheatre, enclosed by a series of ever-diminishing ridges which recede towards the plains of north-west India. In the lower elevations, river-forged valleys lie only a few hundred metres above sea level.

TOURIST OFFICES

The helpful tourist information desk (☎ (011) 301-5346) at New Sikkim House, Chanakyapuri, New Delhi is open Monday to Friday, and every second Saturday, from 10 am to 5 pm. Other tourist offices in India are listed in the Permits section, following.

PERMITS
Tourist & Trekking Permits

The permitted length of stay in Sikkim is 15 days; an extension of 15 days will be granted in exceptional circumstances only (ie don't count on it), and are issued through the Home Office, Government of Sikkim, Tashiding Secretariat, Gangtok. Re-entry into Sikkim within three months is not possible, even if you leave Sikkim before your 15 day permit expires.

With a standard tourist permit you may visit Gangtok, Rumtek, Phodang and Pemayangtse. However, you must stick to the National Highway; you can't deviate from the main routes between centres designated on your permit.

While permits can be obtained through the Indian embassy in your home country when you apply for your Indian visa, they are best obtained in India itself. In India, permits for Sikkim can be obtained either while you wait or within a few hours. You will need your passport and one photo (colour or B&W), plus a photocopy of the front page of your passport (ie with expiry details, etc), and the page on which is stamped your Indian visa; there's no charge. When applying for your permit, you must specify your date of entry into the state. A special endorsement (available from the permit office in Gangtok or the Gangtok Home Office) allows you to visit areas around Pemayangtse, including Khecheopari Lake and Tashiding Gompa.

Permits for Tsongo Lake (valid for a day visit only) and Yumthang (in North Sikkim; a nonextendible five day/four night permit) can only be obtained from the permit office in Gangtok, but as you must join a tour (minimum of four) to visit these two places, it's best to let the travel agency sort out the paper work for you.

The only area open in Sikkim for trekking is in the Dzongri area of West Sikkim. Trekking permits are in addition to the normal tourist permit and are issued at the permit office in Gangtok, or from the Government of Sikkim Tourist Information Centre in New Delhi (see below). To get one, you must be part of a group of at least four people and have made a booking for a trek with a recognised travel agent. The government will arrange for a liaison officer/guide to accompany you. You cannot simply go trekking in this region alone, or without a booking or trekking permit.

For areas not included in the regular tourist or trekking permits, apply to the Ministry of Home Affairs, Grih Mantralaya, New Delhi, 11003. Each application will be considered on its own merits.

Permits are checked and your passport stamped when entering or leaving Sikkim, and at Legship and Yuksom.

Permits can be obtained from any of the following places:

Foreigners' Registration Offices
    Delhi, Mumbai (Bombay), Calcutta, Madras, Darjeeling; see the Facts for the Visitor chapter
Resident Commissioner
    Government of Sikkim, 14 Panchsheel Marg, Chanakyapuri, New Delhi (☎ (011) 301-5346)
Sikkim Tourism Information Centre
    4C Poonam, 5/2 Russel St, Calcutta (☎ (033) 29-7516)
Sikkim Tourist Information Centre
    SNT Bus Compound, Tenzing Norgay Rd, Siliguri, West Bengal (☎ (0353) 43-2646)

Kangchenjunga National Park

Access into the heart of Kangchenjunga National Park, including the vast Zemu Glacier, is generally only permitted to mountaineering expeditions or experienced trekking parties. For permission, you'll need to contact the Indian Embassy in your home country, or apply direct to the Government of India, Ministry of Home Affairs, Grih Mantralaya, New Delhi 11003. If permission is granted, the ministry will contact the Sikkim state government, who will arrange a liaison officer for the expedition. After the permit has been granted, the expedition party needs to obtain permission from the Chief Wildlife Warden, Government of Sikkim, Forest Department, Deorali, Gangtok, Sikkim. This is just a formality, and can be done either before entering Sikkim, or on arrival in Gangtok. Arrangements need to be made through a recognised travel agent; in Gangtok, reputable agents include Tashila Tours & Travels, Sikkim World Expeditions and Yuksam Tours & Travels. See Trekking Outfits and Tour Operators in the Gangtok section for further details.

Mountaineering expeditions interested in climbing peaks over 6000m need to obtain clearance from the Indian Mountaineering Foundation (IMF) (☎ (011) 67-1211; fax 688-3412), Benito Juarez Rd, Anand Niketan, New Delhi 110021.

Festivals of Sikkim
The focus of festivals in Sikkim is Tibetan Buddhism, although the Lepchas and Nepalese Hindus also celebrate certain events. There are also festivals to celebrate the flowering of Sikkim's orchids.

March-April
Bhumchu – This festival is celebrated at Tashiding Gompa in West Sikkim on the 15th day of the first month (March). More information can be found in the Tashiding section. At Khecheopari Lake, devotees make offerings of flowers, fruit and butter lamps.

March-May
International Flower Festival – Held naturally to correspond with the best flowering of Sikkim's orchids, this festival takes place in Gangtok. Other species, including gladioli, rhododendrons and magnolias, are also on display.

April-May
Sikkim Festival – Held in the White Hall at Gangtok in late April/early May, the main focus of this festival is a flower show at which orchids are the chief attraction.

May-June
Saga Dawa – This 'triple blessed festival' is to celebrate Buddha's birth, attainment of buddhahood and of *nirvana* (final release from the cycle of existence). Processions of monks carrying sacred scriptures proceed through the streets of Gangtok and other towns. Saga Dawa falls on the full moon of the fourth lunar month (late May or early June).

June-July
Tse Chu – This important *chaam* (lama dance) depicts the life of Padmasambhava. It takes place at Rumtek Gompa in Sikkim on the 10th day of the fifth month of the Tibetan lunar calendar (July).

July-August
Drukpa Teshi – This festival is to celebrate the first teaching given by the Buddha. It is held on the fourth day of the sixth month (August) of the Tibetan lunar calendar.

August-September
Panglhapsol – This is a uniquely Sikkimese festival, as it is devoted to Kangchenjunga, the guardian deity of Sikkim, and to Yabdu, the 'supreme commander' of Kangchenjunga. The festival is celebrated with dramatic dances, with Kangchenjunga represented by a red mask ringed by five human skulls, and Yabdu by a black mask. Dancing warriors in Sikkimese battledress with helmets, shields and swords, also participate. The highlight of the dance is the entrance of Mahakala (the protector of the Dharma or Buddhist path), who instructs Kangchenjunga and Yabdu to ensure that Sikkim remains peaceful and prosperous. It falls on the 15th day of the seventh month of the Tibetan lunar calendar (late August or early September).

The mask of Kangchenjunga, the guardian deity of Sikkim.

SIKKIM

October-November

Dasain – This is the Nepali Hindus' version of north Indian Dussehra, Delhi's Ram Lila and West Bengal's Durga Puja. It falls in October, and is also the main holiday period. At this time accommodation and transport, particularly in Gangtok and Darjeeling, are in high demand.

Teohar – This three day festival of lights is celebrated 15 days after Dasain.

January-February

Chaam – Lama dances are conducted at Enchey Gompa in Gangtok on the 18th and 19th days of the 12th month of the Tibetan lunar calendar (January).

Kagyat Dance – Held on the 28th and 29th days of the 12th month of the Tibetan lunar calendar (February), this dance festival symbolises the destruction of evil forces. The dances are performed by monks in the gompa courtyard. Prayers are held before the dance. The main centre for the dance is the Tsuk-La-Khang (Royal Chapel) in Gangtok, but dances are also held at Pemayangtse and Phodang gompas.

Losong – This is the Sikkimese New Year, and it falls in the last week of February. It is known as Namsoong by the Lepchas, and is also called Sonam Losar (Farmers' New Year), as it falls around harvest time.

February-March

Losar – This is the Tibetan new year, and two days prior to it, dances are performed by the monks at Pemayangtse and Rumtek gompas. It falls in early March. ■

East Sikkim

Due to its proximity to the Tibetan border, entry to most of East Sikkim by foreigners is prohibited. However, this region does encompass the capital, Gangtok, which is included on the standard tourist permit. Within the city and its immediate environs are some fascinating places to visit, including Rumtek Gompa, 24 km to the west, the head of the Kagyupa order of Tibetan Buddhism.

GANGTOK

Population: 82,000
Telephone Area Code: 03592

The capital of Sikkim, Gangtok (which means 'hilltop'), occupies the west side of a long ridge flanking the Ranipul River. The scenery is spectacular and there are excellent views of the entire Kangchenjunga Range from many points in the environs of the city.

Many people expect Gangtok to be a smaller version of Kathmandu. It's not, but it is an interesting and pleasant place to stay. Gangtok only became the capital in the mid-1800s (previous capitals were at Yuksom and Rabdentse) and the town has undergone rapid modernisation in recent years.

Gangtok has also become something of a hill station resort for holidaying Bengalis. The influx peaks during the 10 day Durga Puja holiday period at the end of September or early October, when Bengalis converge on the town en masse from the plains. It's a good time to give Gangtok a miss as prices rise – especially for accommodation and local transport – and finding a room at *any* price can be a major headache.

Orientation

To the north is Enchey Gompa and the telecommunications tower. The palace of the former chogyal and the impressive Royal Chapel (the Tsuk-La-Khang) are lower down along the ridge. Nearby is the huge Tashiding, or Secretariat complex, and, below it, the relatively recently built Legislative Assembly, both executed in a traditional architectural style.

On a continuation of this ridge but much lower is the Namgyal Institute of Tibetology,

SIKKIM

an Orchid Sanctuary and, not far beyond the institute, a large *chorten* (Tibetan stupa) and adjoining gompa.

All the main facilities – hotels, cafes, bazaars, bus stand, post office, tourist information centre and the Foreigners' Registration Office – are either on, or very near, the main Darjeeling road (National Highway 31A).

Information

Tourist Office The helpful tourist office is at the top (north) end of MG Marg. It's open in the season daily, including holidays, from 8.30 am to 7 pm, and between June and August, Monday to Saturday from 10 am to 4 pm.

Money Most travellers' cheques can be exchanged at the State Bank of India annexe, behind the tourist office.

Post & Communications The main post office is on Paljor Stadium Rd, just past the Hotel Tibet. It's open Monday to Saturday from 9 am to 12.30 pm, and 1 to 5 pm. Parcels can be posted on weekdays from 9 am to 2 pm, and on Saturday, until noon. The telegraph office is in the same building.

Bookshops & Newsagencies The Gangtok General Store Bookshop, on MG Marg, opposite the tourist office, and Jainco Booksellers, diagonally opposite, both have a good range of English-language titles, with books relevant to Sikkim and the eastern Himalaya. You can get English-language national dailies (the day after publication) at either of these places, and the locally printed *Searchlight*, *Sikkim Express*, *Sikkim Observer* and *Gangtok Times* are all published weekly.

Permits Trekking permits for West Sikkim (ie north of Yuksom) can be obtained from the permit office in the same building as the tourist office. It's open Monday to Saturday from 10 am to 4 pm. To visit Tsongo Lake or North Sikkim, you need to be in a group of four and book a package through a travel agency; agencies will arrange requisite permits. Extensions (issued in exceptional circumstances only) can be applied for at the

Home Office, Government of Sikkim, Tashiding Secretariat, Gangtok.

Permits for Fambonglho Wildlife Sanctuary, 25 km from Gangtok, can be obtained from the District Forest Officer (☎ 23-191), Forest Secretariat, Deorali, Gangtok. It's also possible to book accommodation in the park precincts here. See under Fambonglho Wildlife Sanctuary for more details.

For more information on permits for Sikkim, see the permits section at the beginning of this chapter.

Trekking Outfits & Tour Operators There are a number of travel agencies on Paljor Stadium Rd, opposite the Hotel Tibet. Siniolchu Tours & Travels (☎ 24-457; fax ('att: Siniolchu') 22-707) has the usual Tsongo Lake tour (US$12), an Around Gangtok sunrise tour (US$20) and a day tour to Rumtek Gompa and the Eppica Gardens, also for US$20 per person. They also have tours to North Sikkim (Yumthang), and can arrange permits. The cost is US$50 per person for one night/two days, or US$75 for two nights/three days.

There's a four day cultural tour to the gompas of Sikkim, including Pemayangtse, Rumtek, Phodang, Labrang and Sangachoeling. Accommodation is in tents, and food is extra. The cost is US$120, and a minimum of four people is required.

A one day rafting trip on the Teesta River including lunch and transfers, is US$50, or the overnight trip, with accommodation in tents (sleeping bags provided) is US$65. There's also a budget rafting trip for US$20 for 2½ hours, but transfers and meals are not included.

Tours to North Sikkim, including the recently opened Yumthang Valley, can also be booked through Sikkim World Expeditions (☎ 23-494; fax 24-195), Zero Point, National Highway 31A, Blue Sky Tours & Travels (☎ 23-330), on Tibet Rd, opposite the Hotel Lhakpa, and Yuksam Tours & Travels, National Highway 31A. The cost is around US$50 per person per day, and includes accommodation in huts at Yakshey.

Potala Tours & Travels (☎ 22-041) on

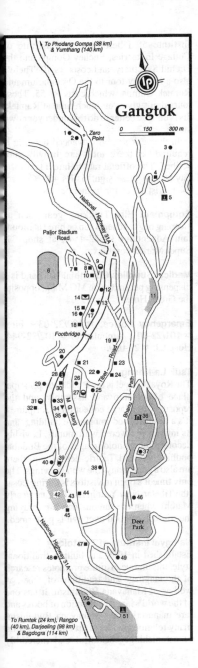

Gangtok

0   150   300 m

To Phodang Gompa (38 km) & Yumthang (140 km)

Zero Point

National Highway 31A

Paljor Stadium Road

Footbridge

Tibet Road

M G Marg

Bhanu Path

National Highway 31A

Deer Park

To Rumtek (24 km), Rangpo (40 km), Darjeeling (98 km) & Bagdogra (114 km)

PLACES TO STAY

4	Siniolchu Lodge
7	Nor-Khill Hotel
8	Hotel Mount View
10	Hotel Lhakhar
15	Hotel Tibet & Charitrust Tibetan Handicraft Emporium
18	Hotel Mayur
19	Hotel Sonam Delek
21	Gangtok Lodge & Gangtok General Store Bookshop
23	Modern Central Lodge
24	Hotel Lhakpa
30	Green Hotel
32	Sunny Guest House
39	Denzong Inn
43	Hotel Tashi Delek & Babu Kazi Sakya & Sons
44	Hotel Soyang
45	Hotel Laden La
47	Pine Ridge Hotel

PLACES TO EAT

13	Hotel Orient & Bar
34	Cook's Inn

OTHER

1	Cottage Industries Emporium
2	Sikkim World Expeditions
3	Telecommunications Tower
5	Enchey Gompa
6	Stadium
9	SNT Bus Stand
11	Ridge Park, Flower Exhibition Centre & White Hall
12	Yuksam Tours & Travels
14	Main Post Office
16	Tibetan Curio Store
17	Siniolchu, Mayur & Potala Tours & Travels
20	Jainco Booksellers
22	Blue Sky Tours & Travels
25	Indian Airlines
26	Chiranjilal Lalchand Dispensary
27	Children's Park Taxi Stand
28	Tourist Office & State Bank of India Annexe
29	Sikkim Tours & Travels
31	Private Bus & Taxi Stands
33	Tashila Tours & Travels
35	Rural Artisans' Marketing Centre
36	Palace
37	Tsuk-La-Khang (Royal Chapel)
38	Foreigners' Registration Office
40	Super Market Complex
41	Lall Market Taxi Stand
42	Lall Market
46	Tashiling (Secretariat Complex)
48	Forest Secretariat
49	Legislative Assembly
50	Namgyal Institute of Tibetology & Orchid Sanctuary
51	Chorten & Gompa

SIKKIM

Paljor Stadium Rd, can arrange the requisite permits for the North Sikkim tour to Yumthang. They also arrange treks including all meals, transfers, accommodation in huts or tents, yaks and porters from US$35 (per person for more than seven people) to US$45 (per person for four people), including a 10 day trek to Goechala, at 4940m, in West Sikkim.

Mayur Travels (☎ 24-462), nearby, has similar packages, and can also arrange treks and sightseeing tours.

Sikkim Tours & Travels (☎ 22-188), Church Rd, near the private bus stand (take the path to the right just below the steps leading down from the overpass) has some interesting tours including bird-watching (US$35 to US$45); a tribal village tour (US$30 to US$35); and a rhododendron tour in Varsey, West Sikkim. Lukendra (Luke) here is a keen photographer, and can also organise tailor-made photography tours.

Mahayana Tours & Travels (☎ 23-772), Room 23 (ground floor), Super Market complex, can arrange gompa tours to West and East Sikkim. Their 12 day trek to Dzongri is US$30 per day, including guide, porter, transport to Yuksom, meals, tent accommodation, sleeping bags and down jackets. They also have an eight day rhododendron trek (US$30 per day), from Yuksom to Bakhim, Dzongri, Phidong and Tsoska.

Tashila Tours & Travels (☎ 22-979; fax 22-155), National Highway 31A, opposite the private bus stand, has the usual trekking and river rafting trips. The friendly tour executive is Alok Raj Pradhan, and he can also arrange special-interest tours such as high-altitude rhododendron and primula tours (the primulas are at their best in May and June).

Tours Local tours operate on a point system, points referring to sites of interest in the environs of Gangtok. A seven point sightseeing trip taking in Enchey and Rumtek gompas, the deer park and the Namgyal Institute of Tibetology, among other places, takes four to five hours and costs Rs 95. A half day five point tour visits the chorten, the

Institute of Tibetology, the Institute of Cottage Industries, Enchey Gompa and the Orchid Sanctuary, and costs Rs 40. There's also a half day tour to the Orchidarium and Rumtek Gompa, which costs Rs 55. These tours don't give you much time at Rumtek, and you'd be better to do this under your own steam.

In the peak season, advanced booking is required, as these tours are heavily subscribed. The official rate to hire a taxi for a day to visit these sights is Rs 450. Contact the tourist office for further details.

Equipment Hire Trekking gear such as sleeping bags and tents can be hired at Mountain Adventures (☎ 22-454), at shop 31, Super Market complex.

Medical Supplies Chiranjilal Lalchand is a dispensing pharmacy on MG Marg, opposite the Green Hotel.

Emergency Police: ☎ 100/22-033; Fire: ☎ 101/22-001; Ambulance: ☎ 102/22-944; Hospital: ☎ 22-059.

Tsuk-La-Khang

The Royal Chapel is the Buddhists' principal place of worship and assembly, and the repository of a large collection of scriptures. It's a beautiful and impressive building, and its interior is covered with murals. Lavishly decorated altars hold images of the Buddha, bodhisattvas and Tantric deities, and there are also a great many fine woodcarvings. The only time it's open to visitors is during Losar (the Tibetan New Year in late February/early March) when the famous dance portraying the triumph of good over evil is performed.

Namgyal Institute of Tibetology

Established in 1958 and built in traditional style, this unique institute promotes research of the language and traditions of Tibet, as well as of Mahayana Buddhism. It has one of the world's largest collection of books and rare manuscripts on Mahayana Buddhism, many religious works of art and a collection of astonishingly beautiful and incredibly finely executed silk-embroidered *thangkas* (religious art produced on cloth).

It also has painted thangkas depicting the eight manifestations of Padmasambhava (also known as Guru Rinpoche, the Indian priest who established Buddhism in Tibet in the 8th century AD). The institute also has the relics of monks from the time of Ashoka, examples of Lepcha script, masks, and ceremonial and sacred objects, such as the *kapali*, a bowl made from a human skull, and the *varku*, a flute made from a thigh bone. The institute also enshrines numerous statues.

The institute has a number of religious art and craft works and books on Tibetan Buddhism for sale. It's open Monday to Friday and every second Saturday from 10 am to 4 pm; entrance is Rs 2. This is a sacred place, and footwear should be removed before entering.

Chorten & Gompa

The gold apex of a huge white chorten, located about 500m beyond the institute, is visible from many points in Gangtok and is surrounded by prayer flags. Next to it is a gompa for young lamas with a shrine containing huge images of Padmasambhava, and his manifestation, Guru Snang-Sid Zilzon. As at other Buddhist gompas, the chorten is surrounded by prayer wheels.

Orchid Sanctuaries

Surrounding the institute and itself enclosed by a peaceful forest is the **Orchid Sanctuary**, where you can see many of the 454 species of orchid found in Sikkim. The best times to visit are April to May and the end of September to the beginning of December.

There is another, much larger, orchid sanctuary, off the main road to Rangpo alongside the Rani Khola, a tributary of the Teesta, called the **Orchidarium**, which is accessible by public bus. It's also usually included on tours to Rumtek Gompa.

Up on top of the ridge, near White Hall is a **Flower Exhibition Centre**, featuring orchids and seasonal flowers, as well as bonsai. It's open from April to June and

September until the end of November from 10 am to 6 pm daily; entry is Rs 2. **White Hall** is the residence of the chief minister, and there are pleasant walks here through fine gardens. It's also a good walk from here to the deer park (see below).

Cottage Industries Emporium

High up on the main road above town, the Cottage Industries Emporium specialises in producing hand-woven carpets, blankets, shawls, Lepcha weaves, patterned decorative paper and Choktse tables, exquisitely carved in relief. It's open daily during the season, and in the off season, daily except Sunday and every second Saturday, from 9 am to 12.30 pm and 1 to 3.30 pm.

Deer Park

This popular viewpoint is on the edge of the ridge next to the Secretariat building. In it, as you might expect, are several varieties of deer, including barking deer and spotted deer. A good time to visit is around 8 am when the deer are fed.

Enchey Gompa

This gompa, three km above Gangtok, was built in 1909, and belongs to the Nyingmapa order. It was built on the site of the hermitage of Lama Druptob Karpo, a Tantric master who performed various extraordinary feats, including flying from South Sikkim to the site of the current gompa. The *chaam* (dance performed by masked lamas) is performed on the 18th and 19th days of the 12th month of the lunar calendar (usually January).

The prayer hall is completely covered with exquisite paintings, and is a feast of colour. The roof, which itself is a riot of colour, is supported by four large red pillars, intricately carved with ornate coloured cornices. The orange ceiling is set off by horizontal bright blue beams. At the *chwa-shyam* (altar) end of the prayer hall is a large Buddha. On the right is Padmasambhava, and on the left, Chenresig, the Tibetan deity of compassion. On the left wall, near the chwa-shyam and behind a class cabinet is an image of Dorje Phurba (Sanskrit: Vajra

SIKKIM

Kila). Dorje is the wild-eyed male part of the image, and Phurba, the female part, is locked in his embrace. Beneath his feet, squashed under his taloned toes, is a tiny demon.

In the vestibule are depicted the Great Kings of the four cardinal directions (see the Rumtek Gompa section for details), who protect not only the gompa, but the universe, from demons.

Lall Market

If you've been to markets in Kathmandu or Darjeeling, this one may come as a disappointment due to its limited range of craft shops, but the vegetable market is certainly colourful and there's plenty of activity.

Places to Stay

There are plenty of places to stay in all price categories in Gangtok. In the winter it's important to enquire about the availability of hot water and heating. A bucket of hot water for showering is available at most places (sometimes for a small extra charge), but heating is a rarity. Where an electric heater is available, it will definitely cost you more. Even some mid-range hotels have no heating. Very few places have single rooms, and there's often no discount for single occupancy of a double room.

Always enquire about off-season discounts wherever you stay. They vary from between 15% to 30%.

Places to Stay – bottom end

Handy to the tourist office on MG Marg is the *Green Hotel* (☎ 23-354). There is a range of rooms, from singles with attached bath for Rs 120, doubles with geyser from Rs 150 to Rs 350, and a triple with common bath for Rs 150. The cheaper rooms are in the old block, and are a little dark, as some have no external windows. There's a popular bar and restaurant here. Hot water is available free in buckets. A 30% discount is offered in the off season.

On Tibet Rd, above MG Marg, is the *Hotel Lhakpa* (☎ 23-002), with very basic singles/doubles with common bath for Rs 40/80, doubles with attached bath (cold

water) for Rs 150, and with geyser, Rs 180. Hot water is available in buckets. The rooms with common bath are at the back of the hotel, and are a little dingy, but fine. There's a groovy little bar downstairs with a good sound system, and the manager is a friendly helpful fellow.

Close by is the popular *Modern Central Lodge* (☎ 24-670), run by two friendly Sikkimese brothers, Sonam and Karma. All rooms have attached baths (other than in the dorm), some with geysers. The brothers are compiling a very useful travellers' comment book, and Sonam has prepared a map of Gangtok for guests. Dorm beds are Rs 30, singles are Rs 50, doubles with attached toilet are Rs 80 (these rooms are a little dark) or Rs 100 with good views, and there are very good doubles with either a bay window or balcony for Rs 120, with attached bath and geyser. The common bathroom has 24 hour hot water. The brothers are also opening a new place, the *Pine Ridge Hotel*, near the Legislative Assembly Building, with comparable prices. There's a snooker room at the Modern Central, and a popular restaurant-cum-bar downstairs.

At the back of the Lall Market is the tiny *Hotel Laden La* (☎ 23-058), with singles/doubles with common bath for Rs 80/150. Rooms are rustic, but appealing, and those at the front have great views down over the busy market. The atmosphere in the fine little saloon-like bar downstairs is somewhat spoilt by the ear-splitting volume of the TV.

Right opposite the SNT bus stand is the *Hotel Lhakhar* (☎ 22-198), with singles/doubles with common bath for Rs 75/150 and doubles/triples with attached bath for Rs 250/300. Hot water is free in buckets. This is a pleasant place, run by a friendly Tibetan couple, with basic, but spotless rooms.

Very cheap, but a long way from the centre and a strenuous hike uphill, is the *Siniolchu Lodge* (☎ 22-074), just below the entrance to Enchey Gompa. Single/double economy rooms with attached bath (cold water; hot water available in buckets) are Rs 50/100, or deluxe rooms with geyser are Rs 80/150. A taxi will charge Rs 15 to take you up here.

GARRY WEARE

RICHARD I'ANSON

MICHELLE COXALL

MICHELLE COXALL

Sikkim

A: Rumtek Gompa, the seat of the Gyalwa Karmapa of the Kagyupa Buddhist order.
B: Tibetan devotees, Tashiding.
C: Khecheopari Gompa festival.
D: Monk at a small gompa of the Nyingmapa Buddhist order, Jorethang.

MICHELLE COXALL

MICHELLE COXALL

Sikkim
Top: Mani stones, Tashiding Gompa.
Bottom: Lall market, Gangtok.

Places to stay – middle

A friendly and central place to stay is the *Gangtok Lodge* (☎ 24-670), upstairs, diagonally opposite the tourist office on MG Marg. Doubles are Rs 280 with attached bath (cold water, but there's a geyser in the common bathroom), or with a view, Rs 300. Good discounts are offered in the off season, and there's a travel desk here.

Opposite the Hotel Tashi Delek on MG Marg is the *Hotel Soyang* (☎ 22-331), with doubles from Rs 550 to Rs 2000. Unfortunately, no advantage is taken of the views as windows are frosted. At Rs 550, rooms are basic but comfortable; rooms from Rs 750 have pleasant Tibetan furnishings and colour TV. A 30% discount is offered in the off season.

On Tibet Rd is the pleasant *Hotel Sonam Delek* (☎ 22-566). Doubles with common bath are Rs 150, or with attached bath, Rs 350 (no view) and Rs 450 (with possibly the best views you'll get in Gangtok). A 20% discount is offered in the off season, and there's a good restaurant here.

Very pleasant, comfortable rooms can be found at Sikkim Tourism's *Hotel Mayur* (☎ 22-825), on Paljor Stadium Rd. Singles/doubles range from Rs 325/400 to Rs 550/700, all with attached bath and geyser. There are some rooms in all price categories with good views, and heaters are supplied free in winter.

Close by is the three-star *Hotel Tibet* (☎ 22-523; fax 22-707), where you'll be welcomed by a doorman in full traditional Tibetan dress. Singles/doubles range from Rs 465/620 to Rs 1160/1550, including breakfast and one other meal. There's 24 hour room service, foreign exchange facilities, a travel desk and a small bookshop with books on Tibetan issues. Most of the cheaper rooms are on the road side, and are a little small and cramped, as are the mid-range rooms on the valley side. The more expensive rooms are very plush, with traditional Tibetan artefacts and a separate sitting area. Its Snow Lion Restaurant has the best food in Gangtok.

Further north along Paljor Stadium Rd is the *Hotel Mount View* (☎ 23-647). All rooms are doubles, but single occupancy is available. Singles/doubles range from Rs 250/375 to Rs 650/850. All have attached baths with 24 hour hot water, and colour TVs, and there are laundry facilities here. Even the cheaper rooms are nicely appointed, with large rugs and pretty bedspreads. The more expensive rooms have great valley views.

At the private bus stand is the *Sunny Guest House* (☎ 22-179). Doubles with common bath (it's right next door) are Rs 150; doubles with attached bath are Rs 250 and Rs 300, the latter with a balcony and good views. This is a friendly place, and not bad value.

The *Denzong Inn* (☎ 22-692) is in the Denzong Cinema complex, just outside Lall Market. Singles/doubles with attached bath and geyser are Rs 300/400, and there's an enormous (small house-sized!) suite for Rs 1500 which could comfortably accommodate four people. Kitchen facilities cost an extra Rs 200 per day, and the hotel can provide utensils and gas. The cheaper rooms are nothing special, but five of them open onto a roof terrace overlooking the Super Market, with great Kangchenjunga views.

Places to Stay – top end

Probably the best place in this price range is the *Hotel Tashi Delek* (☎ 22-991; fax 22-362). Singles/doubles are Rs 2000/2500, or there's a double suite for Rs 2800, and a double-deluxe suite for Rs 3400. Rates include all meals. The tiny ornate doorway on MG Marg opens onto the opulent lobby with traditional Tibetan woodcarving and Tibetan *objets d'art*. The double deluxe suites have great mountain views; the less-expensive rooms are comfortable, but not flash. All rooms have 24 hour room service and colour TV, and there's a pleasant rooftop garden with great views of Kangchenjunga. Nonguests are welcome at the Blue Poppy Restaurant and Dragon Bar.

At the north end of Paljor Stadium Rd, above the stadium, is the *Nor-Khill Hotel* (☎ 23-186; fax 23-187). The guesthouse was built to accommodate guests to Palden Thendup Namgyal's coronation. Single/double rates, which are inclusive of all meals, are Rs 2100/2500, and the double suite is Rs 2900. There's 24 hour room service, a travel desk, gift shop and foreign exchange, and the hotel is set in pretty gardens. With advance reservation, nonguests can dine in the restaurant here.

Places to Eat

There are numerous little seedy and convivial bars in Gangtok, and the prices are refreshingly cheap after West Bengal. A beer will set you back about Rs 28, and a peg of whisky, Rs 8. Note that full-moon and new-moon days are 'dry' days throughout Sikkim. Try *chang* from a chang shop in the market – millet and hot water. The restaurant at the *Green Hotel* is popular, although the food's nothing special. A favourite with locals is *Cook's Inn*, on MG Marg. The chicken ghaytuk is filling and good (Rs 16), and there's other Chinese and Indian cuisine.

Unequivocally the best food in Gangtok is served at the Hotel Tibet's *Snow Lion Restaurant*. It's not too expensive: most veg dishes are under Rs 40, and nonveg dishes are Rs 40 to Rs 70. The delicious and filling chicken korma is Rs 49. The dinner menu features Japanese and Mughlai dishes, as well as Tibetan cuisine and some seafood dishes. The house special is Mandarin fish (Rs 325), but 24 hours advance notice is required. The restaurant is open until 10 pm, and nonguests are welcome without advance notice.

There's an a la carte restaurant at the *Hotel Tashi Delek*. The special dish is chicken a la Tashi, which takes about 30 minutes to prepare. There are also sizzlers (chicken sizzler is Rs 85). Sikkimese cuisine is available, but you need to order it about 12 hours in advance. Veg dishes range from Rs 30 to Rs 65, and nonveg dishes are Rs 70 to Rs 100.

On Paljor Stadium Rd, next door to the Hotel Chumila, is the *Hotel Orient & Bar*, with very cheap Indian and Chinese food. Most main dishes are under Rs 30. On Tibet Rd are the restaurants and bars at the *Hotel Lhakpa* (order Sikkimese dishes one hour in advance) and the *Modern Central Lodge*, where you can get tsampa for Rs 14. Further

up this road is the more up-market *Oyster Restaurant* at the Hotel Sonam Delek. There are continental favourites such as French toast and banana pancakes, as well as Chinese, Indian and Tibetan cuisine. It's not too expensive: the chicken Kashmiri is Rs 35.

The *New Kho-Chi Restaurant & Bar* is in a handy location beneath the Gangtok Lodge on MG Marg. There's an extensive Chinese and Indian menu, with some continental dishes such as pancakes and fritters. Ginger chicken is Rs 48, and chicken ghaytuk is Rs 20.

Down at Lall Market is *Kikis Garden Restaurant*, on the top floor of the Super Market complex. During the season there's a buffet here featuring Sikkimese cuisine, for Rs 60 per person. The restaurant is nothing flash, but there are great views of Kangchenjunga.

In the evening, opposite the tourist office on MG Marg is *Nomad's Plaza* – a mobile dhaba with a limited menu but very cheap favourites such as chicken Manchurian (Rs 23) and ginger chicken (Rs 18). Meals are cooked right in front of your eyes, and it looks fairly hygienic.

Things to Buy

The Rural Artisans' Marketing Centre, about midway along MG Marg, has Tibetan carpets from West Sikkim and handloom products. Carpets range in price from Rs 250 for 38 cm sq rugs, to Rs 2200 for 2.73m x 5.46m, and are made from a blend of New Zealand and Indian wool. All profits go to fund rural development programmes in Sikkim.

The Charitrust Tibetan Handicraft Emporium (beneath the Hotel Tibet on Paljor Stadium Rd) is a Tibetan Government in Exile initiative, with profits used to fund education programmes for economically disadvantaged Tibetan children. Here you'll find brass statues of deities, thangkas, *chubas*, known locally as *bakhus* – the traditional dress worn by Tibetan women – and other Tibetan artefacts.

Directly opposite Potala Tours & Travels, on Paljor Stadium Rd, is the Tibetan Curio Store. Here you can find all things Tibetan, including lengths of fine silk brocade ranging from Rs 200 to Rs 1600, colourful prayer flags (Rs 5 for the small ones, or Rs 20 for the large ones); monks' *thermas* (robes); and *damrhus* (small Tibetan drums from which hangs a tassel called a *chophen*). You might like to carry home a brass *jhemta* – the cymbal used in gompas. They range in price from Rs 900 to Rs 1300. Mr Shyam Sunder Bansal here is happy to explain the items in his shop.

Getting There & Away

Air The closest airport is Bagdogra, 120 km south on the West Bengal plains near Siliguri. (See Getting There & Away in the Siliguri section of the West Bengal Hills chapter for details of flights.) Indian Airlines (☎ 23-099) has an office on Tibet Rd, near the Children's Park taxi stand. It's open daily from 10 am to 1 pm and 2 to 4.45 pm.

The travel desk at Denzong Inn (☎ 22-692),

The Mysterious Zee

Tibetans are known for their beautiful and ornate jewellery, frequently encrusted with turquoise and coral, forming heavy neck pieces and rings. A lesser known ornament is the mysterious *zee*, an off-white, elongated 'stone' featuring black swirls in the form of 'eyes', which are threaded on a string and worn around the neck, or mounted on a ring. This seemingly innocuous little item is highly prized by Tibetans, but if you ask anyone where they come from, generally you'll receive an enigmatic smile and silence. The truth is, no one knows *where* they come from! Some Tibetans claim they are fossilised insects, or segments of fossilised snakes; others believe they are a gift of the gods; still others believe they are a naturally formed stone found only in Tibet. (Some spoilsports reckon they're highly polished and painted pieces of porcelain. Heaven forbid!)

The zee, which is passed down through the family or traded, can range in size from less than a cm to 10 cm long, and is believed to protect the wearer. Belief in the miraculous powers of the zee were apparently confirmed when the survivor of a terrible accident in Taiwan was found to be wearing one. They are allegedly ground down and used in Tibetan medicine, and Tibetans have been heard to vociferously claim that they are put to more sinister use in nuclear warheads!

Zees are found wherever there are Tibetan communities, and those in search of the mysterious zee travel from Taiwan, Nepal and even the Middle East to secure one. There are various types of zee. The *Sakhu nakhu* (sky earth) zee has a solid black square on one side, and an 'eye' on the reverse side. The *thashuma* zee features a zig zag band around the centre, and the *chunchi* features unbroken bands (called *charies*) and no 'eyes'. Eyes are solid black spots encompassed by a white surround; they come in three types: circular, diamond-shaped, and the highly prized (and rare) 'man's eye', which is oval-shaped. A pitch-black eye with a very white background is considered to be particularly auspicious, and commands high prices. To really confuse matters, odd-numbers of eyes are considered to be especially lucky, and no Tibetan will be caught wearing the extremely unlucky four or six eyed zee.

If you're considering buying a zee, bring your chequebook, as a 'genuine' zee can fetch anywhere from between Rs 5000 to Rs 25,000. The cheapest 'genuine' zee has two eyes. Zees can be legally purchased in India (including Sikkim), and Nepal, but it is illegal to purchase a zee in Bhutan. They should be checked for flaws and chips. Vijdy Sakya at Babu Kazi Sakya & Sons, MG Marg, near the Hotel Tashi Delek, is a wealth of knowledge on zees, and may even have a specimen under the counter which he'll show you.

If you can't afford a genuine zee, a porcelain replica will set you back only about Rs 50, and if you get a good one, no one will be able to tell the difference! ■

This zee design features charies and eyes.

near Lall Market, can book flights on Necon Airways from Bhadrapur (just over the West Bengal-Nepal border) to Kathmandu (US$99). The agent for Jet Airways is RNC Enterprises (☎ 23-556), on MG Marg, a few doors up from the Green Hotel.

The local *Searchlight* newspaper (see Bookshops in the Information section) has schedules for flights serving Bagdogra airport on page two.

Bus The SNT bus stand (☎ 22-016) is at the north end of Paljor Stadium Rd. The counter for interstate bookings (advance bookings possible) is open from 6 am to 1 pm and 2 to 3.30 pm. The counter for bookings for destinations within Sikkim (no advance bookings) is open from 6.30 to 8 am and 11.30 to 4 pm. In the season, there are numerous buses to Siliguri between 6 am and 2 pm. Ordinary services are Rs 38, and there are deluxe (2x2) services at 8 am (via Bagdogra, 5½ hours) and 11 am (direct, 4½ hours). There are fewer ordinary services in the off season, and no deluxe services. To Darjeeling there's an ordinary service at 7 am (five hours, Rs 60), and to Kalimpong at 8.30 am and 1.15 pm (four hours, Rs 30). Buses to these places also leave from the private bus stand on National Highway 31A.

Buses for destinations within Sikkim are: Gezing (for Pemayangtse), at 7 am (4½ hours, Rs 40) – buses travel via Singtam, Rablonga, Kewzing and Legship. From Legship there are services to Tashiding and Yuksom (for the Dzongri Trail), Rumtek (4 pm, 1½ hours, Rs 9); Phodang (7 am and 8 am and 1.30 and 4 pm, 2½ hours, Rs 14); and Jorethang (7 am and 2 pm, four hours, Rs 31). Return services depart Gezing at 8 am and 1 pm; Rumtek at 7 am only; Phodang at 3 pm; and Jorethang at 8 am and 2 pm. There is no SNT bus service to Tsongo Lake. There are numerous services between Gezing and Pelling (for Pemayangtse; see under Gezing).

For details of buses to Gangtok from Siliguri, Darjeeling and Kalimpong, see Getting There & Away in those sections of the West Bengal Hills chapter.

Train There's a railway reservation counter at the SNT bus stand on Paljor Stadium Rd. It has a small quota on services from New Jalpaiguri (eight km from Siliguri), and is open Monday to Saturday from 9.30 to 11.30 am and 1.30 to 3 pm. See Getting There & Away in the Siliguri section of the West Bengal Hills chapter for details of interstate trains serving New Jalpaiguri.

Taxi & Jeep Share jeeps are a faster and generally more comfortable alternative to the SNT buses. There are three share-jeep stands: at the private bus stand on National Highway 31A; at Lall Market; and the Children's Park taxi stand, between MG Marg and Tibet Rd.

At the private bus stand you can get share jeeps to Siliguri (every 30 minutes between 6 am and 5 pm, 3½ hours, Rs 80), Darjeeling (7.30 and 8 am, 1 and 1.30 pm, four hours, Rs 100) and Kalimpong (regular departures between 7.30 am and 2 pm, 2½ hours, Rs 46). Times given are scheduled departure times, but at peak periods, more jeeps may leave according to demand.

From Children's Park, jeeps leave for destinations in West Sikkim such as Jorethang (6.45, 7.30 and 8 am, 12.30, 1.30, 3 and 4 pm, three hours, Rs 50), Gezing (7 am, 12.30 and 1 pm, 5½ hours, Rs 70) and on to Pelling (six hours from Gangtok, Rs 90); and in North Sikkim to Phodang (6.30 and 7 am, 12.30, 1 and 1.30 pm, two hours, Rs 30), as well as for Tsongo Lake (two hours, Rs 130, season only).

From Lall Market, you can get share jeeps to Rumtek and Tsongo Lake. During the season, share jeeps for Rumtek leave when full between 2 and 4 pm (one hour, Rs 25), and return between 6 am and 4 pm. In the off season, they leave between 11 am and 3 pm, and return between 6 and 8 am. Share jeeps for Tsongo Lake leave in the season only at 9 am and 2 pm (two hours, Rs 130), and return between noon and 2 pm.

At all of these places you can hire a vehicle, and you should be able to negotiate good discounts in the off season.

For share jeeps to Gangtok from Siliguri, Darjeeling and Kalimpong, see Getting There & Away in those sections of the West Bengal Hills chapter.

Getting Around

All the taxis are new or near-new Maruti vans. Rs 15 will get you just about anywhere around town. To Rumtek you're looking at about Rs 250 return, including about an hour at the gompa. If you want to spend longer there, make sure the driver is aware of this. There's a convenient Maruti stand opposite the tourist office on MG Marg.

AROUND GANGTOK
Rumtek Gompa

Rumtek, on the other side of the Ranipul Valley, is visible from Gangtok though it's 24 km away by road. The gompa is the seat of the Gyalwa Karmapa, the head of the Kagyupa order of Tibetan Buddhism. The order was founded in the 11th century by Lama Marpa, the disciple of the Indian guru Naropa, and later split into several orders, the most important of which are Drukpa, Kagyupa and Karmapa.

The main gompa is a recent structure, built by the 16th Karmapa in strict accordance with traditional designs of his gompa in Tibet. The prayer room enshrines an enormous (three metre high, including the stand) statue of the Buddha, completely plated in gold. Hundreds of tiny Buddhas kept in glass-fronted pigeon holes represent the number of Buddhas who will come to the world.

The walls are richly embellished with paintings, including those of numbers of Tibetan and Indian scholars (if the robe crosses at the neckline, they're Tibetan; those with the robes around the waist are Indian). Ornamentation is restricted to these vibrant paintings; there is little of the intricate woodcarving which features in many gompas.

In the vestibule to the prayer room are four paintings depicting the Great Kings of the four cardinal directions, who guard the universe and the heavens from demons. When facing the prayer hall, they are from left to right: Yulkhor Srung (with a white face, and playing a stringed instrument) – the King of the East; Namthose (the antithesis of the King of the East, with a blue face, fangs, bulging eyes and drawing a sword from a scabbard) – the King of the North; Chenmizang (blood-red face, with a serpent coiled around his arm, and holding a stupa in his hand) – the King of the West; and Yulkhor Srung (yellow face, holding a rat and a banner) – the King of the South.

Visitors are welcome to enter the prayer hall, and there's no objection to your sitting in on the prayer and chanting sessions. You'll even be offered a cup of salted butter tea when it's served to the monks.

Behind the main prayer hall is the Great Golden Reliquary Stupa of the 16th Karmapa, Rangjung Rigpae Dorje, who died in 1981. Around the walls are statues of the 16th Karmapa and his 15 predecessors, and

Will the real Karmapa please step forward?

Since the death of the 16th Karmapa in Chicago in 1981, a dispute has raged over which of two prepubescent boys is his *tulku*, or incarnation, and hence his successor. Before his death, the 16th Karmapa allegedly left instructions in a sealed box which revealed where the new karmapa would be found. A lad answering to the description, by the name of Ugen Thinley Dorje, was located in a remote corner of Tibet, and has been acknowledged by the Dalai Lama as the true karmapa. However, a second candidate, Tenzing Chentse, was discovered in Bhutan, and he is acknowledged as the legitimate successor by a separate group of monks, most of whom hail from Bhutan. A controversy now rages between the two rival factions of monks to which there appears to be no clear end. ∎

SIKKIM

before the stupa, paper prayer wheels constantly rotate by means of the heat generated by butter lamps. From the ceiling are suspended numerous richly embroidered thangkas.

Opposite the stupa is the Karmashri Nalanda Institute of Buddhist Studies. Courses in advanced Buddhist philosophy are run here.

Below the reliquary stupa is the gompa's printing press. The printer (a layperson, not a monk), has been carving wooden blocks with Tibetan script and designs since 1962. The blocks are used for printing prayer books of handmade paper that is made at Rumtek, and prayer flags. You can purchase a set of prayer flags here for Rs 100.

The main chaam known as Tse Chu, is performed on the 10th day of the fifth lunar month (July), and depicts events in the life of Padmasambhava. Another chaam, depicting the battle between good and evil, takes place two days before Losar (Tibetan New Year in February).

Most activity takes place in the late afternoon. At other times you may well find the main door locked, in which case it's a matter of asking around for someone to open it up for you, which they are quite happy to do.

If you follow the tarmac road for two or three km beyond Rumtek, through a gate off to the left you'll find another interesting, but smaller, gompa which was restored in 1983.

Places to Stay & Eat Only two minutes walk from the gompa is the *Sangay Hotel* (no phone). Singles are Rs 50, doubles are between Rs 60 and Rs 80, and triples are Rs 100, all with common bath. Cheap and basic meals are available here. Opposite the main entrance is the *Hotel Kunga Delek* (☎ (0359230) 872), where singles/doubles are Rs 75/150.

Five km from Rumtek, in the village of Martam, is the *Martam Resort*. Singles/doubles cost Rs 1140/1600, or with all meals, an additional Rs 600. It's in a beautiful location in the middle of a paddy field, and staff here can arrange horse riding and treks in the surrounding area. There's also a bar here. Contact the tourist office in Gangtok for more information.

Flanking the road up to the gompa, there are several chai stalls where you can get basic fare.

Getting There & Away There are buses and share jeeps to Rumtek from Gangtok. See Getting There & Away in the Gangtok section for details. If you feel like a bit of exercise, it's a very pleasant 12 km walk (downhill) to the National Highway, from where it's easy to get a ride for the 12 km (uphill!) trip to Gangtok.

Dechenling Cremation Ground & Ngor Gompa

Leaving Gangtok on the road to Tsongo Lake, after two km a road diverges to the right. About 250m along this road, a track to the right leads in a short distance to the Dechenling cremation ground. Visitors are welcome to observe the cremation ritual. From the turn-off to the cremation ground the road proceeds to Ngor Gompa, which overlooks the Bhusuk River. It's not of great architectural interest, but is notable as the only gompa in Sikkim belonging to the Sakyapa order of Tibetan Buddhism.

A taxi will charge about Rs 100 return to visit Ngor Gompa.

Tashi Viewpoint

This viewpoint is eight km to the north of Gangtok, towards Phodang. There are very good views of the east side of Kangchenjunga, as well as those of Siniolchu (6888m), which is considered, along with Nanda Devi in Uttarakhand, to be one of the most beautiful mountains in the world. From Tashi Viewpoint, it's possible to walk to **Ganesh Tok** (*tok* means ridge), in less than an hour. From here, as well as views of Kangchenjunga and Siniolchu, there are fine views back over Gangtok. A taxi to either of these viewpoints from Gangtok will cost about Rs 150 return.

Close to Ganesh Tok is the recently opened **Himalayan Zoological Park**. There are no cages here – it's an open sanctuary covering 205 hectares. The Himalayan black bear, which was previously incarcerated in the Deer Park in Gangtok, has been moved to the more salubrious surroundings here. The park is part of a controlled breeding scheme for wild animals.

Fambonglho Wildlife Sanctuary

This sanctuary is 25 km from Gangtok, and covers an undulating and ecologically diverse area of 5200 hectares. It is home to a variety of mammals, including barking deer, the ungainly serow, and the stocky goral, various types of wild cat, including the marbled leopard and jungle cats, the Himalayan black bear, and the red panda. There are also numerous bird species, such as laughing thrushes, various types of owl and pheasant, and the Nepal tree creeper.

There is a rich variety of flora, with abundant wild orchids, tree ferns, forests of oak and stands of bamboo, and there are magnificent views of the Sikkim Himalaya, including, of course, Kangchenjunga.

As with all wildlife sanctuaries, don't wear brightly coloured clothing or heavy perfume, as this will frighten the animals away. The best time to spot animals is in the early morning and late afternoon.

The sanctuary is open between October and April, and permission is required from the District Forest Officer (see Information, under Gangtok). Permits are issued routinely for foreigners, but you should carry both this and your Sikkim permit with you at all times while in the park. It's necessary to take an assistant wildlife warden or wildlife guard into the park with you. Entry to the park costs Rs 5, and it costs Rs 3 per day to carry a still camera, and Rs 250 for a video camera.

Accommodation is available in rustic *log houses* at Golitar and Tumin, but you'll need to bring food, and water should be carried while you're in the park. Rates are Rs 50 per person.

Tsongo Lake

Lying 35 km north-east of Gangtok, foreigners have recently been permitted to visit this lake; technically you should be in a group of four, and need to join a tour (US$12). Permits are valid for a day visit only. Numerous agencies in Gangtok offer tours to the lake, and can arrange the requisite permit.

North Sikkim

Previously foreigners were only permitted to travel as far north as Phodang, 38 km by road to the north of Gangtok, which is accessible on the standard tourist permit. However, it is now possible to visit Yumthang, 102 km further north via the villages of Mangan and Chungthang. At the time of writing it was necessary to make arrangements through a travel agency in Gangtok and join a tour with a minimum of four people.

PHODANG

Phodang Gompa, north of Gangtok along a winding but largely tarmac road, belongs to the same order (Kagyupa) as Rumtek, but is much smaller and less ornate than that gompa. After the 16th Karmapa fled from Tibet and before he installed himself in Rumtek in 1959, Phodang was the most important of Sikkim's three Kagyupa gompas (the third is Ralang Gompa). Here you can feel the timelessness of a part of Sikkim which tourists rarely visit. The gompa sits high up above the main road to Mangan and there are tremendous views down into the valley below.

Phodang is a fairly recent structure, although the original gompa here was founded, like Rumtek, in 1740. The gompa has a community of about 60 monks, many of them born in India after the Chinese occupation of Tibet. They're very friendly and will take you around and explain the salient features of the gompa. The gompa shelters an image of the 9th Karmapa, Wang Chok Dorje, who allegedly founded this gompa. The chwa-shyam is covered in ornate woodcarvings of two entwined dragons. Murals depict ranks of previous karmapas, and on the right wall (ie when facing the chwa-shyam) is the protective deity of the gompa, Nagpo Chempo. On the back wall is a depiction of Padmasambhava. The ceiling is supported by six large wooden pillars and has beautifully carved cornices.

Behind the chwa-shyam is the Nagpo

Chempo meditation room, which has some disturbing and striking murals of various demonic deities dismembering miscreants in the bowels of hell. When monks are meditating here, access is prohibited to visitors. Monks can spend months alone in this room, with the disturbing murals as meditational prompts, attended only by a young student monk who brings food. Chaams are performed here in December.

Opposite the gompa is a small community of nuns who belong to the same order. **Labrang Gompa**, two km further uphill beyond Phodang Gompa, was established in 1844, and belongs to the Nyingmapa order. Beware of leeches when walking up here.

Places to Stay & Eat

The village of Phodang straddles the main Gangtok to Mangan road, and is about one km north of the turn-off to the gompas towards Mangan. There are a couple of basic places to stay here, including the *Yak & Yeti Lodge*, which has singles/doubles with common bath for Rs 50/70, and doubles with attached bath for Rs 100. Hot water is supplied free in buckets, and with one hour's notice, the family here can probably rustle up a bite to eat. Rooms are spotless, and some have good views down over the valley. *Northway Lodge* has doubles with common bath for Rs 80, some also with good views, and you can also get basic meals here.

You may be offered hospitality by the friendly villagers who live in the gompa grounds.

Getting There & Away

Phodang village is one km beyond the turn-off to the gompa, and buses will drop you here unless you request to be dropped off at the turn-off. From the main road, it's a further one-km walk up to Phodang Gompa. As the main entrance to the gompa compound is at the back of the gompa, remember to walk around to the entrance via the left-hand side (ie in a clockwise direction). Buses from the SNT bus stand in Gangtok leave at 7 and 8 am and 1.30 and 4 pm. You need to set out early from Gangtok if you want to

visit both gompas and return the same day, as the last transport to Gangtok passes through Phodang at about 3 pm. During the season, you may be able to get a share jeep to Phodang from Children's Park taxi stand.

YUMTHANG VALLEY

The Yumthang Valley lies 140 km north of Gangtok, at an elevation of 3564m. This region has recently been opened to foreigners, but trekking is still prohibited. The best time to visit is in April and May, when the rhododendrons are in full bloom. There are hot springs here, covered by a wooden shelter. To get here, you'll need to join a tour (minimum of four people required), and local travel agencies can arrange the requisite permits. The road from Gangtok follows the Teesta River, crossing a spectacular gorge over the Rang Rang suspension bridge. Tour bookings can be made with Blue Sky Tours & Travels, Sikkim World Expeditions and Siniolchu Tours & Travels, all based in Gangtok. See under Information in the Gangtok section for details.

West Sikkim

West Sikkim is attracting more and more visitors. Its main attractions, other than trekking up to Dzongri at the base of Kangchenjunga, are the two old gompas of Pemayangtse and Tashiding, and trekking in the Pemayangtse area.

The roads are sealed for the most part between Jorethang and Legship, but beyond Legship, to Tashiding and Yuksom, they are unsealed, and are subject to landslides.

JORETHANG & NAYA BAZAAR

An important transport hub and administrative centre, Jorethang lies on the east side of the Rangeet River, only 30 km north of Darjeeling, and flanked by its twin city, Naya Bazaar. Jorethang actually lies in the administrative district of South Sikkim – the Rangeet River here marks the boundary between South and West Sikkim. The town is pleasantly sited at the confluence of the Great Rangeet and Rangman rivers, surrounded by wooded hills, and with a colourful market along a strip in the centre of the main road. Inhabitants are engaged in fishing, growing ginger and cultivating orange orchards.

A small staircase opposite the bus stand (enter through the gate here) leads – in a five minute steep walk – to a tiny gompa belonging to the Nyingmapa order. The prayer room shelters small images of Lord Buddha flanked by Avalokitesvara (Chenresig) on the left and Padmasambhava on the right. There are good views from the terrace in front of the gompa.

Places to Stay & Eat

The *Hotel Rangeet Valley*, National Highway, opposite the bus stand, has singles/doubles with attached bath, nets and fans for Rs 100/200; hot water is supplied free in buckets. There's a restaurant here serving Chinese and Indian cuisine.

The *Hotel Walk In*, First Main Rd, two minutes walk from the bus stand, has rooms with nets and fans for Rs 70/150. Singles are a little dark, but the doubles are quite spacious, and the front rooms open onto a balcony.

The best place to stay is the *Hotel Namgyal*, just past the bus stand towards the bridge. Singles/doubles/triples with attached bath are Rs 150/300/350, and are spotless, although there are no nets here. Some of the doubles have balconies overlooking the confluence of the Rangeet and Rangman rivers. The singles are small, but OK. Sikkimese cuisine is available in the restaurant downstairs, and there's a bar here. The *Hotel Shilton* has no rooms, but you can get snacks such as 'water pooches' (poached eggs) and beer here.

Getting There & Away

There are direct buses to Yuksom at 8 and 9.30 am (three hours, Rs 27), and to Legship at 11.30 am and 4.30 pm (one hour, Rs 10), continuing through to Gezing (2½ hours, Rs 15), from Jorethang. There are no direct buses to Tashiding; you have to change at Legship. There are no bus services to Darjeeling. Buses to Siliguri leave at 7 am, 1.30 and 3 pm (3½ hours, Rs 36). Buses to Gangtok depart at 8 am and 2 pm (four hours, Rs 31).

Share jeeps leave regularly for Darjeeling from opposite the bus stand on Main Rd. The journey takes two to three hours, depending on the condition of the road, passing through Singla Bazaar. The checkpost is at Rangman, just beyond Naya Bazaar. Tickets cost Rs 60, and there are no jeeps after 5 pm.

To get to Pemayangtse, you have to change at Gezing, and to Tashiding and Yuksom, change at Legship. Jeeps depart when full between 7 am and 4 pm. It takes one hour to Legship (Rs 20) and 2½ hours to Gezing (Rs 31). To Siliguri, its three hours and Rs 50.

There are numerous share jeeps to Gangtok (three hours, Rs 50).

Rathong River Project

A channel being built on the upper reaches of the Rathong River in the Yuksom area as part of the Rathong River Project has received widespread condemnation by environmental groups and Sikkim's Buddhists.

The project will involve the resettling of many Lepcha and Bhutia villagers, and the project area encompasses a high concentration of sites sacred to Sikkim's Buddhists. Opponents are concerned about the construction of the channel, as this area is subject to landslides, and there is a high possibility of major ecological problems.

Concerned citizens have filed a case against the power department of the Government of Sikkim, and recently a large number of Sikkimese monks marched through Gangtok to protest against the project. ∎

For details of share jeeps to Jorethang from Siliguri and Darjeeling, see Getting There & Away in those sections of the West Bengal Hills chapter.

LEGSHIP

Legship lies 100 km west of Gangtok, and 27 km north of Jorethang, on the banks of the Rangeet River. It's a chaotic and cluttered little burgh surrounded by wooded hills, and has a certain ramshackle appeal, with the colourful produce of fruit and vegie sellers piled in pyramids in wooden shacks flanking the main road.

From Legship you can walk to the hot springs of **Phur Chachu** in about 30 minutes. There is basic accommodation in wooden huts, but you'll need to bring your own food. A cave here is revered as the site where Padmasambhava meditated.

There's a police checkpost in Legship, and only one place to stay, the *Hotel Trishna*, which has five doubles with common bath for Rs 80, charging a hefty Rs 10 for hot water in buckets. A little footbridge spans the river to a small temple sacred to Shiva. High above the north side of the village is the Hing Dam settlement, inhabited by workers on the Rangeet River hydroelectric project.

GEZING

The road from Legship leaves the river and ascends high up above the village for 10 km to Gezing, an important transport junction, but not a very attractive place. The best time to be here is on Friday, when villagers from outlying regions bring their produce into town and a colourful and busy market dominates the main square. There's a small post office next to the Hotel Kanchanzonga, and travellers' cheques can be exchanged at the Central Bank of India, down a lane behind the town square.

Places to Stay & Eat

There are several basic places to stay, including the *Hotel Kanchanzonga*, above the square on the right, which has singles for Rs 40 and doubles from Rs 60 to Rs 80, all with

common bath and free hot water in buckets. There's also a restaurant here.

The *Hotel Chopstick*, behind the chorten at the top of the town square, has doubles for Rs 70 and dorm beds for Rs 25. One of the rooms has good views over the valley, but others are dark and dingy, and should be avoided. Next door is the *Hotel Mayalu*, with basic and rustic doubles/triples for Rs 50/75. Right on the town square is the *Hotel Bamboo Grove*, which has very ramshackle rooms at the top of a rickety staircase. They cost Rs 40/60 with common bath, or Rs 20 in the three bed dorm. There's a bar downstairs.

Getting There & Away

From the SNT bus stand, on the right as you enter Gezing from Gangtok, there are buses to Gangtok via Rablonga at 9 am and 1 pm (four to five hours, Rs 40); to Pelling at 8.30 am, 1 and 2 pm (many more buses on Friday, market day). It takes 30 minutes and costs Rs 4. To Yuksom buses leave at 1 pm via Pelling and at 2 pm via Legship and Tashiding (both four hours, Rs 20).

To Jorethang buses leave at 7, 9 and 10 am, 1 and 4 pm (two hours, Rs 15). The 7 am service continues through to Siliguri (five hours from Gezing, Rs 40). To get to Kalimpong, disembark at either Meli Bazaar or Teesta Bazaar, from both of which there are numerous share taxis and buses to Kalimpong. There's one bus to Tashiding at 2 pm (one hour, Rs 10). There are no buses to Darjeeling. There is no advance booking on SNT buses from Gezing; tickets go on sale 30 minutes prior to departure.

The turn-off for Pemayangtse Gompa is 2½ km before Pelling on the main Gezing to Pelling road. Vehicles will stop here on request, from where it's a steep 10 minute walk uphill to the gompa.

The share jeep office is at the BK Stationery Shop, opposite the Hotel Mayalu. Share jeeps for Gangtok via Jorethang leave at 6.30, 7, 11 and 11.30 am, and via Rablonga at 10.30 am. Both trips take 4½ hours and cost Rs 70. Advance booking is possible (and preferable). There is one share jeep daily for

Tashiding and Yuksom (Rs 40); check times at the share jeep office.

There are numerous share jeeps to Pelling. They leave when full, with more departures in the morning (30 minutes, Rs 10). On market day (Friday) there are numerous vehicles ferrying villagers back to Pelling. There are no direct share jeeps to Darjeeling; you can catch a share jeep to Jorethang (2½ hours, Rs 31), and get a share jeep from there to Darjeeling (two to three hours, Rs 60).

A taxi from the town square will charge Rs 130 to Pelling and Rs 500 to Jorethang.

PELLING
Telephone Area Code: 03593

Pelling is a pleasant base from which to visit points of interest in the area. It is perched high on top of a ridge, and there are magnificent views of the snowy peaks to the north. From here, the perspective is much the same as from Darjeeling. From Pelling, Kangchenjunga (8598m) looks smaller than the distinctive flat-topped Kabru (7338m) to its left, which is closer. To the right of Kangchenjunga is the pyramid-shaped Pandim (6691m). The massive bulk dominating the foreground to the right is Narsingh (5825m).

There are no foreign exchange facilities in Pelling. The closest place to change money is at the Central Bank of India in Gezing.

Cottage Industries Training Centre

About 150 young people are taught traditional handicrafts such as woodcarving, handloom weaving, bamboo canework and carpet weaving at this centre in Lower Pelling. There is a small showroom here where you can buy goods made at the centre. Opposite the centre is a small woollens centre where you can buy handknits such as jumpers, hats and gloves.

Walks Around Pelling

There are some fine walks in the area surrounding Pelling, but unfortunately whenever you leave the main roads, those blood-sucking trekkers' blights, leeches, are lying in wait to secure themselves firmly to any piece of flesh they can grab on to. See the Health section in the Facts for the Visitor chapter for ways of dealing with these tenacious little critters.

It takes about 40 minutes to walk to **Pemayangtse Gompa** (described later in this chapter), 2½ km before Pelling. Follow the main road back towards Gezing until you come to a crossing where there is a large white stupa. A sign here points the direction to the gompa. Behind the stupa is a seat made of stone, known as the **Choeshay Gang**, which is supported by the branches of a tree. The seat was built to commemorate the visit to Sikkim of the Tibetan nun Jaytsun Mingyur Paldon, who delivered a dharma lecture to the monks of Pemayangtse.

A 30 minute walk past the turn-off to Pemayangtse (ie towards Gezing) will bring you to a trail which leads in a few minutes walk to the scattered ruins of the **Rabdentse Palace**. Follow the main road until a curve, from where the trail leads off to the left. The palace was founded by the second king of Sikkim, Tenzung Namgyal, in 1670 AD. From here there are fine views across to the village of Tashiding and Tashiding Gompa.

A 45 minute walk uphill to the west of Pelling will bring you to the **Sangachoeling Gompa** ('Land of the Sacred Spell'), on a ridge above the village. The path commences from behind the soccer field, also known locally as the helipad. It's a beautiful walk along a steep wooded path, with magnificent glimpses of Kangchenjunga and adjacent peaks to the north at intervals, but be prepared for a bloodletting, as it's riddled with leeches. If you reach a grassy ridge, you've passed the gompa; double back towards the wooden buildings behind you.

Dubdi Gompa at Yuksom was the first gompa to be founded in Sikkim; however, Sangachoeling was the first to be built. The original building dated from 1697, but the current building was built after the old gompa was destroyed in an earthquake. Unlike Pemayangtse, which only admitted 'pure monks of pure Tibetan race', Sangachoeling had a much more egalitarian admittance policy, and was open to members of all classes and races, including Bhutias,

Lepchas and Limbus. It was one of the few gompas in Sikkim which admitted women as nuns.

Sangachoeling belongs to the Nyingmapa order, and shelters fine images of Padmasambhava and the Buddha, among others. The walls are of course completely covered in paintings, but the colours are more muted than usual, and the woodcarving in this gompa is less ostentatious than in some larger gompas.

An upstairs room enshrines some less ornate images, as well as cloth-bound sacred texts. In a small room at the back are some of the original clay statues, some of which still retain fragments of colour. Beside the gompa is a Buddhist cremation ground used by Bhutia and Lepcha villagers.

Four hours walk beyond Sangachoeling is the **Rani Dhunga**, or Queen's Stone. Here a large stone is worshipped as the image of the female Buddhist deity Rani Dhunga. It's a very steep walk along an ancient trail once traversed by the king and his courtiers. A 10 km, 1½ hour walk towards Dentam will bring you to the **Changay Waterfalls**. The **Rimbi Waterfalls** are by the roadside on the route to Khecheopari Lake and Yuksom, about 12 km from Pelling.

It takes about four to five hours to walk from Pelling to Tashiding, with some steep ascents along the way, particularly for the last section just before the village. Bring snacks and water, as there's nothing to eat along the way.

Places to Stay & Eat

The *Hotel Garuda* (☎ 50-614) is right at the town's intersection, and is a deservedly popular place to stay. Singles/doubles are Rs 60/120, and four bed rooms are Rs 240, all with common bath. In the eight bed dorm, it's Rs 30, and there are fine Kangchenjunga views from this room. There are also good views from the double with attached bath and geyser (Rs 350). Pemba and Tshering Wangdi here are very helpful and friendly. You can store gear here while you're trekking, and there's a good travellers' comment

book and a noticeboard. Meals are at set times in the dining hall.

The pink building on your right as you walk towards Lower Pelling from the crossroads is the *Hotel Pelling* (☎ 50-707). Doubles with common bath are Rs 100, or Rs 150 on the first floor, and with attached bath, Rs 175 on the ground floor, and Rs 250 on the first floor. There's a triple on the top floor for Rs 350. Some of the rooms are a little dark; the front rooms with views are better.

In Upper Pelling, the *Hotel Pradhan* (☎ 50-615) has double rooms for Rs 100 with common bath. The front rooms have great views, and this place is run by a friendly Nepali family.

The mid-range *Sikkim Tourist Centre* (☎ 50-855) is close to the crossroads in Upper Pelling. Doubles are Rs 650, or Rs 700 with mountain views, and triples with views are Rs 950. These rates include breakfast and either lunch or dinner. There are also room-only rates in the off season only (January to March and mid-June to mid-September). Rooms are not fancy, but are quite comfortable, and all have attached bath with geyser. There's a rooftop restaurant, and nonguests are welcome.

Getting There & Away

As the bus to Siliguri (and Meli Bazaar, for Kalimpong: see the Gezing section) from Gezing leaves at 7 am (five hours, Rs 40), you'll either have to stay overnight in Gezing or walk down to Gezing along the well marked short cut from Pelling opposite the Hotel Garuda (five km, 45 minutes). There's also one share taxi down to Gezing daily (except Sunday) at 6.15 am (Rs 10) which gets you down in time to catch the Siliguri-bound bus (book through Hans Booking Agent, next to the Sikkim Tourist Centre). Later buses from Pelling to Gezing leave at 9 am and 4 pm, except Sunday (30 minutes, Rs 4). The 9 am bus continues to Jorethang (2½ hours from Gezing, Rs 15). To Dentam there's one bus at 4 pm (two hours, Rs 15), passing the Changay Waterfalls en route.

There's one bus daily direct between Pelling and Yuksom at 2.30 pm (three hours,

Rs 15). However, it's a very poor road, and frequently blocked, in which case you'll have to backtrack to Gezing and get the bus at 2 pm from there via Tashiding (one hour to Tashiding, Rs 10, four hours to Yuksom, Rs 20). There are no direct buses to Tashiding from Pelling. There's one bus to Khecheopari at 3 pm (two hours), which returns to Pelling the following morning at 7 am.

There are numerous share jeeps down to Gezing on market day (Friday) in the morning. To hire a jeep down to Gezing costs Rs 200; to Khecheopari, Rs 750 in the season; to Yuksom, Rs 1200; and to Tashiding, Rs 600.

KHECHEOPARI LAKE

Pronounced 'catch a perry', and sometimes spelt Khechepari, Khecheopalri or Khechupherei, this place is a popular objective for trekkers. The sacred lake lies in a depression surrounded by prayer flags and forested hills. Resist the temptation to swim, as it's a holy place. If you feel like a dip, you can swim in the river downhill from Pelling en route to the lake. Take care!

By the lakeshore is the small Lepcha village of **Tsojo**, and about 1½ km above the lake is the Khecheopari Gompa. On the 15th and 16th days of the first month of the Tibetan lunar calendar (around February/March), a festival is held at the lake. There is a *trekkers' hut* and a *pilgrims' hut* at the lake. The trekkers' hut is grimy and dark – not very salubrious. A bed at the pilgrims' hut will cost between Rs 30 and Rs 50. A better bet would be to accept the hospitality offered by villagers, or you might be able to stay at the gompa. There a several chai shops at the lake. It gets very cold here at night, so bring warm gear with you.

By road the lake is about 27 km from Pelling; the walking trail is shorter, but much steeper, and will take about 4½ hours on foot.

From Khecheopari it is possible to continue on foot to Yuksom. The short cut is confusing, so ask for advice whenever you meet anyone en route. It should take three hours to cover the distance between the lake and Yuksom.

There's one bus daily between Pelling and Khecheopari, leaving Pelling at 3 pm (two hours), and returning at 7 am.

PEMAYANGTSE GOMPA

Standing at a height of 2085m and surrounded on two sides by snow-capped mountains, Pemayangtse (Perfect Sublime Lotus) is one of the state's oldest and most important gompas. It was founded in 1705 during the reign of the third chogyal, Chador Namgyal, and its monks enjoyed pre-eminence among the religious community of Sikkim, admittance restricted to those of pure Tibetan race, 'celibate and unde-formed'. They were known as *ta-sang* (pure monks), and the head lama of Pemayangtse was invested with the honour of anointing the chogyal with holy water.

The gompa belongs to the Nyingmapa order, the most common of the Buddhist orders of Sikkim. As with all the gompas of this order in Sikkim, it enshrines a prominent image of Padmasambhava. Here he is framed by an extraordinary woodcarving of serpents entwined around a staff, and there is a particularly gruesome image of Dorje Phurba, and a more equanimous image of Chenresig.

The gompa, damaged in the earthquakes of 1913 and 1960, has been reconstructed several times. It is a plain three storey structure, with an ornate interior. In an upstairs hall, elaborately carved cornices frame the ceiling which is supported by brightly painted beams. The resident monks engage in much drum beating, cymbal clashing, bell ringing, horn blowing and chanting. On the 3rd floor is the *Zandog-palri*, a seven tiered painted wooden model of the abode of Padmasambhava, complete with rainbows, angels and the whole panoply of Buddhas and bodhisattvas. The model was built single-handedly by the late Dungzin Rinpoche in five years.

In February each year the chaam is performed. The exact dates are the 28th and 29th days of the 12th Tibetan lunar month.

Pemayangtse is about six km uphill from Gezing on the Pelling road, 2½ km before Pelling. The SNT buses between Gezing and Pelling pass by the turn-off for Pemayangtse, from where it's a steep 10 minute walk up to the gompa.

Places to Stay & Eat

Just off the approach to the gompa is Sikkim Tourism's *Hotel Mt Pandim* (☎ (03593) 50-756), which has standard doubles for Rs 375, and deluxe doubles (with fantastic views) for Rs 525. There's a dining hall for guests, but nonguests are welcome with advance notice, and there's a bar here. Breakfast is Rs 50, the veg lunch or dinner is Rs 90, or nonveg is Rs 120. This is a very quiet place, and the staff are friendly and attentive.

There is also a budget *trekkers' hut* nearby, but to stay here you require permission from the tourist office in Gangtok.

TASHIDING

To visit this small village, with its beautiful gompa set high above it, technically you require a special endorsement on your tourist or trekking permit. However, at the time of writing, there was no checkpoint here. Nevertheless, it's probably worthwhile taking a few minutes in Gangtok to have your permit endorsed. The village lies 16 km north-east of Legship along a ridge with dramatic valleys falling away on either side, culminating in the cone-shaped hill on which is perched the gompa.

Tashiding Gompa

It's a steep 45 minute walk up to the gompa on the flat terrace of the summit. Hundreds of prayer flags create an ethereal ambience, particularly in the early morning.

Tashiding (the Devoted Central Glory) is a much less ostentatious gompa than Pemayangtse. Originally founded in 1716 by Ngadak Sempa Chempo, it belongs to the Nyingmapa order. It was extended and renovated by the third chogyal, Chador Namgyal.

As you enter the gompa compound, the building immediately to your right surrounded by prayer wheels houses the sacred *bhumpa*, or water vessel. During the annual Bhumchu Festival, celebrated on the 15th day of the first month of the Tibetan lunar calendar (March), the water in the vase is mixed with water from the Rathong and Rangeet rivers and distributed to devotees by the head lama of Tashiding. The bowl is then refilled and locked away for one year. When it is again taken out, the lama makes prognostications according to the amount of water still contained in the vessel. A low level of water is a sign of ill tidings, heralding disease, a poor harvest, drought or famine; if the vessel is full to the brim, there will be bloodshed in Sikkim, but if the vessel is half full, there will be an abundant crop and peace will reign in Sikkim. The building is only opened on special festival days.

The original gompa was dismantled, and six of the eight pillars which supported its ceiling were salvaged and installed in the new building, on which construction commenced in 1987. The main prayer hall enshrines an image of the Buddha flanked by four bodhisattvas on either side.

During the festival of Panghlapsol, celebrated on the 15th day of the seventh lunar month (end of August/early September), the images of Kangchenjunga and Yabdu are brought out to be worshipped, and rich offerings of bread, biscuits, grains and fruit are placed before them.

At the south end of the ridge, beyond the prayer hall and on a lower terrace, are numerous chortens. Remember to circumambulate the chortens in a clockwise direction.

The gompa is surrounded by numerous auxiliary buildings with elaborate facades and ornate wooden fretwork and carving.

Places to Stay & Eat

There are several budget places to stay in Tashiding, all on the left as you walk up the main street from the bus halt. The first place is the *Blue Bird*, which has simple wooden rooms for Rs 40 and simple fare. Next is the *Laxmi*, which has fairly shabby rooms for Rs 30. At the top of the street is the *Siniolchu Guest House*, with good rooms for Rs 50, and meals (dhal bhat) with the family.

Getting There & Away

There is one bus to Gezing at 8.30 am which originates from Yuksom, and a daily bus to

Yuksom at 4 pm. There's a share jeep for the 19 km trip to Yuksom at 3 pm (Rs 20), but as it originates in Gezing, you might have trouble getting a lift – if it's full, it won't stop no matter how wildly you flail your arms around. There's one share jeep to Jorethang at 7.30 am (Rs 50), and a share jeep to Gangtok at 7 am. Your chances of hitching a lift further north along this road are slim.

YUKSOM

Yuksom, 19 km north of Tashiding, is as far north as you can travel in Sikkim by road. Although just a small village in a remote corner of Sikkim, it played a significant role in the former country's history, being the site where pioneer lama Lhatsun Chempo, together with Kathok Rikzin Chempo and Ngadak Sempa Chempo (the last of whom founded the Tashiding Gompa), crossed from Tibet into Sikkim and established the Nyingmapa order of Tibetan Buddhism. Yuksom was originally the capital of the kingdom, and Sikkim's earliest monastic community was founded here, on the site on which Dubdi Gompa was later erected. Most travellers wind up here to undertake the trek to Dzongri. From Yuksom there are fine views of both the north and south peaks of Kabru.

Norbugang Chorten

Norbugang chorten is at the end of a track which branches to the left just before Kathok Lake. It was built with materials brought from all over Sikkim, and commemorates the consecration of the first chogyal, Phuntsog Namgyal, by the three pioneer Tibetan lamas.

Dubdi Gompa

Dubdi (the Hermit's Cell), was founded by Lhatsun Chempo and built in 1701, making it one of Sikkims's oldest gompas. There are no longer monks at Dubdi, and it is only opened during special Buddhist festivals. At other times, you may be able to get permission to enter from the caretaker in the village. Check with locals for his current whereabouts. It takes about 40 minutes to walk up to the gompa along a steep path. Go past the hospital to the end of the motor road, where

you'll pass three disused water-driven prayer wheels. After crossing a bridge, take the track to the right. Beware of leeches in summer.

The first building you'll come to is a double storey stone and wood edifice with intricate carving on the facade, although the once-vibrant paint is fading. Inside this hall are enshrined images of Padmasambhava, Lhatsun Chempo, Chenresig and the first king of Sikkim, Phuntsog Namgyal. The walls are covered with paintings of particularly wrathful deities, and there is a painting of the wheel of life in an upstairs chamber.

The second building is a lovely single storey stone and wood building. The paintings inside are recent.

Places to Stay & Eat

The *Pemthang Lodge*, opposite the Hotel Demazong, is a good place to stay. Singles/doubles with common bath cost Rs 50/100, triples cost Rs 120, and a four bed room is Rs 120. Dorm beds cost Rs 40. Pema Gyaltsen here is a personable fellow and a good source of information on the area.

The *No 1 Forest Rest House* is at the end of a long driveway in the middle of a field behind the Hotel Demazong. *No 2 Forest Rest House* is at Gayshen Busty, 500m north of Yuksom on the Dzongri Trail. Beds at both places are Rs 40, and you need to make bookings for them in Gangtok. There's no hot water at either of these places.

Spacious and comfortable rooms can be found at the *Hotel Demazong*, where doubles cost Rs 150 with common bath. The owners are friendly, and there's a restaurant here with a limited menu.

Getting There & Away

There's one share jeep to Jorethang at 6.30 am (three hours, Rs 50), and one to Gezing (Rs 40), also at 6.30 am. Both go via Tashiding (Rs 20). You can reserve a seat on either jeep through their respective owners. The fellow who operates the Jorethang run lives opposite the Hotel Arpun. The other man lives near the post office on the main road. The SNT bus to Gezing leaves at 7 am (four hours, Rs 20).

TREKKING IN SIKKIM

Pelling-Khecheopari Trek

From Pelling it's possible to do a four day trek taking in Khecheopari, Yuksom, Tashiding and Legship. The first stage takes you to the lake. For the second stage, if you go via a short cut to Yuksom, it takes only three hours, heading downhill for the first stage, and then for the last two hours, ascending gradually to Yuksom. From Yuksom to Tashiding you can follow the road, taking some of the obvious short cuts to cut out some of the loops. Then it's an easy one hour walk along the road to Legship. Bring snacks, as there's not much on offer along the way, and check with locals and other travellers for the best short cuts.

Stage 1	Pelling to Khecheopari (4 hours)
Stage 2	Khecheopari to Yuksom (3 hours)
Stage 2	Yuksom to Tashiding (6 hours)
Stage 3	Tashiding to Legship (1 hour)

Yuksom-Dzongri Trek

The only area open for trekking in Sikkim is in West Sikkim, in the Yuksom area. The most popular trek is from Yuksom to Dzongri. To undertake this trek you must make arrangements through a recognised travel agency in Gangtok. They usually charge from US$40 per person per day. What they provide on the trek will depend on your negotiating skills. Most do not have good sleeping bags or tents and tend to schedule their stages to stay in the state government huts that have been constructed along the trek route. It is imperative not to trek too high too quickly, in particular to Dzongri at 4550m. See the section on Acute Mountain Sickness (AMS) under Health in the Facts for the Visitor chapter.

From Yuksom the trail follows the Rathong Valley through unspoilt forests to the small Lepcha settlement at Bakhim. From Bakhim there is a steep ascent to the village of Tsoska, where a couple of lodges provide overnight accommodation. Above Tsoska the trail enters magnificent rhododendron forests to an intermediary camp at Pethang. A tent must be carried for this stage.

It is a further stage to Dzongri where you gain excellent views of Kangchenjunga (8586m) and many other impressive peaks on the Singalila Range, which marks the border between Sikkim and Nepal.

As an alternative to returning direct from Dzongri to Yuksom, many trekkers opt to continue across the grazing pastures to the Prek Valley and camp at Thansing. From here there are impressive views of the east ridge of Kangchenjunga before returning through pristine rhododendron forests to Pethang and the main trail back to Tsoska and Yuksom.

Stage 1	Yuksom to Bakhim (Tsoska) (5-6 hours)
Stage 2	Bakhim (Tsoska) to Pethang (4-5 hours)
Stage 3	Pethang to Dzongri (2-3 hours)
Stage 4	Dzongri to Thansing (4 hours)
Stage 5	Thansing to Tsoska (6-7 hours)
Stage 6	Tsoska to Yuksom (5-6 hours)

Note Trekking to altitudes above 4200m (ie north of Dzongri) should be avoided between March and April due to winter snows.

Glossary

acharya – revered teacher; originally a spiritual guide or preceptor.

amalaka – stone medallion-shaped flourish featuring fluted edges; it frequently surmounts the *shikhara* of Hindu temples.

amrit – baptism.

ananda – happiness. Ananda was the name of the Buddha's first cousin and favourite disciple.

anna – a 16th of a rupee; it's no longer legal tender but is occasionally referred to in marketplace parlance. (Eight annas are the equivalent of Rs 0.50.)

Arjuna – *Mahabharata* hero and military commander who retired to the Himalaya.

Aryan – Sanskrit for 'noble'; refers to those who migrated from Persia and settled in northern India.

ashram – spiritual community or retreat.

autars – spirits of people who die issueless; they are particularly feared by the Gaddis of Himachal Pradesh.

Avalokitesvara – one of the Buddha's most important disciples; also known as Chenresig.

avataar – incarnation of a deity, usually Vishnu.

ayurveda – Indian herbal medicine.

baba – religious master, father, and a term of respect.

Badri – another name for Vishnu.

bagh – garden.

bakhu – traditional dress worn by women of Tibetan origin in Sikkim. Known as a *chuba* in the western Himalaya.

baksheesh – tip, bribe or donation.

begar – system of unpaid or forced labour.

betel – nut of the betel tree; the leaves and nut are mildly intoxicating and are chewed as a stimulant and digestive.

Bhagavad Gita – Song of the Divine One; Krishna's lessons to Arjuna, the main thrust of which was to emphasise the philosophy of *bhakti* (faith); part of the *Mahabharata*.

bhang – dried leaves and flowering shoots of the marijuana plant.

Bharat – Hindi for India.

Bhim – eldest of the five Pandava brothers and another *Mahabharata* hero, renowned for his great strength and giant stature.

Bodhisattva – one who has almost reached *nirvana*, but who renounces it in order to help others attain it; literally 'one whose essence is perfected wisdom'.

Brahma – the source of all existence and worshipped as the creator. Brahma is depicted as having four heads. His consort is Sarasvati.

Brahmin – a member of the priest caste, the highest Hindu caste.

Buddha – Awakened One; originator of Buddhism

who lived in the 5th century BC; regarded by Hindus as the ninth reincarnation of Vishnu.

bugyal – high-altitude meadow.

caste – one's hereditary station in life.

chaams – lama dances, performed by monks wearing masks during religious celebrations at *gompas*.

chai – tea.

chakra – focus of one's spiritual power; disc-like weapon of Vishnu.

Chamunda – form of the goddess Durga. A real terror, armed with a scimitar, noose and mace, and clothed in elephant hide.

Chandra – the moon, or the moon as a god.

Chandragupta – important ruler of India in the 3rd century BC.

Char Dham – the four sacred shrines in Uttarakhand – Yamunotri, Gangotri, Kedarnath and Badrinath – sacred to the goddesses Yamuna and Ganga, and the gods Shiva and Vishnu respectively.

charpoy – Indian rope bed.

chatti – pilgrims' lodging.

Chenresig – the Tibetan deity of compassion, also known as Avalokitesvara. The Dalai Lama is considered to be an incarnation of Chenresig.

chogyal – Sikkimese king.

choli – sari blouse.

cholo – a dice game which originates from Tibet.

chomo – a Ladakhi term for a Tibetan Buddhist nun.

chorten – Tibetan word for *stupa*; originally reliquaries (chorten means 'receptacle for offerings'), they are now frequently erected as cenotaphs in memory of a Buddhist saint.

chowk – a town square, intersection or marketplace.

chuba – traditional dress worn by Tibetan women. In Sikkim, known as a *bakhu*.

chwa-shyam – the altar, and most sacred part of the *dukhang* in a Buddhist *gompa*. It is here that the ornate images of the deities are enshrined.

Dalit – preferred term for India's casteless class; *see* Untouchable.

darshan – offering or audience with someone; viewing of a deity.

deodar – a type of coniferous tree found in Himalayan regions.

Devi – Shiva's wife. She has a variety of forms.

dhaba – hole-in-the-wall restaurant or snack bar.

dham – religious centre.

dharamsala – pilgrims' lodging.

dharma – Hindu/Buddhist moral code of behaviour.

Dhevbumi – abode of the gods; the Himalaya.

dhobi – person who washes clothes.

dorje – thunderbolt.

Dravidian – a member of one of the aboriginal races of India, pushed south by the Indo-Europeans.

dukhang – the main prayer room or assembly hall of Buddhist *gompas*.

dun (doon) – valley.

Durga – the Inaccessible; a form of Shiva's wife Devi, a beautiful but fierce goddess riding a tiger; major goddess of the Shakti cult.

freaks – westerners wandering India.

Ganesh – god of wisdom and prosperity. Elephant-headed son of Shiva and Parvati. His vehicle is a rat.

Ganga – Ganges River; said to flow through the hair of Shiva; goddess representing the Ganges.

ganj – market.

ganja – dried flowering tips of marijuana plant; highly potent form of cannabis.

garh – fort.

Garuda – man-bird vehicle of Vishnu.

Gayatri – sacred verse of the *Rigveda*, repeated mentally by Brahmins twice a day.

Gelukpa – an order of Tibetan Buddhism founded by the monk Tsongkhapa in the 14th century. The Dalai Lama is the spiritual leader of this order.

getruk – a child student of Tibetan Buddhism.

ghat – steps or landing on a river; range of hills, or road up hills.

gompa – Tibetan Buddhist monastery.

gonda – a decorative hat worn by men and women in Ladakh.

gopis – milkmaids. Krishna was very fond of them.

gudma – a large thick woollen garment made in the Kullu Valley, often used as a blanket.

guru – teacher or holy person (in Sanskrit, literally, *goe* – 'darkness' and *roe* – 'to dispel').

gurudwara – Sikh temple.

Hanuman – monkey god, prominent in the *Ramayana*, follower of Rama.

Harijan – name given by Gandhi to India's Untouchables. This term is, however, no longer considered acceptable. *See* Dalit and Untouchable.

Hinayana – a type of Buddhism which holds that the path to *nirvana* is an individual pursuit; also known as Theravada Buddhism.

IMFL – Indian Made Foreign Liquor; beer or spirits produced in India.

Indra – the most important and prestigious of the Vedic gods of India. God of rain, thunder, lightning and war. His weapons are the *vajra* (thunderbolt), bow, net and *anka* (hook).

jhula – bridge.

ji – honorific that can be added to the end of almost anything; thus Babaji, Gandhiji.

jyoti lingams – the most important Shiva shrines in India, of which there are 12. There are three in the Indian Himalaya, at Kedarnath and Jageshwar, both in Uttarakhand, and at the Vaidyanath Temple in Baijnath, in the Kangra Valley of Himachal Pradesh.

Kagyupa – an order of Tibetan Buddhism; divided into the Drukpa and Drigung orders.

kakkars – the five means by which Sikh men recognise each other: *kesh* – uncut hair; *kangha* – the wooden comb; *kachha* – shorts; *kara* – the steel bracelet; and *kirpan* – the sword.

Kali – the Black; a terrible form of Shiva's wife Diva. Depicted with black skin, dripping with blood, surrounded by snakes and wearing a necklace of skulls.

Kali-Yuga – evil times.

Kalki – the White Horse. Future (10th) incarnation of Vishnu which will appear at the end of Kali-Yuga, when the world ceases to be. Kalki has been compared to Maitreya in Buddhist cosmology.

karma – a law of cause and effect whereby your actions in this life influence the level of your future incarnations.

Kauravas – adversaries of the heroes of the *Mahabharata*, the Pandavas.

Kedar – a name of Shiva.

khadi – homespun cloth; Mahatma Gandhi encouraged people to spin khadi rather than buy English cloth.

kot – fort.

kotwali – police station.

Krishna – Vishnu's eighth incarnation, often coloured blue; a popular Hindu deity, he revealed the *Bhagavad Gita* to Arjuna.

kumbh – pitcher.

kund – lake or tank.

la – a Tibetan word for mountain pass.

Lakshman – half-brother and aide of Rama in the *Ramayana*.

Lakshmi (Laxmi) – Vishnu's consort, goddess of wealth; sprang forth from the ocean holding a lotus. Also referred to as Padma (lotus).

lama – Tibetan Buddhist monk or priest.

lathi – large bamboo stick; a weapon of the Indian police.

lhamo – traditional Tibetan opera, originally performed over several days.

lingam – phallic symbol; symbol of Shiva.

Losong – Sikkimese New Year.

machaan – watchtower (hide) in game reserves from where hunters spied on their prey.

Mahabharata – great epic poem, containing about 10,000 verses, describing the battle between the Pandavas and the Kauravas.

Mahadev – the Great God; a name of Shiva.

Mahadevi – the Great Goddess; a name of Devi, Shiva's wife.

Mahakala – Great Time; a name of Shiva the Destroyer.

maharaja, maharana, maharao – king.

maharani – wife of a princely ruler or a ruler in her own right.

mahatma – literally 'great soul'.

Mahayana – a type of Buddhism which holds that the combined belief of its followers will eventually be great enough to encompass all of humanity and bear it to salvation.

Maheshwara – Great Lord; Shiva.

maidan – open grassed area in a town or city.

Maitreya – Buddha of the future; coming Buddha.

mandala – circle; symbol used in Hindu and Buddhist art to symbolise the universe.

mandapa – pillared pavilion in front of a temple.

mandi – market.

mandir – Hindu or Jain temple.

mani stone – stone carved with the Tibetan Buddhist mantra 'Om Mani Padme Hum', or 'Hail to the jewel in the lotus'.

mantra – sacred word or syllable used by Buddhists and Hindus to aid meditation; metrical psalms of praise found in the *Vedas*.

Mara – Buddhist god of death; has three eyes and holds the wheel of life.

marg – major road.

masjid – mosque. Jama Masjid is the Friday Mosque, or main mosque.

mata – mother.

mataji – female priest.

math – *gompa*, religious seat of learning.

matris – mischievous sprites.

maya – the illusory nature of existence.

mela – a fair.

memsahib – married European lady (from 'madam-sahib').

moksha – salvation.

mudra – ritual hand movements used in Hindu religious dancing; also postures adopted by the Buddha.

Mughal – the Muslim dynasty of Indian emperors from Babur to Aurangzeb.

Namgyal – a kingdom, based in Ladakh, which ruled parts of the region from the 16th to 19th centuries.

Nanda – the cowherd who raised Krishna.

Nanda Devi – the presiding goddess of Uttarakhand. She is revered by all those inhabitants who live within the shadow of the beautiful Nanda Devi mountain, which is believed to be a form of the goddess.

Nandi – bull, vehicle of Shiva. Nandi's images are usually seen before temples dedicated to Shiva.

Narayan – an incarnation of Vishnu the Creator.

Nhilkantha – form of Shiva. His blue throat is a result of swallowing poison that would have destroyed the world.

nirvana – the ultimate aim of Buddhist existence; final release from the cycle of existence.

nulla (nullah) – ditch or small stream; can also mean valley, as in Solang Nullah, near Manali.

Nyingmapa – a Tibetan Buddhist order formed by the followers of the Indian sage Padmasambhava.

Om – sacred invocation representing the absolute essence of the divine principle. For Buddhists, if repeated often enough with complete concentration, it should lead to a state of emptiness.

padma – lotus.

Padmasambhava – highly revered 8th century Indian sage who established Buddhism in Tibet, one of the foremost proponents of Tantric Buddhism.

padmasana – lotus position or posture.

pagoda – Buddhist religious monument composed of a solid hemisphere topped by a spire, containing relics of the Buddha; also known as a *stupa* or *chorten*.

paan – betel nut and leaves plus chewing additives such as lime.

papu – bright, woollen shoes with curled tips worn during festivals and ceremonies by men and women in Ladakh.

Parvati – another form of Shiva's wife.

pashmina – fine wool from a pashmina goat.

pattoo – a thick woollen shawl made in the Kullu Valley and worn by women.

pradesh – state.

pranayama – study of breath control.

prasaad – food offering to the gods.

prayag – sacred confluence; in the Garhwal district of Uttarakhand there are five *(panch)* sacred confluences, known as the Panch Prayag, which are formed by the meeting of the tributaries of the Ganges.

puja – literally 'respect'; offering or prayers.

pujari – person who performs a *puja*; a temple priest.

Puranas – set of 18 encyclopedic Sanskrit stories, written in verse dating from the period of the Guptas (5th century AD).

Radha – favourite mistress of Krishna when he lived as Govinda (or Gopala), the cowherd.

raj – rule or sovereignty.

raja – king.

Rajput – Hindu warrior castes, royal rulers of central India.

rakhi – amulet.

Rama – seventh incarnation of Vishnu. His life story is the central theme of the *Ramayana*.

Ramayana – the story of Rama and Sita and their conflict with Ravana. One of India's most well known legends, it is retold in various forms throughout almost all South-East Asia.

rani – wife of a king.

Ravana – demon king of Lanka (modern-day Sri Lanka). He abducted Sita, and the titanic battle between him and Rama is told in the *Ramayana*.

Rigveda – the original and longest of the four main *Vedas*, or holy Sanskrit texts.

Ringchen Zangpo – known as the Great Translator. He was instrumental in resurrecting Tibetan Buddhism in northern India in the 11th century.

rinpoche – literally 'high in esteem', a title bestowed on highly revered lamas; they are usually incarnate, but need not be.

rishi – originally a sage to whom the hymns of the *Vedas* were revealed; any poet, philosopher or sage.

rumal – finely embroidered handkerchief-sized cloth found in the Chamba district of Himachal Pradesh, used as a covering for sacred texts.

sadar – main.

sadhu – ascetic, or holy person; one who is trying to achieve enlightenment; usually addressed as 'swamaji' or 'babaji'.

sagar – lake, reservoir.

sahib – 'lord', title applied to any gentleman and most Europeans.

Sakyapa – a rare order of Tibetan Buddhism, renowned for its brightly coloured *gompas*.

sal – a type of hardwood tree found at lower elevations in the Himalayan region.

salai – road.

samadhi – an ecstatic state, sometimes defined as 'ecstasy, trance, communion with God'. Also, a place where a holy man has been cremated; usually venerated as a shrine.

sangam – confluence; meeting of two rivers.

sarak – road.

Sarasvati – wife of Brahma, goddess of speech and learning; usually seated on a white swan, holding a *veena* (a stringed instrument).

Sati – wife of Shiva. Became a sati ('honourable woman') by immolating herself. Although banned, the act of sati is occasionally performed.

Shaivaite – follower of Lord Shiva.

Shaivism – the worship of Shiva.

Shakti – goddess; Shiva's consort.

shakti – creative energies perceived as female deities; devotees follow the cult of shaktism.

shaligram – a type of black stone from which idols are often carved; often used in temple architectural elements, such as pillars.

Shankar – Shiva as the Creator.

Shankaracharya – 9th century Hindu theologian who formulated the philosophy of Advaita Vedanta and postulated the concept of *maya*, or the illusory nature of existence. His reforms heralded the revival of Hinduism in India.

shikhara – Hindu temple spire or temple.

singh – literally 'lion'; name of the Rajput caste and adopted by Sikhs as a surname.

Sita – in the *Vedas*, the goddess of agriculture. More commonly associated with the *Ramayana* in which Sita, Rama's wife, is abducted by Ravana and carried off to Lanka.

Shiva – the destroyer; also the Creator, in which form he is worshipped as a *lingam*. Shiva is the presiding deity of the Himalaya.

sri (sree, shri, shree) – honorific; these days the Indian equivalent of Mr or Mrs.

stupa – *see pagoda*.

sudra – low Hindu caste.

Surya – the sun; a major deity in the *Vedas*.

swami – title given to initiated monks; means 'lord of the self'. A title of respect.

tal – lake.

tank – reservoir.

Tantric Buddhism – Tibetan Buddhism with strong sexual and occult overtones.

thakur – Hindu caste.

thangka – rectangular Tibetan painting on cloth.

thepang – distinctive square woollen cap often worn by Kinnauris.

Theravada – *see Hinayana*.

thumpchen – long-stemmed horn played by Buddhist monks; traditionally a Tibetan instrument.

tikka – a mark devout Hindus put on their foreheads.

topi – cap.

tsampa – barley flour, eaten cooked or raw. It is a staple food in more remote parts of Himachal Pradesh and Ladakh.

tso – a Tibetan term meaning lake; used in Ladakh.

Untouchable – lowest caste or 'casteless' for whom the most menial tasks are reserved. The name derives from the belief that higher casts risk defilement if they touch one. Formerly known as *Harijan*, now *Dalit*.

Upanishads – Esoteric doctrine; ancient texts forming part of the *Vedas* (although of a later date), they delve into weighty matters such as the nature of the universe and the soul.

Vaishnavite – follower of Lord Vishnu.

Vedas – the four Hindu sacred books; a collection of hymns composed in pre-classical Sanskrit during the second millennium BC: *Rigveda*, *Yajurveda*, *Samaveda* and *Atharvaveda*.

Vishnu – the third in the Hindu trinity of gods along with Brahma and Shiva. The Preserver and Restorer, who so far has nine avataars.

wallah – literally 'man'. Can be added to other words; thus dhobi-wallah (clothes washer), taxi-wallah, Delhi-wallah.

yatra – pilgrimage.

yoni – vagina; female fertility symbol.

Index

453

LONELY PLANET JOURNEYS

JOURNEYS is a unique collection of travellers' tales – published by the company that understands travel better than anyone else. It is a series for anyone who has ever experienced – or dreamed of – the magical moment when they encountered a strange culture or saw a place for the first time. They are tales to read while you're planning a trip, while you're on the road or while you're in an armchair, in front of a fire.

JOURNEYS books will catch the spirit of a place, illuminate a culture, recount a crazy adventure, or introduce a fascinating way of life. They will always entertain, and always enrich the experience of travel.

ISLANDS IN THE CLOUDS
Travels in the Highlands of New Guinea
Isabella Tree

This is the fascinating account of a journey to the remote and beautiful Highlands of Papua New Guinea and Irian Jaya. The author travels with a PNG Highlander who introduces her to his intriguing and complex world. *Islands in the Clouds* is a thoughtful, moving book, full of insights into a region that is rarely noticed by the rest of the world.

'One of the most accomplished travel writers to appear on the horizon for many years . . . the dialogue is brilliant' – Eric Newby

LOST JAPAN
Alex Kerr

Lost Japan draws on the author's personal experiences of Japan over a period of 30 years. Alex Kerr takes his readers on a backstage tour: friendships with Kabuki actors, buying and selling art, studying calligraphy, exploring rarely visited temples and shrines . . . The Japanese edition of this book was awarded the 1994 Shincho Gakugei Literature Prize for the best work of non-fiction.

'This deeply personal witness to Japan's wilful loss of its traditional culture is at the same time an immensely valuable evaluation of just what that culture was'
– Donald Richie of the Japan Times

THE GATES OF DAMASCUS
Lieve Joris
Translated by Sam Garrett

This best-selling book is a beautifully drawn portrait of day-to-day life in modern Syria. Through her intimate contact with local people, Lieve Joris draws us into the fascinating world that lies behind the gates of Damascus.

'A brilliant book . . . Not since Naguib Mahfouz has the everyday life of the modern Arab world been so intimately described' – William Dalrymple

SEAN & DAVID'S LONG DRIVE
Sean Condon

Sean and David are young townies who have rarely strayed beyond city limits. One day, for no good reason, they set out to discover their homeland, and what follows is a wildly entertaining adventure that covers half of Australia. Sean Condon has written a hilarious, offbeat road book that mixes sharp insights with deadpan humour and outright lies.

'Funny, pithy, kitsch and surreal . . . This book will do for Australia what Chernobyl did for Kiev, but hey you'll laugh as the stereotypes go boom' – Andrew Tuck, Time Out

LONELY PLANET TRAVEL ATLASES

Lonely Planet has long been famous for the number and quality of its guidebook maps. Now we've gone one step further and in conjunction with Steinhart Katzir Publishers produced a handy companion series: Lonely Planet travel atlases – maps of a country produced in book form.

Unlike other maps, which look good but lead travellers astray, our travel atlases have been researched on the road by Lonely Planet's experienced team of writers. All details are carefully checked to ensure the atlas corresponds with the equivalent Lonely Planet guidebook.

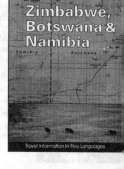

The handy atlas format means no holes, wrinkles, torn sections or constant folding and unfolding. These atlases can survive long periods on the road, unlike cumbersome fold-out maps. The comprehensive index ensures easy reference.

- full-colour throughout
- maps researched and checked by Lonely Planet authors
- place names correspond with Lonely Planet guidebooks
  – no confusing spelling differences
- legend and travelling information in English, French, German, Japanese and Spanish
- size: 230 x 160 mm

Available now:
Thailand; India & Bangladesh; Vietnam; Zimbabwe, Botswana & Namibia

Coming soon:
Chile; Egypt; Israel; Laos; Turkey

LONELY PLANET TV SERIES & VIDEOS

Lonely Planet travel guides have been brought to life on television screens around the world. Like our guides, the programmes are based on the joy of independent travel, and look honestly at some of the most exciting, picturesque and frustrating places in the world. Each show is presented by one of three travellers from Australia, England or the USA and combines an innovative mixture of video, Super-8 film, atmospheric soundscapes and original music.

Videos of each episode – containing additional footage not shown on television – are available from good book and video shops, but the availability of individual videos varies with regional screening schedules.

Video destinations include: Alaska; Australia (Southeast); Brazil; Ecuador & the Galápagos Islands; Indonesia; Israel & the Sinai Desert; Japan; La Ruta Maya (Yucatán, Guatemala & Belize); Morocco; North India (Varanasi to the Himalaya); Pacific Islands; Vietnam; Zimbabwe, Botswana & Namibia.

Coming soon: The Arctic (Norway & Finland); Baja California; Chile & Easter Island; China (Southeast); Costa Rica; East Africa (Tanzania & Zanzibar); Great Barrier Reef (Australia); Jamaica; Papua New Guinea; the Rockies (USA); Syria & Jordan; Turkey.

The Lonely Planet TV series is produced by:
Pilot Productions
Duke of Sussex Studios
44 Uxbridge St
London W8 7TG UK

Lonely Planet videos are distributed by:
IVN Communications Inc
2246 Camino Ramon
California 94583, USA

107 Power Road, Chiswick
London W4 5PL UK

Music from the TV series is available on CD & cassette.
For ordering information contact your nearest Lonely Planet office.

PLANET TALK

Lonely Planet's FREE quarterly newsletter

We love hearing from you and think you'd like to hear from us.

*When...*is the right time to see reindeer in Finland?
*Where...*can you hear the best palm-wine music in Ghana?
*How...*do you get from Asunción to Areguá by steam train?
*What...*is the best way to see India?

For the answer to these and many other questions read PLANET TALK.

Every issue is packed with up-to-date travel news and advice including:

* a letter from Lonely Planet co-founders Tony and Maureen Wheeler
* go behind the scenes on the road with a Lonely Planet author
* feature article on an important and topical travel issue
* a selection of recent letters from travellers
* details on forthcoming Lonely Planet promotions
* complete list of Lonely Planet products

To join our mailing list contact any Lonely Planet office.

Also available: Lonely Planet T-shirts. 100% heavyweight cotton..

LONELY PLANET ONLINE

Get the latest travel information before you leave or while you're on the road

Whether you've just begun planning your next trip, or you're chasing down specific info on currency regulations or visa requirements, check out the Lonely Planet World Wide Web site for up-to-the-minute travel information.

As well as travel profiles of your favourite destinations (including interactive maps and full-colour photos), you'll find current reports from our army of researchers and other travellers, updates on health and visas, travel advisories, and the ecological and political issues you need to be aware of as you travel.

There's an online travellers' forum (the Thorn Tree) where you can share your experiences of life on the road, meet travel companions and ask other travellers for their recommendations and advice. We also have plenty of links to other Web sites useful to independent travellers.

With tens of thousands of visitors a month, the Lonely Planet Web site is one of the most popular on the Internet and has won a number of awards including GNN's Best of the Net travel award.

http://www.lonelyplanet.com

LONELY PLANET PRODUCTS

Lonely Planet is known worldwide for publishing practical, reliable and no-nonsense travel information in our guides and on our web site. The Lonely Planet list covers just about every accessible part of the world. Currently there are eight series: *travel guides*, *shoestring guides*, *walking guides*, *city guides*, *phrasebooks*, *audio packs*, *travel atlases* and *Journeys* – a unique collection of travellers' tales.

EUROPE

Austria • Baltic States & Kaliningrad • Baltic States phrasebook • Britain • Central Europe on a shoestring • Central Europe phrasebook • Czech & Slovak Republics • Denmark • Dublin city guide • Eastern Europe on a shoestring • Eastern Europe phrasebook • Finland • France • Greece • Greek phrasebook • Hungary • Iceland, Greenland & the Faroe Islands • Ireland • Italy • Mediterranean Europe on a shoestring • Mediterranean Europe phrasebook • Paris city guide • Poland • Prague city guide • Russia, Ukraine & Belarus • Russian phrasebook • Scandinavian & Baltic Europe on a shoestring • Scandinavian Europe phrasebook • Slovenia • St Petersburg city guide • Switzerland • Trekking in Greece • Trekking in Spain • Ukrainian phrasebook • Vienna city guide • Walking in Switzerland • Western Europe on a shoestring • Western Europe phrasebook

NORTH AMERICA

Alaska • Backpacking in Alaska • Baja California • California & Nevada • Canada • Hawaii • Honolulu city guide • Los Angeles city guide • Mexico • New England • Pacific Northwest USA • Rocky Mountain States • San Francisco city guide • Southwest USA • USA phrasebook

CENTRAL AMERICA & THE CARIBBEAN

Central America on a shoestring • Costa Rica • Eastern Caribbean • Guatemala, Belize & Yucatán: La Ruta Maya • Jamaica

SOUTH AMERICA

Argentina, Uruguay & Paraguay • Bolivia • Brazil • Brazilian phrasebook • Buenos Aires city guide • Chile & Easter Island • Colombia • Ecuador & the Galápagos Islands • Latin American Spanish phrasebook • Peru • Quechua phrasebook • Rio de Janeiro city guide • South America on a shoestring • Trekking in the Patagonian Andes • Venezuela

ALSO AVAILABLE:

Travel with Children • Traveller's Tales

AFRICA

Arabic (Moroccan) phrasebook • Africa on a shoestring • Cape Town city guide • Central Africa • East Africa • Egypt & the Sudan • Ethiopian (Amharic) phrasebook • Kenya • Morocco • North Africa • South Africa, Lesotho & Swaziland • Swahili phrasebook • Trekking in East Africa • West Africa • Zimbabwe, Botswana & Namibia • Zimbabwe, Botswana & Namibia travel atlas

MAIL ORDER

Lonely Planet products are distributed worldwide. They are also available by mail order from Lonely Planet, so if you have difficulty finding a title please write to us. North American and South American residents should write to Embarcadero West, 155 Filbert St, Suite 251, Oakland CA 94607, USA; European and African residents should write to 10 Barley Mow Passage, Chiswick, London W4 4PH; and residents of other countries to PO Box 617, Hawthorn, Victoria 3122, Australia.

NORTH-EAST ASIA

Beijing city guide • Cantonese phrasebook • China • Hong Kong, Macau & Canton • Hong Kong city guide • Japan • Japanese phrasebook • Japanese audio pack • Korea • Korean phrasebook • Mandarin phrasebook • Mongolia • Mongolian phrasebook • North-East Asia on a shoestring • Seoul city guide • Taiwan • Tibet • Tibet phrasebook • Tokyo city guide

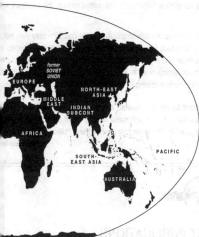

MIDDLE EAST & CENTRAL ASIA

Arab Gulf States • Arabic (Egyptian) phrasebook • Central Asia • Iran • Israel • Jordan & Syria • Middle East • Turkey • Turkish phrasebook • Trekking in Turkey • Yemen

Travel Literature: The Gates of Damascus

ISLANDS OF THE INDIAN OCEAN

Madagascar & Comoros • Maldives & Islands of the East African Ocean • Mauritius, Réunion & Seychelles

INDIAN SUBCONTINENT

Bengali phrasebook • Bangladesh • Delhi city guide • Hindi/Urdu phrasebook • India • India & Bangladesh travel atlas • Indian Himalaya • Karakoram Highway • Nepal • Nepali phrasebook • Pakistan • Sri Lanka • Sri Lanka phrasebook • Trekking in the Indian Himalaya • Trekking in the Nepal Himalaya

SOUTH-EAST ASIA

Bali & Lombok • Bangkok city guide • Burmese phrasebook • Cambodia • Ho Chi Minh city guide • Indonesia • Indonesian phrasebook • Indonesian audio pack • Jakarta city guide • Java • Laos • Lao phrasebook • Malaysia, Singapore & Brunei • Myanmar (Burma) • Philippines • Pilipino phrasebook • Singapore city guide • South-East Asia on a shoestring • Thailand • Thailand travel atlas • Thai phrasebook • Thai audio pack • Thai Hill Tribes phrasebook • Vietnam • Vietnamese phrasebook • Vietnam travel atlas

AUSTRALIA & THE PACIFIC

Australia • Australian phrasebook • Bushwalking in Australia • Bushwalking in Papua New Guinea • Fiji • Fijian phrasebook • Islands of Australia's Great Barrier Reef • Melbourne city guide • Micronesia • New Caledonia • New South Wales & the ACT • New Zealand • Northern Territory • Outback Australia • Papua New Guinea • Papua New Guinea phrasebook • Queensland • Rarotonga & the Cook Islands • Samoa • Solomon Islands • South Australia • Sydney city guide • Tahiti & French Polynesia • Tasmania • Tonga • Tramping in New Zealand • Vanuatu • Victoria • Western Australia

Travel Literature: Islands in the Clouds • Sean & David's Long Drive

THE LONELY PLANET STORY

Lonely Planet published its first book in 1973 in response to the numerous 'How did you do it?' questions Maureen an Tony Wheeler were asked after driving, bussing, hitching, sailing and railing their way from England to Australia.

Written at a kitchen table and hand collated, trimmed and stapled, *Across Asia on the Cheap* became an instant loca bestseller, inspiring thoughts of another book.

Eighteen months in South-East Asia resulted in their second guide, *South-East Asia on a shoestring*, which they put togethe in a backstreet Chinese hotel in Singapore in 1975. The 'yellow bible', as it quickly became known to backpackers aroun the world, soon became *the* guide to the region. It has sold well over half a million copies and is now in its 8th edition, sti retaining its familiar yellow cover.

Today there are over 180 titles, including travel guides, walking guides, language kits & phrasebooks, travel atlases and trave literature. The company is one of the largest travel publishers in the world. Although Lonely Planet initially specialised in guide to Asia, we now cover most regions of the world, including the Pacific, North America, South America, Africa, the Middle East an Europe.

The emphasis continues to be on travel for independent travellers. Tony and Maureen still travel for several months of eac year and play an active part in the writing, updating and quality control of Lonely Planet's guides.

They have been joined by over 70 authors and 170 staff at our offices in Melbourne (Australia), Oakland (USA), Londo (UK) and Paris (France). Travellers themselves also make a valuable contribution to the guides through the feedback w receive in thousands of letters each year.

The people at Lonely Planet strongly believe that travellers can make a positive contribution to the countries they visit, bot through their appreciation of the countries' culture, wildlife and natural features, and through the money they spend. I addition, the company makes a direct contribution to the countries and regions it covers. Since 1986 a percentage of th income from each book has been donated to ventures such as famine relief in Africa; aid projects in India; agricultura projects in Central America; Greenpeace's efforts to halt French nuclear testing in the Pacific; and Amnesty International

'I hope we send the people out with the right attitude about travel. You realise when you travel that there are s many different perspectives about the world, so we hope these books will make people more interested in wha they see. These are guidebooks, but you can't really guide people. All you can do is point them in the right direction
– Tony Wheele

LONELY PLANET PUBLICATIONS

Australia
PO Box 617, Hawthorn 3122, Victoria
tel: (03) 9819 1877 fax: (03) 9819 6459
e-mail: talk2us@lonelyplanet.com.au

USA
Embarcadero West, 155 Filbert St, Suite 251,
Oakland, CA 94607
tel: (510) 893 8555 TOLL FREE: 800 275-8555
fax: (510) 893 8563
e-mail: info@lonelyplanet.com

UK
10 Barley Mow Passage, Chiswick,
London W4 4PH
tel: (0181) 742 3161 fax: (0181) 742 2772
e-mail: 100413.3551@compuserve.com

France:
71 bis rue du Cardinal Lemoine, 75005 Paris
tel: 1 44 32 06 20 fax: 1 46 34 72 55
e-mail: 100560.415@compuserve.com

World Wide Web: http://www.lonelyplanet.com